PLAYER'S HANDBOOK®

Arcane, Divine, and Martial Heroes

ROLEPLAYING GAME CORE RULES

Rob Heinsoo · Andy Collins · James Wyatt

CREDITS

D&D® 4th Edition Design Team
Rob Heinsoo, Andy Collins, James Wyatt

D&D 4th Edition Final Development Strike Team
Bill Slavicsek, Mike Mearls, James Wyatt

Player's Handbook Design
Rob Heinsoo, Andy Collins, James Wyatt

Player's Handbook Development
Andy Collins, Mike Mearls, Stephen Radney-MacFarland,
Peter Schaefer, Stephen Schubert

Player's Handbook Editing
Michele Carter, Jeremy Crawford

Player's Handbook Managing Editing
Kim Mohan

Additional Design and Development
Richard Baker, Greg Bilsland, Logan Bonner, Bart Carroll,
Michele Carter, Jennifer Clarke Wilkes, Bruce R. Cordell,
Jeremy Crawford, Jesse Decker, Michael Donais, Robert
Gutschera, Gwendolyn F. M. Kestrel, Peter Lee, Julia
Martin, Kim Mohan, David Noonan, Christopher Perkins,
Matthew Sernett, Chris Sims, Ed Stark, Rodney Thompson,
Rob Watkins, Steve Winter, Chris Youngs

Director of R&D, Roleplaying Games/Book Publishing
Bill Slavicsek

D&D Story Design and Development Manager
Christopher Perkins

D&D System Design and Development Manager
Andy Collins

D&D Senior Art Director
Stacy Longstreet

Cover Illustration
Wayne Reynolds (front), **Rob Alexander** (back)

Special Thanks to Brandon Daggerhart, keeper of Shadowfell

Graphic Designers
Keven Smith, Leon Cortez, Emi Tanji

Additional Graphic Design
Karin Powell, Mari Kolkowsky, Shauna Narciso,
Ryan Sansaver

Concept Artists
Rob Alexander, Dave Allsop, Christopher Burdett, Adam
Gillespie, Lars Grant-West, David Griffith, Lee Moyer,
William O'Connor

Interior Illustrations
Zoltan Boros & Gabor Szikszai, Matt Cavotta,
Eric Deschamps, Wayne England, David Griffith,
Ralph Horsley, Howard Lyon, Raven Mimura, Lee
Moyer, William O'Connor, Steve Prescott, Dan Scott,
Anne Stokes, Franz Vohwinkel, Eva Widermann

D&D Script Design
Daniel Reeve

D&D Brand Team
Liz Schuh, Scott Rouse, Sara Girard, Kierin Chase,
Martin Durham, Linae Foster

Publishing Production Specialists
Angelika Lokotz, Erin Dorries, Moriah Scholz,
Christopher Tardiff

Prepress Manager
Jefferson Dunlap

Imaging Technicians
Travis Adams, Bob Jordan, Sven Bolen

Production Managers
Cynda Callaway

Building on the Design of Previous Editions by
E. Gary Gygax, Dave Arneson (1st Edition and earlier);
David "Zeb" Cook (2nd Edition); **Jonathan Tweet,
Monte Cook, Skip Williams, Richard Baker, Peter Adkison**
(3rd Edition)

Dedicated to the memory of E. Gary Gygax

620-21736720-001 EN
9 8 7 6 5 4 3 2 1
First Printing: June 2008
ISBN: 978-0-7869-4867-3

U.S., CANADA, ASIA, PACIFIC,
& LATIN AMERICA
Wizards of the Coast, Inc.
P.O. Box 707
Renton WA 98057-0707
+1-800-324-6496

EUROPEAN HEADQUARTERS
Hasbro UK Ltd
Caswell Way
Newport, Gwent NP9 0YH
GREAT BRITAIN
Please keep this address for your records

WIZARDS OF THE COAST, BELGIUM
't Hofveld 6D
1702 Groot-Bijgaarden
Belgium
+32 2 467 3360

VISIT OUR WEBSITE AT WWW.WIZARDS.COM/DND

CONTENTS

CHAPTER 1

HOW TO PLAY

IMAGINE A world of bold warriors, mighty wizards, and terrible monsters.

Imagine a world of ancient ruins, vast caverns, and great wild wastes where only the bravest heroes dare to tread.

Imagine a world of swords and magic, a world of elves and goblins, a world of giants and dragons.

This is the world of the DUNGEONS & DRAGONS® Roleplaying Game (also referred to as D&D), the pinnacle of fantasy roleplaying games. You take on the role of a legendary hero—a skilled fighter, a courageous cleric, a deadly rogue, or a spell-hurling wizard. With some willing friends and a little imagination, you strike out on daring missions and epic quests, testing yourself against an array of daunting challenges and bloodthirsty monsters.

Get ready—the *Player's Handbook* contains everything you need to create a heroic character of your own! To start you on your first adventure, this chapter discusses the following topics.

✦ **A Roleplaying Game:** How the D&D game is different from any other game you've played.

✦ **What's in a D&D Game:** The essential ingredients of the DUNGEONS & DRAGONS game.

✦ **How Do You Play?:** A look at what happens during the game, including a brief example of activity at the game table.

✦ **The Core Mechanic:** The single fundamental rule you need to know for most challenges you face in the game.

RALPH HORSLEY

The DUNGEONS & DRAGONS game is a roleplaying game. In fact, D&D invented the roleplaying game and started an industry.

A roleplaying game is a storytelling game that has elements of the games of make-believe that many of us played as children. However, a roleplaying game such as D&D provides form and structure, with robust gameplay and endless possibilities.

D&D is a fantasy-adventure game. You create a character, team up with other characters (your friends), explore a world, and battle monsters. While the D&D game uses dice and miniatures, the action takes place in your imagination. There, you have the freedom to create anything you can imagine, with an unlimited special effects budget and the technology to make anything happen.

What makes the D&D game unique is the Dungeon Master. The DM is a person who takes on the role of lead storyteller and game referee. The DM creates adventures for the characters and narrates the action for the players. The DM makes D&D infi-nitely flexible—he or she can react to any situation, any twist or turn suggested by the players, to make a D&D adventure vibrant, exciting, and unexpected.

The adventure is the heart of the D&D game. It's like a fantasy movie or novel, except the characters that you and your friends create are the stars of the story. The DM sets the scene, but no one knows what's going to happen until the characters do something—and then anything can happen! You might explore a dark dungeon, a ruined city, a lost temple deep in a jungle, or a lava-filled cavern beneath a mysterious mountain. You solve puzzles, talk with other characters, battle all kinds of fantastic monsters, and discover fabulous magic items and treasure.

D&D is a cooperative game in which you and your friends work together to complete each adventure and have fun. It's a storytelling game where the only limit is your imagination. It's a fantasy-adventure game, building on the traditions of the greatest fantasy stories of all time. In an adventure, you can attempt anything you can think of. Want to talk to the dragon instead of fighting it? Want to disguise yourself as an orc and sneak into the foul lair? Go ahead and give it a try. Your actions might work or they might fail spectacularly, but either way you've contributed to the unfolding story of the adventure and probably had fun along the way.

You "win" the DUNGEONS & DRAGONS game by participating in an exciting story of bold adventurers confronting deadly perils. The game has no real end; when you finish one story or quest, you can start another one. Many people who play the D&D game keep their games going for months or years, meeting with their friends every week to pick up the story where they left off.

Your character grows as the game continues. Each monster defeated, each adventure completed, and each treasure recovered not only adds to your continuing story, but also earns your character new abilities. This increase in power is reflected by your character's level; as you continue to play, your character gains more experience, rising in level and mastering new and more powerful abilities.

From time to time, your character might come to a grisly end, torn apart by ferocious monsters or done in by a nefarious villain. But even when your character is defeated, you don't "lose." Your companions can employ powerful magic to revive your character, or you might choose to create a new character to carry on from where the previous character fell. You might fail to complete the adventure, but if you had a good time and you created a story that everyone remembers for a long time, the whole group wins.

WILLIAM O'CONNOR

A Fantastic World

The world of the Dungeons & Dragons game is a place of magic and monsters, of brave warriors and spectacular adventures. It begins with a basis of medieval fantasy and then adds the creatures, places, and powers that make the D&D world unique.

The world of the D&D game is ancient, built upon and beneath the ruins of past empires, leaving the landscape dotted with places of adventure and mystery. Legends and artifacts of past empires still survive—as do terrible menaces.

The current age has no all-encompassing empire. The world is shrouded in a dark age, between the collapse of the last great empire and the rise of the next, which might be centuries away. Minor kingdoms prosper, to be sure: baronies, holdings, city-states. But each settlement appears as a point of light in the widespread darkness, a haven, an island of civilization in the wilderness that covers the world. Adventurers can rest and recuperate in settlements between adventures. No settlement is entirely safe, however, and adventures break out within (and under) such places as often as not.

During your adventures, you might visit a number of fantastic locations: wide cavern passages cut by rivers of lava; towers held aloft in the sky by ancient magic; forests of strange, twisted trees, with shimmering fog in the air—anything you can imagine, your character might experience as the game unfolds.

Monsters and supernatural creatures are a part of this world. They prowl in the dark places between the points of light. Some are threats, others are willing to aid you, and many fall into both camps and might react differently depending on how you approach them.

Magic is everywhere. People believe in and accept the power that magic provides. However, true masters of magic are rare. Many people have access to a little magic, and such minor magic helps those living within the points of light to maintain their communities. But those who have the power to shape spells the way a blacksmith shapes metal are as rare as adventurers and appear as friends or foes to you and your companions.

At some point, all adventurers rely on magic in one form or another. Wizards and warlocks draw magic from the fabric of the universe, shape it with their will, and hurl it at their foes in explosive blasts. Clerics and paladins call down the wrath of their gods to sear their foes with divine radiance, or they invoke their gods' mercy to heal their allies' wounds. Fighters, rangers, rogues, and warlords don't use obviously magical powers, but their expertise with their magic weapons makes them masters of the battlefield. At the highest levels of play, even nonmagical adventurers perform deeds no mere mortal could dream of doing without magic—swinging great axes in wide swaths that shake the earth around them or cloaking themselves in shadow to become invisible.

THE HISTORY OF D&D

Before roleplaying games, before computer games, before trading card games, there were wargames. Using metal miniatures to re-create famous battles from history, wargamers were the original hobby gamers. In 1971, Gary Gygax created *Chainmail*, a set of rules that added fantastic creatures and magic into the traditional wargame. In 1972, Dave Arneson approached Gygax with a new take; instead of controlling a massive army, each player would play a single character, a hero. Instead of fighting each other, the heroes would cooperate to defeat villains and gain rewards. This combination of rules, miniatures, and imagination created a totally new entertainment experience, and in 1974 Gygax and Arneson published the first set of roleplaying game rules with TSR, Inc.—the Dungeons & Dragons game.

In 1977, the rules were rewritten and repackaged into the Dungeons & Dragons Basic Set, and suddenly D&D was on its way to becoming a phenomenon. A year later, the first edition of Advanced Dungeons & Dragons was published in a series of high-quality hardcover books.

Throughout the 1980s, the game experienced remarkable growth. Novels, a cartoon series, computer games, and the first campaign settings (Forgotten Realms and Dragonlance) were released, and in 1989 the long-awaited second edition

of AD&D took the world by storm. The 1990s started out strong, with the release of more campaign settings (including Ravenloft, Dark Sun, and Planescape), but as the decade was drawing to a close, the D&D juggernaut was losing steam. In 1997, Wizards of the Coast purchased TSR, Inc. and moved its creative staff to Seattle to begin work on the third edition of the original roleplaying game.

In 2000, the third edition of D&D was released, and it was hailed as an innovation in game mechanics. In this period, D&D reached new heights of popularity, celebrated its thirtieth anniversary, and published an amazing collection of rulesbooks, supplements, and adventures. We've seen D&D grow and make its mark on popular culture. It has inspired multiple generations of gamers, writers, computer game designers, filmmakers, and more with its ability to expand the imagination and inspire creativity.

Now we've reached a new milestone. This is the 4th Edition of the Dungeons & Dragons game. It's new. It's exciting. It's bright and shiny. It builds on what has gone before, and firmly establishes D&D for the next decade of play. Whether you were with the game from the beginning or just discovered it today, this new edition is your key to a world of fantasy and adventure.

All DUNGEONS & DRAGONS games have four basic ingredients: at least one player (four or five players is best), a Dungeon Master, an adventure, and game books and dice.

PLAYER CHARACTERS

As a player, you create a character—a heroic adventurer. This adventurer is part of a team that delves into dungeons, battles monsters, and explores the world's dark wilderness. A player-generated character is known as a player character (PC). Like the protagonists of a novel or a movie, player characters are at the center of the game's action.

When you play your D&D character, you put yourself into your character's shoes and make decisions as if you were that character. You decide which door your character opens next. You decide whether to attack a monster, to negotiate with a villain, or to attempt a dangerous quest. You can make these decisions based on your character's personality, motivations, and goals, and you can even speak or act in character if you like. You have almost limitless control over what your character can do and say in the game.

THE DUNGEON MASTER

One person has a special role in a D&D game: the Dungeon Master (DM). The Dungeon Master presents the adventure and the challenges that the players try to overcome. Every D&D game needs a Dungeon Master—you can't play without one.

The Dungeon Master has several functions in the game.

♦ **Adventure Builder:** The DM creates adventures (or selects premade adventures) for you and the other players to play through.

♦ **Narrator:** The DM sets the pace of the story and presents the various challenges and encounters the players must overcome.

♦ **Monster Controller:** The Dungeon Master controls the monsters and villains the player characters battle against, choosing their actions and rolling dice for their attacks.

♦ **Referee:** When it's not clear what ought to happen next, the DM decides how to apply the rules and adjudicate the story.

The Dungeon Master controls the monsters and villains in the adventure, but he isn't your adversary. The DM's job is to provide a framework for the whole group to enjoy an exciting adventure. That means challenging the player characters with interesting encounters and tests, keeping the game moving, and applying the rules fairly.

Many D&D players find that being the Dungeon Master is the best part of the game. Taking on the Dungeon Master role isn't necessarily a permanent post—you and your friends can take turns being the DM from adventure to adventure. If you think you'd like to be the Dungeon Master in your group, you can find all the tools to help you in the *Dungeon Master's Guide.*

THE ADVENTURE

Adventurers need adventures. A DUNGEONS & DRAGONS adventure consists of a series of events. When the players decide which way to go next and

GAME DICE

The game uses polyhedral dice with different numbers of sides, as shown below. You can find dice like these in the store where you bought this book, in any game store, and in many bookstores.

In these rules, the different dice are referred to by the letter "d" followed by the number of sides: d4, d6 (the common six-sided die many games use), d8, d10, d12, and d20.

When you need to roll dice, the rules tell you how many dice to roll, what size they are, and what modifiers to add. For example, "3d8 + 5" means you roll three eight-sided dice and add 5 to the total.

You can use d10s to roll percentages, if you ever need to. Roll 1d10 for the "tens" and 1d10 for the "ones" to generate a number between 1 and 100. Two 10s is 100, but otherwise a 10 on the tens die counts as 0—so a 10 on the tens die and a 7 on the ones die is a result of 7 (not 107!).

d4   d6   d8   d10   d12   d20

how their characters meet the resulting encounters and challenges, they turn the adventure into an exciting story about their characters. D&D adventures feature action, combat, mystery, magic, challenges, and lots of monsters!

Adventures come in three forms:

✦ **Ready to Play:** The DM can buy or obtain professionally written, ready-to-play adventures from a number of sources, including www.dndinsider.com.

✦ **Adventure Hooks and Components:** Most D&D supplements offer pieces of adventures—story ideas, maps, interesting villains or monsters—that the DM can assemble into an adventure. DUNGEON MAGAZINE (www.dndinsider.com) is also a rich source of adventure material.

✦ **Homemade:** Many DMs choose to create their own dungeons and adventures, building challenging encounters and stocking them with monsters from the *Monster Manual* and treasure from the *Player's Handbook*.

An adventure can be a simple "dungeon crawl"—a series of rooms filled with monsters and traps, with little story to explain why the adventurers need to explore them—or as complex as a murder mystery or a tale of political intrigue. It can last for a single game session or stretch out over many sessions of play. For example, exploring a haunted castle might take half a dozen game sessions over the course of a couple of months of real time.

When the same group of player characters plays with the same Dungeon Master through multiple adventures, you've got a campaign. The story of the heroes doesn't end with a single adventure, but continues on for as long as you like!

GAME BOOKS AND DICE

The action of the game takes place mostly in your imagination, but you still need a few "game pieces" to play D&D.

✦ *Player's Handbook:* Every player needs a *Player's Handbook* for reference.

✦ *Dungeon Master's Guide* and *Monster Manual:* The Dungeon Master needs a copy of each of these books (and players might also enjoy perusing the contents).

✦ **Dice:** The DUNGEONS & DRAGONS game requires a special set of game dice (see the sidebar).

✦ **Character Sheet:** To keep track of all the important information about your character, use the character sheet at the back of this book, or check out www.dndinsider.com.

You might find some of the following items and accessories useful at your game table.

✦ **Miniatures:** Each player needs a miniature to represent his or her character, and the DM needs minis for monsters. Official *D&D Miniatures* are custom-made to be used with the D&D game.

✦ **Battle Grid or *Dungeon Tiles*:** Combat in D&D plays out on a grid of 1-inch squares. You can pick up an erasable battle grid at many hobby game stores, or try *D&D Dungeon Tiles*—heavy cardstock tiles that can be set up to create a wide variety of locations—or you can create your own grid.

HOW DO YOU PLAY?

Your "piece" in the DUNGEONS & DRAGONS game is your character. He or she is your representative in the game world. Through your character, you can interact with the game world in any way you want. The only limit is your imagination—and, sometimes, how high you roll on the dice.

Basically, the D&D game consists of a group of player characters taking on an adventure presented by the Dungeon Master. Each adventure is made up of encounters—challenges of some sort that your characters face.

Encounters come in two types.

✦ **Combat encounters** are battles against nefarious foes. In a combat encounter, characters and monsters take turns attacking until one side or the other is defeated.

✦ **Noncombat encounters** include deadly traps, difficult puzzles, and other obstacles to overcome. Sometimes you overcome noncombat encounters by using your character's skills, sometimes you can defeat them with clever uses of magic, and sometimes you have to puzzle them out with nothing but your wits. Noncombat encounters also include social interactions, such as attempts to persuade, bargain with, or obtain information from a nonplayer character (NPC) controlled by the DM. Whenever you decide that your character wants to talk to a person or monster, it's a noncombat encounter.

EXPLORATION

Between encounters, your characters explore the world. You make decisions about which way your character travels and what he or she tries to do next. Exploration is the give-and-take of you telling the DM what you want your character to do, and the DM telling you what happens when your character does it.

For example, let's say the player characters have just climbed down into a dark chasm. The DM tells you that your characters see three tunnels leading from the chasm floor into the gloom. You and the other players decide which tunnel your characters venture into first, and you tell the DM which way your characters are heading. That's exploration. You might try almost anything else: finding a place to hide and set an ambush in case monsters come by, shouting "Hello, any monsters here?" as loud as you can, or searching the chasm floor carefully in case there's anything interesting lying amid the boulders and moss. That's all exploration, too.

Decisions you make as you explore eventually lead to encounters. For example, one tunnel might lead into a nest of hungry gricks—if you decide to go that way, your characters are heading into a combat encounter. Another tunnel might lead to a door sealed by a magic lock that you have to break through—a noncombat encounter.

While exploring a dungeon or other adventure location, you might try to do any of the following actions:

✦ Move down a hallway, follow a passage, cross a room

✦ Listen by a door to determine if you hear anything on the other side

✦ Try a door to see if it's locked

✦ Break down a locked door

✦ Search a room for treasure

✦ Pull levers, push statues or furnishings around

✦ Pick the lock of a treasure chest

✦ Jury-rig a trap

The Dungeon Master decides whether or not something you try actually works. Some actions automatically succeed (you can move around without trouble, usually), some require one or more die rolls, called checks (breaking down a locked door, for example), and some simply can't succeed. Your character is capable of any deeds a strong, smart, agile, and well-armed human action hero can pull off. You can't punch your way through a door of 3-inch-thick iron plate with your bare hands, for example—not unless you have powerful magic to help you out!

Taking Your Turn

In exploration, you don't usually need to take turns. The DM normally prompts you by asking "What do you do?", you answer, and then the DM tells you what happens. You can break in with questions, offer suggestions to other players, or tell the DM a new action any time you like. But try to be considerate of the other players. They want their characters to take actions, too.

In combat encounters, it works differently: The player characters and the monsters all take turns in a fixed rotation, called the initiative order.

Example of Play

Here's a typical D&D game session. The adventurers are exploring the ruins of an old dwarven stronghold, now infested by monsters. The players in this session are:

Dave, the Dungeon Master;

Toby, whose character is the human fighter Ammar;

Cam, playing Isidro, a halfling rogue;

Daneen, whose character is an eladrin wizard named Serissa.

Dave (*DM*): "Old stone steps climb up about 30 feet or so into the mountainside, alongside a cold stream splashing through the cave. The steps end at a landing in front of a big stone door carved with the image of a bearded dwarf face. The door stands open about a foot or so. There's a bronze gong hanging from a bracket in the wall nearby. What do you do?"

Cam (*Isidro*): "I'll creep up and peek through the opening."

Daneen (*Serissa*): "I want to take a closer look at the gong."

Toby (*Ammar*): "I'm going to hang back and keep watch, in case Isidro gets into trouble."

Cam (*Isidro*): "Not a chance, I'm a pro."

Dave (*DM*): "Okay, first Serissa: It's a battered old bronze gong. There's a small hammer hanging beside it."

Toby (*Ammar*): "Don't touch it!"

Daneen (*Serissa*): "I wasn't going to! It looks like the doorbell to me. No sense telling the monsters we're here."

Dave (*DM*): "Okay. Now for Isidro: Since you're trying to be sneaky, Cam, make a Stealth check."

Cam (*rolls a Stealth check for Isidro*): "I got a 22."

Dave (*DM*): "Isidro is pretty stealthy." *Dave compares Isidro's Stealth check result to the Perception check result of the monsters he knows are in the next room. Cam's roll beats the Perception check, so the monsters don't know the halfling is there.*

Daneen (*Serissa*): "So what does he see?"

Dave (*DM*): "You're by the gong, remember? Isidro, you peek in the door's opening, and you see a large stone hall with several thick pillars. There's a large fire pit in the center of the room filled with dimming embers. You see four beastlike humanoids with hyena faces crouching around the fire pit, and a big animal—like a real hyena, but much bigger—dozing on the floor nearby. The hyena-men are armed with spears and axes."

Toby (*Ammar*): "Gnolls! I hate those guys."

Daneen (*Serissa*): "Looks like we'll have to fight our way in. Can we take them?"

Cam (*Isidro*): "No problem, we've got the drop on 'em."

Dave (*DM*): "So are you going through the door?" *The players all agree that they are.* "Show me where your characters are standing right before you go in."

The players arrange their characters' miniatures on the Dungeon Tiles that Dave has prepared for the encounter. They're now on the landing just outside the room with the gnolls.

Toby (*Ammar*): "All right, on the count of three. One . . . two . . . three!"

Dave (*DM*): "You've surprised the gnolls! Everybody roll initiative, and we'll see if you can take these guys or not."

What happens next? Can Ammar, Isidro, and Serissa defeat the gnolls? That depends on how the players play their characters, and how lucky they are with their dice!

THE CORE MECHANIC

How do you know if your sword-swing hurts the dragon, or just bounces off its iron-hard scales? How do you know if the ogre believes your outrageous bluff, or if you can swim the raging river and reach the other side?

All these actions depend on very basic, simple rules: Decide what you want your character to do and tell the Dungeon Master. The DM tells you to make a check and figures out your chance of success (a target number for the check).

You roll a twenty-sided die (d20), add some numbers, and try to hit the target number determined by the DM. That's it!

THE CORE MECHANIC

1. Roll a d20. You want to roll high!
2. Add all relevant modifiers.
3. Compare the total to a target number.

If your check result is higher than or equal to the target number, you succeed. If your check result is lower than the target number, you fail.

If your check succeeds, you determine the outcome. If your check was an attack, you roll damage. If it was a

check to see if you managed to jump across a pit, your check result determines how far you jumped. If you succeed on a check when you're trying to hide, the monsters don't see you.

There's a little more to it than that, but the core mechanic governs all game play. All the rest of the rules in the book are extensions and refinements of this simple mechanic.

THREE BASIC RULES

In addition to the core mechanic, three principles are at the heart of the DUNGEONS & DRAGONS game. Many other rules are based on these assumptions.

SIMPLE RULES, MANY EXCEPTIONS

Every class, race, feat, power, and monster in the D&D game lets you break the rules in some way. These can be very minor ways: Most characters don't know how to use longbows, but every elf does. These exceptions can also appear in very significant ways: A swing with a sword normally does a few points of damage, but a high-level fighter can use a power that can fell multiple monsters in a single blow. All these game elements are little ways of breaking the rules—and most of the books published for the D&D game are full of these game elements.

SPECIFIC BEATS GENERAL

If a specific rule contradicts a general rule, the specific rule wins. For example, a general rule states that you can't use a daily power when you charge. But if you have a daily power that says you can use it when you charge, the power's specific rule wins. It doesn't mean that you can use any daily power when you charge, just that one.

ALWAYS ROUND DOWN

Unless otherwise noted, if you wind up with a fraction as the result of a calculation, round down even if the fraction is 1/2 or larger. For instance, this rule comes into play whenever you calculate one-half your level: If your level is an odd number, you always round down to the next lower whole number.

D&D INSIDER

Think the game ends with the words on these pages? Think again! Check out www.dndinsider.com for all kinds of information, game tools, and community participation in your favorite game. For a nominal subscription, *D&D Insider* unlocks the ongoing content of *Dragon Magazine* and *Dungeon Magazine* online, with issue updates happening multiple times each week. In addition to great articles, adventure hooks, and inside information, *D&D Insider* provides an interactive database of all things D&D, a custom

D&D character builder that helps you create and manage your characters, a suite of powerful tools to help Dungeon Masters manage their adventures and campaigns, and the remarkable D&D Game Table that turns the Internet into your kitchen table so that you can play D&D with distant friends—anytime, anywhere! *D&D Insider* is constantly updated with new material, new stories, new tools, and new features dedicated to the phenomenon that is the D&D experience.

CHAPTER 2

MAKING CHARACTERS

YOUR FIRST step in playing D&D is to imagine and then create a character of your own. Your character is a combination of the fantastic hero in your mind's eye and the different game rules that describe what he or she can do. You choose a race such as elf or dragonborn, a class such as wizard or fighter, and distinct powers such as magic spells or divine prayers. Then you invent a personality, description, and story for your character.

Your character is your representative in the game, your avatar in the D&D world. A character is a combination of game statistics and roleplaying hooks; the statistics define the physical aspects of what the character does in the world, while roleplaying choices define who he or she is.

Throughout this book, we use the word "you" interchangeably with "your character." As far as the rules of the game are concerned, your character is you. You decide what your character does as you move through the world, exploring dungeons, fighting monsters, and interacting with other characters in the game.

This chapter includes the following sections.

✦ **Character Creation:** A guide to the character creation process.

✦ **Ability Scores:** How to generate your character's ability scores.

✦ **Roleplaying:** Elements to help you shape your character, including alignment, deities, personality, appearance, background, and languages.

✦ **Making Checks:** Expanding on the core mechanic to explain the basic die rolls of the game.

✦ **Gaining Levels:** Rules for gaining experience levels and advancing your character.

✦ **Character Sheet:** Explanation of a character sheet and where you can find information for each entry on the sheet.

First, take a minute to imagine your character. Think about the kind of hero you want your character to be. Your character exists in your imagination—all the game statistics do is help you determine what your character can do in the game. Do you like fantasy fiction featuring dwarves or elves? Try building a character of one of those races. Do you want your character to be the toughest adventurer at the table? Try choosing fighter or paladin for your character class. If you don't know where else to begin, take a look at the art that appears throughout this book and the brief character descriptions in each race entry in Chapter 3, and see what catches your interest.

Follow these steps to create your D&D character. You can take these out of order; for example, some people prefer to pick their powers last.

1. **Choose Race.** Decide the race of your character. Your choice of race offers several racial advantages to your character. *Chapter 3.*

2. **Choose Class.** Your class represents your training or profession, and it is the most important part of your character's capabilities. *Chapter 4.*

3. **Determine Ability Scores.** Generate your ability scores. Your ability scores describe the fundamental strengths of your body and mind. Your race adjusts the scores you generate, and different classes rely on different ability scores. *Chapter 2.*

4. **Choose Skills.** Skills measure your ability to perform tasks such as jumping across chasms, hiding from observers, and identifying monsters. *Chapter 5.*

5. **Select Feats.** Feats are natural advantages or special training you possess. *Chapter 6.*

6. **Choose Powers.** Each character class offers a different selection of powers to choose from. *Chapter 4.*

7. **Choose Equipment.** Pick your character's armor, weapons, implements, and basic adventuring gear. At higher levels, you'll be able to find and create magic items. *Chapter 7.*

8. **Fill in the Numbers.** Calculate your hit points, Armor Class and other defenses, initiative, attack bonuses, damage bonuses, and skill check bonuses. *Chapter 2.*

9. **Roleplaying Character Details.** Flesh out your character with details about your personality, appearance, and beliefs. *Chapter 2.*

RACE, CLASS, AND ROLE

The first two decisions you make in character creation are picking your character's race and choosing a class. Together, these describe your basic character concept; for example, dwarf fighter, eladrin wizard, or tiefling warlord. Your choice of character class also determines your character's role—the job your character does when the adventuring party is in a fight.

You should pick the race and class combination that interests you the most. However, sometimes it's a good idea to first consider the role you want your character to fill. For example, if you join an existing game and none of the other players are playing a character in the defender role, you would help them out by playing a fighter or a paladin.

CHARACTER RACE

A variety of fantastic races populate the world of the DUNGEONS & DRAGONS game—people such as dragonborn, dwarves, and elves. In any good-sized town or city, you typically run across at least a few individuals of each race, even if they are simply travelers or wandering mercenaries looking for their next challenge.

Many different intelligent creatures populate the world, creatures such as dragons, mind flayers, and demons. These aren't characters you can play; they're monsters you fight. Your character is an adventurer of one of the civilized races of the world.

Dragonborn are proud, honor-bound draconic humanoids. They wander the world as mercenaries and adventurers. They are strong and possess dragonlike abilities.

Legendary for their toughness and strong will, **dwarves** are indomitable warriors and master artisans. Dwarven kingdoms are mighty mountain citadels, but clans of dwarf crafters can be found in any town or city.

Eladrin are a graceful, magical race born of the Feywild, the realm of Faerie. They love arcane magic, swordplay, and exquisite work in metal and stone. They live in shining cities on the borders of the Feywild.

Kin to the eladrin, **elves** dwell in the deep forests of the world and love the beauty of nature. Many elves (and some eladrin, too) live in wandering companies that visit many lands, staying a season or two in each.

Elves and humans sometimes have children together, giving rise to **half-elves**. With many of the best features of both humans and elves, half-elves have capabilities distinct from both races. They are charismatic and versatile.

Halflings, the smallest of the civilized races, are a plucky, quick, and likable people. Halflings gather in small clans in the marshes and along the rivers of the world, traveling and trading widely with the other races.

Brave and ambitious, **humans** are somewhat more numerous than other races, and their city-states are among the brightest spots in a dark world. However, there still exist vast portions of the world where no human has set foot.

Tieflings are a race descended from ancient humans who bargained with infernal powers. Tieflings are loners who live in the shadows of human society, relying only on trusted allies.

You can learn more about these races in Chapter 3.

Each character race has innate strengths that make it more suited to particular classes. However, you can create any combination you like. There's nothing wrong with playing against type; dwarves aren't usually rogues, but you can create a capable and effective dwarf rogue by choosing your feats and powers carefully.

CHARACTER CLASS

Many different types of heroes and villains inhabit the world: sneaky rogues, clever wizards, burly fighters, and more. Character race defines your basic appearance and natural talents, but character class is your chosen vocation, the specific trade you follow. You can learn more about these classes in Chapter 4.

Cleric: Courageous and devout, clerics are holy warriors and healers. If you want to blast foes with divine powers, bolster your companions with healing and magical power, and lead them to victory with your wisdom and determination, play a cleric.

Fighter: Fighters are experts in armed combat, relying on muscle, training, and pure grit to see them through. If you want to mix it up in close combat, protect your companions, and hack enemies into submission while their attacks rain down fruitlessly on your heavily armored body, be a fighter.

Paladin: Devout warriors and champions of their deities, paladins are divinely inspired knights who fight at the front of a battle. If you want to challenge foes to single combat, fight for a cause, and smite your foes with divine might, then paladin is the class for you.

Ranger: Expert trackers and scouts, rangers are wilderness warriors who excel at hit-and-run fighting. If you want to master both bow and blade, vanish into the woods like a ghost, and bring down your foes before they know you're there, play a ranger.

Rogue: Thieves, scoundrels, dungeon-delvers, jacks-of-all-trades—rogues have a reputation for larceny and trickery. If you want to slip into and out of the shadows on a whim, tumble across the field of battle with little fear of enemy reprisal, and appear from nowhere to plant a blade in your foe's back, be a rogue.

Warlock: Wielders of forbidden lore, warlocks are dangerous practitioners of magic who turn their baleful powers against their enemies. If you want to deal with mysterious powers, scour enemies with potent blasts of eldritch energy, and bedevil them with potent curses, warlock is the best choice for you.

Warlord: Hardy and skilled in close combat, warlords are brilliant leaders who have the gift of inspiration. If you want to lead the battle with the point of your sword, coordinate brilliant tactics with your comrades, and bolster and heal them when they falter, play a warlord.

Wizard: Masters of potent arcane powers, wizards disdain physical conflict in favor of awesome magic. If you want to hurl balls of fire that incinerate your enemies, cast spells that change the battlefield, or research arcane rituals that can alter time and space, you should be a wizard.

CHARACTER ROLE

Each character class specializes in one of four basic functions in combat: control and area offense, defense, healing and support, and focused offense. The roles embodied by these functions are **controller**, **defender**, **leader**, and **striker**. The classic adventuring party includes one character of each role: wizard, fighter, cleric, and rogue.

Character roles identify which classes can stand in for each other. For example, if you don't have a cleric in your party, a warlord serves just as well in the leader role.

Roles also serve as handy tools for building adventuring parties. It's a good idea to cover each role with at least one character. If you have five or six players in your group, it's best to double up on defender first, then striker. If you don't have all the roles covered, that's okay too—it just means that the characters need to compensate for the missing function.

Future volumes of the *Player's Handbook* will introduce additional classes for all these roles.

ATTACK POWERS AND UTILITY POWERS

Every class gives you access to **attack** powers you can use to harm or hinder your enemies and **utility** powers that help you and your allies. Powers in each of these broad categories are further defined by how often you can use them.

You can use **at-will** powers as often as you choose. You can use **encounter** powers many times during a day of adventuring, but you have to rest a few minutes between each use, so you can use them each once per encounter. **Daily** powers are so dramatic and powerful that you can use each one only once a day.

CONTROLLER (WIZARD)

Controllers deal with large numbers of enemies at the same time. They favor offense over defense, using powers that deal damage to multiple foes at once, as well as subtler powers that weaken, confuse, or delay their foes.

DEFENDER (FIGHTER, PALADIN)

Defenders have the highest defenses in the game and good close-up offense. They are the party's front-line combatants; wherever they're standing, that's where the action is. Defenders have abilities and powers that make it difficult for enemies to move past them or to ignore them in battle.

LEADER (CLERIC, WARLORD)

Leaders inspire, heal, and aid the other characters in an adventuring group. Leaders have good defenses, but their strength lies in powers that protect their companions and target specific foes for the party to concentrate on.

Clerics and warlords (and other leaders) encourage and motivate their adventuring companions, but just because they fill the leader role doesn't mean they're necessarily a group's spokesperson or commander. The party leader—if the group has one—might as easily be a charismatic warlock or an authoritative paladin. Leaders (the role) fulfill their function through their mechanics; party leaders are born through roleplaying.

STRIKER (RANGER, ROGUE, WARLOCK)

Strikers specialize in dealing high amounts of damage to a single target at a time. They have the most concentrated offense of any character in the game. Strikers rely on superior mobility, trickery, or magic to move around tough foes and single out the enemy they want to attack.

ABILITY SCORES

After you choose your race and class, determine your ability scores. Six abilities provide a quick description of your character's physical and mental characteristics. Are you muscle-bound and insightful? Brilliant and charming? Nimble and hardy? Your ability scores define these qualities—your strengths as well as your weaknesses.

Strength (Str) measures your character's physical power. It's important for most characters who fight hand-to-hand.

✦ Melee basic attacks are based on Strength.

✦ Clerics, fighters, paladins, rangers, and warlords have powers based on Strength.

✦ Your Strength might contribute to your Fortitude defense.

✦ Strength is the key ability for Athletics skill checks.

Constitution (Con) represents your character's health, stamina, and vital force. All characters benefit from a high Constitution score.

✦ Your Constitution score is added to your hit points at 1st level.

✦ The number of healing surges you can use each day is influenced by your Constitution.

✦ Many warlock powers are based on Constitution.

✦ Your Constitution might contribute to your Fortitude defense.

✦ Constitution is the key ability for Endurance skill checks.

Dexterity (Dex) measures hand-eye coordination, agility, reflexes, and balance.

✦ Ranged basic attacks are based on Dexterity.

✦ Many ranger and rogue powers are based on Dexterity.

✦ Your Dexterity might contribute to your Reflex defense.

✦ If you wear light armor, your Dexterity might contribute to your Armor Class.

✦ Dexterity is the key ability for Acrobatics, Stealth, and Thievery skill checks.

Intelligence (Int) describes how well your character learns and reasons.

✦ Wizard powers are based on Intelligence.

✦ Your Intelligence might contribute to your Reflex defense.

✦ If you wear light armor, your Intelligence might contribute to your Armor Class.

✦ Intelligence is the key ability for Arcana, History, and Religion skill checks.

Wisdom (Wis) measures your common sense, perception, self-discipline, and empathy. You use your Wisdom score to notice details, sense danger, and get a read on other people.

✦ Many cleric powers are based on Wisdom.

✦ Your Wisdom might contribute to your Will defense.

✦ Wisdom is the key ability for Dungeoneering, Heal, Insight, Nature, and Perception skill checks.

Charisma (Cha) measures your force of personality, persuasiveness, and leadership.

✦ Many paladin and warlock powers are based on Charisma.

✦ Your Charisma might contribute to your Will defense.

✦ Charisma is the key ability for Bluff, Diplomacy, Intimidate, and Streetwise skill checks.

Each of your ability scores is a number that measures the power of that ability. A character with a 16 Strength is much stronger than a character with a 6 Strength. A score of 10 or 11 is the normal human average, but player characters are a cut above average in most abilities. As you advance in levels, your ability scores keep getting better.

Your ability score determines an ability modifier that you add to any attack, check, roll, or defense based on that ability. For instance, making a melee attack with a battleaxe is a Strength attack, so you add the ability modifier for your Strength score to your attack rolls and damage rolls. If your score is 17, you're pretty strong; you add +3 to your attack rolls and damage rolls when you make that attack.

Your ability scores also influence your defenses (see page 275), since you add your ability modifier to your defense score.

✦ For **Fortitude defense,** you add the higher of your Strength or Constitution ability modifiers.

✦ For **Reflex defense,** you add the higher of your Dexterity or Intelligence ability modifiers.

✦ For **Will defense,** you add the higher of your Wisdom or Charisma ability modifiers.

✦ If you wear light armor or no armor, you also add the higher of your Dexterity or Intelligence ability modifiers to your **Armor Class.**

ABILITY MODIFIERS

Ability Score	Ability Modifier	Ability Score	Ability Modifier
1	-5	18-19	+4
2-3	-4	20-21	+5
4-5	-3	22-23	+6
6-7	-2	24-25	+7
8-9	-1	26-27	+8
10-11	+0	28-29	+9
12-13	+1	30-31	+10
14-15	+2	32-33	+11
16-17	+3	and so on . . .	

GENERATING ABILITY SCORES

You can use one of three methods to generate ability scores. In each method, you can take the numbers you generate and assign them to whichever ability score you want. Remember, your class determines which ability scores are important to you, and your race modifies certain ability scores.

Ability scores increase as a character gains levels (see the Character Advancement table on page 29). When you assign your initial scores, remember that they'll improve with time.

METHOD 1: STANDARD ARRAY

Take these six numbers and assign them to your abilities any way you like: **16, 14, 13, 12, 11, 10.**

Apply your racial ability adjustments (see Chapter 3) after you assign the scores to your abilities.

METHOD 2: CUSTOMIZING SCORES

This method is a little more complicated than the standard array, but it gives comparable results. With this method, you can build a character who's really good in one ability score, but at the cost of having average scores in the other five.

Start with these six scores: 8, 10, 10, 10, 10, 10. You have 22 points to spend on improving them. The cost of raising a score from one number to a higher number is shown on the table below.

Score	Cost	Score	Cost
9	– (1)*	14	5
10	0 (2)*	15	7
11	1	16	9
12	2	17	12
13	3	18	16

* If your score is 8, you can pay 1 to make it 9 or 2 to make it 10. You must buy your score up to 10 before you can improve it further.

Here are some sample ability arrays you can generate using this method:

14	13	13	13	13	13
14	14	13	13	13	11
14	14	14	12	12	11
14	14	14	14	12	8
15	14	13	12	12	11
15	15	13	12	11	10
16	15	12	11	11	10
16	14	14	12	11	8
16	16	12	10	10	10
16	16	12	11	11	8
17	15	12	11	10	8
17	14	12	11	10	10
18	13	13	10	10	8
18	14	11	10	10	8
18	12	12	10	10	10

Apply your racial ability adjustments (see Chapter 3) after you determine your scores.

METHOD 3: ROLLING SCORES

Some players like the idea of generating ability scores randomly. The result of this method can be really good, or it can be really bad. On average, you'll come out a little worse than if you had used the standard array. If you roll well, you can come out way ahead, but if you roll poorly, you might generate a character who's virtually unplayable. Use this method with caution.

Roll four 6-sided dice (4d6) and add up the highest three numbers. Do that six times, and then assign the numbers you generated to your six ability scores. Apply your racial ability adjustments.

If the total of your ability modifiers is lower than +4 or higher than +8 before racial ability adjustments, your DM might rule that your character is too weak or too strong compared to the other characters in the group and decide to adjust your scores to fit better within his or her campaign preferences.

You can't roll ability scores for a character you plan to use in RPGA® events.

SKILLS, FEATS, POWERS, AND EQUIPMENT

To round out the unique aspects of your character, choose skills, feats, powers, and equipment.

Your class tells you how many skills you start with at 1st level. Some races give you an additional skill choice as well. See Chapter 5 for details on skills.

You also choose one heroic tier feat at 1st level (or two, if you're a human). Some classes grant bonus feats as well. See Chapter 6 for feat descriptions.

Your choice of class powers defines how your character functions in and out of combat. Each class

section in Chapter 4 offers recommendations on choosing powers that reflect your approach.

Finally, consult Chapter 7 to pick your equipment. You begin your career at 1st level with 100 gold pieces, enough to equip yourself with basic gear (and maybe have a few coins left over).

FILL IN THE NUMBERS

Once you've picked all the other aspects of your character, it's time to fill in the numbers. The calculations you need are described on page 30 in the instructions on completing your character sheet.

ROLEPLAYING

The DUNGEONS & DRAGONS game is, first and foremost, a roleplaying game, which means that it's all about taking on the role of a character in the game. Some people take to this playacting naturally and easily; others find it more of a challenge. This section is here to help you out, whether you're comfortable and familiar with roleplaying or you're new to the concept.

Your character is more than a combination of race, class, and feats. He or she is also one of the protagonists in a living, evolving story line. Like the hero of any fantasy novel or film, he or she has ambitions and fears, likes and dislikes, motivations and mannerisms, moments of glory and of failure. The best D&D characters blend the ongoing story of their adventuring careers with memorable characteristics or traits. Jaden the 4th-level human fighter is a perfectly playable character even without any embellishment, but Jaden the Grim's personality—brooding, fatalistic, and honest—suggests a particular approach to negotiating with NPCs or discussing issues with the other characters. A well-crafted character personality expands your experience of the game dramatically.

D&D is a roleplaying game but not necessarily an exercise in improvisational theater. Sometimes, the role you play is defender or leader—the character you're playing is engaged in combat and has a job to do so that your team comes out victorious. Even in combat, though, you can interject bits of personality and dialogue that make your character more than just the statistics on your character sheet.

ALIGNMENT

If you choose an alignment, you're indicating your character's dedication to a set of moral principles: good, lawful good, evil, or chaotic evil. In a cosmic sense, it's the team you believe in and fight for most strongly.

ALIGNMENT

A character's alignment (or lack thereof) describes his or her moral stance:

✦ **Good:** Freedom and kindness.
✦ **Lawful Good:** Civilization and order.
✦ **Evil:** Tyranny and hatred.
✦ **Chaotic Evil:** Entropy and destruction.
✦ **Unaligned:** Having no alignment; not taking a stand.

For the purpose of determining whether an effect functions on a character, someone of lawful good alignment is considered good and someone of chaotic evil alignment is considered evil. For instance, a lawful good character can use a magic item that is usable only by good-aligned characters.

Alignments are tied to universal forces bigger than deities or any other allegiance you might have. If you're a high-level cleric with a lawful good alignment, you're on the same team as Bahamut, regardless of whether you worship that deity. Bahamut is not in any sense the captain of your team, just a particularly important player (who has a large number of supporters). Most people in the world, and plenty of player characters, haven't signed up to play on any team—they're unaligned. Picking and adhering to an alignment represents a distinct choice.

If you choose an alignment for your character, you should pick either good or lawful good. Unless your DM is running a campaign in which all the characters are evil or chaotic evil, playing an evil or chaotic evil

character disrupts an adventuring party and, frankly, makes all the other players angry at you.

Here's what the four alignments (and being unaligned) mean.

THE GOOD ALIGNMENT

Protecting the weak from those who would dominate or kill them is just the right thing to do.

If you're a good character, you believe it is right to aid and protect those in need. You're not required to sacrifice yourself to help others or to completely ignore your own needs, but you might be asked to place others' needs above your own . . . in some cases, even if that means putting yourself in harm's way. In many ways, that's the essence of being a heroic adventurer: The people of the town can't defend themselves from the marauding goblins, so you descend into the dungeon—at significant personal risk—to put an end to the goblin raids.

You can follow rules and respect authority, but you're keenly aware that power tends to corrupt those who wield it, too often leading them to exploit their power for selfish or evil ends. When that happens, you feel no obligation to follow the law blindly. It's better for authority to rest in the members of a community rather than the hands of any individual or social class. When law becomes exploitation, it crosses into evil territory, and good characters feel compelled to fight it.

Good and evil represent fundamentally different viewpoints, cosmically opposed and unable to coexist in peace. Good and lawful good characters, though, get along fine—even if a good character thinks a lawful good companion might be a little too focused on following the law, rather than simply doing the right thing.

THE LAWFUL GOOD ALIGNMENT

An ordered society protects us from evil.

If you're lawful good, you respect the authority of personal codes of conduct, laws, and leaders, and you believe that those codes are the best way of achieving your ideals. Just authority promotes the well-being

ALIGNMENT VS. PERSONALITY

Isn't alignment just another part of your personality? Yes and no.

Certain personality traits have moral weight, particularly those that influence how you interact with others. Cruelty and generosity can be considered personality traits, but they're also manifestations of your beliefs about the importance and worth of other people. A character who aspires to good might have a cruel streak, but if that streak manifests too frequently or in extreme ways, it's hard to say he's really upholding his moral ideals.

Other personality traits have no moral weight at all. A fastidious and well-organized person can just as easily be evil as good. An impulsive prankster can also be good or evil. These quirks of personality are mostly unrelated to alignment, but your alignment might affect the way your personality translates into action. An evil prankster might favor cruel practical jokes that cause personal harm and damage property, while a good one would steer away from such injurious acts.

of its subjects and prevents them from harming one another. Lawful good characters believe just as strongly as good ones do in the value of life, and they put even more emphasis on the need for the powerful to protect the weak and lift up the downtrodden. The exemplars of the lawful good alignment are shining champions of what's right, honorable, and true, risking or even sacrificing their lives to stop the spread of evil in the world.

When leaders exploit their authority for personal gain, when laws grant privileged status to some citizens and reduce others to slavery or untouchable status, law has given in to evil and just authority becomes tyranny. You are not only capable of challenging such injustice, but morally bound to do so. However, you would prefer to work within the system to right such problems rather than resorting to more rebellious and lawless methods.

THE EVIL ALIGNMENT
It is my right to claim what others possess.

Evil characters don't necessarily go out of their way to hurt people, but they're perfectly willing to take advantage of the weakness of others to acquire what they want.

Evil characters use rules and order to maximize personal gain. They don't care whether laws hurt other people. They support institutional structures that give them power, even if that power comes at the expense of others' freedom. Slavery and rigid caste structures are not only acceptable but desirable to evil characters, as long as they are in a position to benefit from them.

THE CHAOTIC EVIL ALIGNMENT
I don't care what I have to do to get what I want.

Chaotic evil characters have a complete disregard for others. Each believes he or she is the only being that matters and kills, steals, and betrays others to gain power. Their word is meaningless and their actions destructive. Their worldviews can be so warped that they destroy anything and anyone that doesn't directly contribute to their interests.

By the standards of good and lawful good people, chaotic evil is as abhorrent as evil, perhaps even more so. Chaotic evil monsters such as demons and orcs are at least as much of a threat to civilization and general well-being as evil monsters are. An evil creature and a chaotic evil creature are both opposed to good, but they don't have much respect for each other either and rarely cooperate toward common goals.

UNALIGNED
Just let me go about my business.

If you're unaligned, you don't actively seek to harm others or wish them ill. But you also don't go out of your way to put yourself at risk without some hope for reward. You support law and order when doing so benefits you. You value your own freedom, without worrying too much about protecting the freedom of others.

A few unaligned people, and most unaligned deities, aren't undecided about alignment. Rather, they've chosen not to choose, either because they see the benefits of both good and evil or because they see themselves as above the concerns of morality. The Raven Queen and her devotees fall into the latter camp, believing that moral choices are irrelevant to their mission since death comes to all creatures regardless of alignment.

DEITIES
Deities are the most powerful immortal creatures, residents of the countless dominions that swirl through the Astral Sea. They appear in dreams and visions to their followers and wear countless different faces, and artwork depicting them shows them in a variety of forms. Their true nature is beyond any physical form. Corellon is often depicted as an eladrin, but he is no more an eladrin than he is a fey panther—he is a god, and he transcends the physical laws that bind even angels to their concrete forms.

Some deities are good or lawful good, some are evil or chaotic evil, and some are unaligned. Each deity has a vision of how the world should be, and the agents of the deities seek to bring that vision to life in the world. Except for the chaotic evil gods (Gruumsh and Lolth), all deities are enemies of the demons, which would rather destroy the world than govern it.

Most people revere more than one deity, praying to different gods at different times. Commoners in a small town might visit a temple that has three altars, where they pray to Bahamut for protection, Pelor for fertile crops, and Moradin to aid their skill at crafting. Clerics and paladins more often serve a single deity, championing that god's particular cause in the world. Other adventurers range across the spectrum, from paying lip service to the whole pantheon, to fervently serving a single god, to ignoring the gods entirely as they pursue their own divine ascension.

Many deities have contradictory versions of how the world should work. Even the agents and worshipers of deities who share an alignment can come into conflict.

Avandra
Good

The god of change, Avandra delights in freedom, trade, travel, adventure, and the frontier. Her temples are few in civilized lands, but her wayside shrines

appear throughout the world. Halflings, merchants, and all types of adventurers are drawn to her worship, and many people raise a glass in her honor, viewing her as the god of luck. Her commandments are few:

✦ Luck favors the bold. Take your fate into your own hands, and Avandra smiles upon you.

✦ Strike back against those who would rob you of your freedom and urge others to fight for their own liberty.

✦ Change is inevitable, but it takes the work of the faithful to ensure that change is for the better.

Bahamut
Lawful Good

Called the Platinum Dragon, Bahamut is the god of justice, protection, nobility, and honor. Lawful good paladins often revere him, and metallic dragons worship him as the first of their kind. Monarchs are crowned in his name. He commands his followers thus:

✦ Uphold the highest ideals of honor and justice.

✦ Be constantly vigilant against evil and oppose it on all fronts.

✦ Protect the weak, liberate the oppressed, and defend just order.

Corellon
Unaligned

The god of spring, beauty, and the arts, Corellon is the patron of arcane magic and the fey. He seeded the world with arcane magic and planted the most ancient forests. Artists and musicians worship him, as do those who view their spellcasting as an art, and his shrines can be found throughout the Feywild. He despises Lolth and her priestesses for leading the drow astray. He urges his followers thus:

✦ Cultivate beauty in all that you do, whether you're casting a spell, composing a saga, strumming a lute, or practicing the arts of war.

✦ Seek out lost magic items, forgotten rituals, and ancient works of art. Corellon might have inspired them in the world's first days.

✦ Thwart the followers of Lolth at every opportunity.

Erathis
Unaligned

Erathis is the god of civilization. She is the muse of great invention, founder of cities, and author of laws. Rulers, judges, pioneers, and devoted citizens revere her, and her temples hold prominent places in most of the world's major cities. Her laws are many, but their purpose is straightforward:

✦ Work with others to achieve your goals. Community and order are always stronger than the disjointed efforts of lone individuals.

✦ Tame the wilderness to make it fit for habitation, and defend the light of civilization against the encroaching darkness.

✦ Seek out new ideas, new inventions, new lands to inhabit, new wilderness to conquer. Build machines, build cities, build empires.

Ioun
Unaligned

Ioun is the god of knowledge, skill, and prophecy. Sages, seers, and tacticians revere her, as do all who live by their knowledge and mental power. Corellon is the patron of arcane magic, but Ioun is the patron of its study. Libraries and wizard academies are built in her name. Her commands are also teachings:

✦ Seek the perfection of your mind by bringing reason, perception, and emotion into balance with one another.

✦ Accumulate, preserve, and distribute knowledge in all forms. Pursue education, build libraries, and seek out lost and ancient lore.

✦ Be watchful at all times for the followers of Vecna, who seek to control knowledge and keep secrets. Oppose their schemes, unmask their secrets, and blind them with the light of truth and reason.

KORD

Unaligned

Kord is the storm god and the lord of battle. He revels in strength, battlefield prowess, and thunder. Fighters and athletes revere him. He is a mercurial god, unbridled and wild, who summons storms over land and sea; those who hope for better weather appease him with prayers and spirited toasts. He gives few commands:

✦ Be strong, but do not use your strength for wanton destruction.

✦ Be brave and scorn cowardice in any form.

✦ Prove your might in battle to win glory and renown.

MELORA

Unaligned

Melora is the god of the wilderness and the sea. She is both the wild beast and the peaceful forest, the raging whirlpool and the quiet desert. Rangers, hunters, and elves revere her, and sailors make offerings to her before beginning their voyages. Her strictures are these:

✦ Protect the wild places of the world from destruction and overuse. Oppose the rampant spread of cities and empires.

✦ Hunt aberrant monsters and other abominations of nature.

✦ Do not fear or condemn the savagery of nature. Live in harmony with the wild.

MORADIN

Lawful Good

Moradin is the god of creation and patron of artisans, especially miners and smiths. He carved the mountains from primordial earth and is the guardian and protector of the hearth and the family. Dwarves from all walks of life follow him. He demands these behaviors of his followers:

✦ Meet adversity with stoicism and tenacity.

✦ Demonstrate loyalty to your family, your clan, your leaders, and your people.

✦ Strive to make a mark on the world, a lasting legacy. To make something that lasts is the highest good, whether you are a smith working at a forge or a ruler building a dynasty.

PELOR

Good

God of the sun and summer, Pelor is the keeper of time. He supports those in need and opposes all that is evil. As the lord of agriculture and the bountiful harvest, he is the deity most commonly worshiped by ordinary humans, and his priests are well received wherever they go. Paladins and rangers are found among his worshipers. He directs his followers thus:

✦ Alleviate suffering wherever you find it.

✦ Bring Pelor's light into places of darkness, showing kindness, mercy, and compassion.

✦ Be watchful against evil.

THE RAVEN QUEEN

Unaligned

The name of the god of death is long forgotten, but she is called the Raven Queen. She is the spinner of fate and the patron of winter. She marks the end of each mortal life, and mourners call upon her during funeral rites, in the hope that she will guard the departed from the curse of undeath. She expects her followers to abide by these commandments:

✦ Hold no pity for those who suffer and die, for death is the natural end of life.

✦ Bring down the proud who try to cast off the chains of fate. As the instrument of the Raven Queen, you must punish hubris where you find it.

✦ Watch for the cults of Orcus and stamp them out whenever they arise. The Demon Prince of the Undead seeks to claim the Raven Queen's throne.

SEHANINE

Unaligned

God of the moon and autumn, Sehanine is the patron of trickery and illusions. She has close ties to Corellon and Melora and is a favorite deity among elves and halflings. She is also the god of love, who sends shadows to cloak lovers' trysts. Scouts and thieves ask for her blessing on their work. Her teachings are simple:

✦ Follow your goals and seek your own destiny.

✦ Keep to the shadows, avoiding the blazing light of zealous good and the utter darkness of evil.

✦ Seek new horizons and new experiences, and let nothing tie you down.

LEE MOYER (6)

EVIL AND CHAOTIC EVIL DEITIES

Your character can worship an evil or a chaotic evil deity without being of the same alignment, but that's walking a fine line. The commandments of these deities exhort their followers to pursue evil ends or commit destructive deeds.

The commandments of evil and chaotic evil deities aren't included here. They're described in the *Dungeon Master's Guide*.

Asmodeus is the evil god of the Nine Hells. He is patron of the powerful, god of tyranny and domination, and the commander of devils.

Bane is the evil god of war and conquest. Militaristic nations of humans and goblins serve him and conquer in his name.

Gruumsh is the chaotic evil god of destruction, lord of marauding barbarian hordes. Where Bane commands conquest, Gruumsh exhorts his followers to slaughter and pillage. Orcs are his most fervent followers.

Lolth is the chaotic evil god of shadow, lies, and spiders. Scheming and treachery are her commands, and her clerics are a constant force of disruption in the otherwise stable society of the evil drow.

Tiamat is the evil god of wealth, greed, and envy. She urges her followers to take vengeance for every slight, and she is the patron of chromatic dragons.

Torog is the evil god of the Underdark, patron of jailers and torturers. Common superstition holds that if his name is spoken, the King that Crawls will burrow up from below and drag the hapless speaker underground to an eternity of imprisonment and torture.

Vecna is the evil god of undead, necromancy, and secrets. He rules that which is not meant to be known and that which people wish to keep secret.

Zehir is the evil god of darkness, poison, and assassins. Snakes are his favored creation, and the yuan-ti revere him above all other gods.

PERSONALITY

DUNGEONS & DRAGONS is a game of heroic extremes, populated by legendary heroes and unrepentant villains. Your character needs only a few personality traits that you can use as roleplaying touchstones, key traits that you can focus on and that are fun to play. A complex background and extensive motivations aren't necessary, although you can flesh out your character's personality as much as you like.

A typical D&D adventure offers many opportunities for your character's personality to shine. Those roleplaying opportunities usually arise in three kinds of situations: social interactions, decision points, and dire straits. The following sections pose questions to help you choose personality traits for your character, which you can write on your character sheet. Select one personality trait for each kind of situation. If you already have a personality in mind for your character, you can skip this section; the information here is for inspiration only.

SOCIAL INTERACTIONS

When you communicate with a nonplayer character outside combat and try to influence that individual, that's a social interaction. You might try to persuade a guardian monster to let you pass, negotiate with a merchant lord to increase the pay offered for a dangerous mission, or question a surly centaur about the goblins that ambush travelers in the forest. The DM plays the part of any NPC you talk to, while you and the other players decide what your characters say, even speaking in character if you like.

How do others perceive you in social interactions?

Cheerful	Talkative	Reserved
Charming	Witty	Relaxed

How optimistic are you?

Enthusiastic	Hopeful	Fatalistic
Grim	Self-assured	Brooding

How trusting are you?

Gullible	Open-minded	Skeptical
Suspicious	Naive	Trusting

DECISION POINTS

When you face tough choices in an adventure, your character's personality can influence the decisions you make. Do you try to sneak past the dragon's cave, approach openly to parley, or storm in with blades drawn and spells blazing? Which of the six stone doors in the entry hall do you open first? Do you save the captives from the trap or pursue the slavers? When your group tries to decide what to do next, how do you approach such conversations?

How assertive are you at a decision point?

Humble	Adaptable	Commanding
Timid	Easygoing	Impatient

How conscientious are you about following rules?

Scrupulous	Pragmatic	Dutiful
Honest	Flexible	Wild

How empathetic are you?

Kind	Stern	Thoughtful
Protective	Hard-hearted	Oblivious

DIRE STRAITS

Some of the most memorable demonstrations of a character's personality appear in dire straits. A character retorts to a villain's threat with a trademark one-liner, shouts a famous battle cry, leaps into harm's way to protect others, or turns and flees in the face of overwhelming odds. Every battle, hazard, or other dire situation offers opportunities for roleplaying, especially if things go awry. When your character lands in a dire situation, how does he or she usually react? Do you follow a code? Do you follow your heart? Do you look out for yourself or others?

How courageous are you in dire straits?

Brave	Competitive	Steady
Cautious	Reckless	Fierce

How do you feel when faced by setbacks?

Stoic	Driven	Happy-go-lucky
Vengeful	Bold	Impassioned

How are your nerves?

Calm	Skittish	Restless
Impulsive	Patient	Unshakable

MANNERISMS

The easiest way to bring your character to life at the gaming table is to adopt distinctive mannerisms—particular patterns of speech or other behaviors that you can take on at the table to convey how your character looks, sounds, and acts. If you are naturally inclined to spin dice or shuffle cards while the game takes place, you might consider incorporating that behavior into your character. Perhaps your character carries a deck of cards that he shuffles when he's bored or nervous, or maybe she crouches to the ground and creates little sculptures out of rubble while she's waiting for her companions to decide where to go next. By contrast, another character might vociferously participate in those deliberations, frequently resorting to exclamations such as "By Kord's right arm!" to emphasize his opinion.

Speech patterns can be even more distinctive. A dwarf who never enters battle without shouting, "The dwarves are upon you!" injects a dose of fun roleplaying just as the die rolling is getting most intense. A wizard who never speaks except in haiku might be carrying the idea of distinctive speech to an extreme, but if you can pull it off (try writing a page full of standbys to cover common situations before the game begins), everyone at the table will remember your character for years!

Another good way to think about speech and other mannerisms is to create specific prompts your character says or does when using certain powers. For example, your paladin might yell, "Feel the might of Bahamut!" every time she uses the *righteous smite* power, and murmur, "Bahamut's healing breath wash over you," when she uses *lay on hands*.

APPEARANCE

Is your character tall, short, or in between? Solid and muscular, or lean and wiry? Male or female? Old or young? These decisions have no real impact on the game, but they might affect the way that nonplayer characters—and even the other players—think about your character.

Each race description in Chapter 3 gives the average height and weight for a character of that race. You can decide for your character to be above or below average.

You should also decide what color skin, hair, and eyes your character has. Most races approximate the human range of coloration, but some races also have unusual coloration, such as the stony gray skin of dwarves or the violet eyes of some elves.

Finally, consider features that distinguish your character from others. Some of these might be inborn, such as an unusual eye color or skin color, while others might be habits of fashion or the scars of past injuries. Jewelry, clothing, tattoos and birthmarks, hairstyles and colors, and posture—one unusual feature from among those choices can make your character stand out in the other players' minds.

BACKGROUND

Your character's background often stays there—in the background. What's most important about your character is what you do in the course of your adventures, not what happened to you in the past. Even so, thinking about your birthplace, family, and upbringing can help you decide how to play your character.

These questions can help you start thinking about your background.

✦ Why did you decide to be an adventurer?

✦ How did you acquire your class? If you're a fighter, for example, you might have been in a militia, come from a family of soldiers, or trained in a martial school, or you might be a self-taught warrior.

✦ How did you acquire your starting equipment? Did you assemble it piece by piece over time? Was it a gift from a parent or a mentor? Do any of your personal items have special significance?

✦ What's the worst event of your life?

✦ What's the best thing that's ever happened to you?

✦ Do you stay in contact with your family? What do your relatives think of you and your chosen career?

Dwarven script

LANGUAGES AND SCRIPTS

Ten languages form the basis of every dialect spoken throughout the D&D game's many worlds. These languages are transcribed in different scripts, most of which are alphabets, from the flowing characters of the Rellanic alphabet to the runes of the Davek alphabet. The Supernal script is a system of hieroglyphics.

Depending on your character's race, you start off knowing two or three languages and the script associated with each. You can learn additional languages by taking the Linguist feat (page 198).

You can't choose the Abyssal or Supernal languages as a 1st-level character.

Language	Spoken by . . .	Script
Common	Humans, halflings, tieflings	Common
Deep Speech	Mind flayers, githyanki, kuo-toas	Rellanic
Draconic	Dragons, dragonborn, kobolds	Iokharic
Dwarven	Dwarves, azer	Davek
Elven	Elves, eladrin, fomorians	Rellanic
Giant	Giants, orcs, ogres	Davek
Goblin	Goblins, hobgoblins, bugbears	Common
Primordial	Efreets, archons, elementals	Barazhad
Supernal	Angels, devils, gods	Supernal
Abyssal	Demons, gnolls, sahuagin	Barazhad

The *Dungeon Master's Guide* has more information about languages and scripts.

MAKING CHECKS

Before you go any further, it's important to understand the use of the core mechanic and how it applies to every aspect of the game.

Every power, skill, and special feature in the game is keyed to one of the six ability scores. You resolve actions by making different kinds of **checks**, all of which use the same core mechanic: roll a d20, add any modifiers, and announce the result. Your Dungeon Master then compares your **check result** against a target number, the **Difficulty Class (DC)** of the test, task, or attack that you're attempting. Most difficulty class numbers are set for the Dungeon Master; for example, an ogre savage has an Armor Class of 19, and climbing a typical dungeon wall has a DC of 15.

Other times, your Dungeon Master estimates the DC of a task that isn't specifically covered by the rules.

The D&D game uses three basic kinds of checks, which are described further below: attack rolls, skill checks, and ability checks.

If you try to hit a monster with a mace, you're making a Strength attack against the monster's AC; if you try to blast a monster with a *fireball* spell, it's an Intelligence attack against Reflex defense; if you try to balance on a tightrope, it's an Acrobatics check against a DC set by the DM; if you try to bash down a door, it's a Strength check against a set DC that depends on the nature of the door. The description of each power and skill tells you what ability you base its check on. Occasionally, you make a check that is compared against someone else's check result. Doing this is called making an **opposed check**.

A **modifier** is any number that adds to or subtracts from a die roll. The most commonly used modifiers are based on your ability scores. A **bonus** refers to positive values. If a feat adds your Dexterity modifier to damage, it won't do anything if your Dexterity modifier isn't positive. A **penalty** is the opposite: It's always negative.

Part of creating a character is figuring out your normal check modifiers for common tasks such as making attacks or using skills. Most checks in the game add additional modifiers, including the following:

+ Your bonus from your weapon proficiency if you're making an attack
+ Your skill training bonus if you're using a skill
+ Special bonuses for feats you've chosen or magic items you're using
+ Bonuses that apply to the circumstances of the check (charge attacks or combat advantage, for example)
+ Penalties that apply to the circumstances (your target has cover, you're attacking while prone, and so on)

Your modifiers reflect everything about you that is relevant to the task at hand: your training, competence, and native ability. The d20 roll represents luck, fate, fortune, and unpredictable opportunities or sudden distractions. A battle is full of frantic action, and the random die roll represents that mayhem.

Elven script

ATTACK ROLLS

Perhaps the most frequent die rolls you make in a D&D game are **attack rolls**. All attack rolls are described in this way:

[Ability] vs. [Defense]

For example, a wizard's *fireball* spell is an Intelligence attack against the target's Reflex defense (written as Intelligence vs. Reflex). A fighter's longsword attack is a Strength attack against Armor Class (or AC). The ability score and the defense involved depend on the attack you're using. If the check result is higher than or equal to your opponent's defense, you hit and (usually) deal damage.

The total of all the modifiers you add to an attack roll is your **base attack bonus**. You can find much more about attack rolls in Chapter 9.

Example: Kiera, an 8th-level elf ranger with a Dexterity of 17 and a +1 *magic bow*, shoots her bow at an ogre savage. Her base attack bonus is +10, which includes +4 for one-half her level, her +3 Dexterity modifier, her +2 bonus for being proficient with the bow, and the bow's +1 enhancement bonus. To see if she hits the ogre, she rolls 1d20 and adds 10. If she rolls an 11, her check result is 21. Since an ogre savage has an Armor Class of 19, she has scored a hit!

ATTACK

To make an attack, roll 1d20 and add the following:

✦ One-half your level
✦ The relevant ability score modifier
✦ All other modifiers (see page 279)

The total is your attack result.

SKILL CHECKS

The knowledge and talents your character has learned are represented by **skill checks**. When you use a skill, you hope for a result higher than the DC of the task.

For example, a cleric's Heal check is a skill check against a specific DC. A rogue's Stealth check is a skill check against a DC equal to the target's Perception check result (an opposed check). If the check result is higher than or equal to the DC, you succeed.

The total of the modifiers you add to a skill check is your **base skill check bonus**. You can find much more about skill checks in Chapter 5.

Example: Alek, a 6th-level human wizard with an Intelligence of 18, is trying to identify a strange creature by using the Arcana skill. His base skill check bonus is +12, which includes +3 for one-half his level, his +4 Intelligence modifier, and a +5 bonus for being trained in Arcana. To see if he identifies the creature, he rolls 1d20 and adds 12. If he rolls a 7, his check result is 19. Since the DC to identify the creature is 15, he realizes it's a quickling.

SKILL CHECK

To make a skill check, roll 1d20 and add the following:

✦ One-half your level
✦ The relevant ability score modifier
✦ All other modifiers (see page 178)

The total is your skill check result.

ABILITY CHECKS

Sometimes you're not making an attack or a skill check, but trying to accomplish a task that doesn't fall into either category. You make an ability check. Ability checks give the DM a way to adjudicate actions when an attack or a skill check isn't appropriate.

ABILITY CHECK

To make an ability check, roll 1d20 and add the following:

✦ One-half your level
✦ The relevant ability score modifier
✦ All other modifiers

The total is your ability check result.

Example: A Strength check to break down a door is 1d20 + one-half your level + your Strength ability modifier. A 4th-level character with a 16 Strength makes a Strength check by rolling 1d20 + 5 (+2 for level, +3 Strength modifier). If he rolls a 16, his result for that Strength check is 21.

ACTIONS AND COMBAT

Combat encounters are played out in rounds. Each round represents about 6 seconds in the game world, regardless of how long it takes to play out the round. Combat starts with initiative checks to determine the order of play for the entire battle. There are four types of actions you can take in any round: standard actions, move actions, minor actions, and free actions. See Chapter 9 for complete rules on combat.

GAINING LEVELS

As you adventure and gain experience, you advance in level. Gaining a level (also called leveling or leveling up) is one of the biggest rewards you'll receive for your success in the game—your character improves in several ways every time you go up a level.

Each time you overcome a noncombat encounter, defeat monsters, or complete a quest, your Dungeon Master awards you **experience points (XP)**. When you earn enough XP, you reach a new level. For more about rewards, see Chapter 8.

The Character Advancement table shows the total XP you need to reach each level and the abilities and other benefits you gain with each new level.

STEP BY STEP

Refer to the Character Advancement table and follow these steps when your character gains a level.

At most levels, you gain access to a new power or a new feat. Refer to your class description in Chapter 4 for the full listing of the powers available to you, and see Chapter 6 for the complete list of feats. The game assumes that you've been learning these powers in your spare time, studying musty tomes or practicing a complicated series of maneuvers. In game terms, though, as soon as you gain a level, you can immediately use your new powers and feats.

1. ABILITY SCORES

Check the Ability Scores column to see if you can improve your ability scores. If you can, choose the abilities you want to increase. At 4th, 8th, 14th, 18th, 24th, and 28th levels, you increase two ability scores by 1 (you can't take both increases in the same score). At 11th and 21st level, you increase each of your ability scores by 1.

If you increase an ability score to an even number, your ability modifier goes up, and that change affects powers, skills, and defenses that rely on that ability score. Make a note of that fact, but don't change any numbers just yet.

2. LEVEL MODIFIER

If your new level is an even number, everything that's based on one-half your level becomes better—your attacks, defenses, initiative, skill checks, and ability checks. In combination with any increased ability modifiers, you now have the information you need to increase those numbers. Go through your character sheet and note those increases.

3. PARAGON AND EPIC

If you just reached 11th or 21st level, you have some exciting decisions to make—you can choose a paragon path or epic destiny, both of which are described in Chapter 4. Make that choice, and make a note of the new power or feature you gain.

4. HIT POINTS

Check your class description in Chapter 4 to see how many hit points you gain with your new level. Add those to your total. If you increased your Constitution score, increase your hit points by 1 (as if you had your new Constitution score when you were 1st level). Also, if you increased your Constitution score to an even number, increase your number of healing surges by one.

5. CLASS FEATURES

When you check your class description for hit points, also check your class features to see if any of your powers or other abilities improve with level. For example, the rogue's Sneak Attack class feature improves at 11th and 21st levels.

6. FEATS

Check the Powers and Features column of the Character Advancement table to see if you learn any new feats. You learn one feat at 1st level, one new feat at every even-numbered level after that, plus one new feat at 11th and 21st levels. If you increased an ability score, you might meet the prerequisites for some feats that you didn't qualify for before. (The Feats Known column on the Character Advancement table enables you to double-check at every level to be sure you have the number of feats you're entitled to.)

7. POWERS

At most levels, you gain access to a new power. You can take each power only once (you can't choose the same power multiple times). Refer to your class description in Chapter 4 for a full listing of the powers available to you.

At-Will Attack Powers: At 1st level, choose two at-will attack powers from the list in your class description. You don't automatically learn new at-will powers as you advance, but as you gain levels you can choose to retrain (see "Retraining," below) and replace an at-will power you know with a new one.

Encounter Attack Powers: At 1st level, select one power from the list of 1st-level encounter attack powers in your class description. At 3rd and 7th levels, you learn a new encounter power of your level or lower.

At 11th level, you learn a new encounter power when you choose a paragon path. The path you choose determines the power you gain.

At 13th, 17th, 23rd, and 27th levels, you can replace any encounter attack power you know from your class with a new one of your new level (or an encounter attack power of a lower level, if you choose).

Daily Attack Powers: At 1st level, choose one power from the list of 1st-level daily attack powers in your class description. You learn a new daily attack power of your level or lower at 5th level and again at 9th level.

At 20th level, you learn a new daily power, determined by your paragon path.

At 15th, 19th, 25th, and 29th levels, you can replace any daily attack power you know from your class with a new daily attack power of your new level (or a daily attack power of a lower level, if you choose).

Utility Powers: At 2nd level, choose one utility power from the list of 2nd-level utility powers in your class description.

You learn a new power chosen from the list of utility powers of your level (or a utility power of a lower level, if you choose) at 6th level and again at 10th, 16th, and 22nd levels.

At 12th level, you learn a new utility power determined by your paragon path. At 26th level, you learn a new utility power from your epic destiny.

Retraining

Sometimes you make decisions when you create or advance your character that you later regret. Perhaps a power you chose isn't working with your character concept, or a feat never comes into play the way you anticipated. Fortunately in such a case, level advancement isn't only a time to learn new powers—it's also an opportunity to change some of those decisions.

Every time you gain a level, you can retrain your character: change one feat, power, or skill selection you made previously. You can make only one change at each level. When your class table tells you to replace a power you know with a different power of a higher level, that doesn't count as retraining—you can still retrain an additional feat, power, or skill as normal.

Feat: You can replace a feat with another feat. You must meet the prerequisites of the new feat. You can't replace a feat if it's a prerequisite for any other attribute you have (another feat or a paragon path, for example), or if the feat is a feature of your class, path, or destiny (as the Ritual Caster feat is a class feature for wizards). You can replace heroic tier feats (see page 193) with higher-tier feats, but only one at a time, once per level you gain. For instance, at 11th level, you gain one feat and you can also retrain one of your heroic tier feats, gaining a paragon tier feat in its place. At 12th level you can do the same, so you can potentially have four paragon tier feats at 12th level. (You might find that many of your heroic tier feats remain worthwhile well into higher levels, however.)

Power: You can replace a power with another power of the same type (at-will attack power, encounter attack power, daily attack power, or utility power), of the same level or lower, and from the same class—a 5th-level attack power for another 5th-level attack

power, for example, or a 22nd-level utility power for a different 22nd-level utility power.

You can't replace a power that's a class feature (such as a cleric's *healing word* or a warlock's *eldritch blast*) or a power gained from a paragon path or epic destiny.

Skill: You can replace a trained skill with another trained skill from your class list. You can't replace a skill if it's required for a feat, a power, or any other attribute you have, or if it's predetermined by your class (such as Arcana for wizards or Religion for clerics). If your class requires you to choose one of two skills (such as the ranger, which requires either Dungeoneering or Nature), you can alter your choice by retraining, but you're limited to replacing one skill with the other.

THE THREE TIERS

The thirty levels of your career are divided into three tiers: the heroic tier (1st level through 10th level), the paragon tier (11th level through 20th level), and the epic tier (21st level through 30th level). When you leave one tier and cross the threshold into a new one, you experience some major increases in power. At the same time, the threats you face in a higher tier are much more lethal.

In the **heroic** tier, your character is already a hero, set apart from the common people by your natural talents, learned skills, and some hint of a greater destiny that lies before you. Your capabilities are largely determined by your choice of character class and to a lesser extent by your race. You move around on foot or on a relatively mundane mount such as a horse. In combat, you might make mighty leaps or incredible climbs, but you're still basically earthbound. The fate of a village might hang on the success or failure of your adventures, to say nothing of the risk to your own life. You navigate dangerous terrain and explore haunted crypts, where you can expect to fight sneaky goblins, savage orcs, ferocious wolves, giant spiders, evil cultists, and bloodthirsty ghouls. If you face a dragon, it is a young one still searching for a lair, one that has not yet found its place in the world. One, in other words, that is much like you.

In the **paragon** tier, your character is a shining example of heroism, set well apart from the masses. Your class still largely determines your capabilities. In addition, you gain extra abilities in your specialty: your paragon path. When you reach 11th level, you choose a path of specialization, a course that defines who you are within a certain narrow range of criteria. You are able to travel more quickly from place to place, perhaps on a hippogriff mount or using a spell to grant your party flight. In combat, you might fly or even teleport short distances. Death becomes a surmountable obstacle, and the fate of a nation or even the world might hang in the balance as you undertake momentous quests. You

CHARACTER ADVANCEMENT

Total XP	Level	Ability Scores	Powers and Features	Feats Known	Total Powers Known (At-will/Encounter/ Daily/Utility)
0	1st	see race	class features; racial traits; gain 1 feat; train starting skills; gain 2 at-will attack powers; gain 1 encounter attack power; gain 1 daily attack power	1†	2/1/1/0
1,000	2nd	–	gain 1 utility power; gain 1 feat	2	2/1/1/1
2,250	3rd	–	gain 1 encounter attack power	2	2/2/1/1
3,750	4th	+1 to two	gain 1 feat	3	2/2/1/1
5,500	5th	–	gain 1 daily attack power	3	2/2/2/1
7,500	6th	–	gain 1 utility power, gain 1 feat	4	2/2/2/2
10,000	7th	–	gain 1 encounter attack power	4	2/3/2/2
13,000	8th	+1 to two	gain 1 feat	5	2/3/2/2
16,500	9th	–	gain 1 daily attack power	5	2/3/3/2
20,500	10th	–	gain 1 utility power, gain 1 feat	6	2/3/3/3
26,000	11th	+1 to all	paragon path features; gain 1 paragon path encounter attack power; gain 1 feat	7	2/4/3/3
32,000	12th	–	gain 1 paragon path utility power; gain 1 feat	8	2/4/3/4
39,000	13th	–	replace 1 encounter attack power	8	2/4*/3/4
47,000	14th	+1 to two	gain 1 feat	9	2/4/3/4
57,000	15th	–	replace 1 daily attack power	9	2/4/3*/4
69,000	16th	–	paragon path feature; gain 1 utility power; gain 1 feat	10	2/4/3/5
83,000	17th	–	replace 1 encounter attack power	10	2/4*/3/5
99,000	18th	+1 to two	gain 1 feat	11	2/4/3/5
119,000	19th	–	replace 1 daily attack power	11	2/4/3*/5
143,000	20th	–	gain 1 paragon path daily attack power; gain 1 feat	12	2/4/4/5
175,000	21st	+1 to all	epic destiny feature; gain 1 feat	13	2/4/4/5
210,000	22nd	–	gain 1 utility power, gain 1 feat	14	2/4/4/6
255,000	23rd	–	replace 1 encounter attack power	14	2/4*/4/6
310,000	24th	+1 to two	epic destiny feature; gain 1 feat	15	2/4/4/6
375,000	25th	–	replace 1 daily attack power	15	2/4/4*/6
450,000	26th	–	gain 1 epic destiny utility power; gain 1 feat	16	2/4/4/7
550,000	27th	–	replace 1 encounter attack power	16	2/4*/4/7
675,000	28th	+1 to two	gain 1 feat	17	2/4/4/7
825,000	29th	–	replace 1 daily attack power	17	2/4/4*/7
1,000,000	30th	–	epic destiny feature; gain 1 feat	18	2/4/4/7

NOTE: In addition to the benefits summarized on this table, you always get more hit points when you gain a level. See your class description for details.

* At these levels you replace a known power with a new power of your new level.

† Humans gain one additional feat at 1st level. Some classes grant additional feats as well.

navigate uncharted regions and explore long-forgotten dungeons, where you can expect to fight sneaky drow, savage giants, ferocious hydras, fearless golems, rampaging barbarian hordes, bloodthirsty vampires, and crafty mind flayers. When you face a dragon, it is a powerful adult who has established a lair and found its place in the world. Again, much like you.

In the **epic** tier, your character's capabilities are truly superheroic. Your class still determines most of your abilities, but your most dramatic powers come from your choice of epic destiny, which you select at 21st level. You travel across nations in the blink of an eye, and your whole party might take to the air in combat. The success or failure of your adventures has far-reaching consequences, possibly determining the fate of millions in this world and even planes beyond. You navigate otherworldly realms and explore never-before-seen caverns of wonder, where you can expect to battle savage pit fiends, the ferocious tarrasque, sinister sorrowsworn deathlords, bloodthirsty lich archmages, and even demon princes. The dragons you encounter are ancient wyrms of truly earthshaking power, whose sleep troubles kingdoms and whose waking threatens the world.

CHARACTER SHEET

You can record information about your character any way you like, but most players prefer to use a character sheet. You can find a blank character sheet at the end of this book.

Reproduced here, at half size, is an example of a typical character sheet. The various sections are keyed with numbers that correspond to the following information.

1. **Character Name:** Choose a name for your character and write it here.

2. **Level/Class/Paragon Path/Epic Destiny:** Record your level and character class. If you're 11th level, you also choose a paragon path associated with your class (see the last few pages of each class description). If you're 21st level, you add an epic destiny.

3. **Total XP:** Keep track of your accumulated experience points here.

4. **Race and Size:** Choose your character race (Chapter 3) and record your size. Most characters are Medium size; halflings are Small.

5. **Age, Gender, Height, Weight:** These details are up to you. Most adventurers begin as young adults—say, 18 to 25 for humans.

6. **Alignment, Deity, Adventuring Company or Other Affiliations:** Record your alignment, your character's patron deity (if you choose one), and the name of the group you belong to (if any).

7. **Initiative:** Determine your initiative modifier and record it here. Note any conditional bonuses in the space provided. See page 267.

8. **Defenses:** Record your Armor Class, Fortitude Defense, Reflex Defense, and Will Defense here. These defenses are equal to 10 + one-half your level + the appropriate ability modifier. You also add the bonus from the armor you wear to your Armor Class. If you wear light armor, you add your Dexterity or Intelligence modifier to your Armor Class as well. Note any conditional bonuses in the space provided. See page 275.

9. **Speed:** Determine your speed and record it here. If you have special movement, record it here.

10. **Ability Scores:** Record your ability scores, ability modifiers, and the total of your ability modifier + one-half your level for each ability here (see "Ability Scores," page 16). If you're 1st level, one-half your level is +0.

11. **Senses:** Determine your passive Perception and passive Insight modifiers and record them here. See page 179. Even if you don't select the Perception and Insight skills, you still have to make these checks often. If your race provides a special sense, record it here.

12. **Attack Workspace:** Use this space to determine your attack bonuses with your most frequent attacks.

13. **Hit Points:** Your hit points are determined by your class and level; see the class descriptions in Chapter 4. Add your Constitution score to your hit points. Your bloodied value is one-half your maximum hit points, and your healing surge value is one-quarter of your maximum hit points. Record the number of healing surges you have per day. Your character class

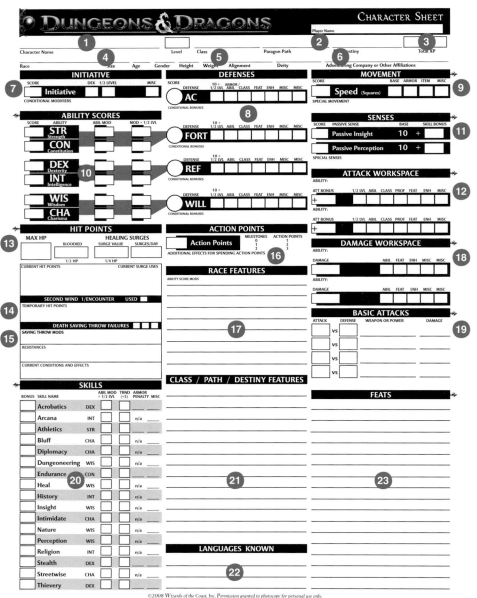

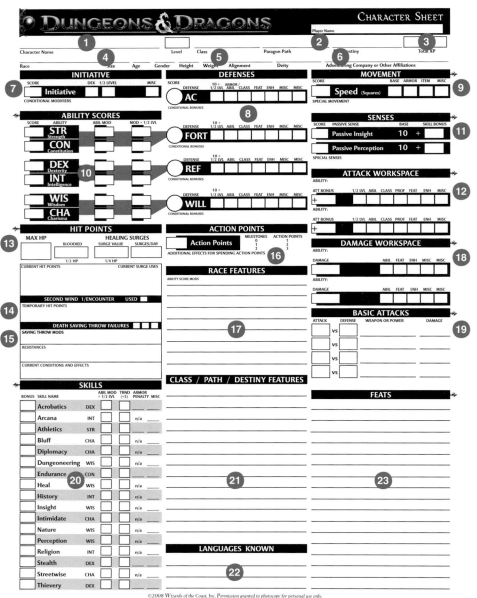©2008 Wizards of the Coast, Inc. Permission granted to photocopy for personal use only.

determines the number of healing surges you get; you add your Constitution modifier to this number. See your class description in Chapter 4. See Chapter 9 for more about hit points and healing.

14. **Second Wind:** Once per encounter, you can spend a healing surge as a standard action. See page 291. Note any temporary hit points in the space provided.

15. **Death Saving Throw Failures:** When you are dying, you make saving throws each round. Mark off each failure; when you have failed three death saving throws, you die. See page 295. Use the boxes to record any saving throw modifiers, resistances to attacks or damage, or current conditions or effects you have.

16. **Action Points:** Note any action points you've earned here. See page 286.

17. **Race Features:** Record the special features and advantages your race provides you. Races are described in Chapter 3.

18. **Damage Workspace:** Use this space to determine your damage with your most frequent attacks.

19. **Basic Attacks:** Record your bonus to attack rolls and the damage you deal when you make a basic attack with the melee weapon and the ranged weapon you normally carry. Use a basic attack when you make an opportunity attack or when a power grants you a basic attack. See page 287.

20. **Skills:** Check off the skills you're trained in and determine your base skill check bonus for each one. You have a +5 bonus to checks using skills you're trained in. See Chapter 5.

21. **Class/Path/Destiny Features:** Record the special features and advantages your class, paragon path, and epic destiny provide you. Classes, paragon paths, and epic destinies are described in Chapter 4.

22. **Languages Known:** Record the languages you know from your race and any you might have learned through a feat here.

23. **Feats:** List the feats you've selected, and note their effects. Feats are described in Chapter 6.

24. **Power Index:** Use this portion of the sheet to list the powers you know, organized by whether they're attack powers or utility powers. (You can also copy your powers onto index cards, if you prefer to keep track of them that way.) Attack powers are divided between at-will, encounter, and daily powers. Make a note of the type of action you have to spend to use the power (free, minor, move, or standard), which ability it's based on, and which defense it attacks. Powers are described in Chapter 4.

25. **Magic Item Index:** Use this portion of your character sheet to list your magic items and any powers they have. (You can also copy your items onto index cards, if you prefer to keep track of them that way.) Magic items are described in Chapter 7.

26. **Character Illustration:** Use this space for a picture of your character, if you wish.

27. **Character Details, Session and Campaign Notes:** Record any notes about the topics in the space provided.

28. **Other Equipment:** List any other equipment you're carrying here.

29. **Rituals:** List the rituals you know here.

30. **Coins and Other Wealth:** Keep track of your hard-earned gains here.

POWER INDEX
List your powers below.
Check the box when the power is used.
Clear the box when the power renews.

AT-WILL POWERS

ENCOUNTER POWERS

DAILY POWERS

UTILITY POWERS

OTHER EQUIPMENT

COINS AND OTHER WEALTH

MAGIC ITEM INDEX
List your powers below.
Check the box when the power is used.
Clear the box when the power renews.

MAGIC ITEMS

WEAPON
WEAPON
WEAPON
WEAPON
ARMOR
ARMS
FEET
HANDS
HEAD
NECK
RING
RING
WAIST

Daily Item Powers Per Day

Heroic (1-10)	☐	Milestone ☐/☐/☐/☐
Paragon (11-20)	☐☐	Milestone ☐/☐/☐/☐
Epic (21-30)	☐☐☐	Milestone ☐/☐/☐/☐

RITUALS

PERSONALITY TRAITS

MANNERISMS AND APPEARANCE

CHARACTER BACKGROUND

COMPANIONS AND ALLIES
NAME   NOTES

SESSION AND CAMPAIGN NOTES

CHAPTER 3

CHARACTER RACES

A VARIETY of cultures and societies populate the world of the DUNGEONS & DRAGONS game, some made up of humans but others made up of fantastic races such as elves, dwarves, and tieflings. Adventurers and heroes can arise from these various peoples. Your choice of character race provides you with a basic set of advantages and special abilities. If you're a fighter, are you a stubborn dwarf monster-slayer, a graceful elf blademaster, or a fierce dragonborn gladiator? If you're a wizard, are you a brave human spell-for-hire or a devious tiefling conjurer? Your character race not only affects your ability scores and powers but also provides the first cues for building your character's story.

RACIAL TRAITS

Each character race offers the following types of benefits.

Ability Scores: Your character race gives you a bonus to a particular ability score or two. Keep these bonuses in mind when you assign your ability scores (see "Ability Scores," page 16).

Speed: Your speed is the number of squares you can normally move when you walk (see "Movement and Position," page 282).

Vision: Most races, including humans, have normal vision. Some races have low-light vision; they see better in darkness than humans do (see "Vision and Light," page 262).

Languages: You start off knowing how to speak, read, and write a few languages. All races speak Common, the language passed on by the last human empire, and some races let you choose a language (see "Languages and Scripts," page 24).

Other Racial Traits: Other traits include bonuses to your skills, weapon training, and a handful of other traits that give you capabilities or bonuses that members of other races don't have.

Racial Power: Several races give you access to a racial power, which is an extra power you gain at 1st level in addition to the powers your class gives you. See page 54 for an explanation of how to read a power description.

MATT CAVOTTA

DRAGONBORN

*Proud, honorable warriors,
born from the blood of an ancient dragon god*

RACIAL TRAITS

Average Height: 6′ 2″–6′ 8″
Average Weight: 220–320 lb.

Ability Scores: +2 Strength, +2 Charisma
Size: Medium
Speed: 6 squares
Vision: Normal

Languages: Common, Draconic
Skill Bonuses: +2 History, +2 Intimidate
Dragonborn Fury: When you're bloodied, you gain a +1 racial bonus to attack rolls.
Draconic Heritage: Your healing surge value is equal to one-quarter of your maximum hit points + your Constitution modifier.
Dragon Breath: You can use *dragon breath* as an encounter power.

Dragon Breath	Dragonborn Racial Power

As you open your mouth with a roar, the deadly power of your draconic kin blasts forth to engulf your foes.

Encounter ✦ Acid, Cold, Fire, Lightning, or **Poison**
Minor Action   Close blast 3
Targets: All creatures in area
Attack: Strength + 2 vs. Reflex, Constitution + 2 vs. Reflex, or Dexterity + 2 vs. Reflex
Hit: 1d6 + Constitution modifier damage.
Increase to +4 bonus and 2d6 + Constitution modifier damage at 11th level, and to +6 bonus and 3d6 + Constitution modifier damage at 21st level.
Special: When you create your character, choose Strength, Constitution, or Dexterity as the ability score you use when making attack rolls with this power. You also choose the power's damage type: acid, cold, fire, lightning, or poison. These two choices remain throughout your character's life and do not change the power's other effects.

Born to fight, dragonborn are a race of wandering mercenaries, soldiers, and adventurers. Long ago, their empire contended for worldwide dominion, but now only a few rootless clans of these honorable warriors remain to pass on their legends of ancient glory.

Play a dragonborn if you want . . .

✦ to look like a dragon.

✦ to be the proud heir of an ancient, fallen empire.

✦ to breathe acid, cold, fire, lightning, or poison.

✦ to be a member of a race that favors the warlord, fighter, and paladin classes.

WILLIAM O'CONNOR

Physical Qualities

Dragonborn resemble humanoid dragons. They're covered in scaly hide, but they don't have tails. They are tall and strongly built, often standing close to 6½ feet in height and weighing 300 pounds or more. Their hands and feet are strong, talonlike claws with three fingers and a thumb on each hand. A dragonborn's head features a blunt snout, a strong brow, and distinctive frills at the cheek and ear. Behind the brow, a crest of hornlike scales of various lengths resembles thick, ropy hair. Their eyes are shades of red or gold.

A typical dragonborn's scales can be scarlet, gold, rust, ocher, bronze, or brown. Rarely do an individual's scales match the hue of a chromatic or metallic dragon, and scale color gives no indication of the type of breath weapon a dragonborn uses. Most dragonborn have very fine scales over most of their body, giving their skin a leathery texture, with regions of larger scales on the forearms, lower legs and feet, shoulders, and thighs.

Young dragonborn grow faster than human children do. They walk hours after hatching, reach the size and development of a 10-year-old human child by the age of 3 and reach adulthood by 15. They live about as long as humans do.

Playing a Dragonborn

To a dragonborn, honor is more important than life itself. First and foremost, honor is tied to battlefield conduct. Adversaries should be treated with courtesy and respect, even if they are bitter enemies. Caution and discretion are key to a warrior's survival, but fear is a disease and cowardice is a moral failing.

The drive to behave honorably extends into the rest of a dragonborn's life: Breaking an oath is the height of dishonor, and attention to honesty extends to every word. A commitment made must be carried out. Ultimately, a dragonborn takes responsibility for his or her actions and their consequences.

A continual drive for self-improvement reveals an additional aspect of dragonborn honor. Dragonborn value skill and excellence in all endeavors. They hate to fail, and they push themselves to extreme efforts before they give up on something. A dragonborn holds mastery of a particular skill as a lifetime goal. Members of other races who share the same commitment find it easy to earn the respect of a dragonborn.

The dragonborn dedication to honor and excellence sometimes leads others to view dragonborn as arrogant and proud. Most dragonborn share a great pride in their race's past and present accomplishments, but they are also quick to admire the accomplishments of others. Even though the tiefling empire of Bael Turath was the enemy of the ancient dragonborn empire of Arkhosia, dragonborn recognize tieflings as worthy companions or opponents, admiring their strength and tenacity as friends or enemies.

Dragonborn seek adventure for the chance to prove their worth, win renown, and perhaps become champions about whom stories will be told for generations. To win everlasting glory through mighty deeds, daring exploits, and supreme skill—that is the dragonborn dream.

Dragonborn Characteristics: Driven, honor-bound, noble, perfectionist, proud, reliable, reserved, rooted in ancient history

Male Names: Arjhan, Balasar, Bharash, Donaar, Ghesh, Heskan, Kriv, Medrash, Nadarr, Patrin, Rhogar, Shamash, Shedinn, Torinn

Female Names: Akra, Biri, Daar, Harann, Kava, Korinn, Mishann, Nala, Perra, Raiann, Sora, Surina, Thava

Dragonborn Adventurers

Three sample dragonborn adventurers are described below.

Bharash is a dragonborn warlord who leads a group of adventurers in search of riches and glory. Inspired by tales of the ancient heroes of Arkhosia, he seeks his destiny in battle. He dreams of someday leading a mighty army against an orc horde or a hobgoblin host, but he is content in the meantime to coordinate strikes against the lesser forces of evil he encounters in dungeons and ruins. He reveres Bahamut as the god of honor.

Harann is a fighter dedicated to the mastery of her chosen weapon, the bastard sword. She rises early every morning to practice combat maneuvers and constantly strives to master new techniques. Excellence with her weapon is symbolic to her; it represents excellence of character, the perfection of her spirit. When she has achieved perfect mastery of the bastard sword, she believes she will be perfect herself.

Donaar is a paladin of Erathis, the god of cities and civilization. He believes that the dragonborn race is destined to rise from the ashes of its ancient empire and to form a new nation carved from the wilderness. And he intends to be instrumental in that process. As a reminder of his heritage, he keeps a piece of the shell from which he hatched in an amulet around his neck. Although he sometimes thinks that pillaging dungeons is a waste of his effort, he occasionally unearths a remnant of the long-lost dragonborn empire. He believes he can put such items to use one day in forging a new empire for his people.

Masters of stone and iron, dauntless and unyielding in the face of adversity

RACIAL TRAITS

Average Height: 4´ 3″–4´ 9″
Average Weight: 160–220 lb.

Ability Scores: +2 Constitution, +2 Wisdom
Size: Medium
Speed: 5 squares
Vision: Low-light

Languages: Common, Dwarven
Skill Bonuses: +2 Dungeoneering, +2 Endurance
Cast-Iron Stomach: +5 racial bonus to saving throws against poison.
Dwarven Resilience: You can use your second wind as a minor action instead of a standard action.
Dwarven Weapon Proficiency: You gain proficiency with the throwing hammer and the warhammer.
Encumbered Speed: You move at your normal speed even when it would normally be reduced by armor or a heavy load. Other effects that limit speed (such as difficult terrain or magical effects) affect you normally.
Stand Your Ground: When an effect forces you to move–through a pull, a push, or a slide–you can move 1 square less than the effect specifies. This means an effect that normally pulls, pushes, or slides a target 1 square does not force you to move unless you want to.

In addition, when an attack would knock you prone, you can immediately make a saving throw to avoid falling prone.

Carved from the bedrock of the universe, dwarves endured an age of servitude to giants before winning their freedom. Their mighty mountain fortress-cities testify to the power of their ancient empires. Even those who live in human cities are counted among the staunchest defenders against the darkness that threatens to engulf the world.

Play a dwarf if you want . . .

✦ to be tough, gruff, and strong as bedrock.
✦ to bring glory to your ancestors or serve as your god's right hand.
✦ to be able to take as much punishment as you dish out.
✦ to be a member of a race that favors the paladin, cleric, and fighter classes.

WILLIAM O'CONNOR

PHYSICAL QUALITIES

Dwarves average about 4½ feet in height and are very broad, weighing as much as an adult human. Dwarves have the same variety of skin, eye, and hair colors as humans, although dwarf skin is sometimes gray or sandstone red and red hair is more common among them. Male dwarves are often bald and braid their long beards into elaborate patterns. Female dwarves braid their hair to show clan and ancestry. Dwarven attire and equipment, including weapons and shields, are decorated with bold geometric shapes, natural gems, and ancestral faces.

Although they reach physical maturity at roughly the same age as humans, dwarves age more slowly and remain vigorous well past 150 years of age, often living to see 200.

PLAYING A DWARF

Proudly proclaiming they were made from the earth itself, dwarves share many qualities with the rock they love. They are strong, hardy, and dependable. They value their ancestral traditions, which they preserve through the ages as fiercely as they defend the carved structures of their mountain homes.

Dwarves believe in the importance of clan ties and ancestry. They deeply respect their elders, and they honor long-dead clan founders and ancestral heroes. They place great value on wisdom and the experience of years, and most are polite to elders of any race.

More so than most other races, dwarves seek guidance and protection from the gods. They look to the divine for strength, hope, and inspiration, or they seek to propitiate cruel or destructive gods. Individual dwarves might be impious or openly heretical, but temples and shrines of some sort are found in almost every dwarven community. Dwarves revere Moradin as their creator, but individual dwarves honor those deities who hold sway over their vocations; warriors pray to Bahamut or Kord, architects to Erathis, and merchants to Avandra—or even to Tiamat, if a dwarf is consumed by the dwarven taste for wealth.

Dwarves never forget their enemies, either individuals who have wronged them or entire races of monsters who have done ill to their kind. Dwarves harbor a fierce hatred for orcs, which often inhabit the same mountainous areas that dwarves favor and which wreak periodic devastation on dwarf communities. Dwarves also despise giants and titans, because the dwarf race once labored as the giants' slaves. They feel a mixture of pity and disgust toward those corrupted dwarves who still have not freed themselves from the giants' yoke—azers and galeb duhrs among them.

To a dwarf, it is a gift and a mark of deep respect to stand beside an ally in battle, and a sign of deepest loyalty to shield that ally from enemy attack. Dwarven legends honor many heroes who gave their lives to save their clans or their friends.

Dwarf Characteristics: Acquisitive, brave, hard-working, loyal, organized, stern, stubborn, tenacious, vengeful

Male Names: Adrik, Baern, Berend, Darrak, Eberk, Fargrim, Gardain, Harbek, Kildrak, Morgran, Orsik, Rangrim, Thoradin, Thorfin, Tordek, Travok, Vondal

Female Names: Artin, Bardryn, Diesa, Eldeth, Falkrunn, Gurdis, Helja, Kathra, Kristryd, Mardred, Riswynn, Torbera, Vistra

DWARF ADVENTURERS

Three sample dwarf adventurers are described below.

Travok is a dwarf paladin committed to the service of Kord. Wearing shining plate armor crafted and proudly worn by his great-grandfather, Travok presents an impenetrable line of defense, defying his enemies to get past him to reach his allies. True to his god and the honor of his ancestors, Travok relishes his physical strength and endurance, vowing that nothing will move him from his place. He is fiercely loyal to his friends, and if the need arises, he will lay down his life to ensure that they live.

Kathra is a dwarf cleric devoted to Moradin, the Great Carver who formed the dwarves out of stone and liberated them from their servitude to the giants. Swinging a warhammer engraved with the hammer-and-anvil symbol of her god, Kathra stands next to her fighter companion, trusting in divine power, the chainmail she made herself, and her own natural resilience to protect her from her enemies. Her dearest hope is to craft a legacy that will last through the ages, as beautiful and enduring as the finest dwarven jewelry—a legacy of peace and justice in this troubled world.

Tordek is a dwarf fighter, last in a long line of noble warriors. Three generations ago, his family's ancestral fortress was overrun by orcs and laid to waste, leaving Tordek with nothing but a signet ring and tales of ancient glory as his birthright. He has sworn that he will rebuild the fortress one day, and that oath drives his every action. In the meantime, his adventuring companions know they can rely on him completely, and someday he will rely on them to help him reclaim his kingdom.

Graceful warriors and wizards at home in the eldritch twilight of the Feywild

RACIAL TRAITS

Average Height: 5′ 5″-6′ 1″
Average Weight: 130-180 lb.

Ability Scores: +2 Dexterity, +2 Intelligence
Size: Medium
Speed: 6 squares
Vision: Low-light

Languages: Common, Elven
Skill Bonuses: +2 Arcana, +2 History
Eladrin Education: You gain training in one additional skill selected from the skill list in Chapter 5.
Eladrin Weapon Proficiency: You gain proficiency with the longsword.
Eladrin Will: You gain a +1 racial bonus to your Will defense.
   In addition, you gain a +5 racial bonus to saving throws against charm effects.
Fey Origin: Your ancestors were native to the Feywild, so you are considered a fey creature for the purpose of effects that relate to creature origin.
Trance: Rather than sleep, eladrin enter a meditative state known as trance. You need to spend 4 hours in this state to gain the same benefits other races gain from taking a 6-hour extended rest. While in a trance, you are fully aware of your surroundings and notice approaching enemies and other events as normal.
Fey Step: You can use *fey step* as an encounter power.

Fey Step	Eladrin Racial Power

With a step, you vanish from one place and appear in another.

Encounter ✦ Teleportation
Move Action   **Personal**
Effect: Teleport up to 5 squares (see "Teleportation," page 286).

Creatures of magic with strong ties to nature, eladrin live in cities in the twilight realm of the Feywild. Their cities lie close enough to the world that they sometimes cross over, appearing briefly in mountain valleys or deep forest glades before fading back into the Feywild.

Play an eladrin if you want . . .

✦ to be otherworldly and mysterious.
✦ to be graceful and intelligent.
✦ to teleport around the battlefield, cloaked in the magic of the Feywild.
✦ to be a member of a race that favors the wizard, rogue, and warlord classes.

ANNE STOKES

PHYSICAL QUALITIES

Eladrin are of human height. They are slim, and even the strongest simply look athletic rather than muscle-bound. They have the same range of complexions as humans, though they are more often fair than dark. Their straight, fine hair is often white, silver, or pale gold, and they wear it long and loose. Their ears are long and pointed, and their eyes are pearly and opalescent orbs of vibrant blue, violet, or green, lacking pupils. Eladrin can't grow facial hair and have little body hair.

Eladrin children grow much as human children do, but their aging process slows to a crawl when they reach maturity. They enjoy youth and health for most of their lives and don't begin to feel the effects of age until the middle of their third century. Most live for over 300 years, and even at the end they suffer few of the infirmities of old age.

PLAYING AN ELADRIN

Eladrin society straddles the boundary between the Feywild and the natural world. Eladrin build their elegant cities and towers in places of striking natural splendor, especially where the veil between the worlds is thin—isolated mountain vales, green islands along wild and storm-wracked coasts, and the deepest recesses of ancient forests. Some eladrin realms exist mostly in the Feywild, only rarely touching the world, while others appear in the world at sunset each day, only to fade back into the Feywild at dawn.

Long-lived and strongly tied to the Feywild, eladrin have a detached view of the world. Eladrin often have difficulty believing that events in the world have much importance to them, and they consider courses of action that can last for centuries.

Their general detachment from the world can make eladrin seem distant and intimidating to other races. Their fey nature also makes them simultaneously alluring and a little frightening. However, eladrin take friendships and alliances to heart and can react with swift fury when their friends are endangered. Combined with their intellect, bravery, and magical power, this loyalty makes them powerful and respected allies.

Eladrin live by an aesthetic philosophy common to the Feywild and personified by Corellon, the god of beauty and patron of the fey. Eladrin seek to exemplify grace, skill, and learning in every part of life, from dance and song to swordplay and magic. Their cities are places of stunning beauty that shape and guide their natural surroundings into elegant forms.

Eladrin are close cousins to the elves and are occasionally called high elves or gray elves. Eladrin favor the Feywild and arcane magic more than elves do, but the two races hold each other in high regard. They share a burning hatred for the third branch of their race—the drow.

The Feywild's most powerful eladrin, called noble eladrin, become so infused with their realm's inherent magic that they transform into entirely new creatures. These noble eladrin take on characteristics of the seasons and other natural phenomena.

Eladrin Characteristics: Aesthetic, deliberative, detached, free, graceful, magical, otherworldly, patient, perceptive

Male Names: Aramil, Arannis, Berrian, Dayereth, Erevan, Galinndan, Hadarai, Immeral, Mindartis, Paelias, Quarion, Riardon, Soveliss

Female Names: Althaea, Anastrianna, Andraste, Bethrynna, Caelynna, Jelenneth, Leshanna, Meriele, Naivara, Quelenna, Sariel, Shanairra, Theirastra, Valenae

ELADRIN ADVENTURERS

Three sample eladrin adventurers are described below.

Meriele is an eladrin wizard. Although her magic favors powers of thunder and lightning, she stands as a point of tranquility in the storm. To her friends, she seems above the world's tumult, present in their midst but clearly apart by her nature. In the evenings, while her companions set up camp and settle in to rest, she slips into a trance and, in her mind, walks among the ageless trees of the Feywild. She smiles at the impatience and impulsiveness of her allies, but they are almost as dear to her as her spellbooks.

Quarion is an eladrin rogue, as comfortable in the shadows of the world as in the twilight of the Feywild. He moves with the grace of a panther and can be uncannily silent when he chooses. In combat, he finds his mind slipping out of time, as though he were watching himself and his foes moving at a snail's pace. His enemies' attacks are easy to calculate, their defenses easy to anticipate and circumvent. Combat is a carefully choreographed dance in his mind, and he savors its elegance.

Anastrianna is an eladrin warlord who once served as the captain of the guard in the castle of a noble eladrin, a ghaele of winter. Banished at the ghaele's angry whim, Anastrianna has turned her back on the Feywild entirely. She is haunted by beautiful visions of herself at the head of a fey army, banners fluttering against a sapphire sky and blood staining the perfect snow, and she imagines that her destiny will lead her against her former lady someday.

Quick, wary archers who freely roam the forests and wilds

RACIAL TRAITS

Average Height: 5´ 4″-6´ 0″
Average Weight: 130-170 lb.

Ability Scores: +2 Dexterity, +2 Wisdom
Size: Medium
Speed: 7 squares
Vision: Low-light

Languages: Common, Elven
Skill Bonuses: +2 Nature, +2 Perception
Elven Weapon Proficiency: You gain proficiency with the longbow and the shortbow.
Fey Origin: Your ancestors were native to the Feywild, so you are considered a fey creature for the purpose of effects that relate to creature origin.
Group Awareness: You grant non-elf allies within 5 squares of you a +1 racial bonus to Perception checks.
Wild Step: You ignore difficult terrain when you shift (even if you have a power that allows you to shift multiple squares).
Elven Accuracy: You can use *elven accuracy* as an encounter power.

Elven Accuracy	Elf Racial Power

With an instant of focus, you take careful aim at your foe and strike with the legendary accuracy of the elves.

Encounter
Free Action   **Personal**
Effect: Reroll an attack roll. Use the second roll, even if it's lower.

Wild and free, elves guard their forested lands using stealth and deadly arrows from the trees. They build their homes in close harmony with the forest, so perfectly joined that travelers often fail to notice that they have entered an elven community until it is too late.

Play an elf if you want . . .

✦ to be quick, quiet, and wild.
✦ to lead your companions through the deep woods and pepper your enemies with arrows.
✦ to be a member of a race that favors the ranger, rogue, and cleric classes.

Physical Qualities

Elves are slender, athletic folk about as tall as humans. They have the same range of complexions as humans, tending more toward tan or brown hues. A typical elf's hair color is dark brown, autumn orange, mossy green, or deep gold. Elves' ears are long and pointed, and their eyes are vibrant blue, violet, or green. Elves have little body hair, but they favor a wild and loose look to their hair.

Elves mature at about the same rate as humans, but show few effects of age past adulthood. The first sign of an elf's advancing age is typically a change in hair color—sometimes graying but usually darkening or taking on more autumnal hues. Most elves live to be well over 200 years old and remain vigorous almost to the end.

Playing an Elf

Elves are a people of deeply felt but short-lived passions. They are easily moved to delighted laughter, blinding wrath, or mournful tears. They are inclined to impulsive behavior, and members of other races sometimes see elves as flighty or impetuous, but elves do not shirk responsibility or forget commitments. Thanks in part to their long life span, elves sometimes have difficulty taking certain matters as seriously as other races do, but when genuine threats arise, elves are fierce and reliable allies.

Elves revere the natural world. Their connection to their surroundings enables them to perceive much. They never cut living trees, and when they create permanent communities, they do so by carefully growing or weaving arbors, tree houses, and catwalks from living branches. They prefer the primal power of the natural world to the arcane magic their eladrin cousins employ. Elves love to explore new forests and new lands, and it's not unusual for individuals or small bands to wander hundreds of miles from their homelands.

Elves are loyal and merry friends. They love simple pleasures—dancing, singing, footraces, and contests of balance and skill—and rarely see a reason to tie themselves down to dull or disagreeable tasks. Despite how unpleasant war can be, a threat to their homes, families, or friends can make elves grimly serious and prompt them to take up arms.

At the dawn of creation, elves and eladrin were a single race dwelling both in the Feywild and in the world, and passing freely between the two. When the drow rebelled against their kin, under the leadership of the god Lolth, the resulting battles tore the fey kingdoms asunder. Ties between the peoples of the Feywild and the world grew tenuous, and eventually the elves and eladrin grew into two distinct races. Elves are descended from those who lived primarily in the world, and they no longer dream of the Feywild. They love the forests and wilds of the world that they have made their home.

Elf Characteristics: Agile, friendly, intuitive, joyful, perceptive, quick, tempestuous, wild

Male Names: Adran, Aelar, Beiro, Carric, Erdan, Gennal, Heian, Lucan, Peren, Rolen, Theren, Varis

Female Names: Adrie, Birel, Chaedi, Dara, Enna, Faral, Irann, Keyleth, Lia, Mialee, Shava, Thia, Valna

Elf Adventurers

Three sample elf adventurers are described below.

Varis is an elf ranger and a devout worshiper of Melora, the god of the wilds. When a goblin army forced his people from their woodland village, the elves took refuge in the nearest human town, walled and guarded by soldiers. Varis now leads other elves and some human townsfolk in raids against the goblins. Although he maintains a cheerful disposition, he frequently stares into the distance, listening, expecting at any moment to hear signs of approaching foes.

Lia is an elf rogue whose ancestral forest burned to the ground decades ago. Lia grew up on the wasteland's fringes in a large human city, unable to quite fit in. Her dreams called her to the forests, while her waking hours were spent in the dirtiest parts of civilization. She joined a group of adventurers after trying to cut a warlock's purse, and she fell in love with the wide world beyond the city.

Heian is an elf cleric of Sehanine, the god of the moon. The elven settlement where he was born still thrives in a forest untouched by the darkness spreading through the world, but he left home years ago, in search of new horizons and adventures. His travels lately have brought rumors to his ears that danger might be brewing in the ancient forest, and he is torn between a desire to seek his own way in the world and a sense of duty to his homeland.

Born heroes and leaders who combine the best features of humans and elves

RACIAL TRAITS

Average Height: 5′ 5″–6′ 2″
Average Weight: 130–190 lb.

Ability Scores: +2 Constitution, +2 Charisma
Size: Medium
Speed: 6 squares
Vision: Low-light

Languages: Common, Elven, choice of one other
Skill Bonuses: +2 Diplomacy, +2 Insight
Dilettante: At 1st level, you choose an at-will power from a class different from yours. You can use that power as an encounter power.
Dual Heritage: You can take feats that have either elf or human as a prerequisite (as well as those specifically for half-elves), as long as you meet any other requirements.
Group Diplomacy: You grant allies within 10 squares of you a +1 racial bonus to Diplomacy checks.

Descended from elves and humans, half-elves are a vital race in which the best features of elves and humans often appear.

Play a half-elf if you want . . .
✦ to be an outgoing, enthusiastic leader.
✦ to be a charismatic hero equally at home in two different cultures.
✦ to be a member of a race that favors the warlord, paladin, and warlock classes.

Physical Qualities

Half-elves tend to be sturdier of build than elves but more slender than most humans. Half-elves have the same range of complexions as humans and elves, and like elves, half-elves often have eye or hair colors not normally found among humans. Male half-elves can grow facial hair, unlike male elves, and often sport thin mustaches, goatees, or short beards. Half-elves' ears are about the size of human ears, but they are tapered, like the ears of their elven ancestors.

Half-elves usually adopt the dress and hairstyles of the society they spend the most time with; for example, a half-elf raised among a barbaric human tribe dresses in the furs and skins favored by the tribe and adopts the tribe's style of braids and face paint. However, it would not be unusual for half-elves raised among humans to seek out articles of elven clothing or jewelry so that they can proudly display signs of their dual heritage.

Half-elves have life spans comparable to humans, but like elves they remain vigorous well into old age.

Playing a Half-Elf

Half-elves are more than just a combination of two races—the combination of human and elf blood produces a unique race with qualities all its own. They share some of the natural grace, athleticism, and keen perceptiveness of elves, along with the passion and drive of humans. But in their own right, they are charismatic, confident, and open-minded and are natural diplomats, negotiators, and leaders.

Half-elves like to be around people, the more diverse the better. They gravitate toward population centers, especially larger settlements where members of many races mingle freely. Half-elves cultivate large networks of acquaintances, as much out of genuine friendliness as for practical purposes. They like to establish relationships with humans, elves, and members of other races so they can learn about them, the way they live, and how they make their way in the world.

Half-elves rarely settle down for any length of time. Their wanderlust makes them natural adventurers, and they quickly make themselves at home wherever they end up. When their paths take them back to a place they have visited before, they track down old friends and renew old contacts.

Ultimately, half-elves are survivors, able to adapt to almost any situation. They are generally well liked and admired by everyone, not just elves and humans. They are empathetic, better at putting themselves in others' shoes than most.

Half-elves naturally inspire loyalty in others, and they return that feeling with deep friendship and a keen sense of responsibility for those who place themselves in their care. Half-elf warlords and generals do not order their followers into danger that they would not face themselves, and they usually lead from the front, trusting their allies to follow.

Half-elves have no culture of their own and are not a numerous people. They usually bear human or elf names, sometimes using one name among elves and a different one among humans. Some are anxious about their place in the world, feeling no kinship with any race, except other half-elves, but most call themselves citizens of the world and kin to all.

Half-Elf Characteristics: Accommodating, adaptable, charming, confident, gregarious, open-minded

Half-Elf Names: Typically elf or human names, though some half-elves have names more typical of other races

Half-Elf Adventurers

Three sample half-elf adventurers are described below.

Daran is a half-elf warlord and an enthusiastic tactician. He has no aspirations to march at the head of an army; he is content leading a small band of friends in a quest for personal glory. Wealth is a welcome benefit of adventuring, and between adventures, he enjoys spending his time and wealth in the world's cities. He wins friends easily, draws on a wide network of contacts to find adventuring opportunities, and can call in favors across the land.

Shuva is a half-elf warlock whose brooding force of personality inspires more fear than loyalty. Unlike many of her kind, she grew up feeling part of neither human nor elven society. She has always been a loner and is accustomed to relying only on herself. Now that she's part of an adventuring group, she's slowly learning to trust her companions.

Calder is a half-elf paladin of Pelor, the god of the sun. A strong sense of compassion leads Calder to aid those in need and alleviate their suffering in any way he can. Often he fights against evil forces that prey on the weak, whether the forces are bandits harrying caravans or gnolls laying waste to farmsteads. He refuses to let fighting define him, however, and spends more time helping the victims of hardship than he does celebrating his successes.

Quick and resourceful wanderers, small in stature but great in courage

RACIAL TRAITS
Average Height: 3′ 10″–4′ 2″
Average Weight: 75–85 lb.

Ability Scores: +2 Dexterity, +2 Charisma
Size: Small
Speed: 6 squares
Vision: Normal

Languages: Common, choice of one other
Skill Bonuses: +2 Acrobatics, +2 Thievery
Bold: You gain a +5 racial bonus to saving throws against fear.
Nimble Reaction: You gain a +2 racial bonus to AC against opportunity attacks.
Second Chance: You can use *second chance* as an encounter power.

Second Chance	Racial Power

Luck and small size combine to work in your favor as you dodge your enemy's attack.

Encounter
Immediate Interrupt **Personal**
Effect: When an attack hits you, force an enemy to roll the attack again. The enemy uses the second roll, even if it's lower.

Halflings are a small race known for their resourcefulness, quick wits, and steady nerves. They are a nomadic folk who roam waterways and marshlands. No people travel farther or see more of what happens in the world than halflings.

Play a halfling if you want . . .
✦ to be a plucky hero who is all too easy to underestimate.
✦ to be likable, warm, and friendly.
✦ to be a member of a race that favors the rogue, ranger, and warlock classes.

BEING SMALL
Small characters follow most of the same rules as Medium ones, with the following exceptions.
✦ You can't use two-handed weapons (page 215), such as greatswords and halberds.
✦ When you use a versatile weapon (page 217), such as a longsword, you must use it two-handed, but you don't deal additional damage for doing so.

DAVID GRIFFITH

Physical Qualities

Halflings stand about 4 feet tall and weigh about 80 pounds. They resemble small humans and are proportioned like human adults. Halflings have the same range of complexions as humans, but most halflings have dark hair and eyes. Halfling males don't have beards, but many have long, full sideburns. Halflings of both genders often wear complicated hairstyles, featuring complex braiding and weaving.

Halflings typically dress in clothes that match their surroundings and prefer earth tones and various shades of green. Their clothing and gear feature woven textures and stitching. Birds, river patterns, boats, and fish are common images in halfling art and decoration.

Halflings have life spans comperable to humans.

Playing a Halfling

Halflings are an affable, warm, and cheerful people. They survive in a world full of larger creatures by avoiding notice or, barring that, avoiding offense. They appear harmless and so have managed to survive for centuries in the shadow of empires and on the edges of wars and political strife.

Halflings are practical and down-to-earth. They concern themselves with basic needs and simple pleasures, harboring few dreams of gold or glory. Adventurers are no more rare among halflings than among other races, but they usually pursue the adventurer's life for reasons of community, friendship, wanderlust, or curiosity. Halfling adventurers are brave and faithful companions, relying on stealth and trickery in battle rather than raw might or magic.

Tight-knit halfling communities are found near the settlements of other races, often along or even on the surface of a body of water. Halflings have never built a kingdom of their own or even held much land. They don't recognize any sort of royalty or nobility of their own, instead looking to family elders to guide them. This emphasis on family and community has enabled halflings to maintain their traditional ways for thousands of years, unaffected by the rise and fall of empires.

According to halfling legend, Melora and Sehanine created the halflings together, giving the race a love of nature and the gift of stealth. When their interest waned, Melora and Sehanine stopped looking after the race, or so the legends go, and halflings made their own way in the world. They say Avandra, the god of luck, admired their resourcefulness and adopted them, favoring them with good fortune. Not all halflings worship Avandra, but nearly all breathe a prayer of thanks to her when fortune favors them.

Halflings are fond of stories and legends such as the myth of Avandra, and their culture is rich in oral tradition. Few members of other races realize that halfling folktales contain a vast amount of lore about people and places long past. Many halflings are able to dredge up knowledge about the history, religion, or culture of other races, but that knowledge is usually wrapped in a fable.

Halfling Characteristics: Brave, curious, determined, down-to-earth, friendly, good-natured, lucky, nimble, optimistic, practical, resourceful, warm

Male Names: Ander, Corrin, Dannad, Errich, Finnan, Garret, Lazam, Lindal, Merric, Nebin, Ostran, Perrin, Reed, Shardon, Ulmo, Wenner

Female Names: Andrey, Bree, Callie, Chenna, Eida, Kithri, Lidda, Nedda, Paela, Shaena, Tryn, Vani, Verna, Wella

Halfling Adventurers

Three sample halfling adventurers are described below.

Lidda is a halfling rogue with a quick wit and an acid tongue. At a young age, she left her family out of a desire to see more of the world and experience firsthand the wonders described in the stories she grew up hearing. She has joined several different adventuring groups during her career, and even though her displays of sarcasm and wry humor at her companions' expense would suggest otherwise, she counts each of them as a close friend.

Garret is a halfling ranger. Several years ago, his grandfather sent him to look for a distant branch of his family that had stopped responding to messages. Garret found the whole clan had been killed, and he returned to bring the sad news to his family. From that time, he has been unable to stay in one place for long. He doesn't know who or what killed his relatives and doesn't dream of vengeance, but he hopes to do some good in the world that might somehow balance out the atrocity of their murders.

Verna is a halfling warlock—and among the most cheerful and gregarious of halflings. The infernal powers she channels seem to leave no mark on her spirit or mind. She takes no delight in killing but uses lethal powers as a practical matter, to protect herself and her allies. She doesn't often talk of the event that propelled her into a life of adventuring and a pact with infernal powers: Without warning, a devil appeared to her and offered her power, in exchange for a favor to be named later. In what she still regards as a moment of folly, she accepted. Nightmares of her unknown future haunt her sleep, but she never speaks of them.

Ambitious, driven, pragmatic—a race of heroes, and also a race of villains

RACIAL TRAITS

Average Height: 5′ 6″–6′ 2″
Average Weight: 135–220 lb.

Ability Scores: +2 to one ability score of your choice
Size: Medium
Speed: 6 squares
Vision: Normal

Languages: Common, choice of one other
Bonus At-Will Power: You know one extra at-will power from your class.
Bonus Feat: You gain a bonus feat at 1st level. You must meet the feat's prerequisites.
Bonus Skill: You gain training in one additional skill from your class skill list.
Human Defense Bonuses: +1 to Fortitude, Reflex, and Will defenses.

Of all the civilized races, humans are the most adaptable and diverse. Human settlements can be found almost anywhere, and human morals, customs, and interests vary greatly.

Play a human if you want . . .

✦ to be a decisive, resourceful hero with enough determination to face any challenge.

✦ to have the most versatility and flexibility of any race.

✦ to be able to excel at any class you choose.

WILLIAM O'CONNOR

PHYSICAL QUALITIES

Humans come in a wide variety of heights, weights, and colors. Some humans have black or dark brown skin, others are as pale as snow, and they cover the whole range of tans and browns in between. Their hair is black, brown, or a range of blonds and reds. Their eyes are most often brown, blue, or hazel.

Human attire varies wildly, depending on the environment and society in which they live. Their clothing can be simple, ostentatious, or anything in between. It's not unusual for several distinct human cultures to live side by side in a particular area and mingle, so human armor, weaponry, and other items incorporate a variety of designs and motifs.

Humans average life spans of about 75 years, though some venerable members of the race live as long as 90 or more years.

PLAYING A HUMAN

Humans are decisive and sometimes rash. They explore the darkest reaches of the world in search of knowledge and power. They hurl themselves into danger, dealing with consequences as they arise. They act first and ponder later, trusting their will to prevail and their native resourcefulness to see them through perilous situations.

Humans always look to the horizon, seeking to expand their influence and their territory. They chase power and want to change the world, for good or for ill. Their settlements are among the brightest lights in a dark and untamed world, and humans constantly seek to explore new lands and settle new frontiers.

Their self-reliance and bravery inclines humans toward martial classes such as fighter, warlord, and rogue. They often prefer to find hidden reserves of strength in themselves rather than trust to the magic of wizards or clerics.

That said, humans tend to be a pious race, worshiping the whole pantheon of gods. Their myths name no god as the creator of the race. Some tales say the gods worked together to create them, infusing them with the best qualities of each race that had come before. Other tales say that humans were the creation of a god whose name is no longer known, a god killed in the war against the primordials or perhaps assassinated by another deity (Asmodeus and Zehir are often accused of the deed).

Humans are tolerant of other races, different beliefs, and foreign cultures. Most human settlements are diverse places where different races live together in relative peace. The human empire of Nerath, the last great world power, united many different peoples. Most of the human towns that have survived the empire's fall are fortified bastions against the encroaching darkness. When elven forests are razed or dwarven mines overrun, the survivors often flee to the nearest human town for protection.

Despite the far reach and power of Nerath, humans in the present day are a scattered and divided people. Dozens of small kingdoms, fiefdoms, and free cities have arisen from Nerath's ruins, and many of these realms are petty, weak, or isolated. Tensions and misunderstandings among them often precipitate skirmishes, espionage, betrayal, and even open warfare.

Human Characteristics: Adaptable, ambitious, bold, corruptible, creative, driven, hardy, pragmatic, resourceful, territorial, tolerant

Male Names: Alain, Alek, Benn, Brandis, Donn, Drew, Erik, Gregg, Jonn, Kris, Marc, Mikal, Pieter, Regdar, Quinn, Samm, Thom, Wil

Female Names: Ana, Cassi, Eliza, Gwenn, Jenn, Kat, Keira, Luusi, Mari, Mika, Miri, Stasi, Shawna, Zanne

HUMAN ADVENTURERS

Three sample human adventurers are described below.

Brandis is a human fighter, a mercenary who has sold his sword arm to every baronet, duke, and princeling from the mountains to the coast. His armor is practical, lacking any decoration, and his sword is intended only for battle, not as a mark of prestige. He prays daily to the Raven Queen—not out of devotion but because he knows that death is inevitable and he hopes to postpone it as long as possible. He began adventuring after a mission ended in disaster. His soldier companions were all dead, and he was captured by hobgoblins and held for a ransom that no one cared enough to pay. He joined the band of adventurers that slew the hobgoblins. He has since found adventuring both more lucrative and more satisfying than his previous life.

Mari is a human ranger, her eyes always on the horizon. She is driven by a passion for exploration and a love of new places. She dreams of ultimately establishing a new settlement in a place where people can live in peace and freedom. She prays to Avandra for protection in her wandering and to Erathis for help in achieving her dream. She is aware of her life's contradiction: She is a creature of the wilderness, but her dream is to tame and cultivate it. A part of her wonders whether she would be able to settle in the village she dreams of founding.

Thom is a human wizard, and his one desire is for power. He adventures in search of arcane lore and ancient artifacts that will increase his mastery of magic. He prays to Ioun because he sees knowledge as the key to power, but he is also drawn to Vecna, wondering what power the god of secrets might offer him in exchange for his devotion.

Heirs of a shattered empire who live in the shadows and do not fear the dark

RACIAL TRAITS

Average Height: 5′ 6″–6′ 2″
Average Weight: 140–230 lb.

Ability Scores: +2 Intelligence, +2 Charisma
Size: Medium
Speed: 6 squares
Vision: Low-light

Languages: Common, choice of one other
Skill Bonuses: +2 Bluff, +2 Stealth
Bloodhunt: You gain a +1 racial bonus to attack rolls against bloodied foes.
Fire Resistance: You have resist fire 5 + one-half your level.
Infernal Wrath: You can use *infernal wrath* as an encounter power.

Infernal Wrath	Tiefling Racial Power

You call upon your furious nature to improve your odds of harming your foe.

Encounter
Minor Action   Personal
Effect: You can channel your fury to gain a +1 power bonus to your next attack roll against an enemy that hit you since your last turn. If your attack hits and deals damage, add your Charisma modifier as extra damage.

Heirs to an ancient, infernal bloodline, tieflings have no realms of their own but instead live within human kingdoms and cities. They are descended from human nobles who bargained with dark powers, and long ago their empire subjugated half the world. But the empire was cast down into ruin, and tieflings were left to make their own way in a world that often fears and resents them.

Play a tiefling if you want . . .

✦ to be a hero who has a dark side to overcome.
✦ to be good at tricking, intimidating, or persuading others to do your will.
✦ to be a member of a race that favors the warlock, warlord, and rogue classes.

PHYSICAL QUALITIES

Tieflings' appearance testifies to their infernal blood-line. They have large horns; thick, nonprehensile tails that range in length from 4 to 5 feet; sharply pointed teeth; and eyes that are solid orbs of black, red, white, silver, or gold. Their skin color covers the whole human range and also extends to reds, from a ruddy tan to a brick red. Their hair, cascading down from behind their horns, is as likely to be dark blue, red, or purple as more common human colors.

Tieflings favor dark colors and reds, leathers and glossy furs, small spikes and buckles. Tiefling-crafted arms and armor often have an archaic style, harkening back to the glory of their long-vanished empire.

PLAYING A TIEFLING

Hundreds of years ago, the leaders of the human empire of Bael Turath made pacts with devils to solidify their hold over its enormous territory. Those humans became the first tieflings, and they governed their empire in the name of their infernal masters. In time, Bael Turath came into conflict with Arkhosia, the ancient empire of the dragonborn, and decades of warfare left both empires in ruins. Bael Turath's grand capital was thrown down in ruin.

Tieflings are the heirs of the surviving noble dynasties that ruled the empire. Their bloodline is tainted by their diabolical connections, passing to their descendants through all generations. In many ways, they are human; they can have children with humans, for example, but their offspring are always tieflings.

Centuries of other races' distrust and outright hatred have made tieflings self-reliant and often too willing to live up to the stereotypes imposed on them. As a race without a homeland, tieflings know that they have to make their own way in the world and that they have to be strong to survive, and they are not quick to trust anyone who claims to be a friend. However, when a tiefling's companions demonstrate that they trust him or her, the tiefling quickly learns to extend the same trust to them. And once a tiefling gives someone trust and loyalty, the tiefling is a firm friend and ally for life.

Although the nobles of Bael Turath subjugated themselves to devils, most present-day tieflings give little thought to gods or patrons, preferring to look out for themselves. Therefore, they do not often follow the path of the divine; tiefling clerics or paladins are rare.

Tieflings are not numerous. Sometimes a tiefling merchant clan that is descended from a Bael Turath dynasty settles as a group in a land where wealth can purchase safety and comfort. But most tieflings are born outside such hidden dynasties and grow up in the roughest quarters of human cities and towns. These tieflings often become swindlers, thieves, or crime lords, who carve out a niche for themselves amid the squalor of their surroundings.

Tiefling Characteristics: Cunning, disquieting, imposing, mysterious, proud, rebellious, self-reliant, sinister, sly, unconventional

Male Names: Akmenos, Amnon, Barakas, Damakos, Ekemon, Iados, Kairon, Leucis, Melech, Morthos, Pelaios, Skamos, Therai

Female Names: Akta, Bryseis, Damaia, Ea, Kallista, Lerissa, Makaria, Nemeia, Orianna, Phelaia, Rieta

Some young tieflings, striving to find a place in the world, choose a name that signifies a concept and then try to embody the concept. For some, the chosen name is a noble quest. For others, it's a grim destiny.

Modern Names: Art, Carrion, Chant, Despair, Fear, Gladness, Hope, Ideal, Music, Nowhere, Open, Poetry, Quest, Random, Reverence, Sorrow, Torment, Weary

TIEFLING ADVENTURERS

Three sample tiefling adventurers are described below.

Akmenos is a tiefling warlock torn between good and evil. He longs to fit into the human society in which he lives and would like to call himself genuinely good. At the same time, he fears that his soul is irretrievably tainted by the touch of evil—both the evil in his blood and the sinister nature of his infernal pact. He feels as if he is on a tightrope between good and evil and might eventually fall either way. His companions recognize the good in his heart and trust him, and that trust has been enough on some days to keep him from sliding into evil. His life is tormented, and though he believes he is called to a great destiny, he is not sure whether he will become a hero or a villain.

Kallista is a tiefling warlord who prays daily that Bahamut will help her keep her commitment to live justly and honorably. She has no love for Bahamut's priests and temples, but she feels a personal connection to the Platinum Dragon, which inspires her to acts of nobility and sacrifice. She leads a group of adventurers in strikes against evil forces but dreams of one day leading an army under Bahamut's banner. In his name, she struggles to keep her violent temper and cruel streak under tight control.

Random is a tiefling rogue, a native of the streets and alleys of a human city and no stranger to poverty, mistrust, or prejudice. As far as he's concerned, good and evil are a matter for priests and philosophers to discuss in their marble temples and universities. The reality of life on the street is survival, and he's willing to do what is necessary to survive. As part of an adventuring group, he has had his first taste of wealth and discovered that he likes it, but he hasn't forgotten his roots. He has also had his first taste of trust and friendship, which are growing on him as well.

CHARACTER CLASSES

YOUR CLASS is the primary definition of what your character can do in the extraordinary magical landscape of the DUNGEONS & DRAGONS world.

A class is more than a profession; it is your character's calling. Your class choice shapes every action you take as you adventure across a spell-tangled, monster-ridden, battle-torn fantasy world.

Will you be a gutsy, youthful sword fighter? A pact-sworn warlock with questionable ties? A gods-worshiping cleric who knows too much? A flamboyant rogue with a dagger up your sleeve? A tattooed wizard with a crystal staff? The choice is yours.

This chapter includes the following material:

+ **Introducing the Classes:** Discussion of the details that make up each class, and your first look at paragon paths and epic destinies.

+ **How to Read a Power:** The specifics on how to understand your class's powers and each power's format and effects.

+ **The Classes:** Class features and complete power descriptions for the cleric, the fighter, the paladin, the ranger, the rogue, the warlock, the warlord, and the wizard, as well as their paragon paths.

+ **Epic Destinies:** A selection of epic destinies that your character can achieve.

DAN SCOTT

This chapter presents full descriptions of the following eight classes:

Cleric (page 60): A divinely inspired warrior.

Fighter (page 75): A master of martial combat.

Paladin (page 89): A champion dedicated to a specific deity.

Ranger (page 103): A ranged or two-weapon combat specialist.

Rogue (page 116): A combatant who uses stealth and slyness to thwart enemies.

Warlock (page 129): A wielder of arcane power gleaned from otherworldly entities.

Warlord (page 143): A commander who leads from the front.

Wizard (page 156): The world's most powerful purveyor of magic.

Each class description opens with a summary of the class's basic traits and an overview of the class's place in the world.

Role: In battle, do members of the class act as defenders, strikers, leaders, or controllers? (See Chapter 2 for an explanation of these roles.) Each class has a role associated with it. Different classes approach their role in different ways, and many classes include limited elements of one or more other roles as well. For example, both the fighter and the paladin are defenders, but the fighter adds some aspects of the striker to his repertoire, while the paladin has some abilities often associated with leaders, such as healing.

Power Source: Each of the eight classes draws its power from the arcane, the divine, or the martial power source.

Key Abilities: Most classes have powers and other features that rely on three different ability scores. Characters of these classes generally want their three best scores in these abilities.

Armor and Weapon Proficiencies: Different classes are proficient with different kinds of armor and weapons, shown in these two entries. An armor or weapon proficiency you gain from a class counts as the appropriate Armor Proficiency or Weapon Proficiency feat (see Chapter 6).

Implement: If the class can use one or more kinds of implements, that information is noted here.

Bonus to Defense: Each class gives you a bonus to one or more of your defenses.

Hit Points: Each class description indicates how many hit points you have at 1st level and how many hit points you gain with each new level you attain.

Healing Surges: Your class determines how many healing surges you can spend in a day.

Trained Skills: Every class has a list of class skills, and you choose a specific number of trained skills from that list. Some classes give you a predetermined trained skill.

The last few lines of the Class Traits section point to later parts of the class entry. Build Options and Class Features are more fully described in the next major sections.

Creating a Character: The next section of a class entry describes each class build in more detail. A build is the theme you think about when choosing your powers and other abilities. The build you choose (if you choose one) suggests what abilities you should prioritize and gives you some guidance as you choose powers, at 1st level and as you gain levels.

A build isn't intended as a constraint, but as a way to help you make informed choices. If you want to be a fighter with a greataxe, rather than wielding a one-handed weapon and a shield, the great weapon fighter build points you toward the powers that are most effective in your hands. You can choose powers intended for the guardian fighter build instead, of course, and they might help your character be a little more balanced. Some of those powers, though, won't be as good for you as they'd be for a fighter with a shield. Builds aren't required; they exist to help guide your decisions.

Each build includes suggestions for choosing feats, skills, and powers for your 1st-level character. These are only suggestions—you are free to choose the feats, skills, and powers that most appeal to you and best fit with your character concept.

Class Features: Class features are abilities shared by every member of the class. Some class features are powers that every member of a class can use, such as the warlock's *eldritch blast* or the cleric's Channel Divinity ability. Others are more like racial traits—they're not so much things you do as things that modify the effects of what you do.

Powers: The longest section of a class description contains full descriptions of all the class's at-will, encounter, and daily attack powers, as well as its utility powers.

CLASS OVERVIEW

A sidebar in each class entry highlights a few key elements of the class.

Characteristics: The features or qualities of the class that make it distinct. This section describes how the class fulfills its role.

Religion: A selection of deities of the D&D pantheon best suited to the class.

Races: The races best suited for each class.

PARAGON PATHS

You have survived and thrived through ten levels of adventure.

You've explored dank dungeons, defeated vile monsters, and learned priceless secrets. You've started making a name for yourself.

Now you're ready to take the next step: you're ready to choose a paragon path.

As your class describes your basic role in the party, your paragon path represents a particular area of expertise within that role. It's a form of specialization beyond even what a build choice represents. You might be a battle cleric and specialize in melee powers, but starting at 11th level you can be a warpriest and specialize in battle prayers.

As shown on the Character Advancement table on page 29, your paragon path gives you new capabilities from 11th level through 20th level. But adopting a paragon path doesn't mean you stop advancing in your class. All the powers and features you gain from your paragon path come *in addition to* your class powers and features, not instead of them. You don't stop being a cleric when you become a radiant servant. Instead, you gain new capabilities that extend, enhance, and complement the abilities of your class.

Paragon paths also broaden the use of action points in different ways. Each paragon path features a different, extra capability that characters can unlock by spending action points. So, once you pick your paragon path, you can still spend an action point to take an extra action. But you'll also have a new capability for action points that is unique to your path. Some of these capabilities come in addition to the extra action you get for spending an action point, some are used instead of getting an extra action.

When you reach 11th level, choose a paragon path. All paths have prerequisites, conditions you have to fulfill before you can adopt that path.

Paragon Multiclassing: You might choose to take on powers from a second class in place of a paragon path. See page 208 for more information on multiclassing.

INTRODUCING THE PARAGON PATHS

Paragon paths are presented in alphabetical order, following the appropriate classes in this chapter. Each paragon path description provides a general overview followed by game rule information.

Prerequisite: If the paragon path has requirements for entry, they are noted here. If a paragon path has a specific class as a prerequisite, you must either be a member of that class or have selected a multiclass feat for the indicated class. For example, you can take the angelic avenger paragon path if you're a cleric or if you have selected a cleric multiclass feat.

Path Features: Every paragon path grants you specific path features, which are similar in nature to the features you gain from your class.

Powers: Your paragon path gives you powers, which are described here.

PARAGON PATHS

Cleric (page 72)	Rogue (page 126)
Angelic avenger	Cat burglar
Divine oracle	Daggermaster
Radiant servant	Master infiltrator
Warpriest	Shadow assassin

Fighter (page 86)	Warlock (page 140)
Iron vanguard	Doomsayer
Kensei	Feytouched
Pit fighter	Life-stealer
Swordmaster	

Paladin (page 100)	Warlord (page 153)
Astral weapon	Battle captain
Champion of order	Combat veteran
Hospitaler	Knight commander
Justiciar	Sword marshal

Ranger (page 113)	Wizard (page 169)
Battlefield archer	Battle mage
Beast stalker	Blood mage
Pathfinder	Spellstorm mage
Stormwarden	Wizard of the Spiral Tower

EPIC DESTINIES

After twenty levels of adventure, what trials could be left to challenge you? You have conquered countless foes and become a hero to common folk everywhere. Deadly dragons and powerful mages alike have fallen to your might. Your gaze has begun to turn to the planes beyond the world, and even to the gods themselves. Finally, you realize there are no heights you cannot achieve.

It's time for you to assume your epic destiny and shape your legend in the universe forevermore.

Like a paragon path, an epic destiny grants special powers in addition to your class powers and features. Unlike paragon paths, epic destinies are not extensions of your class. Instead, they offer extraordinary abilities that represent your journey toward your ultimate fate . . . as you define it.

See page 172 for more about epic destinies.

Epic Destiny	Description
Archmage	Ultimate master of arcane spells
Deadly trickster	A wanderer, thief, pragmatist, and survivor
Demigod	You are on the path to godhood
Eternal seeker	Your destiny finds you

POWER TYPES AND USAGE

Every class has access to a mix of attack powers (used to harm your enemies in combat, more or less directly) and utility powers (used to overcome a variety of obstacles both in and out of combat). Within each type, different powers have different restrictions on how often you can use them: at-will, encounter, or daily.

You can use a power whenever you are able to take the action the power requires. (Certain conditions, as defined in Chapter 9, prohibit you from taking actions.) Your DM might rule that you can't use powers in special circumstances, such as when your hands are tied.

AT-WILL POWERS

You can use your **at-will powers** as often as you want. They represent easy weapon swings or simple magical effects that don't put any unusual strain on you or tax your resources in any way.

ENCOUNTER POWERS

An **encounter power** can be used once per encounter. You need to take a short rest (page 263) before you can use one again. Encounter powers produce more powerful, more dramatic effects than at-will powers. If you're a martial character, they are exploits you've practiced extensively but can pull off only once in a while. If you're an arcane or divine character, these are spells or prayers of such power that they take time to re-form in your mind after you unleash their magic energy.

DAILY POWERS

A **daily power** can be used once per day. Daily powers are the most powerful effects you can produce, and using one takes a significant toll on your physical and mental resources. If you're a martial character, you're reaching into your deepest reserves of energy to pull off an amazing exploit. If you're an arcane magic-user, you're reciting a spell of such complexity that your mind can only hold it

in place for so long, and once it's recited, it's wiped from your memory. If you're a divine character, the divine might that you channel to invoke these powers is so strong that you can harness it only once a day.

Daily powers usually include an effect that takes place regardless of whether the power is used successfully. As a result, these limited resources are at least slightly beneficial every time you use them. Once you use a daily power, you need to take an extended rest (page 263) before you can use it again.

HOW TO READ A POWER

No part of the D&D game has as much variety as the powers that describe what characters can do. Even so, the way that various powers are described follows a structured format. Here's the information you need to understand how a power works.

NAME AND LEVEL

Acid Wave	Wizard Attack 19

The first line of a power description gives the name of the power, the class it's associated with, the kind of power it is (attack or utility), and the power's level (or the fact that it's a class feature). In the above example, *acid wave* is an attack power that a wizard can choose at 19th level.

Some powers, such as the racial powers in Chapter 3 and the feat powers in Chapter 6, carry different information on the right side of this line.

FLAVOR TEXT

A wave of acid dissolves all creatures that stand before you.

The next section of a power description gives a brief explanation of what the power does, sometimes including information about what it looks or sounds like. The flavor text for *acid wave* appears here as an example.

POWER SOURCES

Every class relies on a particular source of energy for the "fuel" that enables members of that class to use powers. The three power sources associated with the classes in this book are arcane, divine, and martial.

Arcane: Drawing on magical energy that permeates the cosmos, the arcane power source can be used for a wide variety of effects, from fireballs to flight to invisibility. Warlocks and wizards, for example, use arcane magic. Each class is the representative of a different tradition of arcane study, and other traditions exist. Arcane powers are called **spells**.

Divine: Divine magic comes from the gods. The gods grant power to their devotees, which clerics and paladins, for example, access through prayers and litanies. Divine magic excels at healing, protection, and smiting the enemies of the gods. Divine powers are called **prayers**.

Martial: Martial powers are not magic in the traditional sense, although some martial powers stand well beyond the capabilities of ordinary mortals. Martial characters use their own strength and willpower to vanquish their enemies. Training and dedication replace arcane formulas and prayers to grant fighters, rangers, rogues, and warlords, among others, their power. Martial powers are called **exploits**.

Other Power Sources: Additional power sources and techniques provide characters of different classes with powers and abilities. These will appear in future *Player's Handbook* volumes. For example, barbarians and druids draw on the primal forces of nature, monks harness the power of their soul energy (or ki), and psions call upon the mind to generate psionic powers. Future power sources include elemental, ki, primal, psionic, and shadow.

A power's flavor text helps you understand what happens when you use a power and how you might describe it when you use it. You can alter this description as you like, to fit your own idea of what your power looks like. Your wizard's *magic missile* spell, for example, might create phantasmal skulls that howl through the air to strike your opponent, rather than simple bolts of magical energy.

When you need to know the exact effect, look at the rules text that follows.

KEYWORDS

At-Will ♦ Martial, Weapon
Encounter ♦ Divine
Daily ♦ Acid, Arcane, Implement

A power's keyword entry gives you important rules information about the power. The first keyword indicates whether the power is an at-will, encounter, or daily power. (One example of each type is given above.) The color used in the line containing the power name also conveys this information: At-will powers have a green bar, encounter powers have a red bar, and daily powers have a black bar.

The other keywords define the fundamental effects of a power. For instance, a power that deals acid damage is an acid effect and thus has the acid keyword. A power that has the poison keyword might deal poison damage, or it might slow the target, immobilize the target, or stun the target. But the poison keyword indicates that it's a poison effect, and other rules in the game relate to that fact in different ways. Dwarves have a bonus to saving throws against poison effects, for example.

Keywords help to determine how, or if, a power works when the target has resistance, vulnerability, or immunity to a damage type or an effect type, or if the power interacts with existing effects. For example, a ritual that forbids teleportation could block a power that has the teleportation keyword.

Resistance or immunity to one keyword of a power does not protect a target from the power's other effects. When damage of a power is described as more than one type, divide the damage evenly between the damage types (round up for the first damage type, round down for all others). For example, a power that deals 25 fire and thunder damage deals 13 fire damage and 12 thunder damage.

If a power allows you to choose the damage type, the power then has that keyword for feats, resistances, and any other information that applies. For example, the wizard spell *elemental maw* does 6d6 + Intelligence modifier damage of a type chosen from the following list: acid, cold, fire, lightning, or thunder. If you choose lightning damage, the Astral Fire feat (+1 feat bonus to damage rolls when you use powers that have the fire or radiant keywords) doesn't add to the power's damage, but the Raging Storm feat (+1 feat bonus

to damage rolls when you use powers that have the lightning or thunder keywords) does.

KEYWORD CATEGORIES

Aside from usage keywords (**at-will**, **encounter**, and **daily**), keywords fall into four categories.

Power Source: The power sources described in this book are **arcane**, **divine**, and **martial**. Basic attacks, racial powers, and epic destiny powers have no power source.

Damage Type: Many powers create energy or a substance that deals damage to their targets.
Acid: Corrosive liquid.
Cold: Ice crystals, arctic air, or frigid liquid.
Fire: Explosive bursts, fiery rays, or simple ignition.
Force: Invisible energy formed into incredibly hard yet nonsolid shapes.
Lightning: Electrical energy.
Necrotic: Purple-black energy that deadens flesh and wounds the soul.
Poison: Toxins that reduce a creature's hit points.
Psychic: Effects that target the mind.
Radiant: Searing white light or shimmering colors.
Thunder: Shock waves and deafening sounds.

Effect Type: Some powers are classified according to how their effects work.
Charm: Mental effects that control or influence the subject's actions.
Conjuration: Powers that create objects or creatures of magical energy.
Fear: Effects that inspire fright.
Healing: Powers that restore hit points.
Illusion: Powers that deceive the senses or the mind.
Poison: Substances that hamper or impede a creature.
Polymorph: Effects that alter a creature's physical form.
Reliable: If you miss when using a reliable power, you don't expend the use of that power.
Sleep: Powers that cause sleep or unconsciousness.
Stance: A stance power lasts until the end of the encounter, for 5 minutes, or until you use another stance power.
Teleportation: Powers that transport creatures instantaneously from one location to another.
Zone: Powers that create lingering effects that extend over an area.

Accessories: These keywords identify items used with the power. If you have a proficiency bonus to attack rolls and damage rolls from your weapon or an enhancement bonus to your attack rolls and damage rolls from a magic weapon or an implement, you add that bonus when you use a power that has the associated keyword.

Implement: Many arcane spells are more effective when used in conjunction with an implement—a wizard's staff, orb, or wand, or a warlock's rod or wand. Many divine prayers use holy symbols as implements. To grant its benefit to a divine character, a holy symbol must represent the character's patron deity or one of a group of deities the character serves. It's not necessary to have an implement in order to use a power that has the implement keyword.

Weapon: Many martial powers, as well as several divine powers, can be used only if you're wielding a weapon. (You can use an unarmed attack as your weapon.) A weapon's reach or range determines the reach or range of a power it's used with.

ACTION TYPE

The next line of a power description begins with what type of action you have to take when you use the power. Most powers require a **standard action**. Some powers are **move actions**, a few are **immediate interrupts** or **immediate reactions**, a handful are **minor actions** or **free actions**, and a scant few require **no action**. Action types are described on page 267.

> **Trigger:** An ally in range is hit by an attack
> **Trigger:** An adjacent enemy moves away from you

Trigger: Some powers come into effect only if a triggering condition occurs. Examples of some typical "Trigger" entries are given above.

ATTACK TYPE AND RANGE

Following a power's action type on the same line is the power's attack type and its range. The four attack types are **melee**, **ranged**, **close**, and **area**. Each of these attack types (fully described in Chapter 9) has rules for range and targeting.

Even though these terms are called "attack types," they apply to utility powers as well as attack powers.

MELEE

A melee power affects a target (or targets) within melee reach. Many melee powers require a weapon. You make a separate attack roll against each target.

Melee weapon: A melee attack power that has a range of "weapon" allows you to attack a target within the reach of the weapon you're wielding. Some weapons extend your reach beyond adjacent squares.

Example: If you use a "Melee weapon" power while you're wielding a dagger, you can attack a target within 1 square of you. If you're wielding a halberd (a reach weapon), you can attack a target within 2 squares of you.

Melee 1: A melee power that has a range of 1 can be used only on an adjacent target.

Melee touch: A melee power that has a range of "touch" can be used on any target you can reach. (Some creatures larger than Medium size have a reach of more than 1 square.)

RANGED

A ranged power affects a target (or targets) at a distance. For details about how ranged attacks work, see page 270.

Ranged weapon: A ranged attack power that has a range of "weapon" allows you to attack a target within your weapon's range (see the table on page 219). If the target is farther away than normal range but within long range, you take a -2 penalty to attack rolls.

Example: If you use a "Ranged weapon" power with a shortbow (normal range 15, long range 30), you take a -2 penalty when attacking targets 16-30 squares away, and you can't attack creatures farther away than 30 squares.

Ranged [number]: A ranged power that has a range expressed as a number can be used on a target within the indicated number of squares.

Ranged sight: A ranged power that has a range of "sight" can be used on any target within line of sight. You still need line of effect to the target.

CLOSE

A close power creates an area of effect (page 272) that originates in a square of your space, and most close powers can hit multiple targets. For details about how close attacks work, see page 271.

Close burst [number]: A close burst power allows you to target creatures or objects within the indicated number of squares from you in all directions. See page 272 for how to determine the area of a burst.

Close blast [number]: A close blast power allows you to target creatures or objects within an adjacent area that is the indicated number of squares on a side. See page 272 for how to determine the area of a blast.

AREA

An area power creates an area of effect (page 272) that can originate in a distant square and hits multiple targets or creates an obstacle. For details about how area attacks work, see page 271.

Area burst [number] within [number] squares: To use an area burst power, choose a square within the range indicated by the second number. The power affects targets in that square or within a number of squares equal to the first number.

Area wall [number] within [number] squares: To use an area wall power, choose a square within the range indicated by the second number to be the wall's origin square (page 272). The first number represents the number of squares the wall occupies (all of its squares must be within range).

PERSONAL

A power that has a range of "personal" affects only you.

PREREQUISITE OR REQUIREMENT

Prerequisite: You must be trained in Stealth.
Requirement: You must be wielding a light blade.

Certain powers are usable only if you meet a predetermined condition.

Prerequisite: You must meet this provision to select this power. If you ever lose a prerequisite for a power (for example, if you use the retraining system to replace training in a skill with training in a different skill), you can't use that power thereafter.

Requirement: You must meet this provision to use this power. You can have the power in your repertoire, but it is not available to you unless you fulfill the requirement.

TARGET

Target: One creature
Target: You or one ally
Target: Each enemy in burst
Targets: One, two, or three creatures
Target: One object or unoccupied square

If a power directly affects one or more creatures or objects, it has a "Target" or "Targets" entry.

When a power's target entry specifies that it affects you and one or more of your allies, then you can take advantage of the power's effect along with your teammates. Otherwise, "ally" or "allies" does not include you, and both terms assume willing targets. "Enemy" or "enemies" means a creature or creatures that aren't your allies (whether those creatures are hostile toward you or not). "Creature" or "creatures" means allies and enemies both, as well as you.

ATTACK

Attack: Strength vs. AC
Attack: Charisma vs. Will
Attack: Constitution vs. Fortitude
Attack: Intelligence + 4 vs. Reflex
Attack: Dexterity vs. AC, one attack per target

Most attack powers that deal damage require you to make an attack roll. The "Attack" entry specifies the kind of attack you make and which of the target's defenses you check against. If you have a modifier to your attack roll, that's mentioned here as well. Example entries are given above.

If your power can attack multiple targets, you make a separate attack roll against each target.

HIT

Hit: 1[W] + Strength modifier damage.
Hit: 3d6 + Intelligence modifier force damage, and the target is dazed until the end of your next turn.
Hit: 5d6 + Intelligence modifier acid damage, and ongoing 10 acid damage (save ends).
Hit: The target is immobilized (save ends).
Hit: 2[W] + Dexterity modifier damage, and the target is slowed and grants combat advantage to you (save ends both).
Hit: 3d6 + Wisdom modifier thunder damage, and you push the target a number of squares equal to 3 + your Charisma modifier.
Hit: 3[W] + Strength modifier damage, and you regain hit points as if you had spent a healing surge.
Hit: 3[W] + Strength modifier damage, and you and each ally within 10 squares of you can spend a healing surge.

Every power that requires an attack roll includes a "Hit" entry, which explains what happens when an attack roll succeeds. Example entries are given above. See "Attacks and Defenses," page 269, for how to make attack rolls, how to deal damage, and how to apply various effects, including conditions and forced movement.

Ongoing damage is a fixed amount rather than an amount determined by a die roll. Ongoing damage is applied to a target each round at the start of the target's turn until the target makes a successful saving throw.

If a "Hit" (or "Effect") entry contains "(save ends)" or "(save ends both)," the indicated consequence of the successful attack persists until the target makes a successful saving throw.

If a hit grants you the ability to compel the target to move, whether through forced movement or teleportation, you can move it any number of squares up to the number specified (or not move it at all, if you so choose).

Some powers add modifiers to attack rolls or damage rolls. These modifiers apply to any roll of the dice, but not to ongoing damage or other static, nonvariable effects. The paladin's *wrath of the gods* prayer, for example, adds her Charisma modifier to her and her allies' damage rolls until the end of the encounter. When her cleric ally invokes *flame strike*, the damage equals 2d10 + Wisdom modifier + the paladin's Charisma modifier fire damage and ongoing 5 fire damage. The ongoing damage doesn't increase, because it's a static effect.

Whenever you affect a creature with a power, that creature knows exactly what you've done to it and what conditions you've imposed. For example, when a paladin uses *divine challenge* against an enemy, the enemy knows that it has been marked and that it will therefore take a penalty to attack rolls and some damage if it attacks anyone aside from the paladin.

Applying a Penalty: When a power description includes wording such as "a penalty to attack rolls equal to your Charisma modifier," that means you subtract the value of your ability modifier from the result or the numerical quantity that's being penalized. If your ability modifier is not a positive number, it does not provide a penalty.

Regaining Hit Points: Some powers allow you or someone else to regain hit points. Sometimes the recipient of this benefit needs to spend a healing surge (page 293), but if a power description includes the wording "as if . . . had spent a healing surge," then the beneficiary gains the appropriate number of hit points but does not spend a healing surge to do so.

Within x Squares of You: When this language appears in a power description, treat the effect it refers to as a close burst for the purpose of determining line of effect.

Duration: Most powers take effect and then end—their effects are instantaneous, perhaps as brief as a single swing of your sword. Some powers last beyond your turn, however—for instance, until the end of the current encounter or until the end of your next turn. If you use a power outside combat, it lasts for 5 minutes unless otherwise noted. Durations are discussed in more detail on page 278.

MISS

Miss: Half damage.
Miss: Half damage, and no ongoing fire damage.
Miss: Half damage, and the target is not pushed or immobilized.

Sometimes the dice are against you, and you miss your target. Missing isn't always the end of the story, however. A miss can indicate a splash effect, a glancing blow, or some other incidental effect of a power. Examples of some typical "Miss" entries are given above.

Half Damage: When you calculate half damage, remember to apply the rule about rounding down (page 11). If a damage roll produces a result of 1, half of that damage is 0.

Secondary Target and Secondary Attack

Secondary Target: One creature within 3 squares of you
Secondary Target: The same or a different target
Secondary Target: Each enemy adjacent to the primary target
Secondary Targets: Two creatures within 10 squares of the primary target

Some powers allow you to make secondary (or even tertiary) attacks. The power description indicates if you can make such an attack after the previous attack was a hit, if that attack was a miss, or regardless of whether the previous attack hits or misses.

Unless otherwise noted, the range of a secondary (or tertiary) attack is the same as for the attack that preceded it.

Effect

Effect: Until the end of your next turn, the target's attack rolls against you take a penalty equal to your Wisdom modifier.
Effect: You become invisible and then teleport 4 squares. The invisibility lasts until the start of your next turn.
Effect: The power's area is difficult terrain until the end of your next turn. You can end this effect as a minor action.
Effect: You gain temporary hit points equal to 2d6 + your Constitution modifier.

Many powers produce effects that take place regardless of whether your attack roll succeeds, and other powers have effects that occur without an attack roll being required. Example entries are given above.

The effects of powers are as varied as the powers themselves. Some effects impose a condition on the power's target. Other effects provide a bonus or a benefit (for you or your allies) or a penalty (for enemies). Still others change the nature of the battlefield or create something that didn't exist a moment ago.

Two kinds of powers—conjurations and zones—produce distinctive effects that are governed by special rules.

Conjurations

Powers that have the conjuration keyword create objects or creatures of magical energy.

Unless a power description says otherwise, a conjuration can't be attacked or physically affected, and allies of the conjuration's creator can move through the space a conjuration occupies, but enemies can't.

A conjuration uses your ability scores and defenses to determine the outcome of attacks it makes and attacks against it (if such attacks are possible).

Environmental phenomena and other forces have no effect on a conjuration unless a power description says otherwise. For example, a conjuration that produces an icy hand functions in a fiery, volcanic cavern without penalty.

If a power allows you to move a conjuration, at least 1 square that the conjuration occupies must remain within the power's range. If you move far enough away from a conjuration that it is no longer in range, its effect immediately ends.

If a conjuration's creator is slain, the conjuration immediately ends.

Zones

The zone keyword applies to powers that create lingering effects that extend over an area. For example, some zones create terrain effects, such as difficult terrain or scorching fire that harms anyone who enters it.

Zones cannot be attacked or otherwise physically affected unless a power description says otherwise. If zones overlap and impose penalties to the same roll or score, creatures in the overlapping area are subject to the worst penalty; the penalties are not cumulative. Similarly, a target in the overlapping area takes damage from whichever zone deals the most damage, regardless of damage type.

Environmental effects, attacks, and other forces have no effect on a zone unless a power description says otherwise. For example, a zone that deals fire damage is in no way diminished by a power that deals cold damage.

If a power allows you to move a zone, at least 1 square that the zone covers must remain within the power's range. If you move far enough away from a zone that it is no longer in range, its effects immediately end.

Unless otherwise specified, a zone fills a power's area of effect. Use the standard rules for areas of effect to determine which squares it fills.

If a zone's creator is slain, the zone immediately ends.

Sustain

Sustain Minor: The zone persists.
Sustain Minor: You slide the target 1 square, whether you hit or miss.
Sustain Minor: When you sustain the power, you make a secondary attack.
Sustain Move: You can sustain this power until the end of the encounter or for 5 minutes.
Sustain Standard: You remain invisible as long as you don't make an attack.

If a power has a "Sustain" entry, you can keep that power active by taking a specified type of action (minor, move, or standard) during your turn. The "Sustain" entry tells you if a power has an effect that occurs when you take the action to sustain it. See "Durations," page 278, for more about sustaining a power.

CLERIC

"Have courage, my friends! Pelor favors us today!"

CLASS TRAITS

Role: Leader. You lead by shielding allies with your prayers, healing, and using powers that improve your allies' attacks.

Power Source: Divine. You have been invested with the authority to wield divine power on behalf of a deity, faith, or philosophy.

Key Abilities: Wisdom, Strength, Charisma

Armor Proficiencies: Cloth, leather, hide, chainmail
Weapon Proficiencies: Simple melee, simple ranged
Implement: Holy symbol
Bonus to Defense: +2 Will

Hit Points at 1st Level: 12 + Constitution score
Hit Points per Level Gained: 5
Healing Surges per Day: 7 + Constitution modifier

Trained Skills: Religion. From the class skills list below, choose three more trained skills at 1st level.
Class Skills: Arcana (Int), Diplomacy (Cha), Heal (Wis), History (Int), Insight (Wis), Religion (Int)

Build Options: Battle cleric, devoted cleric
Class Features: Channel Divinity, Healer's Lore, *healing word*, Ritual Casting

Clerics are battle leaders who are invested with divine power. They blast foes with magical prayers, bolster and heal companions, and lead the way to victory with a mace in one hand and a holy symbol in the other. Clerics run the gamut from humble servants of the common folk to ruthless enforcers of evil gods.

As a cleric, the deity (or deities) you choose to revere goes a long way toward defining you, or at least how other people in the world see you. You could be a platinum-garbed envoy of Bahamut seeking justice throughout the land, a shadowy follower of Sehanine with a roguish streak, a burly disciple of Kord who believes the virtue of strength is sufficient for all challenges, or a dwarf cleric of Moradin bringing honor to the denizens of your mountain home.

Will you protect what is sacred to your god, quest for legendary holy artifacts, pursue a life of evangelical adventuring, or attempt all these deeds and more?

WILLIAM O'CONNOR

CREATING A CLERIC

The cleric has two basic builds to start: the battle cleric and the devoted cleric. Clerics rely on Strength for their melee attacks and Wisdom for their healing and non-melee prayers. Charisma also aids their abilities.

BATTLE CLERIC

If you choose to concentrate on melee, you find a good assortment of strikes to your liking. To achieve this build, make Strength your primary score. Make Wisdom your secondary score and assign Charisma as your tertiary score. Make sure to concentrate on powers that work with melee attacks, since these play to your key ability scores.

Suggested Feat: Weapon Focus (Human feat: Action Surge)

Suggested Skills: Diplomacy, Heal, Insight, Religion

Suggested At-Will Powers: *righteous brand*, *priest's shield*

Suggested Encounter Power: *wrathful thunder*
Suggested Daily Power: *avenging flame*

DEVOTED CLERIC

With this build, you choose to stand back and concentrate your abilities on keeping your fellow adventurers healthy and optimized. To this end, choose powers that grant bonuses and healing, such as *divine glow* and *beacon of hope*. Assign your highest ability score to Wisdom, with Charisma secondary and Strength tertiary. Make sure to concentrate on powers that use Wisdom for attacks, since this is your highest ability score.

Suggested Feat: Channel Divinity feat associated with your deity (Human feat: Human Perseverance)

Suggested Skills: Arcana, Heal, History, Religion

Suggested At-Will Powers: *lance of faith*, *sacred flame*

Suggested Encounter Power: *healing strike*
Suggested Daily Power: *beacon of hope*

CLERIC CLASS FEATURES

Clerics are capable combatants who wield simple weapons in battle—maces and similar weapons have long been symbols of divine authority. In addition, all clerics have the class features described below.

CHANNEL DIVINITY

Once per encounter you can invoke divine power, filling yourself with the might of your patron deity. With the divine might you invoke you can wield special powers, such as *turn undead* and *divine fortune*. Some clerics learn other uses for this feature; for instance, the divinity feats in Chapter 6 grant characters with access to the Channel Divinity class feature the ability to use additional special powers.

Regardless of how many different uses for Channel Divinity you know, you can use only one such ability per encounter. The special ability or power you invoke works just like your other powers.

HEALER'S LORE

Your study of healing allows you to make the most of your healing prayers. When you grant healing with one of your cleric powers that has the healing keyword, add your Wisdom modifier to the hit points the recipient regains.

HEALING WORD

Using the *healing word* power, clerics can grant their comrades additional resilience with nothing more than a short prayer.

RITUAL CASTING

You gain the Ritual Caster feat (page 200) as a bonus feat, allowing you to use magical rituals (see Chapter 10). You possess a ritual book, and it contains two rituals you have mastered: the Gentle Repose ritual and one other 1st-level ritual of your choice.

CLERICS AND DEITIES

All clerics choose a specific faith to which they devote themselves. Usually this faith is the worship of a specific patron deity—for example, Moradin, Pelor, or Erathis. Sometimes clerics are devoted to churches that venerate groups of deities or even philosophies.

As a cleric, your deity does not directly grant you powers. Instead, your ordination or investiture as a cleric grants you the ability to wield divine powers. Clerics are usually formally ordained by existing clerics who perform a special ritual to do so, but on rare occasions a deity moves to directly ordain a worthy worshiper with-

CLERIC OVERVIEW

Characteristics: You are an extremely good healer. You have a mix of melee and ranged powers. Most of your attacks deal only moderate damage, but they safeguard your allies or provide bonuses to their attacks.

Religion: A cleric can choose to worship any deity, but steer clear of choosing an evil or chaotic evil deity unless you have permission from your DM to choose one.

Races: Humans and dwarves make ideal clerics. Elves, half-elves, and dragonborn are good clerics too, but they rarely have the same values of piety and reverence found in many human and dwarven cultures. Certain gods attract a preponderance of clerics of a particular race—for example, many (but not all) clerics of Moradin are dwarves—but in general, all races respect all gods to at least some degree. The race you play and the deity your character worships have little effect on your cleric's ability to utilize divine powers.

out any sort of priestly hierarchy involved. What you do with your powers once you are ordained is up to you, although if you flagrantly and openly defy your deity's tenets, you quickly earn the enmity of the faithful.

GOOD, LAWFUL GOOD, AND UNALIGNED DEITIES

Deity	Alignment	Areas of Influence
Avandra	Good	Change, luck, trade, travel
Bahamut	Lawful good	Justice, honor, nobility, protection
Corellon	Unaligned	Arcane magic, spring, beauty, the arts
Erathis	Unaligned	Civilization, invention, laws
Ioun	Unaligned	Knowledge, prophecy, skill
Kord	Unaligned	Storms, strength, battle
Melora	Unaligned	Wilderness, sea
Moradin	Lawful good	Creation, artisans, family
Pelor	Good	Sun, summer, agriculture, time
Raven Queen	Unaligned	Death, fate, winter
Sehanine	Unaligned	Trickery, moon, love, autumn

EVIL AND CHAOTIC EVIL DEITIES

Deity	Alignment	Areas of Influence
Asmodeus	Evil	Power, domination, tyranny
Bane	Evil	War, conquest
Gruumsh	Chaotic evil	Turmoil, destruction
Lolth	Chaotic evil	Spiders, shadows, lies
Tiamat	Evil	Wealth, greed, vengeance
Torog	Evil	Underdark, imprisonment
Vecna	Evil	Undeath, secrets
Zehir	Evil	Darkness, poison, serpents

You must choose a deity compatible with your alignment: Good clerics serve good deities, lawful good clerics serve lawful good deities, and so on. If a deity is unaligned, your alignment doesn't matter, so a deity such as Melora has good, lawful good, evil, chaotic evil, and unaligned clerics in her service. Similarly, if you're unaligned, you can serve any god. For example, Pelor is served by both good clerics and unaligned clerics, but never by evil, chaotic evil, or lawful good clerics.

For most games, you should choose a good, lawful good, or unaligned deity for your cleric. Ask your Dungeon Master before you select an evil or chaotic evil deity.

IMPLEMENT

Clerics make use of holy symbols to help channel and direct their divine powers. A cleric wearing or holding a magic holy symbol can add its enhancement bonus to the attack rolls and the damage rolls of cleric powers, as well as cleric paragon path powers, that have the implement keyword. Without a holy symbol, a cleric can still use these powers, but he or she doesn't gain the bonus provided by the magic implement.

CLERIC POWERS

Your cleric powers are called prayers. Some are better for the battle cleric and some are better for the devoted cleric, but a cleric can choose any power when making a power selection.

CLASS FEATURES

The cleric has two class features that work like powers: Channel Divinity and *healing word*. The Channel Divinity class feature encompasses multiple powers, two of which (*divine fortune* and *turn undead*) are presented below.

Channel Divinity: Divine Fortune — Cleric Feature

In the face of peril, you hold true to your faith and receive a special boon.

Encounter ✦ Divine
Free Action   Personal
Effect: You gain a +1 bonus to your next attack roll or saving throw before the end of your next turn.

Channel Divinity: Turn Undead — Cleric Feature

You sear undead foes, push them back, and root them in place.

Encounter ✦ Divine, Implement, Radiant
Standard Action   Close burst 2
                    (5 at 11th level, 8 at 21st level)
Target: Each undead creature in burst
Attack: Wisdom vs. Will
Hit: 1d10 + Wisdom modifier radiant damage, and you push the target a number of squares equal to 3 + your Charisma modifier. The target is immobilized until the end of your next turn.
Increase damage to 2d10 + Wisdom modifier at 5th level, 3d10 + Wisdom modifier at 11th level, 4d10 + Wisdom modifier at 15th level, 5d10 + Wisdom modifier at 21st level, and 6d10 + Wisdom modifier at 25th level.
Miss: Half damage, and the target is not pushed or immobilized.

Healing Word — Cleric Feature

You whisper a brief prayer as divine light washes over your target, helping to mend its wounds.

Encounter (Special) ✦ Divine, Healing
Special: You can use this power twice per encounter, but only once per round. At 16th level, you can use this power three times per encounter.
Minor Action   Close burst 5
                    (10 at 11th level, 15 at 21st level)
Target: You or one ally
Effect: The target can spend a healing surge and regain an additional 1d6 hit points.
Increase the amount of additional hit points regained to 2d6 at 6th level, 3d6 at 11th level, 4d6 at 16th level, 5d6 at 21st level, and 6d6 at 26th level.

LEVEL 1 AT-WILL PRAYERS

Lance of Faith — Cleric Attack 1

A brilliant ray of light sears your foe with golden radiance. Sparkles of light linger around the target, guiding your ally's attack.

At-Will ✦ Divine, Implement, Radiant
Standard Action   **Ranged** 5
Target: One creature
Attack: Wisdom vs. Reflex
Hit: 1d8 + Wisdom modifier radiant damage, and one ally you can see gains a +2 power bonus to his or her next attack roll against the target.
Increase damage to 2d8 + Wisdom modifier at 21st level.

Priest's Shield — Cleric Attack 1

You utter a minor defensive prayer as you attack with your weapon.

At-Will ✦ Divine, Weapon
Standard Action   **Melee** weapon
Target: One creature
Attack: Strength vs. AC
Hit: 1[W] + Strength modifier damage, and you and one adjacent ally gain a +1 power bonus to AC until the end of your next turn.
Increase damage to 2[W] + Strength modifier at 21st level.

Righteous Brand — Cleric Attack 1

You smite your foe with your weapon and brand it with a ghostly, glowing symbol of your deity's anger. By naming one of your allies when the symbol appears, you add divine power to that ally's attacks against the branded foe.

At-Will ✦ Divine, Weapon
Standard Action   **Melee** weapon
Target: One creature
Attack: Strength vs. AC
Hit: 1[W] + Strength modifier damage, and one ally within 5 squares of you gains a power bonus to melee attack rolls against the target equal to your Strength modifier until the end of your next turn.
Increase damage to 2[W] + Strength modifier at 21st level.

Sacred Flame — Cleric Attack 1

Sacred light shines from above, searing a single enemy with its radiance while at the same time aiding an ally with its beneficent power.

At-Will ✦ Divine, Implement, Radiant
Standard Action   **Ranged** 5
Target: One creature
Attack: Wisdom vs. Reflex
Hit: 1d6 + Wisdom modifier radiant damage, and one ally you can see chooses either to gain temporary hit points equal to your Charisma modifier + one-half your level or to make a saving throw.
Increase damage to 2d6 + Wisdom modifier at 21st level.

LEVEL 1 ENCOUNTER PRAYERS

Cause Fear — Cleric Attack 1

Your holy symbol ignites with the fury of your god. Uncontrollable terror grips your enemy, causing him to instantly recoil.

Encounter ✦ Divine, Fear, Implement
Standard Action   **Ranged** 10
Target: One creature
Attack: Wisdom vs. Will
Hit: The target moves its speed + your Charisma modifier away from you. The fleeing target avoids unsafe squares and difficult terrain if it can. This movement provokes opportunity attacks.

Divine Glow — Cleric Attack 1

Murmuring a prayer to your deity, you invoke a blast of white radiance from your holy symbol. Foes burn in its stern light, but your allies are heartened and guided by it.

Encounter ✦ Divine, Implement, Radiant
Standard Action   **Close** blast 3
Target: Each enemy in blast
Attack: Wisdom vs. Reflex
Hit: 1d8 + Wisdom modifier radiant damage.
Effect: Allies in the blast gain a +2 power bonus to attack rolls until the end of your next turn.

Healing Strike — Cleric Attack 1

Divine radiance gleams from your weapon. When you smite your enemy, your deity bestows a minor blessing in the form of healing for you or one of your allies.

Encounter ✦ Divine, Healing, Radiant, Weapon
Standard Action   **Melee** weapon
Target: One creature
Attack: Strength vs. AC
Hit: 2[W] + Strength modifier radiant damage, and the target is marked until the end of your next turn. In addition, you or one ally within 5 squares of you can spend a healing surge.

Wrathful Thunder — Cleric Attack 1

Your arm is made strong by the power of your deity. When you strike, a terrible thunderclap smites your adversary and dazes him.

Encounter ✦ Divine, Thunder, Weapon
Standard Action   **Melee** weapon
Target: One creature
Attack: Strength vs. AC
Hit: 1[W] + Strength modifier thunder damage, and the target is dazed until the end of your next turn.

LEVEL 1 DAILY PRAYERS

Avenging Flame — Cleric Attack 1

You slam your weapon into your foe, who bursts into flame. Divine fire avenges each attack your enemy dares to make.

Daily ✦ Divine, Fire, Weapon
Standard Action   **Melee** weapon
Target: One creature
Attack: Strength vs. AC
Hit: 2[W] + Strength modifier damage, and ongoing 5 fire damage (save ends).
Miss: Half damage, and no ongoing fire damage.
Special: If the target attacks on its turn, it can't attempt a saving throw against the ongoing damage.

Beacon of Hope — Cleric Attack 1

A burst of divine energy harms your foes and heals your allies. The radiant energy lingers around your holy symbol and improves your healing powers for the rest of the battle.

Daily ✦ Divine, Healing, Implement
Standard Action   **Close** burst 3
Target: Each enemy in burst
Attack: Wisdom vs. Will
Hit: The target is weakened until the end of its next turn.
Effect: You and all your allies in the burst regain 5 hit points, and your healing powers restore +5 hit points until the end of the encounter.

Cascade of Light — Cleric Attack 1

A burst of divine radiance sears your foe.

Daily ✦ Divine, Implement, Radiant
Standard Action   **Ranged** 10
Target: One creature
Attack: Wisdom vs. Will
Hit: 3d8 + Wisdom modifier radiant damage, and the target gains vulnerability 5 to all your attacks (save ends).
Miss: Half damage, and the target gains no vulnerability.

Guardian of Faith — Cleric Attack 1

You conjure a ghostly guardian, indistinct except for a glowing shield emblazoned with your deity's symbol. A burst of radiance erupts from it to sear foes that move next to it.

Daily ✦ Conjuration, Divine, Implement, Radiant
Standard Action   **Ranged** 5
Effect: You conjure a guardian that occupies 1 square within range. Every round, you can move the guardian 3 squares as a move action. The guardian lasts until the end of the encounter. Any creature that ends its turn next to the conjured guardian is subject to a Wisdom vs. Fortitude attack. On a hit, the attack deals 1d8 + Wisdom modifier radiant damage.

LEVEL 2 UTILITY PRAYERS

Bless — Cleric Utility 2

You beseech your deity to bless you and your allies.

Daily ✦ Divine
Standard Action   **Close** burst 20
Targets: You and each ally in burst
Effect: Until the end of the encounter, all targets gain a +1 power bonus to attack rolls.

Cure Light Wounds — Cleric Utility 2

You utter a simple prayer and gain the power to instantly heal wounds, and your touch momentarily suffuses you or a wounded creature with a dim silver light.

Daily ✦ Divine, Healing
Standard Action   **Melee** touch
Target: You or one creature
Effect: The target regains hit points as if it had spent a healing surge.

Divine Aid — Cleric Utility 2

You beseech your deity to grant you or one of your allies the strength to overcome a hindrance.

Encounter ✦ Divine
Standard Action   **Ranged** 5
Target: You or one ally
Effect: The target makes a saving throw with a bonus equal to your Charisma modifier.

Sanctuary — Cleric Utility 2

You cast a protective ward upon a creature that makes enemies' attacks less effective.

Encounter ✦ Divine
Standard Action   **Ranged** 10
Target: You or one creature
Effect: The target receives a +5 bonus to all defenses. The effect lasts until the target attacks or until the end of your next turn.

Shield of Faith — Cleric Utility 2

A gleaming shield of divine energy appears over you, granting you and nearby allies protection against attacks.

Daily ✦ Divine
Standard Action   **Close** burst 5
Targets: You and each ally in burst
Effect: The targets gain a +2 power bonus to AC until the end of the encounter.

LEVEL 3 ENCOUNTER PRAYERS

Blazing Beacon — Cleric Attack 3

You invoke your deity's name, and holy light envelops your weapon. When you strike your foe, a blazing beacon in the form of a holy rune floats above its head to guide your allies' ranged attacks as well.

Encounter ✦ Divine, Radiant, Weapon
Standard Action   **Melee** weapon
Target: One creature
Attack: Strength vs. AC
Hit: 1[W] + Strength modifier radiant damage, and all ranged attack rolls against the target gain a +4 power bonus until the end of your next turn.

Command — Cleric Attack 3

You utter a single word to your foe, a word that demands obedience. You can choose to drive the foe back, order it closer, or cause the foe to throw itself to the ground.

Encounter ✦ Charm, Divine, Implement
Standard Action   **Ranged** 10
Target: One creature
Attack: Wisdom vs. Will
Hit: The target is dazed until the end of your next turn. In addition, you can choose to knock the target prone or slide the target a number of squares equal to 3 + your Charisma modifier.

Daunting Light — Cleric Attack 3

A burning column of light engulfs your foe. Its brilliance burns and hinders your foe's defense for a short time.

Encounter ✦ Divine, Implement, Radiant
Standard Action   **Ranged** 10
Target: One creature
Attack: Wisdom vs. Reflex
Hit: 2d10 + Wisdom modifier radiant damage.
Effect: One ally you can see gains combat advantage against the target until the end of your next turn.

Split the Sky — Cleric Attack 3

You invoke ancient words of wrath as you attack with your weapon. The thundering power of your melee strike causes your foe to stumble backward and fall.

Encounter ✦ Divine, Thunder, Weapon
Standard Action   **Melee** weapon
Target: One creature
Attack: Strength vs. Fortitude
Hit: 1[W] + Strength modifier thunder damage, and you push the target 2 squares and knock it prone.

LEVEL 5 DAILY PRAYERS

Consecrated Ground — Cleric Attack 5

With a wave of your hand, jagged lines of radiant light spread across the ground around you like a crackling web, moving at your whim. Enemies that stand upon this ground suffer the wrath of your deity.

Daily ✦ Divine, Healing, Radiant, Zone
Standard Action   **Close** burst 1
Effect: The burst creates a zone of sanctified ground that lasts until the end of your next turn. You can move the origin square of the zone 3 squares as a move action. Enemies that start their turns within the zone take 1d6 + your Charisma modifier radiant damage. You and any allies who are bloodied and start their turns within the zone regain hit points equal to 1 + your Charisma modifier.
Sustain Minor: The zone persists.

Rune of Peace — Cleric Attack 5

You smash your weapon into your foe, leaving behind a glowing rune that prevents your foe from making attacks.

Daily ✦ Charm, Divine, Weapon
Standard Action   **Melee** weapon
Target: One creature
Attack: Strength vs. Will
Hit: 1[W] + Strength modifier damage, and the target cannot attack (save ends).
Miss: The target cannot attack you until the end of your next turn.

Spiritual Weapon — Cleric Attack 5

You conjure a glowing weapon adorned with the symbol of your deity. The weapon attacks one of your foes and guides your allies' attacks against the same target.

Daily ✦ Conjuration, Divine, Implement
Standard Action   **Ranged** 10
Target: One creature
Attack: Wisdom vs. AC
Hit: 1d10 + Wisdom modifier damage.
Effect: You conjure a weapon that appears in the target's square and attacks. Your allies gain combat advantage against the target. You can move the weapon up to 10 squares to another enemy's square as a move action. The weapon lasts until the end of your next turn.
Sustain Minor: When you sustain the power, repeat the attack. Your allies continue to gain combat advantage against the weapon's target.

Weapon of the Gods — Cleric Attack 5

Your weapon glows with divine radiance, enhancing your attacks.

Daily ✦ Divine, Radiant, Weapon
Minor Action   **Melee** touch
Target: One held weapon
Effect: Until the end of the encounter, all attacks made with the weapon deal an extra 1d6 radiant damage. When the weapon hits an enemy, the enemy takes a -2 penalty to AC until the end of the weapon wielder's next turn.

LEVEL 6 UTILITY PRAYERS

Bastion of Health — Cleric Utility 6

You invoke a prayer that instantly fortifies one of your allies.

Encounter ✦ Divine, Healing
Minor Action   **Ranged** 10
Target: You or one ally
Effect: The target can spend a healing surge. Add your Charisma modifier to the hit points regained.

Cure Serious Wounds — Cleric Utility 6

You utter a simple prayer and gain the power to instantly heal wounds, and your touch momentarily suffuses you or a wounded creature with bright silver light.

Daily ✦ Divine, Healing
Standard Action   **Melee** touch
Target: You or one creature
Effect: The target regains hit points as if it had spent two healing surges.

Divine Vigor — Cleric Utility 6

You call upon your deity to invigorate you and your battle-weary allies.

Daily ✦ Divine, Healing
Minor Action   **Close** burst 5
Targets: You and each ally in burst
Effect: Each target regains the use of his or her second wind.

Holy Lantern — Cleric Utility 6

A conjured beacon of divine light shines like a lantern, piercing shadows and deception.

At-Will ✦ Conjuration, Divine
Standard Action   **Ranged** 3
Effect: You conjure a lantern that appears in 1 square within range and sheds light 5 squares in all directions. You and allies in the light gain a +2 power bonus to Perception and Insight checks. You can move the lantern up to your speed as a minor action. The lantern lasts for 10 hours, but you can have only a single holy lantern active at a time.

LEVEL 7 ENCOUNTER PRAYERS

Awe Strike — Cleric Attack 7

The supernatural awe and dread that radiates from you as you swing your weapon leaves your foe momentarily frozen in terror.

Encounter ✦ Divine, Fear, Weapon
Standard Action   **Melee** weapon
Target: One creature
Attack: Strength vs. Will
Hit: 1[W] + Strength modifier damage, and the target is immobilized until the end of your next turn.

Break the Spirit — Cleric Attack 7

Calling down the power of your god, you bathe your foe in agonizing radiance, driving strength out of its impending attacks.

Encounter ✦ Charm, Divine, Implement, Radiant
Standard Action   **Ranged** 10
Target: One creature
Attack: Wisdom vs. Will
Hit: 2d8 + Wisdom modifier radiant damage, and the target takes a penalty to attack rolls equal to your Charisma modifier until the end of your next turn.

Searing Light — Cleric Attack 7

You invoke the power of your deity. From your holy symbol a searing ray of light flashes forth, striking and blinding your enemy for a short time.

Encounter ✦ Divine, Implement, Radiant
Standard Action   **Ranged** 10
Target: One creature
Attack: Wisdom vs. Reflex
Hit: 2d6 + Wisdom modifier radiant damage, and the target is blinded until the end of your next turn.

Strengthen the Faithful — Cleric Attack 7

You utter a solemn prayer as you bring your weapon down upon your foe, invoking the power of your deity to physically bolster you and nearby allies.

Encounter ✦ Divine, Healing, Weapon
Standard Action   **Melee** weapon
Target: One creature
Attack: Strength vs. AC
Hit: 2[W] + Strength modifier damage, and you and each ally adjacent to the target can spend a healing surge. Add your Charisma modifier to the hit points regained.

LEVEL 9 DAILY PRAYERS

Astral Defenders — Cleric Attack 9

You conjure two ghostly soldiers, indistinct except for glowing weapons. They lash out with divine radiance against enemies that pass.

Daily ✦ Conjuration, Divine, Implement, Radiant
Standard Action   **Ranged** 10
Effect: You conjure two soldiers, each occupying 1 square within range. The conjured soldiers don't attack normally, but whenever an opportunity attack would be provoked from a conjured soldier, the soldier makes a Wisdom vs. Reflex attack. On a hit, the attack deals 1d10 + Wisdom modifier radiant damage.

You can move one soldier or both a total of 3 squares as a move action. Creatures can move through the spaces occupied by the soldiers. The soldiers last until the end of the encounter.

Blade Barrier
Cleric Attack 9

A barrier of whirling blades appears, slashing at those who come too close or try to pass through.

Daily ✦ Conjuration, Divine, Implement
Standard Action   Area wall 5 within 10 squares
Effect: You conjure a wall of contiguous squares filled with spinning blades of astral energy that lasts until the end of your next turn. The wall can be up to 5 squares long and up to 2 squares high. The spaces occupied by the blade barrier are difficult terrain.
   If a creature enters the barrier's space or starts its turn there, it takes 3d6 + Wisdom modifier damage plus ongoing 5 damage (save ends).
Sustain Minor: The barrier persists.

Divine Power
Cleric Attack 9

You swing your weapon in a wide arc around you, creating a halo of divine energy that drives foes back while fortifying you and your allies.

Daily ✦ Divine, Healing, Radiant, Weapon
Standard Action   Close burst 2
Target: Each enemy in burst you can see
Attack: Strength vs. Fortitude
Hit: 2[W] + Strength modifier radiant damage, and you push the target 1 square.
Effect: Until the end of the encounter, you gain regeneration 5, and you and each ally within the burst gain a +2 power bonus to AC.

Flame Strike
Cleric Attack 9

A column of flame roars downward to engulf your foes.

Daily ✦ Divine, Fire, Implement
Standard Action   Area burst 2 within 10 squares
Target: Each enemy in burst
Attack: Wisdom vs. Reflex
Hit: 2d10 + Wisdom modifier fire damage, and ongoing 5 + Wisdom modifier fire damage (save ends).
Miss: Half damage, and no ongoing fire damage.

Level 10 Utility Prayers

Astral Refuge
Cleric Utility 10

With a touch, you send one of your allies to a sequestered location in the Astral Sea, where he can recuperate for a brief time before rejoining the battle.

Daily ✦ Divine, Healing, Teleportation
Standard Action   Melee touch
Target: One willing ally
Effect: The target is whisked away to a place of safety in the Astral Sea for 3 rounds. While there, the target can spend a healing surge each round but cannot take any other actions. At the end of the effect, the target reappears in the space he or she left or, if the space is not vacant, in the nearest unoccupied space.

Knights of Unyielding Valor
Cleric Utility 10

You conjure four ghostly knights that carry huge shields emblazoned with the symbol of your deity.

Daily ✦ Conjuration, Divine
Standard Action   Ranged 10
Effect: You conjure four ghostly warriors, each occupying 1 square within range. As a move action, you can move any of the knights 2 squares. They can't attack or be attacked or damaged, and they last until the end of the encounter.
   Enemies can't enter a square occupied by a conjured knight, but allies can move through the knights' spaces as if the knights were allies. The conjured knights grant cover to allies but not enemies.

Mass Cure Light Wounds
Cleric Utility 10

With a wave of your hand, healing motes of silver light engulf you and all nearby allies.

Daily ✦ Divine, Healing
Standard Action   Close burst 5
Targets: You and each ally in burst
Effect: The targets regain hit points as if they had spent a healing surge. Add your Charisma modifier to the hit points regained.

Shielding Word
Cleric Utility 10

You invoke a prayer that instantly defends one of your allies.

Encounter ✦ Divine
Immediate Interrupt   Ranged 5
Trigger: An ally in range is hit by an attack
Effect: The ally gains a +4 power bonus to AC until the end of your next turn.

Level 13 Encounter Prayers

Arc of the Righteous
Cleric Attack 13

You channel your god's divine wrath into your weapon, unleashing an arc of lightning with a successful strike that then leaps to another foe within range.

Encounter ✦ Divine, Lightning, Weapon
Standard Action   Melee weapon
Primary Target: One creature
Attack: Strength vs. AC
Hit: 2[W] + Strength modifier lightning damage. Make a secondary attack.
   Secondary Target: One creature within 3 squares of you
   Secondary Attack: Strength vs. AC
   Hit: 1[W] + Strength modifier lightning damage.

Inspiring Strike
Cleric Attack 13

You recite a short verse as you strike your enemy with your weapon. If you hit, the power of the quoted verse brings healing to you or an ally close by.

Encounter ✦ Divine, Healing, Weapon
Standard Action   Melee weapon
Target: One creature
Attack: Strength vs. AC
Hit: 2[W] + Strength modifier damage, and you or an ally within 5 squares regains hit points equal to 15 + your Charisma modifier.

Mantle of Glory — Cleric Attack 13

Whispering a prayer to your deity, you invoke a blast of white radiance from your holy symbol. Foes burn in its glorious light, but your allies are fortified by it.

Encounter ✦ Divine, Healing, Implement, Radiant
Standard Action   **Close** blast 5
Target: Each enemy in blast
Attack: Wisdom vs. Will
Hit: 2d10 + Wisdom modifier radiant damage.
Effect: Allies in the blast can spend a healing surge.

Plague of Doom — Cleric Attack 13

You direct your attention at an enemy, whisper an ancient battle prayer, and send jolts of wracking pain through his body.

Encounter ✦ Divine, Implement
Standard Action   **Ranged** 10
Target: One creature
Attack: Wisdom vs. Fortitude
Hit: 3d8 + Wisdom modifier damage, and the target takes a penalty to all defenses equal to your Charisma modifier until the end of your next turn.

LEVEL 15 DAILY PRAYERS

Holy Spark — Cleric Attack 15

Crackling with heavenly lightning, your weapon hits your foe and engulfs him in glowing arcs. Lightning jumps to other foes that approach the target.

Daily ✦ Divine, Lightning, Weapon
Standard Action   **Melee** weapon
Target: One creature
Attack: Strength vs. Will
Hit: 2[W] + Strength modifier lightning damage, and ongoing 10 lightning damage (save ends). While this power's ongoing damage is in effect, any ally of the target that starts its turn within 3 squares of the target takes 2d10 lightning damage.
Miss: Half damage, and no ongoing lightning damage.

Purifying Fire — Cleric Attack 15

Divine fire engulfs your foes and leaves them burning. Like beacons of holy flame, your burning foes heal your nearby allies while the flames persist.

Daily ✦ Divine, Fire, Healing, Implement
Standard Action   **Area** burst 2 within 10 squares
Target: Each enemy in burst
Attack: Wisdom vs. Reflex
Hit: 3d10 + Wisdom modifier fire damage, and ongoing 10 fire damage (save ends). While this power's ongoing damage is in effect, you and your allies regain hit points equal to 5 + your Charisma modifier when starting a turn adjacent to one or more targets taking the ongoing damage.
Miss: Half damage, and no ongoing fire damage.

Seal of Warding — Cleric Attack 15

You create a circle of faintly glowing divine symbols around you that hinders the movement of enemies caught within it and protects you and your allies from ranged attacks.

Daily ✦ Divine, Implement, Radiant, Zone
Standard Action   **Close** burst 3
Target: Each enemy in burst
Attack: Wisdom vs. Will
Hit: 4d10 + Wisdom modifier radiant damage, and the target is slowed until the end of your next turn.
Miss: Half damage, and the target is not slowed.
Effect: The burst creates a zone of difficult terrain that grants cover to you and your allies against ranged attacks until the end of your next turn.
Sustain Minor: The zone persists.

LEVEL 16 UTILITY PRAYERS

Astral Shield — Cleric Utility 16

You conjure a shimmering silver shield, which you can then move around the battlefield to provide protection where it is needed most.

Encounter ✦ Conjuration, Divine
Standard Action   **Ranged** 5
Effect: You conjure a shield that appears in 1 square within range. You and any allies adjacent to the shield gain a +2 bonus to AC. Every round, you can move the shield up to 3 squares within range as a move action. It can't be attacked or damaged and lasts until the end of the encounter.

Cloak of Peace — Cleric Utility 16

You utter a prayer as you point toward a nearby ally, surrounding him in a mantle of faint silvery light that repels attacks for as long as he does not attack.

Daily ✦ Divine
Standard Action   **Ranged** 10
Target: You or one ally
Effect: The target gains a +5 power bonus to AC and a +10 power bonus to all other defenses until the end of the encounter. This effect ends if the target makes an attack.

Divine Armor — Cleric Utility 16

As you mutter a fervent prayer, the power of your god encases you and healing motes of silver light surround you and all nearby allies.

Daily ✦ Divine, Healing
Standard Action   **Close** burst 3
Targets: You and each ally in burst
Effect: You gain a +2 power bonus to AC, and all targets gain resist 5 to all damage until the end of the encounter.

Hallowed Ground — Cleric Utility 16

You speak a prayer, and the ground around you becomes hallowed, granting you and your allies divine protection.

Daily ✦ Divine, Zone
Standard Action   **Close** burst 5
Effect: The burst creates a zone of hallowed ground. You and any allies gain the following benefits while within the zone: a +2 power bonus to saving throws, a +2 power bonus to all defenses, and a +2 power bonus to attack rolls. The area remains hallowed until the end of the encounter.

LEVEL 17 ENCOUNTER PRAYERS

Blinding Light · Cleric Attack 17

You utter a brief prayer, and a brilliant nimbus of golden light surrounds your weapon, blinding your enemy on impact.

Encounter ✦ Divine, Radiant, Weapon
Standard Action   **Melee** weapon
Target: One creature
Attack: Strength vs. Fortitude
Hit: 2[W] + Strength modifier radiant damage, and the target is blinded until the end of your next turn.

Enthrall · Cleric Attack 17

You begin reciting a verse from some ancient holy text. The truths you speak are enough to wound and hamper your enemies.

Encounter ✦ Charm, Divine, Implement, Psychic
Standard Action   **Area** burst 3 within 10 squares
Target: Each enemy in burst
Attack: Wisdom vs. Will
Hit: 2d10 + Wisdom modifier psychic damage, and the target is immobilized and unable to make attacks against you until the end of your next turn.

Sentinel Strike · Cleric Attack 17

You shout a sacred invocation, and your weapon smolders with silver wisps of divine power. In addition to delivering a stern blow to your enemy, the divine energy clings to your target and foils its attacks for a short time.

Encounter ✦ Divine, Weapon
Standard Action   **Melee** weapon
Target: One creature
Attack: Strength vs. AC
Hit: 3[W] + Strength modifier damage. Choose one ally within 5 squares of you; if the target attacks that ally before the end of your next turn, reduce the target's damage against that ally to 0.

Thunderous Word · Cleric Attack 17

You shout a word that forcefully thrusts your enemies back while allowing your allies to position themselves more advantageously.

Encounter ✦ Divine, Implement, Thunder
Standard Action   **Close** blast 5
Target: Each enemy in blast
Attack: Wisdom vs. Reflex
Hit: 3d6 + Wisdom modifier thunder damage, and you push the target a number of squares equal to 3 + your Charisma modifier.
Effect: Allies in the blast can shift 1 square.

LEVEL 19 DAILY PRAYERS

Fire Storm · Cleric Attack 19

A roiling cloud of fire scours your foes, lingering on the battlefield until you allow it to burn itself out.

Daily ✦ Divine, Fire, Implement, Zone
Standard Action   **Area** burst 5 within 10 squares
Target: Each enemy in burst
Attack: Wisdom vs. Reflex
Hit: 5d10 + Wisdom modifier fire damage.
Miss: Half damage.
Effect: The burst creates a zone of fire that lasts until the end of your next turn. Enemies that start their turn in this zone take 1d10 + Wisdom modifier fire damage.
Sustain Minor: The zone persists.

Holy Wrath · Cleric Attack 19

A burst of furious light washes over your foes and fortifies you with the wrath of your god.

Daily ✦ Divine, Healing, Implement, Radiant
Standard Action   **Close** burst 3
Target: Each enemy in burst
Attack: Strength vs. AC
Hit: 2d10 + Strength modifier radiant damage.
Effect: You gain regeneration 10 and a +2 power bonus to attack rolls until the end of the encounter.

Indomitable Spirit · Cleric Attack 19

The divine power of your mighty attack fortifies your allies.

Daily ✦ Divine, Healing, Weapon
Standard Action   **Melee** weapon
Target: One creature
Attack: Strength vs. AC
Hit: 3[W] + Strength modifier damage.
Miss: Half damage.
Effect: You and each ally within 5 squares of you regain hit points as if you had each spent a healing surge.

Knight of Glory · Cleric Attack 19

You conjure a ghostly warrior clad in the ceremonial armor of your faith. With sword in hand, it attacks your enemies.

Daily ✦ Conjuration, Divine, Implement
Standard Action   **Ranged** 10
Target: One creature adjacent to the ghostly knight
Attack: Wisdom vs. AC
Hit: 3d10 + Wisdom modifier damage.
Effect: You conjure a ghostly knight that occupies 1 square within range, and the knight attacks an adjacent creature. Once per round as a minor action, you can make the knight attack an adjacent creature. Every round, you can move the knight 5 squares as a move action. It lasts until the end of the encounter.

4

Clarion Call of the Astral Sea   Cleric Utility 22

You beseech your deity for aid. A heavenly trumpet sounds, and you or a nearby ally is instantly whisked away to a fortress on the Astral Sea, restored to full health, and returned safely to the battlefield in short order.

Daily ✦ Divine, Healing, Teleportation
Standard Action   Ranged 10
Target: You or one willing ally
Effect: The target teleports away to a safe location in the Astral Sea and regains hit points up to its maximum. While it is away, the target can perceive the surroundings of its previous location, but it can't take any actions. At the start of its next turn, it returns to an unoccupied space chosen by you within 5 squares of its previous location.

Cloud Chariot   Cleric Utility 22

You conjure a white cloud that coalesces into a chariot pulled by a winged horse, both made of solid cloudstuff.

Daily ✦ Conjuration, Divine
Standard Action   Ranged 2
Effect: You conjure a chariot of cloudstuff that occupies a 2-by-2 space within range, and a winged horse of cloudstuff that occupies a 2-by-2 space adjacent to the chariot. The horse and chariot have a speed of fly 8. The chariot can carry up to four Small or Medium creatures, and the horse can hold one Small or Medium rider. The chariot grants cover to its occupants. The chariot and the horse can't attack or be separated, and they can't be attacked or damaged. They remain until you take an extended rest unless you dismiss them (a free action).

Purify   Cleric Utility 22

You wave a hand, releasing golden motes of light that strike nearby allies, ridding them of all lingering afflictions.

Daily ✦ Divine
Standard Action   Close burst 5
Targets: You and each ally in burst
Effect: Every effect that a save can end is removed from the targets.

Spirit of Health   Cleric Utility 22

You conjure an insubstantial spirit that hovers in the air nearby and heals your wounded comrades.

Daily ✦ Conjuration, Divine, Healing
Standard Action   Ranged 10
Effect: You conjure a spirit that appears in 1 square within range. You or any ally adjacent to or in the same square as the spirit can spend a healing surge as a minor action. The spirit can heal one target per round and regains its healing ability at the start of each of your turns. Creatures can move through the spirit's space without impediment. The spirit can't move or be attacked or damaged, and it lasts until the end of the encounter.

LEVEL 22 UTILITY PRAYERS

Angel of the Eleven Winds   Cleric Utility 22

You conjure a luminous winged angel with indistinct features. It hovers 1 foot above the ground and grants others the power of flight.

Daily ✦ Conjuration, Divine
Standard Action   Ranged 10
Effect: You conjure the likeness of an angel that occupies 1 square within range. The angel grants any target you can see a speed of fly 8 and a +4 power bonus to AC against opportunity attacks. Changing the target is a minor action. A creature that no longer benefits from the effect lands on the ground safely. The angel can't move or be attacked or damaged, and it lasts until the end of the encounter.

LEVEL 23 ENCOUNTER PRAYERS

Astral Blades of Death
Cleric Attack 23

You invoke a holy phrase. Merciless blades of silvery light suddenly appear around your enemy and begin hacking at it.

Encounter ✦ Divine, Implement, Radiant
Standard Action   **Ranged** 10
Target: One creature
Attack: Wisdom vs. Reflex
Hit: 6d6 + Wisdom modifier radiant damage.

Divine Censure
Cleric Attack 23

With a hushed prayer, you imbue your weapon with the divine might of your god, such that one hit with the weapon leaves your enemy reeling.

Encounter ✦ Divine, Weapon
Standard Action   **Melee** weapon
Target: One creature
Attack: Strength vs. AC
Hit: 3[W] + Strength modifier damage, and the target takes a –2 penalty to attack rolls until the end of your next turn.

Haunting Strike
Cleric Attack 23

You strike your enemy hard with your weapon and invoke an ancient divine curse that makes him more vulnerable to a subsequent attack.

Encounter ✦ Divine, Weapon
Standard Action   **Melee** weapon
Target: One creature
Attack: Strength + 2 vs. AC
Hit: 4[W] + Strength modifier damage. The next attack roll you make against the target gains a +2 power bonus.

Healing Torch
Cleric Attack 23

You whisper an ancient prayer, igniting your holy symbol with divine light that quickly spreads to engulf your enemies and allies. The light sears your foes and momentarily bathes your allies in a protective, healing glow.

Encounter ✦ Divine, Healing, Implement, Radiant
Standard Action   **Area** burst 5 within 10 squares
Target: Each enemy in burst
Attack: Wisdom vs. Will
Hit: 3d8 + Wisdom modifier radiant damage.
Effect: You and each ally in the burst gain a power bonus to AC equal to your Charisma modifier until the end of your next turn and can spend a healing surge. Add your Charisma modifier to the hit points regained.

LEVEL 25 DAILY PRAYERS

Nimbus of Doom
Cleric Attack 25

Your attack illuminates your foe with a radiant glow, guiding attacks against it.

Daily ✦ Divine, Radiant, Weapon
Standard Action   **Melee** weapon
Target: One creature
Attack: Strength vs. AC
Hit: 6[W] + Strength modifier radiant damage.
Effect: The target takes a –2 penalty to all defenses (save ends).

Sacred Word
Cleric Attack 25

A single word of divine power damages and stuns nearby foes.

Daily ✦ Divine, Implement, Psychic
Standard Action   **Close** burst 5
Target: Each enemy in burst
Attack: Wisdom vs. Fortitude
Hit: 4d10 + Wisdom modifier psychic damage, and the target is stunned until the end of your next turn.
Miss: Half damage, and the target is not stunned.

Seal of Binding
Cleric Attack 25

Faintly glowing symbols encircle your foe, trapping it.

Daily ✦ Divine, Implement
Standard Action   **Ranged** 10
Target: One creature
Attack: Wisdom vs. Will
Hit: 3d10 + Wisdom modifier damage, and the target is stunned and can't be affected by any attack other than this one until the end of your next turn.
Sustain Standard: Each time you sustain the power, you and the target both take 2d10 + Wisdom modifier damage. The target remains stunned and protected against all other attacks. You can't sustain this power if you are bloodied.

Seal of Protection
Cleric Attack 25

You create a circle of faintly glowing symbols that halts your enemies and protects you and your allies from attack.

Daily ✦ Divine, Implement, Radiant, Zone
Standard Action   **Close** burst 2
Target: Each enemy in burst
Attack: Strength vs. Reflex
Hit: 3d10 + Strength modifier radiant damage.
Effect: The burst creates a protected zone until the end of your next turn. You and each ally within the zone gain a +2 bonus to AC. Enemies that enter the zone end their current movement.
Sustain Minor: The zone persists.

LEVEL 27 ENCOUNTER PRAYERS

Punishing Strike
Cleric Attack 27

With a simple prayer, you gain a sudden clarity of purpose and empower your weapon with the indomitable might of your deity.

Encounter ✦ Divine, Weapon
Standard Action   **Melee** weapon
Target: One creature
Attack: Strength + 2 vs. AC
Hit: 4[W] + Strength modifier damage.

Sacrificial Healing
Cleric Attack 27

As you spill the blood of your enemy, you whisper a prayer to your deity, who rewards your battle prowess with a timely blessing upon you and all nearby allies.

Encounter ✦ Divine, Healing, Weapon
Standard Action   **Melee** weapon
Target: One creature
Attack: Strength vs. AC
Hit: 3[W] + Strength modifier damage, and you and each ally within 10 squares of you can spend a healing surge. Add your Charisma modifier to the hit points regained.

Scourge of the Unworthy — Cleric Attack 27

You utter a divine phrase that lashes your enemy, dealing a terrible wound.

Encounter ✦ Divine, Implement, Necrotic
Standard Action   **Ranged** 20
Target: One creature
Attack: Wisdom vs. Reflex
Hit: 4d10 + Wisdom modifier necrotic damage, and the target takes a -2 penalty to attack rolls until the end of your next turn.

Sunburst — Cleric Attack 27

When you invoke an ancient prayer, a brilliant burst of light explodes in front of you, healing your allies and searing your enemies.

Encounter ✦ Divine, Healing, Implement, Radiant
Standard Action   **Area** burst 2 within 10 squares
Target: Each enemy in burst
Attack: Wisdom vs. Will
Hit: 3d8 + Wisdom modifier radiant damage.
Effect: You and each ally in the burst regain hit points equal to 10 + your Charisma modifier and make a saving throw.

LEVEL 29 DAILY PRAYERS

Astral Storm — Cleric Attack 29

You unleash a terrible storm upon your enemies, raining ice, fire, lightning, and thunder down upon them.

Daily ✦ Cold, Divine, Fire, Implement, Lightning, Thunder, Zone
Standard Action   **Area** burst 5 within 20 squares
Target: Each enemy in burst
Attack: Wisdom vs. Reflex
Hit: 6d10 + Wisdom modifier cold, fire, lightning, and thunder damage. Resistance doesn't reduce the damage unless the target has resistance to all four damage types, and only the weakest resistance applies. A target that has vulnerability to any one of the four damage types is subject to that vulnerability.
Miss: Half damage.
Effect: The burst creates a stormy zone until the end of your next turn.
Sustain Minor: When you sustain this power, make a Wisdom vs. Reflex attack against every enemy within the zone, dealing 2d10 + Wisdom modifier lightning damage if you hit and half damage if you miss.

Godstrike — Cleric Attack 29

Your weapon explodes with brilliant light as you swing it at your foe.

Daily ✦ Divine, Radiant, Weapon
Standard Action   **Melee** weapon
Target: One creature
Attack: Strength vs. AC
Hit: 7[W] + Strength modifier radiant damage.
Miss: Half damage.

PARAGON PATHS

ANGELIC AVENGER

"I am as an angel, an avenger for my god."

Prerequisite: Cleric class

You become a special servant of your god, operating with angelic powers to promote the word of your faith. When you use your angelic powers, you briefly take on the aspects of an angel: Your face blurs into angelic blankness, astral wings sprout from your back, and your lower body blurs away.

ANGELIC AVENGER PATH FEATURES

Angelic Action (11th level): When you spend an action point to take an extra action, you also gain a +4 bonus to attack rolls until the start of your next turn.

Astral Vibrance (11th level): Choose an energy form when you gain this feature: lightning, radiant, or thunder. When a bloodied enemy is within 5 squares of you at the start of its turn, it takes energy damage of your chosen type equal to your Charisma modifier.

Weapon Training (11th level): You are proficient with one heavy blade of your choice.

FRANZ VOHWINKEL

Blood and Radiance (16th level): An enemy that bloodies you with an attack is outlined with holy radiance, granting combat advantage to you and your allies until the end of its next turn.

ANGELIC AVENGER PRAYERS

Astral Wave — Angelic Avenger Attack 11

As your angelic visage emerges, a wave of astral energy emanates from you and washes over your enemies with deadly effect.

Encounter ✦ Divine, Implement; Lightning, Radiant, or Thunder
Standard Action   Close burst 8
Target: Each enemy in burst
Attack: Wisdom vs. Will
Hit: 2d8 + Wisdom modifier damage of the energy type you chose for your Astral Vibrance path feature.

Angelic Presence — Angelic Avenger Utility 12

Your features blur into an angel's holy veil, and you are filled with a divine presence.

Daily ✦ Divine, Fear
Minor Action   Personal
Effect: Enemies gain a -2 penalty to attack rolls against you until the end of the encounter or until you are bloodied.

Angel Ascendant — Angelic Avenger Attack 20

You channel divine energy into a single, powerful attack that transforms you into an angelic being. Wings of radiant light spread from your back as your features transform into those of an angel.

Daily ✦ Divine, Weapon
Standard Action   Melee weapon
Attack: Strength vs. AC
Hit: 5[W] + Strength modifier damage.
Effect: You gain a speed of fly 6 (hover) until the end of the encounter. (See the *Dungeon Master's Guide* for rules on hovering.)

DIVINE ORACLE

"I have seen your fate, written in the waves of the Astral Sea."

Prerequisite: Cleric class

You become the voice of your god, full of prophecy and omens. When you use your prophetic powers, your eyes glow with the silvery depths of the Astral Sea.

DIVINE ORACLE PATH FEATURES

Foresight (11th level): You and each ally within 5 squares of you can't be surprised. Also, you roll twice when making an initiative check; use whichever roll you like.

Prophetic Action (11th level): When you spend an action point to take an extra action, you also gain an extra move action that you can use during another turn later in this encounter.

Terrifying Insight (16th level): Whenever you make an attack against Will, you can roll twice and use the higher result. If the attack misses, you are dazed until the end of your next turn.

DIVINE ORACLE PRAYERS

Prophecy of Doom — Divine Oracle Attack 11

You predict dire results for your enemy.

Encounter ✦ Divine
Standard Action   Ranged 5
Target: One creature
Effect: You or an ally who hits the target with an attack can choose to make the attack a critical hit. This power lasts until the end of your next turn or until you or an ally uses it to make an attack a critical hit.

Good Omens — Divine Oracle Utility 12

You peer into the future and predict good fortune for you and your allies.

Daily ✦ Divine
Standard Action   Ranged 10
Targets: You and each ally in range
Effect: The targets gain a +5 power bonus to all d20 rolls until the end of your next turn, but the targets cannot score critical hits while this power is in effect.

Hammer of Fate — Divine Oracle Attack 20

You hammer your foe with prophetic words of power. If your foe avoids the barrage, you can untangle the lines of fate and perform a different action.

Daily ✦ Divine, Implement
Standard Action   Ranged 20
Target: One creature
Attack: Wisdom vs. Will
Hit: 5d10 + Wisdom modifier damage.
Miss: Rewind your turn to the moment before you made the attack, and you don't use this power. Choose a different standard action this turn. You can't use *hammer of fate* again until the next encounter.

RADIANT SERVANT

"I am the light of faith, banishing the darkness."

Prerequisite: Cleric class

You become the light of your god in the world, shining divine illumination into every dark corner and deep shadow. When you use your radiant powers, your countenance glows with the brightness of the sun.

RADIANT SERVANT PATH FEATURES

Illuminating Attacks (11th level): Your powers that have the radiant keyword can now score a critical hit with a natural die roll of 19 or 20.

Radiant Action (11th level): When you spend an action point to take an extra action, you can also choose an enemy within 5 squares of you. That enemy takes ongoing radiant damage equal to your level (save ends).

Lasting Light (16th level): Any saving throws made by demons or undead creatures to remove effects you have placed upon them receive a –2 penalty.

RADIANT SERVANT PRAYERS

Solar Wrath	Radiant Servant Attack 11

Radiant light explodes from you like a solar flare, evaporating shadows and dealing illuminating damage to everything around you.

Encounter ✦ Divine, Radiant
Standard Action   **Close** burst 8
Target: Each enemy in burst
Attack: Wisdom vs. Will
Hit: 3d8 + Wisdom modifier radiant damage. If the target is either an undead creature or a demon, it is also stunned until the end of your next turn.

Healing Sun	Radiant Servant Utility 12

A healing sun shines forth from you, repairing the wounds of your allies while keeping creatures of darkness at bay.

Daily ✦ Divine, Healing, Radiant, Zone
Standard Action   **Close** burst 2
Effect: The burst creates a zone of divine light until the end of your next turn. You and each ally who ends his or her turn within the zone regain hit points equal to 5 + your Charisma modifier. A demon or an undead creature that enters the zone or starts its turn there takes 1d10 + your Charisma modifier radiant damage.
Sustain Standard: The zone persists.
Special: The zone ends at the end of your turn if you are bloodied.

Radiant Brilliance	Radiant Servant Attack 20

You fire a brilliant ray of searing light into a foe, igniting that foe and briefly turning it into a small sun.

Daily ✦ Divine, Implement, Radiant
Standard Action   **Ranged** 20
Target: One creature
Attack: Wisdom vs. Reflex
Hit: 3d10 + Wisdom modifier radiant damage.
Effect: At the start of your next turn, the target is the center of a burst 5 radiant explosion that affects only your enemies: Wisdom vs. Will; 3d10 radiant damage; half damage on a miss.

WARPRIEST

"Let loose the gift of battle!"

Prerequisite: Cleric class

Your god demands battle to accomplish the tenets of your faith, and you are the chosen priest at the forefront of the war. When you call upon your divine powers, your weapons glow with holy light.

WARPRIEST PATH FEATURES

Extra Damage Action (11th level): When you spend an action point to take an extra action, you also add one-half your level to the damage dealt by any of your standard action attacks this turn.

Warpriest's Strategy (11th level): Once per encounter, if you or an adjacent ally rolls a 1 when making a melee attack or a close attack, you can call for a reroll.

Warpriest's Training (11th level): You receive a +1 bonus to AC when wearing heavy armor.

Warpriest's Challenge (16th level): When you hit an enemy with an at-will melee attack, you can choose to mark that enemy for the rest of the encounter. The next time that enemy shifts or attacks a creature other than you, you can make an opportunity attack against that enemy. If you mark a new enemy with this feature, any previous marks you have made with this feature end.

WARPRIEST PRAYERS

Battle Cry	Warpriest Attack 11

You attack every enemy next to you, shouting a revitalizing battle cry that inspires your allies.

Encounter ✦ Divine, Healing, Implement
Standard Action   **Close** burst 1
Target: Each adjacent enemy
Attack: Wisdom vs. Fortitude
Hit: 2[W] + Wisdom modifier
Effect: You and each bloodied ally within 10 squares of you can spend a healing surge.

Battle Favor	Warpriest Utility 12

When you score a critical hit against an enemy, your deity favors you with healing or by renewing one of your prayers.

Daily ✦ Divine, Healing
Free Action   **Personal**
Trigger: You roll a natural 20 when making a melee attack
Effect: Regain hit points as if you had spent two healing surges, or recover one daily power you have already used. Once you use this power, you cannot recover it except by taking an extended rest.

Battle Pyres	Warpriest Attack 20

You call upon a powerful prayer that turns your enemies into pyres ablaze with radiant energy.

Daily ✦ Divine, Implement, Radiant
Standard Action   **Close** burst 5
Primary Target: Each enemy in burst
Attack: Wisdom vs. Will
Hit: 2d8 + Wisdom modifier damage, and ongoing 5 radiant damage (save ends). Make a secondary attack.
Secondary Target: One creature taking ongoing radiant damage within 5 squares of you
Secondary Attack: Wisdom vs. Reflex
Hit: 5d10 + Wisdom modifier damage.
Sustain Standard: You can make the secondary attack in subsequent rounds as long as at least one of your primary targets is taking ongoing radiant damage.

FIGHTER

"You'll have to deal with me first, dragon!"

CLASS TRAITS

Role: Defender. You are very tough and have the exceptional ability to contain enemies in melee.

Power Source: Martial. You have become a master of combat through endless hours of practice, determination, and your own sheer physical toughness.

Key Abilities: Strength, Dexterity, Wisdom, Constitution

Armor Proficiencies: Cloth, leather, hide, chainmail, scale; light shield, heavy shield

Weapon Proficiencies: Simple melee, military melee, simple ranged, military ranged

Bonus to Defense: +2 Fortitude

Hit Points at 1st Level: 15 + Constitution score
Hit Points per Level Gained: 6
Healing Surges per Day: 9 + Constitution modifier

Trained Skills: From the class skills list below, choose three trained skills at 1st level.
Class Skills: Athletics (Str), Endurance (Con), Heal (Wis), Intimidate (Cha), Streetwise (Cha)

Build Options: Great weapon fighter, guardian fighter
Class Features: Combat Challenge, Combat Superiority, Fighter Weapon Talent

Fighters are determined combat adepts trained to protect the other members of their adventuring groups. Fighters define the front line by bashing and slicing foes into submission while reflecting enemy attacks through the use of heavy armor. Fighters draw weapons for gold, for glory, for duty, and for the mere joy of unrestrained martial exercise.

Regardless of your level of skill and the specific weapons you eventually master, your motivations determine who you defend and who you slay. You could be a noble champion who pledges your blade to gallant causes, a calculating mercenary who cares more for the clink of gold than praise, a homeless prince on the run from assassins, or a blood-loving thug looking for the next good fight.

Your future is yours. When you unsheathe your weapon, what battle cry flies from your lips?

CREATING A FIGHTER

You can choose any fighter powers you like for your character, but fighters naturally fall into two basic groups: the great weapon fighter and the guardian fighter. All fighters rely on Strength. Fighters also need Constitution, Dexterity, or Wisdom, depending on which weapon they favor. See "Fighters and Melee Weapons" for more information.

GREAT WEAPON FIGHTER

You're interested in dealing out the most damage you can. You prefer big two-handed weapons such as the greatsword or greataxe. You're more interested in fighting hard than fighting smart. Your best ability score is definitely Strength. A good Constitution improves your ability to use high damage weapons, such as axes and hammers. Plus, extra hit points always help. Select powers that work well with two-handed weapons to make the most of this build.

Suggested Feat: Power Attack (Human feat: Action Surge)
Suggested Skills: Athletics, Endurance, Intimidate
Suggested At-Will Powers: *cleave, reaping strike*
Suggested Encounter Power: *spinning sweep*
Suggested Daily Power: *brute strike*

GUARDIAN FIGHTER

To fight better, you fight smarter. You're willing to trade offense for superior defenses and better ability to control the battlefield around you. You fight with a heavy shield and a good one-handed weapon, such as a longsword, flail, or battleaxe. Like the great weapon fighter, you make Strength your best ability score. After that, prioritize your Dexterity to take advantage of weapons that can be improved by Dexterity-based feats, or your Wisdom to make the most of the combat superiority class feature. You're hard to hurt and hard to move away from. Select powers that make use of your one-handed weapon and shield, as well as take advantage of your higher Dexterity score.

Suggested Feat: Weapon Focus (Human feat: Human Perseverance)
Suggested Skills: Heal, Intimidate, Streetwise
Suggested At-Will Powers: *sure strike, tide of iron*
Suggested Encounter Power: *covering attack*
Suggested Daily Power: *comeback strike*

FIGHTER CLASS FEATURES

Some of your most important characteristics are the ability to wear very good armor, your exceptional hit point total, and your mastery of all military weapons. In addition, you have three unique class features.

COMBAT CHALLENGE

In combat, it's dangerous to ignore a fighter. Every time you attack an enemy, whether the attack hits or misses, you can choose to mark that target. The mark lasts until the end of your next turn. While a target is marked, it takes a –2 penalty to attack rolls for any attack that doesn't include you as a target. A creature can be subject to only one mark at a time. A new mark supersedes a mark that was already in place.

In addition, whenever a marked enemy that is adjacent to you shifts or makes an attack that does not include you, you can make a melee basic attack against that enemy as an immediate interrupt.

COMBAT SUPERIORITY

You gain a bonus to opportunity attacks equal to your Wisdom modifier. An enemy struck by your opportunity attack stops moving, if a move provoked the attack. If it still has actions remaining, it can use them to resume moving.

FIGHTER WEAPON TALENT

Choose either one-handed or two-handed weapons. When using a weapon of your chosen style, you gain a +1 bonus to attack rolls.

FIGHTERS AND MELEE WEAPONS

Fighters master intricacies of melee weapon skill that other characters can't match. Unlike other classes, fighters have many encounter powers that work better when used with specific groups of melee weapons (see the table below). Powers associated with a weapon group favor a particular ability score mix, so that fighters with high Constitution are likely to want to use axes, hammers, or picks, while fighters with high Dexterity are more likely to favor heavy blades, light

---

FIGHTER OVERVIEW

Characteristics: You are extremely tough, with a great Armor Class and lots of hit points. You have extraordinary resilience against physical attack. You don't have much ability to fight at range, but you excel in melee combat. You have special abilities that make it dangerous for enemies to ignore you, so you can contain foes and keep them away from your friends.

Religion: Fighters naturally favor deities of war, combat, adventure, or valor. Bahamut and Kord are popular, as is Avandra. Many unaligned or evil fighters pay homage to Bane, the god of war.

Races: Fighters come from all races. Dragonborn, dwarves, and humans are the most common fighters.

blades, flails, or spears. The weapon feats described in Chapter 6 that provide optimized abilities for specific groups of weapons favor the same ability score mixes, so the list below notes the melee weapon groups and the ability score that is most likely to help you optimize your fighter abilities with that weapon group.

Melee Weapon Groups and Associated Statistics
Axe: Constitution and higher than normal Strength (battleaxe, handaxe, greataxe, halberd)
Flail: Dexterity (flail, heavy flail, spiked chain)
Hammer: Constitution (maul, throwing hammer, warhammer)
Heavy Blade: Dexterity (bastard sword, falchion, glaive, greatsword, longsword, scimitar, scythe)
Light Blade: Dexterity alone is sometimes enough (dagger, katar, rapier, short sword, shuriken, sickle)
Mace: Constitution (club, great club, mace, morningstar)
Pick: Constitution [and rarely Dexterity] (war pick)
Polearm: Wisdom [and rarely Dexterity] (glaive, halberd, longspear)
Spear: Dexterity (javelin, longspear, spear)
Staff: Constitution (quarterstaff)

Most melee weapon groups, with the exception of light blades, require some element of Strength to access the weapon feats that improve their importance. (Light blades have some feats that require only Dexterity, though other light blade feats also require a modicum of Strength.) The list of weapon groups above mentions the ability score *other than Strength* that helps access the feats that improve a specific group of weapons, as well as fighter powers that are tied to specific groups of weapons.

Strength is mentioned in the list only if a weapon group has unusually high requirements for Strength.

A few weapons, including most polearms, are part of multiple groups and can therefore be approached from different optimal ability score builds.

Fighter Powers

Your powers are called exploits. Some work better for great weapon fighters and some work better for guardian fighters, but you can choose any power you like when you reach a level that allows you to choose a new power. The choice of weapon you make also provides benefits to certain fighter powers.

Level 1 At-Will Exploits

Cleave — Fighter Attack 1

You hit one enemy, then cleave into another.

At-Will ✦ Martial, Weapon
Standard Action   Melee weapon
Target: One creature
Attack: Strength vs. AC
Hit: 1[W] + Strength modifier damage, and an enemy adjacent to you takes damage equal to your Strength modifier.
Increase damage to 2[W] + Strength modifier at 21st level.

Reaping Strike — Fighter Attack 1

You punctuate your scything attacks with wicked jabs and small cutting blows that slip through your enemy's defenses.

At-Will ✦ Martial, Weapon
Standard Action   Melee weapon
Target: One creature
Attack: Strength vs. AC
Hit: 1[W] + Strength modifier damage.
Increase damage to 2[W] + Strength modifier at 21st level.
Miss: Half Strength modifier damage. If you're wielding a two-handed weapon, you deal damage equal to your Strength modifier.

Sure Strike — Fighter Attack 1

You trade power for precision.

At-Will ✦ Martial, Weapon
Standard Action   Melee weapon
Target: One creature
Attack: Strength + 2 vs. AC
Hit: 1[W] damage.
Increase damage to 2[W] at 21st level.

Tide of Iron — Fighter Attack 1

After each mighty swing, you bring your shield to bear and use it to push your enemy back.

At-Will ✦ Martial, Weapon
Standard Action   Melee weapon
Requirement: You must be using a shield.
Target: One creature
Attack: Strength vs. AC
Hit: 1[W] + Strength modifier damage, and you push the target 1 square if it is your size, smaller than you, or one size category larger. You can shift into the space that the target occupied.
Increase damage to 2[W] + Strength modifier at 21st level.

Level 1 Encounter Exploits

Covering Attack — Fighter Attack 1

You launch a dizzying barrage of thrusts at your enemy, compelling him to give you all his attention. Under the cover of your ferocious attack, one of your allies can safely retreat from that same foe.

Encounter ✦ Martial, Weapon
Standard Action   Melee weapon
Target: One creature
Attack: Strength vs. AC
Hit: 2[W] + Strength modifier damage, and an ally adjacent to the target can shift 2 squares.

Passing Attack — Fighter Attack 1

You strike at one foe and allow momentum to carry you forward into a second strike against a second foe.

Encounter ✦ Martial, Weapon
Standard Action   Melee weapon
Primary Target: One creature
Attack: Strength vs. AC
Hit: 1[W] + Strength modifier damage, and you can shift 1 square. Make a secondary attack.
  Secondary Target: One creature other than the primary target
  Secondary Attack: Strength + 2 vs. AC
  Hit: 1[W] + Strength modifier damage.

Spinning Sweep — Fighter Attack 1

You spin beneath your enemy's guard with a long, powerful cut, and then sweep your leg through his an instant later to knock him head over heels.

Encounter ✦ Martial, Weapon
Standard Action   Melee weapon
Target: One creature
Attack: Strength vs. AC
Hit: 1[W] + Strength modifier damage, and you knock the target prone.

Steel Serpent Strike — Fighter Attack 1

You stab viciously at your foe's knee or foot to slow him down. No matter how tough he is, he's going to favor that leg for a time.

Encounter ✦ Martial, Weapon
Standard Action   Melee weapon
Target: One creature
Attack: Strength vs. AC
Hit: 2[W] + Strength modifier damage, and the target is slowed and cannot shift until end of your next turn.

Level 1 Daily Exploits

Brute Strike — Fighter Attack 1

You shatter armor and bone with a ringing blow.

Daily ✦ Martial, Reliable, Weapon
Standard Action   Melee weapon
Target: One creature
Attack: Strength vs. AC
Hit: 3[W] + Strength modifier damage.

Comeback Strike — Fighter Attack 1

A timely strike against a hated foe invigorates you, giving you the strength and resolve to fight on.

Daily ✦ Healing, Martial, Reliable, Weapon
Standard Action   Melee weapon
Target: One creature
Attack: Strength vs. AC
Hit: 2[W] + Strength modifier damage, and you can spend a healing surge.

Villain's Menace — Fighter Attack 1

You strike your enemy hard and hound him with skilled parries and stern reprisals.

Daily ✦ Martial, Weapon
Standard Action   Melee weapon
Target: One creature
Attack: Strength vs. AC
Hit: 2[W] + Strength modifier damage, and you gain a +2 power bonus to attack rolls and a +4 power bonus to damage rolls against the target until the end of the encounter.
Miss: Gain a +1 power bonus to attack rolls and a +2 power bonus to damage rolls against the target until the end of the encounter.

Level 2 Utility Exploits

Boundless Endurance — Fighter Utility 2

You shake off the worst of your wounds.

Daily ✦ Healing, Martial, Stance
Minor Action   Personal
Effect: You gain regeneration 2 + your Constitution modifier when you are bloodied.

Get Over Here — Fighter Utility 2

You pull one of your allies into a more advantageous position.

Encounter ✦ Martial
Move Action   Melee 1
Target: One willing adjacent ally
Effect: You slide the target 2 squares to a square that is adjacent to you.

No Opening — Fighter Utility 2

You raise your weapon or shield to block an opening in your defenses.

Encounter ✦ Martial
Immediate Interrupt   Personal
Trigger: An enemy attacks you and has combat advantage against you
Effect: Cancel the combat advantage you were about to grant to the attack.

Unstoppable — Fighter Utility 2

You let your adrenaline surge carry you through the battle.

Daily ✦ Healing, Martial
Minor Action   Personal
Effect: You gain temporary hit points equal to 2d6 + your Constitution modifier.

LEVEL 3 ENCOUNTER EXPLOITS

Armor-Piercing Thrust
Fighter Attack 3

You drive your weapon through a weak point in your foe's defenses.

Encounter ✦ Martial, Weapon
Standard Action   **Melee** weapon
Target: One creature
Attack: Strength vs. Reflex
   Weapon: If you're wielding a light blade or a spear, you gain a bonus to the attack roll equal to your Dexterity modifier.
Hit: 1[W] + Strength modifier damage.
   Weapon: If you're wielding a light blade or a spear, you gain a bonus to the damage roll equal to your Dexterity modifier.

Crushing Blow
Fighter Attack 3

You wind up and deliver a devastating blow with your weapon.

Encounter ✦ Martial, Weapon
Standard Action   **Melee** weapon
Target: One creature
Attack: Strength vs. AC
Hit: 2[W] + Strength modifier damage.
   Weapon: If you're wielding an axe, a hammer, or a mace, you gain a bonus to the damage roll equal to your Constitution modifier.

Dance of Steel
Fighter Attack 3

Weaving your weapon in a graceful figure-eight, you lash out with a sudden attack.

Encounter ✦ Martial, Weapon
Standard Action   **Melee** weapon
Target: One creature
Attack: Strength vs. AC
Hit: 2[W] + Strength modifier damage.
   Weapon: If you're wielding a polearm or a heavy blade, the target is slowed until the end of your next turn.

Precise Strike
Fighter Attack 3

You trade damage for accuracy when you really want to land an attack on your opponent.

Encounter ✦ Martial, Weapon
Standard Action   **Melee** weapon
Target: One creature
Attack: Strength + 4 vs. AC
Hit: 1[W] + Strength modifier damage.

Rain of Blows
Fighter Attack 3

You become a blur of motion, raining a series of blows upon your opponent.

Encounter ✦ Martial, Weapon
Standard Action   **Melee** weapon
Primary Target: One creature
Attack: Strength vs. AC, two attacks
Hit: 1[W] + Strength modifier damage.
   Weapon: If you're wielding a light blade, a spear, or a flail and have Dexterity 15 or higher, make a secondary attack.
   Secondary Target: The same or a different target
   Secondary Attack: Strength vs. AC
   Hit: 1[W] + Strength modifier damage.

Sweeping Blow
Fighter Attack 3

You put all your strength into a single mighty swing that strikes many enemies at once.

Encounter ✦ Martial, Weapon
Standard Action   **Close** burst 1
Target: Each enemy in burst you can see
Attack: Strength vs. AC
   Weapon: If you're wielding an axe, a flail, a heavy blade, or a pick, you gain a bonus to the attack roll equal to one-half your Strength modifier.
Hit: 1[W] + Strength modifier damage.

LEVEL 5 DAILY EXPLOITS

Crack the Shell
Fighter Attack 5

You break through your enemy's armor and deal a painful bleeding wound.

Daily ✦ Martial, Reliable, Weapon
Standard Action   **Melee** weapon
Target: One creature
Attack: Strength vs. AC
Hit: 2[W] + Strength modifier damage, and the target takes ongoing 5 damage and a –2 penalty to AC (save ends both).

Dizzying Blow
Fighter Attack 5

You crack your foe upside the head.

Daily ✦ Martial, Reliable, Weapon
Standard Action   **Melee** weapon
Target: One creature
Attack: Strength vs. AC
Hit: 3[W] + Strength modifier damage, and the target is immobilized (save ends).

Rain of Steel
Fighter Attack 5

You constantly swing your weapon about, slashing and cutting into nearby enemies.

Daily ✦ Martial, Stance, Weapon
Minor Action   **Personal**
Effect: Any enemy that starts its turn adjacent to you takes 1[W] damage, as long as you are able to make opportunity attacks.

LEVEL 6 UTILITY EXPLOITS

Battle Awareness — Fighter Utility 6

No villain or monster can get the drop on you!

Daily ✦ Martial
No Action — **Personal**
Effect: You gain a +10 bonus to your initiative check. Use this power after rolling your initiative.

Defensive Training — Fighter Utility 6

With a soldier's discipline, you fend off attacks that would overcome a lesser person.

Daily ✦ Martial, Stance
Minor Action — **Personal**
Effect: Gain a +2 power bonus to your Fortitude, Reflex, or Will defense.

Unbreakable — Fighter Utility 6

You steel yourself against a brutal attack.

Encounter ✦ Martial
Immediate Reaction — **Personal**
Trigger: You are hit by an attack
Effect: Reduce the damage from the attack by 5 + your Constitution modifier.

LEVEL 7 ENCOUNTER EXPLOITS

Come and Get It — Fighter Attack 7

You call your opponents toward you and deliver a blow they will never forget.

Encounter ✦ Martial, Weapon
Standard Action — **Close** burst 3
Target: Each enemy in burst you can see
Effect: Each target must shift 2 and end adjacent to you, if possible. A target that can't end adjacent to you doesn't move. You can then attack any targets that are adjacent to you (close burst 1).
Attack: Strength vs. AC
Hit: 1[W] + Strength modifier damage.

Griffon's Wrath — Fighter Attack 7

You rain several heavy overhand blows down on your foe. They force him to raise his guard high to meet your attack, exposing a vulnerable spot for your next attack—the underarm, side, or belly.

Encounter ✦ Martial, Weapon
Standard Action — **Melee** weapon
Target: One creature
Attack: Strength vs. AC
Hit: 2[W] + Strength modifier damage, and the target takes a -2 penalty to AC until the end of your next turn.

Iron Bulwark — Fighter Attack 7

You use your weapon or shield to parry one blow after another, denying your foes the satisfaction of getting in a solid hit against you.

Encounter ✦ Martial, Weapon
Standard Action — **Melee** weapon
Target: One creature
Attack: Strength vs. AC
Hit: 2[W] + Strength modifier damage.
Effect: You gain a +1 power bonus to AC (or a +2 bonus if you're using a shield) until the end of your next turn.

Reckless Strike — Fighter Attack 7

You trade precision for power.

Encounter ✦ Martial, Weapon
Standard Action — **Melee** weapon
Target: One creature
Attack: Strength -2 vs. AC
Hit: 3[W] + Strength modifier damage.

Sudden Surge — Fighter Attack 7

You throw your weight into a strike, using the momentum of the swing to surge forward.

Encounter ✦ Martial, Weapon
Standard Action — **Melee** weapon
Target: One creature
Attack: Strength vs. AC
Hit: 2[W] + Strength modifier damage.
Effect: Move a number of squares equal to your Dexterity modifier (minimum 1).

LEVEL 9 DAILY EXPLOITS

Shift the Battlefield — Fighter Attack 9

With supreme skill and great resolve, you beat your enemies back.

Daily ✦ Martial, Weapon
Standard Action — **Close** burst 1
Target: Each enemy in burst you can see
Attack: Strength vs. AC
Hit: 2[W] + Strength modifier damage, and you slide the target 1 square.
Miss: Half damage.

Thicket of Blades — Fighter Attack 9

You sting and hinder nearby foes with a savage flurry of strikes aimed at their legs.

Daily ✦ Martial, Reliable, Weapon
Standard Action — **Close** burst 1
Target: Each enemy in burst you can see
Attack: Strength vs. AC
Hit: 3[W] + Strength modifier damage, and the target is slowed (save ends).

Victorious Surge — Fighter Attack 9

You strike true, and your enemy's howl of pain is like music to your ears, making you forget about your own wounds.

Daily ✦ Healing, Martial, Reliable, Weapon
Standard Action　　　Melee weapon
Target: One creature
Attack: Strength vs. AC
Hit: 3[W] + Strength modifier damage, and you regain hit points as if you had spent a healing surge.

LEVEL 10 UTILITY EXPLOITS

Into the Fray — Fighter Utility 10

You unleash a fierce battle cry as you leap boldly into the fray.

Encounter ✦ Martial
Minor Action　　　Personal
Effect: You can move 3 squares, as long as you can end your move adjacent to an enemy.

Last Ditch Evasion — Fighter Utility 10

Thanks to a combination of skill and luck, you narrowly avoid an attack but leave yourself perilously exposed.

Daily ✦ Martial
Immediate Interrupt　　　Personal
Trigger: You are hit by an attack
Effect: You take no damage from the attack that just hit you. However, you are stunned and take a -2 penalty to all defenses until the end of your next turn.

Stalwart Guard — Fighter Utility 10

Your thoughts turn to defense as you begin using your weapon or shield to protect nearby allies.

Daily ✦ Martial
Minor Action　　　Close burst 1
Target: Each ally in burst
Effect: The targets gain a +1 shield bonus to AC until the end of the encounter. If you are using a shield, increase the bonus to +2 and apply it to your allies' Reflex defense as well.

LEVEL 13 ENCOUNTER EXPLOITS

Anvil of Doom — Fighter Attack 13

Your weapon makes a satisfying clunk as it connects with your enemy's skull.

Encounter ✦ Martial, Weapon
Standard Action　　　Melee weapon
Target: One creature
Attack: Strength vs. AC
Hit: 2[W] + Strength modifier damage, and the target is dazed until the end of your next turn.
　Weapon: If you're wielding a hammer or a mace, the target is stunned rather than dazed.

Chains of Sorrow — Fighter Attack 13

You deliver a ferocious blow and catch your enemy's armor, shield, or claws with your weapon as you draw back for another attack. Your recovery wrenches your enemy out of place.

Encounter ✦ Martial, Weapon
Standard Action　　　Melee weapon
Target: One creature
Attack: Strength vs. AC
Hit: 3[W] + Strength modifier damage, and the target takes a -2 penalty to all defenses until the end of your next turn.
　Weapon: If you're wielding a flail, the target's takes a penalty to all defenses equal to your Dexterity modifier.

Giant's Wake — Fighter Attack 13

You lay about with heavy, sweeping blows, hewing your enemies left and right.

Encounter ✦ Martial, Weapon
Standard Action　　　Melee weapon
Primary Target: One creature
Attack: Strength vs. AC
Hit: 2[W] + Strength modifier damage. Make a secondary attack.
　Weapon: If you're wielding an axe, you gain a bonus to the damage roll equal to your Constitution modifier.
Secondary Target: Each enemy adjacent to the primary target and within your melee reach
Secondary Attack: Strength vs. AC
Hit: 1[W] + Strength modifier damage.
　Weapon: If you're wielding an axe, you gain a bonus to the damage roll equal to your Constitution modifier.

Silverstep — Fighter Attack 13

You trip your enemies, knocking them back. As they recover, you shift to a more advantageous position.

Encounter ✦ Martial, Weapon
Standard Action　　　Melee weapon
Targets: One or two creatures
Attack: Strength vs. AC, one attack per target
Hit: 2[W] + Strength modifier damage, and you push the target 1 square.
　Weapon: If you're wielding a spear or a polearm, you push the target a number of squares equal to your Dexterity modifier.
Effect: You shift 1 square.
　Weapon: If you're wielding a spear or a polearm, you can shift a number of squares equal to your Dexterity modifier.

4

CHAPTER 4 | Character Classes and 81

Storm of Blows — Fighter Attack 13

You duck and weave between your enemies while slashing at them ferociously.

Encounter ✦ Martial, Weapon
Standard Action   **Melee** weapon
Target: One creature
Attack: Strength vs. AC
Hit: 1[W] + Strength modifier damage.
   Weapon: If you're wielding a heavy blade or a light blade, you gain a bonus to the damage roll equal to your Dexterity modifier.
Effect: After the attack, you can shift 1 square and repeat the attack against another target within reach. You can then shift 1 square and repeat the attack against a third target within reach. After the final attack, you can shift 1 square.

Talon of the Roc — Fighter Attack 13

Like the deadly talon of a great raptor, your steel pierces your foe and pins him in place.

Encounter ✦ Martial, Weapon
Standard Action   **Melee** weapon
Target: One creature
Attack: Strength vs. AC
Hit: 3[W] + Strength modifier damage, and the target is slowed until the end of your next turn.
   Weapon: If you're wielding a pick or a spear, the target also cannot shift until the end of your next turn.

LEVEL 15 DAILY EXPLOITS

Dragon's Fangs — Fighter Attack 15

You strike twice in rapid succession.

Daily ✦ Martial, Weapon
Standard Action   **Melee** weapon
Targets: One or two creatures
Attack: Strength vs. AC, two attacks against one target or one attack against each target
Hit: 3[W] + Strength modifier damage.
Miss: Half damage.

Serpent Dance Strike — Fighter Attack 15

You weave through the battlefield, striking like a hungry serpent and sweeping the feet out from under your enemies.

Daily ✦ Martial, Weapon
Standard Action   **Melee** weapon
Target: One creature
Attack: Strength vs. AC
Hit: 2[W] + Strength modifier damage, and the target is knocked prone if it is your size or smaller.
Effect: After the attack, you can shift 1 square and repeat the attack against another target within reach. You can shift and repeat the attack up to three times against different targets.

Unyielding Avalanche — Fighter Attack 15

You twirl your weapon about and test the defenses of nearby foes while expertly parrying their blows.

Daily ✦ Healing, Martial, Stance, Weapon
Minor Action   **Personal**
Effect: You gain regeneration equal to your Constitution modifier, a +1 power bonus to AC, and a +1 power bonus to saving throws. Any enemy that starts its turn adjacent to you takes 1[W] damage and is slowed until the end of its turn, as long as you are able to make opportunity attacks.

LEVEL 16 UTILITY EXPLOITS

Interposing Shield — Fighter Utility 16

Using your weapon or shield, you block an attack made against a close ally.

Encounter ✦ Martial
Immediate Interrupt   **Melee** 1
Trigger: An adjacent ally is hit by an attack
Effect: The ally gains a +2 power bonus to AC and Reflex defense against the triggering attack. If you are using a shield, increase the bonus to +4.

Iron Warrior — Fighter Utility 16

Like a tankard of bad ale, you don't go down easy.

Daily ✦ Healing, Martial
Minor Action   **Personal**
Effect: You spend a healing surge, regain additional hit points equal to 2d6 + your Constitution modifier, and make a saving throw against one effect that a save can end.

Surprise Step — Fighter Utility 16

You dog your enemy's footsteps, refusing to yield.

Encounter ✦ Martial
Immediate Reaction   **Personal**
Trigger: An adjacent enemy moves away from you
Effect: Shift into the square that the enemy vacated. You have combat advantage against that enemy until the end of your next turn.

LEVEL 17 ENCOUNTER EXPLOITS

Exacting Strike   Fighter Attack 17

You trade damage for accuracy to land a much-needed hit on your opponent.

Encounter ✦ Martial, Weapon
Standard Action   **Melee** weapon
Target: One creature
Attack: Strength + 6 vs. AC
Hit: 2[W] + Strength modifier damage.

Exorcism of Steel   Fighter Attack 17

You chop at your foe's hand, causing a grievous injury and forcing him to drop his weapon.

Encounter ✦ Martial, Weapon
Standard Action   **Melee** weapon
Target: One creature
Attack: Strength vs. Reflex
Hit: 2[W] + Strength modifier damage, and the target drops one weapon it is holding. You can choose to catch the dropped weapon in a free hand or have it land on the ground at your feet (in your square).

Harrying Assault   Fighter Attack 17

You frustrate your enemy, landing a calculated blow and then moving away before he can retaliate.

Encounter ✦ Martial, Weapon
Standard Action   **Melee** weapon
Target: One creature
Attack: Strength vs. AC
Hit: 2[W] + Strength modifier damage.
Effect: After the attack, you can move a number of squares equal to your Dexterity modifier and make a melee basic attack after your move.

Mountain Breaking Blow   Fighter Attack 17

You land a ringing blow, then push your enemy back without giving other nearby enemies the opportunity to strike you.

Encounter ✦ Martial, Weapon
Standard Action   **Melee** weapon
Target: One creature
Attack: Strength vs. AC
Hit: 3[W] + Strength modifier damage, and you push the target 3 squares.
Effect: After the attack, you can shift the same distance you pushed the target. You must end your move adjacent to the target.

Vorpal Tornado   Fighter Attack 17

You become a whirling cyclone of death, spinning your weapon about as you strike one foe after another, pushing them back and knocking them down.

Encounter ✦ Martial, Weapon
Standard Action   **Close** burst 1
Target: Each enemy in burst you can see
Attack: Strength vs. AC
Hit: 1[W] + Strength modifier damage. You push the target 1 square, and it is knocked prone.

Warrior's Challenge   Fighter Attack 17

You land a mighty blow that causes your foe to stagger backward. With a wicked grin, you hoist your weapon and flash it menacingly at other enemies nearby.

Encounter ✦ Martial, Weapon
Standard Action   **Melee** weapon
Target: One creature
Attack: Strength vs. AC
Hit: 3[W] + Strength modifier damage, and you push the target 2 squares.
Special: All of your enemies within 2 squares of the target are marked until the end of your next turn.

MATT CAVOTTA

LEVEL 19 DAILY EXPLOITS

Devastation's Wake   Fighter Attack 19

You thrash your foes with a devastating array of strikes, and then unleash your fury a second time against anyone left standing.

Daily ✦ Martial, Weapon
Standard Action   Close burst 1
Primary Target: Each enemy in burst you can see
Attack: Strength vs. AC
Hit: 3[W] + Strength modifier damage.
Miss: Half damage.
Effect: Until the start of your next turn, adjacent enemies are subject to a secondary attack.
Secondary Target: Any enemy that moves adjacent to you or starts its turn adjacent to you
Secondary Attack: Strength vs. AC
Hit: 1[W] + Strength modifier damage.

Reaving Strike   Fighter Attack 19

You swing your weapon in a terrific arc, hitting with such force that your foe stumbles backward.

Daily ✦ Martial, Reliable, Weapon
Standard Action   Melee weapon
Target: One creature
Attack: Strength vs. AC
Hit: 5[W] + Strength damage, and you push the target 1 square.

Strike of the Watchful Guard   Fighter Attack 19

After landing a tremendous blow, you dog your enemy and make him think twice about turning his back on you.

Daily ✦ Martial, Weapon
Standard Action   Melee weapon
Target: One creature
Attack: Strength vs. AC
Hit: 4[W] + Strength modifier damage.
Effect: Until the end of the encounter, you can make a melee basic attack against the target as a free action if you are adjacent to it and it either shifts or attacks one of your allies.

LEVEL 22 UTILITY EXPLOITS

Act of Desperation   Fighter Utility 22

The sight of one of your friends dying propels you into sudden action.

Daily ✦ Martial
Minor Action   Personal
Requirement: An ally within 10 squares is dying.
Effect: You gain an action point that you must spend during your current turn.

No Surrender   Fighter Utility 22

You refuse to go down, turning a death blow into one last chance for victory.

Daily ✦ Healing, Martial
Immediate Reaction   Personal
Trigger: Your hit points drop to 0 or lower
Effect: You regain enough hit points to bring you to one-half your maximum hit points. However, you take a –2 penalty to attack rolls until the end of the encounter.

LEVEL 23 ENCOUNTER EXPLOITS

Cage of Chains   Fighter Attack 23

After landing a decisive blow, you skillfully use your weapon to entangle and restrain your opponent.

Encounter ✦ Martial, Weapon
Standard Action   Melee weapon
Target: One creature
Attack: Strength vs. Reflex
Hit: 4[W] + Strength modifier damage.
   Weapon: If you're wielding a flail and are adjacent to the target at the end of your turn, the target is restrained until the start of your next turn.

Fangs of Steel   Fighter Attack 23

You lunge forward and draw blood from one enemy, then spin around and strike another foe with deadly ferocity.

Encounter ✦ Martial, Weapon
Standard Action   Melee weapon
Primary Target: One creature
Attack: Strength vs. AC
Hit: 3[W] + Strength modifier damage. Make a secondary attack.
   Weapon: If you're wielding a light blade or a heavy blade, you gain a bonus to the damage roll equal to your Dexterity modifier.
Secondary Target: One creature adjacent to the primary target and within your melee reach
Secondary Attack: Strength vs. AC
Hit: 2[W] + Strength modifier damage
   Weapon: If you're wielding a light blade or a heavy blade, you gain a bonus to the damage roll equal to your Dexterity modifier.

Hack 'n' Slash   Fighter Attack 23

You swing your weapon in deadly arcs, mercilessly hacking and slashing at your foe's armor until finally you break through.

Encounter ✦ Martial, Weapon
Standard Action   Melee weapon
Target: One creature
Attack: Strength vs. AC
Hit: 4[W] + Strength modifier damage.
   Weapon: If you're wielding an axe, you gain a bonus to the damage roll equal to your Constitution modifier.

Paralyzing Strike — Fighter Attack 23

With a sharp thrust of your weapon, you leave your enemy nearly paralyzed with pain.

Encounter ✦ Martial, Weapon
Standard Action   **Melee** weapon
Target: One creature
Attack: Strength vs. AC
  Weapon: If you're wielding a pick, a polearm, or a spear, you can score a critical hit on a roll of 18-20.
Hit: 3[W] + Strength modifier damage, and the target is immobilized until the end of your next turn.

Skullcrusher — Fighter Attack 23

You bring your weapon down upon your enemy's skull with a loud crack that leaves him dazed and reeling.

Encounter ✦ Martial, Weapon
Standard Action   **Melee** weapon
Target: One creature
Attack: Strength vs. AC
Hit: 4[W] + Strength modifier damage, and the target is dazed until the end of your next turn.
  Weapon: If you're wielding a hammer or a mace, you gain a bonus to the damage roll equal to your Constitution modifier, and your enemy is blinded until the end of your next turn.

Warrior's Urging — Fighter Attack 23

You call your opponents toward you and strike out with lashing blows.

Encounter ✦ Charm, Martial, Weapon
Standard Action   **Close** burst 4
Target: Each enemy in burst you can see
Effect: Each target must shift 3 and end adjacent to you, if possible. A target that can't end adjacent to you doesn't move. You can then attack any targets that are adjacent to you (close burst 1).
Attack: Strength vs. AC
Hit: 2[W] + Strength modifier damage.

LEVEL 25 DAILY EXPLOITS

Reaper's Stance — Fighter Attack 25

Every enemy within your reach falls victim to the ruthless precision of your attacks and suffers bleeding wounds.

Daily ✦ Martial, Stance, Weapon
Minor Action   **Personal**
Effect: Whenever you use a fighter power, you can score a critical hit on a roll of 19-20, and you gain a power bonus to damage rolls equal to your Dexterity modifier. Any enemy that starts its turn adjacent to you takes 1[W] damage and ongoing 10 damage (save ends), as long as you are able to make opportunity attacks.

Reign of Terror — Fighter Attack 25

After smashing your weapon into a foe with amazing force, you cast your baleful glare upon the enemies that still stand before you.

Daily ✦ Martial, Reliable, Weapon
Standard Action   **Melee** weapon
Target: One creature
Attack: Strength vs. AC
Hit: 6[W] + Strength modifier damage, and all of your enemies you can see are marked until the end of your next turn.

Supremacy of Steel — Fighter Attack 25

Your weapon blurs as you attack your foe a dozen times in the blink of an eye. You have an answer for every parry and every counterattack. Under your incredible assault, your enemy can do little more than defend itself.

Daily ✦ Martial, Reliable, Weapon
Standard Action   **Melee** weapon
Target: One creature
Attack: Strength vs. AC
Hit: 6[W] + Strength modifier damage, and until the end of your next turn the only attacks the target can make are basic attacks.

LEVEL 27 ENCOUNTER EXPLOITS

Adamantine Strike — Fighter Attack 27

Your weapon breaks through shields and armor like they're made of parchment.

Encounter ✦ Martial, Weapon
Standard Action   **Melee** weapon
Target: One creature
Attack: Strength vs. Reflex
Hit: 4[W] + Strength modifier damage, and the target takes a -2 penalty to AC until the end of your next turn.

Cruel Reaper — Fighter Attack 27

You spin your weapon about, carving into adjacent foes and causing them to scream in agony. Without warning, you slip through their blockade and make another spinning sweep.

Encounter ✦ Martial, Weapon
Standard Action   **Close** burst 1
Primary Target: Each enemy in burst you can see
Attack: Strength vs. AC
Hit: 2[W] + Strength modifier damage.
Effect: You can shift 2 squares, and then make a secondary attack.
  Secondary Target: Each enemy in close burst 1
  Secondary Attack: Strength vs. AC
  Hit: 2[W] + Strength modifier damage.

Diamond Shield Defense — Fighter Attack 27

Your shield becomes your staunchest ally.

Encounter ✦ Martial, Weapon
Standard Action   Melee weapon
Requirement: You must be using a shield.
Target: One creature
Attack: Strength vs. AC
Hit: 4[W] + Strength modifier damage, and you take half damage from the target's attacks until the end of your next turn.
Effect: You gain a +2 power bonus to AC until the end of your next turn.

Indomitable Battle Strike — Fighter Attack 27

You will not be denied your enemy's blood, and other foes that witness your savage attack know the ill fate that awaits them.

Encounter ✦ Martial, Weapon
Standard Action   Melee weapon
Target: One creature
Attack: Strength vs. AC
Hit: 4[W] + Strength modifier damage.
Effect: All of your enemies within 10 squares of you are marked until the end of your next turn.

LEVEL 29 DAILY POWERS

Force the Battle — Fighter Attack 29

With the slightest flick of your weapon and minimal movement, you control the battle and turn your enemies' thoughts from conquest to survival.

Daily ✦ Martial, Stance, Weapon
Minor Action   Personal
Effect: You deal an extra 1[W] damage with your at-will and encounter fighter powers. If an enemy starts its turn adjacent to you, you can use an at-will fighter power against it as a free action at the start of its turn, as long as you are able to make opportunity attacks.

No Mercy — Fighter Attack 29

Let nothing stand between a warrior and the object of his wrath.

Daily ✦ Martial, Reliable, Weapon
Standard Action   Melee weapon
Target: One creature
Attack: Strength vs. AC
Hit: 7[W] + Strength modifier damage.

Storm of Destruction — Fighter Attack 29

You knock aside your enemies' weapons, creating holes in their defenses that enable you to strike deadly blows against two of them at once.

Daily ✦ Martial, Weapon
Standard Action   Melee weapon
Targets: One or two creatures
Attack: Strength vs. AC, one attack per target
Hit: 5[W] + Strength modifier damage.
Miss: Half damage.

PARAGON PATHS

IRON VANGUARD

"With every attack I make, I grow stronger and more confident."

Prerequisite: Fighter class

You become a vision of physical perfection, mighty in body and ruthless in your pursuit of victory over every foe. No one defends the front line of battle better than you do, easily taking ground and pushing the enemy to and fro.

IRON VANGUARD PATH FEATURES

Enduring Warrior (11th level): When you drop an enemy to 0 hit points or fewer, you regain hit points equal to your Constitution modifier.

Ferocious Reaction (11th level): When you are reduced to 0 hit points or fewer, as an immediate interrupt before you fall unconscious, you can spend an action point to take an extra action. In addition, whenever you spend an action point to take an extra action, you also gain a +4 bonus to all defenses until the start of your next turn.

Trample the Fallen (16th level): When you push a creature or knock a creature prone, it takes damage equal to your Constitution modifier.

IRON VANGUARD EXPLOITS

Frontline Surge — Iron Vanguard Attack 11

You beat back your enemy, allowing you and your allies to seize new ground.

Encounter ✦ Martial, Weapon
Standard Action   Melee weapon
Target: One creature
Attack: Strength vs. AC
Hit: 2[W] + Strength modifier damage, and you push the target 1 square. You can shift into the square formerly occupied by the target. If you do so, each ally within 2 squares of you can shift 1 square as well.

Inexorable Shift — Iron Vanguard Utility 12

You throw yourself at your enemy and knock him back.

Encounter ✦ Martial
Move Action   Personal
Effect: Shift into any adjacent square. If a creature occupies the square into which you shift, you push that creature 1 square.

Indomitable Strength	Iron Vanguard Attack 20

A mighty blow sends your opponent flying through the air and gives you a few seconds to regain your composure.

Daily ✦ Healing, Martial, Weapon
Standard Action   **Melee** weapon
Target: One creature
Attack: Strength vs. AC
Hit: 4[W] + Strength modifier damage, and you push the target 1 square and it is knocked prone. In addition, the target is dazed until the end of your next turn.
Miss: Half damage.
Effect: You can spend a healing surge.

KENSEI

"My weapon and I are as one."

Prerequisite: Fighter class

You study an ancient form of martial training that makes you one with your chosen weapon, creating a combination of destruction that few foes can long stand against.

KENSEI PATH FEATURES

Kensei Control Action (11th level): You can spend an action point to reroll one attack roll, damage roll, skill check, or ability check, instead of taking an extra action.

Kensei Focus (11th level): You gain a +1 bonus to attack rolls with a melee weapon of your choice.

Kensei Mastery (16th level): You gain a +4 bonus to damage rolls with the same weapon you selected for Kensei Focus. If you ever use a different type of weapon, you lose this benefit, and the benefit for Kensei Focus, until you take a short rest, during which time you reattune yourself to your chosen weapon with a short meditation.

KENSEI EXPLOITS

Masterstroke	Kensei Attack 11

An unerring strike foretells your enemy's demise.

Encounter ✦ Martial, Weapon
Standard Action   **Melee** weapon
Target: One creature
Attack: Strength + 2 vs. AC
Hit: 2[W] + Strength modifier damage.

Ultimate Parry	Kensei Utility 12

With a whirl of your weapon, you expertly deflect an enemy's attack.

Daily ✦ Martial
Immediate Reaction   **Personal**
Trigger: You take damage from an attack
Effect: Reduce the damage by an amount equal to your level.

Weaponsoul Dance	Kensei Attack 20

You leap from one foe to the next, striking with ever-increasing accuracy while negotiating your way through your enemies' thicket of swords.

Daily ✦ Martial, Weapon
Standard Action   **Melee** weapon
Primary Target: One creature
Attack: Strength vs. AC
Hit: 3[W] + Strength modifier damage, and the target is knocked prone and immobilized until the end of your next turn.
Effect: You can shift 5 squares, and then make a secondary attack.
Secondary Target: One creature other than the primary target
Secondary Attack: Strength + 2 vs. AC
Hit: 2[W] + Strength modifier damage, and the target is knocked prone and immobilized until the end of your next turn.
Effect: You can shift 5 squares, and then make a tertiary attack.
Tertiary Target: One creature other than the primary and secondary targets
Tertiary Attack: Strength + 3 vs. AC
Hit: 1[W] + Strength modifier damage, and the target is knocked prone and immobilized until the end of your next turn.

PIT FIGHTER

"I fight dirty, and I fight to win."

Prerequisite: Fighter class

You have learned to fight in dungeons and brawling pits, picking up every survival trick along the way. It might not be the prettiest or most elegant fighting style around, but it gets the job done.

PIT FIGHTER PATH FEATURES

Armor Optimization (11th level): You have learned to make the most of the armor you wear, positioning it to better absorb and deflect blows. You gain a +1 bonus to AC whenever you wear any kind of armor.

Extra Damage Action (11th level): When you spend an action point to take an extra action, you also add one-half your level to the damage dealt by any of your standard action attacks this turn.

Dirty Fighting (16th level): Using tricks and techniques you have learned in constant battles, you know how to add an extra level of pain to every hit you deliver. Increase the damage you deal when using a weapon by a number equal to your Wisdom modifier (minimum +1).

PIT FIGHTER EXPLOITS

All Bets Are Off
Pit Fighter Attack 11

After landing a solid blow, you belt your enemy in the face with your fist.

Encounter ✦ Martial, Weapon
Standard Action   **Melee** weapon
Target: One creature
Attack: Strength vs. AC
Hit: 2[W] + Strength modifier damage. Make a secondary attack against the same target.
  Secondary Attack: Strength + 2 vs. AC
  Hit: 1d6 + Strength modifier damage, and the target is dazed until the end of your next turn.

Deadly Payback
Pit Fighter Utility 12

You react viciously to an enemy that just hurt you.

Daily ✦ Martial, Weapon
Immediate Reaction   **Personal**
Trigger: You take damage from a melee attack
Effect: Until the end of your next turn, you gain a +2 bonus to attack rolls and damage rolls against the enemy that damaged you.

Lion of Battle
Pit Fighter Attack 20

You skewer yet another unworthy foe and let loose a terrifying roar of triumph when he falls.

Daily ✦ Fear, Martial, Weapon
Standard Action   **Melee** weapon
Primary Target: One creature
Attack: Strength vs. AC
Hit: 4[W] + Strength modifier damage. If the target was bloodied before the attack, it takes +2[W] damage.
Miss: Half damage.
Effect: If you reduce the target to 0 hit points or fewer, you can make a secondary attack.
  Secondary Target: Each enemy within 5 squares of you
  Secondary Attack: Strength vs. Will
  Hit: The target moves its speed away from you.

SWORDMASTER

"My blade is exquisite and deadly, as much a work of art as it is a weapon. And in my hands, it is unstoppable."

Prerequisite: Fighter class

You and your blade are as one. You are a master of the sword, able to employ your steel in ways that no lesser warrior can even imagine.

SWORDMASTER PATH FEATURES

Steel Defense Action (11th level): When you spend an action point to take an extra action, you also gain a +4 bonus to AC and Reflex defense until the start of your next turn.

Steel Grace (11th level): When you charge with a light blade or a heavy blade that is not a polearm, you can use Containing Strike or Reaping Strike instead of your melee basic attack.

Steel Blitz (16th level): When you score a critical hit with a light blade or a heavy blade, you regain the use of a fighter encounter power you've already used in the encounter.

SWORDMASTER EXPLOITS

Precision Cut
Swordmaster Attack 11

You slip your blade past your enemy's armor and slice him just so, leaving a bleeding gash.

Encounter ✦ Martial, Weapon
Standard Action (Special)   **Melee** weapon
Special: This power can be used as an opportunity attack.
Target: One creature
Attack: Strength vs. Reflex
Hit: 3[W] + Strength modifier damage.

Fantastic Flourish
Swordmaster Utility 12

With perfect timing, you flick one enemy's blood into the eyes of another.

Encounter ✦ Martial
Minor Action   **Ranged** 5
Requirement: You make a successful melee attack with a light blade or heavy blade (not a polearm)
Target: One enemy other than the one you just hit
Effect: The target is marked until the end of your next turn.

Crescendo Sword
Swordmaster Attack 20

With a tremendous roar, you swing your blade over your head and make lunging strikes at all nearby enemies. At the end of the flurry, you regain some of your power.

Daily ✦ Martial, Weapon
Standard Action   **Close** burst 1
Requirement: You must be wielding a light blade or a heavy blade (not a polearm).
Target: Each enemy in burst you can see
Attack: Strength vs. AC
Hit: 2[W] + Strength modifier damage.
Effect: If you hit at least one of your enemies, you regain one daily power you have already used. If you miss all enemies, you regain one encounter power you have already used.

PALADIN

"*I am the righteous shield of Moradin and a sword in his mighty hand! I fear no evil!*"

CLASS TRAITS

Role: Defender. You are extremely durable, with high hit points and the ability to wear the heaviest armor. You can issue bold challenges to foes and compel them to fight you rather than your allies.

Power Source: Divine. You are a divine warrior, a crusader and protector of your faith.

Key Abilities: Strength, Charisma, Wisdom

Armor Proficiencies: Cloth, leather, hide, chainmail, scale, plate; light shield, heavy shield

Weapon Proficiencies: Simple melee, military melee, simple ranged

Implements: Holy symbol

Bonus to Defense: +1 Fortitude, +1 Reflex, +1 Will

Hit Points at 1st Level: 15 + Constitution score

Hit Points per Level Gained: 6

Healing Surges per Day: 10 + Constitution modifier

Trained Skills: Religion. From the class skills list below, choose three more trained skills at 1st level.
Class Skills: Diplomacy (Cha), Endurance (Con), Heal (Wis), History (Int), Insight (Wis), Intimidate (Cha), Religion (Int)

Build Options: Avenging paladin, protecting paladin

Class Features: Channel Divinity, Divine Challenge, *lay on hands*

Paladins are indomitable warriors who've pledged their prowess to something greater than themselves. Paladins smite enemies with divine authority, bolster the courage of nearby companions, and radiate as if a beacon of inextinguishable hope. Paladins are transfigured on the field of battle, exemplars of divine ethos in action.

To you is given the responsibility to unflinchingly stand before an enemy's charge, smiting them with your sword while protecting your allies with your sacrifice. Where others waver and wonder, your motivation is pure and simple, and your devotion is your strength. Where others scheme and steal, you take the high road, refusing to allow the illusions of temptation to dissuade you from your obligations.

Take up your blessed sword and sanctified shield, brave warrior, and charge forward to hallowed glory!

WILLIAM O'CONNOR

CREATING A PALADIN

Paladins rely on Strength, Charisma, and Wisdom for most of their key abilities and powers. Constitution is useful as well, although no paladin powers are specifically based on Constitution. Paladins start with two common builds: the avenging paladin and the protecting paladin.

AVENGING PALADIN

You burn with the desire to punish the wicked and smite the unbelievers. In your view, the best way to safeguard your allies is to destroy your enemies with divine power and overwhelming attacks. Choose Strength as your highest ability score, since your most damaging attacks are based on Strength. Charisma should be your second-best ability score, and Wisdom your third. Consider wielding a big two-handed weapon such as a greatsword or greataxe, and choose powers that deliver the highest amount of damage.

Suggested Feat: Power Attack (Human Feat: Human Perseverance)
Suggested Skills: Endurance, Heal, Intimidate, Religion
Suggested At-Will Powers: *holy strike, valiant strike*
Suggested Encounter Power: *radiant smite*
Suggested Daily Power: *paladin's judgment*

PROTECTING PALADIN

You emphasize defense, guarding your allies, and healing and bolstering them with a few of your powers. You do not deal as much damage as the avenging paladin, but you are better at dealing with a wider array of situations. Your best ability score should be Charisma. Choose Strength for your second-best score (you'll want a few Strength-based attacks), and

Wisdom as your third-best score. The protecting paladin works best as a shield-carrying warrior, so you should probably use a heavy shield and a one-handed weapon such as a longsword or a warhammer. Select powers that help your allies, along with a few damage-dealing powers for when the need arises.

Suggested Feat: Healing Hands (Human feat: Action Surge)
Suggested Skills: Diplomacy, Heal, Insight, Religion
Suggested At-Will Powers: *bolstering strike, enfeebling strike*
Suggested Encounter Power: *shielding smite*
Suggested Daily Power: *radiant delirium*

IMPLEMENT

Paladins make use of holy symbols to help channel and direct their divine powers. A paladin wearing or holding a magic holy symbol can add its enhancement bonus to the attack rolls and the damage rolls of paladin powers, as well as paladin paragon path powers, that have the implement keyword. Without a holy symbol, a paladin can still use these powers, but he or she doesn't gain the bonus provided by the magic implement.

A *holy avenger*, a special magic weapon, can also be used as an implement for paladin powers, as well as paladin paragon path powers. These weapons are highly sought after by paladins.

PALADINS AND DEITIES

As fervent crusaders in their chosen cause, paladins must choose a deity. Paladins choose a specific faith to serve, as well as an alignment. You must choose an alignment identical to the alignment of your patron deity; a paladin of a good deity must be good, a paladin of a lawful good deity must be lawful good, and a paladin of an unaligned deity must be unaligned. Evil and chaotic evil paladins do exist in the world, but they are almost always villains, not player characters.

PALADIN OVERVIEW

Characteristics: Like the fighter, you are extremely durable. You wear the best armor available, and your defenses are very high. You can force enemies to fight you rather than your weaker allies by using powers to challenge your enemies. Your ranged attack ability is not very good, but you are very capable in melee.

Religion: Warriors wielding divine power can be found in the service of any deity, even evil or chaotic evil ones. However, the majority of paladins serve good or lawful good deities such as Avandra, Bahamut, Moradin, or Pelor.

Races: Most paladins are humans or dwarves. These races have strong traditions of pious warriors choosing to devote themselves to divine service. Dragonborn and half-elves make good paladins, too.

Good, Lawful Good, and Unaligned Deities		
Avandra	Good	Change, luck, trade, travel
Bahamut	Lawful Good	Justice, honor, nobility, protection
Corellon	Unaligned	Arcane magic, spring, beauty, the arts
Erathis	Unaligned	Civilization, invention, laws
Ioun	Unaligned	Knowledge, prophecy, skill
Kord	Unaligned	Storms, strength, battle
Melora	Unaligned	Wilderness, sea
Moradin	Lawful Good	Creation, artisans, family
Pelor	Good	Sun, summer, agriculture, time
Raven Queen	Unaligned	Death, fate, winter
Sehanine	Unaligned	Trickery, moon, love, autumn

Paladins are not granted their powers directly by their deity, but instead through various rites performed when they first become paladins. Most of these rites involve days of prayer, vigils, tests and trials, and ritual purification followed by a knighting ceremony, but each faith has its own methods. This ceremony of investiture gives a paladin the ability to wield divine powers. Once initiated, the paladin is a paladin forevermore. How justly, honorably, or compassionately the paladin wields those powers from that day forward is up to him, and paladins who stray too far from the tenets of their faith are punished by other members of the faithful.

PALADIN CLASS FEATURES

Your armor, your shield, and your weapon are the most important tools of your trade. In addition, you have the following class features.

CHANNEL DIVINITY

Once per encounter you can invoke divine power, filling yourself with the might of your patron deity. With the divine might you invoke you can wield special powers, such as *divine mettle* and *divine strength*. Some paladins learn other uses for this feature; for instance, the divinity feats in Chapter 6 grant characters with access to the Channel Divinity class feature the ability to use additional special powers.

Regardless of how many different uses for Channel Divinity you know, you can use only one such ability per encounter. The special ability or power you invoke works just like your other powers.

DIVINE CHALLENGE

The challenge of a paladin is filled with divine menace. You can use the *divine challenge* power to mark an enemy of your choice.

LAY ON HANDS

Using the *lay on hands* power, paladins can grant their comrades additional resilience with a touch of their hands and a short prayer, though they must give of their own strength to do so.

PALADIN POWERS

Paladin powers are called prayers. In battle, paladins rely on their deities to strengthen their sword-arms and fortify them against the attacks of their enemies.

CLASS FEATURES

The paladin has three class features that work like powers: Channel Divinity, *divine challenge*, and *lay on hands*. The Channel Divinity class feature encompasses multiple powers, two of which (*divine mettle* and *divine strength*) are presented below.

Channel Divinity: Divine Mettle   Paladin Feature

Your unswerving faith in your deity empowers a nearby creature to resist a debilitating affliction.

Encounter ✦ Divine
Minor Action   **Close** burst 10
Target: One creature in burst
Effect: The target makes a saving throw with a bonus equal to your Charisma modifier.

Channel Divinity: Divine Strength   Paladin Feature

You petition your deity for the divine strength to lay low your enemies.

Encounter ✦ Divine
Minor Action   **Personal**
Effect: Apply your Strength modifier as extra damage on your next attack this turn.

Divine Challenge   Paladin Feature

You boldly confront a nearby enemy, searing it with divine light if it ignores your challenge.

At-Will ✦ Divine, Radiant
Minor Action   **Close** burst 5
Target: One creature in burst
Effect: You mark the target. The target remains marked until you use this power against another target, or if you fail to engage the target (see below). A creature can be subject to only one mark at a time. A new mark supersedes a mark that was already in place.

While a target is marked, it takes a -2 penalty to attack rolls for any attack that doesn't include you as a target. Also, it takes radiant damage equal to 3 + your Charisma modifier the first time it makes an attack that doesn't include you as a target before the start of your next turn. The damage increases to 6 + your Charisma modifier at 11th level, and to 9 + your Charisma modifier at 21st level.

On your turn, you must engage the target you challenged or challenge a different target. To engage the target, you must either attack it or end your turn adjacent to it. If none of these events occur by the end of your turn, the marked condition ends and you can't use *divine challenge* on your next turn.

You can use *divine challenge* once per turn.
Special: Even though this ability is called a challenge, it doesn't rely on the intelligence or language ability of the target. It's a magical compulsion that affects the creature's behavior, regardless of the creature's nature. You can't place a divine challenge on a creature that is already affected by your or another character's divine challenge.

Lay on Hands   Paladin Feature

Your divine touch instantly heals wounds.

At-Will (Special) ✦ Divine, Healing
Special: You can use this power a number of times per day equal to your Wisdom modifier (minimum 1), but only once per round.
Minor Action   **Melee** touch
Target: One creature
Effect: You spend a healing surge but regain no hit points. Instead, the target regains hit points as if it had spent a healing surge. You must have at least one healing surge remaining to use this power.

LEVEL 1 AT-WILL PRAYERS

Bolstering Strike — Paladin Attack 1

You attack your foe without mercy or reprieve, and your accuracy is rewarded with a divine gift of vigor.

At-Will ✦ Divine, Weapon
Standard Action   Melee weapon
Target: One creature
Attack: Charisma vs. AC
Hit: 1[W] + Charisma modifier damage, and you gain temporary hit points equal to your Wisdom modifier.
Increase damage to 2[W] + Charisma modifier at 21st level.

Enfeebling Strike — Paladin Attack 1

Your brutal weapon attack leaves your foe weakened.

At-Will ✦ Divine, Weapon
Standard Action   Melee weapon
Target: One creature
Attack: Charisma vs. AC
Hit: 1[W] + Charisma modifier damage. If you marked the target, it takes a -2 penalty to attack rolls until the end of your next turn.
Increase damage to 2[W] + Charisma modifier at 21st level.

Holy Strike — Paladin Attack 1

You strike an enemy with your weapon, which ignites with holy light.

At-Will ✦ Divine, Radiant, Weapon
Standard Action   Melee weapon
Target: One creature
Attack: Strength vs. AC
Hit: 1[W] + Strength modifier radiant damage. If you marked the target, you gain a bonus to the damage roll equal to your Wisdom modifier.
Increase damage to 2[W] + Strength modifier at 21st level.

Valiant Strike — Paladin Attack 1

As you bring your weapon to bear, the odds against you add strength to your attack.

At-Will ✦ Divine, Weapon
Standard Action   Melee weapon
Target: One creature
Attack: Strength + 1 per enemy adjacent to you vs. AC
Hit: 1[W] + Strength modifier damage.
Increase damage to 2[W] + Strength modifier at 21st level.

LEVEL 1 ENCOUNTER PRAYERS

Fearsome Smite — Paladin Attack 1

When you strike a foe with your weapon, the force of the blow causes him to shudder and second-guess his tactics.

Encounter ✦ Divine, Fear, Weapon
Standard Action   Melee weapon
Target: One creature
Attack: Charisma vs. AC
Hit: 2[W] + Charisma modifier damage. Until the end of your next turn, the target takes a penalty to attack rolls equal to your Wisdom modifier.

Piercing Smite — Paladin Attack 1

Silvery spikes cover your weapon, punching through your foe's armor.

Encounter ✦ Divine, Weapon
Standard Action   Melee weapon
Target: One creature
Attack: Strength vs. Reflex
Hit: 2[W] + Strength modifier damage, and the target and a number of enemies adjacent to you equal to your Wisdom modifier are marked until the end of your next turn.

Radiant Smite — Paladin Attack 1

Your weapon glows with a pearly luminescence. Enemies shrink from its pure light, especially creatures of supernatural evil such as demons and devils.

Encounter ✦ Divine, Radiant, Weapon
Standard Action   Melee weapon
Target: One creature
Attack: Strength vs. AC
Hit: 2[W] + Strength modifier + Wisdom modifier radiant damage.

Shielding Smite — Paladin Attack 1

A translucent golden shield forms in front of a nearby ally as you attack with your weapon.

Encounter ✦ Divine, Weapon
Standard Action   Melee weapon
Target: One creature
Attack: Charisma vs. AC
Hit: 2[W] + Charisma modifier damage.
Effect: Until the end of your next turn, one ally within 5 squares of you gains a power bonus to AC equal to your Wisdom modifier.

LEVEL 1 DAILY PRAYERS

On Pain of Death — Paladin Attack 1

You invoke a prayer that wracks your foe with terrible pain and causes further pain whenever he makes an attack.

Daily ✦ Divine, Implement
Standard Action   Ranged 5
Target: One creature
Attack: Charisma vs. Will
Hit: 3d8 + Charisma modifier damage. Once per round, the target takes 1d8 damage after making any attacks on its turn (save ends).
Miss: Half damage. Once per round, the target takes 1d4 damage after making any attacks on its turn (save ends).

Paladin's Judgment — Paladin Attack 1

Your melee attack punishes your enemy and heals an ally.

Daily ✦ Divine, Healing, Weapon
Standard Action   Melee weapon
Target: One creature
Attack: Strength vs. AC
Hit: 3[W] + Strength modifier damage, and one ally within 5 squares of you can spend a healing surge.
Miss: One ally within 5 squares of you can spend a healing surge.

Radiant Delirium — Paladin Attack 1

You engulf your enemy in searing ribbons of radiance.

Daily ✦ Divine, Implement, Radiant
Standard Action   Ranged 5
Target: One creature
Attack: Charisma vs. Reflex
Hit: 3d8 + Charisma modifier radiant damage, and the target is dazed until the end of your next turn. In addition, the target takes a -2 penalty to AC (save ends).
Miss: Half damage, and the target is dazed until the end of your next turn.

LEVEL 2 UTILITY PRAYERS

Astral Speech — Paladin Utility 2

You speak with such compelling conviction that others find it difficult to refute your beliefs and claims.

Daily ✦ Divine
Minor Action   Personal
Effect: You gain a +4 power bonus to Diplomacy checks until the end of the encounter.

Martyr's Blessing — Paladin Utility 2

You step into an attack made against an adjacent ally to save your comrade.

Daily ✦ Divine
Immediate Interrupt   Close burst 1
Trigger: An adjacent ally is hit by a melee or a ranged attack
Effect: You are hit by the attack instead.

Sacred Circle — Paladin Utility 2

You trace a circle around you with your hand, and it quickly expands into a wide circle of faintly glowing runes that glows brightly and protects you and your close allies.

Daily ✦ Divine, Implement, Zone
Standard Action   Close burst 3
Effect: The burst creates a zone that, until the end of the encounter, gives you and allies within it a +1 power bonus to AC.

LEVEL 3 ENCOUNTER PRAYERS

Arcing Smite — Paladin Attack 3

You swing your weapon in a wide arc that strikes not one but two creatures within your reach.

Encounter ✦ Divine, Weapon
Standard Action   Melee weapon
Targets: One or two creatures
Attack: Strength vs. AC, one attack per target
Hit: 1[W] + Strength modifier damage, and the target is marked until the end of your next turn.

Invigorating Smite — Paladin Attack 3

When you hit an enemy with your weapon, you and your allies suddenly feel invigorated by the divine power of your faith.

Encounter ✦ Divine, Healing, Weapon
Standard Action   Melee weapon
Target: One creature
Attack: Charisma vs. Will
Hit: 2[W] + Charisma modifier damage. If you are bloodied, you regain hit points equal to 5 + your Wisdom modifier. Bloodied allies within 5 squares of you also regain hit points equal to 5 + your Wisdom modifier.

Righteous Smite — Paladin Attack 3

Your righteous blow fills you and your nearby allies with preternatural resolve.

Encounter ✦ Divine, Healing, Weapon
Standard Action   Melee weapon
Target: One creature
Attack: Charisma vs. AC
Hit: 2[W] + Charisma modifier damage, and you and each ally within 5 squares of you gain temporary hit points equal to 5 + your Wisdom modifier.

Staggering Smite — Paladin Attack 3

With a mighty swing of your weapon, you knock your enemy back.

Encounter ✦ Divine, Weapon
Standard Action   Melee weapon
Target: One creature
Attack: Strength vs. AC
Hit: 2[W] + Strength modifier damage, and you push the target a number of squares equal to your Wisdom modifier.

LEVEL 5 DAILY PRAYERS

Hallowed Circle — Paladin Attack 5

You wave your hand through the air, and a wide circle of faintly glowing symbols appears around you, damaging enemies and protecting allies within its confines.

Daily ✦ Divine, Implement, Zone
Standard Action   Close burst 3
Target: Each enemy in burst
Attack: Charisma vs. Reflex
Hit: 2d6 + Charisma modifier damage.
Effect: The burst creates a zone of bright light. You and each ally within the zone gain a +1 power bonus to all defenses until the end of the encounter.

Martyr's Retribution — Paladin Attack 5

Divine light engulfs your weapon as you sacrifice your ability to heal in order to strike down your enemy.

Daily ✦ Divine, Radiant, Weapon
Standard Action   Melee weapon
Target: One creature
Attack: Strength vs. AC, and you must spend a healing surge without regaining any hit points
Hit: 4[W] + Strength modifier radiant damage.
Miss: Half damage.

Sign of Vulnerability — Paladin Attack 5

You cause a nearby foe to convulse with pain and render it more susceptible to radiant energy.

Daily ✦ Divine, Implement, Radiant
Standard Action   **Ranged** 5
Target: One creature
Attack: Charisma vs. Fortitude
Hit: 3d8 + Charisma modifier radiant damage, and the target gains vulnerability 5 to radiant damage until the end of the encounter.
Miss: Half damage, and the target gains no vulnerability.

LEVEL 6 UTILITY PRAYERS

Divine Bodyguard — Paladin Utility 6

As your weapon connects with your enemies, so too does the magic of your god connect you to your allies.

Daily ✦ Divine
Minor Action   **Ranged** 5
Effect: Choose an ally within 5 squares of you. You take half that ally's damage until the end of the encounter or until you end the effect as a free action. No power or effect can reduce the damage you take from this power.

One Heart, One Mind — Paladin Utility 6

You and your trusted allies form a telepathic bond.

Daily ✦ Divine
Minor Action   **Close** burst 6
Targets: You and each ally in burst
Effect: Until the end of the encounter, targets can communicate telepathically with each other out to a range of 20 squares, and your aid another actions give a +4 bonus instead of +2.

Wrath of the Gods — Paladin Utility 6

A halo of divine light emanates from you, enabling you and nearby allies to strike down your enemies with greater determination.

Daily ✦ Divine
Minor Action   **Close** burst 1
Targets: You and each ally in burst
Effect: The targets add your Charisma modifier to damage rolls until the end of the encounter.

LEVEL 7 ENCOUNTER PRAYERS

Beckon Foe — Paladin Attack 7

You pull an enemy toward you, dealing grievous wounds as he tries to rebuke you.

Encounter ✦ Divine, Implement
Standard Action   **Ranged** 5
Target: One creature
Attack: Charisma vs. Will
Hit: 2d10 + Charisma modifier damage, and you pull the target a number of squares equal to your Wisdom modifier.

Benign Transposition — Paladin Attack 7

You call upon the power of your deity to switch places with an ally and strike a foe within reach of your new position.

Encounter ✦ Divine, Teleportation, Weapon
Standard Action   **Melee** weapon
Primary Target: One ally within a number of squares equal to your Wisdom modifier
Effect: You and the target swap places. If an enemy is now within your melee reach, you can make a secondary attack against it.
    Secondary Target: One enemy
    Secondary Attack: Charisma vs. AC
    Hit: 2[W] + Charisma modifier damage.

Divine Reverence — Paladin Attack 7

You present yourself with such conviction that your enemies cannot help but be awestruck by the power of your faith.

Encounter ✦ Divine, Implement, Radiant
Standard Action   **Close** burst 1
Target: Each enemy in burst
Attack: Charisma vs. Will
Hit: 1d8 + Charisma modifier radiant damage, and the target is dazed until the end of your next turn.

Thunder Smite — Paladin Attack 7

Your weapon flashes as it strikes, and moments later, a peal of thunder slams into your foe.

Encounter ✦ Divine, Thunder, Weapon
Standard Action   **Melee** weapon
Target: One creature
Attack: Strength vs. AC (can score a critical hit against a marked enemy on a roll of 19-20)
Hit: 2[W] + Strength modifier thunder damage, and the target is knocked prone.

LEVEL 9 DAILY PRAYERS

Crown of Glory — Paladin Attack 9

A scintillating crown of radiant energy appears above your head, then expands suddenly to cripple nearby enemies.

Daily ✦ Divine, Implement, Radiant
Standard Action   **Close** burst 1
Target: Each enemy in burst
Attack: Charisma vs. Will
Hit: 2d8 + Charisma modifier radiant damage.
Effect: Any enemy that starts its turn adjacent to you is slowed until the end of your next turn.
Sustain Minor: You can sustain the power's effect.

One Stands Alone — Paladin Attack 9

Unable to fight alongside your allies, you turn to your faith for protection and press forward undaunted.

Daily ✦ Divine, Implement, Radiant
Standard Action   **Close** burst 1
Target: Each enemy in burst
Attack: Charisma vs. Will
Hit: 2d8 + Charisma modifier radiant damage.
Effect: The targets are weakened (save ends).
Special: You cannot use this power if any allies are within 5 squares of you.

Radiant Pulse — Paladin Attack 9

You target an enemy with a searing, pulsating light that also damages enemies adjacent to him and thrusts them back.

Daily ✦ Divine, Implement, Radiant
Standard Action   **Ranged** 10
Primary Target: One creature
Attack: Charisma vs. Fortitude
Hit: 1d10 + Charisma modifier radiant damage. Make a secondary attack.
   Secondary Target: Each enemy adjacent to the primary target
   Secondary Attack: Charisma vs. Fortitude
   Hit: 1d10 + Charisma modifier radiant damage, and you push the target 3 squares.
   Sustain Minor: When you sustain this power, you can repeat the secondary attack (the primary target is the same each time).
Miss: Half damage, and no secondary attack.

LEVEL 10 UTILITY PRAYERS

Cleansing Spirit — Paladin Utility 10

A translucent outline briefly appears above the creature you designate. The divine spirit gestures, relieving some of the creature's suffering, then fades instantly away.

Encounter ✦ Divine
Minor Action   **Ranged** 5
Target: You or one ally
Effect: The target makes a saving throw with a +2 bonus.

Noble Shield — Paladin Utility 10

You quickly throw up your hand, and a vortex of swirling energy surrounds you and your friends, shielding them from harm at your expense.

Daily ✦ Divine
Immediate Interrupt   **Personal**
Trigger: You are targeted by a close attack or an area attack
Effect: A close attack or an area attack targeting you automatically hits you, and any of your allies who are also hit take only half damage. This power does not change other effects the attack might cause.

Turn the Tide — Paladin Utility 10

You whisper a solemn hymn, and divine light washes gently over you and nearby allies, potentially negating harmful and debilitating afflictions.

Daily ✦ Divine
Standard Action   **Close** burst 3
Targets: You and each ally in burst
Effect: The targets make saving throws against every effect that a save can end.

LEVEL 13 ENCOUNTER PRAYERS

Entangling Smite — Paladin Attack 13

Strands of energy erupt from your weapon as it strikes true, wrapping around your foe and rooting it to the ground.

Encounter ✦ Divine, Weapon
Standard Action   **Melee** weapon
Target: One creature
Attack: Charisma vs. Will
Hit: 2[W] + Charisma modifier damage, and the target is immobilized until the end of your next turn.

Radiant Charge — Paladin Attack 13

You propel yourself through the air toward a nearby foe as brilliant rays of light stream from your weapon.

Encounter ✦ Divine, Radiant, Weapon
Standard Action   **Melee** weapon
Effect: You can fly a number of squares equal to your Wisdom modifier and make an attack.
Target: One creature within your melee reach
Attack: Strength vs. AC
Special: You must charge as part of this attack.
Hit: 3[W] + Strength modifier radiant damage, and the target is marked until the end of your next turn.

Renewing Smite — Paladin Attack 13

As you strike a foe with your weapon, you murmur a prayer of renewal, causing a momentary nimbus of light to engulf and heal a nearby ally.

Encounter ✦ Divine, Healing, Weapon
Standard Action   **Melee** weapon
Target: One creature
Attack: Charisma vs. AC
Hit: 2[W] + Charisma modifier damage, and one ally within 5 squares of you regains hit points equal to 10 + your Wisdom modifier.

Whirlwind Smite — Paladin Attack 13

You sweep your weapon in a full circle, attacking all adjacent enemies in a dazzling display of martial prowess.

Encounter ✦ Divine, Weapon
Standard Action   **Close** burst 1
Target: Each enemy in burst you can see
Attack: Strength vs. AC
Hit: 2[W] + Strength modifier damage, and the target is marked until the end of your next turn.

LEVEL 15 DAILY PRAYERS

Bloodied Retribution — Paladin Attack 15

Battered and bloodied, you call upon the divine power of your deity to deal a retributive blow to your enemy and heal your wounds.

Daily ✦ Divine, Healing, Weapon
Standard Action   **Melee** weapon
Special: You can use this power only when you are bloodied.
Target: One creature
Attack: Strength vs. AC
Hit: 4[W] + Strength modifier damage.
Miss: Half damage.
Effect: You can spend a healing surge.

True Nemesis · Paladin Attack 15

You extend your holy symbol toward a foe, dealing damage and singling him out as the continuing subject of your divine retribution.

Daily ✦ Divine, Implement
Standard Action · **Ranged** 5
Target: One creature
Attack: Charisma vs. Will
Hit: 2d10 + Charisma modifier damage.
Miss: Half damage.
Effect: Until the end of the encounter, whenever the target is within 5 squares of you and attacks you or an ally, you can make a secondary attack against the target as an immediate reaction.
  Secondary Attack: Charisma vs. Will
  Hit: 2d10 + Charisma modifier damage.
  Miss: Half damage.

LEVEL 16 UTILITY PRAYERS

Angelic Intercession · Paladin Utility 16

You teleport to the side of a friend in peril and take the effects of an attack meant for him.

Daily ✦ Divine, Teleportation
Immediate Interrupt · **Personal**
Trigger: An ally within 5 squares of you is hit by an attack
Effect: You teleport adjacent to the ally and are hit by the attack instead.

Death Ward · Paladin Utility 16

You touch a dying creature and share some of your divine inner light, bestowing upon the recipient the power to resist the call of death.

Daily ✦ Divine, Healing
Standard Action · **Melee** touch
Target: One dying creature
Effect: You spend a healing surge but regain no hit points from it. Instead, the target regains hit points as if it had spent two healing surges. Add your Charisma modifier to the hit points regained.

LEVEL 17 ENCOUNTER PRAYERS

Enervating Smite · Paladin Attack 17

With a mighty blow, you leave your foe horribly weakened.

Encounter ✦ Divine, Weapon
Standard Action · **Melee** weapon
Target: One creature
Attack: Charisma vs. Will
Hit: 2[W] + Charisma modifier damage, and the target is weakened until the end of your next turn.

Break the Wall · Paladin Attack 15

You lash out at an enemy with the power of your faith and break down its defenses.

Daily ✦ Divine, Implement
Standard Action · **Ranged** 5
Target: One creature
Attack: Charisma vs. Fortitude
Hit: 3d10 + Charisma damage, and the target takes a -2 penalty to all defenses (save ends).
Miss: Half damage, and the target takes a -1 penalty to all defenses (save ends).

Fortifying Smite — Paladin Attack 17

A symphony of otherworldly music resonates throughout your body, fortifying it to withstand the tests to come.

Encounter ✦ Divine, Weapon
Standard Action   Melee weapon
Target: One creature
Attack: Charisma vs. AC
Hit: 3[W] + Charisma modifier damage. Until the end of your next turn, you gain a power bonus to AC equal to your Wisdom modifier.

Hand of the Gods — Paladin Attack 17

You hold your holy symbol high above your head, and a brilliant flash of divine light explodes from it. The radiance sears your foes and inspires your closest allies.

Encounter ✦ Divine, Implement, Radiant
Minor Action   Close burst 1
Target: Each enemy in burst
Attack: Charisma vs. Fortitude
Hit: 2d10 + Charisma modifier radiant damage, and the target is marked until the end of your next turn.
Effect: Until the end of your next turn, allies in the burst gain a power bonus to attack rolls equal to your Wisdom modifier.

Terrifying Smite — Paladin Attack 17

Striking mercilessly, you hound your foe with waves of divine dread.

Encounter ✦ Divine, Fear, Weapon
Standard Action   Melee weapon
Target: One creature
Attack: Strength vs. AC
Hit: 3[W] + Strength modifier damage, and you push the target a number of squares equal to your Charisma modifier. The target can't move nearer to you on its next turn.

Level 19 Daily Prayers

Corona of Blinding Radiance — Paladin Attack 19

You swing your weapon and brilliant light explodes around you, blinding your enemies.

Daily ✦ Divine, Radiant, Weapon
Standard Action   Close burst 1
Target: Each enemy in burst you can see
Attack: Charisma vs. Reflex
Hit: 3[W] + Charisma modifier radiant damage, and the target is blinded (save ends).
Miss: Half damage, and the target is blinded until the end of your next turn.

Crusader's Boon — Paladin Attack 19

You strike your foe with such conviction that nearby allies can't help but feel inspired.

Daily ✦ Divine, Weapon
Standard Action   Melee weapon
Target: One creature
Attack: Strength vs. AC
Hit: 4[W] + Strength modifier damage.
Miss: Half damage.
Effect: You and allies adjacent to you gain a +1 power bonus to attack rolls until the end of the encounter.

Righteous Inferno — Paladin Attack 19

A raging inferno of holy fire engulfs your enemies and continues to burn those who are drawn to it like moths.

Daily ✦ Divine, Fire, Implement, Zone
Standard Action   Area burst 2 within 10 squares
Target: Each enemy in burst
Attack: Charisma vs. Reflex
Hit: 3d10 + Charisma modifier fire damage, and the target grants combat advantage to you and your allies until the end of your next turn.
Miss: Half damage, and the target does not grant combat advantage.
Effect: The burst creates a zone of fire that lasts until the end of your next turn. Enemies that enter the zone or start their turns there take 1d10 fire damage and grant combat advantage to you and your allies.
Sustain Minor: The zone persists.

Level 22 Utility Prayers

Angelic Rescue — Paladin Utility 22

White wings of astral brilliance envelop an ally in a sparkling cocoon, then disappear. The wings reappear a short distance away and unfold, bringing the ally closer to you.

Daily ✦ Divine, Teleportation
Standard Action   Ranged sight
Target: One willing ally
Effect: The target is teleported from any square you can see to a square within 5 squares of you that is nearer to you than the target's original square.

Cleansing Burst — Paladin Utility 22

Ripples of divine energy wash over you and nearby allies, potentially negating harmful and debilitating afflictions.

Daily ✦ Divine
Minor Action   Close burst 5
Targets: You and each ally in burst
Effect: All targets make a saving throw against each effect that a save can end. Any penalties to attack rolls or defenses affecting the targets are removed.

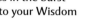

Gift of Life — Paladin Utility 22

You invoke the greatest of all prayers and touch a wounded or recently slain creature, bestowing upon it the gift of life at the expense of your own health.

Daily ✦ Divine, Healing
Standard Action   Melee touch
Target: One creature
Effect: If the target is alive, it regains hit points no greater than one-half your maximum hit points (your choice), and you take an equal amount of damage.
    If the target died since the end of your last turn, it returns to life at 0 hit points, and you take damage equal to one-half your maximum hit points.
    You can't avoid or reduce this damage in any way.

United in Faith — Paladin Utility 22

You utter words of faith, instantly healing yourself and nearby allies.

Daily ✦ Divine, Healing
Minor Action   Close burst 5
Targets: You and each ally in burst
Effect: Each target can spend a healing surge.

LEVEL 23 ENCOUNTER PRAYERS

Here Waits Thy Doom — Paladin Attack 23

You pull an enemy toward you, searing him with radiant energy as he tries to resist.

Encounter ✦ Divine, Implement, Radiant
Standard Action   Ranged 5
Target: One creature
Attack: Charisma vs. Will
Hit: 4d10 + Charisma modifier radiant damage, and you pull the target a number of squares equal to your Wisdom modifier (minimum 1).

Martyr's Smite — Paladin Attack 23

As you assail your foe, you utter a prayer that grants you the power to absorb the damage from your foe's attacks, even when such attacks aren't directed at you.

Encounter ✦ Divine, Weapon
Standard Action   Melee weapon
Target: One creature
Attack: Strength vs. AC
Hit: 4[W] + Strength modifier damage. Until the end of your next turn, any time the target deals damage, you can choose to take that damage. The target's intended victim takes no damage but is subject to any other effects of the attack.

Resounding Smite — Paladin Attack 23

You swing your weapon in a mighty arc, unleashing a peal of thunder that knocks adjacent enemies prone.

Encounter ✦ Divine, Thunder, Weapon
Standard Action   Melee weapon
Primary Target: One creature
Attack: Strength vs. AC
Hit: 3[W] + Strength modifier thunder damage, and the target is knocked prone. Make a secondary attack.
    Secondary Target: Each enemy adjacent to you other than the primary target
    Secondary Attack: Strength vs. AC
    Hit: 1[W] + Strength modifier thunder damage, and the target is knocked prone.

Sublime Transposition — Paladin Attack 23

With a wave of your hand, you teleport an endangered ally to a safer location, teleport yourself to his previous location, and strike a foe within reach.

Encounter ✦ Divine, Teleportation, Weapon
Standard Action   Ranged 5
Primary Target: One willing ally
Effect: You can teleport the target 5 squares. Until the end of your next turn, you grant the target a power bonus to all defenses equal to your Wisdom modifier. In addition, you teleport to the target's original space and make a secondary attack.
    Secondary Target: One creature within your melee reach
    Secondary Attack: Charisma vs. AC
    Hit: 3[W] + Charisma modifier damage.

LEVEL 25 DAILY PRAYERS

Exalted Retribution — Paladin Attack 25

You land a mighty blow, and the symbol of your deity appears above your enemy's head as a glowing red rune that only you can see, flashing brightly to warn you whenever he's about to attack.

Daily ✦ Divine, Weapon
Standard Action   Melee weapon
Target: One creature
Attack: Strength vs. AC
Hit: 4[W] + Strength modifier damage.
Miss: Half damage.
Effect: Until the end of the encounter, the target provokes an opportunity attack from you when it attacks (save ends). You gain a +2 bonus to the opportunity attack roll and deal an extra 1[W] damage.

To the Nine Hells with You — Paladin Attack 25

Divine light explodes out from your holy symbol, blasting and igniting enemies nearby.

Daily ✦ Divine, Fire, Implement
Standard Action   Close burst 5
Target: Each enemy in burst
Attack: Charisma vs. Will
Hit: 6d6 + Charisma modifier damage, and ongoing 10 fire damage (save ends). The target is marked until the end of your next turn.
Miss: Half damage, and ongoing 10 fire damage (save ends). The target is marked until the end of your next turn.

LEVEL 27 ENCOUNTER PRAYERS

Blinding Smite — Paladin Attack 27

Your weapon glows with a pale inner light, and your enemy is struck blind by the force of your blow.

Encounter ✦ Divine, Weapon
Standard Action　　Melee weapon
Target: One creature
Attack: Strength vs. Will
Hit: 3[W] + Strength modifier damage, and the target is blinded until the end of your next turn.

Brand of Judgment — Paladin Attack 27

You touch your holy symbol to an enemy, branding it with the painfully radiant symbol of your deity and causing it to take damage from its own attacks.

Encounter ✦ Divine, Implement, Radiant
Standard Action　　Melee touch
Target: One creature
Attack: Charisma vs. Will
Hit: 4d8 + Charisma modifier radiant damage. If the target makes an attack on its next turn, it takes half damage from its own attack whether it hits or misses.

Deific Vengeance — Paladin Attack 27

You invoke an ancient prayer that unleashes your deity's ire upon a nearby enemy that has just attacked you.

Encounter ✦ Divine, Implement
Immediate Reaction　　Ranged 20
Trigger: A creature within range attacks you
Target: The attacking creature
Attack: Charisma + 2 vs. Fortitude
Hit: 4d10 + Charisma modifier damage, and the target is weakened until the end of your next turn.

Restricting Smite — Paladin Attack 27

You strike your enemy with such resolve that he is blind to all foes except you.

Encounter ✦ Divine, Weapon
Standard Action　　Melee weapon
Target: One creature
Attack: Charisma vs. Will
Hit: 3[W] + Charisma modifier damage, and the target is marked until the end of your next turn. In addition, the target cannot gain line of effect to anyone but you until the end of your next turn.

Stunning Smite — Paladin Attack 27

You swing your weapon in a mighty arc, stunning targets that you hit.

Encounter ✦ Divine, Weapon
Standard Action　　Melee weapon
Primary Target: One creature
Attack: Strength vs. Will
Hit: 2[W] + Strength modifier damage, and the target is stunned until the end of your next turn. Make a secondary attack.
Secondary Target: Each enemy other than the primary target adjacent to you
Secondary Attack: Strength vs. Will
Hit: 1[W] + Strength modifier damage, and the target is stunned until the end of your next turn.

LEVEL 29 DAILY PRAYERS

Even Hand of Justice — Paladin Attack 29

You pronounce a divine sentence upon your enemy and force him to take the damage of his own attacks.

Daily ✦ Divine, Implement
Standard Action　　Ranged 5
Target: One creature
Attack: Charisma vs. Will
Hit: 5d10 + Charisma modifier damage. Whenever the target makes an attack, its attack works as usual, but it takes the full damage and effects of the attack as well (save ends). Saving throws made to end the effect take a -2 penalty.
Miss: 5d10 + Charisma modifier damage.
Special: Many creatures have immunity or resistance to their own attacks. When taking damage from its own attacks resulting from this power, the target does not gain the benefit of any immunities or resistances.

Powerful Faith — Paladin Attack 29

You deal a hard blow to your enemy, and divine arcs of light spring from the tip of your weapon and blind those who stand against you.

Daily ✦ Divine, Weapon
Standard Action　　Melee weapon
Primary Target: One creature
Attack: Strength vs. AC
Hit: 7[W] + Strength modifier damage. Make a secondary attack.
Miss: Half damage, and no secondary attack.
Secondary Target: Each enemy within 10 squares of you
Secondary Attack: Strength vs. Fortitude
Hit: The target is blinded until the end of your next turn.

PARAGON PATHS

ASTRAL WEAPON

"With the power of the Astral Sea flowing through me, and my faith as powerful as a weapon, I fight as my god wills."

Prerequisite: Paladin class

You become a literal weapon for your god, imbued with an extra dose of divine power emanating from the Astral Sea. As an astral weapon, there are no enemies you won't oppose, no challenge you won't take on, for your faith is strong and your weapon sings with power from on high. When you accept this path, the weapon you wield forevermore glows with the silvery light of the Astral Sea.

ASTRAL WEAPON PATH FEATURES

Astral Judgment (11th level): Enemies currently marked by you that attack your allies without attacking you take a -2 penalty to all defenses until they are no longer marked by you.

Astral Rejuvenation Action (11th level): You can spend an action point to regain one paladin encounter power you have already used, instead of taking an extra action.

Courage from on High (16th level): You gain a +2 bonus to saving throws against fear effects.

ASTRAL WEAPON PRAYERS

Carving a Path of Light	Astral Weapon Attack 11

Your weapon glows with astral light, and as it strikes your enemy, that glow spreads to encompass all enemies adjacent to you, temporarily coating them with a glowing target your allies can see.

Encounter ✦ Divine, Weapon
Standard Action   **Melee** weapon
Target: One creature
Attack: Strength vs. AC
Hit: 2[W] + Strength modifier damage, and until the end of your next turn, your allies have combat advantage against any enemy adjacent to you.

Pray for More	Astral Weapon Utility 12

You strike your enemy, but you pray to increase the amount of damage you deal.

Encounter ✦ Divine
Free Action   **Personal**
Effect: If you don't like the damage you have rolled with one of your attacks, reroll your damage. You must use the result of the second roll.

Astral Whirlwind	Astral Weapon Attack 20

Your faith directs you into a whirling attack that strikes out at every foe within reach, instilling them with fear and weakening their defenses.

Daily ✦ Divine, Fear, Weapon
Standard Action   **Close** burst 1
Target: Each enemy in burst you can see
Attack: Strength vs. AC
Hit: 2[W] + Strength modifier damage. In addition, the target takes a -2 penalty to all defenses (save ends).
Special: If this attack kills one or more evil or chaotic evil creatures, roll a d20. On a roll of 10 or higher, you can use this power again during this encounter.

CHAMPION OF ORDER

"The law holds chaos at bay, and I bolster the law with my every action and deed."

Prerequisite: Paladin class

You become a paragon of order, embracing this concept and fulfilling it with every word and deed. The gods of order look favorably upon you as you champion the causes they promote and the ideals they exemplify, turning back the forces of the chaotic evil powers at every opportunity. In the presence of chaotic evil creatures, your weapon glows with radiant light.

CHAMPION OF ORDER PATH FEATURES

Champion's Action (11th level): When you spend an action point to take an extra action, you also flash with radiant light that causes adjacent enemies to take a -1 penalty to all defenses until the start of your next turn.

In Defense of Order (11th level): When you are adjacent to the target of your *divine challenge*, the target provokes an opportunity attack from you if it makes an attack that does not include you. Furthermore, your damage rolls against demons and elemental creatures that you challenge deal an extra 2d6 radiant damage.

Champion's Hammer (16th level): Your attacks ignore the resistances of demons and elemental creatures.

CHAMPION OF ORDER PRAYERS

Certain Justice	Champion of Order Attack 11

You call upon your devotion to law to make your attack strike true.

Encounter ✦ Divine, Weapon
Standard Action   **Melee** weapon
Target: One creature
Attack: Strength + 4 vs. AC
Hit: 1[W] damage. If the target is marked, it is also weakened and dazed by this attack for as long as the mark remains in effect.

None Shall Pass — Champion of Order Utility 12

You contain two foes instead of just one with your divine challenge.

Daily ✦ Divine
Free Action — **Personal**
Effect: Until the end of the encounter, every use of your *divine challenge* targets two enemies rather than one.

Rule of Order — Champion of Order Attack 20

You invoke order through your weapon, causing it to glow as you deliver a punishing blow against an enemy.

Daily ✦ Divine, Radiant, Weapon
Standard Action — **Melee** weapon
Target: One creature
Attack: Strength vs. Fortitude
Special: If the target has scored a critical hit against you or your allies in this encounter, your attack gains a +2 power bonus and deals +2d10 radiant damage.
Hit: 4[W] + Strength modifier damage, and you push the target 1 square. The target is weakened (save ends).
Miss: 1[W] + Strength modifier damage, and the target is weakened (save ends).

HOSPITALER

"I am a healer and a defender, an inspiration to my allies and a fearful visage to my foes."

Prerequisite: Paladin class

Your spiritual path leads you to specialize in the healing arts. You increase the healing you provide to allies as you become a shining beacon of hope on the battlefield. You embody mercy and care, bringing aid to the wounded and cleansing life to those near death—especially when you turn damage against a foe into healing for a friend.

HOSPITALER PATH FEATURES

Hospitaler's Blessing (11th level): When an enemy that you currently challenge attacks one of your allies, whether the attack hits or misses, that ally regains hit points equal to one-half your level + your Wisdom modifier.

Hospitaler's Action (11th level): When you spend an action point to take an extra action, each ally within 5 squares regains hit points equal to your Wisdom modifier.

Hospitaler's Care (16th level): You add your Charisma modifier to the healing provided each time you use your *lay on hands* power.

HOSPITALER PRAYERS

Warding Blow — Hospitaler Attack 11

You strike a foe you have challenged, bringing hope and encouragement to nearby allies.

Encounter ✦ Divine, Weapon
Standard Action — **Melee** weapon
Target: One creature that is marked by you
Attack: Charisma vs. AC
Hit: 2[W] + Charisma modifier damage, and each ally within 5 squares of you can make a saving throw.

WILLIAM O'CONNOR

Healing Font
Hospitaler Utility 12

A short prayer imbues your weapon with healing power, so that whenever it strikes an enemy it heals an ally.

Daily ✦ Divine, Healing
Minor Action   **Personal**
Effect: Until the end of this encounter, when you attack on your turn and hit at least one enemy, you heal an ally. Choose one ally within 10 squares of you. That ally regains a number of hit points equal to 1d6 [ts] your Wisdom modifier.

Life-Giving Smite
Hospitaler Attack 20

You imbue your weapon with radiant power, and as you strike at a foe the power of the attack heals an ally.

Daily ✦ Divine, Healing, Radiant, Weapon
Standard Action   **Melee** weapon
Target: One creature
Attack: Charisma vs. Fortitude
Hit: 4[W] + Charisma modifier radiant damage.
Effect: Choose one ally within 10 squares of you. The ally can spend a healing surge. Add your Charisma modifier to the hit points regained.

JUSTICIAR

"I fight for justice, my faith and my strong arm defending those in need."

Prerequisite: Paladin class

You become the embodiment of justice, a champion of righteousness and fairness—at least as viewed from the perspective of your particular faith. You are granted the ability to shelter and protect your allies and others in need, while also receiving powers that help you do the right thing according to the faith you have embraced.

JUSTICIAR PATH FEATURES

Just Action (11th level): When you spend an action point to take an extra action, each enemy adjacent to you is weakened until the end of its next turn.

Just Spirit (11th level): Each ally adjacent to you can reroll one saving throw at the end of his or her turn.

Just Shelter (16th level): Allies adjacent to you are immune to fear and charm effects and receive a +1 bonus to saving throws.

JUSTICIAR PRAYERS

Just Radiance
Justiciar Attack 11

A burst of light, like purity and justice, explodes from your holy symbol, sending searing pain through enemies you have challenged.

Encounter ✦ Divine, Implement, Radiant
Standard Action   **Close** burst 5
Target: Each enemy marked by you in burst
Attack: Charisma vs. Will
Hit: 2d8 + Charisma modifier radiant damage, and until the end of your next turn, the target cannot make an attack that does not include you.

Strike Me Instead
Justiciar Utility 12

You call upon your innate sense of justice and honor, whisper a short prayer, and redirect an attack so that you take the hit for those you would protect.

Daily ✦ Divine
Immediate Interrupt   **Personal**
Trigger: An ally within 5 squares of you is attacked
Effect: The attack misses all of your allies it targets, but automatically hits you even if you weren't a target of the attack.

Challenge the Unjust
Justiciar Attack 20

Your enemies surround you, and the purity within you cries out for justice. You focus a powerful prayer through your holy symbol, sending forth a radiant burst of punishing force that no enemy can ignore.

Daily ✦ Divine, Implement, Radiant
Standard Action   **Close** burst 10
Target: Each enemy in burst
Attack: Charisma vs. Will
Hit: 3d8 + Charisma modifier radiant damage, and the target is marked until the end of your next turn.
Miss: Half damage, and the target is marked until the end of your next turn.

RANGER

"I'll get the one in the back. That's one hobgoblin who'll regret ever lifting a bow."

CLASS TRAITS

Role: Striker. You concentrate on either ranged attacks or two-weapon melee fighting to deal a lot of damage to one enemy at a time. Your attacks rely on speed and mobility, since you prefer to use hit-and-run tactics whenever possible.

Power Source: Martial. Your talents depend on extensive training and practice, inner confidence, and natural proficiency.

Key Abilities: Strength, Dexterity, Wisdom

Armor Proficiencies: Cloth, leather, hide
Weapon Proficiencies: Simple melee, military melee, simple ranged, military ranged
Bonus to Defense: +1 Fortitude, +1 Reflex

Hit Points at 1st Level: 12 + Constitution score
Hit Points per Level Gained: 5
Healing Surges per Day: 6 + Constitution modifier

Trained Skills: Dungeoneering or Nature (your choice). From the class skills list below, choose four more trained skills at 1st level.
Class Skills: Acrobatics (Dex), Athletics (Str), Dungeoneering (Wis), Endurance (Con), Heal (Wis), Nature (Wis), Perception (Wis), Stealth (Dex)

Build Options: Archer ranger, two-blade ranger
Class Features: Fighting Style, Hunter's Quarry, Prime Shot

Rangers are watchful warriors who roam past the horizon to safeguard a region, a principle, or a way of life. Masters of bow and blade, rangers excel at hit-and-run assaults and can quickly and silently eliminate foes. Rangers lay superb ambushes and excel at avoiding danger.

As a ranger, you possess almost supernaturally keen senses and a deep appreciation for untamed wilderness. With your knowledge of the natural world, you are able to track enemies through nearly any landscape, using the smallest clue to set your course, even sometimes the calls and songs of beasts and birds. Your severe demeanor promises a deadly conclusion to any enemy you hunt.

When you catch sight of your quarry, will the transgressor perish by swift bow shots from a distance, or by the twofold blades that glint and glitter in each of your battle-scarred hands?

WILLIAM O'CONNOR

CREATING A RANGER

Rangers depend on Strength, Dexterity, and Wisdom for most of their powers. Constitution is also useful, since it helps them stand up to damage. The two ranger builds presented here are the archer ranger and the melee ranger.

ARCHER RANGER

You are a master of the bow (or, rarely, the crossbow, sling, or thrown weapon). You prefer ranged attack powers, and you resort to melee only when there are no good targets left for your arrows. Most of your attack powers use Dexterity, so Dexterity should be your highest ability score. You find yourself in melee from time to time, so Strength is a good choice for your second-highest score. Wisdom should be your third-best ability score. Choose powers that reflect your preference for ranged weapons.

Suggested Feat: Agile Hunter (Human feat: Human Perseverance)
Suggested Skills: Endurance, Heal, Nature, Perception, Stealth
Suggested At-Will Powers: *careful attack, nimble strike*
Suggested Encounter Power: *evasive strike*
Suggested Daily Power: *split the tree*

TWO-BLADE RANGER

You like to get up close and rely on the ranger's famous two-weapon fighting style. Naturally, you prefer melee attack powers, and that means Strength should be your highest ability score. For your second ability, Dexterity is a good choice because it improves your AC. Make Wisdom your third choice, since it adds to your Will defense and provides a bonus to many of your

---

powers. Choose powers that reflect your preference for fighting with two melee weapons.

Suggested Feat: Lethal Hunter (Human feat: Action Surge)
Suggested Skills: Acrobatics, Dungeoneering, Endurance, Heal, Perception
Suggested At-Will Powers: *hit and run, twin strike*
Suggested Encounter Power: *dire wolverine strike*
Suggested Daily Power: *jaws of the wolf*

RANGER CLASS FEATURES

Your class features depend largely on the build and fighting style you choose.

FIGHTING STYLE

Choose one of the following fighting styles and gain its benefit.

Archer Fighting Style: Because of your focus on ranged attacks, you gain Defensive Mobility as a bonus feat.

Two-Blade Fighting Style: Because of your focus on two-weapon melee attacks, you can wield a one-handed weapon in your off hand as if it were an off-hand weapon. (Make sure to designate on your character sheet which weapon is main and which is off-hand.) In addition, you gain Toughness as a bonus feat.

HUNTER'S QUARRY

Once per turn as a minor action, you can designate the enemy nearest to you as your quarry.

Once per round, you deal extra damage to your quarry. The extra damage is based on your level. If you can make multiple attacks in a round, you decide which attack to apply the extra damage to after all the attacks are rolled.

The hunter's quarry effect remains active until the end of the encounter, until the quarry is defeated, or until you designate a different target as your quarry.

You can designate one enemy as your quarry at a time.

Level	Hunter's Quarry Extra Damage
1st–10th	+1d6
11th–20th	+2d6
21st–30th	+3d6

PRIME SHOT

If none of your allies are nearer to your target than you are, you receive a +1 bonus to ranged attack rolls against that target.

RANGER OVERVIEW

Characteristics: You combine fast, hard-hitting melee attack power with excellent ranged attack ability, and shift easily from melee to ranged combat. You are moderately resilient in battle, but you prefer hit-and-run attacks or ambushes to prolonged slugging matches. Hit hard, get out; that's the ranger's way.

Religion: Rangers favor deities of nature and of the hunt. They often revere Kord, Melora, or the Raven Queen. Evil or chaotic evil rangers usually worship Gruumsh or Zehir.

Races: Elves are ideal archer rangers. Humans, halflings, dragonborn, and eladrin are all sometimes drawn to the wandering life of a two-blade ranger.

Ranger Powers

Your powers are bold exploits derived from your relentless training in archery and swordplay. At higher levels, you have access to special stance powers (see "Keyword Categories," page 55).

Level 1 At-Will Exploits

Careful Attack   Ranger Attack 1

You study the enemy, looking for a gap in his defenses. Only when you find it do you strike.

At-Will ✦ Martial, Weapon
Standard Action   **Melee** or **Ranged** weapon
Requirement: You must be wielding two melee weapons or a ranged weapon.
Target: One creature
Attack: Strength + 2 vs. AC (melee) or Dexterity + 2 vs. AC (ranged).
Hit: 1[W] damage (melee) or 1[W] damage (ranged).
Increase damage to 2[W] (melee) or 2[W] (ranged) at 21st level.

Hit and Run   Ranger Attack 1

Let the fighter stand toe to toe with the monster. You prefer to make your attack, then withdraw to safer ground.

At-Will ✦ Martial, Weapon
Standard Action   **Melee** weapon
Target: One creature
Attack: Strength vs. AC
Hit: 1[W] + Strength modifier damage
Increase damage to 2[W] + Strength modifier at 21st level.
Effect: If you move in the same turn after this attack, leaving the first square adjacent to the target does not provoke an opportunity attack from the target.

Nimble Strike   Ranger Attack 1

You slink past your enemy's guard to make your attack, or you make your attack and then withdraw to a more advantageous position.

At-Will ✦ Martial, Weapon
Standard Action   **Ranged** weapon
Target: One creature
Special: Shift 1 square before or after you attack
Attack: Dexterity vs. AC
Hit: 1[W] + Dexterity modifier damage.
Increase damage to 2[W] + Dexterity modifier at 21st level.

Twin Strike   Ranger Attack 1

If the first attack doesn't kill it, the second one might.

At-Will ✦ Martial, Weapon
Standard Action   **Melee** or **Ranged** weapon
Requirement: You must be wielding two melee weapons or a ranged weapon.
Targets: One or two creatures
Attack: Strength vs. AC (melee; main weapon and off-hand weapon) or Dexterity vs. AC (ranged), two attacks
Hit: 1[W] damage per attack.
Increase damage to 2[W] at 21st level.

Level 1 Encounter Exploits

Dire Wolverine Strike   Ranger Attack 1

Enemies surround you—much to their chagrin, as you slash them to pieces with the ferocity of a wounded dire wolverine.

Encounter ✦ Martial, Weapon
Standard Action   **Close** burst 1
Requirement: You must be wielding two melee weapons.
Target: Each enemy in burst you can see
Attack: Strength vs. AC
Hit: 1[W] + Strength modifier damage.

Evasive Strike   Ranger Attack 1

You confound enemies by weaving through the battlefield unscathed as you make your attacks.

Encounter ✦ Martial, Weapon
Standard Action   **Melee** or **Ranged** weapon
Target: One creature
Special: You can shift a number of squares equal to 1 + your Wisdom modifier either before or after the attack.
Attack: Strength vs. AC (melee) or Dexterity vs. AC (ranged)
Hit: 2[W] + Strength modifier damage (melee) or 2[W] + Dexterity modifier damage (ranged).

Fox's Cunning   Ranger Attack 1

Using the momentum from your enemy's blow to fall back or slip to one side, you make a sudden retaliatory attack as he stumbles to regain his composure.

Encounter ✦ Martial, Weapon
Immediate Reaction   **Melee** or **Ranged** weapon
Trigger: An enemy makes a melee attack against you
Attack: You can shift 1 square, then make a basic attack against the enemy.
Special: Gain a power bonus to your basic attack roll equal to your Wisdom modifier.

Two-Fanged Strike   Ranger Attack 1

You sink two arrows or both of your blades into the flesh of your enemy, causing it to howl in pain.

Encounter ✦ Martial, Weapon
Standard Action   **Melee** or **Ranged** weapon
Requirement: You must be wielding two melee weapons or a ranged weapon.
Target: One creature
Attack: Strength vs. AC (melee; main weapon and off-hand weapon) or Dexterity vs. AC (ranged), two attacks
Hit: 1[W] + Strength modifier damage (melee) or 1[W] + Dexterity modifier damage (ranged) per attack. If both attacks hit, you deal extra damage equal to your Wisdom modifier.

LEVEL 1 DAILY EXPLOITS

Hunter's Bear Trap — Ranger Attack 1

A well-placed shot to the leg leaves your enemy hobbled and bleeding.

Daily ✦ Martial, Weapon
Standard Action   Melee or **Ranged** weapon
Target: One creature
Attack: Strength vs. AC (melee) or Dexterity vs. AC (ranged)
Hit: 2[W] + Strength modifier damage (melee) or 2[W] + Dexterity modifier damage (ranged), and the target is slowed and takes ongoing 5 damage (save ends both).
Miss: Half damage, no ongoing damage, and the target is slowed until the end of your next turn.

Jaws of the Wolf — Ranger Attack 1

You use your weapons to hedge in your foe and trick him into exposing a weak spot, at which point you strike.

Daily ✦ Martial, Weapon
Standard Action   Melee weapon
Requirement: You must be wielding two melee weapons.
Target: One creature
Attack: Strength vs. AC (main weapon and off-hand weapon), two attacks
Hit: 2[W] + Strength modifier damage per attack.
Miss: Half damage per attack.

Split the Tree — Ranger Attack 1

You fire two arrows at once, which separate in mid-flight to strike two different targets.

Daily ✦ Martial, Weapon
Standard Action   Ranged weapon
Targets: Two creatures within 3 squares of each other
Attack: Dexterity vs. AC. Make two attack rolls, take the higher result, and apply it to both targets.
Hit: 2[W] + Dexterity modifier damage.

Sudden Strike — Ranger Attack 1

You hold your weapons blade-down and slash your foe across the face with one of them. As he spins away and drops his guard, you roll to one side, spring to your feet, and plunge your other blade into his back.

Daily ✦ Martial, Weapon
Standard Action   Melee weapon
Requirement: You must be wielding two melee weapons.
Target: One creature
Attack: Strength vs. AC (off-hand weapon)
Hit: 1[W] damage (off-hand weapon).
Effect: You shift 1 square and make a secondary attack against the target.
  Secondary Attack: Strength vs. AC (main weapon)
  Hit: 2[W] + Strength modifier damage (main weapon), and the target is weakened until the end of your next turn.

LEVEL 2 UTILITY EXPLOITS

Crucial Advice — Ranger Utility 2

You are wise in all things. The sooner your friends realize this, the safer and better off they'll be.

Encounter ✦ Martial
Immediate Reaction   Ranged 5
Trigger: An ally within range that you can see or hear makes a skill check using a skill in which you're trained
Effect: Grant the ally the ability to reroll the skill check, with a power bonus equal to your Wisdom modifier.

Unbalancing Parry — Ranger Utility 2

You deftly block your enemy's strike and turn his momentum against him, causing him to stumble to the side.

Encounter ✦ Martial, Weapon
Immediate Reaction   Melee 1
Trigger: An enemy misses you with a melee attack
Effect: Slide the enemy into a square adjacent to you and gain combat advantage against it until the end of your next turn.

Yield Ground — Ranger Utility 2

Even as your foe connects, you leap backward, out of the way of further harm.

Encounter ✦ Martial
Immediate Reaction   Personal
Trigger: An enemy damages you with a melee attack
Effect: You can shift a number of squares equal to your Wisdom modifier. Gain a +2 power bonus to all defenses until the end of your next turn.

LEVEL 3 ENCOUNTER EXPLOITS

Cut and Run — Ranger Attack 3

You attack twice while maneuvering yourself into the most advantageous position possible.

Encounter ✦ Martial, Weapon
Standard Action   Melee or **Ranged** weapon
Requirement: You must be wielding two melee weapons or a ranged weapon.
Target: One or two creatures
Attack: Strength vs. AC (melee; main weapon and off-hand weapon) or Dexterity vs. AC (ranged), two attacks
Special: After the first or the second attack, you can shift a number of squares equal to 1 + your Wisdom modifier.
Hit: 1[W] + Strength modifier damage (melee) or 1[W] + Dexterity modifier damage (ranged) per attack.

Disruptive Strike — Ranger Attack 3

You thwart an enemy's attack with a timely thrust of your blade or a quick shot from your bow.

Encounter ✦ Martial, Weapon
Immediate Interrupt   Melee or **Ranged** weapon
Trigger: You or an ally is attacked by a creature
Target: The attacking creature
Attack: Strength vs. AC (melee) or Dexterity vs. AC (ranged)
Hit: 1[W] + Strength modifier damage (melee) or 1[W] + Dexterity modifier damage (ranged). The target takes a penalty to its attack roll for the triggering attack equal to 3 + your Wisdom modifier.

Shadow Wasp Strike — Ranger Attack 3

You strike quickly, like a shadow wasp flying out of the darkness, hitting where your foe is most vulnerable.

Encounter ✦ Martial, Weapon
Standard Action   Melee or **Ranged** weapon
Target: One creature that is your quarry
Attack: Strength vs. AC (melee) or Dexterity vs. AC (ranged)
Hit: 2[W] + Strength modifier damage (melee) or 2[W] + Dexterity modifier damage (ranged).

Thundertusk Boar Strike — Ranger Attack 3

You attack twice, causing your foes to stagger backward.

Encounter ✦ Martial, Weapon
Standard Action   Melee or **Ranged** weapon
Requirement: You must be wielding two melee weapons or a ranged weapon.
Targets: One or two creatures
Attack: Strength vs. AC (melee; main weapon and off-hand weapon) or Dexterity vs. AC (ranged), two attacks
Hit: 1[W] + Strength modifier damage (melee) or 1[W] + Dexterity modifier damage (ranged) per attack. With each hit, you push the target 1 square. If both attacks hit the same target, you push the target a number of squares equal to 1 + your Wisdom modifier.

Level 5 Daily Exploits

Excruciating Shot — Ranger Attack 5

One well-placed arrow leaves your enemy hunched over and howling in pain.

Daily ✦ Martial, Weapon
Standard Action   **Ranged** weapon
Target: One creature
Attack: Dexterity vs. AC
Hit: 3[W] + Dexterity modifier damage, and the target is weakened (save ends).
Miss: Half damage, and the target is not weakened.

Frenzied Skirmish — Ranger Attack 5

You leap into the fray and unleash a torrent of steel upon your unsuspecting foes, staggering them with the ferocity of your attacks.

Daily ✦ Martial, Weapon
Standard Action   Melee weapon
Requirement: You must be wielding two melee weapons.
Targets: One or two creatures
Attack: Strength vs. AC (main weapon and off-hand weapon), two attacks
Special: Before or after these attacks, you can move your speed without provoking opportunity attacks.
Hit: 1[W] + Strength modifier damage per attack. If an attack hits, the target is dazed until the end of your next turn. If both attacks hit the same target, it is dazed and slowed until the end of your next turn.

Splintering Shot — Ranger Attack 5

Your arrow burrows into flesh and shatters, sending splinters of wood deep into the wound.

Daily ✦ Martial, Weapon
Standard Action   **Ranged** weapon
Target: One creature
Attack: Dexterity vs. AC
Hit: 3[W] + Dexterity modifier damage, and the target takes a -2 penalty to attack rolls until the end of the encounter.
Miss: Half damage, and the target takes a -1 penalty to attack rolls until the end of the encounter.

Two-Wolf Pounce — Ranger Attack 5

You set upon a foe with weapons bared, then weave to the side and deal a wound to another adversary.

Daily ✦ Martial, Weapon
Standard Action   Melee weapon
Requirement: You must be wielding two melee weapons.
Special: You can shift 2 squares before making this attack.
Primary Target: One creature
Attack: Strength vs. AC, two attacks (main weapon and off-hand weapon)
Hit: 2[W] + Strength modifier damage (main weapon) and 1[W] + Strength modifier damage (off-hand weapon).
Effect: After attacking the primary target, you can shift 2 squares and make a secondary attack.
Secondary Target: One creature other than the primary target
Secondary Attack: Strength vs. AC (off-hand weapon)
Hit: 2[W] damage (off-hand weapon).

Level 6 Utility Exploits

Evade Ambush — Ranger Utility 6

You are the eyes and ears of the group, always alert for the telltale signs of an ambush.

Daily ✦ Martial
No Action   **Ranged** sight
Effect: At the start of a surprise round in which any allies are surprised, use this power to allow a number of allies equal to your Wisdom modifier to avoid being surprised.

Skilled Companion — Ranger Utility 6

Your allies benefit from the things that you have learned.

Daily ✦ Martial
Minor Action   **Ranged** 10
Target: One ally
Effect: Any ally within 10 squares of you who attempts an untrained check with a skill in which you are trained gains a power bonus to checks with a single skill of your choice equal to your Wisdom modifier. The ally must be able to see or hear you to gain this bonus. The benefit lasts until the end of the encounter or for 5 minutes.

Weave through the Fray — Ranger Utility 6

You dodge through the thick of the fight, denying your foes a chance to pin you down in one spot.

Encounter ✦ Martial
Immediate Interrupt   Personal
Trigger: An enemy moves adjacent to you
Effect: You can shift a number of squares equal to your Wisdom modifier.

LEVEL 7 ENCOUNTER EXPLOITS

Claws of the Griffon — Ranger Attack 7

Your steel blades flash menacingly as you taunt your foes with parries and cut deep wounds into their flesh.

Encounter ✦ Martial, Weapon
Standard Action   Melee weapon
Requirement: You must be wielding two melee weapons.
Target: One or two creatures
Attack: Strength vs. AC (main weapon and off-hand weapon), two attacks
Hit: 2[W] + Strength modifier damage (main weapon) and 1[W] + Strength modifier damage (off-hand weapon).

Hawk's Talon — Ranger Attack 7

Like the hawk, you strike with calculated precision.

Encounter ✦ Martial, Weapon
Standard Action   Melee or Ranged weapon
Target: One creature
Attack: Strength vs. AC (melee) or Dexterity vs. AC (ranged). Gain a power bonus to this attack equal to your Wisdom modifier. Ignore any penalties from cover or concealment (but not superior cover or total concealment).
Hit: 2[W] + Strength modifier damage (melee) or 2[W] + Dexterity modifier damage (ranged).

Spikes of the Manticore — Ranger Attack 7

You unleash two arrows in rapid succession.

Encounter ✦ Martial, Weapon
Standard Action   Ranged weapon
Target: One or two creatures
Attack: Dexterity vs. AC, one attack per target
Hit: 2[W] + Dexterity modifier damage (first shot) and 1[W] + Dexterity modifier damage (second shot).

Sweeping Whirlwind — Ranger Attack 7

You slash and stab at surrounding foes with unbound fury, knocking them off balance with thrusts and leg sweeps.

Encounter ✦ Martial, Weapon
Standard Action   Close burst 1
Requirement: You must be wielding two melee weapons.
Target: Each enemy in burst
Attack: Strength vs. AC
Hit: 1[W] + Strength modifier damage, and you push the target a number of squares equal to your Wisdom modifier and it is knocked prone.

LEVEL 9 DAILY EXPLOITS

Attacks on the Run — Ranger Attack 9

Without breaking stride, you make two attacks against a single foe or two different targets.

Daily ✦ Martial, Weapon
Standard Action   Melee or Ranged weapon
Target: One or two creatures
Attack: You can move your speed. At any point during your move, you can make two Strength vs. AC attacks with a melee weapon or two Dexterity vs. AC attacks with a ranged weapon.
Hit: 3[W] + Strength modifier damage (melee) or 3[W] + Dexterity modifier damage (ranged) per attack.
Miss: Half damage per attack.

Close Quarters Shot — Ranger Attack 9

Though menaced by fangs and claws, you calmly unload an arrow into the creature's gaping maw—mere inches from your outstretched arm.

Daily ✦ Martial, Weapon
Standard Action   Ranged 1
Target: One adjacent enemy
Attack: Dexterity vs. AC. This attack does not provoke opportunity attacks.
Hit: 4[W] + Dexterity modifier damage.
Miss: Half damage.

Spray of Arrows — Ranger Attack 9

You fire repeatedly with a short draw, showering arrows at each enemy in front of you.

Daily ✦ Martial, Weapon
Standard Action   Close blast 3
Requirement: You must be wielding a ranged weapon.
Target: Each enemy in blast you can see
Attack: Dexterity vs. AC
Hit: 2[W] + Dexterity modifier damage.
Miss: Half damage.

Swirling Leaves of Steel — Ranger Attack 9

You spin around with blades outstretched, using momentum and skill to slice through enemy defenses.

Daily ✦ Martial, Weapon
Standard Action   Close burst 1
Requirement: You must be wielding two melee weapons.
Target: Each enemy in burst you can see
Attack: Strength vs. AC, one attack per target
Hit: 2[W] + Strength modifier damage.
Miss: Half damage.

LEVEL 10 UTILITY EXPLOITS

Expeditious Stride — Ranger Utility 10

Like a gazelle, you startle allies and enemies alike with your sudden swiftness.

Encounter ✦ Martial
Minor Action   Personal
Effect: Until the end of your next turn, your speed increases by 4, and when you shift, you can shift 1 additional square.

Open the Range — Ranger Utility 10

You keep your distance from an approaching adversary, backpedaling easily away from him.

Daily ✦ Martial
Immediate Interrupt   Personal
Trigger: An enemy moves adjacent to you
Effect: You can shift 1 square and then move a number of squares equal to 1 + your Wisdom modifier. You can't end your move adjacent to the triggering enemy.

Undaunted Stride — Ranger Utility 10

You expertly navigate through difficult terrain.

Daily ✦ Martial, Stance
Minor Action   Personal
Effect: Your movement is not hindered by difficult terrain.

LEVEL 13 ENCOUNTER EXPLOITS

Armor Splinter — Ranger Attack 13

You attack the weak spots in your opponent's armor, not only dealing damage but also leaving your prey vulnerable to later attacks.

Encounter ✦ Martial, Weapon
Standard Action   Melee weapon
Requirement: You must be wielding two melee weapons.
Target: One creature
Attack: Strength vs. AC (main weapon and off-hand weapon), two attacks
Hit: 1[W] + Strength modifier damage per attack. If one attack hits, the target takes a penalty to AC equal to your Wisdom modifier until the end of your next turn. If both attacks hit, the target takes a penalty to AC equal to 2 + your Wisdom modifier until the end of your next turn.

Knockdown Shot — Ranger Attack 13

One shot topples your foe.

Encounter ✦ Martial, Weapon
Standard Action   Ranged weapon
Target: One creature of your size or smaller
Attack: Dexterity vs. Reflex
Hit: 2[W] + Dexterity modifier damage, and the target is knocked prone.

Nimble Defense — Ranger Attack 13

Between strikes, you use both of your weapons to deflect incoming blows.

Encounter ✦ Martial, Weapon
Standard Action   Melee weapon
Requirement: You must be wielding two melee weapons.
Target: One creature
Attack: Strength vs. AC (main weapon and off-hand weapon), two attacks
Hit: 1[W] + Strength modifier damage per attack. If you hit with either attack, you gain a power bonus to AC equal to 2 + your Wisdom modifier until the end of your next turn.

Pinning Strike — Ranger Attack 13

With a well-aimed attack, you pin your foe to the ground or to a nearby wall.

Encounter ✦ Martial, Weapon
Standard Action   Melee or **Ranged** weapon
Requirement: You must be wielding two melee weapons or a ranged weapon.
Targets: One or two creatures
Attack: Strength vs. AC (melee; main weapon and off-hand weapon) or Dexterity vs. AC (ranged), two attacks
Hit: 1[W] + Strength modifier damage (melee) or 1[W] + Dexterity modifier damage (ranged) per attack. The target is immobilized until the start of your next turn.

LEVEL 15 DAILY EXPLOITS

Blade Cascade — Ranger Attack 15

Time seems to slow down as your weapons fall upon your hapless foes like rain from an ominous sky.

Daily ✦ Martial, Weapon
Standard Action   Melee weapon
Requirement: You must be wielding two melee weapons.
Targets: One or more creatures
Attack: Strength vs. AC. Alternate main and off-hand weapon attacks until you miss. As soon as an attack misses, this attack ends.
Hit: 2[W] + Strength modifier damage per attack.

Bleeding Wounds — Ranger Attack 15

Your arrows puncture flesh, and from these wounds blood flows in crimson streams.

Daily ✦ Martial, Weapon
Standard Action   Ranged weapon
Targets: One, two, or three creatures
Attack: Dexterity vs. AC, three attacks
Hit: 1[W] + Dexterity modifier damage per attack, and ongoing 5 damage (save ends). A target hit twice takes ongoing 10 damage (save ends). A target hit three times takes ongoing 15 damage (save ends).
Miss: Half damage per attack, and no ongoing damage.

Confounding Arrows — Ranger Attack 15

Your targets won't know what hit them.

Daily ✦ Martial, Weapon
Standard Action   Ranged weapon
Targets: One, two, or three creatures
Attack: Dexterity vs. AC, three attacks
Hit: 1[W] + Dexterity modifier damage per attack. A target hit once is dazed (save ends). A target hit twice is stunned (save ends). A target hit three times is stunned (save ends) and takes +2[W] damage.
Miss: The target is dazed (save ends).

Stunning Steel — Ranger Attack 15

You fight past your enemies' shields and armor and deal nasty cuts that leave them reeling and unable to react.

Daily ✦ Martial, Weapon
Standard Action   Melee weapon
Requirement: You must be wielding two melee weapons.
Target: One or two creatures
Attack: Strength vs. Fortitude (main weapon and off-hand weapon), two attacks
Hit: 1[W] + Strength modifier damage per attack. If one attack hits, the target is stunned (save ends). If both attacks hit, the target is stunned and immobilized (save ends both).
Miss: Half damage per attack, and the target is not stunned or immobilized.

LEVEL 16 UTILITY EXPLOITS

Evade the Blow — Ranger Utility 16

When your enemy launches his attack, you leap out of the way, leaving your foe to hit nothing but air.

Daily ✦ Martial
Immediate Interrupt   Personal
Trigger: An enemy hits you with a melee attack
Effect: Shift 1 square away from the enemy.

Longstrider — Ranger Utility 16

You have an uncanny knack for being in the right place at the right time.

Daily ✦ Martial, Stance
Minor Action   Personal
Effect: Your speed increases by 2.

Momentary Respite — Ranger Utility 16

Amid the chaos of combat, you're able to calm yourself for an instant and recover from a harmful effect.

Daily ✦ Martial
Standard Action   Personal
Effect: Shift a number of squares equal to your Wisdom modifier and make a saving throw. You are no longer marked by any enemy.

LEVEL 17 ENCOUNTER EXPLOITS

Arrow of Vengeance — Ranger Attack 17

You point your bow at the villain who just wounded your friend and loose a vengeful arrow.

Encounter ✦ Martial, Weapon
Immediate Reaction   Ranged weapon
Trigger: A creature within range attacks your ally
Target: The attacking creature
Attack: Dexterity vs. AC, and gain a power bonus to this attack equal to your Wisdom modifier.
Hit: 2[W] + Dexterity modifier damage.

Cheetah's Rake — Ranger Attack 17

You whirl around with blades outstretched, slashing your foes across the legs and causing them to fall to the ground in mewling heaps.

Encounter ✦ Martial, Weapon
Standard Action   Close burst 1
Requirement: You must be wielding two melee weapons.
Target: Each enemy in burst you can see
Attack: Strength vs. AC
Hit: 1[W] + Strength modifier damage, and the target is immobilized and knocked prone until the end of your next turn.

Triple Shot — Ranger Attack 17

You launch a volley of three arrows, which streak across the battlefield with whispered threats of oblivion.

Encounter ✦ Martial, Weapon
Standard Action   **Ranged** weapon
Targets: One, two, or three creatures
Attack: Dexterity vs. AC, three attacks
Hit: 1[W] + Dexterity modifier damage per attack.

Two-Weapon Eviscerate — Ranger Attack 17

You swing your blades in lethal arcs, dousing the battlefield in your enemy's blood.

Encounter ✦ Martial, Weapon
Standard Action   **Melee** weapon
Requirement: You must be wielding two melee weapons.
Target: One creature
Attack: Strength vs. AC (main weapon and off-hand weapon), two attacks
Hit: 1[W] + Strength modifier damage per attack. If both attacks hit, the target takes an extra 1d10 damage and is weakened until the end of your next turn.

LEVEL 19 DAILY EXPLOITS

Cruel Cage of Steel — Ranger Attack 19

You move swiftly around your enemies, weaving back and forth and delivering a vicious slash with each soft step.

Daily ✦ Martial, Weapon
Standard Action   **Melee** weapon
Requirement: You must be wielding two melee weapons.
Targets: One, two, or three creatures
Attack: Strength + 2 vs. AC, three attacks
Hit: 2[W] + Strength modifier damage (first attack; main), 2[W] + Strength modifier damage (second attack; off-hand), and 1[W] + Strength modifier (third attack; main). A target hit once is dazed until the end of your next turn. A target hit twice is stunned until the end of your next turn. A target hit three times is weakened and stunned until the end of your next turn.
Miss: Half damage per attack, and the target is not dazed, stunned, or weakened.
Effect: After the first attack and after the second attack, you can shift 1 square.

Great Ram Arrow — Ranger Attack 19

You loose an arrow that pierces your foe, hurls him back, and knocks him off his feet.

Daily ✦ Martial, Weapon
Standard Action   **Ranged** weapon
Target: One creature
Attack: Dexterity vs. AC
Hit: 3[W] + Dexterity modifier damage. In addition, you push the target a number of squares equal to your Strength modifier, and it is knocked prone.
Miss: Half damage, and you push the target 1 square and it is knocked prone.

Two-in-One Shot — Ranger Attack 19

The first shot is always the toughest.

Daily ✦ Martial, Weapon
Standard Action   **Ranged** weapon
Target: One creature
Attack: Dexterity vs. AC, two attacks. If the first attack hits, you gain a +5 bonus to the attack roll for the second attack. If the first attack misses, make the second attack normally.
Hit: 2[W] + Dexterity modifier damage per attack.
Miss: Half damage per attack.

Wounding Whirlwind — Ranger Attack 19

Crimson droplets splatter as you slash into all nearby foes.

Daily ✦ Martial, Weapon
Standard Action   **Close** burst 1
Target: Each enemy in burst you can see
Attack: Strength vs. AC (main weapon and off-hand weapon), two attacks per target
Hit: 1[W] + Strength modifier damage per attack. If you hit a target with one weapon, it takes ongoing 5 damage (save ends). If you hit a target with both weapons, it takes ongoing 10 damage (save ends).
Miss: Half damage per attack, and no ongoing damage.

LEVEL 22 UTILITY EXPLOITS

Forest Ghost — Ranger Utility 22

You vanish into your surroundings with such speed and skill that your enemies can't even begin to guess where you might be.

Daily ✦ Illusion, Martial
Standard Action   **Personal**
Effect: When it is not your turn, enemies treat you as invisible if you have cover or concealment from them. An enemy still knows the square you occupy if it saw you in that square at any point during a round. This effect lasts until the end of the encounter or for 5 minutes.

Hit the Dirt — Ranger Utility 22

You throw yourself to the ground, tumble a safe distance, and spring to your feet no worse for wear.

Daily ✦ Martial
Immediate Interrupt   **Personal**
Trigger: You are hit by an area attack or a close attack
Effect: Shift a number of squares equal to your Wisdom modifier.

Master of the Hunt — Ranger Utility 22

You take careful aim with every shot.

Daily ✦ Martial, Stance
Minor Action   **Personal**
Effect: You gain a bonus to damage rolls equal to your Wisdom modifier.

Safe Stride — Ranger Utility 22

You deftly maneuver around your foes as the battle rages on.

Encounter ✦ Martial
Move Action   **Personal**
Effect: Shift a number of squares equal to your Wisdom modifier.

Level 23 Encounter Exploits

Blade Ward
Ranger Attack 23

Your enemy strikes, and as you defend yourself with one blade, you drive the other deep into his gullet.

Encounter ✦ Martial, Weapon
Immediate Interrupt   Melee weapon
Trigger: A creature makes a melee attack against you
Target: The attacking creature
Attack: Strength vs. AC
Hit: [W] + Strength modifier damage.
Effect: Until the end of your next turn, the target's attack rolls against you take a penalty equal to your Wisdom modifier.

Cloak of Thorns
Ranger Attack 23

You stab and slash enemies that come close to you.

Encounter ✦ Martial, Weapon
Standard Action   Melee weapon
Requirement: You must be wielding two melee weapons.
Target: One or two creatures
Attack: Strength vs. AC (main weapon and off-hand weapon), two attacks
Hit: 2[W] + Strength modifier damage per attack. If one attack hits, the target takes a -2 penalty to attack rolls until the end of your next turn. If both attacks hit the same target, this penalty worsens to -4.
Effect: If any adjacent creature makes an attack against you and misses before the start of your next turn, make a melee basic attack against it with both your main weapon and your off-hand weapon as an immediate reaction.

Hammer Shot
Ranger Attack 23

You test the strength of your bowstring as you pull an arrow back as far as it will go and unleash it upon your unsuspecting foe.

Encounter ✦ Martial, Weapon
Standard Action   Ranged weapon
Target: One creature
Attack: Dexterity vs. Fortitude
Hit: 4[W] + Dexterity modifier damage, and you push the target a number of squares equal to 2 + your Wisdom modifier.

Manticore's Volley
Ranger Attack 23

You pepper your foe with arrows.

Encounter ✦ Martial, Weapon
Standard Action   Ranged weapon
Target: One creature
Attack: Dexterity vs. AC, three attacks
Hit: 1[W] + Dexterity modifier damage per attack. If two attacks hit, deal an extra 1[W] damage. If all three attacks hit, deal an extra 2[W] damage.

Level 25 Daily Exploits

Bloodstorm
Ranger Attack 25

With bow or blades, you rain a series of deadly blows on your opponent.

Daily ✦ Martial, Weapon
Standard Action   Melee or Ranged weapon
Requirement: You must be wielding two melee weapons or a ranged weapon.
Target: One creature
Attack: Strength vs. AC (melee; main weapon and off-hand weapon) or Dexterity vs. AC (ranged), two attacks
Hit: 2[W] + Strength modifier damage (melee) or 2[W] + Dexterity modifier damage (ranged) per attack.
Miss: Half damage per attack.
Effect: After making these attacks, you can shift a number of squares equal to your Wisdom modifier.

Tiger's Reflex
Ranger Attack 25

You counter your opponent's attack with a ferocious strike of your own.

Daily ✦ Martial, Stance
Minor Action   Personal
Effect: You can make a basic attack against an enemy you choose as an immediate interrupt if it attacks you.

Unstoppable Arrows
Ranger Attack 25

You loose a volley of arrows with such force that they skewer several nearby enemies.

Daily ✦ Martial, Weapon
Standard Action   Close blast 5
Requirement: You must be wielding a ranged weapon.
Target: Each enemy in blast
Attack: Dexterity vs. AC
Hit: 3[W] + Dexterity modifier damage.
Miss: Half damage.

Level 27 Encounter Exploits

Death Rend
Ranger Attack 27

You plunge your blades into your opponent and rip them out with the ferocity of a tiger, leaving your prey gasping for life.

Encounter ✦ Martial, Weapon
Standard Action   Melee weapon
Requirement: You must be wielding two melee weapons.
Target: One creature
Attack: Strength vs. AC (main weapon and off-hand weapon), two attacks
Hit: 2[W] + Strength modifier damage per attack. If both attacks hit, the target takes an extra 1d10 damage and is stunned until the end of your next turn.

Hail of Arrows — Ranger Attack 27

You launch a barrage of arrows that strike all enemies before you.

Encounter ✦ Martial, Weapon
Standard Action — **Ranged** weapon
Target: Each enemy in range
Attack: Dexterity vs. AC
Hit: 1[W] + Dexterity modifier damage.

Lightning Shot — Ranger Attack 27

As an enemy reels from a terrible wound, you quickly loose an arrow to finish him off.

Encounter ✦ Martial, Weapon
Immediate Reaction — **Ranged** weapon
Trigger: One creature you can see has just taken damage
Target: The creature that took damage
Attack: Dexterity vs. AC
Hit: 2[W] + Dexterity modifier damage, or 3[W] + Dexterity modifier damage if the target is bloodied.

Wandering Tornado — Ranger Attack 27

You strike your enemies in all directions. Then, like a tornado, you weave through the battlefield and unleash a second onslaught of whirling steel.

Encounter ✦ Martial, Weapon
Standard Action — **Close** burst 1
Target: Each enemy in burst you can see
Attack: Strength vs. AC
Hit: 1[W] + Strength modifier damage.
Effect: You can shift a number of squares equal to 1 + your Wisdom modifier, and make another close burst 1 attack (as above).

LEVEL 29 DAILY EXPLOITS

Follow-up Blow — Ranger Attack 29

You follow every strike with a backhanded swipe that breaks through your enemy's defenses.

Daily ✦ Martial, Stance, Weapon
Minor Action — **Personal**
Requirement: You must be wielding two melee weapons.
Effect: You can use your off-hand weapon to make a melee basic attack with a –2 penalty against each enemy you hit using a melee attack power.

Three-in-One Shot — Ranger Attack 29

If you can hit with the first arrow, the others will follow.

Daily ✦ Martial, Weapon
Standard Action — **Ranged** weapon
Target: One creature
Attack: Dexterity vs. AC, three attacks. If the first attack hits, you gain a +5 bonus to the second and third attack rolls. If the first attack misses, roll the second and third attacks normally.
Hit: 2[W] + Dexterity modifier damage per attack.
Miss: Half damage per attack.

Weave a Web of Steel — Ranger Attack 29

Crossing your blades, you form a defense as solid as a mighty shield, ready to riposte if your enemy isn't lucky.

Daily ✦ Martial, Weapon
Immediate Interrupt — **Melee** weapon
Trigger: An enemy hits you with a melee attack
Requirement: You must be wielding two melee weapons.
Target: The triggering enemy
Attack: Strength vs. AC, two attacks (main weapon and off-hand weapon)
Hit: 3[W] + Strength modifier damage (main weapon) and 1[W] + Strength modifier damage (off-hand weapon). If both attacks hit, the target's attack misses.
Miss: Half damage with your main weapon, and no damage with your off-hand weapon.

PARAGON PATHS

BATTLEFIELD ARCHER

"There's no target I can't hit, no matter how far, no matter how small."

Prerequisite: Ranger class, archer fighting style

You become a paragon of marksmanship, an unrivaled archer who remains cool and collected in even the most intense battlefield situations. Your experience and skill show through with every projectile you loose on a target, and every battle goes just a little bit smoother with you in the field.

BATTLEFIELD ARCHER PATH FEATURES

Archer's Action (11th level): You can spend an action point to reroll one ranged attack roll or ranged damage roll, instead of taking an extra action.

Battlefield Experience (11th level): You can designate more than one creature as your quarry at a time, up to a number equal to your Wisdom modifier. In addition, any attack made against a quarry receives a +1 bonus to attack rolls.

Battle Surge (16th level): When you spend an action point to take an extra action or to gain the benefit of your Archer's Action, you also gain a +5 bonus to AC against opportunity attacks until the end of the encounter.

BATTLEFIELD ARCHER EXPLOITS

Combined Fire — Battlefield Archer Attack 11

You combine fire with one of your allies to take down a trouble-some foe.

Encounter ✦ Martial, Weapon
Immediate Reaction — **Ranged** weapon
Trigger: An ally makes a ranged attack or an area attack
Target: One creature attacked by your ally
Attack: Dexterity vs. AC
Hit: 3[W] + Dexterity modifier damage.

Archer's Glory — Battlefield Archer Utility 12

One enemy falls, and those that remain are about to learn what heroism is all about.

Encounter ✦ Martial
Free Action — **Personal**
Trigger: One of your ranged attacks drops an enemy to 0 hit points or fewer
Effect: You gain an action point that you must spend before the end of your next turn.

Quarry's Bane — Battlefield Archer Attack 20

You have multiple quarries in your sights, so you unleash a deadly volley of shots at each of them.

Daily ✦ Martial, Weapon
Standard Action — **Ranged** weapon
Target: Each enemy designated as your quarry
Attack: Dexterity vs. AC
Hit: 3[W] damage.
Miss: The target is knocked prone as it dodges your attack.

BEAST STALKER

"I am the hunter. You are my prey."

Prerequisite: Ranger class, archer fighting style

You become the ultimate hunter of beasts or magical beasts, stalking your chosen prey with deliberate cunning and amazing ease. Against your chosen prey, each arrow hits its mark with unerring accuracy and punishing velocity.

BEAST STALKER PATH FEATURES

Beast Stalker's Action (11th level): When you spend an action point to take an extra action, you also gain a +4 bonus to attack rolls against your quarry until the start of your next turn.

Chosen Prey (11th level): Choose one of the following keywords: beast or magical beast. Your Hunter's Quarry class feature deals an extra 2 damage against creatures of the chosen kind.

Action Shift (16th level): After you spend an action point to take an extra action, you can shift as a minor action until the end of the encounter.

BEAST STALKER EXPLOITS

Pinpointing Arrow — Beast Stalker Attack 11

Your shot is undeterred by obstructions and magical veils.

Encounter ✦ Martial, Weapon
Standard Action — **Ranged** weapon
Target: One creature designated as your quarry
Special: Ignore penalties for cover (but not superior cover), concealment, and total concealment. You can attack an invisible target as if it wasn't invisible.
Attack: Dexterity vs. AC
Hit: 2[W] + Dexterity modifier damage.

Hunter's Grace — Beast Stalker Utility 12

Even as your allies take stock of the enemies pouring in around them, you move into position and set your plans into motion.

Daily ✦ Martial
No Action — **Personal**
Effect: Make a Stealth check and use that as your initiative check result. If you get the first turn in the encounter, you can shift up to your speed as a free action before taking any other actions.

Beast Stalker's Target — Beast Stalker Attack 20

"This foe is my prey!"

Daily ✦ Martial, Weapon
Standard Action — **Ranged** weapon
Target: One creature
Attack: Dexterity vs. AC
Hit: 4[W] + Dexterity modifier damage.
Effect: The target is designated as your quarry until the end of the encounter, and you can designate one additional creature as a quarry following the normal Hunter's Quarry rules.

PATHFINDER

"I can find us a path through that maze of horror, and I can safely lead us to the other end."

Prerequisite: Ranger class, two-blade fighting style

You become the ultimate scout, finding a way through any situation. Sometimes you find the best path, but other times you have to carve that path out of the wilderness with your two blades singing through the air.

PATHFINDER PATH FEATURES

Battlehoned (11th level): You gain two extra healing surges per day.

Pathfinder's Action (11th level): When you spend an action point to take an extra action, you also gain a move action.

Cruel Recovery (16th level): When you hit an enemy and it takes damage from Hunter's Quarry, you gain temporary hit points equal to the amount of damage you dealt from Hunter's Quarry + your Wisdom modifier.

PATHFINDER EXPLOITS

Wrong Step — Pathfinder Attack 11

Your enemy steps unwittingly into your trap, and you catch him by surprise with a sudden, paralyzing thrust.

Encounter ✦ Martial, Weapon
Immediate Interrupt   **Melee** weapon
Trigger: An adjacent enemy shifts or moves
Target: The enemy
Attack: Strength vs. AC
Hit: 1[W] + Strength modifier damage, and the target is immobilized until the end of your next turn.

Act Together — Pathfinder Utility 12

You find it within yourself to capitalize on your comrade's latest act of daring.

Daily ✦ Martial
Immediate Reaction   **Personal**
Trigger: An ally spends an action point to take an extra action
Effect: You gain an action point that you must spend before the end of your next turn.

Slasher's Mark — Pathfinder Attack 20

You fortify yourself, raise your weapons, and carve scarring wounds into the flesh of your enemies.

Daily ✦ Healing, Martial, Weapon
Standard Action   **Melee** weapon
Requirement: You must be wielding two melee weapons.
Special: You can spend a healing surge before attacking.
Primary Target: One creature
Attack: Strength vs. AC (main weapon)
Hit: 3[W] + Strength modifier damage (main weapon).
Effect: The target is marked until the end of the encounter. Make a secondary attack.
   Secondary Target: One creature other than the primary target
   Secondary Attack: Strength vs. AC (off-hand weapon)
Hit: 2[W] + Strength modifier damage (off-hand weapon).
   Effect: The target is marked until the end of the encounter.

STORMWARDEN

"I have accepted the burden of the stormwardens of the Feywild, and this region is under my protection."

Prerequisite: Ranger class, two-blade fighting style

Your role as a warden and defender of the wild takes on new heights as you learn the ancient ways of the stormwardens of the Feywild. These techniques turn your whirling blades into a storm of destruction that rains down punishing blows on your enemies. With each slash of your weapon, the wind howls in anticipation of the coming storm.

STORMWARDEN PATH FEATURES

Blade Storm (11th level): As long as you are armed with a melee weapon and are capable of making an opportunity attack, one adjacent enemy (your choice) takes damage equal to your Dexterity modifier at the end of your turn.

Stormstep Action (11th level): When you spend an action point to take an extra action, you can teleport 3 squares either before or after you use the extra action.

Twin-Blade Storm (16th level): As long as you are armed with a melee weapon and are capable of making an opportunity attack, two adjacent enemies (your choice) take lightning damage equal to your Dexterity modifier at the end of your turn.

STORMWARDEN EXPLOITS

Clearing the Ground — Stormwarden Attack 11

You sweep your blades in mighty arcs around you, cutting foes that get too close and thrusting them back.

Encounter ✦ Martial, Weapon
Standard Action   **Close** burst 1
Requirement: You must be wielding two melee weapons.
Target: Each enemy in burst you can see
Attack: Strength vs. AC
Hit: 1[W] + Strength modifier damage, and you push the target 1 square.

Throw Caution to the Wind — Stormwarden Utility 12

Aw, what the hell. You only live once.

Encounter ✦ Martial, Stance
Minor Action   **Personal**
Effect: You take a -2 penalty to all defenses and gain a +2 bonus to attack rolls.

Cold Steel Hurricane — Stormwarden Attack 20

You rush into the midst of your enemies and, like a freezing wind, flay them alive.

Daily ✦ Martial, Weapon
Standard Action   **Close** burst 1
Requirement: You must be wielding two melee weapons.
Special: Before you attack, shift a number of squares equal to your Wisdom modifier.
Target: Each enemy in burst you can see
Attack: Strength vs. AC (main weapon and off-hand weapon), two attacks per target
Hit: 1[W] + Strength modifier damage per attack.
Effect: You regain your second wind if you have already used it during this encounter.

ROGUE

"You look surprised to see me. If you'd been paying attention, you might still be alive."

CLASS TRAITS

Role: Striker. You dart in to attack, do massive damage, and then retreat to safety. You do best when teamed with a defender to flank enemies.

Power Source: Martial. Your talents depend on extensive training and constant practice, innate skill, and natural coordination.

Key Abilities: Dexterity, Strength, Charisma

Armor Proficiencies: Cloth, leather

Weapon Proficiencies: Dagger, hand crossbow, shuriken, sling, short sword

Bonus to Defense: +2 Reflex

Hit Points at 1st Level: 12 + Constitution score

Hit Points per Level Gained: 5

Healing Surges per Day: 6 + Constitution modifier

Trained Skills: Stealth and Thievery. From the class skills list below, choose four more trained skills at 1st level.

Class Skills: Acrobatics (Dex), Athletics (Str), Bluff (Cha), Dungeoneering (Wis), Insight (Wis), Intimidate (Cha), Perception (Wis), Stealth (Dex), Streetwise (Cha), Thievery (Dex)

Build Options: Brawny rogue, trickster rogue

Class Features: First Strike, Rogue Tactics, Rogue Weapon Talent, Sneak Attack

Rogues are cunning and elusive adversaries. Rogues slip into and out of shadows on a whim, pass anywhere across the field of battle without fear of reprisal, and appear suddenly only to drive home a lethal blade.

As a rogue, you might face others' preconceptions regarding your motivations, but your nature is your own to mold. You could be an agent fresh from the deposed king's shattered intelligence network, an accused criminal on the lam seeking to clear your name, a wiry performer whose goals transcend the theatrical stage, a kid trying to turn around your hard-luck story, or a daredevil thrill-seeker who can't get enough of the adrenaline rush of conflict. Or perhaps you are merely in it for the gold, after all.

With a blade up your sleeve and a concealing cloak across your shoulders, you stride forth, eyes alight with anticipation. What worldly wonders and rewards are yours for the taking?

CREATING A ROGUE

The trickster rogue and the brawny rogue are the two rogue builds, one relying on bluffs and feints, the other on brute strength. Dexterity, Charisma, and Strength are the rogue's most important ability scores.

BRAWNY ROGUE

You like powers that deal plenty of damage, aided by your Strength, and also stun, immobilize, knock down, or push your foes. Your attacks use Dexterity, so keep that your highest ability score. Strength should be a close second—it increases your damage directly, and it can determine other effects of your attacks. Charisma is a good third ability score, particularly if you want to dabble in powers from the other rogue build. Select the brutal scoundrel rogue tactic, and look for powers that pack a lot of damage into every punch.

Suggested Feat: Weapon Focus (Human feat: Toughness)
Suggested Skills: Athletics, Dungeoneering, Intimidate, Stealth, Streetwise, Thievery
Suggested At-Will Powers: *piercing strike, riposte strike*
Suggested Encounter Power: *torturous strike*
Suggested Daily Power: *easy target*

TRICKSTER ROGUE

You like powers that deceive and misdirect your foes. You dart in and out of the fray in combat, dodging your enemies' attacks or redirecting them to other foes. Most of your attack powers rely on Dexterity, so that should be your best ability score. Charisma is important for a few attacks, for Charisma-based skills you sometimes use in place of attacks, and for other effects that depend on successful attacks, so make Charisma your second-best score. Strength is useful if you want to choose powers intended for the other rogue build. Select the artful dodger rogue tactic. Look for powers that take advantage of your high Charisma score, as well as those that add to your trickster nature.

ROGUE OVERVIEW

Characteristics: Combat advantage provides the full benefit of your powers, and a combination of skills and powers helps you gain and keep that advantage over your foes. You are a master of skills, from Stealth and Thievery to Bluff and Acrobatics.

Religion: Rogues prefer deities of the night, luck, freedom, and adventure, such as Sehanine and Avandra. Evil and chaotic evil rogues often favor Lolth or Zehir.

Races: Those with a love for secrets exchanged in shadows and change for its own sake make ideal rogues, including elves, tieflings, and halflings.

Suggested Feat: Backstabber (Human feat: Human Perseverance)
Suggested Skills: Acrobatics, Bluff, Insight, Perception, Stealth, Thievery
Suggested At-Will Powers: *deft strike, sly flourish*
Suggested Encounter Power: *positioning strike*
Suggested Daily Power: *trick strike*

ROGUE CLASS FEATURES

All rogues share these class features.

FIRST STRIKE

At the start of an encounter, you have combat advantage against any creatures that have not yet acted in that encounter.

ROGUE TACTICS

Rogues operate in a variety of ways. Some rogues use their natural charm and cunning trickery to deceive foes. Others rely on brute strength to overcome their enemies.

Choose one of the following options.

Artful Dodger: You gain a bonus to AC equal to your Charisma modifier against opportunity attacks.

Brutal Scoundrel: You gain a bonus to Sneak Attack damage equal to your Strength modifier.

The choice you make also provides bonuses to certain rogue powers. Individual powers detail the effects (if any) your Rogue Tactics selection has on them.

ROGUE WEAPON TALENT

When you wield a shuriken, your weapon damage die increases by one size. When you wield a dagger, you gain a +1 bonus to attack rolls.

SNEAK ATTACK

Once per round, when you have combat advantage against an enemy and are using a weapon from the light blade, the crossbow, or the sling weapon group, an attack you make against that enemy deals extra damage if the attack hits. You decide whether to apply the extra damage after making the damage roll. As you advance in level, your extra damage increases.

Level	Sneak Attack Damage
1st-10th	+2d6
11th-20th	+3d6
21st-30th	+5d6

ROGUE POWERS

Your powers are daring exploits that draw on your personal cunning, agility, and expertise. Some powers reward a high Charisma and are well suited for the trickster rogue, and others reward a high Strength and appeal to the brawny rogue, but you are free to choose any power you like.

LEVEL 1 AT-WILL EXPLOITS

Deft Strike — Rogue Attack 1

A final lunge brings you into an advantageous position.

At-Will ✦ Martial, Weapon
Standard Action   **Melee** or **Ranged** weapon
Requirement: You must be wielding a crossbow, a light blade, or a sling.
Target: One creature
Special: You can move 2 squares before the attack.
Attack: Dexterity vs. AC
Hit: 1[W] + Dexterity modifier damage.
Increase damage to 2[W] + Dexterity modifier at 21st level.

Piercing Strike — Rogue Attack 1

A needle-sharp point slips past armor and into tender flesh.

At-Will ✦ Martial, Weapon
Standard Action   **Melee** weapon
Requirement: You must be wielding a light blade.
Target: One creature
Attack: Dexterity vs. Reflex
Hit: 1[W] + Dexterity modifier damage.
Increase damage to 2[W] + Dexterity modifier at 21st level.

Riposte Strike — Rogue Attack 1

With a calculated strike, you leave your foe vulnerable to an adroit riposte should he dare attack you.

At-Will ✦ Martial, Weapon
Standard Action   **Melee** weapon
Requirement: You must be wielding a light blade.
Target: One creature
Attack: Dexterity vs. AC
Hit: 1[W] + Dexterity modifier damage. If the target attacks you before the start of your next turn, you make your riposte against the target as an immediate interrupt: a Strength vs. AC attack that deals 1[W] + Strength modifier damage.
Increase damage to 2[W] + Dexterity modifier and riposte to 2[W] + Strength modifier at 21st level.

Sly Flourish — Rogue Attack 1

A distracting flourish causes the enemy to forget the blade at his throat.

At-Will ✦ Martial, Weapon
Standard Action   **Melee** or **Ranged** weapon
Requirement: You must be wielding a crossbow, a light blade, or a sling.
Target: One creature
Attack: Dexterity vs. AC
Hit: 1[W] + Dexterity modifier + Charisma modifier damage.
Increase damage to 2[W] + Dexterity modifier + Charisma modifier at 21st level.

LEVEL 1 ENCOUNTER EXPLOITS

Dazing Strike — Rogue Attack 1

An expert strike catches your foe by surprise and leaves him reeling from the pain.

Encounter ✦ Martial, Weapon
Standard Action   **Melee** weapon
Requirement: You must be wielding a light blade.
Target: One creature
Attack: Dexterity vs. AC
Hit: 1[W] + Dexterity modifier damage, and the target is dazed until the end of your next turn.

King's Castle — Rogue Attack 1

It's hard to get to the little guy when he takes cover behind an ally who can crush plate armor in his teeth.

Encounter ✦ Martial, Weapon
Standard Action   **Melee** or **Ranged** weapon
Requirement: You must be wielding a crossbow, a light blade, or a sling.
Target: One creature
Attack: Dexterity vs. Reflex
Hit: 2[W] + Dexterity modifier damage.
Effect: Switch places with a willing adjacent ally.

Positioning Strike — Rogue Attack 1

A false stumble and a shove place the enemy exactly where you want him.

Encounter ✦ Martial, Weapon
Standard Action   **Melee** weapon
Requirement: You must be wielding a light blade.
Target: One creature
Attack: Dexterity vs. Will
Hit: 1[W] + Dexterity modifier damage, and you slide the target 1 square.
   Artful Dodger: You slide the target a number of squares equal to your Charisma modifier.

Torturous Strike — Rogue Attack 1

If you twist the blade in the wound just so, you can make your enemy howl in pain.

Encounter ✦ Martial, Weapon
Standard Action   **Melee** weapon
Requirement: You must be wielding a light blade.
Target: One creature
Attack: Dexterity vs. AC
Hit: 2[W] + Dexterity modifier damage.
   Brutal Scoundrel: You gain a bonus to the damage roll equal to your Strength modifier.

LEVEL 1 DAILY EXPLOITS

Blinding Barrage
Rogue Attack 1

A rapid barrage of projectiles leaves your enemies clearing the blood from their eyes.

Daily ✦ Martial, Weapon
Standard Action   **Close** blast 3
Requirement: You must be wielding a crossbow, a light thrown weapon, or a sling.
Target: Each enemy in blast you can see
Attack: Dexterity vs. AC
Hit: 2[W] + Dexterity modifier damage, and the target is blinded until the end of your next turn.
Miss: Half damage, and the target is not blinded.

Easy Target
Rogue Attack 1

You deal a staggering blow to your enemy, setting it up for future attacks.

Daily ✦ Martial, Weapon
Standard Action   **Melee** or **Ranged** weapon
Requirement: You must be wielding a crossbow, a light blade, or a sling.
Target: One creature
Attack: Dexterity vs. AC
Hit: 2[W] + Dexterity modifier damage, and the target is slowed and grants combat advantage to you (save ends both).
Miss: Half damage, and the target grants combat advantage to you until the end of your next turn.

Trick Strike
Rogue Attack 1

Through a series of feints and lures, you maneuver your foe right where you want him.

Daily ✦ Martial, Weapon
Standard Action   **Melee** or **Ranged** weapon
Requirement: You must be wielding a crossbow, a light blade, or a sling.
Target: One creature
Attack: Dexterity vs. AC
Hit: 3[W] + Dexterity modifier damage, and you slide the target 1 square.
Effect: Until the end of the encounter, each time you hit the target you slide it 1 square.

LEVEL 2 UTILITY EXPLOITS

Fleeting Ghost
Rogue Utility 2

You are stealthy and fleet of foot at the same time.

At-Will ✦ Martial
Move Action   **Personal**
Prerequisite: You must be trained in Stealth.
Effect: You can move your speed and make a Stealth check. You do not take the normal penalty from movement on this check.

Great Leap
Rogue Utility 2

You leap a great distance without a running start.

At-Will ✦ Martial
Move Action   **Personal**
Prerequisite: You must be trained in Athletics.
Effect: Make a high jump or a long jump. Determine the DC of the Athletics check as though you had a running start. The distance you jump can exceed your speed.

Master of Deceit
Rogue Utility 2

The line between truth and deception is thin, and you cross it with ease.

Encounter ✦ Martial
Free Action   **Personal**
Trigger: You roll a Bluff check and dislike the result
Prerequisite: You must be trained in Bluff.
Effect: Reroll the Bluff check. You decide whether to make the reroll before the DM announces the result.

Quick Fingers
Rogue Utility 2

You can pilfer a coin pouch in the blink of an eye.

Encounter ✦ Martial
Minor Action   **Personal**
Prerequisite: You must be trained in Thievery.
Effect: Make a Thievery check as part of this action, even if the check is normally a standard action.

Tumble
Rogue Utility 2

You tumble out of harm's way, dodging the opportunistic attacks of your enemies.

Encounter ✦ Martial
Move Action   **Personal**
Prerequisite: You must be trained in Acrobatics.
Effect: You can shift a number of squares equal to one-half your speed.

LEVEL 3 ENCOUNTER EXPLOITS

Bait and Switch
Rogue Attack 3

You strike and weave, causing your foe to lurch forward so that you can duck around him and slip into his space.

Encounter ✦ Martial, Weapon
Standard Action   **Melee** weapon
Requirement: You must be wielding a light blade.
Target: One creature
Attack: Dexterity vs. Will
Hit: 2[W] + Dexterity modifier damage. In addition, you switch places with the target and can then shift 1 square.
     Artful Dodger: You can shift a number of squares equal to your Charisma modifier.

Setup Strike
Rogue Attack 3

You land a calculated blow that causes your enemy to drop his guard, leaving him vulnerable to subsequent attacks.

Encounter ✦ Martial, Weapon
Standard Action   **Melee** weapon
Requirement: You must be wielding a light blade.
Target: One creature
Attack: Dexterity vs. AC
Hit: 2[W] + Dexterity modifier damage, and the target grants combat advantage to you until the end of your next turn.

Topple Over
Rogue Attack 3

Balance and momentum are your allies as you lunge forward, strike deftly, and knock your opponent to the ground.

Encounter ✦ Martial, Weapon
Standard Action   **Melee** weapon
Requirement: You must be wielding a light blade.
Target: One creature
Attack: Dexterity vs. AC
  Brutal Scoundrel: You gain a bonus to the attack roll equal to your Strength modifier.
Hit: 1[W] + Dexterity modifier damage, and the target is knocked prone.

Trickster's Blade
Rogue Attack 3

You land an expert blow and follow up with a clever series of feints that bewilder your enemies.

Encounter ✦ Martial, Weapon
Standard Action   **Melee** or **Ranged** weapon
Requirement: You must be wielding a crossbow, a light blade, or a sling.
Target: One creature
Attack: Dexterity vs. AC
Hit: 2[W] + Dexterity modifier damage. Add your Charisma modifier to your AC until the start of your next turn.

LEVEL 5 DAILY EXPLOITS

Clever Riposte
Rogue Attack 5

You follow up a fierce attack with a series of quick, painful strikes woven between your enemy's attacks.

Daily ✦ Martial, Weapon
Standard Action   **Melee** weapon
Requirement: You must be wielding a light blade.
Target: One creature
Attack: Dexterity vs. AC
Hit: 2[W] + Dexterity modifier damage.
Effect: Until the end of the encounter, the target takes damage equal to your Dexterity modifier each time it attacks you, and you can shift as an immediate reaction after such an attack.

Deep Cut
Rogue Attack 5

Each drop of blood is another nail in your enemy's coffin.

Daily ✦ Martial, Weapon
Standard Action   **Melee** weapon
Requirement: You must be wielding a light blade.
Target: One creature
Attack: Dexterity vs. Fortitude
Hit: 2[W] + Dexterity modifier damage, and ongoing damage equal to 5 + your Strength modifier (save ends).
Miss: Half damage, and no ongoing damage.

Walking Wounded
Rogue Attack 5

You topple your enemy with a crippling blow and force him to stumble around the battlefield.

Daily ✦ Martial, Weapon
Standard Action   **Melee** or **Ranged** weapon
Requirement: You must be wielding a crossbow, a light blade, or a sling.
Target: One creature
Attack: Dexterity vs. Fortitude
Hit: 2[W] + Dexterity modifier damage, and the target is knocked prone. Until the end of the encounter, if the target moves more than half its speed in a single action, it falls prone at the end of its movement.
Miss: Half damage, and the target is not knocked prone.

LEVEL 6 UTILITY EXPLOITS

Chameleon
Rogue Utility 6

You blend into your surroundings.

At-Will ✦ Martial
Immediate Interrupt   **Personal**
Trigger: You are hidden and lose cover or concealment against an opponent
Prerequisite: You must be trained in Stealth.
Effect: Make a Stealth check. Until the end of your next turn, you remain hidden if a creature that has a clear line of sight to you does not beat your check result with its Perception check. If at the end of your turn you do not have cover or concealment against a creature, that creature automatically notices you.

Ignoble Escape
Rogue Utility 6

With nimble ease, you sidestep one perilous situation after another.

Encounter ✦ Martial
Move Action   **Personal**
Prerequisite: You must be trained in Acrobatics.
Effect: If you are marked, end that condition. You can shift a number of squares equal to your speed.

Mob Mentality
Rogue Utility 6

When it comes to lying, cajoling, or persuading others, your allies follow your lead.

Encounter ✦ Martial
Standard Action   **Close** burst 10
Prerequisite: You must be trained in Intimidate.
Targets: You and each ally in burst
Effect: The targets gain a +2 power bonus to Charisma-based skill and ability checks until the end of your next turn.

Nimble Climb
Rogue Utility 6

You climb surfaces with astounding ease.

At-Will ✦ Martial
Move Action   **Personal**
Prerequisite: You must be trained in Athletics.
Effect: Make an Athletics check to climb a surface. You can move at your full speed during this climb.

Slippery Mind — Rogue Utility 6

You cloud your mind with vague thoughts that shield you against a sudden mental attack.

Encounter ✦ Martial
Immediate Interrupt   Personal
Trigger: You are hit by an attack against your Will defense
Prerequisite: You must be trained in Bluff.
Effect: Gain a +2 power bonus to your Will defense against the triggering attack.

LEVEL 7 ENCOUNTER EXPLOITS

Cloud of Steel — Rogue Attack 7

You shower your enemies in sharp metal.

Encounter ✦ Martial, Weapon
Standard Action   Close blast 5
Requirement: You must be wielding a crossbow, a light thrown weapon, or a sling.
Target: Each enemy in blast you can see
Attack: Dexterity vs. AC
Hit: 1[W] + Dexterity modifier damage.

Imperiling Strike — Rogue Attack 7

You deal a staggering blow, opening a hole in your enemy's defenses.

Encounter ✦ Martial, Weapon
Standard Action   Melee weapon
Requirement: You must be wielding a light blade.
Target: One creature
Attack: Dexterity vs. Fortitude
Hit: 1[W] + Dexterity modifier damage, and the target takes a -1 penalty to AC and Reflex defense until the end of your next turn.
  Brutal Scoundrel: The penalty to AC and Reflex defense is equal to your Strength modifier.

Rogue's Luck — Rogue Attack 7

A gifted rogue can turn failure into fortune.

Encounter ✦ Martial, Weapon
Standard Action   Melee or **Ranged** weapon
Requirement: You must be wielding a crossbow, a light blade, or a sling.
Target: One creature
Attack: Dexterity vs. AC
Hit: 2[W] + Dexterity modifier damage.
Miss: Make a secondary attack against the target.
  Secondary Attack: Dexterity vs. AC
  Artful Dodger: You gain a bonus to the attack roll for the secondary attack equal to your Charisma modifier.
  Hit: 1[W] + Dexterity modifier damage.

Sand in the Eyes — Rogue Attack 7

You scoop up a handful of sand or dirt or pebbles, strike your foe, and throw the grit in his face to blind him.

Encounter ✦ Martial, Weapon
Standard Action   Melee weapon
Requirement: You must be wielding a light blade.
Target: One creature
Attack: Dexterity vs. Reflex
Hit: 1[W] + Dexterity modifier damage, and the target is blinded until the end of your next turn.

LEVEL 9 DAILY EXPLOITS

Crimson Edge — Rogue Attack 9

You deal your enemy a vicious wound that continues to bleed, and like a shark, you circle in for the kill.

Daily ✦ Martial, Weapon
Standard Action   Melee weapon
Requirement: You must be wielding a light blade.
Target: One creature
Attack: Dexterity vs. Fortitude
Hit: 2[W] + Dexterity modifier damage, and the target takes ongoing damage equal to 5 + your Strength modifier and grants combat advantage to you (save ends both).
Miss: Half damage, and no ongoing damage.

Deadly Positioning — Rogue Attack 9

You adroitly outmaneuver your enemy, pushing and baiting him with every stride and strike.

Daily ✦ Martial, Weapon
Standard Action   Melee 1
Requirement: You must be wielding a light blade.
Target: One creature
Attack: You slide the target to any other square adjacent to you, and then make a Dexterity vs. AC attack.
Hit: 3[W] + Dexterity modifier damage.
Effect: Until the end of the encounter, as long as you are adjacent to the target, you slide the target 1 square before making a melee attack against it.

Knockout — Rogue Attack 9

A well-placed blow takes your foe out of the fight.

Daily ✦ Martial, Weapon
Standard Action   Melee weapon
Requirement: You must be wielding a light blade.
Target: One creature
Attack: Dexterity vs. Fortitude
Hit: 2[W] + Dexterity modifier damage, and the target is knocked unconscious (save ends). If the unconscious target takes any damage, it is no longer unconscious.
Miss: Half damage, and the target is dazed until the end of your next turn.

LEVEL 10 UTILITY EXPLOITS

Certain Freedom — Rogue Utility 10

You are as slippery as an eel.

Daily ✦ Martial
Move Action   Personal
Prerequisite: You must be trained in Acrobatics.
Effect: You automatically succeed on an Acrobatics check to escape from a grab or to escape from restraints.

Close Quarters
Rogue Utility 10

You take cover beneath a much larger creature, making it harder for the creature to hit you.

Daily ✦ Martial
Move Action   **Personal**
Prerequisite: You must be trained in Acrobatics.
Effect: Move into the space of an adjacent creature larger than you and at least Large in size. (It gets its usual opportunity attack against you as you leave an adjacent square.) You gain combat advantage against the creature, and it takes a -4 penalty to attack rolls against you. When the creature moves, you move along with it, staying in the same portion of the creature's space. The creature can make a Strength or Dexterity vs. Reflex attack (as a standard action with no penalty) to slide you into an adjacent square and end this effect.
Special: Allies of the target creature can attack you without penalty.

Dangerous Theft
Rogue Utility 10

You snatch an item from an enemy during combat.

Encounter ✦ Martial
Free Action   **Personal**
Prerequisite: You must be trained in Thievery.
Effect: On your next action, ignore the -10 penalty when you make a Thievery check to pick a pocket during combat.

Shadow Stride
Rogue Utility 10

You silently step from shadow to shadow, slipping past your foes unseen and unheard.

At-Will ✦ Martial
Move Action   **Personal**
Prerequisite: You must be trained in Stealth.
Effect: You must be hiding to use this power. You can move your speed. At the end of that movement, if you have cover, you can make a Stealth check with no penalty for moving. If you make the Stealth check, you stay hidden during your movement.

LEVEL 13 ENCOUNTER EXPLOITS

Fool's Opportunity
Rogue Attack 13

You bait your foe into attacking you, and then turn his blow straight back at him.

Encounter ✦ Martial, Weapon
Standard Action   **Melee** weapon
Requirement: You must be wielding a light blade.
Target: One creature
Attack: Dexterity vs. Will
Hit: The target takes damage as if it were hit by its own melee basic attack. If you have combat advantage against the target, you can add your Sneak Attack damage.

Stunning Strike — Rogue Attack 13

A well-timed attack leaves your enemy flailing helplessly for a few critical seconds.

Encounter ✦ Martial, Weapon
Standard Action   **Melee** weapon
Requirement: You must be wielding a light blade.
Target: One creature
Attack: Dexterity vs. AC
Hit: 1[W] + Dexterity modifier damage, and the target is stunned until the end of your next turn.

Tornado Strike — Rogue Attack 13

Your weapon becomes a blur as you make swift, sweeping attacks against two foes, then hastily slip away.

Encounter ✦ Martial, Weapon
Standard Action   **Melee** or **Ranged** weapon
Requirement: You must be wielding a crossbow, a light blade, or a sling.
Targets: One or two creatures
Attack: Dexterity vs. AC, one attack per target
Hit: 2[W] + Dexterity modifier damage, and you slide the target 2 squares.
     Artful Dodger: You slide the target a number of squares equal to 1 + your Charisma modifier.
Effect: You can move 3 squares after making the attack.

Unbalancing Attack — Rogue Attack 13

Ducking and weaving, you land a decisive blow that staggers your foe and sets it up for a tripping attack.

Encounter ✦ Martial, Weapon
Standard Action   **Melee** weapon
Requirement: You must be wielding a light blade.
Target: One creature
Attack: Dexterity vs. AC
Hit: 3[W] + Dexterity modifier damage, and the target cannot shift until the end of your next turn. If the target provokes an opportunity attack from you before the start of your next turn, you gain a bonus to the attack roll and damage roll with the opportunity attack equal to your Strength modifier, and you knock the target prone on a hit.

Level 15 Daily Exploits

Bloody Path — Rogue Attack 15

You dash across the battlefield, leaving bewildered and bleeding enemies in your wake.

Daily ✦ Martial
Standard Action   **Personal**
Effect: You can move your speed. Every enemy that can make an opportunity attack against you as a result of this movement attacks itself with its opportunity attack, rather than you. Any enemy that can make an opportunity attack against you during this movement must do so. It cannot refrain from making the attack to avoid harming itself.

Garrote Grip — Rogue Attack 15

The more your enemy struggles, the less you want to let him go.

Daily ✦ Martial, Reliable, Weapon
Standard Action (Special)   **Melee** weapon
Special: You can use this power as a minor action if you have already grabbed a creature. Doing so requires no attack roll.
Requirement: You must be wielding a light blade.
Target: One creature
Attack: Dexterity vs. Reflex
Hit: 2[W] + Dexterity modifier damage, and you grab the target. Until the target escapes, you have cover, and any melee attack or ranged attack that misses you hits the target instead.
Sustain Minor: Sustain the grab for another round. The third time you sustain the grab after using this power, the target falls unconscious. If an unconscious target takes any damage, it is no longer unconscious.

Slaying Strike — Rogue Attack 15

A ruthless strike yields great rewards, for after death comes the looting.

Daily ✦ Martial, Weapon
Standard Action   **Melee** or **Ranged** weapon
Requirement: You must be wielding a crossbow, a light blade, or a sling.
Target: One creature
Attack: Dexterity vs. AC
Hit: 3[W] + Dexterity modifier damage.
Miss: Half damage.
Special: If the target is bloodied, this attack does 5[W] + Dexterity modifier + Strength modifier damage on a hit (half damage on a miss) and can score a critical hit on a roll of 17–20.

Level 16 Utility Exploits

Foil the Lock — Rogue Utility 16

You tug on a lock a certain way, and just like that, it snaps open.

Daily ✦ Martial
Minor Action   **Personal**
Prerequisite: You must be trained in Thievery.
Effect: On your next action, gain a +10 power bonus when you make a Thievery check to open a lock. If the check succeeds, the lock opens at once.

Hide in Plain Sight — Rogue Utility 16

You stand unseen in the midst of the battle, striking from your place of hiding.

Encounter ✦ Martial
Minor Action   **Personal**
Prerequisite: You must be trained in Stealth.
Effect: You must already be hidden to use this power. You are invisible until you leave your current square. No other action that you perform makes you visible.

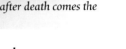

Leaping Dodge
Rogue Utility 16

You leap out of harm's way just in time to avoid an attack.

Encounter ✦ Martial
Immediate Interrupt　　**Personal**
Trigger: An enemy targets you with an attack
Prerequisite: You must be trained in Athletics.
Effect: Make an Athletics check to jump with a +5 power
　bonus and move the appropriate distance.

Raise the Stakes
Rogue Utility 16

You focus on the precision of your attacks, at the expense of hiding the chinks in your own armor.

Daily ✦ Martial
Minor Action　　**Personal**
Prerequisite: You must be trained in Bluff.
Effect: Until the end of your next turn, any of your attacks
　can score a critical hit on a roll of 17-20, and any attack
　against you can score a critical hit on a roll of 19-20.

LEVEL 17 ENCOUNTER EXPLOITS

Dragon Tail Strike
Rogue Attack 17

First you set them up, and then you knock them down.

Encounter ✦ Martial, Weapon
Standard Action　　**Melee** or **Ranged** weapon
Requirement: You must be wielding a crossbow, a light blade,
　or a sling.
Target: One creature
Attack: Dexterity vs. Fortitude
Hit: 3[W] + Dexterity modifier damage. If the target attacks
　you before the start of your next turn, you can attack
　it again as an immediate interrupt and deal 2[W] +
　Dexterity modifier damage if you hit.
　Brutal Scoundrel: The attack you make as an immediate
　　interrupt gains a bonus to the attack roll equal to your
　　Strength modifier.

Hounding Strike
Rogue Attack 17

With snarling ferocity, you attack. Your weapon bites deep into your enemy's flesh, filling his heart with doubt.

Encounter ✦ Martial, Weapon
Standard Action　　**Melee** or **Ranged** weapon
Requirement: You must be wielding a crossbow, a light blade,
　or a sling.
Target: One creature
Attack: Dexterity vs. Will
Hit: 3[W] + Dexterity modifier damage. Until the end of
　your next turn, you gain combat advantage against the
　target and a +1 power bonus to all defenses against its
　attacks.
　Artful Dodger: The power bonus is equal to your Charisma
　　modifier.

Stab and Grab
Rogue Attack 17

Keep your friends close, and your enemies at knifepoint.

Encounter ✦ Martial, Weapon
Standard Action　　**Melee** weapon
Requirement: You must be wielding a light blade.
Target: One creature
Attack: Dexterity vs. Reflex
Hit: 3[W] + Dexterity modifier damage, and you grab
　the target. If you have already grabbed the target, it is
　restrained instead of immobilized until it escapes your
　grab. The target can attempt to escape the grab as normal.

LEVEL 19 DAILY EXPLOITS

Feinting Flurry
Rogue Attack 19

A series of clever feints throws your foe off his game and makes him an easy target.

Daily ✦ Martial, Weapon
Standard Action　　**Melee** or **Ranged** weapon
Requirement: You must be wielding a crossbow, a light blade,
　or a sling.
Target: One creature
Attack: Dexterity vs. Will
Hit: 5[W] + Dexterity modifier damage.
Effect: Until the end of your next turn, all of the target's
　defenses against your attacks take a penalty equal to your
　Charisma modifier.
Sustain Minor: Sustain the penalty for another round.

Flying Foe
Rogue Attack 19

Mastering your foe's reactions allows you to toss him about like a rag doll.

Daily ✦ Martial, Weapon
Standard Action　　**Melee** weapon
Requirement: You must be wielding a light blade.
Target: One creature
Attack: Dexterity vs. Fortitude
Hit: 4[W] + Dexterity modifier damage, and you slide the
　target a number of squares equal to your Strength modi-
　fier. If an obstacle (including a creature) arrests the slide,
　both the target and the obstacle take 1d6 damage and the
　target ends its movement in the square it occupied before
　it collided with the obstacle.
Miss: You slide the target a number of squares equal to your
　Strength modifier, and no damage from obstacles.

Snake's Retreat
Rogue Attack 19

After striking boldly, you frustrate your foe by shifting away just as he's about to attack you.

Daily ✦ Martial, Weapon
Standard Action　　**Melee** or **Ranged** weapon
Requirement: You must be wielding a crossbow, a light blade,
　or a sling.
Target: One creature
Attack: Dexterity vs. AC
Hit: 6[W] + Dexterity modifier damage.
Effect: When the target makes a melee attack or a ranged
　attack against you, you can shift 1 square as an immediate
　interrupt. The target can make a saving throw to end this
　effect.

LEVEL 22 UTILITY EXPLOITS

Cloud Jump — Rogue Utility 22

You leap a phenomenal distance.

Encounter ✦ Martial
Move Action   **Personal**
Prerequisite: You must be trained in Athletics.
Effect: Make two consecutive Athletics checks to jump, with a +5 power bonus to each. You don't have to land between the jumps and can exceed your normal movement.

Dazzling Acrobatics — Rogue Utility 22

With nearly inhuman speed and percision, you slip away from a foe's attack.

Encounter ✦ Martial
Move Action   **Personal**
Prerequisite: You must be trained in Acrobatics.
Effect: You can shift twice your speed. You can climb at full speed as part of this move. If an enemy attacks you while you shift, you gain a +4 bonus to AC against that attack.

Hide from the Light — Rogue Utility 22

As long as you take your time, you can move about the battlefield unseen.

Daily ✦ Martial
Minor Action   **Personal**
Prerequisite: You must be trained in Stealth.
Effect: You must already be hidden to use this power. You are invisible until the end of the encounter or until you end the effect by moving more than 2 squares in a turn or by making any attack other than a basic attack or an at-will attack.

LEVEL 23 ENCOUNTER EXPLOITS

Knave's Gambit — Rogue Attack 23

You make a decisive attack. Failing that, you cause your startled enemy to strike at another nearby foe.

Encounter ✦ Martial, Weapon
Standard Action   **Melee** or **Ranged** weapon
Requirement: You must be wielding a crossbow, a light blade, or a sling.
Target: One creature
Attack: Dexterity vs. AC
Hit: 4[W] + Dexterity modifier damage.
Miss: The target makes a melee basic attack as a free action against an adjacent target other than you. You choose the target of its attack.
Artful Dodger: The attack you cause with a miss gains a bonus to the attack roll and the damage roll equal to your Charisma modifier.

Scorpion Strike — Rogue Attack 23

One of your allies deals a timely blow to your enemy, and like a scorpion, you strike.

Encounter ✦ Martial, Weapon
Immediate Reaction   **Melee** 1
Trigger: An ally damages a creature adjacent to you
Requirement: You must be wielding a light blade.
Target: The creature your ally damaged
Attack: Dexterity vs. AC
Hit: 2[W] + Dexterity modifier damage.
Brutal Scoundrel: Shift a number of squares equal to your Strength modifier after this attack, whether or not you hit.

Steel Entrapment — Rogue Attack 23

Glittering blades pin your foes in place before any of them have a chance to blink, let alone run away.

Encounter ✦ Martial, Weapon
Standard Action   **Close** blast 5
Requirement: You must be wielding a crossbow, a light thrown weapon, or a sling.
Target: Each enemy in blast you can see
Attack: Dexterity vs. Fortitude
Hit: 3[W] + Dexterity modifier damage, and the target is immobilized until the end of your next turn.

LEVEL 25 DAILY EXPLOITS

Biting Assault — Rogue Attack 25

You strike with deadly ferocity to sap your foe's strength.

Daily ✦ Martial, Weapon
Standard Action   **Melee** or **Ranged** weapon
Requirement: You must be wielding a crossbow, a light blade, or a sling.
Target: One creature
Attack: Dexterity vs. Fortitude
Hit: 3[W] + Dexterity modifier damage, and the target takes ongoing 10 damage and is weakened (save ends both).
Miss: Half damage, and the target takes ongoing 10 damage (save ends).

Ghost on the Wind — Rogue Attack 25

You vanish, then strike out of nowhere!

Daily ✦ Martial, Weapon
Standard Action   **Melee** weapon
Requirement: You must be wielding a light blade.
Target: One creature
Attack: Dexterity vs. Will
Hit: 6[W] + Dexterity modifier damage, and you become invisible. You move into any square adjacent to the target and reappear at the start of your next turn. You have combat advantage against the target until the end of your next turn.
Miss: Half damage, you can shift 1 square to another square adjacent to the target, and you have combat advantage against the target until the end of your next turn.

Hamstring
Rogue Attack 25

You hobble your opponent with a ruthless slash across the legs, leaving him barely able to walk.

Daily ✦ Martial, Weapon
Standard Action   **Melee** or **Ranged** weapon
Requirement: You must be wielding a crossbow, a light blade, or a sling.
Target: One creature
Attack: Dexterity vs. AC
Hit: 4[W] + Dexterity modifier damage, and the target takes ongoing 10 damage and is slowed (save ends both).
Miss: Half damage, and the target takes ongoing 5 damage and is slowed (save ends both).

LEVEL 27 ENCOUNTER EXPLOITS

Dance of Death
Rogue Attack 27

You duck and dodge your enemies' attacks, striking as opportunity allows while expertly deflecting attacks made against you.

Encounter ✦ Martial, Weapon
Standard Action   **Close** burst 1
Requirement: You must be wielding a light blade.
Target: Each enemy in burst you can see
Attack: Dexterity vs. AC
Hit: 3[W] + Dexterity modifier damage. If the target makes a melee attack against you before the end of your next turn, you can make it attack another creature of your choice instead, including itself.
  Artful Dodger: The targets gain a bonus to the attack rolls provoked by this power equal to your Charisma modifier.

Hurricane of Blood
Rogue Attack 27

You stab and slash your foe mercilessly, spilling copious amounts of blood.

Encounter ✦ Martial, Weapon
Standard Action   **Melee** weapon
Requirement: You must be wielding a light blade.
Target: One creature
Attack: Dexterity vs. AC
  Brutal Scoundrel: The attack gains a bonus to the attack roll equal to your Strength modifier.
  Hit: 5[W] + Dexterity modifier damage.

Perfect Strike
Rogue Attack 27

Your enemy doesn't know what hit it.

Encounter ✦ Martial, Weapon
Standard Action   **Melee** or **Ranged** weapon
Requirement: You must be wielding a crossbow, a light blade, or a sling.
Target: One creature
Attack: Dexterity vs. AC, Fortitude, Reflex
Special: You make one attack roll, and you hit if the roll equals or exceeds any of the three defenses.
Hit: 4[W] + Dexterity modifier damage. Add an extra 1[W] damage if the attack hits two defenses. The target is also stunned until the end of your next turn if the attack hits all three defenses.

LEVEL 29 DAILY EXPLOITS

Assassin's Point
Rogue Attack 29

A sliced throat or a bolt through the heart—it's all good.

Daily ✦ Martial, Weapon
Standard Action   **Melee** or **Ranged** weapon
Requirement: You must be wielding a crossbow, a light blade, or a sling.
Target: One creature
Attack: Dexterity vs. AC
Hit: 7[W] + Dexterity modifier damage.
Miss: Half damage.
Special: If you have combat advantage against the target, double any extra damage from Sneak Attack or a critical hit.

Immobilizing Strike
Rogue Attack 29

With terrifying ease, you slash at your enemy's exposed tendons and leave him immobilized and whimpering in pain.

Daily ✦ Martial, Weapon
Standard Action   **Melee** or **Ranged** weapon
Requirement: You must be wielding a crossbow, a light blade, or a sling.
Target: One creature
Attack: Dexterity vs. Fortitude
Hit: 5[W] + Dexterity modifier damage, and the target is immobilized (save ends). If the target succeeds on its saving throw, it is slowed (save ends). Saving throws against these effects take a -5 penalty.
Miss: Half damage, and the target is slowed (save ends). Saving throws against this effect take a -5 penalty.

Moving Target
Rogue Attack 29

An attack meant for you hits another creature instead.

Daily ✦ Martial
Immediate Interrupt   **Melee** or **Ranged** weapon
Trigger: A creature makes a melee attack or a ranged attack against you
Requirement: You must be wielding a crossbow, a light blade, or a sling.
Target: The attacking creature
Attack: Charisma vs. Will
Hit: Instead of attacking you, the target attacks a creature you choose within 2 squares of you. You must choose a creature that the target can attack.
Miss: The target's attack is made against you as normal, but deals half damage if it hits.

PARAGON PATHS

CAT BURGLAR

"I am the rogue acrobat, able to leap and roll with amazing agility. I have the grace and quickness of the great cats."

Prerequisite: Rogue class

You hone your body to a razor's edge, adding a higher level of athletic skills to your repertoire of rogue tricks. As a master athlete, you become a rogue of a higher caliber who can surprise adversaries with unbelievable moves and amazing feats of physical stamina while remaining true to your roots as a thief and scoundrel.

Cat Burglar Path Features

Acrobatic Action (11th level): When you spend an action point to take an extra action, you also gain a move action.

Body Control (11th level): Whenever you are affected by a push, a pull, or a slide, you can reduce the number of squares you move by 1 square.

Athletic Master (16th level): Roll twice whenever you make an Athletics check. Use whichever result you prefer.

Cat Burglar Exploits

Cat Burglar's Gambit	Cat Burglar Attack 11

You spring into action, expertly strike, and then sidestep to position yourself for either certain glory or imminent doom.

Encounter ✦ Martial, Weapon
Standard Action   **Melee** weapon
Requirement: You must be wielding a light blade.
Target: One creature
Special: You can shift 3 squares before making the attack.
Attack: Dexterity vs. AC
Hit: 3[W] + Dexterity modifier damage.
Effect: Shift to any square adjacent to the target.

Instant Escape	Cat Burglar Utility 12

With supreme effort, you escape.

Encounter ✦ Martial
Immediate Interrupt   **Personal**
Trigger: You become immobilized, restrained, or slowed
Effect: You end any of the above conditions that currently afflict you. Then you can shift 2 squares.

Redirected Death	Cat Burglar Attack 20

The weapon races toward you, but with a slight move and a flourish of your own blade, you redirect the attack toward a different target.

Daily ✦ Martial, Weapon
Immediate Interrupt   **Melee** weapon
Trigger: An enemy hits you with a melee attack and can reach another enemy
Requirement: You must be wielding a light blade.
Target: The enemy that hit you
Attack: Dexterity vs. Reflex
Hit: The target's attack misses you and hits an enemy of your choice within range of the target's attack.
Miss: 2[W] + Dexterity modifier against the target.
Effect: Shift 1 square.

Daggermaster

"See how the dagger dances along my fingertips, see it spin. I have forgotten more ways to use this dagger than you can ever imagine."

Prerequisite: Rogue class

You and your dagger become one as you master the intricacies of battling with the blade. You are a master of the dagger, able to employ your weapon in ways that no lesser rogue can match.

Daggermaster Path Features

Daggermaster's Action (11th level): You can spend an action point to reroll one attack roll or damage roll you made using a dagger, instead of taking an extra action.

Dagger Precision (11th level): You can score critical hits with daggers on a roll of 18-20.

Dagger Advantage (16th level): When you score a critical hit with a dagger, the target grants combat advantage to you until the end of your next turn.

Daggermaster Exploits

Critical Opportunity	Daggermaster Attack 11

Your first attack deals a critical wound, so you follow the attack with another strike.

Encounter ✦ Martial, Weapon
Minor Action   **Melee** weapon
Requirement: You must be wielding a dagger and have scored a critical hit with a dagger against an enemy during this turn.
Target: The same creature you hit with a critical hit
Attack: Dexterity vs. AC
Hit: 3[W] + Dexterity modifier damage.

Meditation of the Blade	Daggermaster Utility 12

With a moment of concentration, you focus your will into the point of your blade.

Daily ✦ Martial, Weapon
Minor Action   **Personal**
Effect: Until the end of the encounter, your dagger's damage die increases by one size.

Deep Dagger Wound	Daggermaster Attack 20

Your dagger springs forward, plunging deep into your foe.

Daily ✦ Martial, Weapon
Standard Action   **Melee** weapon
Requirement: You must be wielding a dagger.
Target: One creature
Attack: Dexterity vs. AC
Hit: 4[W] + Dexterity modifier damage, and ongoing 10 damage (save ends). On a critical hit, ongoing 20 damage (save ends).
Miss: 2[W] + Dexterity modifier damage, and no ongoing damage.

Master Infiltrator

"I can get in there. No problem."

Prerequisite: Rogue class

You are an expert at getting into and out of places unseen. Furthermore, you have the skills and training you need to handle any infiltration situation that comes your way, from spying and scouting to sniper attacks and assassinations.

MASTER INFILTRATOR PATH FEATURES

Infiltrator's Action (11th level): When you spend an action point to take an extra action, you also gain a move action.

Skillful Infiltrator (11th level): You gain a +2 bonus to Acrobatics, Athletics, and Stealth checks.

Invisible Infiltrator (16th level): When you drop a target that is your level or higher to 0 hit points or fewer, or when you score a critical hit against a target that is your level or higher, you become invisible until the end of your next turn.

MASTER INFILTRATOR EXPLOITS

Distracting Wound   Master Infiltrator Attack 11

You strike from the shadows, delivering a wound that distracts your foe and makes him drop his guard.

Encounter ✦ Martial, Weapon
Standard Action   **Melee** or **Ranged** weapon
Requirement: You must be wielding a crossbow, a light blade, or a sling.
Target: One creature you have combat advantage against
Attack: Dexterity vs. AC
Hit: 2[W] + Dexterity modifier damage, and the target grants combat advantage to you and all your allies until the end of your next turn.

Impossible to Catch   Master Infiltrator Utility 12

With practiced ease, you step into the shadows and disappear from view.

Encounter ✦ Martial
Minor Action   **Personal**
Effect: You become invisible until the start of your next turn.

Painful Puncture   Master Infiltrator Attack 20

Your weapon bites deep, puncturing your enemy and leaving a lingering wound.

Daily ✦ Martial, Weapon
Standard Action   **Melee** or **Ranged** weapon
Requirement: You must be wielding a crossbow, a light blade, or a sling.
Target: One creature
Attack: Dexterity vs. AC
Hit: 3[W] + Dexterity modifier damage, and ongoing 10 damage (save ends).
Miss: Half damage, and no ongoing damage.

SHADOW ASSASSIN

"When you need something dead, you'll be hard pressed to find someone better at the job than me."

Prerequisite: Rogue class

You become a killing machine, striking from the shadows with deadly and bloody efficiency, and turning

attacks against you into pain and suffering for your enemies. You believe in doing unto others before they can do unto you, and you know how to deliver punishment as only a striker can.

SHADOW ASSASSIN PATH FEATURES

Shadow Assassin's Action (11th level): When you spend an action point to take an extra action, you also gain a +4 bonus to attack rolls until the start of your next turn.

Shadow Assassin's Riposte (11th level): Any adjacent enemy that misses you with a melee attack takes damage equal to your Dexterity modifier.

Bloody Evisceration (16th level): Gain an extra 1d6 Sneak Attack damage when attacking a bloodied enemy.

SHADOW ASSASSIN EXPLOITS

Killer's Eye   Shadow Assassin Attack 11

You strike with a killer's eye, seeking to take down your enemy as quickly and efficiently as possible.

Encounter ✦ Martial, Weapon
Standard Action   **Melee** or **Ranged** weapon
Requirement: You must be wielding a crossbow, a light blade, or a sling.
Target: One creature
Attack: Dexterity vs. Reflex
Hit: 2[W] + Dexterity modifier damage.
Special: If this attack is made before the target has acted in the encounter, increase the weapon damage to 3[W].

Bad Idea, Friend   Shadow Assassin Utility 12

The first time an enemy attacks you, that opponent discovers just how bad an idea that is.

Daily ✦ Martial
Immediate Interrupt   Personal
Trigger: An adjacent enemy makes a melee attack against you for the first time during this encounter
Special: If you are granting combat advantage, you cannot use this power.
Effect: Gain a +10 power bonus to all defenses against the enemy's attack. If the attack misses, the enemy takes double your Shadow Assassin's Riposte damage.

Final Blow   Shadow Assassin Attack 20

Your enemy is wounded. This shot will finish it off.

Daily ✦ Martial, Weapon
Standard Action   **Melee** or **Ranged** weapon
Requirement: You must be wielding a crossbow, a light blade, or a sling.
Target: One bloodied creature
Attack: Dexterity vs. Reflex
Hit: 5[W] + Dexterity modifier damage, and you shift a number of squares equal to your Charisma modifier. You must end this movement adjacent to an enemy.
Miss: Half damage, and no shift.

WARLOCK

*"The darkness holds no terror for me, demon!
I curse you now under the Sign of Ill Omen!"*

CLASS TRAITS

Role: Striker. Your attack powers are highly damaging and often weaken or hamper the target in some way. You can elude attacks by flying, teleporting, or turning invisible.

Power Source: Arcane. You gain your magical power from a pact you forge with a powerful, supernatural force or an unnamed entity.

Key Abilities: Charisma, Constitution, Intelligence

Armor Proficiencies: Cloth, leather
Weapon Proficiencies: Simple melee, simple ranged
Implements: Rods, wands
Bonus to Defense: +1 Reflex, +1 Will

Hit Points at 1st Level: 12 + Constitution score
Hit Points per Level Gained: 5
Healing Surges per Day: 6 + Constitution modifier

Trained Skills: From the class skills list below, choose four trained skills at 1st level.
Class Skills: Arcana (Int), Bluff (Cha), History (Int), Insight (Wis), Intimidate (Cha), Religion (Int), Streetwise (Cha), Thievery (Dex)

Build Options: Deceptive warlock, scourge warlock
Class Features: *Eldritch blast*, Eldritch Pact, Prime Shot, Shadow Walk, Warlock's Curse

Warlocks channel arcane might wrested from primeval entities. They commune with infernal intelligences and fey spirits, scour enemies with potent blasts of eldritch power, and bedevil foes with hexing curses. Armed with esoteric secrets and dangerous lore, warlocks are clever and resourceful foes.

However you came to your arcane knowledge, you need not accept the poor reputation warlocks sometimes endure. You could be a libram-toting scholar captivated by ominous lore, a foot-loose wanderer searching for elusive ultimate truths, a devil-touched hunter using infernal spells to eliminate evil, or even a black-clad mercenary who uses sinister trappings to discourage prying strangers and unwanted attention. On the other hand, you could be a true diabolist using your gifts to tyrannize the weak—some warlocks unfortunately are exactly that.

The pacts are complete. The rites have concluded. The signs are drawn in blood, and the seals are broken. Your destiny beckons.

WILLIAM O'CONNOR

CREATING A WARLOCK

The two basic builds of warlock are the deceptive warlock and the scourge warlock. Warlocks rely on Charisma, Constitution, and Intelligence. No warlock powers or class features depend on Strength, Dexterity, or Wisdom.

DECEPTIVE WARLOCK

You prefer spells that deal a little less damage, but that inflict a variety of penalties and negative conditions on your foe. You'd rather fight at range and avoid getting caught in close-up battles. Most of your attack powers depend on Charisma, so that should be your best score. Many of your powers receive a bonus if you have a good Intelligence score, so that should be your second-best score. Constitution should be your third choice since you might want to choose some Constitution-based powers. You need it for a good Fortitude defense anyway.

Deceptive warlocks should choose the fey pact or the star pact (see "Class Features").

Suggested Feat: Improved Misty Step (Human feat: Human Perseverance)
Suggested Skills: Arcana, Bluff, Insight, Thievery
Suggested At-Will Powers: *eldritch blast, eyebite*
Suggested Encounter Power: *witchfire*
Suggested Daily Power: *curse of the dark dream*

SCOURGE WARLOCK

No subtlety here—you want to deal damage. You're tougher than the deceptive warlock, and you've got powers to help you attack and defend in melee, as well as excellent ranged attacks. Your best attack powers depend on Constitution—make that your best ability score. Choose Intelligence second because it provides special bonuses to many of your powers and improves your Reflex defense and AC, too. Charisma is clearly your third choice.

Scourge warlocks should choose the infernal pact or the star pact (see "Class Features").

Suggested Feat: Improved Dark One's Blessing (Human feat: Action Surge)

WARLOCK OVERVIEW

Characteristics: You have excellent short-ranged attack ability, and your powers confuse or weaken your opponent. You can shift easily from ranged attacks to melee attacks. However, you are not very resilient and rely on powers of evasion and concealment to avoid attack.

Religion: Warlocks favor deities of cleverness, arcane power, or secrets. These include Corellon, Ioun, and Sehanine. Evil warlocks often revere Asmodeus or Vecna.

Races: Tieflings are natural warlocks and are drawn to this path. Halflings, half-elves, and humans make formidable warlocks as well.

Suggested Skills: Arcana, History, Intimidate, Streetwise
Suggested At-Will Powers: *eldritch blast, hellish rebuke*
Suggested Encounter Power: *vampiric embrace*
Suggested Daily Power: *flames of Phlegethos*

WARLOCK CLASS FEATURES

You have the following class features.

ELDRITCH BLAST

All warlocks know the *eldritch blast* at-will power. This power can be used as a basic attack. You gain this power as well as another at-will power as determined by your Eldritch Pact.

ELDRITCH PACT

You have forged a pact with mysterious entities that grant you your arcane powers. Choose one of the following pacts: fey pact, infernal pact, or star pact. The pact you choose determines the following warlock abilities:

At-Will Spells: Your pact determines one of the at-will spells you know.

Pact Boon: Each pact includes a pact boon. The pact boon is a granted power you can use to further hex your enemies.

The pact you take also provides bonuses to certain warlock powers. Individual powers detail the effects (if any) your Eldritch Pact selection has on them.

FEY PACT

You have forged a bargain with ancient, amoral powers of the Feywild. Some are primitive earth spirits, grim and menacing; some are capricious wood, sky, or water spirits; and others are incarnations of seasons or natural forces who roam the faerie realm like wild gods. They bestow magic that ranges from feral and savage to wondrous and enchanting.

Eyebite: You know the *eyebite* at-will spell.

Misty Step: You have the Misty Step pact boon. You instantly transform into silver mist that streams a short distance and reforms, allowing you to flee or maneuver to set up a deadly attack.

When an enemy under your Warlock's Curse is reduced to 0 hit points or fewer, you can immediately teleport 3 squares as a free action.

INFERNAL PACT

Long ago a forgotten race of devils created a secret path to power and taught it to the tieflings of old to weaken their fealty to Asmodeus. In his wrath, Asmodeus destroyed the scheming devils and struck their very names from the memory of all beings—but you dare to study their perilous secrets anyway.

Hellish Rebuke: You know the *hellish rebuke* at-will spell.

Dark One's Blessing: You have the Dark One's Blessing pact boon. You instantly gain vitality from a cursed enemy when that enemy falls.

When an enemy under your Warlock's Curse is reduced to 0 hit points or fewer, you immediately gain temporary hit points equal to your level.

STAR PACT

You have mastered the astrologer's art, learning the secret names of the stars and gazing into the Far Realm beyond, gaining great power thereby. You can call upon powers that madden or terrify your enemies, manipulate chance and fate, or scour your foes with icy banes and curses drawn from beyond the night sky.

Dire Radiance: You know the *dire radiance* at-will spell.

Fate of the Void: You have the Fate of the Void pact boon. Your curse intermingles with the lost vitality of a cursed enemy to reveal a glimpse of the future to you.

When an enemy under your Warlock's Curse is reduced to 0 hit points or fewer, you gain a +1 bonus to any single d20 roll you make during your next turn (attack roll, saving throw, skill check, or ability check). If you don't use this bonus by the end of your turn, it is lost.

This bonus is cumulative; if three cursed enemies drop to 0 hit points or fewer before your next turn, you gain a +3 bonus to a d20 roll during your turn.

PRIME SHOT

If none of your allies are nearer to your target than you are, you receive a +1 bonus to ranged attack rolls against that target.

SHADOW WALK

On your turn, if you move at least 3 squares away from where you started your turn, you gain concealment until the end of your next turn.

WARLOCK'S CURSE

Once per turn as a minor action, you can place a Warlock's Curse on the enemy nearest to you that you can see. A cursed enemy is more vulnerable to your attacks. If you damage a cursed enemy, you deal extra damage. You decide whether to apply the extra damage after making the damage roll. You can deal this extra damage once per round.

A Warlock's Curse remains in effect until the end of the encounter or until the cursed enemy drops to 0 hit points or fewer.

You can place a Warlock's Curse on multiple targets over the course of an encounter; each curse requires the use of a minor action. You can't place a Warlock's Curse on a creature that is already affected by your or another character's Warlock's Curse.

As you advance in level, your extra damage increases.

Level	Warlock's Curse Extra Damage
1st–10th	+1d6
11th–20th	+2d6
21st–30th	+3d6

IMPLEMENTS

Warlocks make use of rods and wands to help channel and direct their arcane powers. A warlock wielding a magic rod or wand can add its enhancement bonus to the attack rolls and the damage rolls of warlock powers, as well as warlock paragon path powers, that have the implement keyword. Without a rod or a wand, a warlock can still use these powers, but he or she doesn't gain the bonus provided by the magic implement.

A *pact blade*, a special magic dagger, can also be used as an implement for warlock powers, as well as warlock paragon powers. These daggers are highly sought after by warlocks.

WARLOCK POWERS

Your powers are also known as spells. Each power is associated with one of the three eldritch pacts, but you aren't limited to choosing powers associated with your pact. In fact, most warlocks choose at least a few powers from outside their pact to give themselves a wider range of options.

Spells of the infernal pact use your Constitution score. The dark energy you wield is inherently harmful to the mortal body, and only through sheer physical resolve and discipline can you wield it safely. Fey pact spells rely on Charisma. Your force of will and your ability to bargain with the fey is key to spells of this type. Star pact spells require you to be physically inured to the rigors of otherworldly energy (Constitution), and also ambitious and driven enough to impose your willpower on the strands of fate (Charisma).

LEVEL 1 AT-WILL SPELLS

Dire Radiance — Warlock (Star) Attack 1

You cause a shaft of brilliant, cold starlight to lance down from above, bathing your foe in excruciating light. The nearer he moves toward you, the brighter and more deadly the light becomes.

At-Will ✦ Arcane, Fear, Implement, Radiant
Standard Action — Ranged 10
Target: One creature
Attack: Constitution vs. Fortitude
Hit: 1d6 + Constitution modifier radiant damage. If the target moves nearer to you on its next turn, it takes an extra 1d6 + Constitution modifier damage.
Increase damage and extra damage to 2d6 + Constitution modifier at 21st level.

Eldritch Blast — Warlock (All) Attack 1

You fire a bolt of dark, crackling eldritch energy at your foe.

At-Will ✦ Arcane, Implement
Standard Action   Ranged 10
Target: One creature
Attack: Charisma or Constitution vs. Reflex
Hit: 1d10 + Charisma or Constitution modifier damage. Increase damage to 2d10 + Charisma or Constitution modifier at 21st level.
Special: At 1st level. you determine whether you use Charisma or Constitution to attack with this power. Once you make that choice, you can't change it later.
  This power counts as a ranged basic attack. When a power allows you to make a ranged basic attack, you can use this power.

Eyebite — Warlock (Fey) Attack 1

You glare at your enemy, and your eyes briefly gleam with brilliant colors. Your foe reels under your mental assault, and you vanish from his sight.

At-Will ✦ Arcane, Charm, Implement, Psychic
Standard Action   Ranged 10
Target: One creature
Attack: Charisma vs. Will
Hit: 1d6 + Charisma modifier psychic damage, and you are invisible to the target until the start of your next turn. Increase damage to 2d6 + Charisma modifier at 21st level.

Hellish Rebuke — Warlock (Infernal) Attack 1

You point your finger, and your foe is scoured in hellish flames stoked by your own anger and pain. If you are injured, the flames burst into life one more time before they fade away.

At-Will ✦ Arcane, Fire, Implement
Standard Action   Ranged 10
Target: One creature
Attack: Constitution vs. Reflex
Hit: 1d6 + Constitution modifier fire damage. If you take damage before the end of your next turn, the target takes an extra 1d6 + Constitution modifier fire damage. Increase damage and extra damage to 2d6 + Constitution modifier at 21st level.

LEVEL 1 ENCOUNTER SPELLS

Diabolic Grasp — Warlock (Infernal) Attack 1

You crook your hand into the shape of a claw, and a great talon of sulfurous darkness forms around your enemy. It rakes fiercely at him and drags him a short distance before dissipating again.

Encounter ✦ Arcane, Implement
Standard Action   Ranged 10
Target: One creature of size Large or smaller
Attack: Constitution vs. Fortitude
Hit: 2d8 + Constitution modifier damage, and you slide the target 2 squares.
  Infernal Pact: You slide the target a number of squares equal to 1 + your Intelligence modifier.

Dreadful Word — Warlock (Star) Attack 1

You whisper one word of an unthinkable cosmic secret to your foe. His mind reels in terror.

Encounter ✦ Arcane, Fear, Implement, Psychic
Standard Action   Ranged 5
Target: One creature
Attack: Charisma vs. Will
Hit: 2d8 + Charisma modifier psychic damage, and the target takes a -1 penalty to Will defense until the end of your next turn.
  Star Pact: The penalty to Will defense is equal to 1 + your Intelligence modifier.

Vampiric Embrace — Warlock (Infernal) Attack 1

A ribbon of twisting darkness streams from your hand to your target's heart, feeding on his vital force as you grow stronger.

Encounter ✦ Arcane, Implement, Necrotic
Standard Action   Ranged 5
Target: One creature
Attack: Constitution vs. Will
Hit: 2d8 + Constitution modifier necrotic damage, and you gain 5 temporary hit points.
  Infernal Pact: You gain temporary hit points equal to 5 + your Intelligence modifier.

Witchfire — Warlock (Fey) Attack 1

From the mystic energy of the Feywild, you draw a brilliant white flame and set it in your enemy's mind and body. Rivulets of argent fire stream up into the air from his eyes, mouth, and hands; agony disrupts his very thoughts.

Encounter ✦ Arcane, Fire, Implement
Standard Action   Ranged 10
Target: One creature
Attack: Charisma vs. Reflex
Hit: 2d6 + Charisma modifier fire damage, and the target takes a -2 penalty to attack rolls until the end of your next turn.
  Fey Pact: The penalty to attack rolls is equal to 2 + your Intelligence modifier.

LEVEL 1 DAILY SPELLS

Armor of Agathys — Warlock (Infernal) Attack 1

You surround yourself in a sheath of black ice from a dark and doleful realm. It protects you from attack and radiates fierce cold.

Daily ✦ Arcane, Cold
Standard Action   Personal
Effect: You gain temporary hit points equal to 10 + your Intelligence modifier. Until the end of the encounter, an enemy that starts its turn adjacent to you takes 1d6 + Constitution modifier cold damage.

Curse of the Dark Dream — Warlock (Fey) Attack 1

You inflict a waking nightmare upon your enemy so that he can no longer tell what is real and what exists only in his mind. Under its influence he staggers about, trying to avoid falling from imaginary heights or stepping on unreal serpents.

Daily ✦ Arcane, Charm, Implement, Psychic
Standard Action   **Ranged** 10
Target: One creature
Attack: Charisma vs. Will
Hit: 3d8 + Charisma modifier psychic damage, and you slide the target 3 squares.
Sustain Minor: You slide the target 1 square, whether you hit or miss (save ends).

Dread Star — Warlock (Star) Attack 1

You create a fist-sized orb of painful blue-white radiance that whirls around your enemy, searing him. Fierce rays shoot from it like jabbing daggers of light, fencing him in where he stands.

Daily ✦ Arcane, Fear, Implement, Radiant
Standard Action   **Ranged** 10
Target: One creature
Attack: Charisma vs. Will
Hit: 3d6 + Charisma modifier radiant damage, and the target is immobilized until the end of your next turn.
Effect: The target takes a –2 penalty to Will defense (save ends).

Flames of Phlegethos — Warlock (Infernal) Attack 1

Rivulets of clinging liquid fire appear and cascade over your target. Anything that is flammable ignites at once and burns long after the streams of magic fire fade away.

Daily ✦ Arcane, Fire, Implement
Standard Action   **Ranged** 10
Target: One creature
Attack: Constitution vs. Reflex
Hit: 3d10 + Constitution modifier fire damage.
Effect: The target takes ongoing 5 fire damage (save ends).

LEVEL 2 UTILITY SPELLS

Beguiling Tongue — Warlock (Fey) Utility 2

You channel the grace and glibness of your fey patrons for a time. Your voice gains great power and eloquence.

Encounter ✦ Arcane
Minor Action   **Personal**
Effect: You gain a +5 power bonus to your next Bluff, Diplomacy, or Intimidate check during this encounter.

Ethereal Stride — Warlock (Star) Utility 2

You shift your body out of phase with the world for an instant, teleporting a short distance. When you reappear, you are still somewhat out of phase and difficult to harm or hinder for a short time.

Encounter ✦ Arcane, Teleportation
Move Action   **Personal**
Effect: You can teleport 3 squares, and you gain a +2 power bonus to all defenses until the end of your next turn.

Fiendish Resilience — Warlock (Infernal) Utility 2

You call upon your patron entities to protect you with their fell power. Your flesh is infused with mystic strength, lessening the effect of enemy blows.

Daily ✦ Arcane
Minor Action   **Personal**
Effect: You gain temporary hit points equal to 5 + your Constitution modifier.

Shadow Veil — Warlock (Star) Utility 2

You garb yourself in a pall of murky darkness. While it lasts, you are difficult to see or hear.

Encounter ✦ Arcane, Illusion
Minor Action   **Personal**
Effect: You gain a +5 power bonus to Stealth checks until the end of your next turn.

LEVEL 3 ENCOUNTER SPELLS

Eldritch Rain — Warlock (Fey) Attack 3

You fire purple rays of eldritch power at your foes.

Encounter ✦ Arcane, Implement
Standard Action   **Ranged** 10
Targets: One creature, or two creatures no more than 5 squares apart from each other
Attack: Charisma vs. Reflex, one attack per target
Hit: 1d10 + Charisma modifier damage.
  Fey Pact: Gain a bonus to each attack's damage roll equal to your Intelligence modifier.

Fiery Bolt — Warlock (Infernal) Attack 3

You call up a bolt of golden flame and hurl it at your foe. Anyone standing close to him is burned as well.

Encounter ✦ Arcane, Fire, Implement
Standard Action   **Ranged** 10
Target: One creature
Attack: Constitution vs. Reflex
Hit: 3d6 + Constitution modifier fire damage, and creatures adjacent to the target take 1d6 + Constitution modifier fire damage.
  Infernal Pact: Creatures adjacent to the target take extra fire damage equal to your Intelligence modifier.

Frigid Darkness — Warlock (Star) Attack 3

You create a freezing black shadow around your foe, a small taste of the icy darkness in the depths of the night sky. He is unable to see well enough to defend himself while the shadows cling to him.

Encounter ✦ Arcane, Cold, Fear, Implement
Standard Action   **Ranged** 10
Target: One creature
Attack: Constitution vs. Fortitude
Hit: 2d8 + Constitution modifier cold damage, and the target grants combat advantage to all of your enemies until the end of your next turn.
  Star Pact: The target takes a penalty to AC equal to your Intelligence modifier.

Otherwind Stride — Warlock (Fey) Attack 3

You call up an unseen maelstrom of fey power that lashes nearby creatures . . . and you step into the vortex and emerge somewhere a short distance away.

Encounter ✦ Arcane, Implement, Teleportation
Standard Action   **Close** burst 1
Target: Each creature in burst
Attack: Charisma vs. Fortitude
Hit: 1d8 + Charisma modifier damage, and the target is immobilized until the end of your next turn.
Effect: You teleport 5 squares.
     Fey Pact: You teleport a number of squares equal to 5 + your Intelligence modifier.

LEVEL 5 DAILY SPELLS

Avernian Eruption — Warlock (Infernal) Attack 5

Acrid orange fumes hiss up from beneath the ground, and then suddenly ignite in a thundering detonation. Any creature in the area is burned by the searing flames.

Daily ✦ Arcane, Fire, Implement
Standard Action   **Area** burst 1 within 10 squares
Target: Each creature in burst
Attack: Constitution vs. Reflex
Hit: 2d10 + Constitution modifier fire damage.
Effect: The targets take ongoing 5 fire damage (save ends).

Crown of Madness — Warlock (Fey) Attack 5

You cause an illusory, twisted crown to appear around the target's head. Under its psychic assault, your enemy loses the ability to distinguish friend from foe.

Daily ✦ Arcane, Charm, Implement, Psychic
Standard Action   **Ranged** 10
Target: One creature
Attack: Charisma vs. Will
Hit: 2d6 + Charisma modifier psychic damage.
Miss: Half damage.
Sustain Minor: The target makes a melee basic attack against one of its adjacent allies of your choice (save ends).

Curse of the Bloody Fangs — Warlock (Fey) Attack 5

You call up a pack of ferocious, phantasmal beasts from the darkest and most savage depths of the Feywild. Only their slavering fangs appear in this world, snapping and rending in a mad frenzy at the foe you have cursed.

Daily ✦ Arcane, Implement
Standard Action   **Ranged** 10
Target: One creature
Attack: Charisma vs. AC
Hit: 2d10 + Charisma modifier damage.
Miss: Half damage.
Sustain Minor: The target and any of your enemies adjacent to it take 1d10 damage (save ends).

Hunger of Hadar — Warlock (Star) Attack 5

You create a zone of complete, impermeable darkness filled with flying, fluttering, fanged shadows. The shadows rend at the very life force of creatures caught within.

Daily ✦ Arcane, Implement, Necrotic, Zone
Standard Action   **Area** burst 1 within 10 squares
Effect: The burst creates a zone of darkness until the end of your next turn, blocking line of sight. Creatures that enter the zone or start their turns there take 2d10 necrotic damage.
Sustain Minor: When you sustain the power, you make a secondary attack.
     Secondary Target: Each creature within the zone
     Secondary Attack: Constitution vs. Fortitude
     Hit: 1d6 + Constitution modifier necrotic damage.

LEVEL 6 UTILITY SPELLS

Dark One's Own Luck — Warlock (Star) Utility 6

Refusing the result that fate has decreed for you, you invoke stars of uncertainty and try to rewrite what has been written.

Daily ✦ Arcane
Free Action   **Personal**
Trigger: You make a roll you dislike
Effect: Reroll the attack roll, skill check, ability check, or saving throw, using the higher of the two results.

Fey Switch — Warlock (Fey) Utility 6

You step through the veils of the Feywild to the place where an ally stands and return to the world in that spot. Your ally is instantly whisked back to the place you started from.

Encounter ✦ Arcane, Teleportation
Move Action   **Ranged** 10
Targets: You and one willing ally
Effect: You and your ally trade spaces.

Shroud of Black Steel — Warlock (Infernal) Utility 6

Invoking the power of your dark patrons, you transform your skin into living steel, blackened and hard yet still supple enough to move. Your quickness suffers a bit, but you are much tougher and more resilient.

Daily ✦ Arcane, Polymorph
Minor Action   **Personal**
Effect: You change your skin into living steel. You gain a +2 power bonus to AC and Fortitude defense but take a −2 penalty to speed until the end of the encounter. You can end this effect as a minor action.

Spider Climb — Warlock (Infernal) Utility 6

You bestow on yourself the ability to cling to almost any surface and climb as easily as an insect.

Encounter ✦ Arcane
Move Action   **Personal**
Effect: On this move action, you move with a climb speed equal to your speed.

LEVEL 7 ENCOUNTER SPELLS

Howl of Doom — Warlock (Infernal) Attack 7

You unleash a devastating shout that cracks stone and pulps flesh. Supernatural terror goes with your mighty blast, and your foes are driven back in fright.

Encounter ✦ Arcane, Fear, Implement, Thunder
Standard Action   **Close** blast 3
Target: Each creature in blast
Attack: Constitution vs. Fortitude
Hit: 2d6 + Constitution modifier thunder damage, and you push the target 2 squares.
   Infernal Pact: You push the target a number of squares equal to 1 + your Intelligence modifier.

Infernal Moon Curse — Warlock (Infernal) Attack 7

The shimmer of pale, ghostly silver envelops your foe and lifts him up into the air. Its sinister radiance seeps into his body, a strange and deadly poison.

Encounter ✦ Arcane, Implement, Poison
Standard Action   **Ranged** 10
Target: One creature
Attack: Constitution vs. Fortitude
Hit: 2d8 + Constitution modifier poison damage, and the target is held immobilized 5 feet off the ground until the end of your next turn.
   Infernal Pact: You gain a bonus to the damage roll equal to your Intelligence modifier.

Mire the Mind — Warlock (Fey) Attack 7

You assail your foe's mind with unreal images until he can see nothing else.

Encounter ✦ Arcane, Illusion, Implement, Psychic
Standard Action   **Ranged** 10
Target: One creature
Attack: Charisma vs. Will
Hit: 1d10 + Charisma modifier psychic damage, and you and all of your allies in range are invisible to the target until the end of your next turn.
   Fey Pact: You gain a power bonus to Stealth checks equal to your Intelligence modifier until the end of the encounter.

Sign of Ill Omen — Warlock (Star) Attack 7

You sketch a glowing rune in the air with your fingertip, invoking misfortune upon your enemy. Lines of eldritch power slash across his body as you draw your sign, and fate itself turns against him for a short time.

Encounter ✦ Arcane, Implement
Standard Action   **Ranged** 10
Target: One creature
Attack: Charisma vs. Will
Hit: 2d6 + Charisma modifier damage, and the target must roll twice for its next attack and use the lower of the two rolls.
   Star Pact: When the target rolls twice, it takes a penalty to both rolls equal to your Intelligence modifier.

LEVEL 9 DAILY SPELLS

Curse of the Black Frost — Warlock (Fey) Attack 9

You create a fence of sharp frost-needles around your foe. They slowly freeze him, and if he moves or touches them, they grow longer and sharper.

Daily ✦ Arcane, Cold, Implement
Standard Action   **Ranged** 10
Target: One creature
Attack: Charisma vs. Reflex
Hit: 2d8 + Charisma modifier cold damage.
Effect: If the target moves for any reason, it takes 1d8 cold damage (save ends). If the target saves, you cannot sustain this power.
Sustain Minor: The target takes 2d8 cold damage.

Iron Spike of Dis — Warlock (Infernal) Attack 9

You call up a spear of red iron from the infernal regions and hurl it at your foe. Transfixing clothing, armor, flesh, or skin, it nails him to the spot where he stands.

Daily ✦ Arcane, Implement
Standard Action   **Ranged** 10
Target: One creature
Attack: Constitution vs. Reflex
Hit: 3d10 + Constitution modifier damage, and the target is immobilized (save ends).
Miss: Half damage, and the target is not immobilized.

Summons of Khirad — Warlock (Star) Attack 9

A pale blue flame springs up from your brow as you invoke Khirad, a star of dire portent. Your enemy's mind burns with Khirad's flame, and you teleport him where you wish.

Daily ✦ Arcane, Implement, Psychic, Teleportation
Standard Action   **Ranged** 10
Target: One creature
Attack: Constitution vs. Will
Hit: 2d10 + Constitution modifier psychic damage, and you teleport the target to an unoccupied square within 3 squares of you.
Sustain Minor: Make a Constitution vs. Will attack against the target. On a hit, you teleport the target to an unoccupied square within 3 squares of you. On a miss, the effect ends.

Thief of Five Fates — Warlock (Star) Attack 9

You bind your target's fortunes to five ill-omened stars. Under their dire influence, all sorts of mischance and bad luck befall your enemy.

Daily ✦ Arcane, Implement
Standard Action   **Ranged** 10
Target: One creature
Attack: Charisma vs. Will
Hit: Until the end of your next turn, whenever the target makes a saving throw or an attack roll, you roll a d20 without modifiers. If your result is higher than the target's unmodified die roll, the target's attack misses or the target's saving throw fails.
Sustain Minor: Make a Charisma vs. Will attack against the target. On a hit, the effect continues. On a miss, the effect ends.

Level 10 Utility Spells

Ambassador Imp — Warlock (Infernal) Utility 10

You conjure forth an implike presence from the netherworld and give it a message to deliver to a far-off creature.

Daily ✦ Arcane, Conjuration
Standard Action **Ranged** 100 miles
Effect: You whisper a message into the air, and an implike presence appears next to the creature you wish to speak to and delivers your message. If the creature has a reply, the imp appears adjacent to you at the end of your next turn to utter it. If the creature has no reply or is not within range, the imp appears adjacent to you at the end of your next turn to tell you so. The imp then disappears.

Shadow Form — Warlock (Star) Utility 10

You fly apart into a swarm of batlike shadows.

Daily ✦ Arcane, Polymorph
Minor Action **Personal**
Effect: You assume a shadowy form until the end of the encounter or for 5 minutes. In this form you are insubstantial, gain fly 6, and can't take standard actions. Reverting to your normal form is a minor action.

Shielding Shades — Warlock (Star) Utility 10

You call up a swirling shield of darkness from some far domain, interposing it between yourself and dire peril.

Daily ✦ Arcane
Immediate Reaction **Personal**
Trigger: You are hit by an attack
Effect: Reduce the attack's damage to 0. If the attack targets other creatures, they take damage as normal.

Warlock's Leap — Warlock (Fey) Utility 10

You leap through the mystic veil into the Feywild. An instant later, you return a short distance away and alight without traveling through the intervening air.

Daily ✦ Arcane, Teleportation
Move Action **Personal**
Effect: You teleport 6 squares. You do not need line of sight to the destination, but if you attempt to teleport to a space you can't occupy, you don't move.

Level 13 Encounter Spells

Bewitching Whispers — Warlock (Fey) Attack 13

You whisper words of fey power, words that drive mortals to madness.

Encounter ✦ Arcane, Charm, Implement
Standard Action **Ranged** 10
Target: One creature
Attack: Charisma vs. Will
Hit: Until the end of your next turn, the target treats all creatures as enemies for the purpose of opportunity attacks and must take every opportunity attack possible.
　Fey Pact: The target gains a power bonus to these attack rolls equal to your Intelligence modifier.

Coldfire Vortex — Warlock (Star) Attack 13

You create a spinning vortex of brilliant but frigid energy around your foe. Racing streamers of luminous coldfire lash all creatures nearby.

Encounter ✦ Arcane, Implement; Cold or Radiant
Standard Action **Ranged** 10
Primary Target: One creature
Attack: Constitution vs. Fortitude
Hit: 2d10 + Constitution modifier damage (choose cold or radiant damage). Make a secondary attack.
　Secondary Target: Each creature adjacent to the primary target
　Secondary Attack: Constitution vs. Reflex
　Hit: 1d10 + Constitution modifier damage (choose cold or radiant damage).
　Star Pact: You gain a bonus to damage rolls against the secondary targets equal to your Intelligence modifier.

Harrowstorm — Warlock (Infernal) Attack 13

You call up a churning cyclone from the nether planes. It surrounds your enemy, battering him with deafening claps of thunder and hurling him a short distance.

Encounter ✦ Arcane, Implement, Thunder
Standard Action **Ranged** 10
Target: One creature
Attack: Constitution vs. Fortitude
Hit: 2d10 + Constitution modifier thunder damage, and you slide the target 5 squares.
　Infernal Pact: You slide the target a number of squares equal to 5 + your Intelligence modifier.

Soul Flaying — Warlock (Infernal) Attack 13

You sear your enemy's soul with a bolt of emerald energy, which weakens him greatly for a short time.

Encounter ✦ Arcane, Implement, Necrotic
Standard Action **Ranged** 10
Target: One creature
Attack: Constitution vs. Will
Hit: 2d8 + Constitution modifier necrotic damage, and the target is weakened until the end of your next turn.
　Infernal Pact: The attack deals extra damage equal to your Intelligence modifier.

Level 15 Daily Spells

Curse of the Golden Mist — Warlock (Fey) Attack 15

You lull your enemy into a waking dream. He sees himself in a realm of eldritch beauty, and perceives the real world as a ghostly shadow of itself.

Daily ✦ Arcane, Charm, Implement
Standard Action **Ranged** 10
Target: One creature
Attack: Charisma vs. Will
Hit: The target loses its next standard action.
Sustain Standard: Make a Charisma vs. Will attack against the target. On a hit, the target loses its next standard action. On a miss, the power ends.

Fireswarm Warlock (Infernal) Attack 15

Fiery scorpions crawl out of cracks in the ground and swarm your enemy, stinging madly and spreading out to engulf other nearby creatures.

Daily ✦ Arcane, Fire, Implement, Poison
Standard Action   **Ranged** 10
Target: One creature
Attack: Constitution vs. Reflex
Hit: 4d10 + Constitution modifier fire and poison damage.
Sustain Standard: Make a Constitution vs. Fortitude attack against the target. On a hit, the target and each creature adjacent to it takes 2d10 + Constitution modifier fire and poison damage. On a miss, you deal half damage and the power ends.

Tendrils of Thuban Warlock (Star) Attack 15

From the frozen emerald seas under the star Thuban, you call forth dozens of glimmering green tentacles. Reaching down from overhead, they seize your enemies, draining the heat from their bodies and holding them immobile.

Daily ✦ Arcane, Cold, Implement, Zone
Standard Action   **Area** burst 1 within 10 squares
Target: Each creature in burst
Attack: Constitution vs. Fortitude
Hit: 4d10 + Constitution modifier cold damage, and the target is immobilized (save ends).
Effect: The burst creates a zone of tendrils that lasts until the end of your next turn.
Sustain Minor: Make a Constitution vs. Fortitude attack against all targets within the zone. On a hit, the target takes 1d10 + Constitution modifier cold damage and is immobilized (save ends).

Thirsting Maw Warlock (Infernal) Attack 15

With a flick of your wrist, you create a phantasmal eellike creature from your palm and hurl it at your foe. It latches itself to him and begins to drink his blood . . . and you grow stronger.

Daily ✦ Arcane, Implement
Standard Action   **Ranged** 5
Target: One creature
Attack: Constitution vs. Fortitude
Hit: 4d8 + Constitution modifier damage, and you regain hit points equal to half the amount of damage dealt.
Sustain Minor: The target takes 2d8 damage (save ends). Each time the target takes this damage, you regain hit points equal to half the damage.

LEVEL 16 UTILITY SPELLS

Cloak of Shadow Warlock (Infernal) Utility 16

You briefly become a flying shadow, swift and insubstantial.

Encounter ✦ Arcane
Move Action   **Personal**
Effect: Fly a number of squares equal to your speed + 2. If you don't land at the end of this move, you fall. Until the end of your next turn, you are insubstantial, and you cannot affect, attack, or use powers on creatures or objects.

Eye of the Warlock Warlock (Star) Utility 16

You create upon your forehead a mystical third eye and link that eye's perception to the senses of some other creature nearby.

Daily ✦ Arcane
Minor Action   **Ranged** 10
Target: One creature
Effect: You see through the target's eyes. The target is not aware that you are doing so. You have line of sight and line of effect from the target for your attacks. Your warlock powers can originate in the target's square. Each time you use a power through this link, a mystical third eye briefly appears upon the target's brow (save ends).

Infuriating Elusiveness Warlock (Fey) Utility 16

You will yourself across the boundary between worlds, teleporting a short distance. When you appear from the Feywild, you are surrounded by a glamor of invisibility.

Encounter ✦ Arcane, Illusion, Teleportation
Move Action   **Personal**
Effect: You become invisible and then teleport 4 squares. The invisibility lasts until the start of your next turn.

LEVEL 17 ENCOUNTER SPELLS

Strand of Fate Warlock (Star) Attack 17

You call upon a snaking strand of distilled fate that lances toward your foe. If he can't evade it, terrible misfortune ensues.

Encounter ✦ Arcane, Implement
Standard Action   **Ranged** 10
Target: One creature
Attack: Charisma vs. Reflex
Hit: 1d8 + Charisma modifier damage, and the target gains vulnerability 10 to all attacks until the end of your next turn.
Star Pact: The vulnerability increases to 10 + your Intelligence modifier.

Thirsting Tendrils Warlock (Fey) Attack 17

You lower your hand, and rootlike tendrils shoot from your palm into the ground. An instant later they erupt from the earth beneath your enemy's feet and bore into his flesh, replenishing you with his vital force.

Encounter ✦ Arcane, Healing, Implement
Standard Action   **Ranged** 10
Target: One creature
Attack: Charisma vs. Fortitude
Hit: 3d6 + Charisma modifier damage, and you can spend a healing surge.
Fey Pact: You regain additional hit points equal to twice your Intelligence modifier.

Warlock's Bargain — Warlock (Infernal) Attack 17

You forge a link between your enemy's soul and your own, and then you surrender it to your fiendish patrons. It hurts you, but he suffers more.

Encounter ✦ Arcane, Implement
Standard Action   **Ranged** 5
Target: One creature
Attack: Constitution vs. Fortitude
Hit: You take damage equal to your level, and the target takes 3d10 + Constitution modifier damage plus extra damage equal to one-half your level.
   Infernal Pact: If you hit, you take damage equal to your level minus your Intelligence modifier.

LEVEL 19 DAILY SPELLS

Delusions of Loyalty — Warlock (Fey) Attack 19

Your magic causes your enemy to perceive you as a comrade he must defend, even if he is now at odds with his former allies.

Daily ✦ Arcane, Charm, Implement
Standard Action   **Ranged** 10
Target: One creature
Attack: Charisma vs. Will
Hit: On its next turn, the target uses its standard action to make a basic attack against the last creature to attack you since your last turn. If no one attacked you since your last turn or if the target is unable to attack, the target loses its standard action.
Sustain Minor: When you sustain this power, you can repeat the attack against the target. If you miss, you can no longer sustain the power.

Minions of Malbolge — Warlock (Infernal) Attack 19

You bring forth fire in the shape of small, infernal imps from Malbolge, sixth of the Nine Hells. They hover close around you and hurl themselves upon any enemy that dares to approach, searing with their fiery touch and driving foes away.

Daily ✦ Arcane, Conjuration, Fire, Implement
Standard Action   **Personal**
Effect: You conjure flames in the shape of diabolic imps that appear at your feet. You gain 25 temporary hit points.
   Any enemy that enters a square adjacent to you takes 2d10 fire damage and is pushed 3 squares. This effect applies once per creature per round. It ends when you have no temporary hit points remaining.

Wrath of Acamar — Warlock (Star) Attack 19

You fire a ray of crackling black energy at your enemy. At its touch, he is instantly hurled headlong into the soul-draining depths of Acamar, a dark and distant star.

Daily ✦ Arcane, Implement, Necrotic, Teleportation
Standard Action   **Ranged** 10
Target: One creature
Attack: Charisma vs. Reflex
Hit: 4d10 + Charisma modifier necrotic damage, and the target disappears into a starry realm (save ends).
Special: While in the starry realm, the target cannot take actions, cannot be targeted, and takes 1d10 necrotic damage at the start of its turn. On a save, it returns to the space it was last in. If that space is occupied, the target returns to the nearest unoccupied space of its choice.

LEVEL 22 UTILITY SPELLS

Entropic Ward — Warlock (Star) Utility 22

Fortune favors you; stars portending uncertainty lean in your favor and frown upon your foes.

Encounter ✦ Arcane
Minor Action   **Personal**
Effect: Until the end of your next turn, anyone who attacks you must roll two dice and take the lower result. Each time an attack misses due to this effect, you gain a cumulative +1 power bonus to your next attack roll.

Raven's Glamor — Warlock (Fey) Utility 22

You teleport yourself away from imminent danger, but you leave an illusion of yourself behind, distracting and confusing your foes.

Daily ✦ Arcane, Illusion, Teleportation
Move Action   **Personal**
Effect: You become invisible until the start of your next turn and teleport 20 squares. You leave behind an illusory image of yourself that persists as long as you are invisible. This image stands in place, takes no actions, and uses your defenses if it is attacked. If the illusion is touched or takes any damage, it dissolves into a pile of dead leaves. If you make an attack, you become visible.
Sustain Standard: You remain invisible as long as you don't make an attack.

Wings of the Fiend — Warlock (Infernal) Utility 22

You sprout a large pair of leathery wings from your back.

Daily ✦ Arcane, Polymorph
Minor Action   **Personal**
Effect: You grow wings and gain a fly speed equal to your speed until the end of the encounter or for 5 minutes.

LEVEL 23 ENCOUNTER SPELLS

Dark Transport — Warlock (Star) Attack 23

You forge a short-lived dimensional gate that slices through your opponent. If you wish, you can leap through the gate and take his place while banishing him to the spot you were just in.

Encounter ✦ Arcane, Implement, Teleportation
Standard Action   **Ranged** 10
Target: One creature
Attack: Charisma vs. Will
Hit: 4d10 + Charisma modifier damage, and you can swap places with the target.
   Star Pact: After swapping places with the target, you can teleport a number of squares equal to your Intelligence modifier.

Spiteful Darts — Warlock (Infernal) Attack 23

You create scores of large, infernal darts and send them streaking at your enemies. Each dart that finds flesh pushes the creature it injures out of the place where it stands, moving it to another spot of your choosing.

Encounter ✦ Arcane, Implement
Standard Action   Close blast 5
Target: Each creature in blast
Attack: Constitution vs. Reflex
Hit: 4d8 + Constitution modifier damage, and you push the target 3 squares.
  Infernal Pact: You push each target a number of squares equal to 3 + your Intelligence modifier.

Thorns of Venom — Warlock (Fey) Attack 23

Raising your hands, you call up from the ground thick vines studded with long, poisonous thorns that wrap around your foe. He is held fast and pierced by the deadly thorns.

Encounter ✦ Arcane, Implement, Poison
Standard Action   Ranged 10
Target: One creature
Attack: Charisma vs. Fortitude
Hit: 3d8 + Charisma modifier poison damage, and the target is immobilized and takes a –2 penalty to AC and Reflex defense until the end of your next turn.
  Fey Pact: The penalty to AC and Reflex defense is equal to 1 + your Intelligence modifier.

LEVEL 25 DAILY SPELLS

Curse of the Twin Princes — Warlock (Fey) Attack 25

You begin to steal the very semblance of your target. Those around you and your foe can't distinguish between the two of you any longer.

Daily ✦ Arcane, Illusion, Implement, Psychic
Standard Action   Ranged 5
Target: One creature
Attack: Charisma vs. Will
Hit: 4d10 + Charisma modifier psychic damage. Until the end of the encounter, every time you take damage, you make a Charisma vs. Will attack against the target; if the attack hits, you take half damage and the target takes the other half.
Effect: Until the end of the encounter, whenever you are adjacent to the target, the images of you both begin to flow together, such that anyone who attacks one has a 50% chance of accidentally hitting the other instead.

Tartarean Tomb — Warlock (Infernal) Attack 25

You create a battering storm of rune-scribed black iron plates around your foe. As they whirl and strike, they quickly assemble into a coffinlike prison of iron and shadow.

Daily ✦ Arcane, Implement
Standard Action   Ranged 10
Target: One creature
Attack: Constitution vs. Reflex
Hit: 5d10 + Constitution modifier damage, and the target is entombed (save ends). An entombed target is immobilized and lacks line of sight and line of effect to any space other than its own. All creatures other than you cannot gain line of sight or line of effect to the target.
Miss: Half damage, and the target is immobilized (save ends).

Thirteen Baleful Stars — Warlock (Star) Attack 25

You create thirteen tiny crimson stars that dart and whirl around your enemy, blasting him with countless pinpricks of fire and lashing him with waves of supernatural terror.

Daily ✦ Arcane, Fear, Fire, Implement, Psychic
Standard Action   Ranged 10
Target: One creature
Attack: Constitution vs. Will
Hit: 5d10 + Constitution modifier fire and psychic damage, and the target is stunned until the end of your next turn.
Miss: Half damage, and the target is dazed until the end of your next turn.

LEVEL 27 ENCOUNTER SPELLS

Banish to the Void — Warlock (Star) Attack 27

You hurl your foe screaming into the skies, and he disappears to some remote and terrible corner of the cosmos. When he returns, madness overwhelms him.

Encounter ✦ Arcane, Fear, Implement, Teleportation
Standard Action   Ranged 10
Target: One creature
Attack: Constitution vs. Will
Hit: 2d10 + Constitution modifier damage. The target disappears into a starry realm. At the start of its next turn, the target reappears in its original space. If that space is occupied, the target returns to the nearest unoccupied space (its choice). The target attacks the nearest target on its next turn. Until the end of your next turn, all creatures treat the target as an enemy with respect to provoking opportunity attacks, and the target must take every opportunity attack possible.
  Star Pact: The target gains a power bonus to attack rolls equal to your Intelligence modifier. This bonus applies only to attack rolls it makes due to this power.

Curse of the Fey King — Warlock (Fey) Attack 27

You invoke the power of a mighty fey spirit. A shimmering emerald coil of eldritch power disrupts your foe and steals from him the luck of his next few moments. It's yours if you want it.

Encounter ✦ Arcane, Implement
Standard Action   Ranged 10
Target: One creature
Attack: Charisma vs. Will
Hit: 3d10 + Charisma modifier damage. In addition, the first time the target rolls a d20 on its next turn, you can steal that result. The target rerolls, and you use the stolen result for your next d20 roll.
  Fey Pact: You gain a bonus to the stolen result equal to your Intelligence modifier.

Hellfire Curse — Warlock (Infernal) Attack 27

You level your clenched fist toward your foe and unleash a terrific blast of black flames.

Encounter ✦ Arcane, Fire, Implement
Standard Action   Ranged 10
Target: One creature
Attack: Constitution vs. Fortitude
Hit: 5d10 + Constitution modifier fire damage.
  Infernal Pact: You gain a bonus to the damage roll equal to your Intelligence modifier.

Curse of the Dark Delirium   Warlock (Fey) Attack 29

You trap your enemy's mind with bewildering fey power. He sees what you want him to see, he hears what you want him to hear. Like a sinister puppeteer, you can make him do anything you wish.

Daily ✦ Arcane, Charm, Implement
Standard Action   **Ranged** 10
Target: One creature
Attack: Charisma vs. Will
Hit: On the target's next turn, you dictate its standard, move, and minor actions. The target cannot use immediate actions. It can't use powers other than a basic attack, and it can't take suicidal actions such as leaping off a cliff or attacking itself.
Miss: If the target is adjacent to one of its allies at the start of its next turn, it must begin its turn by using a standard action to make a melee basic attack against that ally.
Sustain Standard: Repeat the attack against the target as long as the target is within range. On a miss, you can't sustain this power.

Doom of Delban   Warlock (Star) Attack 29

A single slanting shaft of frigid starlight strikes your enemy from above and clings to him. Under its unbearable touch, flesh becomes white ice and steel shatters like glass, but you must pay a price to keep Delban's deadly light focused on your foes.

Daily ✦ Arcane, Cold, Fear, Implement
Standard Action   **Ranged** 10
Target: One creature
Attack: Constitution vs. Fortitude
Hit: 5d10 + Constitution modifier cold damage.
Miss: Half damage.
Sustain Standard: You can attack the same target or switch to a new target within range. Make an attack (as above) and increase the cold damage by 1d10 each time this power hits. Each time you sustain this power, you take 2d10 damage.

Hurl through Hell   Warlock (Infernal) Attack 29

You open a short-lived planar rift to the depths of the Nine Hells. It appears as a fiery crevice beneath your enemy's feet, into which he falls screaming, and disappears. A few moments later, a flaming arch appears in the air over the spot where he was standing and disgorges a broken, mewling piece of charred meat.

Daily ✦ Arcane, Fear, Fire, Implement, Teleportation
Standard Action   **Ranged** 10
Target: One creature
Attack: Constitution vs. Will
Hit: 7d10 + Constitution modifier fire damage, and the target disappears into the Nine Hells until the end of your next turn. The target returns to the same square it left, or the nearest unoccupied square, and is prone and stunned.
Sustain Minor: If you spend a minor action to sustain the power, the target's return is delayed until the end of your next turn. You can sustain the power no more than three times.
Miss: Half damage, and the target does not disappear.

PARAGON PATHS

DOOMSAYER

"I speak for the cold darkness beyond the stars. I see the myriad ways that doom comes upon you."

Prerequisite: Warlock class, star pact

You wrap yourself in the fear of the darkness beyond the stars and use it as a shield against your enemies. In addition, you examine the strands of fate to issue proclamations of doom to all who stand against you.

DOOMSAYER PATH FEATURES

Doomsayer's Action (11th level): When you spend an action point to take an extra action, you also deal the extra damage of your Warlock's Curse to all of your enemies currently affected by it.

Doomsayer's Proclamation (11th level): Enemies within 10 squares of you must roll two dice when rolling saving throws against fear effects. They must use the lower of the two rolls.

Doomsayer's Oath (16th level): When you are bloodied, you gain a +2 power bonus to attack rolls when you use a power that has the fear keyword.

DOOMSAYER SPELLS

Fates Entwined   Doomsayer (Star) Attack 11

You lodge a painful psychic shard in your enemy's brain that resonates whenever you take damage.

Encounter ✦ Arcane, Fear, Implement, Psychic
Standard Action   **Ranged** 5
Target: One creature
Attack: Charisma vs. Will
Hit: 2d8 + Charisma modifier psychic damage. Until the end of your next turn, when you take damage, the target takes half that amount of psychic damage.

Accursed Shroud   Doomsayer (Star) Utility 12

You envelop your enemy in an inky cloak of shadow that writhes and coils around him, twisting her attacks against you.

Daily ✦ Arcane
Standard Action   **Ranged** 5
Target: One creature
Effect: You place your Warlock's Curse upon the target. In addition, it must reroll any successful attack it makes while affected by your curse and take the new result.

Long Fall into Darkness   Doomsayer (Star) Attack 20

You point a finger at your foe, and a gaping pit opens beneath him. The pit is merely a figment of his imagination, but he plunges into the darkness nonetheless until, at last, he hits the bottom.

Daily ✦ Arcane, Fear, Illusion, Implement, Psychic
Standard Action   **Ranged** 20
Target: One creature
Attack: Charisma vs. Will
Hit: 4d8 + Charisma modifier psychic damage, and the target is stunned until the end of its next turn and knocked prone.
Miss: Half damage, and the target is dazed until the end of its next turn.

FEYTOUCHED

"I have been touched by the power of the fey, and it drove me mad . . . but the power I gained from the madness has rendered me sane."

Prerequisite: Warlock class, fey pact

Your constant visits to the Feywild and your communion with the fey entity that holds your pact have touched you to your very soul and driven you slightly mad. But within this madness, you have found the power to rise to the next level of your existence. The secrets of the Feywild might be maddening, but they provide you with new opportunities to achieve your goals and defeat your enemies. You relish the madness and can control it, but those you unleash it upon can do nothing but crumble in the wake of the unparalleled majesty of the Feywild.

FEYTOUCHED PATH FEATURES

Feytouched Action (11th level): When you spend an action point to take an extra action, you also gain a +4 bonus to attack rolls until the start of your next turn.

Slashing Wake (11th level): When you leave a square by teleporting, enemies adjacent to that square take damage equal to your Intelligence modifier.

Patron's Favor (16th level): Use Patron's Favor in place of your Misty Step when an enemy under your Warlock's Curse drops to 0 hit points or fewer. Roll 1d6. Use the benefit you rolled or any result lower than that on the list below.

1 or 2: You use your Misty Step as normal.

3: Immediately make a saving throw.

4: Teleport 10 squares as a free action.

5: You gain +2 speed until the end of your next turn.

6: Roll d8s instead of d6s for your Warlock's Curse extra damage until the end of the encounter.

FEYTOUCHED SPELLS

Will of the Feywild   Feytouched (Fey) Attack 11

You bend your enemy's will to your whim. In a blinding flash of golden light, the creature teleports to a location you designate and, in its madness, attacks one of its allies.

Encounter ✦ Arcane, Charm, Implement, Psychic, Teleportation
Standard Action   **Ranged** 10
Target: One creature
Attack: Charisma vs. Will
Hit: 2d8 + Charisma modifier psychic damage. You can teleport the target 5 squares, whereupon it makes a melee basic attack against an adjacent creature of your choice.
Effect: The target is dazed until the end of its next turn.

Twilight Teleport   Feytouched (Fey) Utility 12

An enemy falls to your curse, and another creature appears in its place, surrounded by motes of twilight.

Daily ✦ Arcane, Teleportation
Free Action   **Ranged** 20
Trigger: A creature within range and affected by your Warlock's Curse drops to 0 hit points or fewer
Effect: You teleport yourself or another creature into the triggering creature's space.

Whispers of the Fey   Feytouched (Fey) Utility 20

The disquieting whispers of fey spirits surround you, filling the minds of nearby enemies with deranged thoughts and provoking them to turn on their allies.

Daily ✦ Arcane, Implement, Psychic
Standard Action   **Close** burst 5
Target: Each enemy in burst
Attack: Charisma vs. Will
Hit: The target must make a basic attack against its nearest ally (you choose the target if there are multiple possible targets). If it can't make the attack, the target takes 2d8 + Charisma modifier psychic damage.
Effect: After it makes its attack or takes psychic damage, the target is dazed (save ends).

LIFE-STEALER

"Enemies are all around us, offering their life energy for me to use against them."

Prerequisite: Warlock class, infernal pact

Your pact with infernal powers has given you the ability to steal and utilize the life energy of your enemies. This life energy provides you with a new avenue to power, and you hunger for it as a vampire craves blood.

LIFE-STEALER PATH FEATURES

Infernal Action (11th level): When you spend an action point to take an extra action, if you use your action to make an attack that hits, that hit deals ongoing 5 fire damage (save ends).

Collect Life Spark (11th level): When a creature under your Warlock's Curse drops to 0 hit points or fewer, you take a portion of its life energy by collecting a life spark. As a minor action, you can expend this life spark to gain a benefit based on the creature's origin. At the end of the encounter, any life sparks you have not expended fade away.

Aberrant: You gain a +2 power bonus to all defenses until the end of your next turn.

Immortal: You gain resist 5 to all damage until the end of your next turn.

Elemental: You deal an extra 5 damage to the next target you hit with an attack on your current turn.

Fey: A successful attack you make on your current turn also causes your target to become dazed.

Natural: Regain hit points equal to one-half your level.

Shadow: You become invisible until the end of your next turn.

Sustain Life Spark (16th level): If you have more life sparks at the end of an encounter than you do healing surges, you regain hit points as if you had spent a healing surge.

LIFE-STEALER SPELLS

Soul Scorch	Life-Stealer (Infernal) Attack 11

As black fire immolates your adversary, you release one of your life sparks. Your foe cries out in pain as he feels the life ebb from his body.

Encounter ✦ Arcane, Fire, Implement, Necrotic
Standard Action — **Ranged** 10
Target: One creature
Attack: Constitution vs. Will
Hit: 3d8 + Constitution modifier fire and necrotic damage.
Effect: If the target creature has the same origin as a life spark you possess, you can expend that life spark to deal an extra 10 damage to the target.

Life Spark Summons	Life-Stealer (Infernal) Utility 12

You expend one of your life sparks to fashion an effigy of the creature whose spark you've just released.

Daily ✦ Arcane
Minor Action — **Ranged** 10
Effect: Expend a life spark you possess. Place the creature from which you received that life spark back in the encounter within the power's range. It has 10 hit points and acts on your next turn with a full set of actions as an independent creature that you control. The creature can do nothing except make basic attacks and move. It drops to 0 hit points again, dies, and fades away at the end of your next turn.

Soultheft	Life-Stealer (Infernal) Attack 20

You engulf your enemies in crackling purple energy. As they crumple, blazing motes of soul-light rise up from their bodies and fly into your grasp.

Daily ✦ Arcane, Implement, Necrotic
Standard Action — **Ranged** 5
Targets: One, two, or three creatures
Attack: Constitution vs. Fortitude, one attack per target
Hit: 3d8 + Constitution modifier necrotic damage, and you gain a life spark from any target that drops to 0 hit points or fewer as a result of this attack.
Miss: Half damage, and no life spark.

WARLORD

"Onward to victory! They cannot stand before us!"

CLASS TRAITS

Role: Leader. You are an inspiring commander and a master of battle tactics.

Power Source: Martial. You have become an expert in tactics through endless hours of training and practice, personal determination, and your own sheer physical toughness.

Key Abilities: Strength, Intelligence, Charisma

Armor Proficiencies: Cloth, leather, hide, chainmail; light shield

Weapon Proficiencies: Simple melee, military melee, simple ranged

Bonus to Defense: +1 Fortitude, +1 Will

Hit Points at 1st Level: 12 + Constitution score

Hit Points per Level Gained: 5

Healing Surges per Day: 7 + Constitution modifier

Trained Skills: From the class skills list below, choose four trained skills at 1st level.
Class Skills: Athletics (Str), Diplomacy (Cha), Endurance (Con), Heal (Wis), History (Int), Intimidate (Cha)

Build Options: Inspiring warlord, tactical warlord
Class Features: Combat Leader, Commanding Presence, *inspiring word*

Warlords are accomplished and competent battle leaders. Warlords stand on the front line issuing commands and bolstering their allies while leading the battle with weapon in hand. Warlords know how to rally a team to win a fight.

Your ability to lead others to victory is a direct result of your history. You could be a minor warchief looking to make a name for yourself, a pious knight-commander on leave from your militant order, a youthful noble eager to apply years of training to life outside the castle walls, a calculating mercenary captain, or a courageous marshal of the borderlands who fights to protect the frontier. Regardless of your background, you are a skillful warrior with an uncanny gift for leadership.

The weight of your armor is not a hindrance; it is a familiar comfort. The worn weapon grip molds to your hand as if it were a natural extension of your arm. It's time to fight and to lead.

CREATING A WARLORD

The two warlord builds are inspiring warlord and tactical warlord. Some warlords lean more on their Charisma, while others rely on Intelligence, but Strength is important to every warlord.

INSPIRING WARLORD

You lead by exhortation, encouragement, and inspiration. Your powers help your allies find new surges of courage and endurance within themselves, helping them heal, shrug off debilitating conditions, and defend themselves from attack. Your attack powers rely on Strength, so that should be your best ability score. The benefits you give your allies, though, depend almost entirely on Charisma, so make that second best. Intelligence is your best third choice, so you can dabble in other warlord powers and to help your Reflex defense. Select powers that make the best use of your high Charisma score.

Suggested Feat: Inspired Recovery (Human feat: Toughness)

Suggested Skills: Athletics, Diplomacy, Heal, History

Suggested At-Will Powers: *commander's strike, furious smash*

Suggested Encounter Power: *guarding attack*

Suggested Daily Power: *bastion of defense*

TACTICAL WARLORD

Your leadership takes the form of quick commands, cunning strategies, and tactical superiority. Your powers guide your allies to extra and more powerful attacks, as well as helping them move quickly in combat situations. You also assist your allies by moving your enemies around or knocking them prone. You use Strength for your attack powers, so make that your

best ability score. Intelligence is secondary, because your Intelligence determines just how effective a leader you are. Charisma should be your third best score, so you can dabble in other warlord powers and to improve your Will defense. Select powers that make the best use of your high Intelligence score.

Suggested Feat: Tactical Assault (Human feat: Weapon Focus)

Suggested Skills: Endurance, Heal, History, Intimidate

Suggested At-Will Powers: *viper's strike, wolf pack tactics*

Suggested Encounter Power: *warlord's favor*

Suggested Daily Power: *lead the attack*

WARLORD CLASS FEATURES

All warlords have these class features.

COMBAT LEADER

You and each ally within 10 squares who can see and hear you gain a +2 power bonus to initiative.

COMMANDING PRESENCE

Choose one of the following two benefits.

Inspiring Presence: When an ally who can see you spends an action point to take an extra action, that ally also regains lost hit points equal to one-half your level + your Charisma modifier.

Tactical Presence: When an ally you can see spends an action point to make an extra attack, the ally gains a bonus to the attack roll equal to one-half your Intelligence modifier.

The choice you make also provides bonuses to certain warlord powers. Individual powers detail the effects (if any) your Commanding Presence selection has on them.

INSPIRING WORD

Using the *inspiring word* power, warlords can grant their comrades additional resilience with nothing more than a shout of encouragement.

WARLORD POWERS

Your powers are martial exploits, deeds of extraordinary skill and daring learned through trial and blood-soaked error. Some powers are better for the inspiring warlord and others for the tactical warlord, but you're free to choose any powers you like.

CLASS FEATURE

The warlord's *inspiring word* class feature works like a power and is presented below.

WARLORD OVERVIEW

Characteristics: You are a strong warrior in melee, able to stand beside the fighter or paladin in your party. Your powers grant allies immediate actions (usually moves or attacks), provide bonuses to attack or defense, and grant healing in the midst of battle.

Religion: Warlords favor martial gods such as Bahamut and Kord, and those who have a particular eye for strategy or leadership esteem Ioun or Erathis. Evil and unaligned warlords often worship Bane.

Races: Dragonborn make excellent inspiring warlords, and half-elves are equally inspiring leaders. Eladrin are skilled tactical warlords. Tiefling warlords are versatile, combining powers from both builds, and humans can excel at either path.

Inspiring Word
Warlord Feature

You call out to a wounded ally and offer inspiring words of courage and determination that helps that ally heal.

Encounter (Special) ✦ Martial, Healing
Special: You can use this power twice per encounter, but only once per round. At 16th level, you can use *inspiring word* three times per encounter.
Minor Action   **Close** burst 5
                         (10 at 11th level, 15 at 21st level)
Target: You or one ally in burst
Effect: The target can spend a healing surge and regain an additional 1d6 hit points.
The amount of additional hit points regained is 2d6 at 6th level, 3d6 at 11th level, 4d6 at 16th level, 5d6 at 21st level, and 6d6 at 26th level.

LEVEL 1 AT-WILL EXPLOITS

Commander's Strike
Warlord Attack 1

With a shout, you command an ally to attack.

At-Will ✦ Martial, Weapon
Standard Action   **Melee** weapon
Target: One creature
Attack: An ally of your choice makes a melee basic attack against the target
Hit: Ally's basic attack damage + your Intelligence modifier.

Furious Smash
Warlord Attack 1

You slam your shield into your enemy, bash him with your weapon's haft, or drive your shoulder into his gut. Your attack doesn't do much damage–but your anger inspires your ally to match your ferocity.

At-Will ✦ Martial, Weapon
Standard Action   **Melee** weapon
Target: One creature
Attack: Strength vs. Fortitude
Hit: Deal damage equal to your Strength modifier, and then choose one ally adjacent to either you or the target. This ally applies your Charisma modifier as a power bonus to the attack roll and the damage roll on his or her next attack against the target. If the ally does not attack the target by the end of his or her next turn, the bonus is lost.

Viper's Strike
Warlord Attack 1

You trick your adversary into making a tactical error that gives your comrade a chance to strike.

At-Will ✦ Martial, Weapon
Standard Action   **Melee** weapon
Target: One creature
Attack: Strength vs. AC
Hit: 1[W] + Strength modifier damage.
Increase damage to 2[W] + Strength modifier at 21st level.
Effect: If the target shifts before the start of your next turn, it provokes an opportunity attack from an ally of your choice.

Wolf Pack Tactics
Warlord Attack 1

Step by step, you and your friends surround the enemy.

At-Will ✦ Martial, Weapon
Standard Action   **Melee** weapon
Target: One creature
Special: Before you attack, you let one ally adjacent to either you or the target shift 1 square as a free action.
Attack: Strength vs. AC
Hit: 1[W] + Strength modifier damage.
Increase damage to 2[W] + Strength modifier at 21st level.

LEVEL 1 ENCOUNTER EXPLOITS

Guarding Attack
Warlord Attack 1

With a calculated strike, you knock your adversary off balance and grant your comrade-in-arms some protection against the villain's attacks.

Encounter ✦ Martial, Weapon
Standard Action   **Melee** weapon
Target: One creature
Attack: Strength vs. AC
Hit: 2[W] + Strength modifier damage. Until the end of your next turn, one ally adjacent to either you or the target gains a +2 power bonus to AC against the target's attacks.
  Inspiring Presence: The power bonus to AC equals 1 + your Charisma modifier.

Hammer and Anvil
Warlord Attack 1

You land a ringing blow against your foe, inspiring a nearby ally to strike a blow of his own.

Encounter ✦ Martial, Weapon
Standard Action   **Melee** weapon
Target: One creature
Attack: Strength vs. Reflex
Hit: 1[W] + Strength modifier damage. One ally adjacent to the target makes a melee basic attack against it as a free action. The ally adds your Charisma modifier to the damage.

Leaf on the Wind
Warlord Attack 1

Like a leaf caught in the autumn wind, your foe is driven by the flow of battle. Your fierce attacks force him to give ground.

Encounter ✦ Martial, Weapon
Standard Action   **Melee** weapon
Target: One creature
Attack: Strength vs. AC
Hit: 2[W] + Strength modifier damage. You or an ally adjacent to the target swaps places with the target.

Warlord's Favor
Warlord Attack 1

With a calculated blow, you leave your adversary exposed to an imminent attack from one of your closest allies.

Encounter ✦ Martial, Weapon
Standard Action   **Melee** weapon
Target: One creature
Attack: Strength vs. AC
Hit: 2[W] + Strength modifier damage. One ally within 5 squares of you gains a +2 power bonus to attack rolls against the target until the end of your next turn.
  Tactical Presence: The bonus to attack rolls that you grant equals 1 + your Intelligence modifier.

LEVEL 1 DAILY EXPLOITS

Bastion of Defense   Warlord Attack 1

Honorable warriors never fall!

Daily ✦ Martial, Weapon
Standard Action   **Melee** weapon
Target: One creature
Attack: Strength vs. AC
Hit: 3[W] + Strength modifier damage. Allies within 5
  squares of you gain a +1 power bonus to all defenses until
  the end of the encounter.
Effect: Allies within 5 squares of you gain temporary hit
  points equal to 5 + your Charisma modifier.

Lead the Attack   Warlord Attack 1

*Under your direction, arrows hit their marks and blades drive
home.*

Daily ✦ Martial, Weapon
Standard Action   **Melee** weapon
Target: One creature
Attack: Strength vs. AC
Hit: 3[W] + Strength modifier damage. Until the end of the
  encounter, you and each ally within 5 squares of you gain
  a power bonus to attack rolls against the target equal to 1
  + your Intelligence modifier.
Miss: Until the end of the encounter, you and each ally within
  5 squares of you gain a +1 power bonus to attack rolls
  against the target.

Pin the Foe   Warlord Attack 1

*No matter where your foe turns, one of your allies is waiting for
him.*

Daily ✦ Martial, Weapon
Standard Action   **Melee** weapon
Target: One creature
Attack: Strength vs. AC
Hit: 3[W] + Strength modifier damage.
Effect: Until the end of the encounter, the target cannot
  shift if at least two of your allies (or you and one ally) are
  adjacent to it.

White Raven Onslaught   Warlord Attack 1

*You lead the way with a powerful attack, using your success
to create an opportunity for one of your allies. Each of your
comrades in turn seizes on your example and begins to display
true teamwork.*

Daily ✦ Martial, Weapon
Standard Action   **Melee** weapon
Target: One creature
Attack: Strength vs. AC
Hit: 3[W] + Strength modifier damage, and you slide an
  adjacent ally 1 square. Until the end of the encounter,
  whenever you or an ally within 10 squares of you makes
  a successful attack, the attacker slides an adjacent ally
  1 square.
Miss: Choose one ally within 10 squares. Until the end of
  the encounter, the ally slides an adjacent ally 1 square after
  making a successful attack.

LEVEL 2 UTILITY EXPLOITS

Aid the Injured   Warlord Utility 2

Your presence is both a comfort and an inspiration.

Encounter ✦ Healing, Martial
Standard Action   **Melee** touch
Target: You or one adjacent ally
Effect: The target can spend a healing surge.

Crescendo of Violence   Warlord Utility 2

*A timely critical hit affords you the opportunity to rally a wound-
ed ally.*

Encounter ✦ Martial
Immediate Reaction   **Ranged** 5
Trigger: An ally within range scores a critical hit
Effect: The ally gains temporary hit points equal to your
  Charisma modifier.

Knight's Move   Warlord Utility 2

*With a sharp wave of your arm, you direct one of your allies to a
more tactically advantageous position.*

Encounter ✦ Martial
Move Action   **Ranged** 10
Target: One ally
Effect: The target takes a move action as a free action.

Shake It Off   Warlord Utility 2

You convince yourself or an ally to shake off a debilitating effect.

Encounter ✦ Martial
Minor Action   **Ranged** 10
Target: You or one ally
Effect: The target makes a saving throw with a power bonus
  equal to your Charisma modifier.

LEVEL 3 ENCOUNTER EXPLOITS

Hold the Line   Warlord Attack 3

*With a snap series of commands, you keep your allies in forma-
tion and well defended as you assault your adversary.*

Encounter ✦ Martial, Weapon
Standard Action   **Melee** weapon
Target: One creature
Attack: Strength vs. AC
Hit: 1[W] + Strength modifier damage.
Effect: Until the end of your next turn, allies adjacent to you
  gain a +2 power bonus to AC and cannot be pulled, pushed,
  or slid.

Inspiring War Cry   Warlord Attack 3

*As you strike, you shout a fierce war cry that heartens a nearby
ally. He immediately attempts to shake off whatever condition
troubles him most.*

Encounter ✦ Martial, Weapon
Standard Action   **Melee** weapon
Target: One creature
Attack: Strength vs. AC
Hit: 2[W] + Strength modifier damage.
Effect: One ally who can hear you and is within 5 squares of
  you makes a saving throw.

Steel Monsoon — Warlord Attack 3

You leap into the fray with a wild, whirling attack—but your movements are carefully calculated to distract nearby enemies and give your allies a chance to move into position.

Encounter ✦ Martial, Weapon
Standard Action   Melee weapon
Target: One creature
Attack: Strength vs. AC
Hit: 2[W] + Strength modifier damage, and one ally within 5 squares of you can shift 1 square.
  Tactical Presence: The number of allies who can shift equals your Intelligence modifier.

Warlord's Strike — Warlord Attack 3

One convincing cut is all you need to reveal the enemy's weakness and spur your allies into finishing him off.

Encounter ✦ Martial, Weapon
Standard Action   Melee weapon
Target: One creature
Attack: Strength vs. AC
Hit: 2[W] + Strength modifier damage. Until the end of your next turn, all of your allies gain a +2 bonus to damage rolls against the target.
  Inspiring Presence: The bonus to damage rolls equals 1 + your Charisma modifier.

LEVEL 5 DAILY EXPLOITS

Stand the Fallen — Warlord Attack 5

You will not be denied victory! A determined strike lifts the spirits of your beleaguered allies and restores their fighting spirit.

Daily ✦ Healing, Martial, Weapon
Standard Action   Melee weapon
Target: One creature
Attack: Strength vs. AC
Hit: 3[W] + Strength modifier damage.
Effect: Each ally within 10 squares can spend a healing surge and regains additional hit points equal to your Charisma modifier.

Turning Point — Warlord Attack 5

A well-placed strike catches your foe off guard and allows you or a nearby ally to shake off some effect.

Daily ✦ Martial, Weapon
Standard Action   Melee weapon
Target: One creature
Attack: Strength vs. AC
Hit: 2[W] + Strength modifier damage. You or one ally within 5 squares makes a saving throw.
Miss: You or one ally makes a saving throw against one effect that the target caused and that a save can end.

Villain's Nightmare — Warlord Attack 5

You use weapon thrusts, lunges, and parries to hedge in your adversary, preventing him from moving away from you.

Daily ✦ Martial, Weapon
Standard Action   Melee weapon
Target: One creature
Attack: Strength vs. Reflex
Hit: 3[W] + Strength modifier damage.
Effect: Until the end of the encounter, when you are adjacent to the target and it walks or runs, you can cancel that movement as an immediate interrupt.

LEVEL 6 UTILITY EXPLOITS

Guide the Charge — Warlord Utility 6

You direct your ally's charge, allowing him to strike a deadlier blow and push his foe backward.

Encounter ✦ Martial
Immediate Interrupt   Ranged 10
Trigger: An ally charges
Effect: If the ally hits, he or she adds your Intelligence modifier to the damage roll and pushes the attack's target 2 squares. The ally can shift 2 squares to remain adjacent to the target.

Inspiring Reaction — Warlord Utility 6

As soon as an ally is wounded, you spring forward with help and healing.

Encounter ✦ Healing, Martial
Immediate Reaction   Melee touch
Trigger: You or an adjacent ally takes damage
Effect: You or the ally can spend a healing surge and regain additional hit points equal to your Charisma modifier.

Quick Step — Warlord Utility 6

You spur an ally to move faster.

Daily ✦ Martial
Minor Action   Ranged 10
Target: One ally
Effect: Increase the ally's speed by 2 until the end of the encounter.

Stand Tough — Warlord Utility 6

You fortify your allies with a few words of encouragement.

Daily ✦ Healing, Martial
Minor Action   Close burst 5
Targets: You and each ally in burst
Effect: The targets regain hit points equal to 10 + your Charisma modifier.

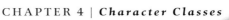

Surprise Attack · Warlord Attack 7

Despite the chaos of battle, you see a golden opportunity for an ally to make a surprising attack.

Encounter ✦ Martial, Weapon
Standard Action **Melee** weapon
Target: One creature
Attack: Strength vs. AC
Hit: 1[W] + Strength modifier damage. An ally within 5 squares of you makes a basic attack with combat advantage as a free action against a target of his or her choice.
  Tactical Presence: The ally gains a bonus to the attack roll equal to your Intelligence modifier.

Surround Foe · Warlord Attack 7

You contain your foe, enabling one of your allies to move around behind him.

Encounter ✦ Martial, Weapon
Standard Action **Melee** weapon
Target: One creature
Attack: Strength vs. AC
Hit: 2[W] + Strength modifier damage.
Effect: You slide one willing ally who is adjacent to the target to any other square adjacent to the target. The ally can move through the target's square.

LEVEL 9 DAILY EXPLOITS

Iron Dragon Charge · Warlord Attack 9

Like a rampaging iron dragon, you hurl yourself at your adversary, landing a terrific blow that inspires your allies to charge as well.

Daily ✦ Martial, Weapon
Standard Action **Melee** weapon
Target: One creature
Attack: Strength vs. AC
Special: You must charge as part of this attack.
Hit: 3[W] + Strength modifier damage.
Effect: Until the end of the encounter, as an immediate reaction, an ally of your choice within 5 squares of you can charge a target that you charge.

Knock Them Down · Warlord Attack 9

The rhythm of your enemies hitting the ground is music to your ears.

Daily ✦ Martial, Weapon
Standard Action **Melee** weapon
Target: One creature
Attack: Strength vs. AC
Hit: 3[W] + Strength modifier damage, and the target is knocked prone. Every ally within 10 squares of you can move 3 squares and make a melee basic attack against one target of his or her choice as a free action. These attacks deal no damage but knock a target prone on a hit.
Miss: Half damage, and the target is knocked prone.

LEVEL 7 ENCOUNTER EXPLOITS

Lion's Roar · Warlord Attack 7

With a bloodcurdling roar, you swing your weapon in a wide, sweeping arc that breaks through your enemy's defenses. The blow reinvigorates you or one of your allies in need.

Encounter ✦ Healing, Martial, Weapon
Standard Action **Melee** weapon
Target: One creature
Attack: Strength vs. AC
Hit: 2[W] + Strength modifier damage.
Effect: You or one ally within 5 squares of you can spend a healing surge.
  Inspiring Presence: Your ally (but not you) gains additional hit points equal to your Charisma modifier.

Sunder Armor · Warlord Attack 7

You probe your opponent's defenses and eventually land a blow that creates a momentary chink in his armor.

Encounter ✦ Martial, Weapon
Standard Action **Melee** weapon
Target: One creature
Attack: Strength vs. AC
Hit: 2[W] + Strength modifier damage. Until the end of your next turn, any attack roll against the target can score a critical hit on a roll of 18–20.

White Raven Strike — Warlord Attack 9

You land a punishing blow that ignites the fire within your allies and keeps them alive on the battlefield.

Daily ✦ Martial, Weapon
Standard Action   Melee weapon
Target: One creature
Attack: Strength vs. AC
Hit: 3[W] + Strength modifier damage.
Effect: One or two allies within 10 squares gain 15 temporary hit points. If you dropped the target to 0 hit points or fewer with this attack, add your Charisma modifier to the temporary hit points your allies gain.

Level 10 Utility Exploits

Defensive Rally — Warlord Utility 10

You marshal your comrades and provide instructions to help them prevail.

Daily ✦ Healing, Martial
Standard Action   Close burst 5
Target: Each ally in burst
Effect: Each target can spend a healing surge and make a saving throw against any single effect that a save can end. In addition, all targets gain a +2 power bonus to all defenses until the end of your next turn.

Ease Suffering — Warlord Utility 10

Your nearby presence is enough to ease the suffering of your allies.

Daily ✦ Martial
Minor Action   Personal
Effect: Allies ignore ongoing damage on any turn they start adjacent to you, neither taking ongoing damage nor making saving throws to end it. This effect persists until the end of the encounter or for 5 minutes.

Tactical Shift — Warlord Utility 10

Your mastery of battle tactics and stern commands allow you to move an ally out of harm's way.

Daily ✦ Martial
Immediate Interrupt   Ranged 10
Trigger: A creature hits your ally with a melee or a ranged attack
Effect: The ally can shift a number of squares equal to 1 + your Intelligence modifier.

Level 13 Encounter Exploits

Beat Them into the Ground — Warlord Attack 13

You sweep the legs out from under your adversary and knock him to the ground with a mighty overhead swing. Your allies, inspired by the sight, follow suit.

Encounter ✦ Martial, Weapon
Standard Action   Melee weapon
Target: One creature
Attack: Strength vs. Fortitude
Hit: 2[W] + Strength modifier damage, and the target is knocked prone. Every ally within 5 squares of you makes a basic attack on one target of his or her choice as a free action. These attacks deal no damage but knock a target prone on a hit.
Tactical Presence: Your allies gain a bonus to the attack rolls granted by this power equal to your Intelligence modifier.

Bolstering Blow — Warlord Attack 13

Your attack inspires a nearby ally, keeping her in the fight.

Encounter ✦ Martial, Weapon
Standard Action   Melee weapon
Target: One creature
Attack: Strength vs. AC
Hit: 3[W] + Strength modifier damage, and you grant 10 temporary hit points to an ally within 5 squares of you.
Inspiring Presence: You grant your ally temporary hit points equal to 10 + your Charisma modifier.

Denying Smite — Warlord Attack 13

No matter how he maneuvers, something comes between the villain and his quarry—and that something is you!

Encounter ✦ Martial, Weapon
Standard Action   Melee weapon
Target: One creature
Attack: Strength vs. AC
Hit: 3[W] + Strength modifier damage.
Effect: Choose one ally within 5 squares of you. The target cannot attack that ally with melee attacks or ranged attacks until the end of your next turn.

Fury of the Sirocco — Warlord Attack 13

The sirocco drives the desert sands in a thousand directions. So too does your furious attack scatter your enemies and drive them where you want them to go.

Encounter ✦ Martial, Weapon
Standard Action   Close burst 1
Target: Each enemy in burst you can see
Attack: Strength vs. AC
Hit: 1[W] + Strength modifier damage, and you slide the target 1 square.

Level 15 Daily Exploits

Make Them Bleed — Warlord Attack 15

You bleed your foe with a wicked strike, exposing a fatal flaw in its armor.

Daily ✦ Martial, Weapon
Standard Action
Target: One creature
Attack: Strength vs. AC
Hit: 3[W] + Strength modifier damage, and ongoing 5 damage (save ends).
Effect: Until the end of the encounter, when you or an ally hits the target, that attack also deals ongoing 5 damage (save ends).

Renew the Troops — Warlord Attack 15

Seeing the beast quail before your onslaught gives your allies the courage to fight on.

Daily ✦ Healing, Martial, Weapon
Standard Action   Melee weapon
Target: One creature
Attack: Strength vs. AC
Hit: 3[W] + Strength modifier damage. Each ally who has line of sight to you regains hit points as if he or she had spent a healing surge. Add your Charisma modifier to the hit points regained.
Miss: Each ally who has line of sight to you regains hit points equal to 10 + your Charisma modifier.

Warlord's Gambit
Warlord Attack 15

You provoke your adversary with a bold stroke. Each time he lunges at you, he recklessly sets up your forces for victory.

Daily ✦ Martial, Weapon
Standard Action   **Melee** weapon
Target: One creature
Attack: Strength vs. AC
Hit: 4[W] + Strength modifier damage.
Effect: The target gains a +2 bonus to attack rolls and damage rolls against you until the end of the encounter. When the target attacks you, an ally of your choice within a number of squares equal to your Intelligence modifier can make a basic attack against the target as an immediate interrupt.

LEVEL 16 UTILITY EXPLOITS

Hero's Defiance
Warlord Utility 16

You fight off an adverse affliction or enable an ally to do the same.

Daily ✦ Martial
Standard Action   **Ranged** 10
Target: You or one ally
Effect: The target succeeds on a saving throw.

Warlord's Banner
Warlord Utility 16

You rally your closest troops before sending them into battle.

Encounter ✦ Healing, Martial
Standard Action   **Close** burst 5
Target: Each ally in burst
Effect: Each target can spend a healing surge. Until the end of your next turn, each target gains a +2 power bonus to attack rolls.

White Raven Formation
Warlord Utility 16

You forego attacks and focus on redirecting your allies.

Daily ✦ Martial
Standard Action   **Close** burst 5
Target: Each ally in burst
Effect: Each target can take a move action.

LEVEL 17 ENCOUNTER EXPLOITS

Battle On
Warlord Attack 17

You rally your forces with a battle cry and a calculated blow against the enemy.

Encounter ✦ Martial, Weapon
Standard Action   **Melee** weapon
Target: One creature
Attack: Strength vs. AC
Hit: 3[W] + Strength modifier damage, and every ally within 5 squares of you makes a saving throw.
    Inspiring Presence: Your allies gain a bonus to the saving throw equal to your Charisma modifier.

Hail of Steel
Warlord Attack 17

You level your weapon at your enemy, then pull it back and lunge forward. As your attack strikes true, your allies rain death down upon him.

Encounter ✦ Martial, Weapon
Standard Action   **Melee** weapon
Target: One creature
Attack: Strength vs. AC
Hit: 2[W] + Strength modifier damage, and every ally within 5 squares of you makes a basic attack against the target.

Thunderous Fury
Warlord Attack 17

The ferocity of your blow quiets the storm of battle for a moment.

Encounter ✦ Martial, Weapon
Standard Action   **Melee** weapon
Target: One creature
Attack: Strength vs. AC
Hit: 3[W] + Strength modifier damage, and the target is dazed until the end of your next turn.
    Tactical Presence: Until the end of your next turn, your allies gain a power bonus to attack rolls against the target equal to your Intelligence modifier.

Warlord's Rush
Warlord Attack 17

Like a wild, terrible storm, you hurl yourself at your foe. Your allies are swept along on the force of your wrath.

Encounter ✦ Martial, Weapon
Standard Action   **Melee** weapon
Target: One creature
Attack: Strength vs. AC
Hit: 3[W] + Strength modifier damage. Allies who have line of sight to you can move their speed.
Miss: One ally who has line of sight to you (your choice) can move his or her speed.

LEVEL 19 DAILY EXPLOITS

Break the Tempo
Warlord Attack 19

You dash about while assailing your foe with a multitude of well-aimed blows, throwing it off balance.

Daily ✦ Martial, Weapon
Standard Action   **Melee** weapon
Target: One creature
Attack: Strength vs. AC
Hit: 4[W] + Strength modifier damage.
Effect: If the target attacks before the end of your next turn, you can use an immediate interrupt to move 4 squares and make a melee basic attack against the target. If you deal damage, the target takes a penalty to its attack roll equal to your Intelligence modifier.
Sustain Minor: The effect continues until the end of your next turn.

Victory Surge — Warlord Attack 19

Victory is within your grasp, so with a mighty roar, you push your allies to seize every opportunity and fight like never before.

Daily ✦ Martial, Weapon
Standard Action   **Melee** weapon
Target: One creature
Attack: Strength vs. AC
Hit: 2[W] + Strength modifier damage. Until the start of your next turn, every ally within 10 squares of you can follow up a standard action with a basic attack made as a free action.
Miss: Until the start of your next turn, one ally of your choice within 10 squares of you can follow up a standard action with a basic attack made as a free action.
Sustain Minor: Until the start of your next turn, one ally of your choice within 10 squares of you can follow up a standard action with a basic attack made as a free action.

Windmill of Doom — Warlord Attack 19

You cleverly maneuver your adversary into a perfect flanking position. As you land the deciding blow, your surrounding allies strike hard from all sides.

Daily ✦ Martial, Weapon
Standard Action   **Melee** weapon
Target: One creature
Attack: Strength vs. AC
Hit: 3[W] + Strength modifier damage. Each ally who is adjacent to the target makes a melee basic attack against it as a free action.
Miss: One ally of your choice adjacent to the target makes a melee basic attack against it as a free action.

Level 22 Utility Exploits

Heart of the Titan — Warlord Utility 22

You level your weapon at your enemies and utter a grim threat that leaves them fearing for their lives. With great words, you turn yourself or an ally into a battle-hardened juggernaut.

Daily ✦ Martial
Standard Action   **Ranged** 10
Target: You or one ally
Effect: The target gains temporary hit points equal to his or her healing surge value + your Charisma modifier. Until the target loses as many temporary hit points as he or she gained from this power, the target adds your Charisma modifier to damage rolls and can't be dazed, immobilized, pulled, pushed, restrained, slid, slowed, stunned, or weakened.

Heroic Surge — Warlord Utility 22

The sight of one of your allies taking a hit fills you with resolve and compassion, and you turn that dark moment into a heroic surge toward victory.

Daily ✦ Healing, Martial
Immediate Reaction   **Close** burst 5
Trigger: You or an ally within 5 squares of you takes damage
Effect: You and each ally in the burst can spend a healing surge. Add your Charisma modifier to the hit points regained.

Own the Battlefield — Warlord Utility 22

Like a puppet master, you position your enemies exactly where you want them.

Daily ✦ Martial
Standard Action   **Close** burst 10
Target: Each enemy in burst you can see
Effect: You slide each target a number of squares equal to your Intelligence modifier.

Level 23 Encounter Exploits

Great Dragon War Cry — Warlord Attack 23

You unleash a terrifying battle cry as you attack. The veins of your foes run cold whenever your allies strike.

Encounter ✦ Fear, Martial, Weapon
Standard Action   **Melee** weapon
Target: One creature
Attack: Strength vs. AC
Hit: 3[W] + Strength modifier damage, and the target is weakened until the end of your next turn.
  Inspiring Presence: Until the end of the encounter, your allies gain a power bonus to their attack rolls against weakened enemies equal to your Charisma modifier.

Pillar to Post — Warlord Attack 23

You strike your foe and send him careening into a waiting ally, who sends the foe stumbling back toward you.

Encounter ✦ Martial, Weapon
Standard Action   **Melee** weapon
Target: One creature flanked by you and an ally
Attack: Strength vs. AC
Hit: 3[W] + Strength modifier damage, and the ally can make a melee basic attack against the target as a free action. If the ally's attack hits, you make a secondary attack against the target.
  Secondary Attack: Strength vs. AC
  Hit: 1[W] + Strength modifier damage.

Rabbits and Wolves — Warlord Attack 23

Between swings and parries, you direct beleaguered allies to safety while calling in fresh reinforcements.

Encounter ✦ Martial, Weapon
Standard Action   **Melee** weapon
Target: One creature
Attack: Strength vs. AC
Hit: 4[W] + Strength modifier damage. Any two allies of your choice within 10 squares of you can shift their speed.

Sudden Assault — Warlord Attack 23

Your slashing blow spurs an ally into action.

Encounter ✦ Martial, Weapon
Standard Action   **Melee** weapon
Target: One creature
Attack: Strength vs. AC
Hit: 1[W] + Strength modifier damage, and an ally of your choice within 5 squares of you takes a standard action.
  Tactical Presence: Your ally gains a power bonus to attack rolls against targets adjacent to you equal to your Intelligence modifier. This bonus applies only to attack rolls made using the standard action granted by this power.

LEVEL 25 DAILY EXPLOITS

Relentless Assault   Warlord Attack 25

You bring your weapon down hard, and your enemy is engulfed by a cloud of crimson mist. A fierce battle cry throws your allies into a blood-stoked frenzy.

Daily ✦ Martial, Weapon
Standard Action   Melee weapon
Target: One creature
Attack: Strength vs. AC
Hit: 5[W] + Strength modifier damage.
Effect: Until the end of the encounter, when you or an ally scores a critical hit, you and each ally can make a basic attack as a free action.

Stir the Hornet's Nest   Warlord Attack 25

"Have at thee, villain! Feel the sting of a thousand angry hornets."

Daily ✦ Martial, Weapon
Standard Action   Ranged weapon
Requirement: You must be weilding a heavy thrown weapon.
Target: One creature
Attack: Strength vs. AC
Hit: 6[W] + Strength modifier damage. Until the end of the encounter, your allies add your Intelligence modifier to attack rolls and damage rolls when making ranged attacks against the target.
Miss: Each ally makes a ranged basic attack against the target as a free action, gaining a bonus to the attack roll and the damage roll equal to your Intelligence modifier.

White Raven's Call   Warlord Attack 25

You unleash a brutal deluge of attacks upon your hated foe, calling out to your allies to stand their ground and shake off their weariness.

Daily ✦ Martial, Weapon
Standard Action   Melee weapon
Target: One creature
Attack: Strength vs. AC
Hit: 6[W] + Strength modifier damage, and you and all of your allies within 10 squares of you make saving throws against any single effect that a save can end.
Miss: Each of your allies within 10 squares of you makes a saving throw against any effect that the target caused and that a save can end.

LEVEL 27 ENCOUNTER EXPLOITS

Chimera Battlestrike   Warlord Attack 27

With a roaring battle cry, you strike nearby foes and thrust them back, changing the complexion of the battlefield.

Encounter ✦ Martial, Weapon
Minor Action   Close burst 1
Target: Each enemy in burst you can see
Attack: Strength vs. Reflex
Hit: 3[W] + Strength modifier damage, and you slide the target 2 squares.
    Tactical Presence: You slide the target a number of squares equal to 1 + your Intelligence modifier.

Devastating Charge   Warlord Attack 27

The fury of your assault is as shocking as the gaping wound you open in your enemy.

Encounter ✦ Martial, Weapon
Standard Action   Melee weapon
Target: One creature
Attack: Strength vs. AC
Special: You must charge as part of this attack.
Hit: 4[W] + Strength modifier damage. Until the end of your next turn, any ally who has line of sight to you gains a bonus to damage rolls equal to your Charisma modifier when he or she makes a melee basic attack as part of a charge.

Incite Heroism   Warlord Attack 27

You deliver a massive blow to your enemy and usher your allies ever closer toward victory. Your words and deeds raise their spirits and inspire them to new acts of heroism.

Encounter ✦ Martial, Weapon
Standard Action   Melee weapon
Target: One creature
Attack: Strength vs. AC
Hit: 4[W] + Strength modifier damage, and each ally in your line of sight gains 20 temporary hit points.
    Inspiring Presence: You grant each ally additional temporary hit points equal to your Charisma modifier.

Warlord's Doom   Warlord Attack 27

You break your adversary's resolve with a ferocious strike.

Encounter ✦ Martial, Weapon
Standard Action   Melee weapon
Target: One creature
Attack: Strength vs. AC
Hit: 4[W] + Strength modifier damage, and until the end of your next turn, you can choose an effect currently on the target. The target fails its next saving throw against that effect.

LEVEL 29 DAILY EXPLOITS

Defy Death   Warlord Attack 29

You leap to your ally's side and spare him from the jaws of death.

Daily ✦ Healing, Martial, Weapon
Immediate Interrupt   Melee weapon
Trigger: A creature attacks your ally
Target: The attacking creature
Special: As part of this action, you can move twice your speed to reach the target without provoking opportunity attacks.
Attack: Strength vs. AC
Hit: 7[W] + Strength modifier damage, and the target's attack misses.
Miss: Half damage, and the target's attack deals half damage if it hits.
Effect: As an immediate reaction, the attacked ally can spend a healing surge.

Stand Invincible — Warlord Attack 29

You throw everything you have at the enemy and become a beacon of strength and perseverance for your allies.

Daily ✦ Martial, Weapon
Standard Action   **Melee** weapon
Target: One creature
Attack: Strength vs. AC
Hit: 7[W] + Strength modifier damage.
Effect: You and each ally within 5 squares of you gain a +4 power bonus to all defenses and resist 5 to all damage until the end of your next turn.
Sustain Minor: The effect continues.

PARAGON PATHS

BATTLE CAPTAIN

"Follow me, and victory will be ours!"

Prerequisite: Warlord class

You become the epitome of the combat leader in action, an inspiring battle captain who easily flows from issuing commands to engaging the enemy and back again as conditions on the battlefield warrant. As a leader who fights as well as he leads, you have earned the loyalty and respect of your allies, and together you have been forged into a cohesive combat team.

BATTLE CAPTAIN PATH FEATURES

Battle Action (11th level): When you spend an action point to take an extra action, your allies gain a +1 bonus to attack rolls until the start of your next turn. Your allies need to be able to see and hear you to gain this bonus.

Cry Havoc (11th level): On the first round of combat (or both the first and the surprise round if your allies gain a surprise round), allies who start their turn within 10 squares of you gain a +2 bonus to attack rolls.

Battle Inspiration (16th level): When you use your *inspiring word* power, allies you heal gain a +1 power bonus to attack rolls and a +1 power bonus to speed until the end of your next turn. If you selected the Tactical Presence class feature, the ally gains bonuses equal to your Intelligence modifier instead.

BATTLE CAPTAIN EXPLOITS

Force Retreat — Battle Captain Attack 11

You hurl yourself into your adversary, knocking him back into his allies and causing them all to stumble away from you.

Encounter ✦ Martial, Weapon
Standard Action   **Melee** weapon
Primary Target: One creature
Attack: Strength vs. Reflex
Hit: 1[W] damage, and you push the target a number of squares equal to your Intelligence modifier. Make a secondary attack.
Secondary Target: Each enemy that was adjacent to the primary target, is its size or smaller, and is within your melee reach
Secondary Attack: Strength vs. Fortitude
Hit: 2d6 + Strength modifier damage, and you push the secondary target 1 square.

ZOLTAN BOROS & GABOR SZIKSZAI

Bolt of Genius — Battle Captain Utility 12

You share a moment of brilliant clarity with a close comrade.

Daily ✦ Martial
Standard Action — **Ranged** 5
Target: One ally
Effect: The target regains an encounter power he or she has already used.

Cunning Flurry — Battle Captain Attack 20

You whirl around like a cyclone of steel terror, slashing at foes. With each landed blow, you knock your enemy prone or send it stumbling backward.

Daily ✦ Martial, Weapon
Standard Action — **Close** burst 1
Target: Each enemy in burst you can see
Attack: Strength vs. AC, one attack per target
Hit: 2[W] + Strength modifier damage, and you push the target 1 square or knock the target prone.
Miss: Half damage, no push, and the target is not knocked prone.

COMBAT VETERAN

"Stick with me. I'll keep us alive, and I may even figure out a way to win this fight while we're at it."

Prerequisite: Warlord class

You are a veteran of many battles, and it shows. You have learned tricks and techniques that can only be picked up on the field of battle, and you have learned how to not only survive—you have learned how to win! Moreover, your combat skills and innate leadership translate to those who fight beside you. You make those around you better, and your allies are happy to have you fighting at their side.

COMBAT VETERAN PATH FEATURES

Combat Veteran's Action (11th level): When you spend an action point to take an extra action, one of your allies within 10 squares of you can take a move action as a free action.

Tough as Nails (11th level): You gain an extra healing surge. When you spend a healing surge, add your Constitution modifier to the hit points you regain.

Battle Healer (16th level): When you use your *inspiring word* power, the target can also make a saving throw.

COMBAT VETERAN EXPLOITS

Skirmish Ploy — Combat Veteran Attack 11

You score a glancing blow, which you turn into an opportunity to thrust your enemy out of position and into the path of a nearby ally.

Encounter ✦ Martial, Weapon
Standard Action — **Melee** weapon
Target: One creature
Attack: Strength vs. Reflex
Hit: 1[W] + Strength modifier damage, and the target is dazed until the end of your next turn. In addition, you slide the target 2 squares, and an ally within 2 squares of you shifts 1 square nearer to the target.

Miss Me Once — Combat Veteran Utility 12

You dodge an enemy's attack, then look at him as though he were already dead.

Encounter ✦ Martial
Immediate Interrupt — **Ranged** 10
Trigger: An enemy within range and in your line of sight misses you with an attack
Effect: The enemy grants combat advantage to each ally who has line of sight to it until the start of its next turn.

Superior Tactics — Combat Veteran Attack 20

Your experience on the battlefield allows you to deal terrible wounds to your enemy and also brings out the best in your allies.

Daily ✦ Martial, Weapon
Standard Action — **Melee** weapon
Target: One creature
Attack: Strength vs. AC
Hit: 3[W] + Strength modifier damage, and you grant an action point to an ally within 10 squares of you. The action point disappears if it's not used by the end of the encounter.
Miss: An ally within 10 squares of you makes a basic attack as a free action.

KNIGHT COMMANDER

"Chivalry and honor are my sword and shield, and strategy and tactics my armor."

Prerequisite: Warlord class, proficiency with heavy armor

Your path as a warlord has led you to take on the role of a knight commander, an armored paragon of leadership and combat who has no fear of leading from the front—and who has the requisite skills and abilities to handle that role. You inspire by example, you press every attack, and you rally your allies with powerful attacks and amazing tactics.

KNIGHT COMMANDER PATH FEATURES

Honor and Glory (11th level): Allies gain a +2 bonus to attack rolls whenever they are adjacent to you.

Knight Commander's Action (11th level): When you spend an action point to take an extra action, your allies gain a +1 bonus to all defenses until the start of your next turn. Your allies need to be able to see and hear you to gain this bonus.

Press of Arms (16th level): You and allies within 3 squares of you gain a bonus to damage rolls when making opportunity attacks equal to your Charisma modifier.

KNIGHT COMMANDER EXPLOITS

Slash and Press — Knight Commander Attack 11

You slash your enemy across the midsection and push it back. You then turn with a snarl and beat back all other nearby foes.

Encounter ✦ Martial, Weapon
Standard Action — Melee weapon
Target: One creature
Attack: Strength vs. AC
Hit: 3[W] + Strength modifier damage.
Effect: After making the attack, you push all adjacent enemies 1 square.

Break Their Nerve — Knight Commander Utility 12

You make your enemy second-guess its decision to face you and your comrades in battle.

Encounter ✦ Martial
Minor Action — Melee 1
Target: One enemy
Effect: The target is marked until the end of your next turn.

Control the Field — Knight Commander Attack 20

You dominate the field of battle to the extent that enemies find your mere presence overwhelming.

Daily ✦ Martial, Weapon
Standard Action — Melee weapon
Target: One creature
Attack: Strength vs. AC
Hit: 3[W] + Strength modifier damage.
Effect: All of your enemies within 5 squares of you are marked until the end of your next turn. All enemies take ongoing damage equal to your Charisma modifier while the mark lasts.

SWORD MARSHAL

"This weapon is my symbol of office, and it shines over the field of battle as I wield it against our enemies."

Prerequisite: Warlord class, proficiency with heavy blade

You have extensively studied the use of light blades and heavy blades, and your weapon of choice has become a symbol of your power and leadership. You never enter a battle without your blade in hand, and your allies know to look for the gleaming weapon when they need help or inspiration.

SWORD MARSHAL PATH FEATURES

Disciplined Blade (11th level): When you miss with a melee attack when using a heavy blade, you gain a +2 bonus to your next attack roll against the same enemy.

Sword Marshal's Action (11th level): You can spend an action point to regain one warlord encounter power you have already used, instead of taking an extra action.

Skewer the Weak (16th level): When you score a critical hit using a heavy blade, you and all your allies gain combat advantage against the enemy you struck until the end of your next turn.

SWORD MARSHAL EXPLOITS

Blade Flurry — Sword Marshal Attack 11

You slash a foe, swoop to one side, and swing your blade against the same foe or another enemy within your reach.

Encounter ✦ Martial, Weapon
Standard Action — Melee weapon
Requirement: You must be wielding a heavy blade.
Primary Target: One creature
Attack: Strength vs. AC
Hit: 2[W] + Strength modifier damage, and you can shift 1 square. Make a secondary attack.
Secondary Target: One creature
Secondary Attack: Strength vs. AC
Hit: 1[W] + Strength modifier damage.

Sword Marshal's Boon — Sword Marshal Utility 12

Warlord, help thyself!

Daily ✦ Martial
Free Action — Personal
Trigger: You use a power that targets your allies but not you
Effect: You are also targeted by the power.

Diamond Blade of Victory — Sword Marshal Attack 20

The presence of stalwart allies adds to the fury of your strike, which slices through the armored shell of your enemy and cuts deep into bone.

Daily ✦ Martial, Weapon
Standard Action — Melee weapon
Requirement: You must be wielding a heavy blade.
Target: One creature
Attack: Strength vs. AC
Hit: 2[W] + Strength modifier damage. For each ally within 2 squares of you, deal an extra 1[W] damage (maximum 6[W] + Strength modifier damage).
Miss: Half damage.

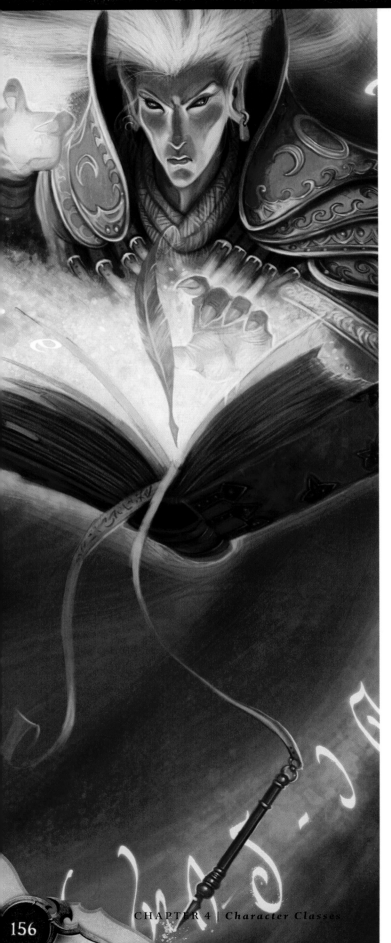

"I am the fire that burns, the choking fog, the storm that rains devastation on our foes."

CLASS TRAITS

Role: Controller. You exert control through magical effects that cover large areas—sometimes hindering foes, sometimes consuming them with fire.

Power Source: Arcane. You channel arcane forces through extensive study, hidden knowledge, and intricate preparation. To you, magic is an art form, an expressive and powerful method by which you seek to control the world around you.

Key Abilities: Intelligence, Wisdom, Dexterity

Armor Proficiencies: Cloth
Weapon Proficiencies: Dagger, quarterstaff
Implements: Orbs, staffs, wands
Bonus to Defense: +2 Will

Hit Points at 1st Level: 10 + Constitution score
Hit Points per Level Gained: 4
Healing Surges per Day: 6 + Constitution modifier

Trained Skills: Arcana. From the class skills list below, choose three more trained skills at 1st level.
Class Skills: Arcana (Int), Diplomacy (Cha), Dungeoneering (Wis), History (Int), Insight (Wis), Nature (Int), Religion (Int)

Build Options: Control wizard, war wizard
Class Features: Arcane Implement Mastery, cantrips, Ritual Casting, spellbook

Wizards are scions of arcane magic. Wizards tap the true power that permeates the cosmos, research esoteric rituals that can alter time and space, and hurl balls of fire that incinerate massed foes. Wizards wield spells the way warriors brandish swords.

Magic lured you into its grasp, and now you seek to master it in turn. You could be a bespectacled sage searching for dusty tomes in forgotten sepulchers, a scarred war mage plying foes with *fireballs* and foul language in equal measure, a disgruntled apprentice who absconded with your master's spellbooks, an eladrin upholding the magical tradition of your race, or even a power-hungry student of magic who might do anything to learn a new spell.

A cloak of spells enfolds you, ancient rituals bolster your senses, and runed implements of your craft hang from your belt. Effervescing arcane lore pulses through your consciousness, a constant pressure craving release. When will you know enough magic to storm the ramparts of reality itself?

CREATING A WIZARD

Wizards have a range of powers, but tend to specialize in one of two character builds: control wizard or war wizard. Every wizard relies on Intelligence for attack powers, and secondarily on Wisdom, Dexterity, and sometimes Constitution.

CONTROL WIZARD

Your favorite powers restrict your enemies in various ways—crushing them in the coils of a lightning serpent, trapping them in a cloud of noxious vapor, or encasing them in ice. Intelligence drives your attack powers, so make it your highest ability score. Wisdom can help you maintain control over your enemies if you choose the orb of imposition form of Implement Mastery, so it should be your second-best score. Make Dexterity your third best score. Putting a good score in Constitution can help you stay alive by increasing your hit points and healing surges, as well as contributing to your Fortitude defense. If you choose the staff of defense form of Implement Mastery, your Constitution can also help your other defenses. Select powers that help you control the battlefield and make the best use of your high Wisdom score.

Suggested Feat: Improved Initiative (Human feat: Human Perseverance)

Suggested Skills: Arcana, Diplomacy, Insight, Nature

Suggested At-Will Powers: *cloud of daggers, thunderwave*

Suggested Encounter Power: *icy terrain*

Suggested Daily Power: *sleep*

WAR WIZARD

Your delight is in powers that deal damage—lots of damage, to many foes at a time. Enormous bursts of fire, searing bolts of lightning, and waves of caustic acid are your weapons. Intelligence is your most important ability score. Dexterity should be your second-best score, and it is important if you choose the wand of accuracy form of Implement Mastery. Make Wisdom your third-best score. You might instead choose the staff of defense form of Implement Mastery, which lets your Constitution aid your defenses against some attacks. Even if you don't, Constitution increases your hit points, healing surges, and Fortitude defense. Select powers that deal lots of damage and that make the best use of your high Dexterity score.

Suggested Feat: Expanded Spellbook (Human feat: Action Surge)

Suggested Skills: Arcana, Dungeoneering, History, Religion

Suggested At-Will Powers: *magic missile, scorching burst*

Suggested Encounter Power: *burning hands*

Suggested Daily Power: *acid arrow*

IMPLEMENTS

Wizards make use of orbs, staffs, and wands to help channel and direct their arcane powers. Every wizard has mastery of one type of implement (see "Class Features"). Without an implement, a wizard can still use his or her powers. A wizard wielding a magic orb, staff, or wand can add its enhancement bonus to the attack rolls and the damage rolls of wizard powers, as well as wizard paragon path powers, that have the implement keyword.

WIZARD CLASS FEATURES

You have the following class features.

ARCANE IMPLEMENT MASTERY

You specialize in the use of one kind of implement to gain additional abilities when you wield it. Choose one of the following forms of implement mastery.

Orb of Imposition: Once per encounter as a free action, you can use your orb to gain one of the following two effects.

You can designate one creature you have cast a wizard spell upon that has an effect that lasts until the subject succeeds on a saving throw. That creature takes a penalty to its saving throws against that effect equal to your Wisdom modifier.

Alternatively, you can choose to extend the duration of an effect created by a wizard at-will spell (such as *cloud of daggers* or *ray of frost*) that would otherwise end at the end of your current turn. The effect instead ends at the end of your next turn.

You must wield an orb to use this ability. Control wizards select this form of mastery because it helps extend the duration of their control effects.

Staff of Defense: A staff of defense grants you a +1 bonus to AC. In addition, once per encounter as an immediate interrupt, you gain a bonus to defense against one attack equal to your Constitution modifier. You can declare the bonus after the Dungeon Master has already told you the damage total. You must wield your staff to benefit from these

---

WIZARD OVERVIEW

Characteristics: Your powers are all about affecting multiple targets at the same time—sometimes two or three foes, sometimes everyone in a room. In addition, you are the master of utility spells that let you avoid or overcome many obstacles, from flying across chasms to halting the flow of time.

Religion: Wizards favor deities of magic, art, knowledge, and secrets, such as Corellon, Ioun, and Vecna.

Races: Eladrin, humans, and half-elves esteem and excel at the practice of arcane magic.

features. This form of mastery is useful for all wizards, particularly if you dabble in both control and damage-dealing spells.

Wand of Accuracy: Once per encounter as a free action, you gain a bonus to a single attack roll equal to your Dexterity modifier. You must wield your wand to benefit from this feature. This form of mastery is good for war wizards because it helps increase their accuracy with damaging powers.

CANTRIPS

Cantrips are minor spells you gain at 1st level. You can use the *ghost sound, light, mage hand,* and *prestidigitation* cantrips as at-will powers.

RITUAL CASTING

You gain the Ritual Caster feat (page 200) as a bonus feat, allowing you to use magical rituals (see Chapter 10).

SPELLBOOK

You possess a spellbook, a book full of mystic lore in which you store your rituals and your daily and utility spells.

Rituals: Your book contains three 1st-level rituals of your choice that you have mastered.

At 5th level, and again at 11th, 15th, 21st, and 25th level, you master two more rituals of your choice and add them to your spellbook. Any ritual you add must be your level or lower.

Daily and Utility Spells: Your spellbook also holds your daily and utility spells. You begin knowing two daily spells, one of which you can use on any given day. Each time you gain a level that lets you select a daily spell or a utility spell, choose two different daily spells or utility spells of that level to add to your book. After an extended rest, you can prepare a number of daily and utility spells according to what you can cast per day for your level. You can't prepare the same spell twice.

If you replace a spell because of gaining a level or through retraining, the previous spell vanishes from your spellbook and is replaced by the new spell.

WIZARDS AND RITUALS

A wizard's spells are potent in combat and useful in a variety of challenge encounters and other situations, but the wizard is also the undisputed master of magical rituals.

As you gain levels, you automatically gain access to new rituals, but you can also buy new rituals or acquire them in the course of your adventures. Higher-level rituals let you seal or open doors, view places or people from a distance, or open portals to other places.

Capacity: A typical spellbook has 128 pages. Each spell takes up 1 page. A ritual takes up a number of pages equal to its level.

WIZARD POWERS

Your arcane powers are called spells, and in the minds of most people in the world, they define what magic is.

CLASS FEATURES

Ghost Sound	Wizard Cantrip

With a wink, you create an illusory sound that emanates from somewhere close by.

At-Will ✦ Arcane, Illusion
Standard Action   **Ranged** 10
Target: One object or unoccupied square
Effect: You cause a sound as quiet as a whisper or as loud as a yelling or fighting creature to emanate from the target. You can produce nonvocal sounds such as the ringing of a sword blow, jingling armor, or scraping stone. If you whisper, you can whisper quietly enough that only creatures adjacent to the target can hear your words.

Light	Wizard Cantrip

With a wave of your hand, you cause a bright light to appear on the tip of your staff, upon some other object, or in a nearby space.

At-Will ✦ Arcane
Minor Action   **Ranged** 5
Target: One object or unoccupied square
Effect: You cause the target to shed bright light. The light fills the target's square and all squares within 4 squares of it. The light lasts for 5 minutes. Putting out the light is a free action.
Special: You can have only one *light* cantrip active at a time. If you create a new light, your previously cast light winks out.

Mage Hand	Wizard Cantrip

You gesture toward an object nearby, and a spectral floating hand lifts the object into the air and moves it where you wish.

At-Will ✦ Arcane, Conjuration
Minor Action   **Ranged** 5
Effect: You conjure a spectral, floating hand in an unoccupied square within range. The hand picks up, moves, or manipulates an adjacent object weighing 20 pounds or less and carries it up to 5 squares. If you are holding the object when you use this power, the hand can move the object into a pack, a pouch, a sheath, or a similar container and simultaneously move any one object carried or worn anywhere on your body into your hand.

As a move action, you can move the hand up to 5 squares. As a free action, you can cause the hand to drop an object it is holding, and as a minor action, you can cause the hand to pick up or manipulate a different object.
Sustain Minor: You can sustain the hand indefinitely.
Special: You can create only one hand at a time.

Prestidigitation · Wizard Cantrip

You perform an amusing magical trick, such as creating a dancing wisp of light, freshening a wilting flower, making a coin invisible, or warming a cold drink.

At-Will ✦ Arcane
Standard Action   **Ranged** 2
Effect: Use this cantrip to accomplish one of the effects given below.

- ✦ Move up to 1 pound of material.
- ✦ Create a harmless sensory effect, such as a shower of sparks, a puff of wind, faint music, or a strong odor.
- ✦ Color, clean, or soil items in 1 cubic foot for up to 1 hour.
- ✦ Instantly light (or snuff out) a candle, a torch, or a small campfire.
- ✦ Chill, warm, or flavor up to 1 pound of nonliving material for up to 1 hour.
- ✦ Make a small mark or symbol appear on a surface for up to 1 hour.
- ✦ Produce out of nothingness a small item or image that exists until the end of your next turn.
- ✦ Make a small, handheld item invisible until the end of your next turn.

Nothing you create with this cantrip can deal damage, serve as a weapon or a tool, or hinder another creature's actions. This cantrip cannot duplicate the effect of any other power.
Special: You can have as many as three prestidigitation effects active at one time.

LEVEL 1 AT-WILL SPELLS

Cloud of Daggers · Wizard Attack 1

You create a small cloud of whirling daggers of force that relentlessly attack creatures in the area.

At-Will ✦ Arcane, Force, Implement
Standard Action   **Area** 1 square within 10 squares
Target: Each creature in square
Attack: Intelligence vs. Reflex
Hit: 1d6 + Intelligence modifier force damage.
Increase damage to 2d6 + Intelligence modifier at 21st level.
Effect: The power's area is filled with sharp daggers of force. Any creature that enters the area or starts its turn there takes force damage equal to your Wisdom modifier (minimum 1). The cloud remains in place until the end of your next turn. You can dispel it earlier as a minor action.

Magic Missile · Wizard Attack 1

You launch a silvery bolt of force at an enemy.

At-Will ✦ Arcane, Force, Implement
Standard Action   **Ranged** 20
Target: One creature
Attack: Intelligence vs. Reflex
Hit: 2d4 + Intelligence modifier force damage.
Increase damage to 4d4 + Intelligence modifier at 21st level.
Special: This power counts as a ranged basic attack. When a power allows you to make a ranged basic attack, you can use this power.

Ray of Frost · Wizard Attack 1

A blisteringly cold ray of white frost streaks to your target.

At-Will ✦ Arcane, Cold, Implement
Standard Action   **Ranged** 10
Target: One creature
Attack: Intelligence vs. Fortitude
Hit: 1d6 + Intelligence modifier cold damage, and the target is slowed until the end of your next turn.
Increase damage to 2d6 + Intelligence modifier at 21st level.

Scorching Burst · Wizard Attack 1

A vertical column of golden flames burns all within.

At-Will ✦ Arcane, Fire, Implement
Standard Action   **Area** burst 1 within 10 squares
Target: Each creature in burst
Attack: Intelligence vs. Reflex
Hit: 1d6 + Intelligence modifier fire damage.
Increase damage to 2d6 + Intelligence modifier at 21st level.

Thunderwave · Wizard Attack 1

You create a whip-crack of sonic power that lashes up from the ground.

At-Will ✦ Arcane, Implement, Thunder
Standard Action   **Close** blast 3
Target: Each creature in blast
Attack: Intelligence vs. Fortitude
Hit: 1d6 + Intelligence modifier thunder damage, and you push the target a number of squares equal to your Wisdom modifier.
Increase damage to 2d6 + Intelligence modifier at 21st level.

LEVEL 1 ENCOUNTER SPELLS

Burning Hands · Wizard Attack 1

A fierce burst of flame erupts from your hands and scorches nearby foes.

Encounter ✦ Arcane, Fire, Implement
Standard Action   **Close** blast 5
Target: Each creature in blast
Attack: Intelligence vs. Reflex
Hit: 2d6 + Intelligence modifier fire damage.

Chill Strike · Wizard Attack 1

You create a bolt of frigid purple energy around your hand and send it hurtling toward your foe.

Encounter ✦ Arcane, Cold, Implement
Standard Action   **Ranged** 10
Target: One creature
Attack: Intelligence vs. Fortitude
Hit: 2d8 + Intelligence modifier cold damage, and the target is dazed until the end of your next turn.

Force Orb — Wizard Attack 1

You hurl an orb of magical force at an enemy. It bursts against the target and throws off razor-sharp shards of force that cut nearby enemies to ribbons.

Encounter ✦ Arcane, Force, Implement
Standard Action   **Ranged** 20
Primary Target: One creature or object
Attack: Intelligence vs. Reflex
Hit: 2d8 + Intelligence modifier force damage. Make a secondary attack.
  Secondary Target: Each enemy adjacent to the primary target
  Secondary Attack: Intelligence vs. Reflex
  Hit: 1d10 + Intelligence modifier force damage.

Icy Terrain — Wizard Attack 1

With frosty breath, you utter a single arcane word that creates a treacherous patch of ice on the ground, hampering your foes.

Encounter ✦ Arcane, Cold, Implement
Standard Action   **Area** burst 1 within 10 squares
Target: Each creature in burst
Attack: Intelligence vs. Reflex
Hit: 1d6 + Intelligence modifier cold damage, and the target is knocked prone.
Effect: The power's area is difficult terrain until the end of your next turn. You can end this effect as a minor action.

Ray of Enfeeblement — Wizard Attack 1

You point three fingers at your foe, curling them like talons. Weird green mist streams from your enemy's flesh, carrying away its strength.

Encounter ✦ Arcane, Implement, Necrotic
Standard Action   **Ranged** 10
Target: One creature
Attack: Intelligence vs. Fortitude
Hit: 1d10 + Intelligence modifier necrotic damage, and the target is weakened until the end of your next turn.

LEVEL 1 DAILY SPELLS

Acid Arrow — Wizard Attack 1

A shimmering arrow of green, glowing liquid streaks to your target and bursts in a spray of sizzling acid.

Daily ✦ Acid, Arcane, Implement
Standard Action   **Ranged** 20
Primary Target: One creature
Attack: Intelligence vs. Reflex
Hit: 2d8 + Intelligence modifier acid damage, and ongoing 5 acid damage (save ends). Make a secondary attack.
  Secondary Target: Each creature adjacent to the primary target
  Secondary Attack: Intelligence vs. Reflex
  Hit: 1d8 + Intelligence modifier acid damage, and ongoing 5 acid damage (save ends).
Miss: Half damage, and ongoing 2 acid damage to primary target (save ends), and no secondary attack.

Flaming Sphere — Wizard Attack 1

You conjure a rolling ball of fire and control where it goes.

Daily ✦ Arcane, Conjuration, Fire, Implement
Standard Action   **Ranged** 10
Target: One creature adjacent to the flaming sphere
Attack: Intelligence vs. Reflex
Hit: 2d6 + Intelligence modifier fire damage.
Effect: You conjure a Medium flaming sphere in an unoccupied square within range, and the sphere attacks an adjacent creature. Any creature that starts its turn next to the flaming sphere takes 1d4 + Intelligence modifier fire damage. As a move action, you can move the sphere up to 6 squares.
Sustain Minor: You can sustain this power until the end of the encounter. As a standard action, you can make another attack with the sphere.

Freezing Cloud — Wizard Attack 1

A pellet shoots from your hand and explodes into a cloud of icy mist at the point of impact.

Daily ✦ Arcane, Cold, Implement
Standard Action   **Area** burst 2 within 10 squares
Target: Each creature in burst
Attack: Intelligence vs. Fortitude
Hit: 1d8 + Intelligence modifier cold damage.
Miss: Half damage.
Effect: The cloud lasts until the end of your next turn. Any creature that enters the cloud or starts its turn there is subject to another attack. You can dismiss the cloud as a minor action.

Sleep — Wizard Attack 1

You exert your will against your foes, seeking to overwhelm them with a tide of magical weariness.

Daily ✦ Arcane, Implement, Sleep
Standard Action   **Area** burst 2 within 20 squares
Target: Each creature in burst
Attack: Intelligence vs. Will
Hit: The target is slowed (save ends). If the target fails its first saving throw against this power, the target becomes unconscious (save ends).
Miss: The target is slowed (save ends).

LEVEL 2 UTILITY SPELLS

Expeditious Retreat — Wizard Utility 2

Your form blurs as you hastily withdraw from the battlefield.

Daily ✦ Arcane
Move Action   **Personal**
Effect: Shift up to twice your speed.

Feather Fall — Wizard Utility 2

You or a creature you choose falls gently, like a feather.

Daily ✦ Arcane
Free Action   **Ranged** 10
Trigger: You or one creature in range falls
Effect: You or the creature takes no damage from the fall, regardless of its distance, and does not fall prone at the end of the fall.

Jump | Wizard Utility 2

You or another creature you choose can suddenly leap great distances.

Encounter ✦ Arcane
Move Action   **Ranged** 10
Target: You or one creature
Effect: The target makes an Athletics check to jump with a +10 power bonus, and the target does not have to move to make a running jump.

Shield | Wizard Utility 2

You throw up your hand, and a shield of arcane energy springs into existence, protecting you against imminent attacks.

Encounter ✦ Arcane, Force
Immediate Interrupt   Personal
Trigger: You are hit by an attack
Effect: You gain a +4 power bonus to AC and Reflex defense until the end of your next turn.

LEVEL 3 ENCOUNTER SPELLS

Color Spray | Wizard Attack 3

A brilliant blast of flashing colors springs from your outstretched fingers, knocking nearby enemies senseless.

Encounter ✦ Arcane, Implement, Radiant
Standard Action   Close blast 5
Target: Each creature in blast
Attack: Intelligence vs. Will
Hit: 1d6 + Intelligence modifier radiant damage, and the target is dazed until the end of your next turn.

Fire Shroud | Wizard Attack 3

With a subtle gesture, you wreathe nearby enemies in flames.

Encounter ✦ Arcane, Fire, Implement
Standard Action   Close burst 3
Target: Each enemy in burst
Attack: Intelligence vs. Fortitude
Hit: 1d8 + Intelligence modifier fire damage, and ongoing 5 fire damage (save ends).

Icy Rays | Wizard Attack 3

You fire two bolts of brilliant blue-white energy. A thin path of frost appears on the ground below each one before fading away.

Encounter ✦ Arcane, Cold, Implement
Standard Action   Ranged 10
Targets: One or two creatures
Attack: Intelligence vs. Reflex, one attack per target
Hit: 1d10 + Intelligence modifier cold damage, and the target is immobilized until the end of your next turn.

Shock Sphere | Wizard Attack 3

You hurl a crackling orb of lightning that explodes at a point you designate, engulfing all nearby creatures in its electric embrace.

Encounter ✦ Arcane, Implement, Lightning
Standard Action   Area burst 2 within 10 squares
Target: Each creature in burst
Attack: Intelligence vs. Reflex
Hit: 2d6 + Intelligence modifier lightning damage.

LEVEL 5 DAILY SPELLS

Bigby's Icy Grasp | Wizard Attack 5

You conjure a giant floating hand made of chiseled ice that clutches foes and freezes them.

Daily ✦ Arcane, Cold, Conjuration, Implement
Standard Action   Ranged 20
Effect: You conjure a 5-foot-tall hand of ice in an unoccupied square within range, and the hand attacks. As a move action, you can move the hand up to 6 squares.
Target: One creature adjacent to the hand
Attack: Intelligence vs. Reflex
Hit: 2d8 + Intelligence modifier cold damage, and the hand grabs the target. If the target attempts to escape, the hand uses your Fortitude or Reflex defense.
Sustain Minor: A target grabbed by the hand takes 1d8 + Intelligence modifier cold damage when you sustain this power. As a standard action, you can attack another target with the hand, but it must release a target it has grabbed.

Fireball | Wizard Attack 5

A globe of orange flame coalesces in your hand. You hurl it at your enemies, and it explodes on impact.

Daily ✦ Arcane, Fire, Implement
Standard Action   Area burst 3 within 20 squares
Target: Each creature in burst
Attack: Intelligence vs. Reflex
Hit: 3d6 + Intelligence modifier fire damage.
Miss: Half damage.

Stinking Cloud | Wizard Attack 5

You call forth a thick cloud of bilious yellow vapors. The foul fumes overwhelm any creature within.

Daily ✦ Arcane, Implement, Poison, Zone
Standard Action   Area burst 2 within 20 squares
Target: Each creature in burst
Attack: Intelligence vs. Fortitude
Hit: 1d10 + Intelligence modifier poison damage.
Effect: The burst creates a zone of poisonous vapor that blocks line of sight until the end of your next turn. Creatures that enter the zone or start their turns there take 1d10 + Intelligence modifier poison damage. As a move action, you can move the zone up to 6 squares.
Sustain Minor: The zone persists.

Web | Wizard Attack 5

You call into being a giant web made of thick magical strands that hang in midair, trapping those within it.

Daily ✦ Arcane, Implement, Zone
Standard Action   Area burst 2 within 20 squares
Target: Each creature in burst
Attack: Intelligence vs. Reflex
Hit: The target is immobilized (save ends).
Effect: The burst creates a zone of webs that fills the area until the end of the encounter or for 5 minutes. The zone is considered difficult terrain. Any creature that ends its move in the web is immobilized (save ends).

Level 6 Utility Spells

Dimension Door — Wizard Utility 6

You trace the outline of a doorway in front of you, step through the portal, and reappear somewhere else nearby.

Daily ✦ Arcane, Teleportation
Move Action — **Personal**
Effect: Teleport 10 squares. You can't take other creatures with you.

Disguise Self — Wizard Utility 6

With a snap of your fingers, you suddenly look like someone else.

Daily ✦ Arcane, Illusion
Minor Action — **Personal**
Effect: You make yourself, your clothing, and your equipment look different. You can take on the appearance of any creature of similar build and size, including a specific individual whom you've seen. You gain neither the abilities or mannerisms of the chosen form, nor the tactile or audible properties of your form or gear. For example, if you took on the illusion of a dwarf fighter in plate armor, anyone touching you would realize you weren't wearing plate armor, and you would not clank, creak, or jingle as you walked. The illusion lasts for 1 hour, although you can end it as a minor action. You must keep the same appearance for the entire duration.

  Anyone who attempts to see through your ruse makes an Insight check opposed by your Bluff check, and you gain a +5 power bonus to your check.

Dispel Magic — Wizard Utility 6

You unleash a ray of crackling arcane energy that destroys a magical effect created by an opponent.

Daily ✦ Arcane
Standard Action — **Ranged 10**
Target: One conjuration or zone
Attack: Intelligence vs. the Will defense of the creator of the conjuration or the zone
Hit: The conjuration or the zone is destroyed. All its effects end, including those that normally last until a target saves.

Invisibility — Wizard Utility 6

A creature you choose vanishes from sight.

Daily ✦ Arcane, Illusion
Standard Action — **Ranged 5**
Target: You or one creature
Effect: The target is invisible until the end of your next turn. If the target attacks, the target becomes visible.
Sustain Standard: If the target is within range, you can sustain the effect.

Levitate — Wizard Utility 6

You hold out your hands, and suddenly you feel air beneath your feet.

Daily ✦ Arcane
Move Action — **Personal**
Effect: You can move 4 squares vertically and remain there, hovering above the ground. While aloft, you are unsteady, taking a –2 penalty to AC and Reflex defense. If some effect, such as a pit opening below you, causes you to be more than 4 squares above the ground, you drop down to 4 squares above the ground. You do not take damage from such a fall.
Sustain Move: You can sustain this power until the end of the encounter or for 5 minutes. When you sustain this power, you can move 3 squares up or down or 1 square horizontally. You cannot go higher than 4 squares above the ground. If you don't sustain the power, you descend to the ground without taking falling damage.

Wall of Fog — Wizard Utility 6

You create a billowing wall of gray fog that obscures vision.

Daily ✦ Arcane, Conjuration
Standard Action — **Area wall 8 within 10**
Effect: You conjure a wall that consists of contiguous squares filled with arcane fog. The wall lasts until the end of your next turn. It can be up to 8 squares long and up to 4 squares high. The fog grants concealment to creatures in its space and blocks line of sight.
Sustain Minor: The wall persists.

Level 7 Encounter Spells

Fire Burst — Wizard Attack 7

A fiery red bead streaks from your finger to the spot you indicate, where it bursts into a great ball of magical flame.

Encounter ✦ Arcane, Fire, Implement
Standard Action — **Area burst 2 within 20 squares**
Target: Each creature in burst
Attack: Intelligence vs. Reflex
Hit: 3d6 + Intelligence modifier fire damage.

Lightning Bolt — Wizard Attack 7

From your outstretched hand erupt brilliant strokes of blue-white lightning.

Encounter ✦ Arcane, Implement, Lightning
Standard Action — **Ranged 10**
Primary Target: One creature
Attack: Intelligence vs. Reflex
Hit: 2d6 + Intelligence modifier lightning damage.
Secondary Targets: Two creatures within 10 squares of the primary target
Secondary Attack: Intelligence vs. Reflex
Hit: 1d6 + Intelligence modifier lightning damage.

Spectral Ram — Wizard Attack 7

You seize your foe with unseen magical force and bash him against the ceiling and walls before dropping him to the ground and hurling him back.

Encounter ✦ Arcane, Force, Implement
Standard Action   **Ranged** 10
Target: One creature
Attack: Intelligence vs. Fortitude
Hit: 2d10 + Intelligence modifier force damage, and you push the target 3 squares and it is knocked prone.

Winter's Wrath — Wizard Attack 7

You raise your hand, and an icy blizzard rains down mercilessly upon an area you designate.

Encounter ✦ Arcane, Cold, Implement
Standard Action   **Area** burst 2 within 10 squares
Target: Each creature in burst
Attack: Intelligence vs. Fortitude
Hit: 2d8 + Intelligence modifier cold damage.
Effect: A blizzard erupts in the designated area and continues until the end of your next turn. It grants concealment, and any creature that starts its turn in the storm takes cold damage equal to your Intelligence modifier. You can end this effect as a minor action.

LEVEL 9 DAILY SPELLS

Ice Storm — Wizard Attack 9

A shower of bitterly cold hailstones pummels a wide swath of ground and covers the area in ice.

Daily ✦ Arcane, Cold, Implement, Zone
Standard Action   **Area** burst 3 within 20 squares
Target: Each creature in burst
Attack: Intelligence vs. Fortitude
Hit: 2d8 + Intelligence modifier cold damage, and the target is immobilized (save ends).
Miss: Half damage, and the target is slowed (save ends).
Effect: The burst creates a zone of ice. The zone is difficult terrain until the end of the encounter or for 5 minutes.

Lightning Serpent — Wizard Attack 9

A crackling bolt of lightning springs from your hand and leaps at a foe, taking serpentine form as it strikes.

Daily ✦ Arcane, Implement, Lightning, Poison
Standard Action   **Ranged** 10
Target: One creature
Attack: Intelligence vs. Reflex
Hit: 2d12 + Intelligence modifier lightning damage, and the target takes ongoing 5 poison damage and is slowed (save ends both).
Miss: Half damage, and the target is slowed (save ends).

Mordenkainen's Sword — Wizard Attack 9

You invoke a sword of crackling golden force that slashes and stabs furiously at the creature you indicate.

Daily ✦ Arcane, Conjuration, Force, Implement
Standard Action   **Ranged** 10
Effect: You conjure a sword of force in an unoccupied square within range, and it attacks. As a move action, you can move the sword to a new target within range. The sword lasts until the end of your next turn.
Target: One creature adjacent to the sword
Attack: Intelligence vs. Reflex
Hit: 1d10 + Intelligence modifier force damage.
Sustain Minor: When you sustain the sword, it attacks again.

Wall of Fire — Wizard Attack 9

A blazing wall of flame erupts from the ground at your command.

Daily ✦ Arcane, Conjuration, Fire, Implement
Standard Action   **Area** wall 8 within 10 squares
Effect: You conjure a wall that consists of contiguous squares filled with arcane fire. It can be up to 8 squares long and up to 4 squares high. The wall lasts until the end of your next turn. Any creature that starts its turn adjacent to the wall takes 1d6 + Intelligence modifier fire damage. If a creature moves into the wall's space or starts its turn there, the creature takes 3d6 + Intelligence modifier fire damage. Entering a square occupied by the wall costs 3 extra squares of movement. The wall blocks line of sight.
Sustain Minor: The wall persists.

LEVEL 10 UTILITY SPELLS

Arcane Gate — Wizard Utility 10

You open a dimensional rift connecting two nearby locations.

Daily ✦ Arcane, Teleportation
Minor Action   **Ranged** 20
Target: Two unoccupied squares
Effect: You create a dimensional rift between the two target squares that lasts until the end of your next turn. Any creature that enters one of the target squares can move to the other target square as if it were adjacent to that square. A creature cannot pass through the rift if either square is occupied by another creature.
Sustain Minor: The rift persists.

Blur — Wizard Utility 10

You cloak yourself with a shimmering aura, making your outline almost impossible to discern.

Daily ✦ Arcane, Illusion
Minor Action   **Personal**
Effect: Until the end of the encounter, you gain a +2 power bonus to all defenses, and enemies 5 or more squares away from you cannot see you.

Mirror Image — Wizard Utility 10

Three duplicate images of you appear, imitating your actions perfectly and confusing your enemies.

Daily ✦ Arcane, Illusion
Minor Action — **Personal**
Effect: Three duplicate images of yourself appear in your space, and you gain a +6 power bonus to AC. Each time an attack misses you, one of your duplicate images disappears and the bonus granted by this power decreases by 2. When the bonus reaches 0, all your images are gone and the power ends. Otherwise, the effect lasts for 1 hour.

Resistance — Wizard Utility 10

You make yourself or another creature in range resistant to a particular kind of damage.

Daily ✦ Arcane
Minor Action — **Ranged** 10
Target: You or one creature
Effect: Against a particular damage type chosen by you, the target gains resistance equal to your level + your Intelligence modifier until the end of the encounter or for 5 minutes. Choose the damage type from the following list: acid, cold, fire, force, lightning, necrotic, poison, psychic, radiant, or thunder.

LEVEL 13 ENCOUNTER SPELLS

Frostburn — Wizard Attack 13

You whisper a word of elemental power and hurl a flaming ball of ice. Waves of fire and ice explode outward from the point of impact.

Encounter ✦ Arcane, Cold, Fire, Implement
Standard Action — **Area** burst 2 within 20 squares
Target: Each creature in burst
Attack: Intelligence vs. Fortitude
Hit: 3d6 + Intelligence modifier cold and fire damage.
Effect: This power's area is difficult terrain until the end of your next turn. Any creature that starts its turn in the area takes 5 cold and fire damage. You can dismiss the effect as a minor action.

Mesmeric Hold — Wizard Attack 13

You immobilize your foes by commanding them to remain still.

Encounter ✦ Arcane, Charm, Implement, Psychic
Standard Action — **Ranged** 10
Targets: One, two, or three creatures
Attack: Intelligence vs. Will, one attack per target
Special: If you target only one creature with this power, you gain a +4 power bonus to the attack roll.
Hit: 2d6 + Intelligence modifier psychic damage, and the target is immobilized until the end of your next turn.

Prismatic Burst — Wizard Attack 13

You lob a fist-sized orb of pulsating white light some distance away, blasting creatures in the area with rays of multicolored light.

Encounter ✦ Arcane, Implement, Radiant
Standard Action — **Area** burst 2 within 20 squares
Target: Each creature in burst
Attack: Intelligence vs. Will
Hit: 3d6 + Intelligence modifier radiant damage, and the target is blinded until the end of your next turn.

Thunderlance — Wizard Attack 13

A thunderous pulse of concussive energy rolls from your hand, bowling over your enemies.

Encounter ✦ Arcane, Implement, Thunder
Standard Action — **Close** blast 5
Target: Each creature in blast
Attack: Intelligence vs. Reflex
Hit: 4d6 + Intelligence modifier thunder damage, and you push the target 4 squares.

LEVEL 15 DAILY SPELLS

Bigby's Grasping Hands — Wizard Attack 15

Two hands of glowing golden force materialize, grab a couple of your foes, and slam them together.

Daily ✦ Arcane, Conjuration, Force, Implement
Standard Action — **Ranged** 10
Effect: You conjure two 5-foot-tall hands of force, each one occupying 1 square within range. Each hand attacks one adjacent creature. A hand that is not grabbing a target can be moved and made to attack a new target within range as a move action. The hands last until the end of your next turn.
Targets: One or two creatures
Attack: Intelligence vs. Reflex
Hit: 2d10 + Intelligence modifier force damage, and the hand grabs the target. If the target attempts to escape, the hand uses your Fortitude or Reflex defense.
Special: If the hands have each grabbed an enemy, you can slam the enemies into each other as a standard action, dealing 2d10 + Intelligence modifier force damage to each grabbed target. After the attack, each hand returns to its original square with its grabbed target.
Sustain Minor: The hands persist.

Blast of Cold — Wizard Attack 15

You create a tremendous blast of supernatural cold, freezing your enemies.

Daily ✦ Arcane, Cold, Implement
Standard Action — **Close** blast 5
Target: Each enemy in blast
Attack: Intelligence vs. Reflex
Hit: 6d6 + Intelligence modifier cold damage, and the target is immobilized (save ends).
Miss: Half damage, and the target is slowed (save ends).

Otiluke's Resilient Sphere
Wizard Attack 15

You trap your enemy in a transparent, immobile globe of impenetrable force.

Daily ✦ Arcane, Conjuration, Force, Implement
Standard Action   Ranged 10
Target: One creature
Attack: Intelligence vs. Reflex
Hit: You conjure a sphere of force that fills the target's entire space until the end of your next turn. The target is immobilized and can't attack anything outside its own space. Creatures outside the sphere can't attack the target, and the sphere blocks objects and creatures attempting to pass through it.
　The sphere, though impenetrable, is not impervious to damage. Attacks against the sphere automatically hit, and it has 100 hit points.
Sustain Minor: If your attack roll was successful, you can sustain the sphere.
Miss: The target is immobilized (save ends).
Special: Instead of attacking an enemy, you can put the sphere around yourself or a willing ally within range without making an attack roll.

Prismatic Beams
Wizard Attack 15

Scintillating beams of rainbow-colored light spring from your outstretched hand, affecting your foes in unpredictable ways.

Daily ✦ Arcane, Fire, Implement, Poison
Standard Action   Close burst 5
Target: Each enemy in burst
Attack: Intelligence vs. Fortitude, Reflex, Will
Hit (Fortitude): If the attack hits the target's Fortitude defense, the target takes 2d6 + Intelligence modifier poison damage, and ongoing 5 poison damage (save ends).
Hit (Reflex): If the attack hits the target's Reflex defense, the target takes 2d6 + Intelligence modifier fire damage, and ongoing 5 fire damage (save ends).
Hit (Will): If the attack hits the target's Will defense, the target is dazed (save ends).
Special: You make only one attack per target, but compare that attack result against all three defenses. A target might be subject to any, all, or none of the effects depending on how many of its defenses were hit. The target must make a saving throw against each ongoing effect separately.

Wall of Ice
Wizard Attack 15

A wall of glittering, jagged ice appears at your command.

Daily ✦ Arcane, Cold, Conjuration, Implement
Standard Action   Area wall 12 within 10 squares
Effect: You conjure a solid wall of contiguous squares filled with arcane ice. The wall can be up to 12 squares long and up to 6 squares high.
　Any creature that starts its turn adjacent to the wall takes 2d6 + Intelligence modifier cold damage. The wall blocks line of sight and prevents movement. No creature can enter a square containing the wall.
Special: As a standard action, a creature can attack one square of the wall. Each square has 50 hit points. Any creature that makes a melee attack against the wall takes 2d6 cold damage. The wall has vulnerability 25 to fire. If the wall is not destroyed, it melts away after 1 hour.

LEVEL 16 UTILITY SPELLS

Displacement
Wizard Utility 16

The recipient of this spell appears to be standing slightly to the left or right of his actual position, making it harder for enemies to hit him.

Encounter ✦ Arcane, Illusion
Immediate Interrupt   Ranged 5
Trigger: A ranged or a melee attack hits you or one ally in range
Effect: The attacker must reroll the attack roll.

Fly
Wizard Utility 16

You leap into the air and don't look back.

Daily ✦ Arcane
Standard Action   Personal
Effect: You gain a speed of fly 8 until the end of your next turn.
Sustain Minor: You can sustain this power until the end of the encounter or for 5 minutes. If you don't sustain it, you float to the ground without taking falling damage.

Greater Invisibility
Wizard Utility 16

With a wave of your hand, you or another creature nearby fades away, becoming invisible.

Daily ✦ Arcane, Illusion
Standard Action   Ranged 20
Target: You or one creature
Effect: The target is invisible until the end of your next turn. If the target attacks, the power ends.
Sustain Minor: If the target is within range, you can sustain the effect.

Stoneskin

Wizard Utility 16

You sprinkle a tiny pinch of diamond dust over the subject, and his skin turns gray and hard as granite.

Daily ✦ Arcane
Standard Action   **Melee** touch
Target: You or one ally
Effect: The target gains resist 10 to all damage until the end of the encounter or for 5 minutes.

LEVEL 17 ENCOUNTER SPELLS

Combust

Wizard Attack 17

You cause several foes to spontaneously burst into flame.

Encounter ✦ Arcane, Fire, Implement
Standard Action   **Area** burst 2 within 20 squares
Target: Each creature in burst
Attack: Intelligence vs. Reflex
Hit: 5d6 + Intelligence modifier fire damage.

Crushing Titan's Fist

Wizard Attack 17

You clench your fist, and crushing force seizes your enemies like the fist of an invisible titan.

Encounter ✦ Arcane, Force, Implement
Standard Action   **Area** burst 2 within 20 squares
Target: Each creature in burst
Attack: Intelligence vs. Reflex
Hit: 3d8 + Intelligence modifier force damage, and the target is immobilized until the end of your next turn.
Effect: Entering a square within the power's area costs 4 extra squares of movement. This effect ends at the end of your next turn, and you can dismiss it as a minor action.

Force Volley

Wizard Attack 17

Silvery missiles spring from your fingertips and streak across the battlefield, striking your enemies with staggering force.

Encounter ✦ Arcane, Force, Implement
Standard Action   **Ranged** 20
Targets: One, two, or three creatures
Attack: Intelligence vs. Reflex, one attack per target
Special: If you target only one creature with this power, you gain a +4 power bonus to the attack roll.
Hit: 3d6 + Intelligence modifier force damage, and the target is dazed until the end of your next turn.

Ice Tomb

Wizard Attack 17

You target an enemy with a freezing ray that briefly traps him in an icy sarcophagus.

Encounter ✦ Arcane, Cold, Implement
Standard Action   **Ranged** 20
Target: One creature
Attack: Intelligence vs. Reflex
Hit: 3d10 + Intelligence modifier cold damage, and the target is entombed in ice. While entombed, the target is stunned, and attacks cannot gain line of effect against it. This effect lasts until the end of your next turn.

LEVEL 19 DAILY SPELLS

Acid Wave

Wizard Attack 19

A wave of acid dissolves all creatures that stand before you.

Daily ✦ Acid, Arcane, Implement
Standard Action   **Close** blast 5
Target: Each creature in blast
Attack: Intelligence vs. Reflex
Hit: 5d6 + Intelligence modifier acid damage, and ongoing 10 acid damage (save ends).
Miss: Half damage, and ongoing 5 acid damage (save ends).

Cloudkill

Wizard Attack 19

Yellow-green vapors emerge from the ground with a hiss, forming a thick, toxic cloud.

Daily ✦ Arcane, Implement, Poison, Zone
Standard Action   **Area** burst 5 within 20 squares
Target: Each creature in burst
Hit: 1d10 + Intelligence modifier poison damage.
Effect: The burst creates a zone of poisonous vapors that lasts until the end of your next turn. A creature that enters the zone or starts its turn there takes 1d10 + Intelligence modifier poison damage. As a move action, you can move the zone 3 squares.
Sustain Minor: The zone persists.

Disintegrate

Wizard Attack 19

You fire a green ray from your wand. Whatever the emerald beam hits disappears in a puff of gray dust.

Daily ✦ Arcane, Implement
Standard Action   **Ranged** 10
Target: One creature or object
Attack: Intelligence vs. Reflex
Special: You don't need to make an attack roll to hit an unattended object with this power.
Hit: 5d10 + Intelligence modifier damage, and ongoing 10 damage (save ends). If the target saves, it takes ongoing 5 damage (save ends).
Miss: 3d10 + Intelligence modifier damage, and ongoing 5 damage (save ends).

Evard's Black Tentacles

Wizard Attack 19

Wriggling, ebon tentacles of necrotic energy erupt from the ground, grasping toward every creature within reach.

Daily ✦ Arcane, Implement, Necrotic, Zone
Standard Action   **Area** burst 4 within 10 squares
Target: Each creature in burst
Attack: Intelligence vs. Reflex
Hit: 2d10 + Intelligence modifier necrotic damage, and the target is immobilized (save ends).
Effect: The burst creates a zone of difficult terrain that lasts until the end of your next turn.
Sustain Minor: When you sustain the power, repeat the attack against any creature within the zone that is not immobilized, and deal 1d10 necrotic damage to creatures that are immobilized.

Level 22 Utility Spells

Mass Fly — Wizard Utility 22

White motes of light fly from your fingertips and swirl about, lifting you and your allies off the ground and granting each of you the power of flight.

Daily ✦ Arcane
Standard Action   **Close** burst 5
Targets: You and each ally in burst
Effect: All targets gain a speed of fly 8 until the end of your next turn.
Sustain Minor: You can sustain this power until the end of the encounter or for 5 minutes. If you don't sustain this power, all targets float to the ground without taking falling damage.

Mordenkainen's Mansion — Wizard Utility 22

You trace the outline of a door, and a shimmering portal appears, leading to a space accessible only by you and your allies.

Daily ✦ Arcane, Conjuration, Teleportation
Standard Action   **Melee** touch
Effect: You conjure a spacious extradimensional dwelling that can hold up to fifty Medium creatures. It is reached through a single doorway that you trace on a surface or in the air. Only you and those you designate can pass through it. You can close the entrance and make it invisible after you enter the mansion, and only someone inside the mansion can open the portal once it's closed. The mansion contains comfortable furnishings and enough food and drink to satisfy its denizens. The furniture and food disappear if removed from the mansion. The mansion lasts for 8 hours, and any creatures still in the mansion when the power ends reappear in unoccupied squares outside the entrance portal.

Time Stop — Wizard Utility 22

Everything around you slows to a halt, frozen in time. Then, after a few moments, everything starts to speed up again, returning to normal time.

Daily ✦ Arcane
Minor Action   **Personal**
Effect: You gain two extra standard actions, which you can't use to attack other creatures.

Level 23 Encounter Spells

Acid Storm — Wizard Attack 23

You create a thick black cloud filled with pelting drops of acid.

Encounter ✦ Acid, Arcane, Implement
Standard Action   **Area** burst 4 within 10 squares
Target: Each creature in burst
Attack: Intelligence vs. Fortitude
Hit: 4d6 + Intelligence modifier acid damage.
Effect: The cloud blocks line of sight, providing total concealment to creatures inside it. Any creature that enters the cloud or starts its turn there takes 10 acid damage. The cloud lasts until the end of your next turn, or you can dismiss it as a minor action.

Chain Lightning — Wizard Attack 23

From your fingertips springs a tremendous stroke of blinding purple-white lightning that leaps from one enemy to another.

Encounter ✦ Arcane, Implement, Lightning
Standard Action   **Ranged** 20
Primary Target: One creature
Attack: Intelligence vs. Reflex
Hit: 4d6 + Intelligence modifier lightning damage.
Secondary Targets: Two creatures within 5 squares of the primary target
Secondary Attack: Intelligence vs. Reflex
Hit: 2d6 + Intelligence modifier lightning damage.
Tertiary Targets: All other enemies within 20 squares of you
Attack: Intelligence vs. Reflex
Hit: 1d6 + Intelligence modifier lightning damage.

Thunderclap — Wizard Attack 23

You tap your staff on the ground, and a peal of thunder rocks and stuns a distant enemy.

Encounter ✦ Arcane, Implement, Thunder
Standard Action   **Ranged** 20
Target: One creature
Attack: Intelligence vs. Fortitude
Hit: 3d6 + Intelligence modifier thunder damage, and the target is stunned until the end of your next turn.

Level 25 Daily Spells

Elemental Maw — Wizard Attack 25

You call up a spinning vortex of elemental energy that inexorably draws everything around it toward seeming destruction.

Daily ✦ Arcane, Implement, Teleportation; Acid, Cold, Fire, Lightning, or Thunder
Standard Action   **Area** burst 4 within 20 squares
Target: Each creature in burst
Attack: Intelligence vs. Reflex
Hit: 6d6 + Intelligence modifier damage of a type chosen from the following list: acid, cold, fire, lightning, or thunder. In addition, the target is pulled 2 squares toward the maw's origin square.
Miss: Half damage, and no pull.
Effect: This attack's origin square becomes a vortex of energy. The burst creates an area of difficult terrain. The effect remains until the end of your next turn. Any creature that is pulled into the vortex takes 3d6 + Intelligence modifier damage of a type chosen from the following list: acid, cold, fire, lightning, or thunder. In addition, you teleport that creature to a square within 20 squares of you. The creature arrives at its destination prone and dazed until the start of your next turn.

Maze
Wizard Attack 25

You trap an enemy in an extradimensional vault resembling a maze. He vanishes from sight, caught in your maze until he can find an escape.

Daily ✦ Arcane, Implement, Psychic, Teleportation
Standard Action   Ranged 10
Target: One creature
Attack: Intelligence vs. Will
Hit: 3d12 + Intelligence modifier psychic damage.
Effect: You trap the target in an extradimensional maze. While caught in the maze, the target cannot see, move, or affect the world outside in any way. Similarly, no one can see or attack the creature in the maze. The maze remains visible as a faintly glowing sigil or rune in the square the trapped creature occupied; it is harmless to all other beings, and creatures can move through or attack through that square without penalty. On its turn each round, the target can attempt an Intelligence check against your Will defense to escape as a standard action. The target gains a cumulative +5 bonus to this check each time it fails. Upon leaving the maze, the creature returns to the space it occupied (or, if occupied, the nearest available unoccupied space of its choice), and the maze ends.

Necrotic Web
Wizard Attack 25

You cover your enemies in a giant web made from strands of black, life-draining energy.

Daily ✦ Arcane, Implement, Necrotic, Zone
Standard Action   Area burst 3 within 20 squares
Target: Each creature in burst
Attack: Intelligence vs. Reflex
Hit: 4d6 + Intelligence modifier necrotic damage, and the target is immobilized (save ends).
Effect: The burst creates a web-filled zone until the end of the encounter or for 5 minutes. The zone is difficult terrain. Any creature in the web at the start of its turn takes 4d6 necrotic damage. Any creature that ends its move in the web is immobilized (save ends).

Prismatic Spray
Wizard Attack 25

A dazzling spray of multicolored light springs from your hands, enveloping your enemies.

Daily ✦ Arcane, Fear, Fire, Implement, Poison
Standard Action   Close burst 5
Target: Each enemy in burst
Attack: Intelligence vs. Fortitude, Reflex, Will
Hit (Fortitude): If the attack hits the target's Fortitude defense, the target takes 3d6 + Intelligence modifier poison damage and is slowed (save ends).
Hit (Reflex): If the attack hits the target's Reflex defense, the target takes 3d6 + Intelligence modifier fire damage, and ongoing 15 fire damage (save ends).
Hit (Will): If the attack hits the target's Will defense, the target is stunned (save ends).
Special: You make only one attack per target, but compare that attack result against all three defenses. A target might be subject to any, all, or none of the effects depending on how many of its defenses were hit. The target must make a saving throw against each ongoing effect separately.

LEVEL 27 ENCOUNTER SPELLS

Black Fire
Wizard Attack 27

A blast of crackling black fire erupts from your hand, charring the flesh and burning the souls of your foes.

Encounter ✦ Arcane, Fire, Implement, Necrotic
Standard Action   Close blast 5
Target: Each enemy in blast
Attack: Intelligence vs. Reflex
Hit: 6d6 + Intelligence modifier fire and necrotic damage.

Confusion
Wizard Attack 27

You magically compel an enemy to attack its nearest ally.

Encounter ✦ Arcane, Charm, Implement, Psychic
Standard Action   Ranged 20
Target: One creature
Attack: Intelligence vs. Will
Hit: 3d10 + Intelligence modifier psychic damage. On the target's next turn, you control its actions: You can move it a number of squares equal to your Wisdom modifier, and it then makes a basic attack against its nearest ally.

Forcecage
Wizard Attack 27

Around your foe you erect an invisible cage made of unbreakable bars of force, effectively imprisoning it.

Encounter ✦ Arcane, Force, Implement
Standard Action   Ranged 20
Target: One creature
Attack: Intelligence vs. Reflex
Hit: 3d10 + Intelligence modifier force damage. The target is confined in the forcecage until the end of your next turn. While confined, it is immobilized, grants combat advantage, and cannot gain line of effect against nonadjacent enemies.

LEVEL 29 DAILY SPELLS

Greater Ice Storm
Wizard Attack 29

A storm of bitterly cold hailstones pummels a wide swath of ground and covers the area in ice.

Daily ✦ Arcane, Cold, Implement, Zone
Standard Action   Area burst 5 within 20 squares
Target: Each creature in burst
Attack: Intelligence vs. Fortitude
Hit: 4d8 + Intelligence modifier cold damage, and the target is immobilized (save ends).
Miss: Half damage, and the target is slowed (save ends).
Effect: The burst creates a zone of ice. The zone is difficult terrain until the end of the encounter or for 5 minutes.

Legion's Hold
Wizard Attack 29

Your eyes darken, becoming black orbs as you command your enemies to stop in their tracks.

Daily ✦ Arcane, Charm, Implement, Psychic
Standard Action   Close burst 20
Target: Each enemy in burst
Attack: Intelligence vs. Will
Hit: 2d10 + Intelligence modifier psychic damage, and the target is stunned (save ends).
Miss: Half damage, and the target is dazed (save ends).

Meteor Swarm	Wizard Attack 29

Fiery orbs rain down from above, shrieking loudly as they fall. They smash into your foes, obliterating them in a storm of fire and scorching the ground.

Daily ✦ Arcane, Fire, Implement
Standard Action   **Area** burst 5 within 20 squares
Target: Each creature in burst
Attack: Intelligence vs. Reflex
Hit: 8d6 + Intelligence modifier fire damage.
Miss: Half damage.

PARAGON PATHS

BATTLE MAGE

"You think I'm just a simple scholar, my head buried amid my scrolls and books? Think again!"

Prerequisite: Wizard class

You didn't leave behind the thrill of battle when you took up the mantle of wizard, so why should you stand back and let the fighters have all the fun? You have developed skills and techniques that have turned you into a true battle mage, ready to deal damage up close and personal or from afar, depending on the situation and how the mood strikes you. You have even learned of a technique for using arcane energy to temporarily stave off death—and you can't wait to try it out in battle!

BATTLE MAGE PATH FEATURES

Arcane Riposte (11th level): Imbued with magical might, your hands bristle with arcane energy in the heat of battle. When a creature provokes an opportunity attack from you, make an opportunity attack with one of your hands (Dexterity vs. AC). Choose cold, fire, force, or lightning. You deal 1d8 + Intelligence modifier damage of that type with this attack.

Battle Mage Action (11th level): When you spend an action point to take an extra action, you also gain a +4 bonus to attack rolls until the start of your next turn.

Battle Edge (16th level): When you first become bloodied in an encounter, you can use any at-will power you know as an immediate reaction.

BATTLE MAGE SPELLS

Forceful Retort	Battle Mage Attack 11

The power and certainty of your words knock your enemies off their feet.

Encounter ✦ Arcane, Implement
Standard Action   **Close** burst 1
Target: Each enemy in burst
Attack: Intelligence vs. Fortitude
Hit: 3d8 + Intelligence modifier force damage, and you push the target 1 square and it is knocked prone.

Arcane Rejuvenation	Battle Mage Utility 12

In a bad spot, you draw on arcane energy to help you stay on your feet.

Daily ✦ Arcane, Healing
Immediate Interrupt   Personal
Trigger: You are reduced to 0 hit points or fewer
Effect: You regain hit points equal to your level + your Intelligence modifier.

Closing Spell	Battle Mage Attack 20

You save the best for last—a devastating display of pure elemental power that your enemies aren't likely to see again.

Daily ✦ Arcane, Implement; Cold, Fire, Lightning, or Thunder
Standard Action   **Area** burst 5 within 20 squares
Target: Each enemy in burst
Attack: Intelligence vs. Reflex
Hit: 3d10 + Intelligence modifier damage of a particular damage type, chosen by you from the following list: cold, fire, lightning, or thunder. Add 5d10 damage of the same damage type if you have no other daily powers remaining.
Miss: Half damage.

BLOOD MAGE

"My blood courses with arcane power, as you are about to see."

Prerequisite: Wizard class

You have learned to combine blood with arcane formulas to cast more powerful spells—your own blood. Your blood is your life, but it is also your source of power. Few wizards step upon this path to arcane mastery, because it is a path steeped in pain and soaked in blood. But you have embraced the way of blood and magic, and you have become more powerful because of it.

BLOOD MAGE PATH FEATURES

Blood Action (11th level): When you spend an action point to take an extra action, if you use your action to make an attack that hits, that attack deals ongoing 10 damage (save ends).

Bolstering Blood (11th level): You learn to turn your own pain into additional pain for your enemies. When you use a wizard encounter power, a wizard daily power, or a blood mage power that deals damage, you can, once per turn as a free action just prior to using the power, deal either a minor wound or a severe wound to yourself.

A minor wound deals 1d10 damage to you.

A severe wound deals 2d10 damage to you.

When the power you use damages a target, you deal extra psychic damage equal to the damage you dealt to yourself.

Burning Blood (16th level): When you use your second wind, enemies within 10 squares of you take psychic damage equal to your Constitution modifier. If those enemies are currently suffering from an effect that you caused, add your Intelligence modifier. They also take ongoing 5 fire damage (save ends).

BLOOD MAGE SPELLS

Blood Pulse
Blood Mage Attack 11

A mote of crimson plasma springs from your hand, streaks across the battlefield, and detonates amid your enemies, covering them in a blood-red shroud.

Encounter ✦ Arcane, Implement
Standard Action   **Area** burst 3 within 20 squares
Target: Each enemy in burst
Attack: Intelligence vs. Will
Hit: 2d6 + Intelligence modifier damage, and until the end of your next turn the target takes 1d6 damage for every square it leaves.

Soul Burn
Blood Mage Utility 12

You trade your recuperative ability for more arcane power.

Daily ✦ Arcane
Minor Action   **Personal**
Effect: You spend a healing surge. Instead of regaining hit points, you regain one encounter power you have already used.

Destructive Salutation
Blood Mage Attack 20

You greet your enemies with a psychic wave that scrambles their minds and leaves them stunned.

Daily ✦ Arcane, Implement, Psychic
Standard Action   **Area** burst 3 within 20 squares
Target: Each enemy in burst
Attack: Intelligence vs. Will
Hit: 6d6 + Intelligence modifier psychic damage, and the target takes ongoing 10 psychic damage and is stunned (save ends both).
Miss: Half damage, no ongoing damage, and the target is stunned until the end of your next turn.

SPELLSTORM MAGE

"I stand in the center of a storm you cannot see, a storm of arcane spells waiting to be snatched from the maelstrom and used as I see fit."

Prerequisite: Wizard class

To you, the arcane energy flowing through the world is like a raging storm that only you can see. Moreover, you can shape and control this arcane storm to accomplish amazing things. The storm consists of individual spells, like each drop of rain in the maelstrom, and you can pluck these spells free and direct them as you will. You are a spellstorm mage, and you stand among the arcane torrent and use it to enhance the power that you wield.

SPELLSTORM MAGE PATH FEATURES

Extra Damage Action (11th level): When you spend an action point to take an extra action, you also add one-half your level to the damage dealt by any of your standard action attacks this turn.

Storm Spell (11th level): Once per day, you can reach into the spellstorm and extract a spell you have already used so that you can use it again. Make a Wisdom check. The result indicates the kind of spell you can extract. You can instead extract a spell using a lower result than the result you rolled, if you so choose.

1-10: Encounter utility spell.
11-15: Encounter attack spell.
16-20: Daily utility spell.
21 or higher: Daily attack spell.

Storm Fury (16th level): When you first become bloodied in an encounter, you unleash a burst of arcane energy that deals 5 + your Wisdom modifier lightning damage to all your enemies within 10 squares of you.

SPELLSTORM MAGE SPELLS

Storm Cage
Spellstorm Mage Attack 11

You trap your enemies in a cage made of lightning and filled with roaring thunder.

Encounter ✦ Arcane, Conjuration, Implement, Lightning, Thunder
Standard Action   **Area** burst 2 within 20 squares
Target: Each creature in burst
Attack: Intelligence vs. Reflex
Hit: 4d6 + Intelligence modifier lightning and thunder damage.
Effect: You conjure a wall in the 16 outer squares of the burst (forming a square enclosure). Any creature that starts its turn adjacent to the wall or moves into a wall square takes 10 lightning damage. Moving into a wall square costs 1 extra square of movement. The wall does not grant cover or concealment. It lasts until the end of your next turn.

Sudden Storm
Spellstorm Mage Utility 12

With a wave of your hand, you create an area of torrential rain that creatures have difficulty passing through.

Daily ✦ Arcane, Zone
Standard Action   **Area** burst 2 within 20 squares
Effect: The burst creates a zone of wind and rain that lasts until the end of your next turn. Squares in the zone are difficult terrain and are lightly obscured. As a move action, you can move the zone up to 5 squares.
Sustain Minor: The zone persists.

Maelstrom of Chaos
Spellstorm Mage Attack 20

Arcane winds and a hailstorm of force energy surrounds you, battering your enemies and teleporting them from one place to another.

Daily ✦ Arcane, Force, Implement, Teleportation
Standard Action   **Close** burst 10
Target: Each enemy in burst
Attack: Intelligence vs. Fortitude
Hit: 3d8 + Intelligence modifier force damage, and you can teleport the target to a location of your choice within the burst.
Miss: Half damage, and no teleportation.

WIZARD OF THE SPIRAL TOWER

"I have taken on the robes of the Spiral Tower, studied beside eladrin mages in the Feywild, and adopted the arcane approach of Corellon's followers as my own."

Prerequisite: Wizard class, proficiency with longsword

You have decided to adopt the traditions of the Spiral Tower, the arcane teachings of the followers of Corellon. This links your use of arcane power firmly to the Feywild and the arcane-focused eladrin traditions. As a wizard of the Spiral Tower, Corellon's longsword becomes your arcane implement and the secrets of the Feywild become pages in your spellbook. As a wizard of the Spiral Tower, you carry a longsword that glows with the arcane beauty of the Feywild.

WIZARD OF THE SPIRAL TOWER PATH FEATURES

Corellon's Implement (11th level): Choose an arcane implement that you specialize in, whether the wand, staff, or orb. You can use a longsword as if it were that type of arcane implement when casting your spells.

Spiral Tower Action (11th level): You can spend an action point to regain one wizard encounter power you have already used, instead of taking an extra action.

Radiant Censure (16th level): When an enemy attacks your Will defense, the enemy takes radiant damage equal to your Charisma modifier (minimum 1).

WIZARD OF THE SPIRAL TOWER SPELLS

The One Sword — Wizard of the Spiral Tower Attack 11

Your blade flashes with the twilight power of the Feywild as you strike your foe.

Encounter ✦ Arcane, Weapon
Standard Action   **Melee** weapon
Target: One creature
Attack: Intelligence vs. Reflex
Hit: 2[W] + Intelligence modifier damage. Make a secondary attack against the target.
     Secondary Attack: Intelligence vs. Will
     Hit: The target is dazed until the end of your next turn, and this power is not expended.

Shape the Dream — Wizard of the Spiral Tower Utility 12

You alter reality slightly, so that an attack your foe assumed it had made didn't actually happen.

Daily ✦ Arcane, Implement
Immediate Interrupt   **Personal**
Trigger: You are hit by an attack against your Will defense
Effect: The attack doesn't occur, as if the creature that attacked you chose to do nothing with its action.

Corellon's Blade — Wizard of the Spiral Tower Attack 20

You swing your glowing longsword around you, striking nearby enemies with the flat of the blade and banishing them into the Feywild.

Daily ✦ Arcane, Radiant, Teleportation, Weapon
Standard Action   **Close** burst 1
Target: Each enemy in burst you can see
Attack: Intelligence + 4 vs. Will
Hit: 3[W] + Intelligence modifier radiant damage. In addition, the target is transported to a remote but nonthreatening corner of the Feywild until the end of your next turn. Return the creature to its original space. If that space is occupied, the target returns to the nearest unoccupied space (its choice).
Miss: Half damage.

Your epic destiny describes the mythic archetype you aspire to achieve. Some characters have a clear epic destiny in mind from the moment they began adventuring, while others discover their epic destiny somewhere along the way.

Most people don't ever come close to achieving an epic destiny. Whether they simply failed in their journey, or whether the universe never intended them to gain such lofty heights, is unknown and unknowable.

Your epic destiny sets you apart from such individuals—you know you're destined for greatness and you have every opportunity to achieve it.

EXTRAORDINARY POWER

Compared to a class or paragon path, an epic destiny grants few benefits, but those it bestows are exceptional. Certain laws of the universe work differently for you—and some don't apply at all.

Your race, class, path, and other character elements might define what you can do, but your epic destiny defines your place in the universe.

IMMORTALITY

Each epic destiny defines your lasting impact on the world or even the universe: how people forever afterward remember and talk about you.

Some people achieve lasting fame or notoriety without achieving an epic destiny, but that's a fleeting thing. Inevitably, those people are forgotten, lost in the murky depths of history. Your epic destiny ensures that your name and exploits live on forever.

THE END

Perhaps most important, your epic destiny describes your character's exit from the world at large (and more specifically, from the game) once you've completed your final adventure. It lays out why, after so many adventures, you finally take your leave of the mortal realm—and where you go next.

GAINING AN EPIC DESTINY

Epic destiny abilities accrue from 21st to 30th level. As shown on the Character Advancement table in Chapter 2, your epic abilities pick up where paragon path benefits leave off.

After gaining all other benefits of reaching 21st level (including class features, ability score increases, and the like), you can choose an epic destiny.

Epic destinies are broader in scope than a class or paragon path. Though most have certain requirements to enter, even these typically apply to a wide range of characters with various backgrounds, talents, and powers.

If you don't choose an epic destiny at 21st level, you can choose one at any level thereafter. You retroactively gain all benefits of the epic destiny appropriate to your current level.

FULFILLING YOUR EPIC DESTINY

The "Immortality" feature of your destiny is not gained at 30th level. Instead, it is gained when you and your allies complete their Destiny Quest. This is described more thoroughly in the *Dungeon Master's Guide*, but essentially, your Destiny Quest is the final grand adventure of the campaign, during which you face the greatest challenges of your characters' careers.

This quest might actually begin before 30th level (in fact, most do), but the climax of the quest can only occur after all participants have reached 30th level. Upon completing your Destiny Quest, your adventuring career—and your life as a normal mortal being—effectively ends. Your DM might give your character a little time to put affairs in order before moving on, or it can occur spontaneously upon completion of the quest. Work with your DM to determine the appropriate timing based on your character, your destiny, and the quest.

Once you've completed your Destiny Quest and initiated your ascension to immortality, your character's story has ended. He lives on in legend, but he no longer takes part in mortal events. Instead, it's time to create a new group of adventurers and begin a new story.

GROWING INTO YOUR CHARACTER'S DESTINY

Epic destinies are as much about a player character's place in the world and the cosmos as they are about gaining new abilities. Therefore, campaigns that intend to play through the epic tier often weave PCs' expected epic destinies into the storyline before 21st level. A character working to become a Demigod might conduct herself differently from a character who believes he is destined to be a Deadly Trickster.

DESTINY QUESTS

The Destiny Quest is a dangerous epic adventure tied to a particular epic destiny (or perhaps to multiple epic destinies in the group) that a high-level adventuring party can undertake to complete the storyline (or storylines) of epic characters. It's entirely possible that a DM's campaign plans don't lead through any Destiny Quests. But if a DM doesn't have solid plans for their campaign during the epic tier, orienting several sessions around quests tied to each PC's epic destiny is an excellent route to explore.

Destiny Quests and Immortality

Groups that want a definite endpoint to their PCs' adventures can use Destiny Quests as a springboard for showing how their 30th-level character eventually leaves the mortal world and ascends into the world of gods and legends. This type of endpoint obviously won't appeal to all groups. Many DMs will have their own ideas of how their campaign should end. Other groups will prefer to keep their 30th-level characters around as options for high-level play. Therefore, the notes that appear in each of the epic destinies below are entirely optional. We present them mainly to help you get in the mood for what an epic character's final destiny might look like, with the understanding that you or your DM might have other plans for your PC's final destiny.

Introducing the Epic Destinies

Epic Destinies are presented in alphabetical order. Each destiny description provides a general overview, followed by game rule information.

Prerequisites: If the epic destiny has requirements for entry, they are listed here.

Destiny Features: Every epic destiny has a unique mix of features described in this section. Upon choosing an epic destiny, you gain the destiny feature listed for 21st level.

Powers: A full description of the power or powers granted by the epic destiny appears here.

Immortality: This entry describes your particular form of immortality once you've completed your Destiny Quest.

Archmage

As the Archmage, you lay claim to being the world's preeminent wizard.

Prerequisite: 21st-level wizard

Your lifelong perusal of grimoires, librams, tomes, and spellbooks has finally revealed the foundation of reality to you: Spells are each tiny portions of a larger arcane truth. Every spell is part of some far superior working, evoking just a minuscule fraction of that ultimate formula. As you continue your studies, you advance your mastery of spells so much that they begin to infuse your flesh, granting you a facility in their use undreamed of by lesser practitioners.

You are often called to use your knowledge to defend the world from supernormal threats. Seeking ever greater enlightenment and the magical power that accompanies it, you are at times tempted by questionable relics, morally suspect spells, and ancient artifacts. Your destiny remains yours to choose—will you be archmage or archfiend?

Immortality, of a Sort

Archmages are an idiosyncratic lot. There's no telling what choices the preeminent wizard of the age will make when he has completed his destiny. The following section details a path several Archmages have walked, but your path might vary.

Arcane Seclusion: When you complete your final quest, you retreat from the world to give your full time and attention to the study of the ultimate arcane formula, the Demispell, whose hyperplanar existence encompasses all the lesser spells there ever were or ever will be.

To aid your study, you build a sanctum sanctorum. At your option, your retreat provides you complete seclusion, and thus could take the form of a tower lost somewhere in the Elemental Chaos. However, you might desire to retain a tie to the world, and thus build a sanctum with a connection to the world. In such a case, you might found a new order of mages for which you serve as the rarely seen High Wizard. Alternatively, you might found a school of magic, for which you serve as the rarely seen headmaster.

Regardless of your retreat's physical form or temporal connection, your contemplation of the arcanosphere persists. As the years flow onward, your study of the fundamental, deep structure of the cosmos removes you from the normal flow of time. Eventually your material shell fades as you merge into the Demispell itself.

Thereafter, your name becomes tied to powerful spells and rituals used by lesser wizards.

Archmage Features

All Archmages have the following features.

Spell Recall (21st level): At the beginning of each day, choose one daily spell that you know (and have prepared today, if you prepare spells). You can use that spell two times that day, rather than only once.

Arcane Spirit (24th level): Once per day, when you die, you can detach your spirit from your body. In arcane spirit form, you heal to maximum hit points and gain the insubstantial and phasing qualities. You can cast encounter spells and at-will spells while in arcane spirit form, but you can't cast daily spells, activate magic items, or perform rituals. If you die in arcane spirit form, you're dead.

At the end of the encounter, after a short rest, your arcane spirit rejoins your body, if your body is still present. Your current hit point total is unchanged, but you no longer experience the other benefits and drawbacks of being in arcane spirit form.

If your body is missing, you will need other magic to return to life, but can continue adventuring in arcane spirit form if you like.

Archspell (30th level): Your comprehension of the ultimate arcane formula and of the spells that constitute it reaches a new threshold. Choose one daily spell that you know. You can now cast that spell as an encounter spell (rather than as a daily spell).

ARCHMAGE POWER

Shape Magic	Archmage Utility 26

You reach into the ebb and flow of arcane energy and pluck a spell you have already used out of the invisible tide, instantly recalling it to memory.

Daily
Standard Action   **Personal**
Effect: You regain one arcane power you have already used.

DEADLY TRICKSTER

The universe is a vast stage set up to amuse you and spark your curiosity, and you are the ultimate trickster—amusing, unrivaled, and deadly.

Prerequisites: 21st level; Dexterity 21 or Charisma 21; training in Acrobatics, Bluff, Stealth, or Thievery

As a Deadly Trickster, you might be a wanderer, thief, cheat, pragmatist, or survivor. Or you might be something stranger still—a hero. You delight in ever-stranger wonders, from the loftiest heights of the celestial spheres to the ash-strewn depths of the encircling chaos. As you take a firmer grasp on your destiny, you alternately scandalize, charm, upset, reward, and confound those around you.

Some prophecies predict the Deadly Trickster will eventually betray his comrades and, in so doing, tumble princes, kingdoms, and perhaps even celestial realms. However, conflicting divinatory writs foretell the trickster's unexpected but vital aid, thus forestalling ultimate disaster and helping to create a new era of prosperity.

Rogues and warlocks are the most likely characters to become Deadly Tricksters, but they have also appeared from the most unlikely of origins.

IMMORTALITY?

Deadly Tricksters have to resist the temptation to take the dark path. Here's an example of how a campaign might present that choice.

Travel by Crooked Paths: When you complete your final quest, your legendary reputation is assured. The stories of your convoluted exploits live forever.

If you stand with your companions and see them through their final quest, embracing their cause as yours, you are acclaimed a true hero. You are acquitted of past transgressions, if any, and you are commended for conquering your erratic temperament when it counted most. You are invited into the realm of the entity you most admire and provided a palace, riches, true friends, and a legacy told and retold for a

thousand years describing how the Trickster's changeable nature burned steady and pure in the finally tally.

If, however, you betray your comrades and disrupt the completion of their final quest (or merely fail to aid them), you are cast out by all who once loved or trusted you. Your worst enemies welcome you to their courts as a newfound friend, and your name becomes a dark curse, forever despised by all who hear it.

DEADLY TRICKSTER FEATURES

All Deadly Tricksters have the following class features.

Sly Fortune's Favor (21st level): You have a knack for getting out of tough situations. Three times per day, as a free action, you can reroll a d20 roll (attack roll, skill check, ability check, or saving throw).

Trickster's Control (24th level): If you roll an 18 or higher on the d20 when making the first attack roll for an encounter or daily attack power, that power is not expended.

Trickster's Disposition (30th level): Once per day, you can tell the DM to treat the result of a d20 roll he just made as a 1. No rerolls are possible.

DEADLY TRICKSTER POWER

Epic Trick	Deadly Trickster Utility 26

When the need is great, you pull an amazing trick out of thin air.

Daily ✦ Healing
Minor Action   **Personal**
Effect: Regain all of your hit points and healing surges, automatically save against all effects on you, recover all expended encounter powers, or recover all expended daily powers except this one. Once you use this power, you cannot recover it except by taking an extended rest.

DEMIGOD

A divine spark ignites your soul, setting you on the path to apotheosis.

Prerequisite: 21st level

Your flesh becomes more than mortal and partakes of the divine vigor enjoyed by the gods themselves. Your epic-level companions are fast, strong, and smart, but you have the spark of godhood that sets you ever so slightly above all mortals.

Deities from every plane eventually learn your name, your nature, and your goals. Some might monitor your progress to observe whether you possess the mettle of a true demigod, and a few could throw roadblocks in your path. It is in your hands to impress the lords of creation, or disappoint them.

If you survive, overcome all challenges put before you, and reach the heights of ability achieved by few mortals, you are worthy to ascend to the ranks of the divine.

Exarch or Free Agent?

One or more gods might ask that you serve them as a probationary exarch while you work toward your own divine goals. You do not gain any additional abilities for accepting such a position, though you do gain access to a divine connection that might grant you information helpful for completing your quests. On the other hand, you might be required to perform tasks that delay your own goals, or even work at cross-purposes to your goals. No one said godhood would be easy, and acting as a free agent has its own problems as various astral beings take your measure.

Route to Immortality

At least one Demigod has chosen the path to ascension outlined below. Your own route to divinity might be different.

Divine Ascension: When you complete your final quest, your divine nature yearns to complete your apotheosis. Upon ordering your mortal affairs, the astral flame smoldering within you detonates, consuming all that remains of your mortal flesh.

The astral flame leaves behind a fledgling god, flush with the power only the truly divine can comprehend and wield. You ascend, blazing like the sunrise (or darkening the skies like an eclipse, if your inclinations run dark). Streaking into the Astral Sea, you are taken up into the realm of an established god who welcomes your strength. You join that god's pantheon and take on an aspect of the god's portfolio.

Soon enough, your transcendent senses discern mortal prayers directed at you.

Demigod Features

All Demigods have the following class features.

Divine Spark (21st level): Increase two ability scores of your choice by 2 each.

Divine Recovery (24th level): The first time you are reduced to 0 hit points or fewer each day, you regain hit points equal to half your maximum hit points.

Divine Miracle (30th level): When you have expended your last remaining encounter power, you regain the use of one encounter power of your choice. In this way, you never run out of encounter powers.

Demigod Power

Divine Regeneration — Demigod Utility 26

You ignite the divine spark that glows within you, unleashing a wave of regenerating energy for a short time.

Daily ✦ Healing
Minor Action — Personal
Effect: You gain regeneration equal to your highest ability score until the end of the encounter.

Eternal Seeker

You continue to search for your ultimate destiny, but that doesn't stop you from participating (some say interfering) in world-shaking events.

Prerequisite: 21st level

You might be a hero whose destiny is still unfolding. Maybe you're a free spirit who wants to experience everything the universe has to offer before tying yourself to a particular piece of the cosmos. You might be a rebel who hates the concept of having a singular destiny and therefore claims that you're not even interested in having a destiny. Or you may just want to avoid taking a side. Whatever the case, you're carving such a wide swath through events that your destiny will have no problem finding you when the time is right.

Seeking Immortality?

No one can predict your final destination. Compared to many other epic characters, your destiny has the advantage of being entirely mutable, so you might end up forging your own destiny by helping your friends accomplish theirs.

Eternal Seeker Features

All Eternal Seekers have the following class features.

Seeker of the Many Paths (21st level): When you gain a class encounter or daily power by gaining a level, you can choose your new power from any class.

Learning a power doesn't necessarily equip you with all the attributes required to use the power. For example, a fighter who learns a wizard spell as an Eternal Seeker would not gain the ability to use implements that make casting wizard spells more effective. Therefore, you're usually better off learning powers that are compatible with what you already know.

Eternal Action (24th level): When you spend an action point to take an extra action, you also gain an extra action on your next turn. The extra action you take on your next turn doesn't benefit from any abilities (such as many paragon path features) that affect what happens when you spend an action point.

Seeker's Lore (26th level): You gain one 22nd-level utility power from any class.

Seeking Destiny (30th level): You gain the 24th-level epic destiny feature from any other epic destiny that you qualify for.

CHAPTER 5

SKILLS

HAS YOUR character studied ancient tomes that describe the nature of magic and the structure of the universe? Do you have a golden tongue that can pass off the most outrageous lies as truth? Do you have a knack for getting information out of people, or have you trained in balance and tumbling? These capabilities are represented in the game by skills.

As an adventurer, you have a basic level of competence in every skill, and you get more competent as you advance in level. Your ability scores affect your use of skills; a halfling rogue with a high Dexterity is better at Acrobatics than a clumsy dwarf paladin with a lower Dexterity. Your aptitude at a skill is measured in the game with a skill check—a d20 roll that determines whether and sometimes how well you succeed at any skill-based task you might attempt.

This chapter tells you everything you need to know about skills:

+ **Skill Training:** How skill training works, including how you learn additional trained skills.
+ **Using Skills:** How you make a skill check, what your target number is, and how to make a check without rolling a die.
+ **Knowledge Skills:** General rules for the skills that determine how much you know about the D&D universe and the creatures that populate it.
+ **Skill Descriptions:** Descriptions of what you can do with the game's skills, from Acrobatics to Thievery.

FRANZ VOHWINKEL

SKILL TRAINING

Training in a skill means that you have some combination of formal instruction, practical experience, and natural aptitude using that skill.

When you select a skill to be trained in, you gain a permanent +5 bonus to that skill. You can't gain training in a skill more than once.

The entry for your class in Chapter 4 tells you how many skills you're trained in and what skills you can choose at 1st level. For example, if you're a 1st-level warlock, you can pick four skills from a list of eight. You can take the Skill Training feat to gain training in a skill even if it's not on your class skill list. Some multiclass feats also give skill training.

The table below shows the skills available in the game, the ability modifier you use when you make that kind of skill check, and which classes have that skill as a class skill.

Key Skill	Ability	Class Skill for . . .
Acrobatics	Dex	Ranger, rogue
Arcana	Int	Cleric, warlock, wizard
Athletics	Str	Fighter, ranger, rogue, warlord
Bluff	Cha	Rogue, warlock
Diplomacy	Cha	Cleric, paladin, warlord, wizard
Dungeoneering	Wis	Ranger, rogue, wizard
Endurance	Con	Fighter, paladin, ranger, warlord
Heal	Wis	Cleric, fighter, paladin, ranger, warlord
History	Int	Cleric, paladin, warlock, warlord, wizard
Insight	Wis	Cleric, paladin, rogue, warlock, wizard
Intimidate	Cha	Fighter, paladin, rogue, warlock, warlord
Nature	Wis	Ranger, wizard
Perception	Wis	Ranger, rogue
Religion	Int	Cleric, paladin, warlock, wizard
Stealth	Dex	Ranger, rogue
Streetwise	Cha	Fighter, rogue, warlock
Thievery	Dex	Rogue, warlock

USING SKILLS

When you use a skill, you make a skill check. This check represents your training, your natural talent (your ability modifier), your overall experience (one-half your level), other applicable factors (relevant bonuses), and sheer luck (a die roll).

The DM tells you if a skill check is appropriate in a given situation or directs you to make a check if circumstances call for one.

SKILL CHECK BONUSES

When you create your character, you should determine your base skill check bonus for each skill you know. Your base skill check bonus for a skill includes the following:

✦ One-half your level
✦ Your ability score modifier (each skill is based on one of your ability scores)
✦ A +5 bonus if you're trained in the skill

In addition, some or all of the following factors might apply to your base skill check bonus:

✦ Armor check penalty, if you're wearing some kinds of armor (see Chapter 7) and making a check using Strength, Dexterity, or Constitution as the key ability
✦ Racial or feat bonuses
✦ An item bonus from a magic item
✦ A power bonus
✦ Any untyped bonus that might apply

SKILL CHECK

To make a skill check, roll 1d20 and add the following:

✦ Your base skill check bonus with the skill
✦ All situational modifiers that apply
✦ Bonuses and penalties from powers affecting you

The total is your check result.

DIFFICULTY CLASS

When you make skill checks, high results are best. You're always trying to meet or beat a certain number. Often, that's a fixed number, called a Difficulty Class (DC). The DC depends on what you're trying to accomplish and is ultimately set by the Dungeon Master. The skill entries in this chapter give sample DCs for each skill. The DM sets the DCs for specific situations based on level, conditions, and circumstances, as detailed in the *Dungeon Master's Guide*. All DCs assume acting in situations that are far from mundane; the DM should call for checks only in dramatic situations.

OPPOSED CHECKS

Sometimes, you make a skill check as a test of your skill in one area against another character's skill in the same area or in a different one. When you use Stealth, for example, you're testing your ability to hide against someone else's ability to spot hidden things (the Perception skill). These skill contests are called opposed checks. When you make an opposed check, both characters roll, and the higher check result wins. If there's a tie, the character with the higher check modifier wins. If it's still a tie, both sides roll again to break the tie.

CHECKS WITHOUT ROLLS

In some situations, luck does not affect whether you succeed or fail. In a calm environment (outside an encounter), when dealing with a mundane task, you can rely on sheer ability to achieve results.

TAKE 10

When you're not in a rush, not being threatened or distracted (when you're outside an encounter), and when you're dealing with a mundane task, you can choose to take 10. Instead of rolling a d20, determine your skill check result as if you had rolled the average (10). When you take 10, your result equals your skill modifiers (including one-half your level) + 10. For mundane tasks, taking 10 usually results in a success.

> **TAKE 10**
> Your check result when you take 10 is equal to 10 + your base skill check bonus for a particular skill.

PASSIVE CHECKS

When you're not actively using a skill, you're assumed to be taking 10 for any opposed checks using that skill. Passive checks are most commonly used for Perception checks and Insight checks, but the DM might also use your passive check result with skills such as Arcana or Dungeoneering to decide how much to tell you about a monster at the start of an encounter.

For example, if you're walking through an area you expect to be safe and thus aren't actively looking around for danger, you're taking 10 on your Perception check to notice hidden objects or enemies. If your Perception check is high enough, or a creature rolls poorly on its Stealth check, you might notice the creature even if you aren't actively looking for it.

COOPERATION

In some situations, you and your allies can work together to use a skill; your allies can help you make a skill check by making a check themselves. Each ally who gets a result of 10 or higher gives you a +2 bonus to your check. Up to four allies can help you, for a maximum bonus of +8. If you have a choice, let the character in your group who has the highest base skill check bonus take the lead, while the other characters cooperate to give bonuses to the check. See "Aid Another," page 287, for how to cooperate in combat.

SKILL CHALLENGES

A skill challenge is an encounter in which your skills, rather than your combat abilities, take center stage. In contrast to an obstacle that requires one successful skill check, a skill challenge is a complex situation in which you must make several successful checks, often using a variety of skills, before you can claim success in the encounter.

The *Dungeon Master's Guide* contains rules for skill challenges, and each encounter has its own guidelines and requirements. In one skill challenge, you might use a Diplomacy check to entreat a duke to send soldiers into a mountain pass, a History check to remind him what happened when his ancestors neglected the pass's defense, and an Insight check to realize that having your fighter companion lean on the duke with an Intimidate check wouldn't help your cause. In another skill challenge, you might use Nature checks and Perception checks to track cultists through a jungle, a Religion check to predict a likely spot for their hidden temple, and an Endurance check to fight off the effects of illness and exhaustion over the course of days in the jungle.

Whatever the details of a skill challenge, the basic structure of a skill challenge is straightforward. Your goal is to accumulate a specific number of victories (usually in the form of successful skill checks) before you get too many defeats (failed checks). It's up to you to think of ways you can use your skills to meet the challenges you face.

KNOWLEDGE SKILLS

Some skills deal with knowledge about a particular topic: Arcana, Dungeoneering, History, Nature, and Religion. You can use such a skill to remember a useful bit of information in its field of knowledge or to recognize a clue related to it. You can also use such a skill to identify certain kinds of monsters, as noted in a skill's description.

The check DC increases based on the specific topic and how common the knowledge is. The check DC increases based on the specific topic and how common the knowledge is. Sometimes your DM might decide that the information you seek is available only to characters trained in an appropriate knowledge skill.

Paragon and Epic Tiers: If the knowledge pertains to the paragon tier or the epic tier, the DC increases as shown on the tables later in this section.

KNOWLEDGE CHECKS

Regardless of the knowledge skill you're using, refer to the rules here when making a knowledge check.

Common Knowledge: This includes the kind of general information that is commonly known about a given topic.

Expert Knowledge: This includes the kind of specialized information that only an expert in the field of study could possibly know.

Master Knowledge: This includes the kind of esoteric information that only a master in the field of study could possibly know.

> **Knowledge Skill:** No action required—either you know the answer or you don't.
> - ✦ **DC:** See the table.
> - ✦ **Success:** You recall a useful bit of information in your field of knowledge or recognize a clue related to it.
> - ✦ **Failure:** You don't recall any pertinent information. The DM might allow you to make a new check if further information comes to light.

Level of Knowledge	DC
Common	15
Expert	20
Master	25
Paragon tier	+10
Epic tier	+15

MONSTER KNOWLEDGE CHECKS

Regardless of the knowledge skill you're using, refer to the rules here when making a check to identify a monster.

> **Monster Knowledge:** No action required—either you know the answer or you don't.
> - ✦ **DC:** See the table.
> - ✦ **Success:** You identify a creature as well as its type, typical temperament, and keywords. Higher results give you information about the creature's powers, resistances, and vulnerabilities.
> - ✦ **Failure:** You don't recall any pertinent information. The DM might allow you to make a new check if further information comes to light.

Monster Knowledge	DC
Name, type, and keywords	15
Powers	20
Resistances and vulnerabilities	25
Paragon tier creature	+5
Epic tier creature	+10

SKILL DESCRIPTIONS

The first line of a skill description shows the name of the skill, followed by the key ability for that skill. You use the ability modifier for that ability score to figure out your base skill check bonus.

For skills based on Strength, Constitution, and Dexterity, the description includes a reminder that your armor check penalty applies to that skill.

The skill description explains the different ways you can use the skill and provides typical DCs. Each description also specifies what kind of action is required to use the skill.

ACROBATICS (DEXTERITY)

Armor Check Penalty

You can perform an acrobatic stunt, keep your balance while walking on narrow or unstable surfaces, slip free of a grab or restraints, or take less damage from a fall.

ACROBATIC STUNT

Make an Acrobatics check to swing from a chandelier, somersault over an opponent, slide down a staircase on your shield, or attempt any other acrobatic stunt that you can imagine and that your DM agrees to let you try. The DM sets the DC based on the complexity of the stunt and the danger of the situation. If the stunt fails, you fall prone in the square where you began the stunt (the DM might change where you land, depending on the specific stunt and situation). Your DM always has the right to say that a stunt won't work in a particular situation or to set a high DC.

> **Acrobatic Stunt:** Standard action or move action, depending on the stunt.
> - ✦ **DC:** Base DC 15.
> - ✦ **Success:** You perform an acrobatic stunt.
> - ✦ **Failure:** You fail to pull off the stunt and might fall or suffer some other consequence.

BALANCE

Make an Acrobatics check to move across a surface less than 1 foot wide (such as a ledge or a tightrope) or across an unstable surface (such as a wind-tossed rope bridge or a rocking log).

> **Balance:** Part of a move action.
> - ✦ **DC:** See the table.
> - ✦ **Success:** You can move one-half your speed across a narrow or unstable surface.
> - ✦ **Fail by 4 or Less:** You stay in the square you started in and lose the rest of your move action, but you don't fall. You can try again as part of a move action.
> - ✦ **Fail by 5 or More:** You fall off the surface (see "Falling," page 284) and lose the rest of your move action. If you are trying to move across an unstable surface that isn't narrow, you instead fall prone in the square you started in. You can try again as part of a move action if you're still on the surface.
> - ✦ **Grant Combat Advantage:** While you are balancing, enemies have combat advantage against you.
> - ✦ **Taking Damage:** If you take damage, you must make a new Acrobatics check to remain standing.

Surface	Acrobatics DC
Narrow or unstable	20
Very narrow (less than 6 inches)	+5
Narrow and unstable	+5

ESCAPE FROM A GRAB

Make an Acrobatics check to wriggle out of a grab (see "Escape," page 288). You can also make escape attempts to get away from other immobilizing effects, as directed by your DM.

ESCAPE FROM RESTRAINTS

Make an Acrobatics check to slip free of restraints.

Escape from Restraints: 5 minutes.
+ **DC:** Base DC 20. The DC is determined by the type of restraint and its quality, as set by the DM.
+ **Fast Escape:** You can make an escape attempt as a standard action, but the DC increases by 10.
+ **Success:** You slip free of a physical restraint.
+ **Failure:** You can try again only if someone else aids you.

REDUCE FALLING DAMAGE (TRAINED ONLY)

If you fall or jump down from a height, you can make an Acrobatics check to reduce the amount of falling damage you take.

Reduce Falling Damage: Free action if you fall or a move action if you jump down.
+ **Damage Reduced:** Make an Acrobatics check, and reduce the amount of falling damage you take by one-half your check result (round down).

Example: The floor beneath Kora swings open over a pit, and she makes an Acrobatics check to reduce the falling damage. The pit is 40 feet deep, resulting in 24 points of damage (from a roll of 4d10). Her Acrobatics check result is 21, which reduces the damage by 10. She takes 14 points of damage from the fall.

ARCANA (INTELLIGENCE)

You have picked up knowledge about magic-related lore and magic effects. This knowledge extends to information about the following planes of existence, including the creatures native to those planes: the Elemental Chaos, the Feywild, and the Shadowfell.

If you have selected this skill as a trained skill, your knowledge represents academic study, either formalized or as a hobby. Also, those trained in the skill have a chance to know something about the mysterious Far Realm (but not about its creatures, which fall under Dungeoneering).

ARCANA KNOWLEDGE

Make an Arcana check to recall a useful bit of magic-related knowledge or to recognize a magic-related clue. See "Knowledge Checks," page 180.

You must be trained in Arcana to remember information about the Far Realm, which requires master knowledge (DC 25) at least.

MONSTER KNOWLEDGE

Elemental, Fey, and Shadow
Make an Arcana check to identify a creature that has the elemental, the fey, or the shadow origin (a creature of the Elemental Chaos, the Feywild, or the Shadowfell), or is a construct. See "Monster Knowledge Checks," page 180.

DETECT MAGIC (TRAINED ONLY)

Your knowledge of magic allows you to identify magical effects and sense the presence of magic.

Identify Conjuration or Zone: Minor action.
+ **DC:** DC 15 + one-half the power's level. You must be able to see the effect of the conjuration or zone.
+ **Success:** You identify the power used to create the effect and its power source and keywords.
+ **Failure:** You can't try to identify the effect again during this encounter.

Identify Ritual: Standard action.
+ **DC:** DC 20 + one-half the ritual's level. You must be able to see or otherwise detect the ritual's effects.
+ **Success:** You identify the ritual and its category.
+ **Failure:** You can't try to identify the ritual again until after an extended rest.

Identify Magical Effect: Standard action.
+ **DC:** DC 20 + one-half the effect's level, if any. You must be able to see or otherwise detect the effect.
+ **Not a Power or a Ritual:** The magical effect must be neither from a magic item nor the product of a power or a ritual.
+ **Success:** You learn the effect's name, power source, and keywords, if any of those apply.
+ **Failure:** You can't try to identify the effect again until after an extended rest.

Sense the Presence of Magic: 1 minute.
+ **DC:** DC 20 + one-half the level of a magic item, power (conjuration or zone), ritual, or magical phenomenon within range.
+ **Area of Detection:** You can detect magic within a number of squares equal to 5 + your level in every direction, and you can ignore any sources of magical energy you're already aware of. Ignore all barriers; you can detect magic through walls, doors, and such.

- **Success:** You detect each source of magical energy whose DC you meet. You learn the magic's power source, if any. If the source of magical energy is within line of sight, you pinpoint its location. If it's not within line of sight, you know the direction from which the magical energy emanates, but you don't know the distance to it.
- **Failure:** Either you detected nothing or there was nothing in range to detect. You can't try again in this area until after an extended rest.

ATHLETICS (STRENGTH)

Armor Check Penalty

Make an Athletics check to attempt physical activities that rely on muscular strength, including climbing, escaping from a grab, jumping, and swimming.

CLIMB

Make an Athletics check to climb up or down a surface. Different circumstances and surfaces make climbing easier or harder.

Climb: Part of a move action.
- **DC:** See the table. If you use a climber's kit, you get a +2 bonus to your Athletics check. If you can brace yourself between two surfaces, you get a +5 bonus to your check.
- **Success:** You climb at one-half your speed. When you climb to reach the top of a surface, such as when you climb out of a pit, the distance to reach the top includes allowing you to arrive in the square adjacent to the surface. The last square of movement places you on that square.
- **Fail by 4 or Less:** You stay where you started and lose the rest of your move action, but you don't fall. You can try again as part of a move action.
- **Fail by 5 or More:** You fall (see "Falling," page 284) and lose the rest of your move action.
- **Grant Combat Advantage:** While you are climbing, all enemies have combat advantage against you.
- **Uses Movement:** Count the number of squares you climb as part of your move.
- **Taking Damage:** If you take damage while climbing, you must make a Climb check using the DC for the surface you're climbing. If that damage makes you bloodied, increase the DC by 5. If you fail the check, you fall from your current height. If you try to catch hold when you fall, add the damage you take to the DC to catch yourself.
- **Catch Hold:** If you fall while climbing, you can make an Athletics check as a free action to catch hold of something to stop your fall. The base DC to catch hold of something is the DC of the surface you were climbing plus 5, modified by circumstances. You can make one check to catch hold. If you fail, you can't try again unless the DM rules otherwise.

- **Climb Speed:** While climbing, creatures that have a climb speed (such as monstrous spiders) use that speed, ignore difficult terrain, do not grant combat advantage because of climbing, and do not make Athletics checks to climb.

Surface	Athletics DC
Ladder	0
Rope	10
Uneven surface (cave wall)	15
Rough surface (brick wall)	20
Slippery surface	+5
Unusually smooth surface	+5

ESCAPE FROM A GRAB

Make an Athletics check to muscle out of a grab (see "Escape," page 288). You can also make escape attempts to get away from other immobilizing effects, as directed by your DM.

JUMP

Make an Athletics check to jump vertically to reach a dangling rope or a high ledge or to jump horizontally to leap across a pit, a patch of difficult terrain, a low wall, or some other obstacle.

High Jump: Part of a move action.
- **Distance Jumped Vertically:** Make an Athletics check and divide your check result by 10 (round down). This is the number of feet you can leap up. The result determines the height that your feet clear with a jump. To determine if you can reach something while leaping, add your character's height plus one-third rounded down (a 6-foot-tall character would add 8 feet to the final distance, and a 4-foot-tall character would add 5 feet).
- **Running Start:** If you move at least 2 squares before making the jump, divide your check result by 5, not 10.
- **Uses Movement:** Count the number of squares you jump as part of your move. If you run out of movement, you fall. You can end your first move in midair if you double move (page 284).

Example: Marc, a 6-foot-tall human, attempts a high jump to catch a rope dangling 12 feet overhead. His check result is 26. With a running start, he leaps the distance (26 ÷ 5 = 5 feet, plus his height and one-third for a final reach of 13 feet). If Marc leaps from a standing position, he can't quite reach the end of the rope (26 ÷ 10 = 2 feet for a final reach of 10 feet).

Long Jump: Part of a move action.
- **Distance Jumped Horizontally:** Make an Athletics check and divide your check result by 10 (don't round the result). This is the number of squares you

can leap across. You land in the square determined by your result. If you end up over a pit or a chasm, you fall and lose the rest of your move action.

✦ **Distance Cleared Vertically:** The vertical distance you clear is equal to one-quarter of the distance you jumped horizontally. If you could not clear the vertical distance of an obstacle along the way, you hit the obstacle, fall prone, and lose the rest of your move action.

✦ **Running Start:** If you move at least 2 squares before making the jump, divide your check result by 5, not 10.

✦ **Uses Movement:** Count the number of squares you jump as part of your move. If you run out of movement, you fall. You can end your first move in midair if you double move (page 284).

Example: Marc attempts a long jump to clear a 5-foot-high wall of thorns and the 10-foot-wide pit beyond it. His check result is 24. With a running start, he easily jumps the distance (24 ÷ 5 = 4.8 squares or 24 feet) and clears the wall (24 ÷ 4 = 6 feet). If Marc jumps from a standing position, he can't quite make it across the pit (24 ÷ 10 = 2.4 squares or 12 feet) and doesn't clear the wall (12 ÷ 4 = 3 feet). He hits the wall of thorns and falls prone before reaching the pit.

SWIM

Make an Athletics check to swim or to tread water. Different conditions make swimming harder. See the Endurance skill for information on swimming or treading water for an hour or more.

Swim or Tread Water: Part of a move action.
✦ **DC:** See the table.
✦ **Success:** You swim at one-half your speed, or you stay afloat and tread water.
✦ **Fail by 4 or Less:** Stay where you are and lose the rest of your move action. You can try again as part of a move action.
✦ **Fail by 5 or More:** Sink 1 square and risk suffocation by drowning (details are in Chapter 9 of the *Dungeon Master's Guide*).
✦ **Uses Movement:** Count the number of squares you swim as part of your move.
✦ **Swim Speed:** While swimming, creatures that have a swim speed (such as sahuagin) use that speed and do not make Athletics checks to swim.

Water	Athletics DC
Calm	10
Rough	15
Stormy	20

BLUFF (CHARISMA)

You can make what's false appear to be true, what's outrageous seem plausible, and what's suspicious seem ordinary. You make a Bluff check to fast-talk a guard, con a merchant, gamble, pass off a disguise or fake documentation, and otherwise tell lies.

Your Bluff check is opposed by an observer's Insight check. Your check might be opposed by multiple Insight checks, depending on how many observers can see and hear you and care about what's going on. During a skill challenge, you might need to beat your observers' Insight checks multiple times to succeed at bluffing them.

Bluff: Standard action in combat or part of a skill challenge.
✦ **Opposed Check:** Bluff vs. Insight.
✦ **Gain Combat Advantage:** Once per combat encounter, you can try to gain combat advantage against an adjacent enemy by feinting. As a standard action, make a Bluff check opposed by the enemy's Insight check. If you succeed, you gain combat advantage against the enemy until the end of your next turn.
✦ **Create a Diversion to Hide:** Once per combat encounter, you can create a diversion to hide. As a standard action, make a Bluff check opposed by the Insight check of an enemy that can see you (if multiple enemies can see you, your Bluff check is opposed by each enemy's Insight check). If you succeed, you create a diversion and can immediately make a Stealth check to hide.

DIPLOMACY (CHARISMA)

You can influence others with your tact, subtlety, and social grace. Make a Diplomacy check to change opinions, to inspire good will, to haggle with a patron, to demonstrate proper etiquette and decorum, or to negotiate a deal in good faith.

A Diplomacy check is made against a DC set by the DM. The target's general attitude toward you (friendly or unfriendly, peaceful or hostile) and other conditional modifiers (such as what you might be seeking to accomplish or what you're asking for) might apply to the DC. Diplomacy is usually used in a skill challenge that requires a number of successes, but the DM might call for a Diplomacy check in other situations.

DUNGEONEERING (WISDOM)

You have picked up knowledge and skills related to dungeoneering, including finding your way through dungeon complexes, navigating winding caverns, recognizing dungeon hazards, and foraging for food in the Underdark.

If you have selected this skill as a trained skill, your knowledge represents formalized study or extensive experience, and you have a better chance of knowing esoteric information in this field. Also, those trained in the skill can identify creatures of the Far Realm that lair and hunt in dungeons and underground settings.

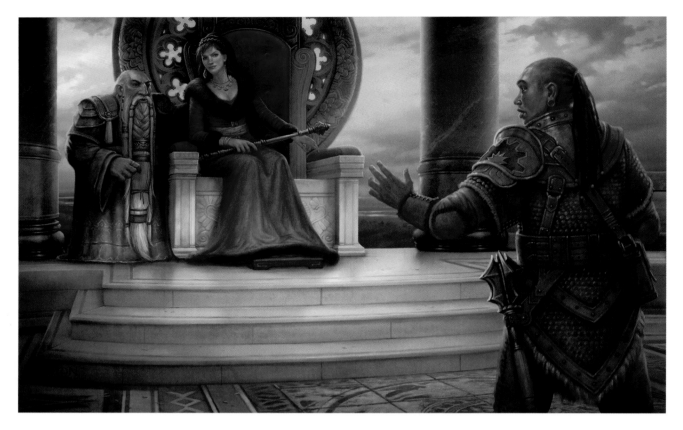

DUNGEONEERING KNOWLEDGE

Make a Dungeoneering check to remember a useful bit of knowledge about an underground environment or to recognize an underground hazard or clue. See "Knowledge Checks," page 180.

Examples of dungeoneering knowledge include determining cardinal directions while underground (common), recognizing a dangerous underground plant (expert), or spotting new construction or noticing a change in depth while exploring an area (expert).

FORAGE

Make a Dungeoneering check to locate and gather enough food and water to last for 24 hours. You can do this only in underground environments that approximate outdoor wilderness—caverns or underground complexes containing pools of water, edible fungus or lichen, small vermin, and the like.

Forage: 1 hour.
✦ **DC:** DC 15 to find food and water for one person, DC 25 for up to five people. The DM might adjust the DC in different environments (5 lower in a cultivated environment or 5 higher in a barren one).
✦ **Success:** You find enough food and water for 24 hours.
✦ **Failure:** You find no food or water. You can forage again but in a different area.

MONSTER KNOWLEDGE

Aberrant

Make a Dungeoneering check to identify a creature that has the aberrant origin (a creature of the Far Realm). See "Monster Knowledge Checks," page 180.

ENDURANCE (CONSTITUTION)

Armor Check Penalty

Make an Endurance check to stave off ill effects and to push yourself beyond normal physical limits. You can hold your breath for long periods of time, forestall the debilitating effects of hunger and thirst, and swim or tread water for extended periods.

Some environmental hazards—including extreme temperatures, violent weather, and diseases—require you to make an Endurance check to resist and delay debilitating effects.

Chapter 3 of the *Dungeon Master's Guide* contains rules for enduring extreme weather, disease, and hunger and thirst.

Endurance: No action required.
✦ **DC:** See the table. The check DC varies based on the situation and the level of a hazard.
✦ **Success:** You endure a particular situation.
✦ **Failure:** You can't try again until circumstances change or a certain amount of time has elapsed.

Task	Endurance DC
Endure extreme weather	Base 15
Resist disease	Varies
Ignore hunger	10 + 2 per day
Ignore thirst	15 + 4 per day
Hold breath (each round after 5)	10 + 1 per round
Swim or tread water (after 1 hour)	15 + 2 per hour

HEAL (WISDOM)

You know how to help someone recover from wounds or debilitating conditions, including disease.

FIRST AID

Make a Heal check to administer first aid.

> **First Aid:** Standard action.
> ✦ **DC:** Varies depending on the task you're attempting.
> ✦ **Use Second Wind:** Make a DC 10 Heal check to allow an adjacent character to use his or her second wind (page 291) without the character having to spend an action. The character doesn't gain the defense bonuses normally granted by second wind.
> ✦ **Stabilize the Dying:** Make a DC 15 Heal check to stabilize an adjacent dying character. If you succeed, the character can stop making death saving throws until he or she takes damage. The character's current hit point total doesn't change as a result of being stabilized.
> ✦ **Grant a Saving Throw:** Make a DC 15 Heal check. If you succeed, an adjacent ally can immediately make a saving throw, or the ally gets a +2 bonus to a saving throw at the end of his or her next turn.

TREAT DISEASE

Make a Heal check to treat a character suffering from a disease. Chapter 3 of the *Dungeon Master's Guide* has more information about disease.

> **Treat Disease:** Part of the diseased character's extended rest. You must attend the character periodically throughout the extended rest, and you make your Heal check when the rest ends.
> ✦ **Replaces Endurance:** Your Heal check result determines the disease's effects if the result is higher than the diseased character's Endurance check result.

HISTORY (INTELLIGENCE)

You have picked up knowledge related to the history of a region and beyond, including the chronological record of significant events and an explanation of their causes. This includes information pertaining to royalty and other leaders, wars, legends, significant personalities, laws, customs, traditions, and memorable events.

If you have selected this skill as a trained skill, your knowledge represents academic study, either formalized or as a hobby, and you have a better chance of knowing esoteric information in this field.

Make a History check to remember a useful bit of historical knowledge or to recognize a historical clue. See "Knowledge Checks," page 180.

INSIGHT (WISDOM)

You can discern intent and decipher body language during social interactions. You make an Insight check to comprehend motives, to read between the lines, to get a sense of moods and attitudes, and to determine how truthful someone is being.

You use Insight to counter a Bluff check, and Insight is used as the social counterpart to the Perception skill. In skill challenges that require a number of successes, use Insight checks to oppose someone's Bluff checks. Insight can also be used to gain clues, figure out how well you might be doing in a social situation, and to determine if someone is under the influence of an outside force.

Whenever you use Insight, you're making a best guess as to what you think a motive or attitude is or how truthful a target is being. Insight is not an exact science or a supernatural power; it represents your ability to get a sense of how a person is behaving.

> **Insight:** No action required when countering a Bluff check, minor action in combat, or part of a skill challenge. Requires some amount of interaction to get a read on a target.
> ✦ **DC:** See the table. If you're trying to see through a bluff, this is an opposed check against your opponent's Bluff check.
> ✦ **Success:** You counter a Bluff check, gain a clue about a social situation, sense an outside influence on someone, or recognize an effect as illusory.
> ✦ **Failure:** You can't try again until circumstances change.
> ✦ **Recognizing an Effect as Illusory:** The DM might use your passive Insight check to determine if you notice the telltale signs of an illusion effect. Noticing such an effect doesn't break the illusion, but you recognize the effect as illusory.

Task	Insight DC
Sense motives, attitudes	10 + creature's level
Sense outside influence	25 + effect's level
Recognize effect as illusory	15 + effect's level

5

INTIMIDATE (CHARISMA)

Make an Intimidate check to influence others through hostile actions, overt threats, and deadly persuasion.

Intimidate can be used in combat encounters or as part of a skill challenge that requires a number of successes. Your Intimidate checks are made against a target's Will defense or a DC set by the DM. The target's general attitude toward you and other conditional modifiers (such as what you might be seeking to accomplish or what you're asking for) might apply to the DC.

Intimidate: Standard action in combat or part of a skill challenge.
+ **Opposed Check:** Intimidate vs. Will (see the table for modifiers to your target's defense). If you can't speak a language your target understands, you take a –5 penalty to your check. If you attempt to intimidate multiple enemies at once, make a separate Intimidate check against each enemy's Will defense. Each target must be able to see and hear you.
+ **Success:** You force a bloodied target to surrender, get a target to reveal secrets against its will, or cow a target into taking some other action.
+ **Failure:** If you attempted to intimidate the target during combat, you can't try again against that target during this encounter.
+ **Target Becomes Hostile:** Using Intimidate usually makes a target hostile toward you, even if you don't succeed on the check.

Enemy is . . .	Will Defense Modifier
Hostile	+10
Unfriendly	+5

NATURE (WISDOM)

You have picked up knowledge and skills related to nature, including finding your way through the wilderness, recognizing natural hazards, dealing with and identifying natural creatures, and living off the land.

If you have selected this skill as a trained skill, your knowledge represents formalized study or extensive experience, and you have a better chance of knowing esoteric information in this field.

FORAGE

Make a Nature check to locate and gather enough food and water to last for 24 hours.

Forage: 1 hour.
+ **DC:** DC 15 to find food and water for one person, DC 25 for up to five people. The DM might adjust the DC in different environments (5 lower in a cultivated environment or 5 higher in a barren one).
+ **Success:** You find enough food and water for 24 hours.
+ **Failure:** You find no food or water. You can forage again but in a different area.

HANDLE ANIMAL

Make a Nature check to calm down a natural beast, teach a natural beast some tricks, or otherwise handle a natural beast. Handling a natural beast is usually part of a skill challenge that requires a number of successes.

NATURE KNOWLEDGE

Make a Nature check to remember a useful bit of knowledge about the natural world—about terrain, climate, weather, plants, and seasons—or to recognize a nature-related clue. See "Knowledge Checks," page 180.

Examples of Nature knowledge include determining cardinal directions or finding a path (common), recognizing a dangerous plant or another natural hazard (master), or predicting a coming change in the weather (expert).

MONSTER KNOWLEDGE

Natural

Make a Nature check to identify a creature that has the natural origin (a creature of the natural world). See "Monster Knowledge Checks," page 180.

PERCEPTION (WISDOM)

Make a Perception check to notice clues, detect secret doors, spot imminent dangers, find traps, follow tracks, listen for sounds behind a closed door, or locate hidden objects.

This skill is used against another creature's Stealth check or against a DC set by the DM. In most situations, the DM uses your passive Perception check result to determine if you notice a clue or an imminent danger.

Perception: No action required—either you notice something or you don't. Your DM usually uses your passive Perception check result. If you want to use the skill actively, you need to take a standard action or spend 1 minute listening or searching, depending on the task.
+ **Opposed Check:** Perception vs. Stealth when trying to spot or hear a creature using Stealth. Your check might be modified by distance or if you're listening through a door or a wall (see the table).
+ **DC:** See the table for DCs when you're trying to hear or spot something, searching an area, or looking for tracks.
+ **Success:** You spot or hear something.
+ **Failure:** You can't try again unless circumstances change.

✦ **Searching:** When actively searching an area or looking for something specific, assume you're searching each adjacent square. The DM might allow you to do this as a standard action, but usually searching requires at least 1 minute.

Listen	Perception DC
Battle	0
Normal conversation	10
Whispers	20
Through a door	+5
Through a wall	+10
More than 10 squares away	+2

Spot or Search	Perception DC
Barely hidden	10
Well hidden	25
More than 10 squares away	+2

Find Tracks	Perception DC
Soft ground (snow, loose dirt, mud)	15
Hard ground (wood or stone)	25
Rain or snow since tracks were made	+10
Each day since tracks were made	+2
Quarry obscured its tracks	+5
Huge or larger creature	-5
Group of ten or more	-5

RELIGION (INTELLIGENCE)

You have picked up knowledge about gods, religious traditions and ceremonies, divine effects, holy symbols, and theology. This knowledge extends to information about the undead and the Astral Sea, including the creatures of that plane.

If you have selected this skill as a trained skill, your knowledge represents academic study, either formalized or as a hobby, and you have a better chance of knowing esoteric information in this field.

RELIGION KNOWLEDGE

Make a Religion check to remember a useful bit of religious knowledge or to recognize a religion-related clue. See "Knowledge Checks," page 180.

MONSTER KNOWLEDGE

Immortal or Undead
Make a Religion check to identify a creature that has the immortal origin (a creature of the Astral Sea) or the undead keyword. See "Monster Knowledge Checks," page 180.

STEALTH (DEXTERITY)

Armor Check Penalty

Make a Stealth check to conceal yourself from enemies, slink past guards, slip away without being noticed, and sneak up on people without being seen or heard.

This skill is used against another creature's Perception check or against a DC set by the DM.

Stealth: Part of whatever action you are trying to perform stealthily.
- **Opposed Check:** Stealth vs. Perception (see the table for modifiers to your check). If there are multiple observers, your Stealth check is opposed by each observer's Perception check.
- **Cover or Concealment:** Unless a creature is distracted, you must have cover against or concealment from the creature to make a Stealth check. You have to maintain cover or concealment to remain unnoticed. If a creature has unblocked line of sight to you (that is, you lack any cover or concealment), the creature automatically sees you (no Perception check required).
- **Superior Cover or Total Concealment:** If you have superior cover or total concealment, a creature can't see you and can't be sure of your exact location. If its Perception check beats your Stealth check, though, it knows you are present, knows the direction to your location, and has a vague idea of the distance between the two of you. If its Perception check beats your Stealth check by 10 or more, the creature can pinpoint your location until the end of your next turn, even if you move.
- **Distracted Creature:** If a creature is distracted, you can attempt to hide from that creature even when you don't have cover or concealment. In combat, creatures are assumed to be paying attention in all directions. Outside combat, a creature might be paying attention to something in a certain direction, allowing you to hide behind the creature's back. You make a Stealth check as normal to avoid the creature's notice, since it might hear you.
- **Success:** You avoid notice, unheard and hidden from view. If you later attack or shout, you're no longer hidden.
- **Failure:** You can't try again unless observers become distracted or you manage to obtain cover or concealment.
- **Combat Advantage:** You have combat advantage against a target that isn't aware of you.
- **Light Source:** Observers automatically see you if you're carrying a light source.

You . . .	Stealth Modifier
Speak	-5
Move more than 2 squares	-5
Run	-10

STREETWISE (CHARISMA)

When in a settlement—a village, a town, or a city—make a Streetwise check to find out what's going on, who the movers and shakers are, where to get what you need (and how to get there), and where not to go.

Streetwise: Using this skill takes 1 hour and might be part of a skill challenge.
- **DC:** See the table.
- **Success:** You collect a useful bit of information, gather rumors, find out about available jobs, or locate the best deal.
- **Failure:** You can try again, but you might draw attention to yourself if you keep chasing after the same information.

Settlement and Information	Streetwise DC
Typical settlement	15
Hostile settlement	20
Totally alien settlement	30
Information is readily available	-2
Information is hard to come by	+5
Information is secret or closely guarded	+10

THIEVERY (DEXTERITY)

Armor Check Penalty

You have picked up thieving abilities and can perform tasks that require nerves of steel and a steady hand: disabling traps, opening locks, picking pockets, and sleight of hand.

The DM might decide that some uses of this skill are so specialized that you are required to be trained in it to have a chance of succeeding.

DISABLE TRAP

Make a Thievery check to prevent a trap from triggering. You need to be aware of a trap to try to disable it. Make a Perception check to find a hidden trap.

Disable Trap: Standard action in combat or part of a skill challenge.
- **DC:** See the table. You get a +2 bonus to the check if you use thieves' tools.
- **Delay Trap:** You get a +5 bonus to the check if you try to delay a trap, rather than disable it.
- **Success:** You disable or delay the trap. Disabling a trap makes it harmless until it resets. Delaying a trap makes the trapped area safe for passage until the end of your next turn.
- **Fail by 4 or Less:** Nothing happens. You can try again as a new action.
- **Fail by 5 or More:** You trigger the trap.

Trap	Thievery DC
Heroic tier	20
Paragon tier	30
Epic tier	35

OPEN LOCK

Make a Thievery check to pick a lock.

> **Open Lock:** Standard action in combat or part of a skill challenge.
> - ✦ **DC:** See the table. You get a +2 bonus to the check if you use thieves' tools.
> - ✦ **Success:** You pick the lock.
> - ✦ **Failure:** You can try again as a new action.

Lock	Thievery DC
Heroic tier	20
Paragon tier	30
Epic tier	35

PICK POCKET

Make a Thievery check to lift a small object (such as a purse or an amulet) from a creature without that creature being aware of the theft. It must be an object that the creature isn't holding.

> **Pick Pocket:** Standard action.
> - ✦ **DC:** DC 20 + your target's level. If in combat, you take a -10 penalty to your check.
> - ✦ **Success:** You lift a small object from the target without the target noticing.
> - ✦ **Fail by 4 or Less:** You don't get the object, but the target didn't notice. You can try again as a new action.
> - ✦ **Fail by 5 or More:** You don't get the object, and the target notices your failed attempt.

SLEIGHT OF HAND

Make a Thievery check to palm an unattended object small enough to fit into your hand (such as a coin or a ring) or to perform an act of legerdemain.

> **Sleight of Hand:** Standard action in combat or part of a skill challenge.
> - ✦ **DC:** Base DC 15.
> - ✦ **Success:** You palm an unattended, small object or perform an act of legerdemain.
> - ✦ **Failure:** You can still pick up the object, but onlookers see you pick it up, or they see through your act of legerdemain.

RAVEN MIMURA

CHAPTER 6

FEATS

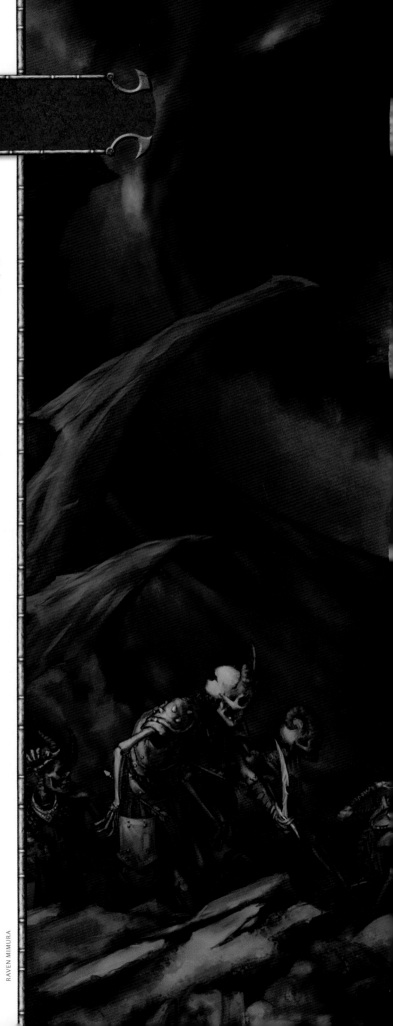

AS YOU advance in level, you gain a number of benefits that improve your capabilities. These benefits are called feats. Typically, a feat doesn't give you a new ability, but instead improves something you're already able to do. A feat might provide a bonus to a skill check, grant a bonus to one of your defense scores, or allow you to ignore a particular restriction or penalty in certain situations. Some feats also allow you to use skills in different ways, alter the effects of your powers, improve your racial traits, or even grant you capabilities from another class.

This chapter discusses all aspects of feats:

✦ **Choosing Feats:** How you gain feats and how they work.
✦ **Feat Descriptions:** Full explanation of each feat and what it does.
✦ **Multiclass Feats:** Discussion of the multiclassing rules and the feats involved.

RAVEN MIMURA

CHOOSING FEATS

When you create a 1st-level character, you select one feat. (If you're human, you have an additional feat at 1st level, so you start with two feats.) You gain an additional feat at every even-numbered level and at 11th and 21st levels. When you choose a feat, you must meet the feat's prerequisites.

Generally, you can't take the same feat more than once, and most of the time you wouldn't want to. A few feats, however, specify that you can take the same feat multiple times. That means you can apply the bonus from the feat to more than one situation—multiple weapon groups, powers you know, and so on.

How Feats Work

Most feats give you small, static bonuses to one of the numbers on your character sheet. When picking feats, there's one important rule to remember about these bonuses: Bonuses of the same type don't add together (or stack).

Some of these bonuses apply in any situation. These are defined as feat bonuses: Great Fortitude gives you a +2 feat bonus to your Fortitude defense, and that bonus is always in effect. If you have two feat bonuses that apply to the same number, only the higher bonus applies—the bonuses don't add together. So if you have both Alertness (which gives you a +2 feat bonus to Perception checks) and Dragonborn Senses (which gives you a +1 feat bonus to Perception checks), you have only a +2 bonus—the bonuses don't add up to +3.

A bonus that's untyped (such as one expressed as simply a "+2 bonus") usually applies only in certain situations. These situational bonuses reward particular combat tactics. For example, Combat Reflexes gives you a +1 bonus to attack rolls with opportunity attacks. Unlike feat bonuses, however, untyped bonuses stack with themselves. If you have both Defensive Advantage (which gives you a +2 bonus to your AC against a foe when you have combat advantage) and Defensive Mobility (a feat that gives you a +2 bonus to your AC against opportunity attacks), you have a +4 bonus as long as both circumstances apply.

Bonuses of different types stack as well. If you have Fleet-Footed and Fast Runner, you have a +1 feat bonus to your speed all the time (from Fleet-Footed), and an additional +2 bonus when you charge or run (from Fast Runner). So your speed when you charge is 3 higher than it would be if you had neither feat.

For more details, see "Bonuses and Penalties," page 275.

Feats and Keywords: When a feat provides a benefit related to using a power that has a keyword, that benefit applies when you use a power of a magic item, as well as when you use a power granted by your class, your race, or another feat.

Types of Feats

A few types of feats have special rules that apply to all feats of the same category.

Class Feats

Class feats help characters of a specific class improve their class features and powers, or specialize their capabilities along the lines of their builds. A class feat is denoted by the name of a class in brackets after the name of the feat: Expanded Spellbook [Wizard] is a feat that only wizards can take.

Class feats are also available to characters who have taken a multiclass feat in the class the feat is associated with. For example, if you're a fighter who has the Sneak of Shadows feat, you can take Press the Advantage, which is a rogue feat.

Divinity Feats

Divinity feats grant characters who have the Channel Divinity class feature (clerics and paladins) the use of special powers from their deity. The power associated with each of these feats follows the feat description. A divinity feat is denoted by "Divinity" in brackets after the name of the feat.

Multiclass Feats

Multiclass feats are a special category of feats. The complete rules for multiclassing and the associated feats are found on page 208. Most multiclass feats are denoted by a bracketed phrase that includes "Multiclass" followed by the name of a class: Student of Battle [Multiclass Warlord], for example, is the feat that lets you gain a feature of the warlord class.

Three of the multiclass feats in this book are of a different sort—they allow you to exchange a class power you have from your primary class for a power of the same type from the class you have chosen to multiclass in. These feats are denoted by a bracketed phrase that includes "Multiclass" followed by the type of power (Encounter, Utility, or Daily) that can be exchanged.

Racial Feats

Racial feats are available only to characters of a specific race. They build on the innate talents of each race and help you create a character who feels like an ideal representative of your race. A racial feat is denoted by the name of a race in brackets after the name of the feat: Lost in the Crowd [Halfling] is a feat that only halflings can take.

FEAT DESCRIPTIONS

The feats in this chapter are presented in the format described below.

LINGUIST
Prerequisite: Int 13
Benefit: Choose three languages. You can now speak, read, and write those languages fluently.
Special: You can take this feat more than once. Each time you select this feat, choose three new languages to learn.

In the header that gives the name of the feat, the type of feat (if appropriate) appears in brackets after the name.

PREREQUISITE(S)
You must meet these additional requirements to take the feat. If you ever lose a prerequisite for a feat (for example, if you use the retraining system to replace training in a prerequisite skill with training in a different skill), you can't use that feat thereafter. If this entry is absent, the feat has no prerequisites.

BENEFIT
This section (which might be more than one paragraph) describes the advantage you gain when you take the feat.

SPECIAL
Occasionally, special rules apply to a feat. This entry specifies whether you can take the same feat multiple times and any provisions that apply if you do so. It also can indicate any other requirement for using the feat.

HEROIC TIER FEATS

Any feat in the following section is available to a character of any level who meets the prerequisites. Heroic tier feats are the only feats you can take if you are 10th level or lower.

ACTION SURGE [HUMAN]
Prerequisite: Human
Benefit: You gain a +3 bonus to attack rolls you make during any action you gained by spending an action point.

AGILE HUNTER [RANGER]
Prerequisites: Dex 15, ranger, Hunter's Quarry class feature
Benefit: When you score a critical hit with a melee attack against the target of your Hunter's Quarry, you can shift as a free action, and the enemy takes a -2 penalty on attack rolls against you until the end of your next turn.

ALERTNESS
Benefit: You don't grant enemies combat advantage during surprise rounds.
You also gain a +2 feat bonus to Perception checks.

ARMOR OF BAHAMUT [DIVINITY]
Prerequisites: Channel Divinity class feature, must worship Bahamut
Benefit: You can invoke the power of your deity to use *armor of Bahamut*.

Channel Divinity: Armor of Bahamut — Feat Power
Bahamut protects you or a friend from devastating harm.
Encounter ✦ Divine
Immediate Interrupt — **Ranged** 5
Trigger: An enemy scores a critical hit on you or an ally
Effect: Turn a critical hit against you or an ally within range into a normal hit.
Special: You must take the Armor of Bahamut feat to use this power.

ARMOR PROFICIENCY (CHAINMAIL)
Prerequisites: Str 13, Con 13, training with leather or hide armor
Benefit: You gain training with chainmail.

ARMOR PROFICIENCY (HIDE)
Prerequisites: Str 13, Con 13, training with leather armor
Benefit: You gain training with hide armor.

ARMOR PROFICIENCY (LEATHER)
Benefit: You gain training with leather armor.

ARMOR PROFICIENCY (PLATE)
Prerequisites: Str 15, Con 15, training with scale armor
Benefit: You gain training with plate armor.

ARMOR PROFICIENCY (SCALE)
Prerequisites: Str 13, Con 13, training with chainmail
Benefit: You gain training with scale armor.

ASTRAL FIRE
Prerequisites: Dex 13, Cha 13
Benefit: You gain a +1 feat bonus to damage rolls when you use a power that has the fire or radiant keyword.
At 11th level, this bonus increases to +2. At 21st level, it increases to +3.

Avandra's Rescue [Divinity]

Prerequisites: Channel Divinity class feature, must worship Avandra

Benefit: You can invoke the power of your deity to use *Avandra's rescue*.

Channel Divinity: Avandra's Rescue — Feat Power

Avandra smiles upon you and helps you rescue a friend in need.

Encounter ✦ Divine
Move Action   **Melee** 1
Target: One ally
Effect: Shift into the space of an adjacent ally; that ally simultaneously shifts into your space. Your space and your ally's space must be the same size.
Special: You must take the Avandra's Rescue feat to use this power.

Backstabber [Rogue]

Prerequisites: Rogue, Sneak Attack class feature

Benefit: The extra damage dice from your Sneak Attack class feature increase from d6s to d8s.

Blade Opportunist

Prerequisites: Str 13, Dex 13

Benefit: You gain a +2 bonus to opportunity attack rolls with a heavy blade or a light blade.

Burning Blizzard

Prerequisites: Int 13, Wis 13

Benefit: You gain a +1 feat bonus to damage rolls when you use a power that has the acid or cold keyword.

At 11th level, this bonus increases to +2. At 21st level, it increases to +3.

Combat Reflexes

Prerequisite: Dex 13

Benefit: You gain a +1 bonus to opportunity attack rolls.

Corellon's Grace [Divinity]

Prerequisites: Channel Divinity class feature, must worship Corellon

Benefit: You can invoke the power of your deity to use *Corellon's grace*.

Channel Divinity: Corellon's Grace — Feat Power

Corellon's grace allows you to move when others take action.

Encounter ✦ Divine
Immediate Interrupt   **Ranged** 10
Trigger: Another creature within range spends an action point to take an extra action
Effect: You take a move action.
Special: You must take the Corellon's Grace feat to use this power.

Dark Fury

Prerequisites: Con 13, Wis 13

Benefit: You gain a +1 feat bonus to damage rolls when you use a power that has the necrotic or psychic keyword.

At 11th level, this bonus increases to +2. At 21st level, it increases to +3.

Defensive Mobility

Benefit: You gain a +2 bonus to AC against opportunity attacks.

Distracting Shield [Fighter]

Prerequisites: Wis 15, fighter, Combat Challenge class feature

Benefit: If you hit a foe with an attack granted by your Combat Challenge class feature, the target takes a -2 penalty to attack rolls until the start of your next turn.

Special: You must have a shield equipped to benefit from this feat.

Dodge Giants [Dwarf]

Prerequisite: Dwarf

Benefit: You gain a +1 bonus to AC and Reflex defense against the attacks of Large or larger foes.

Dragonborn Frenzy [Dragonborn]

Prerequisite: Dragonborn

Benefit: While you are bloodied, you gain a +2 bonus to damage rolls.

Dragonborn Senses [Dragonborn]

Prerequisite: Dragonborn

Benefit: You gain low-light vision.
You gain a +1 feat bonus to Perception checks.

Durable

Benefit: Increase your number of healing surges by two.

Dwarven Weapon Training [Dwarf]

Prerequisite: Dwarf

Benefit: You gain proficiency and a +2 feat bonus to damage rolls with axes and hammers.

Eladrin Soldier [Eladrin]

Prerequisite: Eladrin

Benefit: You gain proficiency with all spears and a +2 feat bonus to damage rolls with longswords and all spears.

Elven Precision [Elf]

Prerequisites: Elf, *elven accuracy* racial power

Benefit: When you use the *elven accuracy* power, you gain a +2 bonus to the new attack roll.

ENLARGED DRAGON BREATH [DRAGONBORN]

Prerequisites: Dragonborn, *dragon breath* racial power

Benefit: When you use your *dragon breath* power, you can choose to make it blast 5 instead of blast 3.

ESCAPE ARTIST

Prerequisite: Trained in Acrobatics

Benefit: You can attempt to escape a grab as a minor action, instead of as a move action.

You gain a +2 feat bonus to Acrobatics checks.

EXPANDED SPELLBOOK [WIZARD]

Prerequisites: Wis 13, wizard

Benefit: Choose one daily wizard attack spell of every level you know. Add this spell to your spellbook.

Each time you gain a new level of daily wizard attack spells, you learn one extra spell of that level (in other words, add three spells to your spellbook instead of only two).

This feat doesn't change the number of daily attack spells you can prepare each day.

FAR SHOT

Prerequisite: Dex 13

Benefit: When you use a projectile weapon such as a bow or a crossbow, increase both the normal range and the long range by 5 squares.

FAR THROW

Prerequisite: Str 13

Benefit: When you use a thrown weapon such as a dagger or a javelin, increase both the normal range and the long range by 2 squares.

FAST RUNNER

Prerequisite: Con 13

Benefit: You gain a +2 bonus to speed when you charge or run.

FEROCIOUS REBUKE [TIEFLING]

Prerequisites: Tiefling, *infernal wrath* racial power

Benefit: When you use the *infernal wrath* power and hit with an attack, you can push the target 1 square in addition to any damage you deal.

GROUP INSIGHT [HALF-ELF]

Prerequisite: Half-elf

Benefit: You grant allies within 10 squares of you a +1 racial bonus to Insight checks and initiative checks.

HALFLING AGILITY [HALFLING]

Prerequisites: Halfling, *second chance* racial power

Benefit: When you use your halfling second chance ability, the attacker takes a –2 penalty to the new attack roll.

HARMONY OF ERATHIS [DIVINITY]

Prerequisites: Channel Divinity class feature, must worship Erathis

Benefit: You can invoke the power of your deity to use *harmony of Erathis*.

Channel Divinity: Harmony of Erathis Feat Power

Erathis brings harmony of purpose to like-minded allies.

Encounter ✦ Divine

Minor Action   **Ranged** 10

Target: One ally

Effect: If you have at least three allies within range, grant one of those allies a +2 power bonus to the first attack roll he or she makes before the start of your next turn.

Special: You must take the Harmony of Erathis feat to use this power.

HEALING HANDS [PALADIN]

Prerequisites: Paladin, *lay on hands* power

Benefit: When you use the *lay on hands* power, the affected ally regains additional hit points equal to your Charisma modifier.

HELLFIRE BLOOD [TIEFLING]

Prerequisite: Tiefling

Benefit: You gain a +1 feat bonus to attack rolls and damage rolls when you use a power that has the fire or fear keyword.

EVA WIDERMANN

HEROIC TIER FEATS

6

HEROIC TIER FEATS

Name	Prerequisites	Benefit
Action Surge	Human	+3 to attacks when you spend an action point
Agile Hunter	Dex 15, ranger, Hunter's Quarry class feature	Shift as a free action after scoring a critical hit
Alertness	—	No combat advantage when surprised, +2 to Perception
Armor of Bahamut	Channel Divinity class feature, must worship Bahamut	Use Channel Divinity to invoke *armor of Bahamut*
Armor Proficiency (Chainmail)	Str 13, Con 13, training with leather or hide armor	Training with chainmail armor
Armor Proficiency (Leather)	—	Training with leather armor
Armor Proficiency (Hide)	Str 13, Con 13, training with leather armor	Training with hide armor
Armor Proficiency (Plate)	Str 15, Con 15, training with scale armor	Training with plate armor
Armor Proficiency (Scale)	Str 13, Con 13, training with chainmail	Training with scale armor
Astral Fire	Dex 13, Cha 13	+1 damage with fire or radiant power
Avandra's Rescue	Channel Divinity class feature, must worship Avandra	Use Channel Divinity to invoke *Avandra's rescue*
Backstabber	Rogue, Sneak Attack class feature	Sneak Attack dice increase to d8s
Blade Opportunist	Str 13, Dex 13	+2 to opportunity attacks with heavy blade or light blade
Burning Blizzard	Int 13, Wis 13	+1 damage with acid or cold power
Combat Reflexes	Dex 13	+1 to opportunity attacks
Corellon's Grace	Channel Divinity class feature, must worship Corellon	Use Channel Divinity to invoke Corellon's grace
Dark Fury	Con 13, Wis 13	+1 damage with necrotic or psychic power
Defensive Mobility	—	+2 to AC against opportunity attacks
Distracting Shield	Wis 15, fighter, Combat Challenge class feature	Target hit by opportunity attack takes -2 to attack rolls
Dodge Giants	Dwarf	+1 to AC and Reflex against attacks of Large or larger foes
Dragonborn Frenzy	Dragonborn	+2 damage when bloodied
Dragonborn Senses	Dragonborn	Low-light vision, +1 to Perception
Durable	—	Increase number of healing surges by 2
Dwarven Weapon Training	Dwarf	+2 damage and proficiency with axes and hammers
Eladrin Soldier	Eladrin	+2 damage and proficiency with longswords and spears
Elven Precision	Elf	+2 to reroll with *elven accuracy*
Enlarged Dragon Breath	Dragonborn, *dragon breath* racial power	Dragon breath becomes blast 5
Escape Artist	Trained in Acrobatics	Escape a grab as minor action, +2 to Acrobatics
Expanded Spellbook	Wis 13, wizard	Add additional daily spell to spellbook
Far Shot	Dex 13	Increase projectile weapon range by 5 squares
Far Throw	Str 13	Increase thrown weapon range by 2 squares
Fast Runner	Con 13	+2 to speed when you charge or run
Ferocious Rebuke	Tiefling, *infernal wrath* racial power	Push 1 square with *infernal wrath*
Group Insight	Half-Elf	Grant allies +1 to Insight and initiative
Halfling Agility	Halfling, *second chance* racial power	Attacker takes a -2 penalty with *second chance* reroll
Harmony of Erathis	Channel Divinity class feature, must worship Erathis	Use Channel Divinity to invoke *harmony of Erathis*
Healing Hands	Paladin, *lay on hands* power	Add Cha modifier to damage healed with *lay on hands*
Hellfire Blood	Tiefling	+1 attack and damage with fire and fear powers
Human Perseverance	Human	+1 to saving throws
Improved Dark One's Blessing	Con 15, warlock, infernal pact	Pact boon grants 3 additional temporary hit points
Improved Fate of the Void	Con 13 or Cha 13, warlock, star pact	Pact boon grants additional +1 bonus to die roll

Name	Prerequisites	Benefit
Improved Initiative	—	+4 to initiative checks
Improved Misty Step	Int 13, warlock, fey pact	Pact boon grants additional 2 squares of teleport
Inspired Recovery	Warlord, Inspiring Presence class feature	Grant ally saving throw with Cha modifier bonus
Ioun's Poise	Channel Divinity class feature, must worship Ioun	Use Channel Divinity to invoke *Ioun's poise*
Jack of All Trades	Int 13	+2 to untrained skill checks
Kord's Favor	Channel Divinity class feature, must worship Kord	Use Channel Divinity to invoke *Kord's favor*
Lethal Hunter	Ranger, Hunter's Quarry class feature	Hunter's Quarry damage dice increase to d8s
Light Step	Elf	Add to overland speed of group, +1 to Acrobatics and Stealth
Linguist	Int 13	Learn three new languages
Long Jumper	Trained in Athletics	Make standing jumps as if from a running start, +1 to Athletics
Lost in the Crowd	Halfling	+2 to AC when adjacent to at least two larger enemies
Melora's Tide	Channel Divinity class feature, must worship Melora	Use Channel Divinity to invoke *Melora's tide*
Moradin's Resolve	Channel Divinity class feature, must worship Moradin	Use Channel Divinity to invoke *Moradin's resolve*
Mounted Combat	—	Gain access to the special abilities of your mount
Nimble Blade	Dex 15	+1 to attacks with light blade and combat advantage
Pelor's Radiance	Channel Divinity class feature, must worship Pelor	Use Channel Divinity to invoke *Pelor's radiance*
Potent Challenge	Con 15, fighter, Combat Challenge class feature	Add Con modifier damage to target hit with opportunity attack
Power Attack	Str 15	+2 damage for -2 to attack
Powerful Charge	Str 13	+2 damage, +2 to bull rush on a charge
Precise Hunter	Wis 15, ranger, Hunter's Quarry class feature	Allies gain +1 attack against target hit by critical hit
Press the Advantage	Cha 15, rogue	Retain combat advantage with a critical hit
Quick Draw	Dex 13	Draw a weapon with attack action, +2 to initiative
Raging Storm	Con 13, Dex 13	+1 damage with lightning or thunder power
Raven Queen's Blessing	Channel Divinity class feature, must worship the Raven Queen	Use Channel Divinity to invoke *Raven Queen's blessing*
Ritual Caster	Trained in Arcana or Religion	Master and perform rituals
Sehanine's Reversal	Channel Divinity class feature, must worship Sehanine	Use Channel Divinity to invoke *Sehanine's reversal*
Shield Proficiency (Heavy)	Str 15, Shield Proficiency (Light)	Proficiency with heavy shields
Shield Proficiency (Light)	Str 13	Proficiency with light shields
Shield Push	Fighter, Combat Challenge class feature	Push 1 square to target hit by Combat Challenge attack
Skill Focus	Training in chosen skill	+3 to checks with chosen skill
Skill Training	—	Gain training in one skill
Sure Climber	Trained in Athletics	Climb at normal speed on any surface, +1 to Athletics
Surprise Knockdown	Str 15, rogue	Knock target prone with critical hit
Tactical Assault	Warlord, Tactical Presence class feature	Ally gains bonus to damage equal to your Int modifier
Toughness	—	Gain 5 additional hit points per tier
Two-Weapon Defense	Dex 13, Two-Weapon Fighting	+1 to AC and Reflex while holding a weapon in each hand
Two-Weapon Fighting	Dex 13	+1 damage while holding a melee weapon in each hand
Weapon Focus	—	+1 damage with chosen weapon group
Weapon Proficiency	—	Gain proficiency with the weapon of your choice
Wintertouched	—	Gain combat advantage against foe vulnerable to cold

6

Human Perseverance [Human]

Prerequisite: Human

Benefit: You gain a +1 feat bonus to saving throws.

Improved Dark One's Blessing [Warlock]

Prerequisites: Con 15, warlock, infernal pact

Benefit: Your Dark One's Blessing now gives you 3 additional temporary hit points.

Improved Fate of the Void [Warlock]

Prerequisites: Con 13 or Cha 13, warlock, star pact

Benefit: Your Fate of the Void grants an additional +1 bonus to the d20 roll.

Improved Initiative

Benefit: You gain a +4 feat bonus to initiative checks.

Improved Misty Step [Warlock]

Prerequisites: Int 13, warlock, fey pact

Benefit: Your Misty Step now allows you to teleport an additional 2 squares.

Inspired Recovery [Warlord]

Prerequisites: Warlord, Inspiring Presence class feature

Benefit: When an ally who can see you spends an action point to gain an extra standard action, that ally can roll a saving throw as a free action, adding your Charisma modifier to the roll.

Ioun's Poise [Divinity]

Prerequisites: Channel Divinity class feature, must worship Ioun

Benefit: You can invoke the power of your deity to use *Ioun's poise*.

Channel Divinity: Ioun's Poise	Feat Power

Ioun grants strength of will to those she favors.

Encounter ✦ Divine

Minor Action   **Ranged 5**

Target: You or one ally

Effect: The target gains a +5 power bonus to Will defense until the start of your next turn.

Special: You must take the Ioun's Poise feat to use this power.

Jack of All Trades

Prerequisite: Int 13

Benefit: You gain a +2 feat bonus to all untrained skill checks.

Kord's Favor [Divinity]

Prerequisites: Channel Divinity class feature, must worship Kord

Benefit: You can invoke the power of your deity to use *Kord's favor*.

Channel Divinity: Kord's Favor	Feat Power

Kord favors a strong hit in combat with healing.

Encounter ✦ Divine, Healing

Free Action   **Ranged 5**

Trigger: You or an ally within range scores a critical hit with a melee attack

Effect: You or the ally can spend a healing surge.

Special: You must take the Kord's Favor feat to use this power.

Lethal Hunter [Ranger]

Prerequisites: Ranger, Hunter's Quarry class feature

Benefit: The extra damage dice from your Hunter's Quarry class feature increase from d6s to d8s.

Light Step [Elf]

Prerequisite: Elf

Benefit: For the purpose of hourly or daily travel rates, add 1 to your overland speed and the speed of all allies in your traveling group.

Add 5 to the DC required to find or follow your tracks. If traveling with allies, you can share this benefit with up to five other characters.

You gain a +1 feat bonus to Acrobatics checks and Stealth checks.

Linguist

Prerequisite: Int 13

Benefit: Choose three languages. You can now speak, read, and write those languages fluently.

Special: You can take this feat more than once. Each time you select this feat, choose three new languages to learn.

Long Jumper

Prerequisite: Trained in Athletics

Benefit: You can make all long jumps as if you had a running start.

You also gain a +1 feat bonus to Athletics checks.

Lost in the Crowd [Halfling]

Prerequisite: Halfling

Benefit: You gain a +2 bonus to AC when you are adjacent to at least two enemies larger than you.

Melora's Tide [Divinity]

Prerequisites: Channel Divinity class feature, must worship Melora

Benefit: You can invoke the power of your deity to use *Melora's tide*.

Channel Divinity: Melora's Tide — Feat Power

Melora sends a tide of healing energy to aid you or a bloodied friend.

Encounter ✦ Divine, Healing
Minor Action   Ranged 5
Target: You or one ally; bloodied target only
Effect: The target gains regeneration 2 until the end of the encounter or until he or she is no longer bloodied.
    If you are 11th level or higher, this power grants regeneration 4 instead. If you are 21st level or higher, this power grants regeneration 6 instead.
Special: You must take the Melora's Tide feat to use this power.

MORADIN'S RESOLVE [DIVINITY]

   Prerequisites: Channel Divinity class feature, must worship Moradin

   Benefit: You can invoke the power of your deity to use *Moradin's resolve*.

Channel Divinity: Moradin's Resolve — Feat Power

Moradin's blessing puts the small on more equal footing with the large.

Encounter ✦ Divine
Minor Action   Personal
Effect: Until the end of your next turn, you gain a +2 bonus to attack rolls against Large or larger creatures.
Special: You must take the Moradin's Resolve feat to use this power.

MOUNTED COMBAT

   Benefit: When you ride a creature, you gain access to any special mount abilities it confers to its rider. Not every creature has these abilities. The *Dungeon Master's Guide* has more information on mounts and mounted combat.

   While you are riding a creature, the creature can make any Athletics, Acrobatics, Endurance, or Stealth checks using your base skill check bonus rather than its own if yours is higher.

NIMBLE BLADE

   Prerequisite: Dex 15

   Benefit: When you attack with a light blade and you have combat advantage, you gain a +1 bonus to attack rolls.

PELOR'S RADIANCE [DIVINITY]

   Prerequisites: Channel Divinity class feature, must worship Pelor

   Benefit: You can invoke the power of your deity to use *Pelor's radiance*.

Channel Divinity: Pelor's Radiance — Feat Power

When undead creatures abound, Pelor's radiance shines to aid the faithful.

Encounter ✦ Divine, Implement, Radiant
Standard Action   Close burst 1
               (3 at 11th level, 5 at 21st level)
Target: Each undead creature in burst
Attack: Wisdom vs. Will
Hit: 1d12 + Wisdom modifier radiant damage, and the target is stunned until the end of your next turn.
Increase damage to 2d12 at 5th level, 3d12 at 11th, 4d12 at 15th, 5d12 at 21st, and 6d12 at 25th.
Special: You must take the Pelor's Radiance feat to use this power.

POTENT CHALLENGE [FIGHTER]

   Prerequisites: Con 15, fighter, Combat Challenge class feature

   Benefit: If you hit a foe with an attack granted by your Combat Challenge class feature, add your Constitution modifier to the damage roll.

   Special: This benefit applies only to attacks made with two-handed weapons.

POWER ATTACK

   Prerequisite: Str 15

   Benefit: When making a melee attack, you can take a –2 penalty to the attack roll. If the attack hits, you gain a +2 bonus to the damage roll (or a +3 bonus to the damage roll with a two-handed weapon).

   This extra damage increases by level, as shown on the table below, but the attack penalty remains the same.

Level	Extra Damage (Two-Handed Weapon)
1st-10th	+2 (+3)
11th-20th	+4 (+6)
21st-30th	+6 (+9)

POWERFUL CHARGE

   Prerequisite: Str 13

   Benefit: When you charge, you gain a +2 bonus to damage and a +2 bonus to bull rush attempts.

PRECISE HUNTER [RANGER]

   Prerequisites: Wis 15, ranger, Hunter's Quarry class feature

   Benefit: When you score a critical hit against the target of your Hunter's Quarry with a ranged attack, your allies gain a +1 bonus to attack rolls against that target until the start of your next turn.

PRESS THE ADVANTAGE [ROGUE]

   Prerequisites: Cha 15, rogue

   Benefit: If you score a critical hit while you have combat advantage, you gain combat advantage against the target until the end of your next turn.

Channel Divinity: Raven Queen's Blessing
Feat Power

The Raven Queen grants a boon to those who send the dead on their way.

Encounter ✦ Divine, Healing
Free Action   **Ranged** 10
Trigger: Your attack drops an enemy within range to 0 hit points or fewer
Effect: You or an ally within 5 squares of the enemy can spend a healing surge.
Special: You must take the Raven Queen's Blessing feat to use this power.

Ritual Caster
Prerequisite: Trained in Arcana or Religion
Benefit: You can master and perform rituals of your level or lower. See Chapter 10 for information on acquiring, mastering, and performing rituals. Even though some rituals use the Heal skill or the Nature skill, the Arcana skill or the Religion skill is required to understand how to perform rituals.

Sehanine's Reversal [Divinity]
Prerequisites: Channel Divinity class feature, must worship Sehanine
Benefit: You can invoke the power of your deity to use *Sehanine's reversal*.

Channel Divinity: Sehanine's Reversal
Feat Power

Sehanine's blessing turns the powers of your enemies against them.

Encounter ✦ Divine
No Action   **Ranged** 5
Trigger: You roll a natural 20 on a saving throw
Effect: Choose an enemy within range; that creature gains the condition you just saved against.
Special: You must take the Sehanine's Reversal feat to use this power.

Shield Proficiency (Heavy)
Prerequisites: Str 15, Shield Proficiency (Light)
Benefit: You gain proficiency with heavy shields.

Shield Proficiency (Light)
Prerequisite: Str 13
Benefit: You gain proficiency with light shields.

Shield Push [Fighter]
Prerequisites: Fighter, Combat Challenge class feature
Benefit: If you hit a foe with an attack granted by your Combat Challenge class feature, you push the target 1 square after dealing damage.
Special: You must carry a shield to benefit from this feat.

Quick Draw
Prerequisite: Dex 13
Benefit: You can draw a weapon (or an object stored in a belt pouch, bandolier, or similar container, such as a potion) as part of the same action used to attack with the weapon or use the object.

You also gain a +2 feat bonus to initiative checks.

Raging Storm
Prerequisites: Con 13, Dex 13
Benefit: You gain a +1 feat bonus to damage rolls when you use a power that has the lightning or thunder keyword.

At 11th level, this bonus increases to +2. At 21st level, it increases to +3.

Raven Queen's Blessing [Divinity]
Prerequisites: Channel Divinity class feature, must worship the Raven Queen
Benefit: You can invoke the power of your deity to use *Raven Queen's blessing*.

FRANZ VOHWINKEL

Skill Focus

Prerequisite: Training in chosen skill
Benefit: Choose a skill in which you have training. You have a +3 feat bonus to checks with that skill.
Special: You can take this feat more than once. Each time you select this feat, choose a different skill.

Skill Training

Benefit: You gain training in one skill. The skill need not be on your class skill list.
Special: You can take this feat more than once. Each time you select this feat, choose a skill in which you are not trained.

Sure Climber

Prerequisite: Trained in Athletics
Benefit: A successful Athletics check allows you to climb at your normal speed, rather than half speed.
You also gain a +1 feat bonus to Athletics checks.

Surprise Knockdown [Rogue]

Prerequisites: Str 15, rogue
Benefit: If you score a critical hit while you have combat advantage, you knock the target prone.

Tactical Assault [Warlord]

Prerequisites: Warlord, Tactical Presence class feature
Benefit: When an ally who can see you spends an action point to make an attack, the attack's damage roll gains a bonus equal to your Intelligence modifier.

Toughness

Benefit: When you take this feat, you gain additional hit points. You gain an additional 5 hit points at each tier of play (at 1st, 11th, and 21st level).

Two-Weapon Defense

Prerequisites: Dex 13, Two-Weapon Fighting
Benefit: While holding a melee weapon in each hand, you gain a +1 shield bonus to AC and Reflex.

Two-Weapon Fighting

Prerequisite: Dex 13
Benefit: While holding a melee weapon in each hand, you gain a +1 bonus to damage rolls with your main weapon.

Weapon Focus

Benefit: Choose a specific weapon group, such as spears or heavy blades. You gain a +1 feat bonus to damage rolls with your chosen weapon group. At 11th level, this bonus increases to +2. At 21st level, it increases to +3.
Special: You can take this feat more than once. Each time you select this feat, choose another weapon group.

Weapon Proficiency

Benefit: You gain proficiency in a single weapon of your choice.
Special: You can take this feat more than once. Each time you select this feat, choose another weapon.

Wintertouched

Benefit: When attacking a creature that is vulnerable to cold, you gain combat advantage when you use a power that has the cold keyword.

Paragon Tier Feats

Any feat in the following section is available to a character of 11th level or higher who meets the prerequisites.

Action Recovery [Human]

Prerequisite: Human

Benefit: When you spend an action point to gain an extra standard action, you can immediately roll a saving throw against each condition affecting you that a save can end.

Agile Athlete

Benefit: When you make an Acrobatics check or an Athletics check, roll twice and use the higher result.

Arcane Reach

Prerequisite: Dex 15

Benefit: When using a close arcane attack power, you can choose a square within 2 squares of yours as the origin square. The power still follows the rules for close attacks.

Armor Specialization (Chainmail)

Prerequisites: Dex 15, training with chainmail

Benefit: You gain a +1 feat bonus to AC while wearing chainmail. You reduce the check penalty incurred by chainmail by 1.

Armor Specialization (Hide)

Prerequisites: Con 15, training with hide armor

Benefit: You gain a +1 feat bonus to AC when wearing hide armor. You reduce the check penalty incurred by hide armor by 1.

Armor Specialization (Plate)

Prerequisites: Con 15, training with plate armor

Benefit: You gain a +1 feat bonus to AC when wearing plate armor.

Armor Specialization (Scale)

Prerequisites: Dex 15, training with scale armor

Benefit: You gain a +1 feat bonus to AC when wearing scale armor. You ignore the speed penalty normally incurred by scale armor.

Back to the Wall

Benefit: Whenever you are adjacent to a wall, you gain a +1 bonus to melee attack rolls, melee damage rolls, and AC.

Blood Thirst

Benefit: You gain a +2 bonus to melee damage rolls against bloodied foes.

Combat Anticipation

Benefit: You gain a +1 feat bonus to all defenses against ranged, area, and close attacks.

Combat Commander [Warlord]

Prerequisites: Warlord, Combat Leader class feature

Benefit: The bonus to initiative granted by your Combat Leader class feature is now equal to your Charisma modifier or your Intelligence modifier, whichever is higher.

Danger Sense

Benefit: When you make an initiative check, roll twice and take the higher of the two rolls.

Deadly Axe

Prerequisites: Str 17, Con 13

Benefit: You treat all axes as high crit weapons.

Defensive Advantage

Prerequisite: Dex 17

Benefit: When you have combat advantage against an enemy, you gain a +2 bonus to AC against that enemy's attacks.

Devastating Critical

Benefit: When you score a critical hit, you deal an extra 1d10 damage.

Distant Shot

Benefit: You ignore the –2 penalty for making ranged attacks at long range.

Dwarven Durability [Dwarf]

Prerequisite: Dwarf

Benefit: Increase your number of healing surges by two and your healing surge value by your Constitution modifier.

Empowered Dragon Breath [Dragonborn]

Prerequisites: Dragonborn, *dragon breath* racial power

Benefit: Use d10s for the damage roll of your *dragon breath* power instead of d6s.

Evasion

Prerequisite: Dex 15

Benefit: When an area or close attack targeting your AC or Reflex defense misses you but deals damage on a miss, you take no damage from the attack.

FEYWILD PROTECTION [ELADRIN]

Prerequisites: Eladrin, *fey step* racial power
Benefit: When you use your *fey step* power, you gain a +2 bonus to all your defenses until the end of your next turn.

FIERY REBUKE [TIEFLING]

Prerequisites: Tiefling, *infernal wrath* racial power
Benefit: When you use your *infernal wrath* power and hit with an attack, the target takes fire damage equal to 5 + one-half your level in addition to any other damage the attack deals.

FLEET-FOOTED

Benefit: You gain a +1 feat bonus to your speed.

GREAT FORTITUDE

Benefit: You gain a +2 feat bonus to your Fortitude defense.

HAMMER RHYTHM

Prerequisites: Str 15, Con 17
Benefit: If you miss with a melee attack with a hammer or a mace and you wouldn't otherwise still deal damage on the miss, you deal damage to your original target equal to your Constitution modifier. This damage receives no modifiers or other benefits you normally gain to weapon damage.

HEAVY BLADE OPPORTUNITY

Prerequisites: Str 15, Dex 15
Benefit: When you make an opportunity attack with a heavy blade, you can use an at-will attack that has the weapon keyword instead of a basic attack.

IMPROVED SECOND WIND

Benefit: When you use your second wind, you heal an additional 5 hit points.

INESCAPABLE FORCE

Benefit: When you use a power that has the force keyword, you deal full damage (instead of half damage) against insubstantial creatures, and that power deals an extra 1d10 damage to such creatures.

IRON WILL

Benefit: You gain a +2 feat bonus to your Will defense.

LASTING FROST

Benefit: Any target you hit with a power that has the cold keyword gains vulnerable cold 5 until the end of your next turn.

6

LEE MOYER

PARAGON TIER FEATS

Name	Prerequisites	Benefit
Action Recovery	Human	Gain extra saving throws by spending action point
Agile Athlete	–	Roll twice with Acrobatics and Athletics checks
Arcane Reach	Dex 15	Choose square within 2 as origin with close attack power
Armor Specialization (Chainmail)	Dex 15, training with chainmail	+1 to AC with chainmail, reduce check penalty by 1
Armor Specialization (Hide)	Con 15, training with hide armor	+1 to AC with hide armor, reduce check penalty by 1
Armor Specialization (Plate)	Con 15, training with plate armor	+1 to AC with plate armor
Armor Specialization (Scale)	Dex 15, training with scale armor	Ignore speed penalty of scale armor
Back to the Wall	–	+1 to melee attack, damage, AC when adjacent to a wall
Blood Thirst	–	+2 to damage against bloodied foes
Combat Anticipation	–	+1 to defenses against ranged, area, close attacks
Combat Commander	Warlord, Combat Leader class feature	Bonus to Combat Leader equals Cha or Int modifier
Danger Sense	–	Roll twice for initiative, use the higher result
Deadly Axe	Str 17, Con 13	Treat all axes as high crit weapons
Defensive Advantage	Dex 17	+2 AC when you have combat advantage against enemy
Devastating Critical	–	Deal additional 1d10 damage on a critical hit
Distant Shot	–	Ignore -2 penalty for long range
Dwarven Durability	Dwarf	Increase number of healing surges, healing surge value
Empowered Dragon Breath	Dragonborn, *dragon breath* racial power	*Dragon breath* uses d10s
Evasion	Dex 15	No damage from missed area or close attack
Feywild Protection	Eladrin, *fey step* racial power	+2 to defenses when you use *fey step*
Fiery Rebuke	Tiefling, *infernal wrath* racial power	Cause fire damage with *infernal wrath*
Fleet-Footed	–	+1 to speed
Great Fortitude	–	+2 to Fortitude defense
Hammer Rhythm	Str 15, Con 17	Damage with hammer or mace on a miss
Heavy Blade Opportunity	Str 15, Dex 15	Use at-will power with opportunity attack
Improved Second Wind	–	Heal 5 additional damage with second wind
Inescapable Force	–	Force powers ignore insubstantial, deal additional damage

LIGHT BLADE PRECISION

Prerequisites: Dex 13, Small or Medium size
Benefit: You gain a +2 bonus to damage rolls with light blades against Large or larger targets.

LIGHTNING ARC

Benefit: When you score a critical hit with a power that has the lightning keyword, you can choose to treat the attack as a normal hit instead of a critical hit. If you do, choose another target within 10 squares of the original target that was not already targeted or affected by the power. That target takes damage equal to the damage dealt to the original target.

LIGHTNING REFLEXES

Benefit: You gain a +2 feat bonus to your Reflex defense.

METTLE

Benefit: When an area or close attack targeting your Fortitude or Will defense misses you and still deals damage on a miss, you take no damage from the attack.

POINT-BLANK SHOT

Benefit: If you make a ranged attack against a foe within 5 squares of you, your attack ignores cover and concealment, including superior cover but not total concealment.

POLEARM GAMBLE

Prerequisites: Str 15, Wis 15
Benefit: When a nonadjacent enemy enters a square adjacent to you, you can make an opportunity attack with a polearm against that enemy, but you grant combat advantage to that enemy until the end of the enemy's turn.

PARAGON TIER FEATS CONT.

Name	Prerequisites	Benefit
Iron Will	—	+2 to Will defense
Lasting Frost	—	Target hit with cold power gains vulnerable cold 5
Light Blade Precision	Dex 13, Small or Medium size	+2 damage against Large or larger targets
Lightning Arc	—	Affect second target with lightning power on critical hit
Lightning Reflexes	—	+2 to Reflex defense
Mettle	—	No damage from missed area or close attacks
Point-Blank Shot	—	Ignore cover and concealment within 5 squares
Polearm Gamble	Str 15, Wis 15	Make opportunity attack against adjacent enemy
Psychic Lock	—	Target hit with psychic power takes -2 on next attack roll
Resounding Thunder	—	Add 1 to size of blast or burst with thunder keyword
Running Shot	Elf	No attack penalty to ranged attacks after you run
Scimitar Dance	Str 15, Dex 17	Deal Dex modifier damage on miss
Second Implement	Wizard, Arcane Implement Mastery class feature	Gain mastery with second arcane implement
Secret Stride	Trained in Stealth	No penalty to Stealth with move while hiding or sneaking
Seize the Moment	Dex 17	Gain combat advantage over foe with lower initiative
Shield Specialization	Dex 15, Shield Proficiency (Heavy or Light)	+1 to AC and Reflex when using a shield
Sly Hunter	Wis 15	+3 damage with bow against isolated target
Solid Sound	Con 13	+2 to defense after you use thunder or force power
Spear Push	Str 15, Dex 13	Add 1 square to distance pushed with spear or polearm
Spell Focus	Cha 13, wizard	-2 to saves against your wizard spells
Steady Shooter	Con 15	+3 damage with crossbow if you don't move
Sweeping Flail	Str 15, Dex 15	+2 to attacks with flail against foe with a shield
Twofold Curse	Warlock, Warlock's Curse class feature	Curse the two nearest enemies
Uncanny Dodge	Wis 15	Enemies denied bonus to attack from combat advantage
Underfoot	Halfling, trained in Acrobatics	Move through spaces of Large or larger creatures

PSYCHIC LOCK

Benefit: Any target you hit with a power that has the psychic keyword takes a -2 penalty to its next attack roll.

RESOUNDING THUNDER

Benefit: You can add 1 to the size of any blast or burst that has the thunder keyword.

RUNNING SHOT [ELF]

Prerequisite: Elf

Benefit: You don't take any attack penalty to ranged attacks after you use the run action.

SCIMITAR DANCE

Prerequisites: Str 15, Dex 17

Benefit: If you miss with a melee attack with a scimitar and you wouldn't otherwise still deal damage on the miss, you deal damage to your original target equal to your Dexterity modifier. This damage receives no modifiers or other benefits you normally gain on weapon damage.

SECOND IMPLEMENT [WIZARD]

Prerequisites: Wizard, Arcane Implement Mastery class feature

Benefit: You gain a second Arcane Implement Mastery class feature.

SECRET STRIDE

Prerequisite: Trained in Stealth

Benefit: You do not incur penalties to your Stealth checks if you move at full speed while hiding or sneaking. You still take the full penalty if you run.

SEIZE THE MOMENT

Prerequisite: Dex 17

Benefit: During the first round of combat and during surprise rounds, you automatically gain combat advantage over a foe whose initiative result is lower than yours.

SHIELD SPECIALIZATION

Prerequisites: Dex 15, Shield Proficiency (Heavy or Light)

Benefit: You gain a +1 feat bonus to AC and Reflex when using a shield with which you are proficient.

SLY HUNTER

Prerequisite: Wis 15

Benefit: You gain a +3 bonus to damage rolls with bow attacks against any target that has no creature within 3 squares of it.

SOLID SOUND

Prerequisite: Con 13

Benefit: Until the end of your next turn, you gain a +2 bonus to Fortitude, Reflex, or Will after you use any power that has the thunder or force keyword. Choose the defense when you use the power.

SPEAR PUSH

Prerequisites: Str 15, Dex 13

Benefit: When you push a foe with a polearm or spear attack, you can add 1 square to the distance pushed.

SPELL FOCUS [WIZARD]

Prerequisites: Cha 13, wizard

Benefit: Creatures that attempt saving throws against your wizard powers take a -2 penalty to the rolls.

STEADY SHOOTER

Prerequisite: Con 15

Benefit: You gain a +3 bonus to damage rolls with crossbow attacks if you haven't moved since the end of your last turn.

SWEEPING FLAIL

Prerequisites: Str 15, Dex 15

Benefit: When making a melee attack with a flail against a foe carrying a shield, you gain a +2 bonus to the attack roll.

TWOFOLD CURSE [WARLOCK]

Prerequisites: Warlock, Warlock's Curse class feature

Benefit: When you use your Warlock's Curse class feature, you can curse the two nearest enemies.

UNCANNY DODGE

Prerequisite: Wis 15

Benefit: Enemies do not gain the normal +2 bonus to attack rolls against you when they have combat advantage. Any other benefits derived from combat advantage still apply.

UNDERFOOT [HALFLING]

Prerequisites: Halfling, trained in Acrobatics

Benefit: You can move through the space of a creature two or more sizes larger than you (Large or larger) without provoking opportunity attacks from that creature. You don't provoke when you leave an adjacent square to enter the target creature's space, or when you leave the target creature's space to enter an adjacent square.

You still provoke attacks from other creatures. You can't end your move in another creature's space.

EPIC TIER FEATS

Any feat in the following section is available to a character of 21st level or higher who meets the prerequisites.

ARCANE MASTERY [WIZARD]

Prerequisite: Wizard

Benefit: Once per encounter, you can spend an action point to regain the use of a daily wizard power you've already used today, instead of taking an extra action.

AXE MASTERY

Prerequisites: Str 21, Con 17

Benefit: When you make a melee weapon attack with an axe, you can score a critical hit on a natural roll of 19 or 20.

BLIND-FIGHT

Prerequisite: Wis 13 or trained in Perception

Benefit: Adjacent creatures do not gain the benefit of concealment or invisibility against you. This means you can make opportunity attacks against creatures you can't see.

BLUDGEON MASTERY

Prerequisites: Str 19, Con 19

Benefit: When you make a melee weapon attack with a hammer, mace, or staff, you can score a critical hit on a natural roll of 19 or 20.

EPIC RESURGENCE

Benefit: The first time you score a critical hit during an encounter, you regain the use of one encounter attack power of your choice. If you use an attack that targets multiple foes, you gain this feat's benefit only on the first attack roll you make.

FLAIL MASTERY

Prerequisites: Str 19, Dex 19

Benefit: When you make a melee weapon attack with a flail, you can score a critical hit on a natural roll of 19 or 20.

EPIC TIER FEATS

Name	Prerequisites	Benefit
Arcane Mastery	Wizard	Regain daily spell by spending action point
Axe Mastery	Str 21, Con 17	Critical hit with axe melee attack roll of 19 or 20
Blind-Fight	Wis 13 or trained in Perception	Adjacent creatures aren't concealed or invisible to you
Bludgeon Mastery	Str 19, Con 19	Critical hit with bludgeoning melee attack roll of 19 or 20
Epic Resurgence	—	Regain encounter attack power on critical hit
Flail Mastery	Str 19, Dex 19	Critical hit with flail melee attack roll of 19 or 20
Flanking Maneuver	Dex 17, trained in Acrobatics	Move diagonally and through enemies' spaces
Font of Radiance	—	Target illuminated with critical hit, takes radiant damage
Heavy Blade Mastery	Str 21, Dex 17	Critical hit with heavy blade melee attack roll of 19 or 20
Irresistible Flame	—	Decrease target's resist fire by 20
Light Blade Mastery	Str 17, Dex 21	Critical hit with light blade melee attack roll of 19 or 20
Pick Mastery	Str 21, Con 17	Critical hit with pick melee attack roll of 19 or 20
Spear Mastery	Str 19, Dex 19	Critical hit with spear melee attack roll of 19 or 20
Spell Accuracy	Wizard	Omit squares from any area or close wizard power
Triumphant Attack	—	Target at -2 to attacks and defenses after a critical hit
Two-Weapon Flurry	Dex 19, Two-Weapon Fighting	Make opportunity attack with off-hand melee weapon
Unfettered Stride	Trained in Acrobatics	Ignore the effect of difficult terrain on your movement

FLANKING MANEUVER

Prerequisites: Dex 17, trained in Acrobatics

Benefit: You can move diagonally even if a wall corner normally blocks such movement.

You can move through enemies' spaces. You provoke opportunity attacks for this movement as normal. You can't end your move in an enemy's space.

FONT OF RADIANCE

Benefit: When you score a critical hit with a power that has the radiant keyword, the target begins to glow brightly (save ends).

The target's space and all squares adjacent to it are illuminated by bright light. Invisible creatures become visible while they are in affected squares, and attack rolls against creatures in those squares take no penalty for concealment. Any foe that ends its turn in an affected square (including the original target) takes 3d6 radiant damage.

HEAVY BLADE MASTERY

Prerequisites: Str 21, Dex 17

Benefit: When you make a melee weapon attack with a heavy blade, you can score a critical hit on a natural roll of 19 or 20.

IRRESISTIBLE FLAME

Benefit: Treat your target's resist fire as 20 fewer than normal when determining damage for your attacks.

LIGHT BLADE MASTERY

Prerequisites: Str 17, Dex 21

Benefit: When you make a melee weapon attack with a light blade, you can score a critical hit on a natural roll of 19 or 20.

PICK MASTERY

Prerequisites: Str 21, Con 17

Benefit: When you make a melee weapon attack with a pick, you can score a critical hit on a natural roll of 19 or 20.

SPEAR MASTERY

Prerequisites: Str 19, Dex 19

Benefit: When you make a melee weapon attack with a spear, you can score a critical hit on a natural roll of 19 or 20.

SPELL ACCURACY [WIZARD]

Prerequisite: Wizard

Benefit: You can omit a number of squares from the area of effect of any of your area or close wizard powers. This number can't exceed your Wisdom modifier.

TRIUMPHANT ATTACK

Benefit: If you score a critical hit with a melee attack, the target of your attack takes a -2 penalty to attack rolls and defenses for the rest of the encounter (save ends).

TWO-WEAPON FLURRY

Prerequisites: Dex 19, Two-Weapon Fighting

Benefit: While holding a melee weapon in each hand, if you make a successful opportunity attack with your primary weapon, you can also make an opportunity attack with your off-hand weapon against the same target (but with a -5 penalty to the attack roll).

UNFETTERED STRIDE

Prerequisite: Trained in Acrobatics

Benefit: You can ignore the effect of difficult terrain on your movement.

Multiclass feats allow you to dabble in the class features and powers of another class. You might be a fighter who dips his toe into wizardry, or a warlock who wants a smattering of rogue abilities. Each class has a class-specific multiclass feat that gives you access to features from that class.

CLASS-SPECIFIC FEATS

There are two restrictions on your choice of a class-specific multiclass feat. First, you can't take a multiclass feat for your own class. Second, once you take a multiclass feat, you can't take a class-specific feat for a different class. You can dabble in a second class but not a third.

A character who has taken a class-specific multiclass feat counts as a member of that class for the purpose of meeting prerequisites for taking other feats and qualifying for paragon paths. For example, a character who takes Initiate of the Faith counts as a cleric for the purpose of selecting feats that have cleric as a prerequisite. These feats can qualify you for other feats; for example, a warlock who takes Sneak of Shadows can use the rogue's Sneak Attack class feature, which means that he meets the prerequisite for the Backstabber feat.

INITIATE OF THE FAITH
[MULTICLASS CLERIC]
Prerequisite: Wis 13
Benefit: You gain training in the Religion skill.
Once per day, you can use the cleric's *healing word* power.
In addition, you can use a holy symbol as an implement when using a cleric power or a cleric paragon path power.

STUDENT OF THE SWORD
[MULTICLASS FIGHTER]
Prerequisite: Str 13
Benefit: You gain training in one skill from the fighter's class skill list.
Choose either one-handed melee weapons or two-handed melee weapons. Once per encounter as a free action, you can add a +1 bonus to the next attack roll you make with a weapon of that category. Whether the attack hits or misses, you mark the target until the end of your next turn.

SOLDIER OF THE FAITH
[MULTICLASS PALADIN]
Prerequisites: Str 13, Cha 13
Benefit: You gain training in one skill from the paladin's class skill list.

Once per encounter, you can use the paladin's *divine challenge* power.
In addition, you can use a holy symbol or a *holy avenger* as an implement when using a paladin power or a paladin paragon path power.

WARRIOR OF THE WILD
[MULTICLASS RANGER]
Prerequisite: Str 13 or Dex 13
Benefit: You gain training in one skill from the ranger's class skill list.
Once per encounter, you can use the ranger's Hunter's Quarry class feature.

SNEAK OF SHADOWS
[MULTICLASS ROGUE]
Prerequisite: Dex 13
Benefit: You gain training in the Thievery skill.
Once per encounter, you can use the rogue's Sneak Attack class feature.

PACT INITIATE
[MULTICLASS WARLOCK]
Prerequisite: Cha 13
Benefit: You gain training in one skill from the warlock's class skill list.
Choose a warlock pact. You gain the pact's at-will power as an encounter power, and you can pursue the warlock paragon path based on that pact.
In addition, you can use a rod, a wand, or a *pact blade* as an implement when using a warlock power or a warlock paragon path power.

STUDENT OF BATTLE
[MULTICLASS WARLORD]
Prerequisite: Str 13
Benefit: You gain training in one skill from the warlord's class skill list.
Once per day, you can use the warlord's *inspiring word* power.

ARCANE INITIATE
[MULTICLASS WIZARD]
Prerequisite: Int 13
Benefit: You gain training in the Arcana skill.
Choose a 1st-level wizard at-will power. You can use that power once per encounter.
In addition, you can use an orb, a staff, or a wand as an implement when using a wizard power or a wizard paragon path power.

MULTICLASS FEATS

Name	Prerequisites	Benefit
Initiate of the Faith	Wis 13	Cleric: Religion skill, *healing word* 1/day
Student of the Sword	Str 13	Fighter: skill training, +1 to attack and mark 1/encounter
Soldier of the Faith	Str 13, Cha 13	Paladin: skill training, *divine challenge* 1/encounter
Warrior of the Wild	Str 13 or Dex 13	Ranger: skill training, designate prey 1/encounter
Sneak of Shadows	Dex 13	Rogue: Thievery skill, Sneak Attack 1/encounter
Pact Initiate	Cha 13	Warlock: skill training, *eldritch blast* 1/encounter
Student of Battle	Str 13	Warlord: skill training, *inspiring word* 1/day
Arcane Initiate	Int 13	Wizard: Arcana skill, wizard power 1/encounter
Novice Power	Any class-specific multiclass feats, 4th level	Swap one encounter power with one of multiclass
Acolyte Power	Any class-specific multiclass feats, 8th level	Swap one utility power with one of multiclass
Adept Power	Any class-specific multiclass feats, 10th level	Swap one daily power with one of multiclass

POWER-SWAP FEATS

The Novice Power, Acolyte Power, and Adept Power feats give you access to a power from the class for which you took a class-specific multiclass feat. That power replaces a power you would normally have from your primary class. When you take one of these power-swap feats, you give up a power of your choice from your primary class and replace it with a power of the same level or lower from the class you have multi-classed in.

Any time you gain a level, you can alter that decision. Effectively, pretend you're choosing the power-swap feat for the first time at the new level you've just gained. You gain back the power that you gave up originally from your primary class, lose the power that you chose from your second class, and make the trade again. You give up a different power from your primary class and replace it with a new power of the same level from your second class.

You can't use power-swap feats to replace powers you gain from your paragon path or epic destiny.

If you use retraining to replace a power-swap feat with another feat, you lose any power gained from the power-swap feat and regain a power of the same level from your primary class.

NOVICE POWER
[MULTICLASS ENCOUNTER]

Prerequisites: Any class-specific multiclass feat, 4th level

Benefit: You can swap one encounter attack power you know for one encounter attack power of the same level or lower from the class you multiclassed into.

ACOLYTE POWER
[MULTICLASS UTILITY]

Prerequisites: Any class-specific multiclass feat, 8th level

Benefit: You can swap one utility power you know for one utility power of the same level or lower from the class you multiclassed into.

ADEPT POWER [MULTICLASS DAILY]

Prerequisites: Any class-specific multiclass feat, 10th level

Benefit: You can swap one daily attack power you know for one daily attack power of the same level or lower from the class you multiclassed into.

PARAGON MULTICLASSING

If you have the Novice Power, Acolyte Power, and Adept Power feats for a class, you can choose to continue to gain powers from that class rather than take a paragon path. If you choose this option, you gain several benefits.

At 11th level, you can choose to replace one of your at-will powers with an at-will power from your second class.

In place of the paragon path encounter power gained at 11th level, you can select any encounter power of 7th level or lower from your second class.

In place of the paragon path utility power gained at 12th level, you can select any utility power of 10th level or lower from your second class.

In place of the paragon path daily power gained at 20th level, you can select any daily power of 19th level or lower from your second class.

CHAPTER 7

EQUIPMENT

WHEN YOU leave the safety of a city or other refuge for the wilderness and the unknown, you must be prepared. Being ready means you need protection, arms, and tools to see you through potential challenges, dangers, and hardships. An unprepared explorer all too often winds up injured or lost—or worse—so gear up for the hazards you expect on your adventures.

When you create a 1st-level character, you start with basic clothing and 100 gold pieces to spend on armor, weapons, and adventuring gear. This is an abstraction; your character probably doesn't walk into a store one day with a bag of coins—unless you just came into an inheritance or won a tournament of some sort. Rather, the items you start with, and any gold you have left over, might come your way as gifts from family, gear used during military service, equipment issued by a patron, or even something you made yourself.

As you go up in level, you acquire more gold that you can spend, not just on mundane gear, but on fabulous magic items as well.

Here's an overview of the contents of this chapter.

✦ **Armor and Shields:** Essential gear for protection in combat.

✦ **Weapons:** The basic tools of combat for many characters, from swords to polearms.

✦ **Adventuring Gear:** The tools of the adventuring trade. Look in this section for everburning torches, flasks of oil, backpacks, and spellbooks. This section also discusses arcane implements and holy symbols, useful for the powers of some classes.

✦ **Magic Items:** When you have the gold to spend on magic items, this section shows you what's available. You'll find magic weapons, armor, and more.

Armor provides a barrier between you and your foes—or, put more bluntly, between you and death. Every class provides access to one or more armor proficiencies, and it's in your best interest to wear the finest armor you can. This section includes information on shields, which improve your defensive capabilities.

ARMOR TYPES

Armor is grouped into categories. These categories can help you decide what armor is best for you.

Your class tells you what kinds of armor you're proficient with. You can take feats to learn the proper use of other kinds of armor. If you wear armor you're not proficient with, it makes you clumsy and uncoordinated: You take a -2 penalty to attack rolls and to your Reflex defense.

Putting on a suit of armor always takes at least 5 minutes, which means that it's an activity you can undertake only outside combat (likely while you're taking a short rest).

Armor is defined as either light or heavy. **Light armor** is easy to move in if you're proficient with it. Cloth armor, leather armor, and hide armor are light armor. When you wear light armor, you add either your Intelligence or your Dexterity modifier to your Armor Class, whichever is higher. **Heavy armor** is more restrictive, so your natural agility matters less. When you wear heavy armor, you don't add an ability score

modifier to your AC. Chainmail, scale armor, and plate armor are heavy armor.

Certain kinds of armor are made according to arcane and esoteric methods that involve weaving magic into the substance of the armor. These **masterwork armors** never appear except as magic armor (see page 227), and even then only at the highest levels (16th and above). The various kinds of masterwork armor fall into the same categories as mundane armor and have similar statistics, but they have a higher armor bonus than their mundane counterparts. The cost of masterwork armor is included in the cost of magic armor.

Cloth Armor: Jackets, mantles, woven robes, and padded vests don't, by themselves, provide any significant protection. However, you can imbue them with protective magic. Cloth armor doesn't slow you down or hinder your movement at all. All characters are proficient with cloth armor. Feyweave armor is woven with techniques perfected by the eladrin. Starweave armor is fashioned after patterns created in the divine dominions of the Astral Sea.

Leather Armor: Leather armor is sturdier than cloth armor. It protects vital areas with multiple layers of boiled-leather plates, while covering the limbs with supple leather that provides a small amount of protection. Feyleather armor is cured by an elven method that leaves the armor supple but tougher than normal leather. Starleather armor is infused with the raw spiritual matter of the Astral Sea, making it light and strong.

Hide Armor: Thicker and heavier than leather, hide armor is composed of skin from any creature that

COINS AND CURRENCY

Merchants and adventurers alike use the gold piece (gp) as the standard unit of currency for most transactions. The exchange of large amounts of money might be handled by letters of credit or gems and jewelry, but the value is always measured in gold pieces.

The common people of the world deal more widely in the silver piece (sp) and the copper piece (cp). A gold piece is worth 10 silver pieces, and a silver piece is worth 10 copper pieces.

People use copper, silver, and gold coins daily. Many of the world's ancient empires also minted platinum pieces, and merchants still accept them even if most people never see them. They're most common in ancient treasure hoards. A platinum piece is worth 100 gold pieces.

A coin is about an inch across, and weighs about a third of an ounce (50 coins to the pound).

Gems and jewelry are a more portable form of wealth favored by adventurers. Among commoners, "portable wealth" usually means cattle (with one cow worth about 10 gp in trade).

Astral Diamonds: In fantastic realms beyond the natural world—in the City of Brass in the Elemental Chaos, the Bright City in the Astral Sea, the city of Sigil, and similar markets—the astral diamond (ad) is used as currency for transactions involving staggering amounts of wealth. One astral diamond is worth 100 platinum pieces, or 10,000 gold pieces.

An astral diamond weighs one-tenth as much as a coin (500 astral diamonds weigh 1 pound).

Monetary Unit	Exchange Value					Weight
	cp	sp	gp	pp	ad	
Copper piece (cp)	1	1/10	1/100	1/10,000	1/1,000,000	1/50 lb.
Silver piece (sp)	10	1	1/10	1/1,000	1/100,000	1/50 lb.
Gold piece (gp)	100	10	1	1/100	1/10,000	1/50 lb.
Platinum piece (pp)	10,000	1,000	100	1	1/100	1/50 lb.
Astral diamond (ad)	1,000,000	100,000	10,000	100	1	1/500 lb.

1. Cloth armor; 2. Leather armor; 3. Hide armor; 4. Chainmail; 5. Scale armor; 6. Plate armor; 7. Light shield, 8. Heavy shield

has a tough hide, such as a bear, a griffon, or a dragon. Hide armor can bind and slightly hinder your precision, but it's light enough that it doesn't affect your speed. Darkhide armor is a superior tiefling armor cured in fire and infused with shadow. Elderhide armor involves scouring with elemental forces.

Chainmail: Metal rings woven together into a shirt, leggings, and a hood make up a suit of chainmail. Chainmail grants good protection, but it's cumbersome, so it reduces your mobility and agility. Forgemail armor is made with superior metallurgy and a chain-making technique mastered by dwarves. Spiritmail

armor is made with techniques from the divine dominions of the Astral Sea.

Scale Armor: Overlapping pieces of highly durable material, such as steel or even dragon scales, make up scale armor. Despite its heaviness, scale is surprisingly easy to wear; its straps and buckles make it adjustable and able to fit snugly on the body, allowing flexibility and agility. Mundane scale armor uses metal plates. Wyrmscale is made using ancient techniques the dragonborn invented to mimic the strength of overlapping dragon scales, and elderscale is a similar armor scoured with elemental forces.

Plate Armor: The heaviest type of armor, made up of shaped plates of metal or similarly resilient material, plate provides the most armor protection. The cost for its superior fortification is mobility and agility. Legend holds that Moradin made the first godplate armor, and ancient dwarf smiths copied his patterns imperfectly to make warplate armor.

SHIELD TYPES

As with armor, you need the proper shield proficiency to use a shield effectively. When you use a shield, you strap it to an arm and sometimes use the hand on that arm—your shield arm and shield hand. Shields grant a shield bonus that you add to your AC and to your Reflex defense. If you're not proficient with a shield,

CHOOSING ARMOR

There are a few different aspects to determining your armor choice. Decide what you want your character to be able to do within your class role, and think about your ability scores and how they affect your Armor Class. Take a look at an armor's encumbrance (light or heavy), and think about its check penalty and speed. You might be able to have the same AC with more mobility, which could be a better choice for your character and your party. Your decision to use a shield rather than a two-handed weapon, or vice versa, might also influence whether you choose a certain suit of armor, so include that factor in your decision making.

ARMOR

Cloth Armor (Light)	Armor Bonus	Minimum Enhancement Bonus	Check	Speed	Price (gp)	Weight
Cloth armor (basic clothing)	–	+0	–	–	1	4 lb.
Feyweave armor	+1	+4	–	–	special	5 lb.
Starweave armor	+2	+6	–	–	special	3 lb.

Leather Armor (Light)	Armor Bonus	Minimum Enhancement Bonus	Check	Speed	Price (gp)	Weight
Leather armor	+2	–	–	–	25	15 lb.
Feyleather armor	+3	+4	–	–	special	15 lb.
Starleather armor	+4	+6	–	–	special	15 lb.

Hide Armor (Light)	Armor Bonus	Minimum Enhancement Bonus	Check	Speed	Price (gp)	Weight
Hide armor	+3	–	-1	–	30	25 lb.
Darkhide armor	+4	+4	-1	–	special	25 lb.
Elderhide armor	+5	+6	-1	–	special	25 lb.

Chainmail (Heavy)	Armor Bonus	Minimum Enhancement Bonus	Check	Speed	Price (gp)	Weight
Chainmail	+6	–	-1	-1	40	40 lb.
Forgemail	+9	+4	-1	-1	special	40 lb.
Spiritmail	+12	+6	-1	-1	special	40 lb.

Scale Armor (Heavy)	Armor Bonus	Minimum Enhancement Bonus	Check	Speed	Price (gp)	Weight
Scale armor	+7	–	–	-1	45	45 lb.
Wyrmscale armor	+10	+4	–	-1	special	45 lb.
Elderscale armor	+13	+6	–	-1	special	45 lb.

Plate Armor (Heavy)	Armor Bonus	Minimum Enhancement Bonus	Check	Speed	Price (gp)	Weight
Plate armor	+8	–	-2	-1	50	50 lb.
Warplate armor	+11	+4	-2	-1	special	50 lb.
Godplate armor	+14	+6	-2	-1	special	50 lb.

Shields	Shield Bonus	Minimum Enhancement Bonus	Check	Speed	Price (gp)	Weight
Light shield	+1	–	–	–	5	6 lb.
Heavy shield	+2	–	-2	–	10	15 lb.

you don't gain the shield bonus to your AC or Reflex defense.

Light Shield: You need to use your shield hand to wield a light shield properly. You can still use that hand to hold another item, to climb, or the like. However, you can't use your shield hand to make attacks.

Heavy Shield: When you use a heavy shield, you gain a greater bonus to your AC and Reflex defense, but you can't use your shield hand for any other task.

READING THE ARMOR TABLE

An armor or a shield entry on the Armor table contains the following information.

Armor Bonus: Armor provides this bonus to AC.

Shield Bonus: Shields provide this bonus to AC and Reflex defense.

Minimum Enhancement Bonus: Masterwork armor requires a minimum enhancement bonus, as shown in this entry.

Check: You take this penalty to all Strength-, Dexterity-, and Constitution-based skill checks when you wear the armor. You don't take the penalty to ability checks (such as a Strength check to break down a door or a Dexterity check to determine initiative in combat).

Speed: You take this penalty to your speed (in squares) when wearing the armor.

Price: The item's cost in gold pieces. See individual magic items for their base market price and appropriate levels. The cost of masterwork armor is included in the cost of magic armor of 16th level or higher.

Weight: The armor's weight.

WEAPONS

When you confront villains and monsters in their lairs, you often end up in situations that can be resolved only with arms and magic. If you don't have magical powers, you had better have a weapon or two. In fact, you might want a weapon to back up or even augment your powers.

WEAPON CATEGORIES

Weapons fall into four categories. **Improvised weapons** aren't weapons you train with–they're objects you pick up to hit someone with. Punching or kicking someone is also considered an improvised weapon. **Simple weapons** are basic, requiring little more skill than lifting and hitting with the business end. **Military weapons** are designed for skilled users. Balance and precision are important factors when using military weapons, and someone without the proper training can't use them effectively. **Superior weapons** are even more effective than military weapons but require special training to use. You can learn to use a superior weapon by taking the Weapon Proficiency feat.

Weapons in all four categories are further categorized as **melee weapons**, which you use to attack foes within reach of the weapon, or **ranged weapons**, which you use to fire at more distant enemies. You can't use a ranged weapon as a melee weapon. A melee weapon with the heavy thrown or the light thrown property counts as a ranged weapon when thrown and can be used with ranged attack powers that have the weapon keyword.

Finally, weapons are classified as either **one-handed** or **two-handed**. A one-handed weapon is light enough or balanced enough to be used in one hand. A two-handed weapon is too heavy or unbal-

anced to use without two hands. Bows and some other weapons require two hands because of their construction.

Some one-handed weapons are light enough for you to use in your off hand while holding another one-handed weapon in your other hand. Doing this doesn't let you make multiple attacks in a round (unless you have powers that let you do so), but you can attack with either weapon. Other one-handed weapons are large enough that you can keep a good grip on them with two hands and deal extra damage by using them as two-handed weapons.

WEAPON GROUPS

Weapon groups are families of weapons that share certain properties. They're wielded similarly and are equally suited to certain kinds of attacks. In game terms, some powers and feats work only when you're attacking with a weapon in a specific group.

If a weapon falls into more than one group, you can use it with powers that require a weapon from any of its groups. For example, the halberd is both an axe and a polearm, so you can use it with powers that give you an additional benefit when you wield an axe or a polearm.

Axe: Axes are weapons that have bladed, heavy heads and deal vicious cuts. An axe's weight makes it fine for delivering crushing blows.

Bow: A bow is a shaft of strong, supple material with a string stretched between its two ends. It's a projectile weapon that you use to fire arrows. Bows take training to use effectively, and they can be extremely deadly in expert hands.

Crossbow: Essentially a small metal bow mounted on a stock and equipped with a mechanical trigger, a crossbow is a point-and-shoot projectile weapon. Crossbows are popular because they require little training to master, yet the heavy pull of the metal bow gives them substantial power.

Flail: Weapons in the flail group have a flexible material, usually a length of chain, between a solid handle and the damage-dealing end of the weapon.

Hammer: A hammer has a blunt, heavy head with one or more flat striking surfaces attached to a haft.

Heavy Blade: Blades are balanced edged weapons. Heavy blades share some of the precision of light blades and some of the mass of axes. Heavy blades are used primarily for slashing cuts rather than stabs and thrusts.

Light Blade: Light blades reward accuracy as much as force. Pinpoint attacks, lunges, and agile defenses are the strong points of these weapons.

Mace: Much like hammers, maces are blunt weapons that have a heavier head than handle, but they're more balanced than hammers. They're useful for delivering crushing blows.

CHOOSING WEAPONS

If you belong to a class whose powers don't include weapon keywords, just pick weapons that you're proficient with and that you'd like to use. If you're a fighter or a member of any other class that has powers linked to particular weapon groups, you care more about weapons than other characters might. Be sure to consider the powers you'd like to use when choosing your weapons, and vice versa.

You want to have an option for melee combat as well as ranged combat, even if you're not as effective at one or the other. Be sure to choose at least one of each kind of weapon. When that flying monster makes its getaway, you don't want to be left standing around with nothing to do but hurl insults at it.

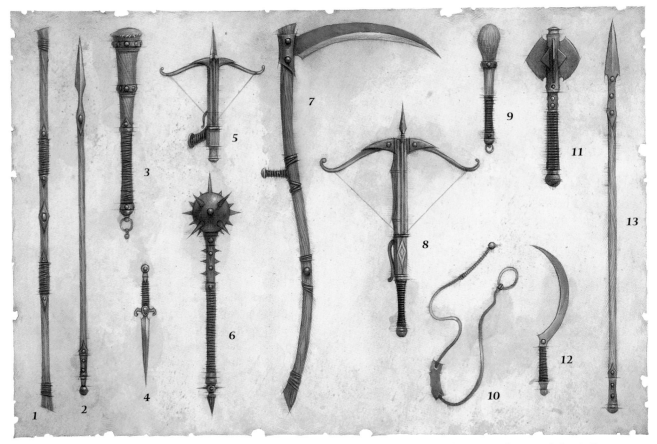

1. Quarterstaff; 2. Javelin; 3. Greatclub; 4. Dagger; 5. Hand crossbow; 6. Morningstar; 7. Scythe; 8. Crossbow; 9. Club; 10. Sling; 11. Mace; 12. Sickle; 13. Spear

Pick: Weighted toward the top like a mace or an axe, a pick has a long, pointed head made to pierce and create deep wounds.

Polearm: Polearms are weapons mounted at the end of long hafts. All polearms also fall into another category of weapon, usually axe, heavy blade, or spear. Polearms are reach weapons.

Sling: Slings are leather straps used to hurl stones or metal pellets. They are projectile weapons.

STRENGTH OR DEXTERITY?

As a rule, the attack you're making determines the ability you use with the attack. When you use a power, the power tells you whether you're making a Strength attack, a Dexterity attack, or an attack based on a different ability. When you make a basic attack, though, the ability you use depends on the weapon you're wielding.

A basic attack with a melee weapon is always a Strength attack. A basic attack with a ranged weapon is usually a Dexterity attack, unless the weapon you're using has the heavy thrown property (see "Weapon Properties").

Spear: Consisting of a stabbing head on the end of a long shaft, a spear is great for lunging attacks.

Staff: In its most basic form, a staff is a long piece of wood or some other substance, roughly the same diameter along its whole length.

Unarmed: When you punch, kick, elbow, knee, or even head butt an opponent, you're making an unarmed strike. A simple unarmed attack is treated as an improvised weapon. Creatures that have natural weapons such as claws or bite attacks are proficient with those natural weapons.

WEAPON PROPERTIES

Weapon properties define additional characteristics shared by weapons that might be in different groups.

Heavy Thrown: You hurl a thrown weapon from your hand, rather than using it to loose a projectile. A ranged basic attack with a heavy thrown weapon uses your Strength instead of your Dexterity for the attack and damage rolls.

1. *Halberd*; 2. *Longbow*; 3. *Handaxe*; 4. *Short sword*; 5. *Shortbow*; 6. *Longsword*; 7. *Maul*; 8. *Greataxe*; 9. *War pick*; 10. *Bastard sword*;
11. *Warhammer*; 12. *Flail*; 13. *Battleaxe*; 14. *Throwing hammer*; 15. *Scimitar*; 16. *Glaive*

High Crit: A high crit weapon deals more damage when you score a critical hit with it. A critical hit deals maximum weapon damage and an extra 1[W] at 1st-10th levels, an extra 2[W] at 11th-20th levels, and an extra 3[W] at 21st-30th levels. This extra damage is in addition to any critical damage the weapon supplies if it is a magic weapon.

Light Thrown: A ranged basic attack with a light thrown weapon uses your Dexterity. Light thrown weapons don't deal as much damage as heavy thrown weapons, but some powers let you hurl several of them at once or in rapid succession.

Load: Ranged weapons that loose projectiles, including bows, crossbows, and slings, take some time to load. When a weapon shows "load free" on the Ranged Weapons table, that means you draw and load ammunition as a free action, effectively part of the action used to attack with the weapon. Any weapon that has the load property requires two hands to load, even if you can use only one hand to attack with it. (The sling, for example, is a one-handed weapon, but you need a free hand to load it.) The crossbow is "load minor," which means it requires a minor action to load a bolt into the weapon. If a power allows you to hit multiple targets, the additional load time is accounted for in the power.

Off-Hand: An off-hand weapon is light enough that you can hold it and attack effectively with it while holding a weapon in your main hand. You can't attack with both weapons in the same turn, unless you have a power that lets you do so, but you can attack with either weapon.

Reach: With a reach weapon, you can attack enemies that are 2 squares away from you as well as adjacent enemies, with no attack penalty. You can still make opportunity attacks only against adjacent enemies. Likewise, you can flank only an adjacent enemy.

Small: This property describes a two-handed or a versatile weapon that a Small character can use in the same way a Medium character can. A halfling can use a shortbow, for example, even though half-lings can't normally use two-handed weapons.

Versatile: Versatile weapons are one-handed, but you can use them two-handed. If you do, you deal an extra 1 point of damage when you roll damage for the weapon.

A Small character such as a halfling must use a versatile weapon two-handed and doesn't deal extra damage.

MELEE WEAPONS

SIMPLE MELEE WEAPONS

One-Handed

Weapon	Prof.	Damage	Range	Price	Weight	Group	Properties
Club	+2	1d6	–	1 gp	3 lb.	Mace	–
Dagger	+3	1d4	5/10	1 gp	1 lb.	Light blade	Off-hand, light thrown
Javelin	+2	1d6	10/20	5 gp	2 lb.	Spear	Heavy thrown
Mace	+2	1d8	–	5 gp	6 lb.	Mace	Versatile
Sickle	+2	1d6	–	2 gp	2 lb.	Light blade	Off-hand
Spear	+2	1d8	–	5 gp	6 lb.	Spear	Versatile

Two-Handed

Weapon	Prof.	Damage	Range	Price	Weight	Group	Properties
Greatclub	+2	2d4	–	1 gp	10 lb.	Mace	–
Morningstar	+2	1d10	–	10 gp	8 lb.	Mace	–
Quarterstaff	+2	1d8	–	5 gp	4 lb.	Staff	–
Scythe	+2	2d4	–	5 gp	10 lb.	Heavy blade	–

MILITARY MELEE WEAPONS

One-Handed

Weapon	Prof.	Damage	Range	Price	Weight	Group	Properties
Battleaxe	+2	1d10	–	15 gp	6 lb.	Axe	Versatile
Flail	+2	1d10	–	10 gp	5 lb.	Flail	Versatile
Handaxe	+2	1d6	5/10	5 gp	3 lb.	Axe	Off-hand, heavy thrown
Longsword	+3	1d8	–	15 gp	4 lb.	Heavy blade	Versatile
Scimitar	+2	1d8	–	10 gp	4 lb.	Heavy blade	High crit
Short sword	+3	1d6	–	10 gp	2 lb.	Light blade	Off-hand
Throwing hammer	+2	1d6	5/10	5 gp	2 lb.	Hammer	Off-hand, heavy thrown
Warhammer	+2	1d10	–	15 gp	5 lb.	Hammer	Versatile
War pick	+2	1d8	–	15 gp	6 lb.	Pick	High crit, versatile

Two-Handed

Weapon	Prof.	Damage	Range	Price	Weight	Group	Properties
Falchion	+3	2d4	–	25 gp	7 lb.	Heavy blade	High crit
Glaive	+2	2d4	–	25 gp	10 lb.	Heavy blade, polearm	Reach
Greataxe	+2	1d12	–	30 gp	12 lb.	Axe	High crit
Greatsword	+3	1d10	–	30 gp	8 lb.	Heavy blade	–
Halberd	+2	1d10	–	25 gp	12 lb.	Axe, polearm	Reach
Heavy flail	+2	2d6	–	25 gp	10 lb.	Flail	–
Longspear	+2	1d10	–	10 gp	9 lb.	Polearm, spear	Reach
Maul	+2	2d6	–	30 gp	12 lb.	Hammer	–

SUPERIOR MELEE WEAPONS

One-Handed

Weapon	Prof.	Damage	Range	Price	Weight	Group	Properties
Bastard sword	+3	1d10	–	30 gp	6 lb.	Heavy blade	Versatile
Katar	+3	1d6	–	3 gp	1 lb.	Light blade	Off-hand, high crit
Rapier	+3	1d8	–	25 gp	2 lb.	Light blade	–

Two-Handed

Weapon	Prof.	Damage	Range	Price	Weight	Group	Properties
Spiked chain	+3	2d4	–	30 gp	10 lb.	Flail	Reach

IMPROVISED MELEE WEAPONS

One-Handed

Weapon	Prof.	Damage	Range	Price	Weight	Group	Properties
Any*	n/a	1d4	–	–	1-5 lb.	None	–
Unarmed attack	n/a	1d4	–	–	–	Unarmed	–

Two-Handed

Weapon	Prof.	Damage	Range	Price	Weight	Group	Properties
Any*	n/a	1d8	–	–	6-12 lb.	None	–

* Improvised weapons include anything you happen to pick up, from a rock to a chair.

RANGED WEAPONS

SIMPLE RANGED WEAPONS

One-Handed

Weapon	Prof.	Damage	Range	Price	Weight	Group	Properties
Hand crossbow	+2	1d6	10/20	25 gp	2 lb.	Crossbow	Load free
Sling	+2	1d6	10/20	1 gp	0 lb.	Sling	Load free

Two-Handed

Weapon	Prof.	Damage	Range	Price	Weight	Group	Properties
Crossbow	+2	1d8	15/30	25 gp	4 lb.	Crossbow	Load minor

MILITARY RANGED WEAPONS

Two-Handed

Weapon	Prof.	Damage	Range	Price	Weight	Group	Properties
Longbow	+2	1d10	20/40	30 gp	3 lb.	Bow	Load free
Shortbow	+2	1d8	15/30	25 gp	2 lb.	Bow	Load free, small

SUPERIOR RANGED WEAPONS

One-Handed

Weapon	Prof.	Damage	Range	Price	Weight	Group	Properties
Shuriken (5)	+3	1d4	6/12	1 gp	1/2 lb.	Light blade	Light thrown

IMPROVISED RANGED WEAPONS

One-Handed

Weapon	Prof.	Damage	Range	Price	Weight	Group	Properties
Any*	n/a	1d4	5/10	–	1 lb.	None	–

* Improvised weapons include anything you happen to pick up, from a rock to a chair.

READING THE WEAPON TABLES

A weapon entry contains the following information, organized in columns on the weapon tables.

Weapon: The weapon's name.

Prof.: Proficiency with a weapon gives you a proficiency bonus to attack rolls, which appears in this column if applicable. Some weapons are more accurate than others, as reflected here. If you're not proficient with the weapon, you don't gain this bonus.

Damage: The weapon's damage die. When a power deals a number of weapon damage dice (such as 4[W]), you roll the number of the dice indicated by this entry. If the weapon's damage die is an expression of multiple dice, roll that number of dice the indicated number of times. For example, a falchion (which has a damage die of 2d4) deals 8d4 damage when used with a power that deals 4[W] on a hit.

Range: Weapons that can strike at a distance have range. The number before the slash indicates the normal range (in squares) for an attack. The number after the slash indicates the long range for an attack; an attack at long range takes a –2 penalty to the attack roll. Squares beyond the second number are considered to be out of range and can't be targeted with this weapon. If a melee weapon has a range entry, it can be thrown and belongs to either the light thrown or the heavy thrown category. An entry of "–" indicates that the weapon can't be used at range.

Price: The weapon's cost in gold pieces. An entry of "–" indicates that the item has no cost.

Weight: The weapon's weight in pounds.

Group and Properties: These terms are explained on pages 215-217.

1. *Spiked chain;* 2. *Rapier;* 3. *Shuriken;* 4. *Greatsword;*
5. *Falchion;* 6. *Katar*

Weapons and Size

The weapon tables assume a Medium wielder, which includes almost all player characters. Characters and creatures that are smaller or larger than Medium have special rules.

Small characters use the same weapons that Medium creatures do. However, a Small character (such as a halfling) can't use a two-handed weapon. When a Small character uses a versatile weapon, he or she must wield it two-handed and doesn't deal any extra damage for doing so.

Large, Huge, and Gargantuan creatures use weapons that are specially sized for them. Each size category larger than Medium increases the weapon's damage die by one size.

One-Handed							
1d4 → 1d6 → 1d8 → 1d10 → 1d12 → 2d6 → 2d8 → 2d10							

Two-Handed							
1d8 → 2d4 → 1d10 → 1d12 → 2d6 → 2d8 → 2d10							

Thus, a longsword sized for a Large fire giant deals 1d10 weapon damage instead of 1d8, and a Large quarterstaff deals 2d4 weapon damage.

Large creatures can use two-handed weapons intended for creatures one size category smaller than themselves and treat them as one-handed weapons. A fire giant (Large) can use a human's greatsword with one hand, and a fire titan (Huge) can use a fire giant's greatsword with one hand. A creature can't use an undersized one-handed weapon at all; its hand is too large to effectively hold the weapon's small grip.

Creatures can't use weapons designed for creatures larger than themselves. A human can't fit his or her hands properly around the hilt of a fire giant's dagger, let alone use it as an effective weapon.

When a creature that has a natural reach uses a reach weapon, the weapon increases the creature's natural reach by 1 square.

Silvered Weapons

Some monsters, such as werewolves, are susceptible to attacks made by silvered weapons. A single weapon, 30 arrows, 10 crossbow bolts, 20 sling bullets, or 5 shuriken can be silvered at a cost of 500 gp. This cost represents not only the price of the silver, but the time and expertise needed to add silver to a weapon without making it less effective.

Selling Equipment

You cannot sell mundane armor, weapons, or adventuring gear unless your DM allows, in which case you receive one-fifth of an item's market price. Art objects or fine goods that have a specific value, such as a gold dagger worth 100 gp, bring their full price.

ADVENTURING GEAR

From meals to torches, adventuring gear is essential to your party's success. You're assumed to start with basic clothing, and before your first adventure, you should equip yourself with weapons, armor, and other gear.

Standard Adventurer's Kit: This kit includes all the items grouped beneath its entry on the table: a backpack, a bedroll, flint and steel, a belt pouch, two sunrods, ten days' worth of trail rations, 50 feet of hempen rope, and a waterskin.

Ammunition: Arrows come in a quiver that holds thirty, crossbow bolts come in a case that holds twenty, and sling bullets come in a pouch that holds twenty. Ammunition is used up when you fire it from a projectile weapon.

Arcane Implement: Wizards use orbs, staffs, or wands as focus items for their spells, while warlocks use rods or wands. Using a nonmagical implement confers no benefit. You can purchase a magic implement to gain an enhancement bonus to attack rolls and damage rolls with your arcane powers. A staff implement can also function as a quarterstaff.

Climber's Kit: This kit includes all the items grouped beneath its entry: a grappling hook, a small hammer, and ten pitons. When you use a climber's kit, you gain a +2 bonus to Athletics checks for climbing.

Everburning Torch: This torch never stops burning. It sheds magical light but no heat, so you can stow it in a bag or a pouch. You can't set fire to anything with it.

Holy Symbol: This is a finely crafted symbol of precious metal that clerics and paladins use as a focus for their prayers. Using a nonmagical holy symbol confers no benefit. You can purchase a magic holy symbol to gain an enhancement bonus to attack rolls and damage rolls when using your divine powers.

Journeybread: This magic bread fills the stomach and provides all necessary nutrients with only a few small bites, so you can carry food for a long journey without weighing yourself down.

Ritual Book: Ritual casters use a ritual book to store the rituals they have mastered.

Ritual Components: These items are needed by ritual casters. You purchase as many gold pieces worth of components as you need or can afford. See Chapter 10 for more information.

Spellbook: Wizards keep the daily spells, the utility spells, and the rituals they've learned in a spellbook.

Sunrod: This minor magic item sheds bright light to a radius of 20 squares for 4 hours before burning out.

Thieves' Tools: To use the Thievery skill properly, you need the right picks and pries, skeleton keys, clamps, and so on. Thieves' tools grant a +2 bonus to Thievery checks to open a lock or to disarm a trap.

DAVID GRIFFITH

7

ADVENTURING GEAR

Item	Price	Weight
Standard adventurer's kit	15 gp	33 lb.
Backpack (empty)	2 gp	2 lb.
Bedroll	1 sp	5 lb.
Flint and steel	1 gp	–
Pouch, belt (empty)	1 gp	1/2 lb.
Rations, trail (10 days)	5 gp	10 lb.
Rope, hempen (50 ft.)	1 gp	10 lb.
Sunrods (2)	4 gp	2 lb.
Waterskin	1 gp	4 lb.
Ammunition		
Arrows (30)	1 gp	3 lb.
Crossbow bolts (20)	1 gp	2 lb.
Sling bullets (20)	1 gp	5 lb.
Arcane implement		
Orb	15 gp	2 lb.
Rod	12 gp	2 lb.
Staff	5 gp	4 lb.
Wand	7 gp	–
Candle	1 cp	–
Chain (10 ft.)	30 gp	2 lb.
Chest (empty)	2 gp	25 lb.
Climber's kit	2 gp	11 lb.
Grappling hook	1 gp	4 lb.
Hammer	5 sp	2 lb.
Pitons (10)	5 sp	5 lb.
Everburning torch	50 gp	1 lb.
Fine clothing	30 gp	6 lb.
Flask (empty)	3 cp	1 lb.
Holy symbol	10 gp	1 lb.
Journeybread (10 days)	50 gp	1 lb.
Lantern	7 gp	2 lb.
Ritual book	50 gp	3 lb.
Ritual components	Varies	–
Rope, silk (50 ft.)	10 gp	5 lb.
Spellbook	50 gp	3 lb.
Tent	10 gp	20 lb.
Thieves' tools	20 gp	1 lb.
Torch	1 sp	1 lb.

Food, Drink, and Lodging

When you're not traveling in the wilderness, you can enjoy the comforts of a village or a town—a soft bed at an inn and hot meals brought to your table.

Item	Price
Food	
Meal, common	2 sp
Meal, feast	5 gp
Drink	
Ale, pitcher	2 sp
Wine, bottle	5 gp
Inn stay (per day)	
Typical room	5 sp
Luxury room	2 gp

Mounts and Transport

As described in Chapter 8, mounts and vehicles can improve your speed or increase the amount you can carry when you travel. This table shows the price for various kinds of transport, as well as the weight of each can carry. For mounts, the carrying capacity shown is the normal load, heavy load, and maximum drag load for the creature (see "Carrying, Lifting, and Dragging," below). For vehicles, it's the maximum amount of goods you can haul with the vehicle.

Mount or Transport	Cost	Carrying Capacity
Cart or wagon	20 gp	1 ton
Riding horse*	75 gp	237/475/1,187 lb.
Rowboat	50 gp	600 lb.
Sailing ship	10,000 gp	150 tons
Warhorse*	680 gp	262/525/1,312 lb.

* Quadrupeds can carry 25 percent more than bipeds.

Carrying, Lifting, and Dragging

Adventurers carry a lot of gear. When that quantity becomes extreme, it might be enough to slow you down and otherwise hamper your capabilities. The amount you carry should rarely be an issue, and you don't need to calculate the weight your character is hauling around unless it's likely to matter.

More often, you'll need to know how much weight you can push or drag along the ground—are you strong enough to slide the statue covering the trapdoor? This information is contained in your Strength score.

Multiply your Strength score by 10. That's the weight, in pounds, that you can carry around without penalty. This amount of weight is considered a **normal load**.

Double that number (Strength × 20). That's the maximum weight you can lift off the ground. If you try to carry that weight, though, you're slowed. Carrying such a load requires both hands, so you're not particularly effective while you're doing so. This amount of weight is considered a **heavy load**.

Five times your normal load (Strength × 50) is the most weight you can push or drag along the ground. You're slowed if you try to push or drag more weight than you can carry without penalty, and you can't push or drag such a heavy load over difficult terrain. This amount of weight is referred to as your **maximum drag load**.

Your DM might rule that you can't carry certain objects at full speed no matter what your Strength score is, just because they're so bulky or unwieldy. Your DM can also ask you to make a Strength check to push or to lift something heavy in a stressful situation, such as in the middle of combat.

MAGIC ITEMS

As you gain levels, the mundane equipment you purchased as a starting character becomes less important; it's overshadowed by the magic items you acquire on your adventures. Magic armor that can cloak you in shadow, magic weapons that burst into flame, magic rings that turn you invisible, or *Ioun stones* that orbit your head to grant you great capabilities—these items enhance and supplement the powers you gain from your class and enhance your attacks and defenses.

Magic items have levels, just as characters, powers, and monsters do. An item's level is a general measure of its power and translates to the average level of character using that item. In practice, your character will end up with some items that are three or four levels above your level and others that are several levels below. There's no restriction on using or acquiring items based on their level, except that you can't use the Enchant Magic Item ritual (page 304) to create an item above your level. If, for some reason, your 10th-level character finds a 20th-level magic sword, you can use it to full effect.

You can sometimes buy magic items just as you can mundane equipment. It's rare to find a shop or a bazaar that routinely sells magic items, except perhaps the lowest-level items. Some fantastic places, such as the legendary City of Brass in the heart of the Elemental Chaos, have such markets, but those are the exception rather than the rule. Your DM might say that you can track down a seller for the item you want to buy or that you might have to do some searching, but in general you can buy any item you can afford.

You can also use the Enchant Magic Item ritual to create an item of your level or lower. In terms of the economic transaction, creating an item is the same as buying it: You spend money equal to the market price of the item and acquire the item. Some DMs prefer to have characters enchant their own items rather than buy them, particularly for more powerful items.

As you adventure, you'll come across magic items as part of the treasure you acquire. Often, these are magic items much higher than your level—items you can't enchant and can't easily afford to buy. Ideally, these are items that someone in your party can use effectively, which makes them very rewarding treasure.

If you find a magic item you don't want to keep, or you find an item that replaces an item you already have, you might end up either selling the item or disenchanting it (with the Disenchant Magic Item ritual; see page 304). This isn't a favorable transaction for you—the sale price of a magic item, or the value of *residuum* you get from disenchanting it, is only one-fifth the normal price of the item. That means selling an item gives you enough money or *residuum* to buy or enchant an item that's five levels lower than the original item.

IDENTIFYING MAGIC ITEMS

Most of the time, you can determine the properties and powers of a magic item during a short rest. In the course of handling the item for a few minutes, you discover what the item is and what it does. You can identify one magic item per short rest.

Some magic items might be a bit harder to identify, such as cursed or nonstandard items, or powerful magical artifacts. Your DM might ask for an Arcana check to determine their properties, or you might even need to go on a special quest to find a ritual to identify or to unlock the powers of a unique item.

PRICES

The purchase price of a permanent magic item depends on its level, as shown on the table below. The purchase price of a consumable item (such as a potion or an elixir) is much lower than the price of a permanent item of the same level. The sale price of a magic item (the amount a PC gets from either selling

MAGIC ITEM PRICES

Item Level	Purchase Price (gp)	Sale Price (gp)*
1	360	72
2	520	104
3	680	136
4	840	168
5	1,000	200
6	1,800	360
7	2,600	520
8	3,400	680
9	4,200	840
10	5,000	1,000
11	9,000	1,800
12	13,000	2,600
13	17,000	3,400
14	21,000	4,200
15	25,000	5,000
16	45,000	9,000
17	65,000	13,000
18	85,000	17,000
19	105,000	21,000
20	125,000	25,000
21	225,000	45,000
22	325,000	65,000
23	425,000	85,000
24	525,000	105,000
25	625,000	125,000
26	1,125,000	225,000
27	1,625,000	325,000
28	2,125,000	425,000
29	2,625,000	525,000
30	3,125,000	625,000

* Or equivalent gold piece value of *residuum* acquired from disenchanting an item

or disenchanting an item) is one-fifth of the purchase price.

Prices shown are the base market price for the items. The actual cost to purchase a magic item depends on supply and demand and might be 10 to 40 percent more than the base market price.

Magic Item Categories

Magic items fall into seven broad categories: armor, weapons, implements, clothing, rings, wondrous items, and potions. Items in a particular category have similar effects—all magic weapons give you bonuses when you attack with them, and all magic boots have powers relating to movement. Aside from those broad generalities, though, magic items possess a wide variety of powers and properties.

Within the broad category of clothing, items are grouped by kind of clothing—whether you wear the item on your head or your feet, for example. These are called **item slots**, and they provide a practical limit to the number of magic items you can wear and use. You can benefit from only one magic item that you wear in your arms slot even if, practically speaking, you can wear bracers and carry a shield at the same time. You benefit from the item you put on first; any other item you put in the same item slot doesn't function for you

until you take off the first item. Sometimes there are physical limitations as well—you can't wear two helms at the same time.

Wondrous items include a variety of useful tools, from a *bag of holding* to a *flying carpet*. Each item's description indicates how a character accesses its effects.

All magic armor gives you an enhancement bonus to your Armor Class. All magic weapons and implements give you an enhancement bonus to your attack rolls and damage rolls when you use them to make an attack. All magic cloaks, amulets, and other neck slot items give you an enhancement bonus to your Fortitude, Reflex, and Will defenses. Other magic items don't generally give you bonuses to these numerical statistics, though there are some exceptions.

The rest of this chapter describes a broad selection of magic items of all levels, presented alphabetically within each category.

Reading a Magic Item

Here's a sample magic item, the *holy avenger* weapon:

Holy Avenger	Level 25+

The most prized weapon of any paladin.

Lvl 25   +5   625,000 gp   Lvl 30   +6   3,125,000 gp

Weapon: Axe, Hammer, Heavy Blade

Enhancement: Attack rolls and damage rolls

Critical: +1d6 radiant damage per plus, and you can spend a healing surge

Property: A holy avenger deals an extra 1d10 radiant damage when the power you use to make the attack has the radiant keyword.

Power (Daily): Minor Action. You and each ally within 10 squares of you gain a +5 power bonus to Fortitude, Reflex, and Will defenses until the end of your next turn.

Special: A *holy avenger* can be used as a holy symbol. It adds its enhancement bonus to attack rolls and damage rolls and the extra damage granted by its property (if applicable) when used in this manner. You do not gain your weapon proficiency bonus to the attack roll when using a *holy avenger* as an implement.

Name and Level

The name of the magic item and the item's level appear on the first line of the description. If an item's level line ends with a plus sign, that item is available at more than one level, with higher-level versions having a greater enhancement bonus or more potent powers and properties.

The *holy avenger* is available as a 25th-level item and also comes in a higher-level version.

Description

The next entry gives a brief description of the item, sometimes explaining what it does in plain language, other times offering flavorful information about its appearance, origin, effect, or place in the world. This material isn't rules text; when you need to know the exact effect, look at the rules text below.

CATEGORY AND PRICE

The next line or lines indicate the magic item's various levels and enhancement bonus (if applicable) and the price for each version of the item. For weapons, the line beneath this information tells you which weapon groups can be enchanted with that set of qualities, and for armor, it notes the same for the five types of armor (plus clothing). For implements, it shows the specific kind of implement. For clothing items, the entry appears as "Item Slot:" followed by the appropriate slot.

The magic item's purchase price is either a single number (for an item with a fixed level) or a list of values, as in the example of *flamedrinker armor*.

The price of a *holy avenger* (as well as its enhancement bonus) depends on its level. The 25th-level version is a +5 weapon and costs 625,000 gp, and the 30th-level version is a +6 weapon and costs 3,125,000 gp. It's a weapon, and its characteristics can be applied to axes, hammers, and heavy blades.

ENHANCEMENT

For items that give an enhancement bonus, this entry specifies what that bonus applies to: AC, other defenses, or attack rolls and damage rolls.

Magic weapons and implements grant their enhancement bonus to attack rolls and damage rolls only when you use powers delivered through the weapon or the implement (or directly from the weapon or the implement, for items that have attack powers).

For example, a fighter's attack powers are delivered through a weapon, so he or she adds a magic weapon's enhancement bonus to attack rolls and damage rolls. A wizard's attack powers are delivered through an implement (orb, staff, or wand), so he or she adds an implement's enhancement bonus to attack rolls and damage rolls with those powers.

A power's description indicates if it functions through the use of a weapon or an implement. Each class description in Chapter 4 indicates which imple-

ments (if any) a character of that class is allowed to use when delivering powers. For example, a cleric can wear a holy symbol to use implement powers, while a warlock can wield either a rod or a wand.

A magic item's level and its enhancement bonus are associated. An item that has a +2 bonus is always between level 6 and level 10.

Item Level	Enhancement Bonus
1–5	+1
6–10	+2
11–15	+3
16–20	+4
21–25	+5
26–30	+6

Because a *holy avenger* is a magic weapon, its enhancement bonus applies to the user's weapon attack rolls and damage rolls.

CRITICAL

For magic weapons and implements, this entry describes what happens when you score a critical hit using that item. Just as with an enhancement bonus, this effect only applies for attacks that are delivered through the weapon or the implement. (A wizard's *magic missile* can't benefit from the critical hit effect noted for the magic dagger she carries, for example.)

All magic weapons and implements deal one or more extra dice of damage on a critical hit. The number of extra dice is equal to the item's enhancement bonus, and the die rolled depends on the particular weapon or implement. (The normal critical die is a d6.) Unless noted otherwise, the damage type of this extra damage is the same as the normal damage type for the weapon.

In addition to extra damage, some magic weapons or implements produce other effects on a critical hit. This information is noted in the weapon's description. An attack that does not deal damage still does not deal damage on a critical hit.

A *holy avenger* deals an extra 5d6 or an extra 6d6 (depending on its enhancement bonus) damage on a critical hit and also allows the wielder to spend a healing surge.

PROPERTY

Some magic items have a special property that is constantly active (or active under certain conditions). A property doesn't normally require any action to use, although some properties allow you to turn them off (or on again).

When you're wielding a *holy avenger*, all your radiant powers deal extra damage when you use the weapon to deliver them. You don't need to turn this property on or off.

RESIDUUM

Residuum is the magical substance that results from using the Disenchant Magic Item ritual on an item. It's a fine, silvery dust that some describe as concentrated magic, useful as a generic component for rituals (see Chapter 10). In some exotic locales, *residuum* is traded as currency, measured by weight and carried in small metal vials. It's a convenient way to transport large sums of wealth; 10,000 gp worth of *residuum* weighs as much as a single gold piece and takes up only slightly more space, so 1 pound of *residuum* is worth 500,000 gp and fits in a belt pouch.

POWER

Some magic items have a special power. This entry, when present in an item description, includes the action required to use the power and the effect of the power. In some cases, it might also indicate the specific conditions under which you can use the power (for instance, only if you're bloodied).

In general, magic item powers follow the same rules as other powers (in that they have ranges, shapes, and so forth). See "How to Read a Power," page 54, for details.

Like racial powers and class powers, magic item powers often have keywords that indicate their damage or effect types. When you use a magic item as part of a racial power or a class power, the keywords of the item's power and the other power all apply. For instance, if a paladin uses a *flaming sword* to attack with a power that deals radiant damage, the power deals both fire damage and radiant damage.

Like other powers, magic item powers are sometimes at-will powers, sometimes encounter powers, and sometimes daily powers. Magic item powers have two other categories as well: Healing surge powers are usable every time you spend a healing surge, and consumable powers appear in one-use magic items.

At-Will: These powers can be used as often as their action types allow.

Encounter: These powers can be used once per encounter and are renewed when their user takes a short rest.

Daily: A magic item's daily power can be used once per day and is renewed when its user takes an extended rest. As with daily powers provided by your class, there is a limit to the number of magic item daily powers you can use on any given day. This limit depends on your level.

At 1st–10th level, you can use one magic item daily power per day.

At 11th–20th level, you can use two magic item daily powers per day.

At 21st–30th level, you can use three magic item daily powers per day.

Each use of a magic item daily power must come from a different magic item. At 11th level, for example, you can use the daily powers provided by two different magic items, but you can't use two different daily powers from the same magic item. Your character sheet includes boxes to help you keep track of these uses.

Each time you reach a milestone (see page 259), you gain one additional use of a magic item daily power. This benefit can be used to activate any magic item daily power that you have not already used this day (even if you've already used a different daily power from that magic item).

After you take an extended rest, all of your magic item daily powers are renewed, and you start fresh with regard to the number of magic item daily powers you can use per day.

Healing Surge: You begin with one use of the power per day, like a daily power. You can renew this item's power by taking a standard action to funnel your vitality into the item, spending a healing surge in the process. Spending a healing surge in this way doesn't restore hit points, and this standard action is separate from the action required to activate the item's power.

Consumable: Some items, particularly potions and elixirs, contain one-use powers that are expended when you use them.

Once per day, you can use a *holy avenger* to increase the defenses of you and your allies. This power renews when you take an extended rest.

SPECIAL

If any special rules or restrictions on the item's use exist, here's where you'll find them.

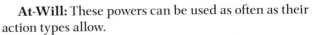

ZOLTAN BOROS & GABOR SZIKSZAI

ARMOR

Magic armor adds an enhancement bonus to AC, so a set of +5 *black iron dragonscale* adds a total of 15 to the wearer's Armor Class (10 from the scale armor and 5 from the enhancement bonus). If you're not proficient with the armor type, you take –2 penalty to attack rolls and to your Reflex defense but still gain the enhancement bonus of the magic armor.

The category determines what kind of armors can be enchanted with that particular set of qualities. "Any" includes all armors: cloth, leather, hide, chain, scale, and plate.

You can resize magic armor with the Enchant Magic Item ritual (see page 304).

Angelsteel Armor — Level 19+

The links in this armor glow with the silvery light of the Astral Sea.

Lvl 19	+4	105,000 gp	Lvl 29	+6	2,625,000 gp
Lvl 24	+5	525,000 gp			

Armor: Chain
Enhancement: AC
Power (Daily): Immediate Reaction. You can use this power when you are hit by an attack. Gain a +2 power bonus to the defense that attack targeted until the end of the encounter.

Barkskin Armor — Level 5+

The enchantment placed upon this armor toughens the material and provides it with a rough texture like tree bark.

Lvl 5	+1	1,000 gp	Lvl 20	+4	125,000 gp
Lvl 10	+2	5,000 gp	Lvl 25	+5	625,000 gp
Lvl 15	+3	25,000 gp	Lvl 30	+6	3,125,000 gp

Armor: Hide, Scale
Enhancement: AC
Power (Daily): Minor Action. Gain a +2 power bonus to AC until the end of the encounter. Each time an attack hits your AC, reduce this bonus by 1 (minimum 0).
Level 15 or 20: Gain a +3 power bonus.
Level 25 or 30: Gain a +4 power bonus.

Battleforged Armor — Level 5+

The dwarves and the dragonborn argue over which race invented this enchanted armor.

Lvl 5	+1	1,000 gp	Lvl 20	+4	125,000 gp
Lvl 10	+2	5,000 gp	Lvl 25	+5	625,000 gp
Lvl 15	+3	25,000 gp	Lvl 30	+6	3,125,000 gp

Armor: Plate
Enhancement: AC
Property: If you use your second wind when you are bloodied, regain an extra 1d10 hit points.
Level 15 or 20: Regain an extra 2d10 hit points.
Level 25 or 30: Regain an extra 3d10 hit points.

Black Iron Armor — Level 4+

The black metal of this armor glows red when violence flares.

Lvl 4	+1	840 gp	Lvl 19	+4	105,000 gp
Lvl 9	+2	4,200 gp	Lvl 24	+5	525,000 gp
Lvl 14	+3	21,000 gp	Lvl 29	+6	2,625,000 gp

Armor: Scale, Plate
Enhancement: AC
Property: Resist 5 fire and resist 5 necrotic.
Level 14 or 19: Resist 10 fire and resist 10 necrotic.
Level 24 or 29: Resist 15 fire and resist 15 necrotic.

Bloodcut Armor — Level 4+

This armor has a crimson tinge that flares blood red when its power is activated.

Lvl 4	+1	840 gp	Lvl 19	+4	105,000 gp
Lvl 9	+2	4,200 gp	Lvl 24	+5	525,000 gp
Lvl 14	+3	21,000 gp	Lvl 29	+6	2,625,000 gp

Armor: Leather, Hide
Enhancement: AC
Power (Healing Surge): Minor Action. While you are bloodied, use this armor to gain resist 10 to all damage until the end of your next turn.
Level 14 or 19: Resist 15 to all damage.
Level 24 or 29: Resist 20 to all damage.

Bloodthread Armor — Level 5+

Eladrin master tailors magically weave threads of enchanted blood into the supple cloth used to create this robe or jacket.

Lvl 5	+1	1,000 gp	Lvl 20	+4	125,000 gp
Lvl 10	+2	5,000 gp	Lvl 25	+5	625,000 gp
Lvl 15	+3	25,000 gp	Lvl 30	+6	3,125,000 gp

Armor: Cloth
Enhancement: AC
Property: When you are bloodied, you gain a +2 item bonus to AC and saving throws.

Curseforged Armor — Level 3+

In ancient days, the tieflings poured their bitterness into their forges as a lesson to those who would betray them.

Lvl 3	+1	680 gp	Lvl 18	+4	85,000 gp
Lvl 8	+2	3,400 gp	Lvl 23	+5	425,000 gp
Lvl 13	+3	17,000 gp	Lvl 28	+6	2,125,000 gp

Armor: Chain, Scale
Enhancement: AC
Power (Daily): Immediate Reaction. You can use this power when an enemy hits you with an attack. That enemy takes a –2 penalty to attack rolls (save ends). When the enemy saves against the penalty, the enemy takes a –1 penalty to attack rolls (save ends).
Level 13 or 18: –3 penalty.
Level 23 or 28: –4 penalty.

MAGIC ARMOR

Lvl	Name	Price (gp)	Categories
1	Magic +1	360	Any
2	Dwarven +1	520	Chain, Scale, Plate
2	Razor +1	520	Scale
3	Curseforged +1	680	Chain, Scale
3	Delver's +1	680	Any
3	Eladrin +1	680	Chain
3	Fireburst +1	680	Cloth
3	Sylvan +1	680	Cloth, Leather, Hide
4	Black Iron +1	840	Scale, Plate
4	Bloodcut +1	840	Leather, Hide
4	Darkleaf +1	840	Cloth, Leather, Hide
5	Barkskin +1	1,000	Hide, Scale
5	Battleforged +1	1,000	Plate
5	Bloodthread +1	1,000	Cloth
5	Deathcut +1	1,000	Leather, Hide
5	Exalted +1	1,000	Chain
6	Magic +2	1,800	Any
7	Dwarven +2	2,600	Chain, Scale, Plate
7	Razor +2	2,600	Scale
7	Sunleaf +2	2,600	Cloth, Leather, Hide
8	Curseforged +2	3,400	Chain, Scale
8	Delver's +2	3,400	Any
8	Eladrin +2	3,400	Chain
8	Elven battle +2	3,400	Leather, Hide
8	Fireburst +2	3,400	Cloth
8	Mountain +2	3,400	Plate
8	Sylvan +2	3,400	Cloth, Leather, Hide
9	Black Iron +2	4,200	Scale, Plate
9	Bloodcut +2	4,200	Leather, Hide
9	Darkleaf +2	4,200	Cloth, Leather, Hide
9	Ghostphase +2	4,200	Cloth
10	Barkskin +2	5,000	Hide, Scale
10	Battleforged +2	5,000	Plate
10	Bloodthread +2	5,000	Cloth
10	Deathcut +2	5,000	Leather, Hide
10	Exalted +2	5,000	Chain

MAGIC ARMOR CONT.

Lvl	Name	Price (gp)	Categories
11	Magic +3	9,000	Any
12	Dwarven +3	13,000	Chain, Scale, Plate
12	Razor +3	13,000	Scale
12	Sunleaf +3	13,000	Cloth, Leather, Hide
13	Curseforged +3	17,000	Chain, Scale
13	Delver's +3	17,000	Any
13	Eladrin +3	17,000	Chain
13	Elven battle +3	17,000	Leather, Hide
13	Fireburst +3	17,000	Cloth
13	Hydra +3	17,000	Scale
13	Mountain +3	17,000	Plate
13	Shadowflow +3	17,000	Cloth, Leather
13	Sylvan +3	17,000	Cloth, Leather, Hide
14	Black Iron +3	21,000	Scale, Plate
14	Bloodcut +3	21,000	Leather, Hide
14	Darkleaf +3	21,000	Cloth, Leather, Hide
14	Flamedrinker +3	21,000	Plate
14	Ghostphase +3	21,000	Cloth
14	Tombforged +3	21,000	Chain
15	Barkskin +3	25,000	Hide, Scale
15	Battleforged +3	25,000	Plate
15	Bloodthread +3	25,000	Cloth
15	Deathcut +3	25,000	Leather, Hide
15	Exalted +3	25,000	Chain
15	Trollskin +3	25,000	Hide, Scale
16	Magic +4	45,000	Any
17	Dwarven +4	65,000	Chain, Scale, Plate
17	Razor +4	65,000	Scale
17	Sunleaf +4	65,000	Cloth, Leather, Hide
18	Curseforged +4	85,000	Chain, Scale
18	Delver's +4	85,000	Any
18	Eladrin +4	85,000	Chain
18	Elven battle +4	85,000	Leather, Hide
18	Fireburst +4	85,000	Cloth
18	Hydra +4	85,000	Scale
18	Mountain +4	85,000	Plate

Darkleaf Armor — Level 4+

Darkleaves from the gravetrees of the Shadowfell give this armor its protective properties.

Lvl 4	+1	840 gp	Lvl 19	+4	105,000 gp
Lvl 9	+2	4,200 gp	Lvl 24	+5	525,000 gp
Lvl 14	+3	21,000 gp	Lvl 29	+6	2,625,000 gp

Armor: Cloth, Leather, Hide
Enhancement: AC
Property: Gain a +2 item bonus to AC against the first attack made against you in each encounter.

Deathcut Armor — Level 5+

Crafted from the hides of creatures slain by necromantic magic, this armor radiates unease and offers protection against similar magic.

Lvl 5	+1	1,000 gp	Lvl 20	+4	125,000 gp
Lvl 10	+2	5,000 gp	Lvl 25	+5	625,000 gp
Lvl 15	+3	25,000 gp	Lvl 30	+6	3,125,000 gp

Armor: Leather, Hide
Enhancement: AC
Property: Resist 5 necrotic and resist 5 poison.
Power (Daily ✦ Necrotic): Immediate Reaction. You can use this power when an enemy hits you with a melee attack. Deal 1d10 + Charisma modifier necrotic damage to that enemy.
Level 15 or 20: 2d10 + Charisma modifier necrotic damage.
Level 25 or 30: 3d10 + Charisma modifier necrotic damage.

Lvl	Name	Price (gp)	Categories
18	Shadowflow +4	85,000	Cloth, Leather
18	Sylvan +4	85,000	Cloth, Leather, Hide
19	Angelsteel +4	105,000	Chain
19	Black Iron +4	105,000	Scale, Plate
19	Bloodcut +4	105,000	Leather, Hide
19	Darkleaf +4	105,000	Cloth, Leather, Hide
19	Flamedrinker +4	105,000	Plate
19	Ghostphase +4	105,000	Cloth
19	Soulforged +4	105,000	Plate
19	Tombforged +4	105,000	Chain
20	Barkskin +4	125,000	Hide, Scale
20	Battleforged +4	125,000	Plate
20	Bloodthread +4	125,000	Cloth
20	Deathcut +4	125,000	Leather, Hide
20	Exalted +4	125,000	Chain
20	Trollskin +4	125,000	Hide, Scale
21	Magic +5	225,000	Any
22	Dwarven +5	325,000	Chain, Scale, Plate
22	Razor +5	325,000	Scale
22	Sunleaf +5	325,000	Cloth, Leather, Hide
23	Curseforged +5	425,000	Chain, Scale
23	Delver's +5	425,000	Any
23	Eladrin +5	425,000	Chain
23	Elven battle +5	425,000	Leather, Hide
23	Fireburst +5	425,000	Cloth
23	Hydra +5	425,000	Scale
23	Mantle of the Seventh Wind +5	425,000	Cloth
23	Mountain +5	425,000	Plate
23	Shadowflow +5	425,000	Cloth, Leather
23	Sylvan +5	425,000	Cloth, Leather, Hide
24	Angelsteel +5	525,000	Chain
24	Black Iron +5	525,000	Scale, Plate
24	Bloodcut +5	525,000	Leather, Hide
24	Darkleaf +5	525,000	Cloth, Leather, Hide
24	Flamedrinker +5	525,000	Plate
24	Ghostphase +5	525,000	Cloth
24	Soulforged +5	525,000	Plate
24	Tombforged +5	525,000	Chain
25	Barkskin +5	625,000	Hide, Scale
25	Battleforged +5	625,000	Plate
25	Bloodthread +5	625,000	Cloth
25	Deathcut +5	625,000	Leather, Hide
25	Exalted +5	625,000	Chain
25	Trollskin +5	625,000	Hide, Scale
26	Magic +6	1,125,000	Any
27	Dwarven +6	1,625,000	Chain, Scale, Plate
27	Razor +6	1,625,000	Scale
27	Sunleaf +6	1,625,000	Cloth, Leather, Hide
28	Curseforged +6	2,125,000	Chain, Scale
28	Delver's +6	2,125,000	Any
28	Eladrin +6	2,125,000	Chain
28	Elven battle +6	2,125,000	Leather, Hide
28	Fireburst +6	2,125,000	Cloth
28	Hydra +6	2,125,000	Scale
28	Mountain +6	2,125,000	Plate
28	Mantle of the Seventh Wind +6	2,125,000	Cloth
28	Shadowflow +6	2,125,000	Cloth, Leather
28	Sylvan +6	2,125,000	Cloth, Leather, Hide
29	Angelsteel +6	2,625,000	Chain
29	Black Iron +6	2,625,000	Scale, Plate
29	Bloodcut +6	2,625,000	Leather, Hide
29	Darkleaf +6	2,625,000	Cloth, Leather, Hide
29	Flamedrinker +6	2,625,000	Plate
29	Ghostphase +6	2,625,000	Cloth
29	Soulforged +6	2,625,000	Plate
29	Tombforged +6	2,625,000	Chain
30	Barkskin +6	3,125,000	Hide, Scale
30	Battleforged +6	3,125,000	Plate
30	Bloodthread +6	3,125,000	Cloth
30	Deathcut +6	3,125,000	Leather, Hide
30	Exalted +6	3,125,000	Chain
30	Trollskin +6	3,125,000	Hide, Scale

Delver's Armor — Level 3+

A popular armor among adventurers, it is relatively easy to make.

Lvl 3	+1	680 gp	Lvl 18	+4	85,000 gp
Lvl 8	+2	3,400 gp	Lvl 23	+5	425,000 gp
Lvl 13	+3	17,000 gp	Lvl 28	+6	2,125,000 gp

Armor: Any
Enhancement: AC
Power (Daily): Free Action. Gain a +2 power bonus to a saving throw you just rolled; use the new result.

Dwarven Armor — Level 2+

Crafted by the finest dwarf armorsmiths, this armor was once only available to dwarves, though now some armorsmiths will create a set for whoever can pay the price.

Lvl 2	+1	520 gp	Lvl 17	+4	65,000 gp
Lvl 7	+2	2,600 gp	Lvl 22	+5	325,000 gp
Lvl 12	+3	13,000 gp	Lvl 27	+6	1,625,000 gp

Armor: Chain, Scale, Plate
Enhancement: AC
Property: Gain an item bonus to Endurance checks equal to the armor's enhancement bonus.
Power (Daily ✦ Healing): Free Action. Regain hit points as if you had spent a healing surge.

Eladrin Armor   Level 3+

Crafted by master eladrin armorsmiths, the fine links of this chainmail sparkle in even the faintest light.

Lvl 3	+1	680 gp	Lvl 18	+4	85,000 gp
Lvl 8	+2	3,400 gp	Lvl 23	+5	425,000 gp
Lvl 13	+3	17,000 gp	Lvl 28	+6	2,125,000 gp

Armor: Chain
Enhancement: AC
Property: Add 1 square to the maximum distance of any teleport you make.
   This armor has no speed or skill check penalties.
   Level 13 or 18: +2 squares to teleport distance.
   Level 23 or 28: +3 squares to teleport distance.

Elven Battle Armor   Level 8+

There's no mistaking the forest motif woven into elven battle armor.

Lvl 8	+2	3,400 gp	Lvl 23	+5	425,000 gp
Lvl 13	+3	17,000 gp	Lvl 28	+6	2,125,000 gp
Lvl 18	+4	85,000 gp			

Armor: Leather, Hide
Enhancement: AC
Property: Gain a +5 item bonus to saving throws against being slowed or immobilized.
Power (Encounter): Minor Action. Gain a +2 power bonus to speed until the end of your next turn.

Exalted Armor   Level 5+

Clerics and warlords often seek out exalted armor because of its properties that improve their healing powers.

Lvl 5	+1	1,000 gp	Lvl 20	+4	125,000 gp
Lvl 10	+2	5,000 gp	Lvl 25	+5	625,000 gp
Lvl 15	+3	25,000 gp	Lvl 30	+6	3,125,000 gp

Armor: Chain
Enhancement: AC
Power (Daily ✦ Healing): Minor Action. Until the end of your turn, each character healed by one of your encounter powers or daily powers regains additional hit points equal to 1d10 + your Charisma modifier.

Fireburst Armor   Level 3+

Eladrin master tailors magically weave threads of arcane fire into the supple cloth used to make this robe or jacket.

Lvl 3	+1	680 gp	Lvl 18	+4	85,000 gp
Lvl 8	+2	3,400 gp	Lvl 23	+5	425,000 gp
Lvl 13	+3	17,000 gp	Lvl 28	+6	2,125,000 gp

Armor: Cloth
Enhancement: AC
Property: You automatically succeed on saving throws against ongoing fire damage.
Power (Daily ✦ Fire): Minor Action. Until the end of your next turn, any creature that hits you with a melee attack takes 1d8 + Charisma modifier fire damage.
   Level 13 or 18: 2d8 + Charisma modifier fire damage.
   Level 23 or 28: 3d8 + Charisma modifier fire damage.

Flamedrinker Armor   Level 14+

This well-crafted plate armor absorbs flames, providing some protection against fire.

| Lvl 14 | +3 | 21,000 gp | Lvl 24 | +5 | 525,000 gp |
| Lvl 19 | +4 | 105,000 gp | Lvl 29 | +6 | 2,625,000 gp |

Armor: Plate
Enhancement: AC
Property: Resist 10 fire.
   Level 24 or 29: Resist 15 fire.
Power (Daily): Immediate Interrupt. You can use this power when you are hit by an attack that has the fire keyword. You and each ally within 5 squares of you gain resist 20 fire until the start of your next turn.
   Level 24 or 29: Resist 30 fire.

Ghostphase Armor   Level 9+

This thin white-and-gray mantle fades away near the bottom.

Lvl 9	+2	4,200 gp	Lvl 24	+5	525,000 gp
Lvl 14	+3	21,000 gp	Lvl 29	+6	2,625,000 gp
Lvl 19	+4	105,000 gp			

Armor: Cloth
Enhancement: AC
Property: None.
   Level 14: Resist 5 necrotic.
   Level 19 or 24: Resist 10 necrotic.
   Level 29: Resist 15 necrotic.
Power (Daily): Minor Action. Become insubstantial until the end of your next turn.
   Level 24 or 29: Become insubstantial and gain phasing until the end of your next turn.

Hydra Armor   Level 13+

The scales of the mighty hydra are used to craft this armor.

| Lvl 13 | +3 | 17,000 gp | Lvl 23 | +5 | 425,000 gp |
| Lvl 18 | +4 | 85,000 gp | Lvl 28 | +6 | 2,125,000 gp |

Armor: Scale
Enhancement: AC
Property: When an enemy scores a critical hit against you, gain regeneration 5 until the end of the encounter.
   Level 23 or 28: Gain regeneration 10.

Magic Armor   Level 1+

A set of basic yet effective enchanted armor.

Lvl 1	+1	360 gp	Lvl 16	+4	45,000 gp
Lvl 6	+2	1,800 gp	Lvl 21	+5	225,000 gp
Lvl 11	+3	9,000 gp	Lvl 26	+6	1,125,000 gp

Armor: Any
Enhancement: AC

Mantle of the Seventh Wind   Level 23+

This enchanted robe or jacket catches the fickle wind to bear you aloft.

| Lvl 23 | +5 | 425,000 gp | Lvl 28 | +6 | 2,125,000 gp |

Armor: Cloth
Enhancement: AC
Property: You have a fly speed equal to your speed, but you must end each turn on a solid surface or you fall.

Mountain Armor — Level 8+

Dwarf armorsmiths combine the elemental earth of their mountain homes with other metals to craft this heavy armor.

Lvl 8	+2	3,400 gp	Lvl 23	+5	425,000 gp
Lvl 13	+3	17,000 gp	Lvl 28	+6	2,125,000 gp
Lvl 18	+4	85,000 gp			

Armor: Plate

Enhancement: AC

Power (Encounter): Immediate Interrupt. You can use this power when you are subjected to a pull, a push, or a slide effect. Reduce the forced movement by 1 square.
Level 18 or 23: Reduce the forced movement by 2 squares.
Level 28: Reduce the forced movement by 3 squares.

Razor Armor — Level 2+

Jutting spikes and sharp edges cover each scale set into this armor.

Lvl 2	+1	520 gp	Lvl 17	+4	65,000 gp
Lvl 7	+2	2,600 gp	Lvl 22	+5	325,000 gp
Lvl 12	+3	13,000 gp	Lvl 27	+6	1,625,000 gp

Armor: Scale

Enhancement: AC

Property: When an enemy scores a melee critical hit against you, that enemy takes 1d10 + Dexterity modifier damage.
Level 12 or 17: 2d10 + Dexterity modifier damage.
Level 22 or 27: 3d10 + Dexterity modifier damage.

Shadowflow Armor — Level 13+

Inky tendrils of night seep from this pure black armor.

Lvl 13	+3	17,000 gp	Lvl 23	+5	425,000 gp
Lvl 18	+4	85,000 gp	Lvl 28	+6	2,125,000 gp

Armor: Cloth, Leather

Enhancement: AC

Property: Gain an item bonus to Stealth checks equal to the armor's enhancement bonus.

Power (Encounter): Minor Action. Gain concealment until the start of your next turn.
Level 23 or 28: Gain invisibility until the start of your next turn.

Soulforged Armor — Level 19+

A bit of your own life force flows through this plate armor, granting you a moment of respite where others would succumb to the wounds of battle.

Lvl 19	+4	105,000 gp	Lvl 29	+6	2,625,000 gp
Lvl 24	+5	525,000 gp			

Armor: Plate

Enhancement: AC

Property: When reduced to 0 hit points or fewer, you remain conscious until the end of your next turn. If you are still at 0 hit points or fewer at that point, you fall unconscious (or die) as normal.

Sunleaf Armor — Level 7+

Elf master crafters use the leaves of the sun tree to create radiant armor of cloth, leather, or hide.

Lvl 7	+2	2,600 gp	Lvl 22	+5	325,000 gp
Lvl 12	+3	13,000 gp	Lvl 27	+6	1,625,000 gp
Lvl 17	+4	65,000 gp			

Armor: Cloth, Leather, Hide

Enhancement: AC

Property: Resist 5 radiant.
Level 17 or 22: Resist 10 radiant.
Level 27: Resist 15 radiant.

Power (Daily ✦ Radiant): Free Action. You can use this power when an enemy hits you with an opportunity attack. Deal 1d10 + Dexterity modifier radiant damage to that enemy.
Level 12 or 17: 2d10 + Dexterity modifier radiant damage.
Level 22 or 27: 3d10 + Dexterity modifier radiant damage.

Sylvan Armor — Level 3+

This brown and gray armor is favored by those who want to move like a leaf carried along on a forest breeze.

Lvl 3	+1	680 gp	Lvl 18	+4	85,000 gp
Lvl 8	+2	3,400 gp	Lvl 23	+5	425,000 gp
Lvl 13	+3	17,000 gp	Lvl 28	+6	2,125,000 gp

Armor: Cloth, Leather, Hide

Enhancement: AC

Property: Gain an item bonus to Athletics checks and Stealth checks equal to the armor's enhancement bonus.

Tombforged Armor — Level 14+

This armor is constructed around a single link from the burial armor of a hero dead at least 100 years.

Lvl 14	+3	21,000 gp	Lvl 24	+5	525,000 gp
Lvl 19	+4	105,000 gp	Lvl 29	+6	2,625,000 gp

Armor: Chain

Enhancement: AC

Property: Resist 10 necrotic.
Level 24 or 29: Resist 15 necrotic.

Power (Daily ✦ Healing): Immediate Interrupt. You can use this power when an ally within 5 squares of you takes damage. You spend a healing surge but regain no hit points. Instead, the ally regains hit points as if he or she had spent a healing surge.
Level 24 or 29: Ally within 10 squares of you.

Trollskin Armor — Level 15+

Trolls hate everyone, but especially you and your warty green armor.

Lvl 15	+3	25,000 gp	Lvl 25	+5	625,000 gp
Lvl 20	+4	125,000 gp	Lvl 30	+6	3,125,000 gp

Armor: Hide, Scale

Enhancement: AC

Power (Daily ✦ Healing): Standard Action. Gain regeneration 5 until the end of the encounter or until you drop to 0 hit points or fewer.
If you take acid or fire damage, the regeneration is suppressed until the end of your next turn.
Level 25 or 30: Regeneration 10.

MAGIC WEAPONS

Lvl	Name	Price (gp)	Categories
1	Magic +1	360	Any
2	Resounding +1	520	Hammer, Flail, Mace, Sling, Staff
2	Vicious +1	520	Any
3	Duelist's +1	680	Light Blade
3	Flameburst +1	680	Any ranged
3	Frost +1	680	Any
3	Pact Blade +1	680	Light Blade
3	Thundering +1	680	Any
4	Terror +1	840	Axe, Hammer, Heavy Blade
4	Thunderburst +1	840	Any ranged
5	Flaming +1	1,000	Any
5	Lifedrinker +1	1,000	Any melee
5	Lightning +1	1,000	Any
6	Magic +2	1,800	Any
7	Resounding +2	2,600	Hammer, Flail, Mace, Sling, Staff
7	Vicious +2	2,600	Any
8	Duelist's +2	3,400	Light Blade
8	Flameburst +2	3,400	Any ranged
8	Frost +2	3,400	Any
8	Pact Blade +2	3,400	Light Blade
8	Thundering +2	3,400	Any
9	Dragonslayer +2	4,200	Any
9	Terror +2	4,200	Axe, Hammer, Heavy Blade
9	Thunderburst +2	4,200	Any ranged
10	Berserker +2	5,000	Axe, Heavy Blade

MAGIC WEAPONS CONT.

Lvl	Name	Price (gp)	Categories
10	Flaming +2	5,000	Any
10	Lifedrinker +2	5,000	Any melee
10	Lightning +2	5,000	Any
11	Magic +3	9,000	Any
12	Resounding +3	13,000	Hammer, Flail, Mace, Sling, Staff
12	Vicious +3	13,000	Any
13	Duelist's +3	17,000	Light Blade
13	Flameburst +3	17,000	Any ranged
13	Frost +3	17,000	Any
13	Pact Blade +3	17,000	Light Blade
13	Thundering +3	17,000	Any
14	Dragonslayer +3	21,000	Any
14	Phasing +3	21,000	Any ranged
14	Terror +3	21,000	Axe, Hammer, Heavy Blade
14	Thunderburst +3	21,000	Any ranged
15	Berserker +3	25,000	Axe, Heavy Blade
15	Flaming +3	25,000	Any
15	Lifedrinker +3	25,000	Any melee
15	Lightning +3	25,000	Any
16	Magic +4	45,000	Any
17	Resounding +4	65,000	Hammer, Flail, Mace, Sling, Staff
17	Vicious +4	65,000	Any
18	Duelist's +4	85,000	Light Blade
18	Flameburst +4	85,000	Any ranged
18	Frost +4	85,000	Any
18	Pact Blade +4	85,000	Light Blade

Weapons

A magic weapon adds an enhancement bonus to attack rolls and damage rolls, so a +3 *flameburst longbow* adds +3 to all attack rolls and damage rolls made with the bow. This bonus does not apply to any ongoing damage or other damage that might be applied to the attack.

If you're not proficient with the weapon type, you don't gain the proficiency bonus to attack rolls, but you still gain the enhancement bonus of the magic weapon.

The category determines what kind of weapons can be enchanted with that particular set of qualities. "Any ranged" includes projectile weapons and weapons with the heavy thrown or the light thrown property. "Any" or "Any melee" includes all applicable categories.

Ammunition: Ranged weapons such as bows, crossbows, and slings impart their magic to appropriate ammunition fired from them. Ammunition (such as arrows, bolts, or sling stones) doesn't come in magical versions. You can't craft (or find) a *+1 flameburst arrow* or a *+3 sling stone*.

Thrown Weapons: Any magic light thrown or heavy thrown weapon, from the lowly *+1 shuriken* to a *+6 perfect hunter's spear*, automatically returns to its wielder's hand after a ranged attack with the weapon is resolved.

Catching a returning thrown weapon is a free action; if you do not wish (or are unable) to catch the weapon, it falls at your feet in your space.

Berserker Weapon — Level 10+

A weapon of pure rage.

Lvl 10	+2	5,000 gp	Lvl 25	+5	625,000 gp
Lvl 15	+3	25,000 gp	Lvl 30	+6	3,125,000 gp
Lvl 20	+4	125,000 gp			

Weapon: Axe, Heavy Blade
Enhancement: Attack rolls and damage rolls
Critical: +1d10 damage per plus
Power (Daily): Minor Action. Gain a +2 power bonus to attack rolls and damage rolls with this weapon and take a –5 penalty to all defenses. You also gain resist 5 to all damage. The effects last until the end of the encounter or until you fall unconscious.
Level 20 or 25: Resist 10 to all damage.
Level 30: Resist 15 to all damage.

Lvl	Name	Price (gp)	Categories
18	Thundering +4	85,000	Any
19	Dragonslayer +4	105,000	Any
19	Phasing +4	105,000	Any ranged
19	Terror +4	105,000	Axe, Hammer, Heavy Blade
19	Thunderburst +4	105,000	Any ranged
20	Berserker +4	125,000	Axe, Heavy Blade
20	Dancing +4	125,000	Heavy Blade, Light Blade
20	Flaming +4	125,000	Any
20	Lifedrinker +4	125,000	Any melee
20	Lightning +4	125,000	Any
21	Magic +5	225,000	Any
22	Resounding +5	325,000	Hammer, Flail, Mace, Sling, Staff
22	Vicious +5	325,000	Any
23	Duelist's +5	425,000	Light Blade
23	Flameburst +5	425,000	Any ranged
23	Frost +5	425,000	Any
23	Pact Blade +5	425,000	Light Blade
23	Thundering +5	425,000	Any
24	Dragonslayer +5	525,000	Any
24	Phasing +5	525,000	Any ranged
24	Terror +5	525,000	Axe, Hammer, Heavy Blade
24	Thunderburst +5	525,000	Any ranged
25	Berserker +5	625,000	Axe, Heavy Blade
25	Dancing +5	625,000	Heavy Blade, Light Blade

Lvl	Name	Price (gp)	Categories
25	Flaming +5	625,000	Any
25	Holy Avenger +5	625,000	Axe, Hammer, Heavy Blade
25	Lifedrinker +5	625,000	Any melee
25	Lightning +5	625,000	Any
26	Magic +6	1,125,000	Any
27	Resounding +6	1,625,000	Hammer, Flail, Mace, Sling, Staff
27	Vicious +6	1,625,000	Any
28	Duelist's +6	2,125,000	Light Blade
28	Flameburst +6	2,125,000	Any ranged
28	Frost +6	2,125,000	Any
28	Pact Blade +6	2,125,000	Light Blade
28	Thundering +6	2,125,000	Any
29	Dragonslayer +6	2,625,000	Any
29	Phasing +6	2,625,000	Any ranged
29	Terror +6	2,625,000	Axe, Hammer, Heavy Blade
29	Thunderburst +6	2,625,000	Any ranged
30	Berserker +6	3,125,000	Axe, Heavy Blade
30	Dancing +6	3,125,000	Heavy Blade, Light Blade
30	Flaming +6	3,125,000	Any
30	Holy Avenger +6	3,125,000	Axe, Hammer, Heavy Blade
30	Lifedrinker +6	3,125,000	Any melee
30	Lightning +6	3,125,000	Any
30	Perfect Hunter's +6	3,125,000	Any ranged
30	Vorpal +6	3,125,000	Axe, Heavy Blade

Dancing Weapon — Level 20+

This blade floats beside you, cutting through the air as a dancer glides across a ballroom.

| Lvl 20 | +4 | 125,000 gp | Lvl 30 | +6 | 3,125,000 gp |
| Lvl 25 | +5 | 625,000 gp | | | |

Weapon: Heavy Blade, Light Blade
Enhancement: Attack rolls and damage rolls
Critical: +1d6 damage per plus
Power (Daily): Minor Action. You release the dancing weapon, and it hovers near you until the end of your next turn or until you drop to 0 hit points or fewer.

You can deliver basic attacks and attack powers through the dancing weapon as if you were holding it yourself (including all attack and damage modifiers you'd normally apply).

If you do not attack with a dancing weapon before the end of your turn, it makes a melee basic attack against an enemy of your choice within 2 squares of you as if you were wielding it. A dancing weapon cannot make opportunity attacks.

Except during brief moments when it is attacking, a dancing weapon remains in your space, even if you move away or are teleported. It automatically resists any attempts by other creatures to take hold of it.

At any time during the encounter, you can take hold of the weapon again. This ends the effect.

Sustain Minor: The sword continues to hover and fight near you until the end of your next turn.

Dragonslayer Weapon — Level 9+

The bane of dragonkind.

Lvl 9	+2	4,200 gp	Lvl 24	+5	525,000 gp
Lvl 14	+3	21,000 gp	Lvl 29	+6	2,625,000 gp
Lvl 19	+4	105,000 gp			

Weapon: Any
Enhancement: Attack rolls and damage rolls
Critical: +1d8 damage per plus, or +1d12 damage per plus against dragons
Property: This weapon provides resistance against dragon breath attacks, as shown below.
Level 9: Resist 5
Level 14 or 19: Resist 10
Level 24 or 29: Resist 15
Power (Daily): Minor Action. Your next attack with this weapon against a dragon, if made before the end of your turn, gains a +5 power bonus to the attack roll and automatically ignores any resistance the dragon has.

Flaming Weapon

Level 5+

You can will this weapon to burst into flame.

Lvl 5	+1	1,000 gp	Lvl 20	+4	125,000 gp
Lvl 10	+2	5,000 gp	Lvl 25	+5	625,000 gp
Lvl 15	+3	25,000 gp	Lvl 30	+6	3,125,000 gp

Weapon: Any

Enhancement: Attack rolls and damage rolls

Critical: +1d6 fire damage per plus

Power (At-Will ✦ Fire): Free Action. All damage dealt by this weapon is fire damage. Another free action returns the damage to normal.

Power (Daily ✦ Fire): Free Action. Use this power when you hit with the weapon. Deal an extra 1d6 fire damage, and the target takes ongoing 5 fire damage (save ends).
Level 15 or 20: 2d6 fire damage and ongoing 10 fire damage.
Level 25 or 30: 3d6 fire damage and ongoing 15 fire damage.

Frost Weapon

Level 3+

A thin layer of frost coats the business end of this weapon.

Lvl 3	+1	680 gp	Lvl 18	+4	85,000 gp
Lvl 8	+2	3,400 gp	Lvl 23	+5	425,000 gp
Lvl 13	+3	17,000 gp	Lvl 28	+6	2,125,000 gp

Weapon: Any

Enhancement: Attack rolls and damage rolls

Critical: +1d6 cold damage per plus

Power (At-Will ✦ Cold): Free Action. All damage dealt by this weapon is cold damage. Another free action returns the damage to normal.

Power (Daily ✦ Cold): Free Action. Use this power when you hit with the weapon. The target takes an extra 1d8 cold damage and is slowed until the end of your next turn.
Level 13 or 18: 2d8 cold damage.
Level 23 or 28: 3d8 cold damage.

Holy Avenger

Level 25+

The most prized weapon of any paladin.

| Lvl 25 | +5 | 625,000 gp | Lvl 30 | +6 | 3,125,000 gp |

Weapon: Axe, Hammer, Heavy Blade

Enhancement: Attack rolls and damage rolls

Critical: +1d6 radiant damage per plus, and you can spend a healing surge

Property: A holy avenger deals an extra 1d10 radiant damage when the power you use to make the attack has the radiant keyword.

Power (Daily): Minor Action. You and each ally within 10 squares of you gain a +5 power bonus to Fortitude, Reflex, and Will defenses until the end of your next turn.

Special: A *holy avenger* can be used as a holy symbol. It adds its enhancement bonus to attack rolls and damage rolls and the extra damage granted by its property (if applicable) when used in this manner. You do not gain your weapon proficiency bonus to an attack roll when using a *holy avenger* as an implement.

Duelist's Weapon

Level 3+

The favorite weapon of a rogue.

Lvl 3	+1	680 gp	Lvl 18	+4	85,000 gp
Lvl 8	+2	3,400 gp	Lvl 23	+5	425,000 gp
Lvl 13	+3	17,000 gp	Lvl 28	+6	2,125,000 gp

Weapon: Light Blade

Enhancement: Attack rolls and damage rolls

Critical: +1d6 damage per plus, or +1d8 damage per plus if you have combat advantage

Power (Daily): Minor Action. You have combat advantage against the next creature you attack with this weapon on this turn.

Flameburst Weapon

Level 3+

This ranged weapon packs a fiery surprise.

Lvl 3	+1	680 gp	Lvl 18	+4	85,000 gp
Lvl 8	+2	3,400 gp	Lvl 23	+5	425,000 gp
Lvl 13	+3	17,000 gp	Lvl 28	+6	2,125,000 gp

Weapon: Any ranged

Enhancement: Attack rolls and damage rolls

Critical: +1d6 fire damage per plus

Power (Daily ✦ Fire): Minor Action. The next ranged basic attack you make with this weapon before the end of your turn becomes a burst 1 centered on the target. Use your normal attack bonus for the basic attack, but against Reflex. Instead of normal damage, each target hit takes ongoing 5 fire damage (save ends).
Level 13 or 18: Burst 2; ongoing 10 fire damage.
Level 23 or 28: Burst 3; ongoing 15 fire damage.

Lifedrinker Weapon · Level 5+

This weapon transfers an enemy's vitality to you.

Lvl 5	+1	1,000 gp	Lvl 20	+4	125,000 gp
Lvl 10	+2	5,000 gp	Lvl 25	+5	625,000 gp
Lvl 15	+3	25,000 gp	Lvl 30	+6	3,125,000 gp

Weapon: Any melee

Enhancement: Attack rolls and damage rolls

Critical: +1d6 necrotic damage per plus

Property: When you drop an enemy to 0 hit points or fewer with a melee attack made with this weapon, gain 5 temporary hit points.
  Level 15 or 20: Gain 10 temporary hit points.
  Level 25 or 30: Gain 15 temporary hit points.

Lightning Weapon · Level 5+

This weapon crackles with dancing lightning.

Lvl 5	+1	1,000 gp	Lvl 20	+4	125,000 gp
Lvl 10	+2	5,000 gp	Lvl 25	+5	625,000 gp
Lvl 15	+3	25,000 gp	Lvl 30	+6	3,125,000 gp

Weapon: Any

Enhancement: Attack rolls and damage rolls

Critical: +1d6 lightning damage per plus

Power (At-Will ✦ Lightning): Free Action. All damage dealt by this weapon is lightning damage. Another free action returns the damage to normal.

Power (Daily ✦ Lightning): Free Action. Use this power when you hit with the weapon. The target and each enemy within 2 squares of the target take 1d6 lightning damage.
  Level 15 or 20: 2d6 lightning damage.
  Level 25 or 30: 3d6 lightning damage.

Magic Weapon · Level 1+

A basic enchanted weapon.

Lvl 1	+1	360 gp	Lvl 16	+4	45,000 gp
Lvl 6	+2	1,800 gp	Lvl 21	+5	225,000 gp
Lvl 11	+3	9,000 gp	Lvl 26	+6	1,125,000 gp

Weapon: Any

Enhancement: Attack rolls and damage rolls

Critical: +1d6 damage per plus

Pact Blade · Level 3+

Warlocks favor this wickedly sharp blade.

Lvl 3	+1	680 gp	Lvl 18	+4	85,000 gp
Lvl 8	+2	3,400 gp	Lvl 23	+5	425,000 gp
Lvl 13	+3	17,000 gp	Lvl 28	+6	2,125,000 gp

Weapon: Light Blade (usually daggers and sickles)

Enhancement: Attack rolls and damage rolls

Critical: +1d6 damage per plus

Property: This blade functions as a warlock implement, adding its enhancement bonus to attack rolls and damage rolls for warlock powers that use implements.

Property: When a creature you have cursed with your Warlock's Curse makes a melee attack against you, deal damage to the creature equal to the *pact blade*'s enhancement bonus.

Special: You do not gain your weapon proficiency bonus to the attack roll when using a *pact blade* as an implement.

Perfect Hunter's Weapon · Level 30

This weapon ignores cover and concealment when its magic is activated.

Lvl 30	+6	3,125,000 gp

Weapon: Any ranged

Enhancement: Attack rolls and damage rolls

Critical: +1d12 damage per plus

Power (Daily): Standard Action. When you use this power, you automatically pinpoint the location of all creatures within 10 squares of you, even if line of sight or line of effect to those creatures would normally be blocked. This pinpointing lasts until the end of your turn. You can target any one of those creatures as if it did not have cover or concealment. You can then make a ranged basic attack with this weapon with a +5 bonus to the attack roll.

Phasing Weapon · Level 14+

This weapon's projectiles phase in and out of reality when fired, slipping through cover as if it weren't there.

Lvl 14	+3	21,000 gp	Lvl 24	+5	525,000 gp
Lvl 19	+4	105,000 gp	Lvl 29	+6	2,625,000 gp

Weapon: Any ranged

Enhancement: Attack rolls and damage rolls

Critical: +1d6 damage per plus

Property: Your ranged attacks with the weapon ignore the penalty to attack rolls for cover or superior cover.

7

Resounding Weapon — Level 2+

A thundering peal sounds when this weapon hits, dazing its target.

Lvl 2	+1	520 gp	Lvl 17	+4	65,000 gp
Lvl 7	+2	2,600 gp	Lvl 22	+5	325,000 gp
Lvl 12	+3	13,000 gp	Lvl 27	+6	1,625,000 gp

Weapon: Hammer, Flail, Mace, Sling, Staff
Enhancement: Attack rolls and damage rolls
Critical: +1d6 thunder damage per plus
Power (Daily): Free Action. Use this power when you hit with the weapon. The target is dazed until the end of your next turn.

Terror Weapon — Level 4+

The bite of this weapon sends waves of fear through its target.

Lvl 4	+1	840 gp	Lvl 19	+4	105,000 gp
Lvl 9	+2	4,200 gp	Lvl 24	+5	525,000 gp
Lvl 14	+3	21,000 gp	Lvl 29	+6	2,625,000 gp

Weapon: Axe, Hammer, Heavy Blade
Enhancement: Attack rolls and damage rolls
Critical: +1d8 damage per plus
Power (Daily ✦ Fear): Free Action. Use this power when you hit with the weapon. The target takes a -2 penalty to all defenses (save ends).

Thunderburst Weapon — Level 4+

Suddenly, the projectile explodes in a burst of violent sound.

Lvl 4	+1	840 gp	Lvl 19	+4	105,000 gp
Lvl 9	+2	4,200 gp	Lvl 24	+5	525,000 gp
Lvl 14	+3	21,000 gp	Lvl 29	+6	2,625,000 gp

Weapon: Any ranged
Enhancement: Attack rolls and damage rolls
Critical: +1d6 thunder damage per plus
Power (Daily ✦ Thunder): Minor Action. The next ranged basic attack you make with this weapon before the end of your turn becomes a burst 1 centered on the target. Use your normal attack bonus for the basic attack, but against Fortitude. Each target hit takes thunder damage equal to the normal damage you would deal with a ranged basic attack with the weapon.
Level 14 or 19: Burst 2.
Level 24 or 29: Burst 3.

Thundering Weapon — Level 3+

You can unleash a clap of thunder when this weapon hits, carrying your foe away on a wave of deadly sound.

Lvl 3	+1	680 gp	Lvl 18	+4	85,000 gp
Lvl 8	+2	3,400 gp	Lvl 23	+5	425,000 gp
Lvl 13	+3	17,000 gp	Lvl 28	+6	2,125,000 gp

Weapon: Any
Enhancement: Attack rolls and damage rolls
Critical: +1d6 thunder damage per plus
Power (Daily ✦ Thunder): Free Action. Use this power when you hit with the weapon. Deal an extra 1d8 thunder damage and push the target 1 square.
Level 13 or 18: 2d8 extra thunder damage.
Level 23 or 28: 3d8 extra thunder damage.

Vicious Weapon — Level 2+

Some wielders claim this weapon takes pleasure in dealing pain.

Lvl 2	+1	520 gp	Lvl 17	+4	65,000 gp
Lvl 7	+2	2,600 gp	Lvl 22	+5	325,000 gp
Lvl 12	+3	13,000 gp	Lvl 27	+6	1,625,000 gp

Weapon: Any
Enhancement: Attack rolls and damage rolls
Critical: +1d12 damage per plus

Vorpal Weapon — Level 30

There is nothing as sharp as the bite of a vorpal blade.

Lvl 30	+6	3,125,000 gp

Weapon: Axe, Heavy Blade
Enhancement: Attack rolls and damage rolls
Critical: +1d12 damage per plus
Property: Whenever you roll the maximum result on any damage die for this weapon, roll that die again and add the additional result to the damage total. If a reroll results in another maximum damage result, roll it again and keep adding.
Power (Daily): Free Action. Use this power when you hit with the weapon. Deal an extra 3d12 damage with the attack.

HOLY SYMBOLS

If you are a member of a class that can use a holy symbol as an implement, you can apply the enhancement bonus of a holy symbol to the attack rolls and the damage rolls of any of your powers from that class that have the implement keyword, and you can use a holy symbol's properties and powers. Members of other classes gain no benefit from wearing or holding a holy symbol.

A holy symbol represents your deity and takes the shape of an aspect of the god. (See pages 21-22 for the symbols of the good, lawful good, and unaligned deities.) As with most other implements, you can't make melee attacks with a holy symbol.

Unlike other implements, you need only to wear a holy symbol for its property or power to function. If you are wearing or holding more than one holy symbol, none of your symbols function.

Magic Holy Symbol — Level 1+

A holy symbol of your god, enchanted with magical power.

Lvl 1	+1	360 gp	Lvl 16	+4	45,000 gp
Lvl 6	+2	1,800 gp	Lvl 21	+5	225,000 gp
Lvl 11	+3	9,000 gp	Lvl 26	+6	1,125,000 gp

Implement (Holy Symbol)
Enhancement: Attack rolls and damage rolls
Critical: +1d6 damage per plus

Symbol of Battle — Level 5+

This holy symbol is favored by battle clerics and warpriests.

Lvl 5	+1	1,000 gp	Lvl 20	+4	125,000 gp
Lvl 10	+2	5,000 gp	Lvl 25	+5	625,000 gp
Lvl 15	+3	25,000 gp	Lvl 30	+6	3,125,000 gp

Implement (Holy Symbol)

Enhancement: Attack rolls and damage rolls

Critical: +1d8 damage per plus

Power (Daily): Free Action. Use this power when you hit with an attack using this holy symbol. Deal an extra 1d10 damage.
Level 15 or 20: 2d10 extra damage.
Level 25 or 30: 3d10 extra damage.

Symbol of Hope — Level 3+

The power of your faith makes it easier for allies to recover from debilitating effects.

Lvl 3	+1	680 gp	Lvl 18	+4	85,000 gp
Lvl 8	+2	3,400 gp	Lvl 23	+5	425,000 gp
Lvl 13	+3	17,000 gp	Lvl 28	+6	2,125,000 gp

Implement (Holy Symbol)

Enhancement: Attack rolls and damage rolls

Critical: +1d6 damage per plus

Power (Daily): Immediate Reaction. You can use this power when you or an ally within 5 squares of you is hit by an effect that a save can end. You or the ally gains a +5 power bonus to saving throws against the effect.

Symbol of Life — Level 2+

The power of your faith adds energy to your healing prayers.

Lvl 2	+1	520 gp	Lvl 17	+4	65,000 gp
Lvl 7	+2	2,600 gp	Lvl 22	+5	325,000 gp
Lvl 12	+3	13,000 gp	Lvl 27	+6	1,625,000 gp

Implement (Holy Symbol)

Enhancement: Attack rolls and damage rolls

Critical: +1d6 damage per plus

Power (Daily ✦ Healing): Minor Action. Until the end of your turn, any character healed by one of your encounter powers or daily powers regains an additional 1d6 hit points.
Level 12 or 17: Regains an additional 2d6 hit points.
Level 22 or 27: Regains an additional 3d6 hit points.

Symbol of Power — Level 7+

The power of your faith makes it harder for enemies to recover from debilitating effects.

Lvl 7	+2	2,600 gp	Lvl 22	+5	325,000 gp
Lvl 12	+3	13,000 gp	Lvl 27	+6	1,625,000 gp
Lvl 17	+4	65,000 gp			

Implement (Holy Symbol)

Enhancement: Attack rolls and damage rolls

Critical: +1d6 damage per plus

Property: When you use this symbol to deliver an effect that a save can end, the target takes a -2 penalty to saving throws against the effect.

HOLY SYMBOLS

Lvl	Name	Price (gp)
1	Magic holy symbol +1	360
2	Symbol of life +1	520
3	Symbol of hope +1	680
5	Symbol of battle +1	1,000
6	Magic holy symbol +2	1,800
7	Symbol of power +2	2,600
7	Symbol of life +2	2,600
8	Symbol of hope +2	3,400
9	Symbol of victory +2	4,200
10	Symbol of battle +2	5,000
11	Magic holy symbol +3	9,000
12	Symbol of power +3	13,000
12	Symbol of life +3	13,000
13	Symbol of hope +3	17,000
14	Symbol of victory +3	21,000
15	Symbol of battle +3	25,000
16	Magic holy symbol +4	45,000
17	Symbol of power +4	65,000
17	Symbol of life +4	65,000
18	Symbol of hope +4	85,000
19	Symbol of victory +4	105,000
20	Symbol of battle +4	125,000
21	Magic holy symbol +5	225,000
22	Symbol of power +5	325,000
22	Symbol of life +5	325,000
23	Symbol of hope +5	425,000
23	Symbol of radiance +5	425,000
24	Symbol of victory +5	525,000
25	Symbol of battle +5	625,000
26	Magic holy symbol +6	1,125,000
27	Symbol of power +6	1,625,000
27	Symbol of life +6	1,625,000
28	Symbol of hope +6	2,125,000
28	Symbol of radiance +6	2,125,000
29	Symbol of victory +6	2,625,000
30	Symbol of battle +6	3,125,000

Symbol of Radiance — Level 23+

This symbol glows with the power of your faith.

Lvl 23	+5	425,000 gp	Lvl 28	+6	2,125,000 gp

Implement (Holy Symbol)

Enhancement: Attack rolls and damage rolls

Critical: +1d6 radiant damage per plus

Power (Daily ✦ Healing): Free Action. Use this power when using the symbol to attack with a power that has the radiant keyword. One ally of your choice within 10 squares of you can spend a healing surge.

Symbol of Victory — Level 9+

Your god helps those who help themselves.

Lvl 9	+2	4,200 gp	Lvl 24	+5	525,000 gp
Lvl 14	+3	21,000 gp	Lvl 29	+6	2,625,000 gp
Lvl 19	+4	105,000 gp			

Implement (Holy Symbol)
Enhancement: Attack rolls and damage rolls
Critical: +1d8 damage per plus
Power (Daily): Free Action. You can use this power when you or an ally within 5 squares of you scores a critical hit. That character gains an action point.

ORBS

If you are a member of a class that can use an orb as an implement, you can apply the enhancement bonus of an orb to the attack rolls and the damage rolls of any of your powers from that class that have the implement keyword, and you can use an orb's properties and powers. Members of other classes gain no benefit from wielding an orb.

An orb is a heavy, round object, usually made of glass or crystal, of a size to fit comfortably in the palm of your hand. Orbs range in color, from clear glass to solid ebony, with storms of color erupting deep within their depths. As with most other implements, you can't make melee attacks with an orb.

Magic Orb — Level 1+

A standard crystal orb, enchanted to channel arcane energy.

Lvl 1	+1	360 gp	Lvl 16	+4	45,000 gp
Lvl 6	+2	1,800 gp	Lvl 21	+5	225,000 gp
Lvl 11	+3	9,000 gp	Lvl 26	+6	1,125,000 gp

Implement (Orb)
Enhancement: Attack rolls and damage rolls
Critical: +1d6 damage per plus

Orb of Drastic Resolutions — Level 13+

A sphere of brilliant purple glass, alight with ribbons of crimson dancing beneath its smooth surface.

Lvl 13	+3	17,000 gp	Lvl 23	+5	425,000 gp
Lvl 18	+4	85,000 gp	Lvl 28	+6	2,125,000 gp

Implement (Orb)
Enhancement: Attack rolls and damage rolls
Critical: +1d6 damage per plus
Power (Daily): Free Action. You can use this power when an enemy within 10 squares of you drops to 0 hit points or fewer. Immobilize (save ends) or weaken (save ends) a different enemy within 10 squares of you.

Orb of Indisputable Gravity — Level 7+

A sphere of sky blue crystal.

Lvl 7	+2	2,600 gp	Lvl 22	+5	325,000 gp
Lvl 12	+3	13,000 gp	Lvl 27	+6	1,625,000 gp
Lvl 17	+4	65,000 gp			

Implement (Orb)
Enhancement: Attack rolls and damage rolls
Critical: +1d6 damage per plus
Power (Daily): Minor Action. Until the end of your next turn, any attack that hits a flying creature within 10 squares of you also forces that creature to gently fall 10 squares. If a descent of that distance would bring the creature to ground, it lands prone but takes no damage from the fall.

Orb of Inevitable Continuance — Level 3+

A sphere of gray crystal that appears as a ball of solid mist.

Lvl 3	+1	680 gp	Lvl 18	+4	85,000 gp
Lvl 8	+2	3,400 gp	Lvl 23	+5	425,000 gp
Lvl 13	+3	17,000 gp	Lvl 28	+6	2,125,000 gp

Implement (Orb)
Enhancement: Attack rolls and damage rolls
Critical: +1d6 damage per plus
Power (Daily): Minor Action. One of your powers that is due to end at the end of this turn instead lasts until the end of your next turn.

Orb of Invasive Fortune — Level 20+

A sphere of crystal consisting of swirls of gold and orange.

Lvl 20	+4	125,000 gp	Lvl 30	+6	3,125,000 gp
Lvl 25	+5	625,000 gp			

Implement (Orb)
Enhancement: Attack rolls and damage rolls
Critical: +1d8 damage per plus
Power (Daily): Immediate Interrupt. You can use this power when an enemy within 10 squares of you successfully recharges a power. Instead, the recharge fails and you regain the use of an expended encounter power.

Orb of Reversed Polarities — Level 9+

A sphere of polished crystal that appears as a ball of stormy sky.

Lvl 9	+2	4,200 gp	Lvl 24	+5	525,000 gp
Lvl 14	+3	21,000 gp	Lvl 29	+6	2,625,000 gp
Lvl 19	+4	105,000 gp			

Implement (Orb)
Enhancement: Attack rolls and damage rolls
Critical: +1d6 damage per plus
Power (Daily): Minor Action. Until the end of your next turn, your attacks treat any resistance possessed by a target as vulnerable 5 to the same damage type.
Level 14 or 19: Vulnerable 10.
Level 24 or 29: Vulnerable 15.

ORBS

Lvl	Name	Price (gp)
1	*Magic orb* +1	360
3	*Orb of inevitable continuance* +1	680
5	*Orb of sanguinary repercussions* +1	1,000
6	*Magic orb* +2	1,800
7	*Orb of indisputable gravity* +2	2,600
8	*Orb of inevitable continuance* +2	3,400
9	*Orb of reversed polarities* +2	4,200
10	*Orb of sanguinary repercussions* +2	5,000
11	*Magic orb* +3	9,000
12	*Orb of indisputable gravity* +3	13,000
13	*Orb of drastic resolutions* +3	17,000
13	*Orb of inevitable continuance* +3	17,000
14	*Orb of reversed polarities* +3	21,000
15	*Orb of sanguinary repercussions* +3	25,000
16	*Magic orb* +4	45,000
17	*Orb of indisputable gravity* +4	65,000
18	*Orb of drastic resolutions* +4	85,000
18	*Orb of inevitable continuance* +4	85,000
19	*Orb of reversed polarities* +4	105,000
20	*Orb of invasive fortune* +4	125,000
20	*Orb of sanguinary repercussions* +4	125,000
21	*Magic orb* +5	225,000
22	*Orb of indisputable gravity* +5	325,000
23	*Orb of drastic resolutions* +5	425,000
23	*Orb of inevitable continuance* +5	425,000
24	*Orb of reversed polarities* +5	525,000
25	*Orb of invasive fortune* +5	625,000
25	*Orb of sanguinary repercussions* +5	625,000
26	*Magic orb* +6	1,125,000
27	*Orb of indisputable gravity* +6	1,625,000
28	*Orb of drastic resolutions* +6	2,125,000
28	*Orb of inevitable continuance* +6	2,125,000
29	*Orb of reversed polarities* +6	2,625,000
30	*Orb of invasive fortune* +6	3,125,000
30	*Orb of sanguinary repercussions* +6	3,125,000

Orb of Sanguinary Repercussions — Level 5+

A sphere of brilliant crimson.

Lvl 5	+1	1,000 gp	Lvl 20	+4	125,000 gp
Lvl 10	+2	5,000 gp	Lvl 25	+5	625,000 gp
Lvl 15	+3	25,000 gp	Lvl 30	+6	3,125,000 gp

Implement (Orb)

Enhancement: Attack rolls and damage rolls

Critical: +1d6 damage per plus, or +1d10 damage per plus against bloodied creatures

Power (Daily): Minor Action. Deal 1d6 + Intelligence modifier damage to each bloodied creature within 5 squares of you.
  Level 15 or 20: 2d6 + Intelligence modifier damage.
  Level 25 or 30: 3d6 + Intelligence modifier damage.

RODS

If you are a member of a class that can use a rod as an implement, you can apply its enhancement bonus to the attack and damage rolls of any of your powers from that class that have the implement keyword, and you can use a rod's properties and powers. Members of other classes gain no benefit from wielding a rod.

A rod is a short, heavy cylinder, typically covered in mystic runes or inscribed crystals. As with most other implements, you can't make melee attacks with a rod.

Magic Rod — Level 1+

A standard rod, enchanted so as to channel arcane energy.

Lvl 1	+1	360 gp	Lvl 16	+4	45,000 gp
Lvl 6	+2	1,800 gp	Lvl 21	+5	225,000 gp
Lvl 11	+3	9,000 gp	Lvl 26	+6	1,125,000 gp

Implement (Rod)

Enhancement: Attack rolls and damage rolls

Critical: +1d6 damage per plus

Rod of Corruption — Level 3+

This rod magnifies and multiplies your Warlock's Curse.

Lvl 3	+1	680 gp	Lvl 18	+4	85,000 gp
Lvl 8	+2	3,400 gp	Lvl 23	+5	425,000 gp
Lvl 13	+3	17,000 gp	Lvl 28	+6	2,125,000 gp

Implement (Rod)

Enhancement: Attack rolls and damage rolls

Critical: +1d6 damage per plus

Property: Whenever your pact boon is triggered, instead of taking its normal benefit you can transfer your Warlock's Curse to each enemy within 5 squares of the original target.

Rod of Dark Reward — Level 2+

This rod channels your Warlock's Curse while adding to your defenses.

Lvl 2	+1	520 gp	Lvl 17	+4	65,000 gp
Lvl 7	+2	2,600 gp	Lvl 22	+5	325,000 gp
Lvl 12	+3	13,000 gp	Lvl 27	+6	1,625,000 gp

Implement (Rod)

Enhancement: Attack rolls and damage rolls

Critical: +1d6 damage per plus

Property: Whenever you place a Warlock's Curse on an enemy, you gain a +1 power bonus to AC until the start of your next turn.

Rod of Death's Grasp — Level 23+

A rod that ripples with necrotic energy.

Lvl 23	+5	425,000 gp	Lvl 28	+6	2,125,000 gp

Implement (Rod)

Enhancement: Attack rolls and damage rolls

Critical: Ongoing 10 necrotic damage (save ends), and you gain 10 temporary hit points
  Level 28: Ongoing 15 necrotic damage (save ends), and you gain 15 temporary hit points

Power (Daily ✦ Necrotic): Free Action. Use this power when you place your Warlock's Curse on a target. The target takes ongoing 10 necrotic damage (save ends). Each time this damage is dealt, you gain 10 temporary hit points.
  Level 28: Ongoing 15 necrotic damage (save ends), and you gain 15 temporary hit points.

RODS

Lvl	Name	Price (gp)
1	*Magic rod +1*	360
2	*Rod of dark reward +1*	520
3	*Rod of corruption +1*	680
5	*Rod of reaving +1*	1,000
6	*Magic rod +2*	1,800
7	*Rod of dark reward +2*	2,600
8	*Rod of corruption +2*	3,400
8	*Rod of first blood +2*	3,400
10	*Rod of reaving +2*	5,000
10	*Rod of the pyre +2*	5,000
11	*Magic rod +3*	9,000
12	*Rod of dark reward +3*	13,000
13	*Rod of corruption +3*	17,000
13	*Rod of first blood +3*	17,000
14	*Rod of harvest +3*	21,000
15	*Rod of reaving +3*	25,000
15	*Rod of the pyre +3*	25,000
16	*Magic rod +4*	45,000
17	*Rod of dark reward +4*	65,000
18	*Rod of corruption +4*	85,000
18	*Rod of first blood +4*	85,000
19	*Rod of harvest +4*	105,000
20	*Rod of reaving +4*	125,000
20	*Rod of the pyre +4*	125,000
21	*Magic rod +5*	225,000
22	*Rod of dark reward +5*	325,000
23	*Rod of corruption +5*	425,000
23	*Rod of death's grasp +5*	425,000
23	*Rod of first blood +5*	425,000
24	*Rod of harvest +5*	525,000
25	*Rod of reaving +5*	625,000
25	*Rod of the pyre +5*	625,000
26	*Magic rod +6*	1,125,000
27	*Rod of dark reward +6*	1,625,000
28	*Rod of corruption +6*	2,125,000
28	*Rod of death's grasp +6*	2,125,000
28	*Rod of first blood +6*	2,125,000
29	*Rod of harvest +6*	2,625,000
30	*Rod of reaving +6*	3,125,000
30	*Rod of the pyre +6*	3,125,000

Rod of First Blood — Level 8+

This rod demands to strike first in any battle.

Lvl 8	+2	3,400 gp	Lvl 23	+5	425,000 gp
Lvl 13	+3	17,000 gp	Lvl 28	+6	2,125,000 gp
Lvl 18	+4	85,000 gp			

Implement (Rod)
Enhancement: Attack rolls and damage rolls
Critical: +1d6 damage per plus, or +1d8 damage per plus against creatures that have maximum hit points
Property: When you hit a creature that has maximum hit points with an attack using this rod, deal 1d8 extra damage.
Level 13 or 18: 2d8 extra damage.
Level 23 or 28: 3d8 extra damage.

Rod of Harvest — Level 14+

This rod stores the power of your pact boon so that you can unleash it when you want to.

Lvl 14	+3	21,000 gp	Lvl 24	+5	525,000 gp
Lvl 19	+4	105,000 gp	Lvl 29	+6	2,625,000 gp

Implement (Rod)
Enhancement: Attack rolls and damage rolls
Critical: +1d6 damage per plus
Property: When your pact boon is triggered, you can store its effect within your rod instead of using it immediately. Your rod can hold only one pact boon effect at a time.
Power (Encounter): Minor Action. Use the pact boon effect stored within your rod.

Rod of Reaving — Level 5+

This rod enhances the damage dealt to those suffering your Warlock's Curse.

Lvl 5	+1	1,000 gp	Lvl 20	+4	125,000 gp
Lvl 10	+2	5,000 gp	Lvl 25	+5	625,000 gp
Lvl 15	+3	25,000 gp	Lvl 30	+6	3,125,000 gp

Implement (Rod)
Enhancement: Attack rolls and damage rolls
Critical: +1d8 damage per plus
Property: When you place your Warlock's Curse on a target, the creature takes damage equal to the rod's enhancement bonus.

Rod of the Pyre — Level 10+

This rod crackles with arcane fire.

Lvl 10	+2	5,000 gp	Lvl 25	+5	625,000 gp
Lvl 15	+3	25,000 gp	Lvl 30	+6	3,125,000 gp
Lvl 20	+4	125,000 gp			

Implement (Rod)
Enhancement: Attack rolls and damage rolls
Critical: +1d6 fire damage per plus
Power (Daily): Free Action. When you place your Warlock's Curse on a target, the creature gains vulnerability 2 fire until the end of your next turn.
Level 15: Vulnerability 3 fire.
Level 20: Vulnerability 4 fire.
Level 25: Vulnerability 5 fire.
Level 30: Vulnerability 6 fire.

STAFFS

A staff is a shaft of wood as tall or slightly taller than you are, sometimes crowned with a decorative crystal or some other arcane fetish. Fashioned either as a quarterstaff or a walking staff, it is also imbued with arcane enchantments so that you can channel your spells through it. Unlike other implements, a staff also functions as a melee weapon (treat it as a quarterstaff). When used in melee, a staff applies its enhancement bonus and critical damage dice just as a weapon does.

However, you must be a member of a class that can use a staff as an implement to apply the enhancement bonus of a staff to the attack rolls and the damage rolls of any of your powers from that class that have the

STAFFS

Lvl	Name	Price (gp)
1	Magic staff +1	360
2	Staff of fiery might +1	520
3	Staff of the war mage +1	680
4	Staff of winter +1	840
5	Staff of storms +1	1,000
6	Magic staff +2	1,800
7	Staff of fiery might +2	2,600
8	Staff of the war mage +2	3,400
8	Thunderwave staff +2	3,400
9	Staff of winter +2	4,200
10	Staff of storms +2	5,000
11	Magic staff +3	9,000
12	Staff of fiery might +3	13,000
13	Staff of the war mage +3	17,000
13	Thunderwave staff +3	17,000
14	Staff of winter +3	21,000
15	Staff of storms +3	25,000
16	Magic staff +4	45,000
17	Staff of fiery might +4	65,000
18	Staff of the war mage +4	85,000
18	Thunderwave staff +4	85,000
19	Staff of power +4	105,000
19	Staff of winter +4	105,000
20	Staff of storms +4	125,000
21	Magic staff +5	225,000
22	Staff of fiery might +5	325,000
23	Staff of the war mage +5	425,000
23	Thunderwave staff +5	425,000
24	Staff of power +5	525,000
24	Staff of winter +5	525,000
25	Staff of storms +5	625,000
26	Magic staff +6	1,125,000
27	Staff of fiery might +6	1,625,000
28	Staff of the war mage +6	2,125,000
28	Thunderwave staff +6	2,125,000
29	Staff of power +6	2,625,000
29	Staff of winter +6	2,625,000
30	Staff of storms +6	3,125,000

implement keyword and to use a staff's properties and powers. If your class can't normally use staffs as implements, or if you're not using an implement power, a staff is simply a magic quarterstaff.

For example, a cleric could pick up and use a +3 *staff of fiery might* as a melee weapon: He would add 3 to his melee attack rolls and damage rolls, and if he scored a critical hit with the staff, he would add 3d10 fire damage. However, he couldn't use the staff's power in conjunction with a cleric power that had the fire keyword, because cleric powers can't be cast through staffs.

Magic Staff — Level 1+

A basic staff, enchanted to channel arcane energy.

Lvl 1	+1	360 gp	Lvl 16	+4	45,000 gp
Lvl 6	+2	1,800 gp	Lvl 21	+5	225,000 gp
Lvl 11	+3	9,000 gp	Lvl 26	+6	1,125,000 gp

Implement (Staff)
Enhancement: Attack rolls and damage rolls
Critical: +1d6 damage per plus

Staff of Fiery Might — Level 2+

This staff is engraved with fire symbols and is warm to the touch. It makes fire spells more potent.

Lvl 2	+1	520 gp	Lvl 17	+4	65,000 gp
Lvl 7	+2	2,600 gp	Lvl 22	+5	325,000 gp
Lvl 12	+3	13,000 gp	Lvl 27	+6	1,625,000 gp

Implement (Staff)
Enhancement: Attack rolls and damage rolls
Critical: 1d8 fire damage per plus
Power (Daily): Free Action. Use this power when using a power that has the fire keyword. After rolling damage, you can reroll a number of damage dice equal to or less than the staff's enhancement bonus. You must keep the new results, and you can't reroll any die more than once.

RAVEN MIMURA

Staff of Power — Level 19+

This staff, topped by a clawed hand holding a blue crystal, allows you to cast a spell twice.

Lvl 19	+4	105,000 gp		Lvl 29	+6	2,625,000 gp
Lvl 24	+5	525,000 gp				

Implement (Staff)
Enhancement: Attack rolls and damage rolls
Critical: +1d10 damage per plus
Power (Daily): Free Action. Use this power when you score a critical hit using an encounter power or a daily power. That power is not expended.

Staff of Storms — Level 5+

This staff, covered in lightning runes, enhances the power of lightning and thunder spells.

Lvl 5	+1	1,000 gp		Lvl 20	+4	125,000 gp
Lvl 10	+2	5,000 gp		Lvl 25	+5	625,000 gp
Lvl 15	+3	25,000 gp		Lvl 30	+6	3,125,000 gp

Implement (Staff)
Enhancement: Attack rolls and damage rolls
Critical: +1d6 lightning or thunder damage per plus
Power (Daily ✦ Lightning, Thunder): Free Action. Use this power when using a power that has the lightning or the thunder keyword. After resolving the power, deal 1d8 lightning and thunder damage to every creature in a close blast 3.
Level 15 or 20: 2d8 lightning and thunder damage.
Level 25 or 30: 3d8 lightning and thunder damage.

Staff of the War Mage — Level 3+

This staff, topped with a red crystal, enhances the size of your blast and burst spells.

Lvl 3	+1	680 gp		Lvl 18	+4	85,000 gp
Lvl 8	+2	3,400 gp		Lvl 23	+5	425,000 gp
Lvl 13	+3	17,000 gp		Lvl 28	+6	2,125,000 gp

Implement (Staff)
Enhancement: Attack rolls and damage rolls
Critical: +1d8 damage per plus
Power (Daily): Free Action. Use this power when using a power that has a blast or a burst effect. Increase the size of the blast or the burst by 1.

Staff of Winter — Level 4+

This staff is engraved with winter symbols and is cold to the touch. It adds to the effect of your cold spells.

Lvl 4	+1	840 gp		Lvl 19	+4	105,000 gp
Lvl 9	+2	4,200 gp		Lvl 24	+5	525,000 gp
Lvl 14	+3	21,000 gp		Lvl 29	+6	2,625,000 gp

Implement (Staff)
Enhancement: Attack rolls and damage rolls
Critical: +1d6 cold damage per plus
Power (Daily): Free Action. Use this power when using a power that has the cold keyword. After you resolve the power, all enemies within 3 squares of you are immobilized (save ends).

Thunderwave Staff — Level 8+

This rune-covered staff emits waves of thunder that deal damage and knock enemies prone.

Lvl 8	+2	3,400 gp		Lvl 23	+5	425,000 gp
Lvl 13	+3	17,000 gp		Lvl 28	+6	2,125,000 gp
Lvl 18	+4	85,000 gp				

Implement (Staff)
Enhancement: Attack rolls and damage rolls
Critical: +1d8 thunder damage per plus
Power (Daily ✦ Thunder): Free Action. Use this power when you would push one or more creatures with one of your powers. Instead of pushing those creatures, knock them prone and deal xd6 thunder damage to each one, where x equals the number of squares you would normally push each one.
Level 13 or 18: xd8 thunder damage.
Level 23 or 28: xd10 thunder damage.

WANDS

A wand is a slender, tapered piece of wood, enchanted to channel arcane energy. If you are a member of a class that can use a wand as an implement, you can apply the enhancement bonus of a wand to the attack rolls and the damage rolls of any of your powers from that class that have the implement keyword, and you can use a wand's properties and powers. Members of other classes gain no benefit from wielding a wand.

Using a wand's power works like using the power normally. To do so, you need to be able to use at least one power from the same power source as the wand. For example, a rogue who has picked up at least one wizard power through multiclassing feats could use a wizard power in a wand, since each knows one power that uses the arcane power source. Several wands appear below, but you can also design your own.

A wand can contain an encounter power of any class capable of using wands. When you craft a wand, you can choose any encounter power that you know or that is available to your class. You can't choose anything other than a class power (you can't choose a paragon path power, for instance).

Wand Level	Power Level
3	1
8	2* or 3
13	6* or 7
18	10* or 13
23	16* or 17
28	22* or 23

*Indicates utility power.

Magic Wand — Level 1+

A basic wand, enchanted so as to channel arcane energy.

Lvl 1	+1	360 gp		Lvl 16	+4	45,000 gp
Lvl 6	+2	1,800 gp		Lvl 21	+5	225,000 gp
Lvl 11	+3	9,000 gp		Lvl 26	+6	1,125,000 gp

Implement (Wand)
Enhancement: Attack rolls and damage rolls
Critical: +1d6 damage per plus

WANDS

Lvl	Name	Price (gp)
1	*Magic wand +1*	360
3	*Wand of (power level 1) +1*	680
3	*Wand of ray of enfeeblement +1*	680
3	*Wand of witchfire +1*	680
6	*Magic wand +2*	1,800
8	*Wand of (power level 3 or lower) +2*	3,400
8	*Wand of eldritch rain +2*	3,400
8	*Wand of fiery bolt +2*	3,400
8	*Wand of icy rays +2*	3,400
8	*Wand of ray of enfeeblement +2*	3,400
8	*Wand of shield +2*	3,400
8	*Wand of witchfire +2*	3,400
11	*Magic wand +3*	9,000
13	*Wand of (power level 7 or lower) +3*	17,000
13	*Wand of eldritch rain +3*	17,000
13	*Wand of fiery bolt +3*	17,000
13	*Wand of fire burst +3*	17,000
13	*Wand of icy rays +3*	17,000
13	*Wand of ray of enfeeblement +3*	17,000
13	*Wand of shield +3*	17,000
13	*Wand of witchfire +3*	17,000
16	*Magic wand +4*	45,000
18	*Wand of (power level 13 or lower) +4*	85,000
18	*Wand of eldritch rain +4*	85,000
18	*Wand of fiery bolt +4*	85,000
18	*Wand of fire burst +4*	85,000

WANDS Cont.

Lvl	Name	Price (gp)
18	*Wand of icy rays +4*	85,000
18	*Wand of ray of enfeeblement +4*	85,000
18	*Wand of shield +4*	85,000
18	*Wand of soul flaying +4*	85,000
18	*Wand of witchfire +4*	85,000
21	*Magic wand +5*	225,000
23	*Wand of (power level 17 or lower) +5*	425,000
23	*Wand of eldritch rain +5*	425,000
23	*Wand of fiery bolt +5*	425,000
23	*Wand of fire burst +5*	425,000
23	*Wand of icy rays +5*	425,000
23	*Wand of ray of enfeeblement +5*	425,000
23	*Wand of shield +5*	425,000
23	*Wand of soul flaying +5*	425,000
23	*Wand of witchfire +5*	425,000
26	*Magic wand +6*	1,125,000
28	*Wand of (power level 23 or lower) +6*	2,125,000
28	*Wand of eldritch rain +6*	2,125,000
28	*Wand of fiery bolt +6*	2,125,000
28	*Wand of fire burst +6*	2,125,000
28	*Wand of icy rays +6*	2,125,000
28	*Wand of ray of enfeeblement +6*	2,125,000
28	*Wand of shield +6*	2,125,000
28	*Wand of soul flaying +6*	2,125,000
28	*Wand of witchfire +6*	2,125,000

Wand of Eldritch Rain — Level 8+

This wand carries the warlock spell eldritch rain.

Lvl 8	+2	3,400 gp	Lvl 23	+5	425,000 gp
Lvl 13	+3	17,000 gp	Lvl 28	+6	2,125,000 gp
Lvl 18	+4	85,000 gp			

Implement (Wand)

Enhancement: Attack rolls and damage rolls

Critical: +1d6 damage per plus

Power (Daily ✦ Arcane, Implement): Standard Action. As the warlock's *eldritch rain* power.

Wand of Fiery Bolt — Level 8+

This wand carries the warlock spell fiery bolt.

Lvl 8	+2	3,400 gp	Lvl 23	+5	425,000 gp
Lvl 13	+3	17,000 gp	Lvl 28	+6	2,125,000 gp
Lvl 18	+4	85,000 gp			

Implement (Wand)

Enhancement: Attack rolls and damage rolls

Critical: +1d6 damage per plus

Power (Daily ✦ Arcane, Fire, Implement): Standard Action. As the warlock's *fiery bolt* power.

Wand of Fire Burst — Level 13+

This wand carries the wizard spell fire burst.

| Lvl 13 | +3 | 17,000 gp | Lvl 23 | +5 | 425,000 gp |
| Lvl 18 | +4 | 85,000 gp | Lvl 28 | +6 | 2,125,000 gp |

Implement (Wand)

Enhancement: Attack rolls and damage rolls

Critical: +1d6 damage per plus

Power (Daily ✦ Arcane, Fire, Implement): Standard Action. As the wizard's *fire burst* power.

Wand of Icy Rays — Level 8+

This wand carries the wizard spell icy rays.

Lvl 8	+2	3,400 gp	Lvl 23	+5	425,000 gp
Lvl 13	+3	17,000 gp	Lvl 28	+6	2,125,000 gp
Lvl 18	+4	85,000 gp			

Implement (Wand)

Enhancement: Attack rolls and damage rolls

Critical: +1d6 damage per plus

Power (Daily ✦ Arcane, Cold, Implement): Standard Action. As the wizard's *icy rays* power.

Wand of Ray of Enfeeblement — Level 3+

This wand carries the wizard spell *ray of enfeeblement*.

Lvl 3	+1	680 gp	Lvl 18	+4	85,000 gp
Lvl 8	+2	3,400 gp	Lvl 23	+5	425,000 gp
Lvl 13	+3	17,000 gp	Lvl 28	+6	2,125,000 gp

Implement (Wand)

Enhancement: Attack rolls and damage rolls

Critical: +1d6 damage per plus

Power (Daily ✦ Arcane, Implement, Necrotic): Standard Action. As the wizard's *ray of enfeeblement* power.

Wand of Shield — Level 8+

This wand carries the wizard spell *shield*.

Lvl 8	+2	3,400 gp	Lvl 23	+5	425,000 gp
Lvl 13	+3	17,000 gp	Lvl 28	+6	2,125,000 gp
Lvl 18	+4	85,000 gp			

Implement (Wand)

Enhancement: Attack rolls and damage rolls

Critical: +1d6 damage per plus

Power (Daily ✦ Arcane, Force): Immediate Interrupt. As the wizard's *shield* power.

Wand of Soul Flaying — Level 18+

This wand carries the warlock spell *soul flaying*.

Lvl 18	+4	85,000 gp	Lvl 28	+6	2,125,000 gp
Lvl 23	+5	425,000 gp			

Implement (Wand)

Enhancement: Attack rolls and damage rolls

Critical: +1d6 damage per plus

Power (Daily ✦ Arcane, Implement, Necrotic): Standard Action. As the warlock's *soul flaying* power.

Wand of Witchfire — Level 3+

This wand carries the warlock spell *witchfire*.

Lvl 3	+1	680 gp	Lvl 18	+4	85,000 gp
Lvl 8	+2	3,400 gp	Lvl 23	+5	425,000 gp
Lvl 13	+3	17,000 gp	Lvl 28	+6	2,125,000 gp

Implement (Wand)

Enhancement: Attack rolls and damage rolls

Critical: +1d6 damage per plus

Power (Daily ✦ Arcane, Fire, Implement): Standard Action. As the warlock's *witchfire* power.

ARMS SLOT ITEMS

Shields and bracers contain powers that protect you from harm or that turn an attack against you into an immediate attack against your enemy. A set of qualities that pertains to a magic shield can be applied to either a light shield or a heavy shield.

Bashing Shield — Level 5+

This stout shield can be used to force your opponents back.

Lvl 5	1,000 gp	Lvl 25	625,000 gp
Lvl 15	25,000 gp		

Item Slot: Arms

Power (Daily): Free Action. Use this power when you hit an enemy with a melee attack. Push the enemy 1d4 squares after applying the attack's effects.
 Level 15: Push 2d4 squares.
 Level 25: Push 3d4 squares.

Bracers of Defense — Level 7+

These enchanted armbands can be activated to reduce the damage you take from a single attack.

Lvl 7	2,600 gp	Lvl 27	1,625,000 gp
Lvl 17	65,000 gp		

Item Slot: Arms

Power (Daily): Immediate Interrupt. You can use this power when you are hit by a melee attack. Reduce the damage dealt to you by the attack by 10.
 Level 17: Reduce the damage dealt by 20.
 Level 27: Reduce the damage dealt by 30.

Bracers of Mighty Striking — Level 2+

These enchanted armbands increase the damage you deal with a melee attack.

Lvl 2	520 gp	Lvl 22	325,000 gp
Lvl 12	13,000 gp		

Item Slot: Arms

Property: When you hit with a melee basic attack, you gain a +2 item bonus to the damage roll.
 Level 12: +4 item bonus.
 Level 22: +6 item bonus.

Bracers of the Perfect Shot — Level 3+

These enchanted armbands increase the damage you deal with a ranged attack.

Lvl 3	680 gp	Lvl 23	425,000 gp
Lvl 13	17,000 gp		

Item Slot: Arms

Property: When you hit with a ranged basic attack, you gain a +2 item bonus to the damage roll.
 Level 13: +4 item bonus.
 Level 23: +6 item bonus.

ARMS SLOT ITEMS

Lvl	Name	Price (gp)
2	Bracers of mighty striking (heroic tier)	520
3	Bracers of the perfect shot (heroic tier)	680
3	Shield of protection (heroic tier)	680
5	Bashing shield (heroic tier)	1,000
7	Bracers of defense (heroic tier)	2,600
8	Shield of defiance (heroic tier)	3,400
10	Guardian shield (heroic tier)	5,000
12	Bracers of mighty striking (paragon tier)	13,000
12	Shield of deflection (paragon tier)	13,000
13	Bracers of the perfect shot (paragon tier)	17,000
13	Shield of protection (paragon tier)	17,000
14	Shield of warding (paragon tier)	21,000
15	Bashing shield (paragon tier)	25,000
16	Dragondaunt shield (paragon tier)	45,000
17	Bracers of defense (paragon tier)	65,000
18	Shield of defiance (paragon tier)	85,000
20	Guardian shield (paragon tier)	125,000
22	Bracers of mighty striking (epic tier)	325,000
22	Shield of deflection (epic tier)	325,000
23	Bracers of the perfect shot (epic tier)	425,000
23	Shield of protection (epic tier)	425,000
24	Shield of warding (epic tier)	525,000
25	Bashing shield (epic tier)	625,000
26	Dragondaunt shield (epic tier)	1,125,000
27	Bracers of defense (epic tier)	1,625,000
28	Shield of defiance (epic tier)	2,125,000
30	Guardian shield (epic tier)	3,125,000

Dragondaunt Shield — Level 16+

This ornate shield provides extra protection against dragon attacks and can be activated to reduce the damage of an area attack.

Lvl 16	45,000 gp	Lvl 26	1,125,000 gp

Item Slot: Arms

Property: You gain resist 5 to all attacks of dragons.
　Level 26: Resist 10 to all attacks of dragons.

Power (Daily): Immediate Interrupt. You can use this power when you are hit by an area or a close attack. Reduce the damage dealt by the attack to you and each adjacent ally by 10.
　Level 26: Reduce damage by 15.

Guardian Shield — Level 10+

Activate the power of this shield to defend an ally from attack.

Lvl 10	5,000 gp	Lvl 30	3,125,000 gp
Lvl 20	125,000 gp		

Item Slot: Arms

Power (Daily): Immediate Interrupt. You can use this power when an adjacent ally is hit by an attack. You are hit by the attack instead. You then gain resistance to all damage equal to half the damage dealt by the attack (if any) until the start of your next turn.
　Level 20: Protect an ally within 5 squares of you.
　Level 30: Protect an ally within 10 squares of you.

Shield of Defiance — Level 8+

This enchanted shield provides immediate healing after you receive a critical hit.

Lvl 8	3,400 gp	Lvl 28	2,125,000 gp
Lvl 18	85,000 gp		

Item Slot: Arms

Power (Daily ✦ Healing): Immediate Reaction. You can use this power when a critical hit is scored on you. You can spend a healing surge.
　Level 18: Regain an additional 2d6 hit points.
　Level 28: Regain an additional 4d6 hit points.

Shield of Deflection — Level 12+

This enchanted shield reduces the damage you suffer from ranged attacks.

Lvl 12	13,000 gp	Lvl 22	325,000 gp

Item Slot: Arms

Property: Gain resist 5 to damage from all ranged attacks.
　Level 22: Resist 10 to damage from all ranged attacks.

Shield of Protection — Level 3+

This enchanted shield can be activated to provide you and an ally with magical protection for a short time.

Lvl 3	680 gp	Lvl 23	425,000 gp
Lvl 13	17,000 gp		

Item Slot: Arms

Power (Daily): Standard Action. You and an adjacent ally gain resist 10 to all damage until the end of your next turn.
　Level 13: Resist 15 to all damage.
　Level 23: Resist 20 to all damage.

Shield of Warding — Level 14+

Activate the power of this shield to reduce the damage an ally suffers.

Lvl 14	21,000 gp	Lvl 24	525,000 gp

Item Slot: Arms

Power (Daily): Immediate Interrupt. You can use this power when an adjacent ally is hit by an attack. That ally gains resist 15 to any damage from the attack.
　Level 24: Resist 20 to any damage from the attack.

Feet Slot Items

Boots and greaves contain powers that enhance your speed, provide additional movement, or otherwise assist you in movement-related situations.

FEET SLOT ITEMS

Lvl	Name	Price (gp)
2	Acrobat boots	520
3	Catstep boots	680
4	Wavestrider boots	840
5	Boots of spider climbing	1,000
7	Dwarven greaves	2,600
9	Boots of striding	4,200
11	Elven boots	9,000
12	Battlestrider greaves	13,000
13	Winged boots	17,000
14	Boots of striding and springing	21,000
16	Eladrin boots	45,000
22	Boots of balance	325,000
28	Boots of the infinite stride	2,125,000

Acrobat Boots — Level 2

These enchanted boots enhance your acrobatic skills.

Item Slot: Feet   520 gp
Property: Gain a +1 item bonus to Acrobatics checks.
Power (At-Will): Minor Action. Stand up from prone.

Battlestrider Greaves — Level 12

This enchanted leg armor increases your speed when wearing heavy armor.

Item Slot: Feet   13,000 gp
Property: Gain a +1 item bonus to speed while wearing heavy armor.

Boots of Balance — Level 22

These enchanted boots greatly increase your acrobatic skills.

Item Slot: Feet   325,000 gp
Property: Gain a +5 item bonus to Acrobatics checks.
Power (Daily): Free Action. Reroll an Acrobatics check you just made. Use the new result.

Boots of the Infinite Stride — Level 28

These enchanted boots allow you to teleport once per day.

Item Slot: Feet   2,125,000 gp
Property: Gain a +1 item bonus to speed.
Power (Daily ✦ Teleportation): Move Action. Teleport up to 1 mile (line of sight and line of effect to the destination are required).

Boots of Spider Climbing — Level 5

These enchanted boots enhance your ability to climb.

Item Slot: Feet   1,000 gp
Property: When you make an Athletics check to climb, you can climb at your normal speed instead of one-half your speed.
Power (Daily): Move Action. On this move action, you move with a climb speed equal to your speed.

Boots of Striding — Level 9

These enchanted boots increase your speed if you wear light armor or no armor.

Item Slot: Feet   4,200 gp
Property: Gain a +1 item bonus to speed when wearing light or no armor.

Boots of Striding and Springing — Level 14

These enchanted boots increase your speed if you wear light armor or no armor and enhance your jumping capability.

Item Slot: Feet   21,000 gp
Property: Gain a +1 item bonus to speed when wearing light or no armor.
Property: Gain a +2 item bonus to Athletics checks made to jump.

Catstep Boots — Level 3

These enchanted boots reduce falling damage and enhance your acrobatics and athletics skills.

Item Slot: Feet   680 gp
Property: When you fall or jump down, you take only half normal falling damage and always land on your feet.
Power (Daily): Free Action. Gain a +5 power bonus to your next Acrobatics check or Athletics check.

Dwarven Greaves — Level 7

This enchanted leg armor, crafted in the dwarven tradition, can be activated to negate a pull, a push, or a slide effect.

Item Slot: Feet   2,600 gp
Power (Daily): Immediate Interrupt. You can use this power when you are hit by a power that has a pull, a push, or a slide effect. You negate the forced movement.

Eladrin Boots — Level 16

These enchanted boots, crafted in the eladrin tradition, increase your teleport distance.

Item Slot: Feet   45,000 gp
Property: Add 2 to the maximum range of any teleport you make (other than that provided by these boots).
Power (Daily ✦ Teleportation): Move Action. Teleport up to 5 squares (or up to 10 if you're an eladrin).

Elven Boots — Level 11

These enchanted boots, crafted in the elven tradition, can be activated to increase your speed and to enhance your stealth for a short time.

Item Slot: Feet   9,000 gp
Power (Encounter): Minor Action. Gain a +2 power bonus to speed and Stealth checks until the end of your turn.

Wavestrider Boots — Level 4

These enchanted boots allow you to walk across liquid as if it were solid land.

Item Slot: Feet   840 gp
Property: If you begin your turn standing on a solid surface, you can move across liquid as if it were normal terrain. If you are still on liquid at the end of your turn, you fall in.
Power (Daily): Minor Action. You can move across liquid surfaces as if they were normal terrain until the end of the encounter.

Winged Boots — Level 13

These enchanted boots protect you from falling damage and can be activated to allow you to fly for a short time.

Item Slot: Feet   17,000 gp

Property: You take no damage from a fall and always land on your feet.

Power (Daily): Move Action. Fly a number of squares equal to your speed. At the end of your turn, you float down to the ground if you aren't already there.

HANDS SLOT ITEMS

Gloves and gauntlets contain powers that assist with skill checks, increase attack and damage rolls, and even allow you to reroll in some situations.

Burglar's Gloves — Level 1

These fingerless black gloves are embroidered with dark red sigils and improve your thievery skills.

Item Slot: Hands   360 gp

Property: Gain a +1 item bonus to Thievery checks.

Gauntlets of Destruction — Level 18

These armored gloves enable you to deal more than minimum damage when you make a melee attack.

Item Slot: Hands   85,000 gp

Property: When rolling damage on melee attacks, reroll all 1s until they come up as something other than a 1.

Gauntlets of Ogre Power — Level 5

These oversized armored gloves increase your strength and can be activated to increase your damage.

Item Slot: Hands   1,000 gp

Property: Gain a +1 item bonus to Athletics checks and Strength ability checks (but not Strength attacks).

Power (Daily): Free Action. Use this power when you hit with a melee attack. Add a +5 power bonus to the damage roll.

Gauntlets of the Ram — Level 8

These armored gloves bear the symbol of a ram's head.

Item Slot: Hands   3,400 gp

Property: Add 1 square to the distance of any push effect you create.

Gloves of Piercing — Level 3

These enchanted gloves can be activated to ignore an opponent's resistances for a short time.

Item Slot: Hands   680 gp

Power (Daily): Minor Action. Until the end of the encounter, your attacks ignore any resistance of 10 or lower.

HANDS SLOT ITEMS

Lvl	Name	Price (gp)
1	Burglar's gloves	360
3	Gloves of piercing	680
5	Gauntlets of ogre power	1,000
6	Shadowfell gloves (heroic tier)	1,800
8	Gauntlets of the ram	3,400
12	Rogue's gloves	13,000
16	Shadowfell gloves (paragon tier)	45,000
18	Gauntlets of destruction	85,000
23	Guildmaster's gloves	425,000
26	Shadowfell gloves (epic tier)	1,125,000

Guildmaster's Gloves — Level 23

These stylish black gloves greatly improve your thievery skills.

Item Slot: Hands   425,000 gp

Property: Gain a +5 item bonus to Thievery checks.

Power (Daily): Minor Action. Each time you make a Thievery check during this encounter, roll twice and take the higher result.

Rogue's Gloves — Level 12

These enchanted black gloves moderately improve your thievery skills.

Item Slot: Hands   13,000 gp

Property: Gain a +3 item bonus to Thievery checks.

Power (Daily): Minor Action. Each time you make a Thievery check during this turn, roll twice and take the higher result.

Shadowfell Gloves — Level 6+

These supple black gloves, woven with Shadowfell thread, are highly prized by wizards and warlocks.

| Lvl 6 | 1,800 gp | Lvl 26 | 1,125,000 gp |
| Lvl 16 | 45,000 gp | | |

Item Slot: Hands

Power (Daily ✦ Necrotic): Minor Action. Change the damage type dealt by the next arcane power you use to necrotic. Add 1d6 to the damage dealt by that power (if any).
Level 16: Add 2d6 to the damage dealt.
Level 26: Add 3d6 to the damage dealt.

HEAD SLOT ITEMS

These items contain powers that enhance Intelligence-based and Wisdom-based skills, increase damage, and enhance senses.

Basilisk Helm — Level 18

This helm, carved to resemble a basilisk, can be activated to immobilize an enemy.

Item Slot: Head   85,000 gp

Power (Daily): Immediate Reaction. You can use this power when an enemy within 5 squares of you makes a melee or a ranged attack against you. That enemy is immobilized (save ends).

Circlet of Authority — Level 7

This simple metal headband improves your diplomatic and intimidation skills.

Item Slot: Head   2,600 gp

Property: You gain a +2 item bonus to Diplomacy checks and Intimidate checks.

Crown of Command — Level 17

This ornate crown greatly enhances your diplomatic and intimidation skills.

Item Slot: Head   65,000 gp

Property: Gain a +4 item bonus to Diplomacy checks and Intimidate checks.

Power (Daily): Free Action. You can use this power when you or an ally within 5 squares of you rolls a poor Diplomacy or Intimidate check. You or the ally rerolls the check and uses the new result.

Diadem of Acuity — Level 8

This metal headband enhances your insight and perception skills.

Item Slot: Head   3,400 gp

Property: Gain a +2 item bonus to Insight checks and Perception checks.

Goggles of Night — Level 14

This eyewear provides you with darkvision.

Item Slot: Head   21,000 gp

Property: Gain darkvision.

Halo of Fallen Stars — Level 25

Tiny motes of sparkling light circle around your head like orbiting stars, enhancing your healing, nature, and religion skills.

Item Slot: Head   625,000 gp

Property: Gain a +5 item bonus to Heal checks, Nature checks, and Religion checks.

Power (Daily ✦ Radiant): Immediate Interrupt. You can use this power when an enemy makes a melee attack or a ranged attack against you. That enemy takes 5d6 + Charisma modifier radiant damage and is blinded (save ends).

HEAD SLOT ITEMS

Lvl	Name	Price (gp)
6	*Horned helm (heroic tier)*	1,800
7	*Circlet of authority*	2,600
8	*Diadem of acuity*	3,400
9	*Helm of battle (heroic tier)*	4,200
10	*Helm of heroes (heroic tier)*	5,000
12	*Helm of the eagle*	13,000
14	*Goggles of night*	21,000
16	*Horned helm (paragon tier)*	45,000
17	*Crown of command*	65,000
18	*Basilisk helm*	85,000
19	*Helm of battle (paragon tier)*	105,000
20	*Helm of heroes (paragon tier)*	125,000
22	*Helm of ghostly defense*	325,000
23	*Phoenix helm*	425,000
25	*Halo of fallen stars*	625,000
26	*Horned helm (epic tier)*	1,125,000
27	*Iron of spite*	1,625,000
28	*Ioun stone of true sight*	2,125,000
29	*Helm of battle (epic tier)*	2,625,000
30	*Helm of heroes (epic tier)*	3,125,000

Helm of Battle — Level 9+

This simple helmet enhances the initiative of you and your allies.

Lvl 9   4,200 gp   Lvl 29   2,625,000 gp
Lvl 19   105,000 gp

Item Slot: Head

Property: You and each ally within 5 squares of you gain a +1 item bonus to initiative checks.
Level 19: +2 item bonus.
Level 29: +3 item bonus.

Helm of the Eagle — Level 12

This helm, carved to resemble an eagle, enhances your perception and can be activated to improve a ranged attack.

Item Slot: Head   13,000 gp

Property: Gain a +3 item bonus to Perception checks.

Power (Daily): Minor Action. Gain a +2 power bonus to your next ranged attack roll this turn.

Helm of Ghostly Defense — Level 22

This misty helmet allows you to resist some necrotic damage and can be activated to turn you insubstantial for a short time.

Item Slot: Head   325,000 gp

Property: Gain resist 10 necrotic.

Power (Encounter): Immediate Interrupt. You can use this power when you are hit by an attack. You become insubstantial until the start of your next turn.

Helm of Heroes — Level 10+

This ornate helmet makes you and your allies less susceptible to fear effects and can be activated to improve an ally's attack.

Lvl 10	5,000 gp	Lvl 30	3,125,000 gp
Lvl 20	125,000 gp		

Item Slot: Head
Property: You and each ally within 10 squares of you gain a +2 item bonus to saving throws against fear effects.
  Level 30: +5 item bonus.
Power (Daily): Free Action. Use this power when you grant an ally a basic attack. That ally can take a standard action instead. The ally gains a +2 power bonus to any damage rolls made during that standard action.
  Level 20: +5 power bonus to damage rolls.
  Level 30: +10 power bonus to damage rolls.

Horned Helm — Level 6+

This horned helmet increases the damage you deal when making a charge attack.

Lvl 6	1,800 gp	Lvl 26	1,125,000 gp
Lvl 16	45,000 gp		

Item Slot: Head
Property: Your charge attacks deal an extra 1d6 damage.
  Level 16: 2d6 extra damage.
  Level 26: 3d6 extra damage.

Ioun Stone of True Sight — Level 28

This dark blue rhomboid stone floats lightly in the air, granting you darkvision and greatly enhanced insight and perception.

Item Slot: Head   2,125,000 gp
Property: Gain darkvision and a +6 item bonus to Insight checks and Perception checks.
Power (Daily): Minor Action. You can see invisible creatures as if they were visible.
  Sustain Minor: The power remains in effect.

Iron of Spite — Level 27

A spiked metal sphere, slightly smaller than your fist, hovers near your shoulder and gives off black sparks. It greatly enhances your arcana and intimidate skills.

Item Slot: Head   1,625,000 gp
Property: Gain a +6 item bonus to Arcana checks and Intimidate checks.
Property: Any enemy that hits you with a melee attack takes 1d10 necrotic damage.

Phoenix Helm — Level 23

This helm, carved to resemble a phoenix, increases your perception and can be activated to improve a ranged attack.

Item Slot: Head   425,000 gp
Property: Gain a +5 item bonus to Perception checks.
Power (Daily ✦ Fire): Minor Action. Gain a +2 power bonus to your next ranged attack roll this turn. If that attack hits, it deals an extra 2d8 fire damage.

NECK SLOT ITEMS

Amulets and cloaks grant an enhancement bonus to Fortitude, Reflex, and Will defense.

Amulet of False Life — Level 9+

This dark blue amulet with a crimson center increases your defenses and can be activated to grant you temporary hit points.

Lvl 9	+2	4,200 gp	Lvl 24	+5	525,000 gp
Lvl 14	+3	21,000 gp	Lvl 29	+6	2,625,000 gp
Lvl 19	+4	105,000 gp			

Item Slot: Neck
Enhancement: Fortitude, Reflex, and Will
Power (Daily): Minor Action. Use this power when you are bloodied to gain temporary hit points equal to your healing surge value.

Amulet of Health — Level 3+

This golden amulet increases your defenses and resists poison.

Lvl 3	+1	680 gp	Lvl 18	+4	85,000 gp
Lvl 8	+2	3,400 gp	Lvl 23	+5	425,000 gp
Lvl 13	+3	17,000 gp	Lvl 28	+6	2,125,000 gp

Item Slot: Neck
Enhancement: Fortitude, Reflex, and Will
Property: Gain resist 5 poison.
  Level 13 or 18: Resist 10 poison.
  Level 23 or 28: Resist 15 poison.

Amulet of Protection — Level 1+

This light blue amulet increases your defenses.

Lvl 1	+1	360 gp	Lvl 16	+4	45,000 gp
Lvl 6	+2	1,800 gp	Lvl 21	+5	225,000 gp
Lvl 11	+3	9,000 gp	Lvl 26	+6	1,125,000 gp

Item Slot: Neck
Enhancement: Fortitude, Reflex, and Will

Cloak of Feywild Escape — Level 20+

This cloak of dark green swirls increases your defenses and can be activated to allow you to briefly gain respite in the Feywild.

Lvl 20	+4	125,000 gp	Lvl 30	+6	3,125,000 gp
Lvl 25	+5	625,000 gp			

Item Slot: Neck
Enhancement: Fortitude, Reflex, and Will
Power (Daily): Move Action. Choose an ally you can see. You disappear from the world until the start of your next turn, at which point you appear in any unoccupied space within 5 squares of the chosen ally.

Cloak of Invisibility — Level 23+

This gold-hemmed cloak increases your defenses and can be activated to turn you invisible for a short time.

Lvl 23	+5	425,000 gp	Lvl 28	+6	2,125,000 gp

Item Slot: Neck
Enhancement: Fortitude, Reflex, and Will
Power (Daily ✦ Illusion): Standard Action. You become invisible until the end of the encounter or until you are hit by a melee attack or a ranged attack.

CHAPTER 7 | Equipment

249

NECK SLOT ITEMS

Lvl	Name	Price (gp)
1	Amulet of protection +1	360
2	Cloak of resistance +1	520
3	Amulet of health +1	680
3	Safewing amulet +1	680
6	Amulet of protection +2	1,800
7	Cloak of resistance +2	2,600
7	Elven cloak +2	2,600
8	Amulet of health +2	3,400
8	Safewing amulet +2	3,400
9	Amulet of false life +2	4,200
9	Cloak of survival +2	4,200
11	Amulet of protection +3	9,000
12	Cloak of resistance +3	13,000
12	Elven cloak +3	13,000
13	Amulet of health +3	17,000
13	Periapt of wisdom +3	17,000
13	Safewing amulet +3	17,000
14	Amulet of false life +3	21,000
14	Cloak of survival +3	21,000
15	Stormwalker's cloak +3	25,000
16	Amulet of protection +4	45,000
17	Cloak of resistance +4	65,000
17	Elven cloak +4	65,000
18	Amulet of health +4	85,000
18	Periapt of wisdom +4	85,000
18	Safewing amulet +4	85,000
19	Amulet of false life +4	105,000
19	Cloak of survival +4	105,000

NECK SLOT ITEMS CONT.

Lvl	Name	Price (gp)
20	Cloak of feywild escape +4	125,000
20	Guardian's cape +4	125,000
20	Stormwalker's cloak +4	125,000
21	Amulet of protection +5	225,000
22	Cloak of resistance +5	325,000
22	Elven cloak +5	325,000
23	Amulet of health +5	425,000
23	Cloak of invisibility +5	425,000
23	Periapt of wisdom +5	425,000
23	Safewing amulet +5	425,000
24	Amulet of false life +5	525,000
24	Cloak of survival +5	525,000
25	Cloak of feywild escape +5	625,000
25	Guardian's cape +5	625,000
25	Stormwalker's cloak +5	625,000
26	Amulet of protection +6	1,125,000
27	Cloak of resistance +6	1,625,000
27	Elven cloak +6	1,625,000
28	Amulet of health +6	2,125,000
28	Cloak of invisibility +6	2,125,000
28	Periapt of wisdom +6	2,125,000
28	Safewing amulet +6	2,125,000
29	Amulet of false life +6	2,625,000
29	Cloak of survival +6	2,625,000
30	Cloak of feywild escape +6	3,125,000
30	Guardian's cape +6	3,125,000
30	Scarab of invulnerability +6	3,125,000
30	Stormwalker's cloak +6	3,125,000

Cloak of Resistance — Level 2+

This crimson-hemmed cloak can be activated to provide minor resistance to all attacks.

Lvl 2	+1	520 gp	Lvl 17	+4	65,000 gp
Lvl 7	+2	2,600 gp	Lvl 22	+5	325,000 gp
Lvl 12	+3	13,000 gp	Lvl 27	+6	1,625,000 gp

Item Slot: Neck

Enhancement: Fortitude, Reflex, and Will

Power (Daily): Minor Action. Gain resist 5 to all damage until the start of your next turn.
   Level 12 or 17: Resist 10 to all damage.
   Level 22 or 27: Resist 15 to all damage.

Cloak of Survival — Level 9+

This brown cloak can be activated to increase your endurance and provide resistance to cold and fire.

Lvl 9	+2	4,200 gp	Lvl 24	+5	525,000 gp
Lvl 14	+3	21,000 gp	Lvl 29	+6	2,625,000 gp
Lvl 19	+4	105,000 gp			

Item Slot: Neck

Enhancement: Fortitude, Reflex, and Will

Property: Gain an item bonus to Endurance checks equal to the cloak's enhancement bonus. Gain resist 5 cold and resist 5 fire.
   Level 19 or 24: Resist 10 cold and resist 10 fire.
   Level 29: Resist 15 cold and resist 15 fire.

Elven Cloak — Level 7+

This cloak of swirling leaves, crafted in the elven tradition, increases your stealth.

Lvl 7	+2	2,600 gp	Lvl 22	+5	325,000 gp
Lvl 12	+3	13,000 gp	Lvl 27	+6	1,625,000 gp
Lvl 17	+4	65,000 gp			

Item Slot: Neck

Enhancement: Fortitude, Reflex, and Will

Property: Gain an item bonus to Stealth checks equal to the cloak's enhancement bonus.

Guardian's Cape — Level 20+

This dark blue cape can be activated to allow you to teleport and switch places with an ally.

Lvl 20	+4	125,000 gp	Lvl 30	+6	3,125,000 gp
Lvl 25	+5	625,000 gp			

Item Slot: Neck

Enhancement: Fortitude, Reflex, and Will

Power (Daily ✦ Teleportation): Move Action. Teleport to the space of an ally within 10 squares of you; that ally simultaneously teleports to your original space. You need not have line of sight or line of effect to the ally's space.

Periapt of Wisdom — Level 13+

This silver amulet increases your wisdom and can be activated to greatly enhance the strength of your will.

Lvl 13	+3	17,000 gp	Lvl 23	+5	425,000 gp
Lvl 18	+4	85,000 gp	Lvl 28	+6	2,125,000 gp

Item Slot: Neck

Enhancement: Fortitude, Reflex, and Will

Property: Gain a +1 item bonus to Wisdom ability checks and Wisdom-based skill checks (but not Wisdom attacks). Level 23 or 28: +2 item bonus.

Power (Daily): Immediate Interrupt. You can use this power when you are hit by an attack that targets your Will defense. Gain a +5 power bonus to Will against the attack.

Safewing Amulet — Level 3+

This orange amulet reduces the damage you suffer when falling.

Lvl 3	+1	680 gp	Lvl 18	+4	85,000 gp
Lvl 8	+2	3,400 gp	Lvl 23	+5	425,000 gp
Lvl 13	+3	17,000 gp	Lvl 28	+6	2,125,000 gp

Item Slot: Neck

Enhancement: Fortitude, Reflex, and Will

Property: When falling, reduce the distance by 10 feet for every plus (-10 feet for +1, -20 feet for +2, and so on) for the purpose of calculating damage. You always land on your feet after a fall.

Scarab of Invulnerability — Level 30

This night black amulet can be activated to make you invulnerable for a short time.

Lvl 30	+6	3,125,000 gp

Item Slot: Neck

Enhancement: Fortitude, Reflex, and Will

Power (Daily): Minor Action. You have immunity to damage until the end of your next turn.

Stormwalker's Cloak — Level 15+

This dark gray cloak with lightning-bolt edging provides protection from lightning and thunder damage and can be activated to deal such damage to your opponents for a short time.

Lvl 15	+3	25,000 gp	Lvl 25	+5	625,000 gp
Lvl 20	+4	125,000 gp	Lvl 30	+6	3,125,000 gp

Item Slot: Neck

Enhancement: Fortitude, Reflex, and Will

Property: Gain resist 10 lightning and resist 10 thunder. Level 25 or 30: Resist 15 lightning and resist 15 thunder.

Power (Daily ✦ Lightning, Thunder): Minor Action. Until the end of your next turn, each time you are hit by a melee attack the attacker takes 3d6 lightning damage or 3d6 thunder damage (your choice).
Level 20: 4d6 lightning damage or 4d6 thunder damage.
Level 25: 5d6 lightning damage or 5d6 thunder damage.
Level 30: 6d6 lightning damage or 6d6 thunder damage.

RINGS

Magic rings provide properties and powers that aid characters in a variety of ways, from healing and skill use to flying and teleportation. A character can wear and gain the benefit of up to two magic rings (one on each hand). If you are wearing more than two magic rings, none of your magic rings function.

RINGS

Lvl	Name	Price (gp)
14	*Iron ring of the dwarf lords*	21,000
15	*Ring of freedom of movement*	25,000
17	*Ring of protection*	65,000
18	*Ring of invisibility*	85,000
19	*Ring of true seeing*	105,000
20	*Ring of flight*	125,000
21	*Ring of wizardry*	225,000
24	*Ring of regeneration*	525,000
26	*Star opal ring*	1,125,000

Iron Ring of the Dwarf Lords — Level 14

This solid iron ring bears the geometric patterns of the dwarf lords.

Item Slot: Ring   21,000 gp

Property: Gain one healing surge.

Power (Daily): Immediate Interrupt. You can use this power when you are hit by a power that has a pull, a push, or a slide effect. You negate the forced movement.
If you've reached at least one milestone today, you also gain immunity to pull, push, and slide effects (unless you are willing to be moved) until the end of your next turn.

Ring of Flight — Level 20

This delicate silver ring bears a feathery pattern.

Item Slot: Ring   125,000 gp

Property: You take no damage from a fall and always land on your feet.

Power (Daily): Minor Action. Gain a fly speed equal to your speed until the end of your turn.
If you've reached at least one milestone today, this lasts until the end of your next turn instead.

Ring of Freedom of Movement — Level 15

This sky blue band seems to shimmer and move around your finger.

Item Slot: Ring   25,000 gp

Property: Gain a +2 item bonus to Acrobatics checks.

Power (Daily): Minor Action. Until the end of the encounter, gain a +5 power bonus to checks made to escape a grab and a +5 power bonus to saving throws to end the immobilized, restrained, or slowed conditions.
If you've reached at least one milestone today, you can also move across difficult terrain as if it were normal until the end of the encounter.

Ring of Invisibility — Level 18

This simple golden ring bears Elven runes etched lightly across its surface.

Item Slot: Ring 85,000 gp

Property: Gain a +2 item bonus to Stealth checks.

Power (Daily ✦ Illusion): Standard Action. Become invisible until the end of your next turn.

    If you've reached at least one milestone today, using this power requires only a minor action.

Ring of Protection — Level 17

This simple ring of white gold is engraved with a tiny shield.

Item Slot: Ring 65,000 gp

Property: Gain a +1 item bonus to saving throws.

Power (Daily): Immediate Interrupt. You can use this power when you are hit by an attack. Gain a +2 power bonus to a single defense score against the attack.

    If you've reached at least one milestone today, this bonus lasts until the start of your next turn instead.

Ring of Regeneration — Level 24

This ring of plain silver is adorned with a blood red ruby.

Item Slot: Ring 525,000 gp

Property: Gain a +3 item bonus to your healing surge value.

Power (Daily ✦ Healing): Minor Action. Regain one healing surge you've already used today.

    If you've reached at least one milestone today, you also gain regeneration 10 until the end of the encounter or until you spend a healing surge.

Ring of True Seeing — Level 19

This gold band sports a white pearl that appears like an eye upon your finger.

Item Slot: Ring 105,000 gp

Property: Gain a +2 item bonus to Perception checks.

Power (Daily): Minor Action. Until the end of your turn, you can see invisible creatures as if they were visible. You also ignore the attack penalty for concealment or total concealment.

    If you've reached at least one milestone today, this lasts until the end of your next turn instead.

Ring of Wizardry — Level 21

This silver band is engraved with powerful arcane symbols.

Item Slot: Ring 225,000 gp

Property: Gain a +3 item bonus to Arcana checks.

Power (Daily): Minor Action. Regain the use of an arcane encounter utility power that you've already used (as if you hadn't used it this encounter).

    If you've reached at least one milestone today, you can instead regain the use of an arcane encounter attack power.

Star Opal Ring — Level 26

This black band sports a star opal that glows softly.

Item Slot: Ring 1,125,000 gp

Property: Gain a +1 item bonus to speed.

Power (Daily ✦ Radiant, Teleportation): Move Action. Teleport up to 10 squares.

    If you've reached at least one milestone today, a brilliant explosion bursts from your starting square after you complete the teleport: Close burst 3; Charisma attack (with a +5 bonus) vs. Reflex; 4d8 + Charisma modifier radiant damage (half on a miss).

WAIST SLOT ITEMS

Belts contain powers that improve Strength-based skills, healing, and resistances.

WAIST SLOT ITEMS

Lvl	Name	Price (gp)
2	*Belt of vigor (heroic tier)*	520
5	*Ironskin belt (heroic tier)*	1,000
7	*Belt of sacrifice (heroic tier)*	2,600
9	*Dynamic belt (heroic tier)*	4,200
12	*Belt of vigor (paragon tier)*	13,000
15	*Belt of giant strength*	25,000
15	*Ironskin belt (paragon tier)*	25,000
17	*Belt of sacrifice (paragon tier)*	65,000
19	*Dynamic belt (paragon tier)*	105,000
22	*Belt of vigor (epic tier)*	325,000
25	*Belt of titan strength*	625,000
25	*Ironskin belt (epic tier)*	625,000
27	*Belt of sacrifice (epic tier)*	1,625,000
29	*Dynamic belt (epic tier)*	2,625,000

Belt of Giant Strength — Level 15

This rugged leather belt is inset with numerous chunks of polished gray stone. It improves your athletic skills and melee damage.

Item Slot: Waist 25,000 gp

Property: Gain a +2 item bonus to Athletics checks and Strength ability checks (but not Strength attacks).

Power (Daily): Free Action. Use this power when you hit with a melee attack. Add a +10 power bonus to the damage roll.

Belt of Sacrifice — Level 7+

This belt of leather allows you to help others heal.

Lvl 7 2,600 gp   Lvl 27 1,625,000 gp
Lvl 17 65,000 gp

Item Slot: Waist

Property: Each ally within 5 squares of you gains a +1 item bonus to his or her healing surge value.

    Level 17: +2 item bonus.

    Level 27: +3 item bonus.

Power (Daily ✦ Healing): Minor Action. Lose two healing surges. An ally within 5 squares of you regains one healing surge.

Belt of Titan Strength
Level 25

This rugged leather belt is inset with numerous chunks of polished obsidian. It greatly improves your athletic skills and melee damage.

Item Slot: Waist   625,000 gp

Property: Gain a +3 item bonus to Athletics checks and Strength ability checks (but not Strength attacks).

Power (Daily): Free Action. Gain a +10 power bonus to all melee damage rolls until the start of your next turn.

Belt of Vigor
Level 2+

This chain metal belt improves your recuperative abilities.

Lvl 2	520 gp	Lvl 22	325,000 gp
Lvl 12	13,000 gp		

Item Slot: Waist

Property: You gain a +1 item bonus to your healing surge value.

Level 12: +2 item bonus.

Level 22: +3 item bonus.

Dynamic Belt
Level 9+

This intricately woven mesh belt improves your acrobatics and athletics skills.

Lvl 9	4,200 gp	Lvl 29	2,625,000 gp
Lvl 19	105,000 gp		

Item Slot: Waist

Property: Gain a +2 item bonus to Acrobatics checks and Athletics checks.

Level 19: +4 item bonus.

Level 29: +6 item bonus.

Power (Daily): Free Action. Reroll an Acrobatics check or an Athletics check you just rolled. Use the new result.

Ironskin Belt
Level 5+

The first of these belts of chain links was forged by a dwarf armorsmith enslaved by fire giants. It can be activated to provide protection against weapon attacks.

Lvl 5	1,000 gp	Lvl 25	625,000 gp
Lvl 15	25,000 gp		

Item Slot: Waist

Power (Daily): Minor Action. Gain resist 5 to all weapon damage until the end of your next turn.

Level 15: Resist 10 to all weapon damage.

Level 25: Resist 15 to all weapon damage.

WONDROUS ITEMS

This category includes some of the most useful and interesting items in the game. They don't take up item slots and don't fall into any other classification.

WONDROUS ITEMS

Lvl	Name	Price (gp)
4	*Everlasting provisions*	840
5	*Bag of holding*	1,000
10	*Handy haversack*	5,000
10	*Rope of climbing*	5,000
11	*Ritual candle*	9,000
11	*Sending stones* (pair)	9,000
12	*Keoghtom's ointment*	13,000
13	*Dust of appearance*	17,000
14	*Feather boat*	21,000
17	*Dimensional shackles*	65,000
19	*Portable hole*	105,000
20	*Flying carpet*	125,000
20	*Revenant ankh*	125,000

Bag of Holding
Level 5

This item appears to be a simple sack of brown canvas.

Wondrous Item   1,000 gp

Property: This bag can hold up to 200 pounds in weight or 20 cubic feet in volume, but it always weighs only 1 pound. Drawing an item from a *bag of holding* is a minor action.

Dimensional Shackles
Level 17

These manacles of solid energy glow a brilliant blue when placed upon a foe, effectively shackling the creature to the here and now.

Wondrous Item   65,000 gp

Power (Daily): Standard Action. To place *dimensional shackles* on an adjacent creature, you make a Strength or a Dexterity melee attack against the target's Reflex. You must have combat advantage against a target to use shackles on it.

A creature held by these shackles is restrained and also can't teleport or be teleported. Escaping from the shackles requires a DC 35 Acrobatics check.

The shackles automatically adjust to fit any size or shape of creature. As a standard action, any creature other than the one in the shackles can remove them from an adjacent creature.

Dust of Appearance
Level 13

This plain pouch holds a single handful of sparkling dust, which it periodically renews.

Wondrous Item   17,000 gp

Power (Encounter): Standard Action. Pull a handful of dust from the pouch and throw it into the air (close blast 3). Doing this creates a zone that lasts until the end of the encounter. Invisible creatures and objects within or entering the zone become visible and can't become invisible again until the end of the encounter.

Everlasting Provisions — Level 4

This plain basket radiates delicious smells.

Wondrous Item 840 gp

Property: After an extended rest, you open the basket, creating enough food and water to feed five Medium or Small creatures (or one Large creature) for 24 hours.

Feather Boat — Level 14

The secrets of the feather boat, first created by noble eladrin explorers, have long since passed on to other races.

Wondrous Item 21,000 gp

Power (Daily): Standard Action. By placing this feather in water, you cause the feather to become a long swan-shaped boat. This boat can hold up to five Medium or Small creatures (or two Large creatures). It can be rowed by two creatures at a speed of 4. After 12 hours, or when its user wills it (a minor action), the boat returns to its feather form.

Flying Carpet — Level 20

This 4-foot square of carpet is woven with intricate stitching and strange runes.

Wondrous Item 125,000 gp

Power (At-Will): Move Action. A character on a *flying carpet* can mentally command it to fly 6 squares. The carpet has a maximum altitude of 10 squares. If no rider is upon it, it hovers in place 1 foot above the ground if it is unrolled or sits on the ground if it is rolled up.

  The carpet's flight isn't entirely stable; while on the carpet, a rider takes a -2 penalty to AC and Reflex defense. The carpet can carry one Medium or Small character of no more than 300 pounds. If more than 300 pounds are placed on it, the carpet (and all it carries) falls to the ground, and the character and all objects the carpet was holding take falling damage.

Handy Haversack — Level 10

This ordinary-looking backpack is surprisingly light.

Wondrous Item 5,000 gp

Property: This backpack can hold up to 1,000 pounds in weight or 100 cubic feet in volume, but it always weighs only 1 pound.

  Drawing an item from a *handy haversack* is a minor action.

Keoghtom's Ointment — Level 12

This tiny jar magically creates a dollop of potent healing unguent each day.

Wondrous Item 13,000 gp

Power (Daily ✦ Healing): Standard Action. Apply this substance to yourself or an adjacent ally. That creature automatically ends one disease or poison effect that a save can end or regains one healing surge (your choice).

Portable Hole — Level 19

This handkerchief-sized black circle becomes a great hole when placed on a flat surface.

Wondrous Item 105,000 gp

Power (At-Will): Standard Action. Place a *portable hole* on a wall, a floor, or a ceiling. (The surface must be flat for the item to function.) The *portable hole* instantly creates a 5-foot-wide, 5-foot-deep hole in that surface. With a standard action, any creature adjacent to a *portable hole* can pick it up, provided there are no creatures or objects inside it.

Revenant Ankh — Level 20

This powerful ankh temporarily imbues an ally with life force, allowing him to return to battle.

Wondrous Item   125,000 gp

Power (Daily): Standard Action. Choose an ally within your line of sight who died since the end of your last turn. That ally returns to maximum hit points and is dazed.

　　The ally can't regain hit points, gain temporary hit points, or recover from the dazed condition. At the start of each of the ally's turns, the ally takes damage equal to his or her level. The ally dies again when reduced to 0 hit points or fewer or when the encounter ends.

　　No character can be affected by a *revenant ankh* more than once per day.

Ritual Candle — Level 11

This candle of rune-carved purple wax gives off a clear, bright glow when lit.

Wondrous Item   9,000 gp

Property: This candle never burns down (except as noted).

Power (Daily): Standard Action. Light the candle before beginning to perform a ritual. You gain a +2 power bonus to any skill checks made as part of the ritual.

　　The candle automatically extinguishes at the end of the ritual and can be used again the following day.

Rope of Climbing — Level 10

A coil of golden rope.

Wondrous Item   5,000 gp

Property: This 100-foot-long rope has 100 hit points and can hold up to 2,500 pounds (roughly 10 Medium creatures and their gear).

Power (At-Will): Minor Action. The rope moves up to 10 squares along a horizontal or a vertical surface. As part of the same action, it can tie itself around an object to create a secure point for climbing. It can't tie itself to or otherwise affect a creature.

　　Anyone holding the rope can activate its power. On command, the rope unties itself as a minor action.

Sending Stones (pair) — Level 11

Each fist-sized round stone bears a Dwarven rune that translates as "Speak."

Wondrous Item   9,000 gp

Power (At-Will): Standard Action. Until the end of your next turn, any person speaking into one stone can be heard by those near the other stone as though he or she were standing in the other stone's place. At the end of your next turn, both stones are exhausted. With a minor action, any character touching a single stone renews the set.

Special: *Sending stones* normally come in a matched pair attuned to one another. Larger sets of stones attuned to each other can be created (add 50 percent to the base price for each additional stone).

POTIONS

A potion is a magic liquid that produces its effects when imbibed. Drinking a potion is usually a minor action. Administering a potion to an unconscious creature is usually a standard action. Drawing a potion out of your pack is a minor action.

　　Potions that restore health or even life are useful to adventurers in dire emergencies. These consumables are not as effective as the healing powers of a cleric or a warlord, but many adventurers find it useful to carry one or two healing potions with them on their journeys.

POTIONS

Lvl	Name	Price (gp)
5	*Potion of healing*	50
15	*Potion of vitality*	1,000
25	*Potion of recovery*	25,000
30	*Potion of life*	125,000

Potion of Healing — Level 5

This simple potion draws on the body's natural healing ability to cure your wounds.

Potion   50 gp

Power (Consumable ✦ Healing): Minor Action. Drink this potion and spend a healing surge. Instead of the hit points you would normally regain, you regain 10 hit points.

Potion of Life — Level 30

This fabled potion not only heals wounds but can even bring back the recently deceased.

Potion   125,000 gp

Power (Consumable ✦ Healing): Standard Action. If this potion is administered to a character who died since the end of your last turn, that character is restored to life at 50 hit points.

　　If consumed by a living creature, this potion instead functions as a *potion of recovery*.

Potion of Recovery — Level 25

This mighty potion uses your own stamina to restore your hit points and to help you shrug off harm.

Potion   25,000 gp

Power (Consumable ✦ Healing): Minor Action. Drink the potion and spend a healing surge. Instead of the hit points you would normally regain, you regain 50 hit points and make a saving throw against each effect on you that a save can end.

Potion of Vitality — Level 15

This potent curative heals wounds and can even fix other ailments.

Potion   1,000 gp

Power (Consumable ✦ Healing): Minor Action. Drink the potion and spend a healing surge. Instead of the hit points you would normally regain, you regain 25 hit points and make one saving throw against an effect that a save can end.

CHAPTER 8

ADVENTURING

EXPLORE THE ruins of an ancient drow city, delve into miles of winding tunnels and vast caverns far below the surface, uncover the wicked vizier's plot to overthrow the baron, travel to the fabled City of Brass in search of a long-forgotten ritual—these are the kinds of adventures you might have when you play the DUNGEONS & DRAGONS game.

Now that you've created and equipped your character, it's time to get into the details of what happens during a game session and a campaign. This chapter explains the following topics:

✦ **Quests:** An introduction to quests and how they can lead you into adventure.

✦ **Encounters:** A look at the game's two kinds of encounters and the types of things you can do during an encounter.

✦ **Rewards:** Information about experience points, action points, treasure, and other rewards your character can win by completing quests and encounters.

✦ **Exploration:** Rules for moving through a dungeon or a trackless wilderness. This section covers the basics of movement, as well as vision and light and dealing with obstacles that block your path.

✦ **Rest and Recovery:** Details on recovering hit points, healing surges, and powers, and on keeping watch while you rest.

STEVE PRESCOTT

Most adventures have a goal, something you have to do to complete the adventure successfully. The goal might be a personal one, a cause shared by you and your allies, or a task you have been hired to perform. A goal in an adventure is called a quest.

Quests connect a series of encounters into a meaningful story. The simplest adventures revolve around a single quest. For example, your quest might be to thwart goblin raiders in nearby ruins, to rescue a kidnapped merchant, or to behead the red dragon Kharathas.

Most adventures are more complex, involving multiple quests. A single major quest might drive your adventure. For example, a high priest of Pelor calls upon you to venture into the Fortress of the Iron Ring to retrieve the ancient artifact called the Adamantine Scepter. Any number of minor quests could complicate that task. A wizard, hearing of your journey, offers to pay handsomely for one of the magic rings said to be found within the fortress. One of your friends believes that his mother, a paladin of Pelor, died while exploring the fortress, and he seeks to recover her remains for a proper burial. Once you approach the fortress, you discover that the slaads living around it hold a number of human prisoners, and you might decide to free those prisoners.

Sometimes a quest is spelled out for you at the start of an adventure. The town mayor might implore you to find the goblin raiders' lair, or the priest of Pelor might relate the history of the Adamantine Scepter, before sending you on your quest. Other times, you figure out your quests while adventuring. Once you assemble clues you find, they might turn into new quests.

You can also, with your DM's approval, create a quest for your character. Such a quest can tie into your character's background. For instance, perhaps *your* mother is the person whose remains lie in the Fortress of the Iron Ring. Quests can also relate to individual goals, such as a ranger searching for a magic bow to wield. Individual quests give you a stake in a campaign's unfolding story and give your DM ingredients to help develop that story.

When you complete quests, you earn rewards, including experience points, treasure, and possibly other kinds of rewards. The *Dungeon Master's Guide* includes guidelines for your DM about creating quests, evaluating player-created quests, and assigning rewards for completing quests.

ENCOUNTERS

Encounters are where the action of the D&D game takes place, whether the encounter is a life-or-death battle against monstrous foes, a high-stakes negotiation with a duke and his vizier, or a death-defying climb up the Cliffs of Desolation.

LEE MOYER

Encounters serve many purposes. They are the times when D&D is most like a game, rather than an exercise in cooperative storytelling. They are when you most often bring your powers and skills to bear, when the information on your character sheet is most important. Even so, they should advance the story of an adventure; a pitched battle should have a reason and consequences that relate to your overall quest.

In an encounter, either you succeed in overcoming a challenge or you fail and have to face the consequences. When an encounter begins, everyone has something to do, and it's important for the whole group to work together to achieve success.

Two kinds of encounters occur in most D&D adventures: combat and noncombat encounters.

COMBAT ENCOUNTERS

Combat encounters rely on your attack powers, movement abilities, skills, feats, and magic items—just about every bit of rules material that appears on your character sheet. A combat encounter might include elements of a noncombat encounter. Chapter 9 provides the rules for combat encounters.

NONCOMBAT ENCOUNTERS

Noncombat encounters focus on skills, utility powers, and your own wits (not your character's), although sometimes attack powers can come in handy as well. Such encounters include dealing with traps and hazards, solving puzzles, and a broad category of situations called **skill challenges**.

A skill challenge occurs when exploration (page 260) or social interaction becomes an encounter, with serious consequences for success or failure. When you're making your way through a dungeon or across the trackless wilderness, you typically don't take turns or make checks. But when you spring a trap or face a serious obstacle or hazard, you're in a skill challenge. When you try to persuade a dragon to help you against an oncoming orc horde, you're also in a skill challenge.

In a skill challenge, your goal is to accumulate a certain number of successful skill checks before rolling too many failures. Powers you use might give you bonuses on your checks, make some checks unnecessary, or otherwise help you through the challenge. Your DM sets the stage for a skill challenge by describing the obstacle you face and giving you some idea of the options you have in the encounter. Then you describe your actions and make checks until you either successfully complete the challenge or fail.

Chapter 5 describes the sorts of things you can attempt with your skills in a skill challenge. You can use a wide variety of skills, from Acrobatics and Athletics to Nature and Stealth. You might also use combat powers and ability checks. The *Dungeon Master's Guide* contains rules for designing and running skill challenges.

REWARDS

Although encounters involve risk, they also hold the promise of great rewards. Every successful encounter brings experience, measured in experience points (XP). As you adventure, you also gain action points, treasure, and perhaps rewards of reputation, status, or other intangibles.

This table summarizes the rewards you gain as you adventure.

Frequency	Reward
Every encounter	XP
Every milestone	Action point
Every few encounters	Treasure
Every quest	XP, treasure, other
After about ten encounters	A new level

EXPERIENCE POINTS

Experience points are a measure of your character's learning and growth. When you complete an encounter or a quest, the DM awards you experience points (XP). The amount of XP depends on the difficulty of the encounter or the quest. Completing a major quest is comparable to completing an encounter, while minor quests bring smaller rewards.

A 1st-level character starts with 0 XP. You accumulate XP from each encounter, quest, and adventure, always adding to your XP total. You never lose XP, and your total never resets to 0.

As you accumulate XP, you gain levels. The amount of XP you need for each level varies. For example, you need 1,000 XP to reach 2nd level but 2,250 to reach 3rd. When you gain 1,000,000 XP, you reach 30th level, the pinnacle of accomplishment. See "Gaining Levels," page 27, for all you need to know about level advancement.

The *Dungeon Master's Guide* contains guidelines for your DM on awarding experience points.

MILESTONES

You gain certain benefits when you reach a milestone—when you complete two encounters without stopping for an extended rest (see page 263).

ACTION POINTS

Your character starts with 1 action point. No more than once per encounter, you can spend an action point to take an extra action (see page 286), use certain feats, or use paragon path powers.

When you spend an action point, it's gone, but you can gain more in two ways: by reaching a milestone or by taking an extended rest. Each time you reach a milestone, you gain an action point. After you take an extended rest, you lose any action points you haven't spent, but you start fresh with 1 action point.

Magic Items

Each time you reach a milestone, you gain one additional use of a magic item daily power (see page 226). Some magic items, particularly rings, also grow more powerful after you reach a milestone. See "Magic Items," page 223, for more information.

Treasure

Treasure comes in a variety of forms, but it falls into two basic categories: magic items you can use, and money you can spend to acquire items and services. Money can be coins, gemstones, fine art, or magic items you sell instead of use.

You don't necessarily receive treasure at the completion of each encounter. Treasure is usually a reward for completing several encounters, a quest, or an adventure. Some creatures might carry—and use—magic items that become treasure after you defeat the creatures. Other creatures might keep chests of gold, or you might find treasure suspended in the slimy body of a gelatinous cube. Sometimes you find treasure locked in a vault, stockpiled in an armory, or heaped in a dragon's hoard.

As your group finds treasure, having one person keep track of the items can be helpful. When the treasure includes an item that a character wants to use, that character can take the item, but make a note of the item on the group treasure list. Ideally, you end up with a fair distribution of magic items among the characters in your group.

You don't need to divide the remaining treasure until you get back to town or until some other opportunity arises to spend your hard-earned spoils. Before dividing up the treasure, you might want to use it to pay for group expenses. Group expenses might include the cost for a ritual to resurrect a dead companion or to remove a curse. It's up to your group to decide what is and isn't a group expense.

When the time comes to divide your treasure, parcel it out as evenly as you can after paying for group expenses. Sell or disenchant magic items that no one wants, and add the value to the monetary treasure you found. Then, you can approach the distribution of monetary treasure in one of two ways:

1. Divide monetary treasure evenly among all the party members.
2. Divide monetary treasure among only the characters who didn't get magic items.

Intangible Rewards

Intangible rewards include noble titles, medals and honors, favors, and reputation. Such rewards appear most often as quest rewards, as recognition of your work in completing a quest. If you save the baron's son from kidnappers, the baron might reward you with a medal or even a minor noble title, in addition to granting some monetary reward. If you retrieve a magic orb from the bleak ruins of Havoc Hall and bring it to the mysterious wizard who sent you there, he might promise you a later favor, along with the money he promised you up front. When you save a village from goblin raiders, the village honors you as local heroes, and word of your deeds begins to spread.

You can't buy anything with intangible rewards, and they don't grant any combat bonuses. But they can be important in the campaign's story, and they can help you out in social encounters. Don't overlook the importance of contacts, favors, and fame, even if they don't translate directly into fortune.

EXPLORATION

A significant part of D&D adventures is exploration, which takes place between encounters. Exploration includes making your way through unmapped dungeon corridors, untracked wilderness, or a sprawling city and exploring the environment's dangers and wonders.

Exploration usually involves movement, so this section covers the rules for moving when you're not in an encounter. When you're exploring, you need to know what you can see, particularly in a dark dungeon, so a discussion of vision and light follows the movement rules. During exploration, you interact with your environment in various ways: pushing objects around, fiddling with levers, searching rooms, picking locks, and smashing open chests. The last part of this section includes rules for doing such things.

Movement

Movement is what gets you from encounter to encounter and from one place to another within an encounter. This section provides rules for movement between encounters, whereas "Movement and Position," page 282, explains movement during a combat encounter.

Often a DM can summarize your movement, without figuring out exact distances or travel times: "You travel for three days and reach the dungeon entrance." Even in a dungeon, particularly a large dungeon or a cave network, your DM can summarize movement between encounters: "After killing the guardian at the entrance to the ancient dwarven stronghold, you wander through miles of echoing corridors before you arrive at a chasm bridged by a narrow stone arch, which is broken in the middle."

Your DM might evocatively describe the terrain you pass over, but the encounters along the way are the focus of your adventures. Sometimes it's important, however, to know how long it takes to get from one encounter to another, whether the answer is in days, hours, or minutes. The rules to figure out travel time depend on two factors: your speed and the terrain you're moving over.

Speed

The Base Overland Speed table shows how much distance a character who has a given speed covers in a day, an hour, or a minute of travel. A group of travelers moves at the slowest traveler's pace, so most groups use the table's first row (to accommodate the group's dwarves and heavily armored members).

BASE OVERLAND SPEED

Speed	Per Day	Per Hour	Per Minute
5	25 miles	2½ miles	250 ft.
6	30 miles	3 miles	300 ft.
7	35 miles	3½ miles	350 ft.

Speed per Day: Player characters can sustain a normal walking pace for 10 hours of travel a day without tiring out. The *Dungeon Master's Guide* explains what happens if you travel for more than 10 hours. Ordinary people can't walk for more than 6 or 8 hours in a day, so their travel rate is more like 15 to 25 miles per day.

Speed per Hour: Your speed per hour on the Base Exploration Speed table assumes a walking pace. You can move overland at twice this speed, but it's hard to sustain that pace. Rules in the *Dungeon Master's Guide* cover what happens if you push yourself too hard.

Speed per Minute: Your speed per minute on the Base Exploration Speed table assumes a walking pace and is intended for travel that takes less than an hour. If you're in a hurry, you can move overland at twice this speed.

Terrain

The distances on the Base Exploration Speed table assume relatively clear terrain—roads, open plains, or dungeon corridors that aren't choked with rubble. Other terrain does slow your progress. How much? That depends on the prevalence of difficult terrain in the area.

TERRAIN AND MOVEMENT

Distance Multiplier	Terrain
× ½	**Mostly difficult terrain: dense forests, mountains, deep swamps, rubble-choked ruins**
× ¾	**Extensive difficult terrain: forests, hills, swamps, crumbling ruins, natural caves, cities**
× 1	**Very little difficult terrain: open fields, plains, roads, clear dungeon corridors**

To figure out how far you travel per day, hour, or minute, multiply the distance you travel, as shown on the Base Exploration Speed table, by the distance multiplier shown on the Terrain and Movement table.

Flying creatures, when airborne, ignore distance multipliers for difficult terrain.

Mounts and Vehicles

When traveling long distances outdoors, you can use mounts or vehicles to increase your speed, your carrying capacity, or both. This table shows the effective speed of common mounts and vehicles. The table assumes a day of travel is 10 hours long, although sailing ships can sail 24 hours a day if properly crewed. For mount and vehicle carrying capacities, see page 222.

MOUNTS AND VEHICLES

Mount/Vehicle	Speed	Per Day	Per Hour
Riding horse	10	50 miles	5 miles
Warhorse	8	40 miles	4 miles
Cart or wagon	5	25 miles	2½ miles
Rowboat	3	15 miles	1½ miles
Downstream	4-6	20-30 miles	2-3 miles
Sailing ship	7	84 miles	3½ miles

Marching Order

It's a good idea for your group to establish a standard marching order, the way your characters are normally arranged when traveling. You can change your marching order any time, but having it set out before you get into an encounter lets the DM know exactly where everyone is when the encounter begins.

You can record your marching order any way you like: Write it on paper or a whiteboard, or arrange your miniatures on the battle grid to show your relative position. You can also create different marching orders for different situations—one marching order for corridors that are 2 squares wide and one for open areas, for example.

Danger in a dungeon environment often comes from the front, so it's a good idea to put a defender at the front of the marching order, protecting your controllers. Leaders make a good choice for the back of the group, since they're tough enough to withstand an attack if you get ambushed from behind. Strikers might scout ahead, but most prefer to stay nearer to the middle of a group.

Find a balance between clustering and spreading out. Staying close ensures that everyone can get to the action quickly when an encounter begins, but being bunched up leaves you vulnerable to area attacks from traps or ambushers.

Vision and Light

As you explore an adventure environment, the DM tells you what you see, from the obvious, such as the dimensions of a corridor, to the hidden, such as a pit trap.

You automatically see the obvious, but you use the Perception skill (page 186) to try to see the hidden. If you aren't actively searching an area, the DM determines whether you see hidden objects or creatures by using your passive Perception check (see page 186).

You can't see anything without some light. Many dungeons are illuminated, since only a few monsters are at home in utter darkness.

Dungeons are often illuminated by torches (sometimes magic torches that never stop burning), ceiling panels magically imbued with light, great oil-filled braziers or stone channels that burn continuously, or even globes of light that drift through the air.

Caverns might be filled with phosphorescent fungi or lichen, extraordinary mineral veins that glimmer in the dark, streams of glowing lava, or eerie auroralike veils of magic fire undulating high above a cavern floor.

Categories of Light

Light in the D&D game is defined in three categories: bright light, dim light, and darkness.

Bright Light: This category includes the light provided by most portable light sources, daylight, and the light cast by surrounding fires or lava. There are no special rules for vision in bright light.

Dim Light: This category includes the light provided by a candle or another dim light source, moonlight, indirect illumination (such as in a cave interior whose entrance is nearby or in a subterranean passageway that has narrow shafts extending to the surface), and the light cast by things such as phosphorescent fungi. Characters who have normal vision can't see well in dim light: Creatures in the area have concealment (page 281). Characters who have low-light vision or darkvision see normally in dim light.

Darkness: Darkness prevails outside on a moonless night or in rooms with no light sources. Characters who have normal vision or low-light vision can't see creatures or objects in darkness. Characters who have darkvision can see without penalty.

Light Sources

Even though many dungeons are adequately lit, the cautious adventurer brings a torch or a sunrod when venturing into a cavern or an underground complex.

Assuming nothing blocks your view, you can see most light sources from at least a quarter-mile away, and you can see exceptionally bright sources from up to a mile away.

Typical light sources are described on the following table.

Source	Radius	Brightness	Duration
Candle	2	dim	1 hour
Torch	5	bright	1 hour
Lantern	10	bright	8 hours/pint of oil
Campfire	10	bright	8 hours
Sunrod	20	bright	4 hours

Radius: A light source illuminates its square (your square if you're carrying the light source) and all squares within the range shown on the table. For example, if you carry a torch, bright light illuminates your square and 5 squares in every direction from you.

Brightness: Most light sources provide an area of bright light around them.

Duration: A light source lasts only so long because it requires a fuel source.

Interacting with the Environment

A typical adventure environment is full of dangers, surprises, and puzzles. A dungeon room might hold a complex bank of mysterious levers, a statue positioned over a trap door, a locked chest, or a teleportation circle. Sometimes you need to cut through a rope, break a chain, bash down a door, lift a portcullis, or smash the Golden Orb of Khadros the Reaver before the villain can use it.

Your character's interaction with the environment is often simple to resolve in the game. You tell the DM that you're moving the lever on the right, and the DM tells you what happens, if anything. The lever might be part of a fiendishly clever puzzle that requires you to pull several levers in the right order before the room completely fills with water, testing your ingenuity to the limit, but rules aren't necessary for pulling a lever. You simply tell the DM which lever you pull.

DCS TO BREAK OR BURST COMMON ITEMS

Strength Check to:	DC
Break down wooden door	16
Break down barred door	20
Break down iron door	25
Break down adamantine door	29
Force open wooden portcullis	23
Force open iron portcullis	28
Force open adamantine portcullis	33
Burst rope bonds	26
Burst iron chains	30
Burst adamantine chains	34
Smash wooden chest	19
Smash iron box	26
Smash adamantine box	32
Break through wooden wall (6 in. thick)	26
Break through masonry wall (1 ft. thick)	35
Break through hewn stone wall (3 ft. thick)	43

If a lever is rusted in position, though, you might need to force it. In such a situation, the DM might ask you to make an ability check (see page 26); no particular skill is involved, just a raw test of your Strength.

Similarly, the DM might call for Strength checks to see if you can break through a barred door or lift an adamantine portcullis. This table shows DCs to break through, break down, or break open some common dungeon features.

When you're a 1st-level character, breaking down a wooden door is a challenge well within reach if you have a high Strength score. When you reach epic levels, you can sometimes break through a masonry wall with a single blow, and with time, you can force your way through 3 feet of solid stone!

REST AND RECOVERY

Sooner or later, even the toughest adventurers need to rest. When you're not in an encounter, you can take one of two types of rest: a short rest or an extended rest.

About 5 minutes long, a short rest consists of stretching your muscles and catching your breath after an encounter. At least 6 hours long, an extended rest includes relaxation, sometimes a meal, and usually sleep.

SHORT REST

A short rest allows you to renew your encounter powers and spend healing surges to regain hit points.

SHORT REST

- **Duration:** A short rest is about 5 minutes long.
- **No Limit per Day:** You can take as many short rests per day as you want.
- **No Strenuous Activity:** You have to rest during a short rest. You can stand guard, sit in place, ride on a wagon or other vehicle, or do other tasks that don't require much exertion.
- **Renew Powers:** After a short rest, you renew your encounter powers, so they are available for your next encounter.
- **Spend Healing Surges:** After a short rest, you can spend as many healing surges as you want (see "Healing," page 293). If you run out of healing surges, you must take an extended rest to regain them.
- **Using Powers while You Rest:** If you use an encounter power (such as a healing power) during a short rest, you need another short rest to renew it so that you can use it again.
- **Interruptions:** If your short rest is interrupted, you need to rest another 5 minutes to get the benefits of a short rest.

EXTENDED REST

Once per day, you can gain the benefits of an extended rest.

EXTENDED REST

- **Duration:** An extended rest is at least 6 hours long.
- **Once per Day:** After you finish an extended rest, you have to wait 12 hours before you can begin another one.
- **No Strenuous Activity:** You normally sleep during an extended rest, though you don't have to. You can engage in light activity that doesn't require much exertion.
- **Regain Hit Points and Healing Surges:** At the end of an extended rest, you regain any hit points you have lost and any healing surges you have spent.
- **Powers:** At the end of an extended rest, you regain all your encounter powers and daily powers.
- **Action Points:** At the end of an extended rest, you lose any unspent action points, but you start fresh with 1 action point.
- **Interruptions:** If anything interrupts your extended rest, such as an attack, add the time spent dealing with the interruption to the total time you need to spend in the extended rest.

SLEEPING AND WAKING UP

You need at least 6 hours of sleep every day to keep functioning at your best. If, at the end of an extended rest, you haven't slept at least 6 hours in the last 24, you gain no benefit from that extended rest.

When you're asleep, you're unconscious (see "Conditions," page 277). You wake up if you take damage or if you make a successful Perception check (with a -5 penalty) to hear sounds of danger. An ally can wake you up by shaking you (a standard action) or by shouting (a free action).

KEEPING WATCH

Adventurers typically take turns keeping watch while their companions sleep. If five characters are in your group, each of you can take a turn on watch duty for 1½ hours and sleep for 6 hours, so that you spend a total of 7½ hours resting.

When it's your turn on watch, you actively look for signs of danger. When you start your shift on watch, make a Perception check. If something occurs during your watch, the DM uses the result of your Perception check to determine whether you notice.

If your entire group sleeps at the same time without setting a watch, the DM uses your individual passive Perception scores, counting the -5 penalty for being asleep, to determine whether you hear approaching danger and wake up.

CHAPTER 9

COMBAT

WHETHER IT'S a skirmish against a handful of orcs or an all-out battle with Orcus, Demon Prince of the Undead, combat is a staple of a DUNGEONS & DRAGONS adventure.

Combat encounters usually begin when you enter an area containing monsters. Sometimes the monsters enter your area instead—when werewolves attack your camp at night, for example—or you and the monsters stumble upon each other. You might meet on a road, or you might be exploring a dungeon when you run into a hostile patrol.

This chapter details the rules for combat.

✦ **The Combat Sequence:** The sequence of rounds and turns that make up a battle. Includes rules for rolling initiative.

✦ **Action Types:** The different types of actions that you can take on your turn and on other combatants' turns.

✦ **Taking Your Turn:** What to do at the start of your turn, during your turn, and at the end of your turn.

✦ **Attacks and Defenses:** How to choose a target, make an attack roll, deal damage, inflict various effects on your enemies, and make saving throws.

✦ **Attack Modifiers:** Various factors that affect attack rolls, including combat advantage, cover, and concealment.

✦ **Movement and Position:** Rules for speed, creature size, difficult terrain, obstacles, flanking, teleportation, and forced movement.

✦ **Actions in Combat:** The most common actions in a battle, from spending an action point to walking.

✦ **Healing:** Rules on hit points, healing surges, temporary hit points, and regeneration.

✦ **Death and Dying:** What happens when you drop to 0 hit points or fewer and how to escape death.

MATT CAVOTTA

THE COMBAT SEQUENCE

A typical combat encounter is a clash between two sides, a flurry of weapon swings, feints, parries, footwork, and spellcasting. The DUNGEONS & DRAGONS game organizes the chaos of combat into a cycle of rounds and turns.

ROUNDS AND TURNS

- **Round:** In a round, every combatant takes a turn. A round represents about 6 seconds in the game world.

- **Turn:** On your turn, you take actions: a standard action, a move action, a minor action, and any number of free actions, in any order you wish. See "Action Types," page 267, for what you can do with these different actions.

The actions in a combat encounter happen almost simultaneously in the game world, but to make combat manageable, combatants take turns acting–like taking turns in a board game. If your turn comes up before an enemy's, your actions take place before the enemy's actions do. The order of turns is determined at the beginning of a combat encounter, when combatants roll initiative.

A combat encounter follows these steps:

1. **Determine surprise.** The DM determines whether any combatants are surprised. If any combatants notice enemy combatants without being noticed in return, the aware combatants gain a surprise round.

2. **Establish positions.** The DM decides where the combatants are positioned on the battle grid. For example, if the PCs have just opened a door into a room, the DM might draw or arrange a depiction of the door and the room on the battle grid and then ask the players to arrange their miniatures near the door. Then the DM places miniatures that represent the monsters in the room.

3. **Roll initiative.** Everyone involved in a combat encounter rolls initiative, determining the order of combatants' turns. You roll initiative only at the beginning of a combat encounter.

4. **Take surprise round actions.** If any combatants gained a surprise round, they act in initiative order, each one taking a single action. (Surprised combatants take no actions during the surprise round.) The surprise round then ends, and the first regular round of combat begins.

5. **Take turns.** In initiative order, every combatant takes a turn, which includes various actions.

VISUALIZING THE ACTION

When a combat encounter starts, it's time to turn your attention to the **battle grid**. The combat rules assume that you use D&D *Dungeon Tiles*, a poster map, a gridded white board, or an erasable, gridded mat to show the area where a battle takes place. The rules also assume that you use D&D Miniatures to represent the adventurers and the enemies they face.

A combat encounter can be played without such visual representations, but there are good reasons to use them.

- **Position is everything.** With a battle grid, you can easily determine whether your character can see a monster, whether the monster has cover, and whether you flank the monster.

- **Combat can be complex.** With five player characters and a bunch of monsters involved, having miniatures on the table helps everyone remember which monsters are down, who's attacking whom, and where everyone is.

- **Terrain matters.** An exciting combat encounter includes terrain features and hazards that make the environment an important part of the encounter. If you want to claim the magic circle or avoid the cursed stone, you need to know where they are.

- **Imagination sometimes needs help.** Your DM might describe a room with bubbling lava, a narrow stone bridge, overlooking ledges, and acid pits. It's a great scene, but sometimes it's a little hard to imagine how all those pieces fit together. The battle grid helps by showing you exactly where all the elements of the scene are in relation to one another.

A 1-inch square on the battle grid represents a 5-foot square in the game world. So a dungeon room that is 40 feet by 50 feet would be 8 squares by 10 squares, which is a huge room but a good size for a busy combat encounter.

Characters and monsters are represented on the grid with miniature figures. If you don't have miniatures available, you can use coins, beads, or cardboard markers. You can use a creature in the game without having the exact miniature for it. If your character is a dwarf fighter with a mace, and all your dwarf miniatures have axes or swords (or you don't have any dwarf miniatures), choose the figure you like best. Just make sure that everyone at the table knows which object on the table stands for which combatant.

Miniatures for human-sized characters and monsters are a little more than 1 inch tall (about 32 millimeters) and stand on a base that fits in a 1-inch square. Plenty of creatures in the D&D game aren't human-sized, though. Larger creatures take up more space on the battle grid. For information about creature sizes on the battle grid, see "Creature Size and Space," page 282.

(Combatants can also take certain actions on one another's turns.)

6. **Begin the next round.** When every combatant has had a turn, the round ends. Begin the next round with the combatant who has the highest initiative.

7. **End the encounter.** Repeat steps 5 and 6 until the the combatants on one side are captured, fleeing, unconscious, or dead. The encounter ends when the other side then takes a short rest or an extended rest.

INITIATIVE

Before the first round of combat, you roll initiative. Rolling initiative is a Dexterity check and follows the normal rules for ability checks. The DM rolls initiative for your enemies.

Throughout a battle, combatants act in order, from highest initiative result to lowest. The order in which combatants take their turns is called the **initiative order.** The initiative order remains the same from round to round, although a combatant's position in the order can change after delaying (page 288) or readying an action (page 291).

ROLLING INITIATIVE

To determine a combat encounter's initiative order, roll initiative. To do so, make a Dexterity check.

Roll 1d20 and add the following:
+ One-half your level
+ Your Dexterity modifier
+ Any bonuses or penalties that apply

The result is your initiative for this encounter.

When combatants have the same initiative, the combatant with the higher initiative bonus (the total of one-half your level, your Dexterity modifier, and any bonuses) goes before the other. If their bonuses are the same, they can roll a die or flip a coin to break the tie.

THE SURPRISE ROUND

Some battles begin with a surprise round. A surprise round occurs if any combatants are unaware of enemy combatants' presence or hostile intentions. For example, if you fail your Perception check to notice concealed enemies, you're surprised. Or if supposed allies spring an attack and you failed your Insight check to notice the attackers' traitorous intentions, you're surprised. But if any of your allies made their Perception or Insight checks, they're not surprised.

When any combatants achieve surprise, they act in initiative order during the surprise round. Surprised combatants don't act at all during the surprise round.

THE SURPRISE ROUND

Two special rules apply to the surprise round.

+ **Limited Action:** If you get to act in the surprise round, you can take a standard action, a move action, or a minor action (see "Action Types"). You can also take free actions, but you can't spend action points. After every nonsurprised combatant has acted, the surprise round ends, and you can act normally in subsequent rounds.

+ **Surprised:** If you're surprised, you can't take any actions (not even free actions, immediate actions, or opportunity actions), and you grant combat advantage (page 279) to all attackers. As soon as the surprise round ends, you are no longer surprised.

ACTION TYPES

A combat round is made up of actions. Firing an arrow, casting a spell, running across a room, opening a door—each of these activities, along with many others, is considered an action. You use different action types to do different things. For example, most attack powers are standard actions, and moving from one spot on the battlefield to another is normally a move action. (A few powers don't require an action to use.) See "Actions in Combat," page 286, for rules on many specific actions.

THE MAIN ACTION TYPES

A typical combat round includes actions of four types: standard actions, move actions, minor actions, and free actions.

THE MAIN ACTION TYPES

+ **Standard Action:** Standard actions are the core of combat. You can normally take one standard action on your turn. *Examples:* most attack powers, charging an enemy, using your second wind.

+ **Move Action:** Move actions involve movement from one place to another. You can normally take them only on your turn. *Examples:* walking, shifting.

+ **Minor Action:** Minor actions are enabling actions, simple actions that usually lead to more exciting actions. You can normally take them only on your turn. *Examples:* pulling an item from a pouch or a sheath, opening a door or a treasure chest, picking up an item in your space or in an unoccupied square within reach.

+ **Free Action:** Free actions take almost no time or effort. You can take as many free actions as you want during your or another combatant's turn. The DM can restrict the number of free actions in a turn. *Examples:* speaking a few sentences, dropping a held item, letting go of a grabbed enemy.

TRIGGERED ACTION TYPES

Two action types–opportunity actions and immediate actions–require triggers. A **trigger** is an action, an event, or an effect that allows you to use a triggered action. (Some powers require a trigger but are free actions or aren't actions at all.)

OPPORTUNITY ACTION

✦ **Trigger:** Opportunity actions allow you to take an action in response to an enemy letting its guard down. The one type of opportunity action that every combatant can take is an opportunity attack (page 290). Opportunity attacks are triggered by an enemy leaving a square adjacent to you or by an adjacent enemy making a ranged attack or an area attack.

✦ **Once per Combatant's Turn:** You can take no more than one opportunity action on each other combatant's turn. You can't take an opportunity action on your own turn.

✦ **Interrupts Action:** An opportunity action interrupts the action that triggered it.

There are two kinds of immediate actions: interrupts and reactions. Certain rules govern all immediate actions, whether they're immediate interrupts or immediate reactions.

IMMEDIATE ACTION

✦ **Trigger:** Each immediate action—usually a power—defines its specific trigger. The one type of immediate action that every combatant can take is a readied action (see "Ready an Action," page 291).

✦ **Once per Round:** You can take only one immediate action per round, either an immediate interrupt or an immediate reaction. If you haven't taken an immediate action since the end of your last turn, you can take one when a trigger allows you to. You can't take an immediate action on your own turn.

✦ **Interrupt:** An immediate interrupt lets you jump in when a certain trigger condition arises, acting before the trigger resolves. If an interrupt invalidates a triggering action, that action is lost. For example, an enemy makes a melee attack against you, but you use a power that lets you shift away as an immediate interrupt. If your enemy can no longer reach you, the enemy's attack action is lost.

✦ **Reaction:** An immediate reaction lets you act in response to a trigger. The triggering action, event, or condition occurs and is completely resolved before you take your reaction, except that you can interrupt a creature's movement. If a creature triggers your immediate reaction while moving (by coming into range, for example), you take your action before the creature finishes moving but after it has moved at least 1 square.

An immediate reaction might interrupt other actions a combatant takes after its triggering action. For example, if a power lets you attack as an immediate reaction when an attack hits you, your action happens before the monster that hit you can take any other action. If a monster has a power that lets it make two attack rolls against you as a standard action, and the first one hits, you can use an immediate reaction before the next attack roll.

TAKING YOUR TURN

When your turn comes up in the initiative order, it's time for you to act. Your turn has three parts: the start of your turn, the actions on your turn, and the end of your turn.

THE START OF YOUR TURN

Before you act, you keep track of certain effects. The start of your turn always takes place, even if you're unconscious, and it takes no time in the game world.

THE START OF YOUR TURN

✦ **Ongoing Damage:** If you're suffering ongoing damage (page 278), you take the damage now.

✦ **Regeneration:** If you have regeneration (page 293), you regain hit points now.

✦ **Other Effects:** Deal with any other effects that occur at the start of your turn.

✦ **End Effects:** Some effects end automatically at the start of your turn.

✦ **No Actions:** You can't take any actions at the start of your turn.

SUBSTITUTING ACTIONS

On your turn, you can take a move action or a minor action instead of a standard action, and you can take a minor action instead of a move action. Because you can substitute actions in this way, the three actions you get on your turn (in addition to any free actions) can vary.

Option A
Standard action
Move action
Minor action

Option B
Standard action
Two minor actions

Option C
Two move actions
Minor action

Option D
Move action
Two minor actions

Option E
Three minor actions

ACTIONS ON YOUR TURN

During your turn, you can take a few actions. You decide what to do with each, considering how your actions can help you and your allies achieve victory. See "Action Types," above, for definitions of the different actions you can take.

ACTIONS ON YOUR TURN

✦ **Your Actions:** You get the following three actions on your turn:

> Standard action
>
> Move action
>
> Minor action

✦ **Free Actions:** You can take any number of free actions on your turn.

✦ **Any Order:** You can take your actions in any order you wish, and you can skip any of them.

✦ **Substitute Actions:** You can take a move action or a minor action instead of a standard action, and you can take a minor action instead of a move action.

✦ **Extra Action:** You can take an extra action by spending an action point (page 286).

✦ **Other Combatants' Actions:** Other combatants can take free actions on your turn, and you might take actions that trigger immediate actions or opportunity actions from other combatants.

THE END OF YOUR TURN

After you act, you keep track of any effects that stop at the end of your turn or that continue. The end of your turn always takes place, even if you're unconscious, and it takes no time in the game world.

THE END OF YOUR TURN

✦ **Saving Throws:** You now make a saving throw (page 279) against any effect on you that a save can end.

✦ **Check Actions Spent:** Some powers and effects can be sustained for multiple turns (see "Durations," page 278). Check that you spent the action required to sustain a power or an effect during your turn. If you didn't spend the action, the power or effect ends now.

✦ **End Effects:** Some effects end automatically at the end of your turn.

✦ **No Actions:** You can't take any actions at the end of your turn.

ACTIONS ON OTHER TURNS

Most of your actions take place on your turn. But you can take free actions on anyone's turn, and an event or another combatant's actions might provide an opportunity for you to take an immediate action or an opportunity action on someone else's turn. See "Action Types," above, for definitions of the different actions you can take.

ACTIONS ON OTHER TURNS

✦ **Opportunity Actions:** You can take one opportunity action on each other combatant's turn. An opportunity action must be triggered by an enemy's action.

✦ **Immediate Actions:** You can take one immediate action per round, either an immediate interrupt or an immediate reaction. An immediate action must be triggered by an event or an action on another combatant's turn.

✦ **Free Actions:** You can take any number of free actions on other combatants' turns.

ATTACKS AND DEFENSES

Battles in the D&D game are won through cleverly chosen attacks, able defenses, and luck. On a typical turn, you'll use your standard action to make an attack, whether you're a stalwart fighter, a wily rogue, or a devout cleric. And your defenses will be frequently tested by your foes' attacks.

When you attack, you make an attack roll to determine whether your attack hits your target. You roll a d20, add a bonus for whatever attack you're using, and compare the result to one of the target's four defenses: Armor Class, Fortitude, Reflex, or Will.

Each character has a number of attacks to choose from, including a basic attack (page 287). The exact attacks you have available depend on which powers you select for your character (see Chapter 4).

MAKING AN ATTACK

All attacks follow the same basic process:

1. Choose the attack you'll use. Each attack has an **attack type.**

2. Choose **targets** for the attack (page 272). Each target must be within **range** (page 273). Check whether you can **see** and **target** your enemies (page 273).

3. Make an **attack roll** (page 273).

4. Compare your attack roll to the target's **defense** (page 274) to determine whether you **hit** or **miss.**

5. Deal **damage** and apply other effects (page 276).

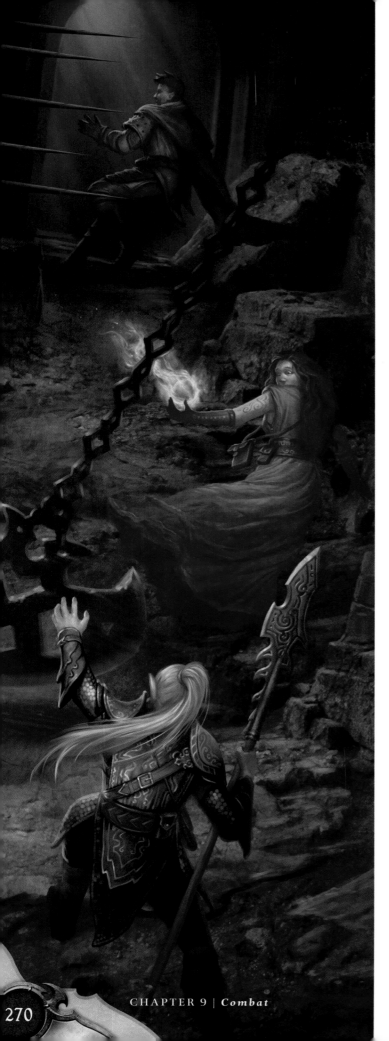

Attack Types

Attacks in the Dungeons & Dragons world take many forms. A fighter swings a greatsword at a foe. A ranger looses an arrow at a distant target. A dragon exhales a blast of fire. A wizard creates a burst of lightning. These examples illustrate the four attack types: melee, ranged, close, and area.

Melee Attack

A melee attack usually uses a weapon and targets one enemy within your melee reach (your reach is usually determined by the weapon you're wielding). Attacking with a longsword or a polearm is a melee attack. Some powers allow you to make multiple melee attacks, against either multiple enemies or a single enemy.

MELEE ATTACK

- ✦ **Targeted:** Melee attacks target individuals. A melee attack against multiple enemies consists of separate attacks, each with its own attack roll and damage roll. Melee attacks don't create areas of effect (page 272).
- ✦ **Range:** A melee attack's range usually equals your melee reach. (Sometimes a power specifies that it affects only adjacent targets, though, so even if you're using a reach weapon, you can't attack more distant targets with that power.)
- ✦ **Reach:** Most characters have a reach of 1 square. Certain powers, feats, and weapons can increase your reach.

Simply wielding a weapon in each hand doesn't allow you to make two attacks in a round. If you hold two melee weapons, you can use either one to make a melee attack.

Ranged Attack

A ranged attack is a strike against a distant target. A ranged attack usually targets one creature within its range. Shooting a bow or casting a *magic missile* is a ranged attack.

RANGED ATTACK

- ✦ **Targeted:** Ranged attacks target individuals. A ranged attack against multiple enemies consists of separate attacks, each with its own attack roll and damage roll. Ranged attacks don't create areas of effect (page 272).

  If you're using a projectile weapon to make a ranged attack against multiple targets, you need one piece of ammunition for each target, and if you're using thrown weapons, you need one for each target.

- **Range:** Some powers set a specific range ("Ranged 10") or allow you to attack any target you can see ("Ranged sight"). If you're using a weapon, the attack's range is the range of your weapon, as shown on the Ranged Weapons table in Chapter 7.

  Long Range: If you use a ranged weapon and your target is farther away than the weapon's normal range but within its long range, you take a -2 penalty to your attack roll. You can't hit a target beyond the weapon's long range. A ranged power that doesn't use a weapon has a normal range but no long range.

- **Provoke Opportunity Attacks:** If you use a ranged power while adjacent to an enemy, that enemy can make an opportunity attack against you.

CLOSE ATTACK

A close attack is an area of effect that comes directly from you; its origin square is within your space. Swinging your sword in an arc to hit every enemy next to you with one blow, creating a blast of fire from your hands, or causing radiant energy to burst from your holy symbol—these are all examples of close attacks.

Close attacks include two basic categories of powers: weapon attacks that damage multiple enemies with one swing, and powers created from energy that flows directly from your body or an object you carry.

CLOSE ATTACK

- **Area of Effect:** A close attack creates an area of effect, usually a blast or a burst. A close attack affects certain targets within its area of effect, which has a certain size. A close attack's area of effect and targets are specified in its power description (see Chapter 4).

- **Origin Square:** A close attack's area of effect defines the attack's origin square, which is the attack's starting point. A close burst uses your space as its origin square. A close blast uses a square within your space as its origin square. For a target to be affected by a close attack, there must be line of effect from the origin square to the target (see "Seeing and Targeting," page 273).

- **Multiple Attack Rolls but One Damage Roll:** When you make a close attack, you make a separate attack roll against each target in the area of effect, but you make a single damage roll that affects all the targets. A Large or larger creature hit by a close attack is affected only once by the attack, even if multiple squares of the creature's space are in the area of effect.

  If you're using a projectile weapon to make a close attack, you need one piece of ammunition for each target, and if you're using thrown weapons, you need one for each target.

AREA ATTACK

Area attacks are similar to close attacks, except that the origin square can be some distance away from you. An area attack's area of effect sets the shape of the attack and the targets it affects. A ball of fire that streaks across the battlefield and explodes is an example of an area attack. A magical wall of fog that springs from the ground to obscure a dungeon corridor is another example.

Area attacks include two categories of powers: projectiles that detonate in their origin squares and effects that appear far away from you and fill an area.

AREA ATTACK

- **Area of Effect:** An area attack creates an area of effect, usually a burst or a wall, within range. An area attack affects certain targets within its area of effect, which has a certain size. An area attack's area of effect, range, and targets are specified in its power description (see Chapter 4).

- **Origin Square:** You choose a square within an area attack's range as the attack's origin square, which is where you center or start the area of effect. You need line of effect from a square in your space to the origin square (see "Seeing and Targeting," page 273). For a target to be affected by an area attack, there needs to be line of effect from the origin square to the target. You don't have to be able to see the origin square or the target, and concealment (page 281) between the origin square and the target doesn't apply.

- **Multiple Attack Rolls but One Damage Roll:** When you make an area attack, you make a separate attack roll against each target in the area of effect, but you make a single damage roll that affects all the targets. A Large or larger creature hit by an area attack is affected only once by the attack, even if multiple squares of the creature's space are in the area of effect.

  If you're using a projectile weapon to make an area attack, you need one piece of ammunition for each target, and if you're using thrown weapons, you need one for each target.

- **Provoke Opportunity Attacks:** If you use an area power while adjacent to an enemy, that enemy can make an opportunity attack against you.

9

AREAS OF EFFECT

Most area attacks and close attacks have one of three areas of effect: a blast, a burst, or a wall.

AREAS OF EFFECT

✦ **Blast:** A blast fills an area adjacent to you that is a specified number of squares on a side. For example, the wizard power *thunderwave* is a blast 3, which means the power affects a 3-square-by-3-square area adjacent to you. The blast must be adjacent to its origin square, which is a square in your space. The origin square is not affected by the blast. A blast affects a target only if the target is in the blast's area and if there is line of effect from the origin square to the target.

✦ **Burst:** A burst starts in an origin square and extends in all directions to a specified number of squares from the origin square. For example, the cleric power *flame strike* is a burst 2 within 10 squares of you, which means the power originates in a square up to 10 squares away from you and affects the origin square and every square within 2 squares of it (a 5-square-by-5-square area). Unless a power description notes otherwise, a close burst you create does not affect you. However, an area burst you create does affect you. A burst affects a target only if there is line of effect from the burst's origin square to the target.

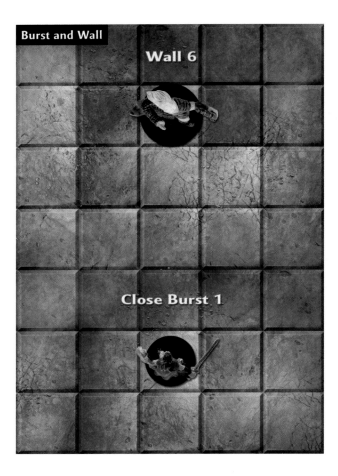

Burst and Wall

Wall 6

Close Burst 1

✦ **Wall:** A wall fills a specified number of contiguous squares within range, starting from an origin square. Each square of the wall must share a side—not just a corner—with at least one other square of the wall, but a square can share no more than two sides with other squares in the wall (this limitation does not apply when stacking squares on top of each other). You can shape the wall however you like within those limitations. A solid wall, such as a wall of ice, cannot be created in occupied squares.

CHOOSING TARGETS

If you want to use a power against an enemy, the enemy must be within the range of your power, and you have to be able to target the enemy. Many powers allow you to target multiple enemies. Each of these enemies must be an eligible target.

When you use a melee attack or a ranged attack, you can target a square instead of an enemy. This tactic is useful when an enemy has total concealment (page 281) and you have to guess its location.

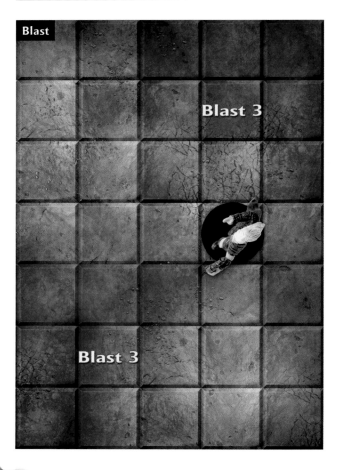

Blast

Blast 3

Blast 3

RANGE

The first step in choosing targets for an attack is to check the attack's range. Range is the distance from you to a target (or to the attack's origin square). The range of each power is noted in its description.

To determine the range between you and a target, count the number of squares between you, including at least one square that the target occupies. If a target's space is larger than 1 square, you can target that enemy if any square of its space is within range or within the area of effect of your attack.

Counting Distance: When counting the distance from one square to another, start counting from any adjacent square (even one that is diagonally adjacent but around a corner) and then count around solid obstacles that fill their squares. You must choose the most direct path to a target when counting squares for range or when determining the extent of an area of effect.

Adjacent Squares: Two squares are adjacent if a side or a corner of one touches a side or a corner of the other. Two creatures or objects are adjacent if one of them occupies a square adjacent to a square occupied by the other.

Nearest Creature or Square: To determine the nearest creature or square to you, count distance normally. When two or more squares or creatures are equally close, you can pick either one as the nearest.

Personal: When you use a power with a range of personal, you affect only yourself. Examples include creating magic armor on yourself or giving yourself the ability to fly.

SEEING AND TARGETING

Cluttered dungeon chambers, dense forests, or brooding ruins offer plenty of places for your enemies to hide. Figuring out whether you see and target a particular enemy from where you're standing is often important.

Line of Sight: The first question is what you can see in an encounter area—that is, what is in your line of sight.

To determine whether you can see a target, pick a corner of your space and trace an imaginary line from that corner to any part of the target's space. You can see the target if at least one line doesn't pass through or touch an object or an effect—such as a wall, a thick curtain, or a cloud of fog—that blocks your vision.

Even if you can see a target, objects and effects can still partially block your view. If you can see a target but at least one line passes through an obstruction, the target has cover or concealment

(page 280). You can see a gnoll archer crouching behind a rock wall, but the wall makes him more difficult to hit, because the wall gives him cover. You can see a goblin standing at the edge of a fog cloud, but the fog makes him a shadowy figure, giving him concealment.

Line of Effect: You can target a creature or a square if there's an unblocked path between it and you—that is, if you have line of effect to it. If every imaginary line you trace to a target passes through or touches a solid obstacle, you don't have line of effect to the target.

Fog, darkness, and other types of obscured squares block vision, but they don't block line of effect. If you hurl a fireball into a pitch-black room, you don't have to see your enemies for the fireball to hit them. In contrast, you can see through a transparent wall of magical force, but you don't have line of effect through it. You can see the snarling demon on the other side, but the wall blocks attacks.

You need line of effect to any target you attack and to any space in which you wish to create an effect. When you make an area attack, you need line of effect to the attack's origin square. To hit a target with the attack, there must be line of effect from the origin square to the target.

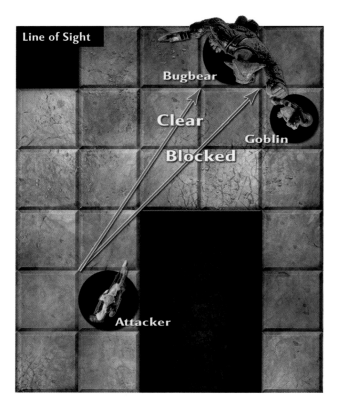

Line of Sight

Bugbear

Clear

Goblin

Blocked

Attacker

ATTACK ROLL

To determine whether an attack succeeds, you make an attack roll. You roll a d20 and add your base attack bonus for that power. A power's base attack bonus measures your accuracy with that attack and is the total of all modifiers that normally apply to it.

ATTACK ROLL

Roll 1d20 and add the following:

✦ The attack power's base attack bonus

✦ Situational attack modifiers (page 279) that apply

✦ Bonuses and penalties from powers affecting you

The power you use dictates which ability modifier adds to your base attack bonus and which of your target's defenses you compare the result against. For example:

Melee basic attack	**Strength vs. AC**
Ranged basic attack	**Dexterity vs. AC**
Stunning steel	**Strength vs. Fortitude**
Fireball	**Intelligence vs. Reflex**
Cause fear	**Wisdom vs. Will**

Your base attack bonus can change temporarily in certain circumstances, such as when you're affected by a power that gives you an attack bonus or penalty, when a feat or a magic item gives you a bonus in certain circumstances, or when attack modifiers apply (page 279).

ATTACK BONUSES

When you create your character, you should determine your base attack bonus for each power you know, including your basic attacks. Your base attack bonus for a power includes the following:

✦ One-half your level

✦ The ability score modifier used for the attack (the power you use specifies which ability)

In addition, any of the following factors might apply to an attack's base attack bonus:

✦ Your weapon's proficiency bonus (if you're using a weapon you're proficient with)

✦ Racial or feat bonuses

✦ An enhancement bonus (usually from a magic weapon or an implement)

✦ An item bonus

✦ A power bonus

✦ Untyped bonuses

Example: Melech, a 7th-level tiefling wizard, attempts to hit three enemies with *fireball*, an Intelligence vs. Reflex attack. His attack roll against each target gets a +10 bonus, which includes +3 for one-half his level, his +5 Intelligence modifier, the +1 feat bonus from Hellfire Blood, and the +1 enhancement bonus from his +1 *wand of witchfire*. He could add a +2 bonus from his Wand of Accuracy class feature against one of his targets and a +1 racial bonus against any bloodied targets from his Bloodhunt racial trait.

DEFENSES

Your ability to avoid injury and other ill effects is measured by four defenses: Armor Class, Fortitude, Reflex, and Will. Your defense scores rate how hard it is for an enemy to affect you with attacks.

Armor Class (AC) measures how hard it is for your enemies to land a significant blow on you with a weapon or a magical effect that works like a weapon. Some characters have a high AC because they are extremely quick or intelligent and able to dodge well, while other characters have a high AC because they wear heavy protective armor that is difficult to penetrate.

Fortitude measures the inherent toughness, mass, strength, and resilience of your physique. It is the key defense against attacks that include effects such as disease, poison, and forced movement.

Reflex measures your ability to predict attacks or to deflect or dodge an attack. It's useful against areas of effect such as dragon breath or a *fireball* spell.

Will is your defense against effects that daze, disorient, confuse, or overpower your mind. It measures your strength of will, self-discipline, and devotion.

DEFENSE SCORES

You determine your defense scores as follows.

- **Base Defense:** All defenses start with 10 + one-half your level.
- **Armor Class:** Add the armor bonus of the armor you wear and the shield bonus of the shield you carry. If you're wearing light armor or no armor, also add your Dexterity modifier or Intelligence modifier, whichever is higher.
- **Fortitude:** Add your Strength modifier or Constitution modifier, whichever is higher.
- **Reflex:** Add your Dexterity modifier or Intelligence modifier, whichever is higher. If you're using a shield, add its shield bonus.
- **Will:** Add your Wisdom modifier or Charisma modifier, whichever is higher.

Also add any of the following that apply:

- Racial or feat bonuses
- An enhancement bonus (usually from a neck slot magic item)
- An item bonus
- A power bonus
- Untyped bonuses

Your defenses can change temporarily in certain circumstances—for instance, if you're affected by a power or condition that increases or lowers your defense scores, or if a feat or a magic item gives you a bonus under certain circumstances.

Example: Brandis, a 23rd-level human fighter, has the following defenses.

AC 38 = 10 + 11 (one-half level) + 11 (armor bonus from warplate armor) + 2 (shield bonus from a heavy shield) + 4 (enhancement bonus from +4 *battleforged armor*).

Reflex 31 = 10 + 11 (one-half level) + 1 (racial bonus) + 2 (Dexterity modifier) + 2 (shield bonus from a heavy shield) + 5 (enhancement bonus from *cloak of resistance* +5).

Fortitude 35 = 10 + 11 (one-half level) + 1 (racial bonus) + 2 (fighter class) + 6 (Strength modifier) + 5 (enhancement bonus from *cloak of resistance* +5)

Will 31 = 10 + 11 (one-half level) + 1 (racial bonus) + 2 (Wisdom modifier) + 2 (feat bonus from Iron Will) + 5 (enhancement bonus from *cloak of resistance* +5)

When Brandis's warlord ally uses her *hallowed ground* power, he gains a +2 power bonus to all defenses when he stands within the power's zone.

BONUSES AND PENALTIES

Attack rolls, damage rolls, defenses, skill checks, and ability checks are often modified by bonuses and penalties.

Bonuses: There's one important rule for bonuses: Don't add together bonuses of the same type to the same roll or score. If you have two bonuses of the same type that apply to the same roll or score, use the higher bonus.

An **armor bonus** is granted by your armor. The bonus applies as long as you wear the armor.

An **enhancement bonus** augments your attack rolls and damage rolls or your defenses. You gain an enhancement bonus to AC when wearing magic armor, an enhancement bonus to attack rolls and damage rolls when wielding a magic weapon or implement, and an enhancement bonus to Fortitude, Reflex, and Will when wearing a magic item that occupies the neck item slot (see page 249). You can benefit from a magic weapon, magic armor, and a magic cloak at the same time, since their enhancement bonuses add to different rolls or scores.

A **feat bonus** is granted by a feat. The bonus applies as long as you have the feat.

An **item bonus** is granted by certain magic items. The bonus applies as long as you wear the item.

A **power bonus** derives from a power or a class feature. Power bonuses are usually temporary or situational.

The **proficiency bonus** gained from proficiency with a weapon applies to attack rolls made using that weapon. You gain the proficiency bonus only when using powers that have the weapon keyword.

A **racial bonus** is granted by your race. An elf's Group Awareness trait, for example, grants non-elf allies within 5 squares a +1 racial bonus to Perception checks.

A **shield bonus** is granted by your shield. Shield bonuses apply to AC and Reflex defense. Powers, feats, or magic items might provide a shield bonus; these typically help only characters who aren't using shields.

Some bonuses are **untyped** ("a +2 bonus"). Most of these are situational and add together with other bonus you have, including other untyped bonuses.

Penalties: Unlike bonuses, penalties don't have types. Penalties add together, unless they're from the same power. If two monsters attack you with the same power and each causes you to take a penalty to a particular roll or score, you don't add the penalties together; you take the worst penalty.

A penalty might be effectively canceled by a bonus and vice versa. If you gain a +2 bonus to attack rolls and take a –2 penalty to attack rolls at the same time, you end up with a +0 modifier.

ATTACK RESULTS

You resolve an attack by comparing the total of your attack roll (1d20 + base attack bonus + attack modifiers) to the appropriate defense score. If your roll is higher than or equal to the defense score, you hit. Otherwise, you miss.

When you hit, you usually deal damage and sometimes produce some other effect. When you're using a power, the power description tells you what happens when you hit. Some descriptions also say what happens when you miss or when you score a critical hit.

ATTACK RESULTS

When you make an attack, compare your attack roll to the appropriate defense score of the target.

- ✦ **Hit:** If the attack roll is higher than or equal to the defense score, the attack hits and deals damage, has a special effect, or both.
  Automatic Hit: If you roll a natural 20 (the die shows a 20), your attack automatically hits.
  Critical Hit: If you roll a natural 20 (the die shows a 20), your attack might be a critical hit (page 278). A critical hit deals maximum damage, and some powers and magic items have an extra effect on a critical hit.
- ✦ **Miss:** If your attack roll is lower than the defense score, the attack misses. Usually, there's no effect. Some powers have an effect on a miss, such as dealing half damage.
  Automatic Miss: If you roll a natural 1 (the die shows a 1), your attack automatically misses.

DAMAGE

When you hit with an attack, you normally deal damage to your target, reducing the target's hit points. The damage you deal depends on the power you use for the attack. Most powers deal more damage than basic attacks do, and high-level powers generally deal more damage than low-level ones. If you use a weapon to make the attack, your weapon also affects your damage. If you use a greataxe to deliver a power, you deal more damage than if you use a dagger with the same power.

DAMAGE ROLLS

- ✦ Roll the damage indicated in the power description. If you're using a weapon for the attack, the damage is some multiple of your weapon damage dice.
- ✦ Add the ability modifier specified in the power description. Usually, this is the same ability modifier you used to determine your base attack bonus for the attack.

In addition, any of the following factors might apply to a damage roll:

- ✦ Racial or feat bonuses
- ✦ An enhancement bonus (usually from a magic weapon or an implement)
- ✦ An item bonus
- ✦ A power bonus
- ✦ Untyped bonuses

Weapon Damage Dice: A [W] in a damage expression stands for your weapon's damage dice. (The weapon tables on pages 218–219 show damage dice for all weapons.) The number before the [W] indicates the number of times you roll your weapon dice. If a power's damage is "2[W] + Strength modifier" and you use a dagger (1d4 damage), roll 2d4, then add your Strength modifier. If you use a heavy flail (2d6 damage) with the same power, roll 4d6, then add your Strength modifier.

Damage Types: In addition to normal damage, such as the damage a weapon or a monster's claws deal, powers and other effects can deal specific types of damage. For example, a hell hound's breath deals fire damage, a scorpion's sting deals poison damage, a mind flayer's telepathic blast deals psychic damage, and a wraith's touch deals necrotic damage.

When a power deals a specific type of damage, the power description specifies the type before the word "damage." A *fireball* deals 3d6 + Intelligence modifier fire damage, for example. All the damage it deals is fire damage. If a power doesn't specify a damage type, the damage has no type.

Example: Valenae. a 12th-level eladrin paladin, hits a foe with *thunder smite*. The attack deals 2[W] + Strength modifier thunder damage and knocks the target prone. The damage would be 2d8 (longsword's 1d8 × 2) + 7. The +7 bonus includes her +3 Strength modifier, a +2 feat bonus (Weapon Focus), and a +2 enhancement bonus (from her +2 *thundering longsword*).

If she scores a critical hit, she deals maximum damage of 23 points and adds 2d6 thunder damage from her *thundering longsword*. If she wanted to use her *thundering longword*'s encounter power on this hit, she would add 10 thunder damage and push 1.

RESISTANCE AND VULNERABILITY

Some creatures are resistant or vulnerable to certain types of damage. Some powers can grant you a similar resistance, or impose vulnerability on an enemy.

Resist: Resistance means you take less damage from a specific damage type. If you have resist 5 fire, then any time you take fire damage, you reduce that damage by 5. (An attack can't do less than 0 damage to you.)

Vulnerable: Being vulnerable to a damage type means you take extra damage from that damage type.

If you have vulnerable 5 fire, then any time you take fire damage, you take an additional 5 fire damage.

Some creatures have additional weaknesses tied to damage types. For example, if you use cold against an elemental made of magma, you might slow it or otherwise hinder its moves or attacks.

CONDITIONS

Powers, monsters, traps, and the environment can all cause conditions. A condition imposes a penalty, a vulnerability, a hindrance, or a combination of effects.

The Remove Affliction ritual (page 311) can be useful for eliminating a long-lasting condition that affects you.

BLINDED
+ You grant combat advantage.
+ You can't see any target (your targets have total concealment).
+ You take a -10 penalty to Perception checks.
+ You can't flank an enemy.

DAZED
+ You grant combat advantage.
+ You can take either a standard action, a move action, or a minor action on your turn (you can also take free actions). You can't take immediate actions or opportunity actions.
+ You can't flank an enemy.

DEAFENED
+ You can't hear anything.
+ You take a -10 penalty to Perception checks.

DOMINATED
+ You're dazed.
+ The dominating creature chooses your action. The only powers it can make you use are at-will powers.

DYING
+ You're unconscious.
+ You're at 0 or negative hit points.
+ You make a death saving throw every round.

HELPLESS
+ You grant combat advantage.
+ You can be the target of a coup de grace.
Note: Usually you're helpless because you're unconscious.

IMMOBILIZED
+ You can't move from your space, although you can teleport and can be forced to move by a pull, a push, or a slide.

MARKED
+ You take a -2 penalty to attack rolls for any attack that doesn't target the creature that marked you.

PETRIFIED
+ You have been turned to stone.
+ You can't take actions.

+ You gain resist 20 to all damage.
+ You are unaware of your surroundings.
+ You don't age.

PRONE
+ You grant combat advantage to enemies making melee attacks against you.
+ You get a +2 bonus to all defenses against ranged attacks from nonadjacent enemies.
+ You're lying on the ground. (If you're flying, you safely descend a distance equal to your fly speed. If you don't reach the ground, you fall.)
+ You take a -2 penalty to attack rolls.
+ You can drop prone as a minor action.

RESTRAINED
+ You grant combat advantage.
+ You're immobilized.
+ You can't be forced to move by a pull, a push, or a slide.
+ You take a -2 penalty to attack rolls.

SLOWED
+ Your speed becomes 2. This speed applies to all your movement modes, but it does not apply to teleportation or to a pull, a push, or a slide. You can't increase your speed above 2, and your speed doesn't increase if it was lower than 2. If you're slowed while moving, stop moving if you have already moved 2 or more squares.

STUNNED
+ You grant combat advantage.
+ You can't take actions.
+ You can't flank an enemy.

SURPRISED
+ You grant combat advantage.
+ You can't take actions, other than free actions.
+ You can't flank an enemy.

UNCONSCIOUS
+ You're helpless.
+ You take a -5 penalty to all defenses.
+ You can't take actions.
+ You fall prone, if possible.
+ You can't flank an enemy.

WEAKENED
+ Your attacks deal half damage. Ongoing damage you deal is not affected.

INSUBSTANTIAL

Some creatures, such as wailing ghosts, are insubstantial, and some powers can make you insubstantial. When you are insubstantial, you take half damage from any attack that deals damage to you. Ongoing damage is also halved.

ONGOING DAMAGE

Some powers deal extra damage on consecutive turns after the initial attack. An efreet might hit you with a burst of fire that sets you alight, dealing ongoing fire damage. When a snake's venom courses through your blood, it deals ongoing poison damage. A mummy's rotting touch deals ongoing necrotic damage, and a kruthik's corrosive spittle deals ongoing acid damage.

ONGOING DAMAGE

+ **Start of Your Turn:** You take the specified damage at the start of your turn. *Example:* If you're taking ongoing 5 fire damage, you take 5 points of fire damage at the start of your turn.

+ **Saving Throw:** Each round at the end of your turn, make a saving throw (page 279) against ongoing damage. If you succeed, you stop taking the ongoing damage.

+ **Different Types of Ongoing Damage:** If effects deal ongoing damage of different types, you take damage from each effect every round. You make a separate saving throw against each damage type.

+ **The Same Type of Ongoing Damage:** If effects deal ongoing damage of the same type, or if the damage has no type, only the higher number applies. *Example:* You're taking ongoing 5 damage (no type) when a power causes you to take ongoing 10 damage. You're now taking ongoing 10 damage, not 15.

CRITICAL HITS

When you roll a natural 20 and your total attack roll is high enough to hit your target's defense, you score a critical hit, also known as a crit.

CRITICAL HIT DAMAGE

+ **Natural 20:** If you roll a 20 on the die when making an attack roll, you score a critical hit if your total attack roll is high enough to hit your target's defense. If your attack roll is too low to score a critical hit, you still hit automatically.

+ **Precision:** Some class features and powers allow you to score a critical hit when you roll numbers other than 20 (only a natural 20 is an automatic hit).

+ **Maximum Damage:** Rather than roll damage, determine the maximum damage you can roll with your attack. This is your critical damage. (Attacks that don't deal damage still don't deal damage on a critical hit.)

+ **Extra Damage:** Magic weapons and implements, as well as high crit weapons, can increase the damage you deal when you score a critical hit. If this extra damage is a die roll, it's not automatically maximum damage; you add the result of the roll.

You automatically score a critical hit when you deal a coup de grace (page 288).

FORCING MOVEMENT

Some powers allow you to force your target to move in specific ways. Depending on the power, you can pull, push, or slide your target (see "Pull, Push, and Slide," page 285).

DURATIONS

Many powers take effect and then end; their effects are instantaneous, perhaps as brief as a single swing of your sword. Some powers last beyond your turn, however.

Unless otherwise noted, a power is instantaneous and has no lasting effect. The two types of durations are conditional and sustained.

DURATIONS

+ **Conditional Durations:** These effects last until a specified event occurs.

   Until the Start of Your Next Turn: The effect ends when your next turn starts.

   Until the End of Your Next Turn: The effect ends when your next turn ends.

   Until the End of the Encounter: The effect ends when you take a rest (short or extended) or after 5 minutes.

   Save Ends: The effect ends when the target makes a successful saving throw against it.

+ **Sustained Durations:** An effect that has a "sustain standard," a "sustain move," or a "sustain minor" duration lasts as long as you sustain it. Starting on the turn after you create an effect, you sustain the effect by taking the indicated action: a standard action, a move action, or a minor action. (You can sustain an effect once per turn.) Some effects do something, such as attack, when you sustain them. A power's description indicates what happens when you sustain it or let it lapse. At the end of your turn, if you haven't spent the required action to sustain the effect, the effect ends.

+ **Overlapping Durations:** If a target is affected by multiple powers that have the same effect but end at different times, the effect with the most time remaining applies.

Unless a description says otherwise, you can sustain a power with a sustained duration for as long as 5 minutes. However, you can't rest while sustaining a power, so you can't regain the use of your encounter powers or second wind until you stop sustaining a power.

Rituals (see Chapter 10) can create effects that last for hours, days, or years.

Saving Throws

When you're under a persistent effect or condition that can be ended by a save ("save ends"), you have a chance to escape the effect each round at the end of your turn. You do that by making a saving throw, which is a d20 roll unmodified by your level or ability modifiers. A successful saving throw is called a **save**.

SAVING THROWS

- **End of Turn:** At the end of your turn, you make a saving throw against each effect on you that a save can end. Roll a d20, with one of the following results:

  Lower than 10: Failure. The effect continues.

  10 or higher: Success. The effect ends.

- **Choose Order:** Whenever you make a saving throw, you choose which effect to roll against first, which effect to roll against second, and so on.

- **Modifiers:** A saving throw normally doesn't include modifiers; it's just a d20 roll. Some powers, feats, or racial traits might modify a saving throw.

A saving throw gives you slightly better than even odds to shake off an effect. Most of the time, you can't improve the odds, and your chance of success doesn't have anything to do with an effect's severity. What makes a giant snake's poison worse than a normal snake's is not how hard it is to shake off the poison's effects, but how easily it affects you in the first place (its attack bonus) and what it does to you while it remains in your system (its ongoing damage or other effect).

Each round, at the end of your turn, you roll a saving throw against each effect on you. Sometimes an effect is a single condition or one type of ongoing damage (page 278). Another kind of effect is like an imp's hellish poison, which includes both ongoing poison damage and a -2 penalty to Will defense. You don't make separate saving throws against the ongoing poison damage and the Will defense penalty; you make a single saving throw each round against the hellish poison itself.

Some powers create effects that require multiple saving throws to fully escape. These powers include aftereffects that apply after you save against the initial effect. For example, a power might knock you unconscious until you save but have an aftereffect that slows you. Once you save against the unconscious condition, you need to save against the slowed condition before you've fully escaped the power's effects.

An aftereffect doesn't begin until after you've rolled all your saving throws at the end of your turn. This means you can't make a saving throw against an aftereffect at the end of the same turn when you saved against the initial effect.

ATTACK MODIFIERS

Combat rarely consists of foes standing toe to toe and bashing each other. Movement and position are key; if one archer can fire from behind a tree at an enemy archer out in the open, the one using the tree for cover enjoys an advantage. Similarly, the use of magic or special abilities often creates opportunities you can exploit. If your wizard ally turns you invisible, you can easily evade your enemies, but if an enemy wizard stuns you with a spell, you drop your guard, and your enemies can easily gang up on you.

Temporary advantages and disadvantages in combat are reflected in a set of common attack modifiers. An attack modifier is a bonus or a penalty that applies to your attack roll. Add the modifier to your base attack bonus when you make an attack.

ATTACK MODIFIERS

Circumstance	Modifier
Combat advantage against target	+2
Attacker is prone	-2
Attacker is restrained	-2
Target has cover	-2
Target has superior cover	-5
Target has concealment (melee and ranged only)	-2
Target has total concealment (melee and ranged only)	-5
Long range (weapon attacks only)	-2
Charge attack (melee only)	+1

Combat Advantage

One of the most common attack modifiers is combat advantage. Combat advantage represents a situation in which the defender can't give full attention to defense. The defender is pressed by multiple enemies at the same time, stunned, distracted, or otherwise caught off guard. When you have combat advantage against a target, you gain a +2 bonus to your attack rolls against that target.

Some powers require you to have combat advantage in order to use them against a target, and other powers have a better effect against a target you have combat advantage against. If a feat, power, or other ability grants you a benefit when you have combat advantage, that benefit applies only against a target you have combat advantage against.

COMBAT ADVANTAGE

- **+2 Bonus to Attack Rolls:** You gain a +2 bonus to your attack roll when you have combat advantage against the target of your attack.

- **Able to See Target:** You must be able to see a target to gain combat advantage against it.

The following situations give an attacker combat advantage against a defender.

When a defender is . . .
    Balancing (page 180)
    Blinded (page 277)
    Climbing (page 182)
    Dazed (page 277)
    Flanked by the attacker (page 285)
    Helpless (page 277)
    Prone (melee attacks only) (page 277)
    Restrained (page 277)
    Running (page 291)
    Squeezing (page 292)
    Stunned (page 277)
    Surprised (page 277)
    Unable to see the attacker (page 281)
    Unaware of you (page 188)
    Unconscious (page 277)

Once per encounter, you can try to gain combat advantage against a target by making a Bluff check (page 183).

Combat advantage is relative. In any given pair of combatants, either, both, or neither might have combat advantage against the other. It's possible for a single creature to be adjacent to one enemy that has combat advantage against it and a second enemy that does not.

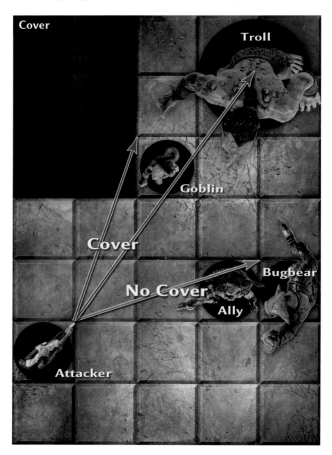

COVER AND CONCEALMENT

Many types of terrain offer you places to hide or obstructions you can duck behind in order to avoid attacks. Solid obstructions that can physically deflect or stop objects are considered cover. Objects or effects that don't physically impede an attack but instead hide you from an enemy's view are considered concealment.

COVER

Enemies behind a low wall, around a corner, or behind a tree enjoy some amount of cover; you can't hit them as easily as you normally could.

COVER

✦ **Cover (-2 Penalty to Attack Rolls):** The target is around a corner or protected by terrain. For example, the target might be in the same square as a small tree, obscured by a small pillar or a large piece of furniture, or behind a low wall.

✦ **Superior Cover (-5 Penalty to Attack Rolls):** The target is protected by a significant terrain advantage, such as when fighting from behind a window, a portcullis, a grate, or an arrow slit.

✦ **Area Attacks and Close Attacks:** When you make an area attack or a close attack, a target has cover if there is an obstruction between the origin square and the target, not between you and the target.

✦ **Reach:** If a creature that has reach attacks through terrain that would grant cover if the target were in it, the target has cover. For example, even if you're not in the same square as a small pillar, it gives you cover from the attack of an ogre on the other side of the pillar.

✦ **Creatures and Cover:** When you make a ranged attack against an enemy and other enemies are in the way, your target has cover. Your allies never grant cover to your enemies, and neither allies nor enemies give cover against melee, close, or area attacks.

✦ **Determining Cover:** To determine if a target has cover, choose a corner of a square you occupy (or a corner of your attack's origin square) and trace imaginary lines from that corner to every corner of any one square the target occupies. If one or two of those lines are blocked by an obstacle or an enemy, the target has cover. (A line isn't blocked if it runs along the edge of an obstacle's or an enemy's square.) If three or four of those lines are blocked but you have line of effect, the target has superior cover.

CONCEALMENT

If you can't get a good look at your target, it has concealment from you, which means your attack rolls take a penalty against that target. You might be fighting in an area of dim light (see "Vision and Light," page 262), in an area filled with smoke or mist, or among terrain features that get in the way of your vision, such as foliage.

OBSCURED SQUARES

✦ **Lightly Obscured:** Squares of dim light, foliage, fog, smoke, heavy falling snow, or rain are lightly obscured.

✦ **Heavily Obscured:** Squares of heavy fog, heavy smoke, or heavy foliage are heavily obscured.

✦ **Totally Obscured:** Squares of darkness are totally obscured.

Effects that cause concealment obscure vision without preventing attacks.

CONCEALMENT

✦ **Concealment (–2 Penalty to Attack Rolls):** The target is in a lightly obscured square or in a heavily obscured square but adjacent to you.

✦ **Total Concealment (–5 Penalty to Attack Rolls):** You can't see the target. The target is invisible, in a totally obscured square, or in a heavily obscured square and not adjacent to you.

✦ **Melee Attacks and Ranged Attacks Only:** Attack penalties from concealment apply only to the targets of melee or ranged attacks.

Part of the challenge of attacking a target you can't see is knowing where to direct your attack. You have to choose a square to attack, and the target might not

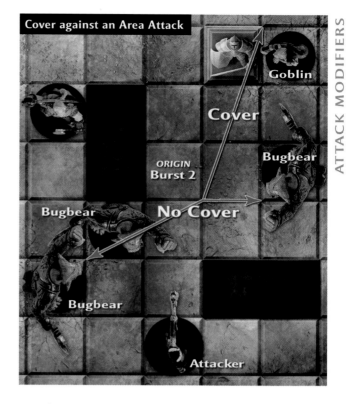

Cover against an Area Attack

even be in that square (see "Targeting What You Can't See," below).

A variety of powers and other effects can render you invisible, effectively giving you total concealment.

INVISIBLE

✦ You can't be seen by normal forms of vision.

✦ You have combat advantage against any enemy that can't see you.

✦ You don't provoke opportunity attacks from enemies that can't see you.

TARGETING WHAT YOU CAN'T SEE

If you're fighting a creature you can't see—when a creature is invisible, you're blinded, or you're fighting in darkness you can't see through—you have to target a square rather than the creature. You also have to figure out which square to attack. Here's how it works.

Invisible Creature Uses Stealth: At the end of a concealed creature's turn, it makes a Stealth check opposed by your passive Perception check. If you beat it, you know there's a creature present that you can't see, and you know the direction to its location. If you beat it by 10 or more, you know exactly what square the creature ended its turn in. The concealed creature also makes a Stealth check if it takes an immediate action or an opportunity action.

Make a Perception Check: On your turn, you can make an active Perception check as a minor action, comparing

the result to the concealed creature's last Stealth check. If you win, you know the direction to the creature's location, or its exact location if you beat it by 10 or more.

Pick a Square and Attack: Choose a square to attack, using whatever information you've gleaned so far about the target's location. Roll the attack normally (taking the –5 penalty for attacking a creature that has total concealment). If you pick the wrong square, your attack automatically misses, but only the DM knows whether you guessed the wrong square or your attack just missed.

Close or Area Attacks: You can make a close attack or an area attack that includes the square you think (or know) the concealed creature is in. Your attack roll doesn't take a penalty from the target's concealment.

During a pitched battle, heroes and monsters are in constant motion. The rogue skirts the melee, looking for a chance to set up a deadly flanking attack. The wizard keeps a distance from the enemy and tries to find a position to make the best use of area attacks, while goblin archers move to get clear shots with their bows. You can increase your effectiveness in battle by learning how to use movement and position to your advantage.

CREATURE SIZE AND SPACE

Each creature falls into one of six size categories, which correspond to the number of squares a creature occupies on the battle grid. A creature's space is an expression of the number of squares it occupies.

SPECIAL RULES FOR SIZE

Creatures smaller than Small or larger than Medium have special rules relating to position and attacking.

- ✦ **Tiny:** Four individual Tiny creatures can fit in a square, but a swarm of Tiny creatures might consist of hundreds, or even thousands, of them in a square. Most Tiny creatures can't attack, and if they can, they can't attack adjacent targets. They can attack only targets in the space they occupy. They can enter and end their turn in a larger creature's space.

- ✦ **Small:** Small creatures occupy the same amount of space as Medium creatures. However, Small creatures cannot use two-handed weapons. If a one-handed weapon can be used two-handed for extra damage, a Small creature must use it two-handed and doesn't extra damage by doing so.

- ✦ **Large, Huge, and Gargantuan:** Very large creatures take up more than 1 square. For example, an ogre takes up a space 2 squares by 2 squares. Most Large and larger creatures have melee reach greater than 1 square—that is, they can make melee attacks against creatures that aren't adjacent to them. A creature's basic body shape usually determines its reach—a Large ogre has a reach of 2, but a Large horse has a reach of 1.

Size	Example	Space	Reach
Tiny	Rat	1/2*	0
Small	Goblin	1	1
Medium	Human	1	1
Large	Troll	2 × 2	1-2
Huge	Death titan	3 × 3	2-3
Gargantuan	Ancient dragon	4 × 4 or larger	3-4

*Four individual Tiny creatures can fit in a square. More can fit if the creatures are a swarm.

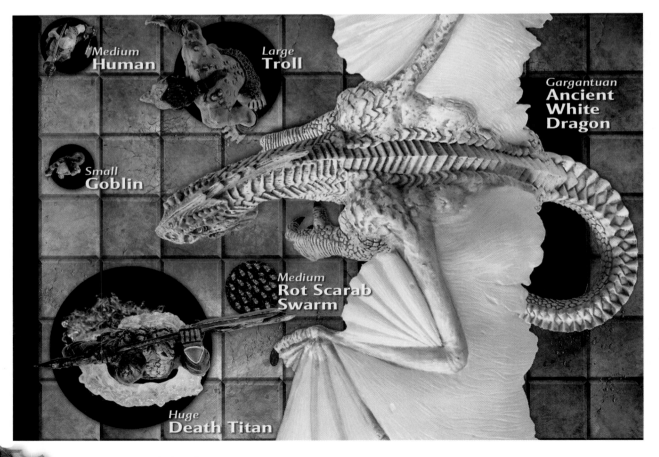

Medium **Human**

Large **Troll**

Gargantuan **Ancient White Dragon**

Small **Goblin**

Medium **Rot Scarab Swarm**

Huge **Death Titan**

SPEED

Your speed is measured in squares on the battle grid, with each 1-inch square representing a 5-foot square in the game world. A character who has a speed of 6 can move up to 6 squares (or 30 feet) on the battle grid by using a move action. Your speed is determined by your race and the armor you wear.

DETERMINING SPEED
Determine your speed as follows:
✦ Start with your race's speed.
✦ Take your armor's speed penalty, if applicable.
✦ Add any bonuses that apply.

Your speed is your base walking speed, in contrast to your speed while swimming or, if you're affected by a power, flying.

TACTICAL MOVEMENT

During your turn, you can use a move action to move some distance across the battlefield and still use a standard action to launch an attack. See "Actions in Combat," page 286, for various move actions you can use in combat. All move actions are governed by the following rules.

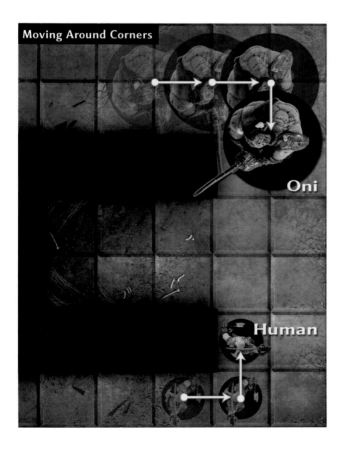
Moving Around Corners
Oni
Human

DIAGONAL MOVEMENT

Moving diagonally works the same as other movement, except you can't cross the corner of a wall or another obstacle that fills the corner between the square you're in and the square you want to move to. You can move diagonally past most creatures, since they don't completely fill their squares.

OCCUPIED SQUARES

A creature is considered to occupy the square or squares within its space.

MOVING THROUGH OCCUPIED SQUARES
✦ **Ally:** You can move through a square occupied by an ally.
✦ **Enemy:** You normally can't move through an enemy's space unless that enemy is helpless or two size categories larger or smaller than you.
    Moving into a nonhelpless enemy's space provokes an opportunity attack from that enemy, because you left a square adjacent to the enemy. (Some powers let you move through an enemy's square without provoking an opportunity attack.)
✦ **Ending Movement:** You can end your movement in an ally's square only if the ally is prone. You can end your movement in an enemy's square only if the enemy is helpless. However, Tiny creatures can end their movement in a larger creature's square. If you don't have enough movement remaining to reach a square you are allowed to be in, your move ends in the last square you could occupy.
✦ **Standing Up:** If you're prone and in the same square as another creature, see "Stand Up," page 292, for how to stand up.

TERRAIN AND OBSTACLES

Most battles don't take place in bare rooms or plains. Adventurers fight in boulder-strewn caverns, briar-choked forests, and steep staircases. Each battleground offers its own combination of cover, concealment, and poor footing.
    This section explains how terrain affects movement. For information about how it affects vision and defense, see "Cover and Concealment," page 280.

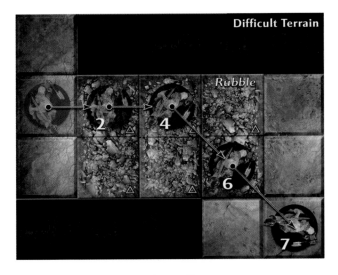

Difficult Terrain

Rubble

DIFFICULT TERRAIN

Rubble, undergrowth, shallow bogs, steep stairs, and all sorts of other impediments are difficult terrain that hampers movement.

- ✦ **Costs 1 Extra Square:** Each square of difficult terrain you enter costs 1 extra square of movement.
- ✦ **Large, Huge, and Gargantuan Creatures:** If such a creature enters two or more squares with different types of terrain, count that square of movement according to the most difficult terrain. Count only squares it is entering for the first time, not squares it already occupies.
- ✦ **Ending Movement:** If you don't have enough movement remaining to enter a square of difficult terrain, you can't enter it.
- ✦ **Flying:** Creatures are not hampered by difficult terrain when flying.
- ✦ **Terrain Walk:** Some creatures have a special ability to ignore difficult terrain in specific kinds of environments. For example, dryads have forest walk, which allows them to ignore difficult terrain in forests.

Because difficult terrain costs 1 extra square of movement to enter, you can't normally shift into a square of difficult terrain. On the other hand, if a power lets you shift 2, you can shift into a square of difficult terrain.

OBSTACLES

Like difficult terrain, obstacles can hamper movement.

- ✦ **Obstacles Filling Squares:** An obstacle such as a large tree, a pillar, or a floor-to-ceiling wall blocks a square entirely by completely filling it. You can't enter a square that is filled by an obstacle.
  Corners: When an obstacle fills a square, you can't move diagonally across the corner of that square (page 283).
- ✦ **Obstacles Between Squares:** Some obstacles run along the edges of squares instead of through squares. An obstacle such as a low wall between two squares makes moving from one square to the other just like entering a square of difficult terrain, even if the squares on each side of the wall are not difficult.

DOUBLE MOVE

On your turn, you can move twice if you take a move action instead of a standard action. If you take the same move action twice in a row—two walks, two runs, two shifts, two crawls—you're taking a double move.

DOUBLE MOVE

- ✦ **Same Move Action:** To double move, you have to take the same move action twice in a row on the same turn.
- ✦ **One Speed:** When you double move, add the speeds of the two move actions together and then move.
- ✦ **Occupied Squares:** When you double move, your first move action can end in an ally's space, because you're not stopping. Your second move action can't end in an ally's space, as normal.
- ✦ **Difficult Terrain:** When you double move, you can sometimes move over more squares of difficult terrain than normal, because you add the speeds of the two move actions together and then move. For example, if your speed is 5, you can enter only 2 squares of difficult terrain when you walk. If you double move by walking twice in a row, you can enter 5 squares of difficult terrain, not 4.

FALLING

Some kinds of terrain present a unique danger: a precipitous drop. When you fall at least 10 feet, you take damage.

FALLING

- ✦ **Falling Damage:** You take 1d10 damage for each 10 feet you fall.
  Fast Alternative: If you fall more than 50 feet, take 25 damage per 50 feet, plus 1d10 per 10 extra feet.
- ✦ **Prone:** You fall prone when you land, unless you take no damage from the fall.
- ✦ **Jumping Down:** If you are trained in Acrobatics, you can make a check to reduce the amount of damage you take from a fall. See page 181.
- ✦ **Catching Yourself:** If a power or a bull rush (page 287) forces you over a precipice or into a pit, you can immediately make a saving throw to avoid going over the edge. This saving throw works just like a normal saving throw, except you make it as soon as you reach the edge, not at the end of your turn.

Lower than 10: Failure. You fall over the edge.

10 or higher: Success. You fall prone at the edge, in the last square you occupied before you would have fallen. The forced movement ends.

✦ **Large, Huge, and Gargantuan Creatures:** If only part of a creature's space is over a pit or a precipice, the creature doesn't fall.

FLANKING

One of the simplest combat tactics is for you and an ally to move to flanking positions adjacent to an enemy.

FLANKING

✦ **Combat Advantage:** You have combat advantage (page 279) against an enemy you flank.

✦ **Opposite Sides:** To flank an enemy, you and an ally must be adjacent to the enemy and on opposite sides or corners of the enemy's space.

When in doubt about whether two characters flank an enemy, trace an imaginary line between the centers of the characters' squares. If the line passes through opposite sides or corners of the enemy's space, the enemy is flanked.

✦ **Must Be Able to Attack:** You and your ally must be able to attack the enemy, whether you're armed or unarmed. If there's no line of effect between your enemy and either you or your ally, you don't flank. If you're affected by an effect that prevents you from taking opportunity actions, you don't flank.

✦ **Large, Huge, and Gargantuan Creatures:** If a flanking creature's space takes up more than 1 square, the creature gains combat advantage if any square it occupies counts for flanking.

PULL, PUSH, AND SLIDE

Certain powers and effects allow you to pull, push, or slide a target.

PULL, PUSH, AND SLIDE

✦ **Pull:** When you pull a creature, each square you move it must bring it nearer to you.

✦ **Push:** When you push a creature, each square you move it must place it farther away from you.

✦ **Slide:** When you slide a creature, there's no restriction on the direction you can move it.

Whether you're pulling, pushing, or sliding a target, certain rules govern all forced movement.

FORCED MOVEMENT

✦ **Line of Effect:** You must have line of effect to any square you pull, push, or slide a creature into.

✦ **Distance in Squares:** The power you're using specifies how many squares you can move a target. You can choose to move the target fewer squares or not to move it at all. You can't move the target vertically.

✦ **Specific Destination:** Some powers don't specify a distance in squares but instead specify a destination, such as "adjacent" (a square adjacent to you).

✦ **No Opportunity Attacks:** Forced movement does not provoke opportunity attacks or other opportunity actions.

✦ **Ignore Difficult Terrain:** Forced movement isn't hindered by difficult terrain.

✦ **Not a Move:** Forced movement doesn't count against a target's ability to move on its turn. A target's speed is irrelevant to the distance you move it.

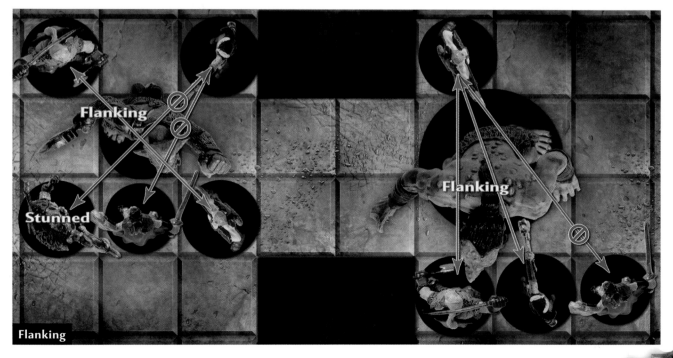

Flanking

Stunned

Flanking

Flanking

Flanking

- ✦ **Clear Path:** Forced movement can't move a target into a space it couldn't enter by walking. The target can't be forced into an obstacle or made to squeeze into a space.
- ✦ **Catching Yourself:** If you're forced over a precipice or a pit, you can try to catch yourself before you fall. See "Falling," page 284.
- ✦ **Swapping Places:** Some powers let you swap places with a target. You slide the target so that its space overlaps your space, and then you shift so your space includes at least one square that the target just left.

TELEPORTATION

Many powers and rituals allow you to teleport—to move instantaneously from one point to another. Unless a power or a ritual specifies otherwise, teleportation follows these rules.

TELEPORTATION
- ✦ **Line of Sight:** You have to be able to see your destination.
- ✦ **No Line of Effect:** You can teleport to a place you can see even if you don't have line of effect to it.
- ✦ **No Opportunity Attacks:** Your movement doesn't provoke opportunity attacks.
- ✦ **Destination:** Your destination must be a space you can occupy without squeezing.
- ✦ **Instantaneous:** When you teleport, you disappear from the space you occupy and immediately appear in a new space you choose. Creatures, objects, and terrain between you and your destination don't hinder your movement in any way.
- ✦ **Immobilized:** Being immobilized doesn't prevent you from teleporting. If you were immobilized because of a physical effect, such as a creature grabbing you, you can teleport away and are no longer immobilized or restrained, if applicable. If you were immobilized because of an effect on your mind or body, teleporting does not end that effect; you're still immobilized when you reach your destination.

PHASING

Some creatures, such as shadow snakes, have a special ability called phasing, and some powers allow you to phase. When you are phasing, you ignore difficult terrain, and you can move through obstacles and other creatures but must end your movement in an unoccupied space.

ACTIONS IN COMBAT

During your turn, you can choose from a wide variety of actions. Usually, the most important decision you make in combat is what to do with your standard action each turn. Do you use one of your powers? If so, which one? Or does the situation demand a different approach, such as using your standard action to drink a healing potion, try to call a parley and talk to your foes, or instead get a second move action this turn? This section describes how to perform the most common actions that are available to you on your turn.

The list isn't exhaustive—you can try to do anything you can imagine your character doing in the game world. The rules in this section cover the most common actions, and they can serve as a guide for figuring out what happens when you try something not in the rules.

ACTION POINTS

Once per encounter, you can spend an action point. When you spend an action point, it's gone, but you can earn more.

EARNING ACTION POINTS
- ✦ You start with 1 action point. (Monsters usually have no action points.)
- ✦ You gain 1 action point when you reach a milestone (page 259).
- ✦ After you take an extended rest (page 263), you lose any unspent action points, but you start fresh with 1 action point.

Most often, you spend an action point to take an extra action during your turn.

SPEND AN ACTION POINT: FREE ACTION
- ✦ **During Your Turn:** You can spend an action point only during your turn, but never during a surprise round.
- ✦ **Gain an Extra Action:** You gain an extra action this turn. You decide if the action is a standard action, a move action, or a minor action.
- ✦ **Once per Encounter:** After you spend an action point, you must take a short rest (page 263) before you can spend another. (Some monsters can spend more than 1 action point per encounter.)

If you spend an action point to take an extra action and are within sight of an allied warlord, the warlord's Commanding Presence grants you a benefit.

Instead of taking an extra action when you spend an action point, you can use a paragon path feature or a feat that requires an action point. Whatever you use an action point for, you can spend only 1 per encounter.

AID ANOTHER

You use your action to aid another character. You can aid an ally's attack roll against one enemy or grant an ally a bonus against an enemy's next attack. You can also use this action to aid someone else's skill check or ability check.

AID ANOTHER: STANDARD ACTION

✦ **Attack Roll:** Choose a target within your melee reach and make a melee basic attack vs. AC 10. If you succeed, deal no damage, but choose one ally. That ally gets a +2 bonus to his or her next attack roll against the target or to all defenses against the target's next attack. This bonus ends if not used by the end of your next turn.

✦ **Skill or Ability Check:** You can instead aid a skill check or an ability check made by an adjacent ally. Make a DC 10 skill check or ability check. If you succeed, you give a +2 bonus to your ally's next check using the same skill or ability. This bonus ends if not used by the end of the ally's next turn.

BASIC ATTACK

A basic attack is an at-will attack power that everyone possesses, regardless of class. The power comes in two forms: melee and ranged. You calculate the attack bonuses of a basic attack like those of any other attack power (page 274).

When a power allows you to make a basic attack, you can make either a melee basic attack or a ranged basic attack. If a power specifically calls for a melee basic attack or a ranged basic attack, you must use that type.

You use a melee basic attack to make an opportunity attack, and some powers or effects (especially warlord powers) give you the ability to make a basic attack when it isn't your turn.

Melee Basic Attack	Basic Attack

You resort to the simple attack you learned when you first picked up a melee weapon.

At-Will ✦ Weapon
Standard Action Melee weapon
Target: One creature
Attack: Strength vs. AC
Hit: 1[W] + Strength modifier damage.
Increase damage to 2[W] + Strength modifier at 21st level.
Special: You can use an unarmed attack as a weapon to make a melee basic attack.

Ranged Basic Attack	Basic Attack

You resort to the simple attack you learned when you first picked up a ranged weapon.

At-Will ✦ Weapon
Standard Action Ranged weapon
Target: One creature
Attack: Dexterity vs. AC
Hit: 1[W] + Dexterity modifier damage.
Increase damage to 2[W] + Dexterity modifier at 21st level.
Special: Weapons with the heavy thrown property (see page 216) use Strength instead of Dexterity for attack rolls and damage rolls.
Special: Warlocks can use *eldritch blast* as a ranged basic attack, and wizards can use *magic missile* as a ranged basic attack.

Like other ranged attacks, ranged basic attacks provoke opportunity attacks.

BULL RUSH

You try to push an enemy away. This tactic is useful for forcing an enemy out of a defensive position or into a dangerous one, such as in a pool of lava or over a cliff.

BULL RUSH: STANDARD ACTION

✦ **Target:** You can bull rush a target adjacent to you that is smaller than you, the same size category as you, or one category larger than you.

✦ **Strength Attack:** Make a Strength attack vs. Fortitude defense. Do not add any modifiers for the weapon you use.
  Hit: Push the target 1 square, and shift into the vacated space.

✦ **Impossible Push:** If there's no square you can push the target into, your bull rush has no effect.

CHARGE

You throw yourself into the fight, dashing forward and launching an attack.

CHARGE: STANDARD ACTION

✦ **Move and Attack:** Move your speed as part of the charge and make a melee basic attack or a bull rush at the end of your move.

✦ **+1 Bonus to the Attack Roll:** You gain a +1 bonus to the attack roll of your basic attack or bull rush.

✦ **Movement Requirements:** You must move at least 2 squares from your starting position, and you must move directly to the nearest square from which you can attack the enemy. You can't charge if the nearest square is occupied. Moving over difficult terrain costs extra squares of movement as normal.

- **Provoke Opportunity Attacks:** If you leave a square adjacent to an enemy, that enemy can make an opportunity attack against you.
- **No Further Actions:** After you resolve a charge attack, you can't take any further actions this turn, unless you spend an action point to take an extra action.

COUP DE GRACE

Sometimes, you have the opportunity to attack a foe who is completely defenseless. It's not chivalrous to do so, but it is viciously effective. This action is known as a coup de grace.

COUP DE GRACE: STANDARD ACTION

- **Helpless Target:** You can deliver a coup de grace against a helpless enemy adjacent to you. Use any attack power you could normally use against the enemy, including a basic attack.
  Hit: You score a critical hit.
- **Slaying the Target Outright:** If you deal damage greater than or equal to the target's bloodied value, the target dies.

CRAWL

When you are prone, you can crawl.

CRAWL: MOVE ACTION

- **Prone:** You must be prone to crawl.
- **Movement:** Move up to half your speed.
- **Provoke Opportunity Attacks:** If you leave a square adjacent to an enemy, that enemy can make an opportunity attack against you.

DELAY

You can choose to wait to take your turn until later in the round. You can wait until after your allies take actions so you can plan out tactics, or you can wait for enemies to move into range.

DELAY: NO ACTION

- **Delay Entire Turn:** You must delay your entire turn, so you can't delay if you've already taken an action on your turn. You also can't delay if you're dazed or if you're unable to take actions.

- **Coming Back into the Initiative Order:** After any other combatant has completed a turn, you can step back into the initiative order. Perform your actions as desired and adjust your initiative to your new position in the order.
- **Losing a Delayed Turn:** If you don't take your delayed turn before your initiative comes up, you lose the delayed turn and your initiative remains where it was.
- **Start of Your Turn:** At the moment you delay, carry out the start of your turn normally.
- **End of Your Turn:** You don't have a normal end of your turn (page 269). Instead, the things you do at the end of your turn happen at two separate times.
  End Beneficial Effects when You Delay: At the moment you delay, end effects that last until the end of your turn and that are beneficial to you or your allies. For example, if on your previous turn you stunned an enemy until the end of your next turn, the stunned condition ends. You can't prolong a beneficial effect by delaying.
  End Sustained Effects when You Delay: You can't sustain a power if you delay. At the moment you delay your action, the "check actions spent" part of the end of your turn occurs. Because you haven't spent an action to sustain any active powers, sustainable effects end.
  End Harmful Effects after You Act: After you return to the initiative order and take your actions, end effects that last until the end of your turn and that are harmful to you. For example, if an enemy stunned you until the end of your next turn, the stunned condition ends. You can't avoid a harmful effect by delaying.
  Make Saving Throws after You Act: After you return to the initiative order and take your actions, you make saving throws against effects on you.

ESCAPE

You attempt to escape from an enemy who has grabbed you (see "Grab"). Other immobilizing effects might let you make escape attempts.

ESCAPE: MOVE ACTION

- **Acrobatics or Athletics:** Make an Acrobatics check vs. Reflex or an Athletics check vs. Fortitude against the creature or effect that immobilized you.
- **Check:** Resolve your check.
  Success: You end the grab and can shift as part of this move action.
  Failure: You're still grabbed.

ACTIONS IN COMBAT

STANDARD ACTIONS

Action	Description
Administer a potion	Help an unconscious creature consume a potion
Aid another	Improve an ally's attack roll, defense, skill check, or ability check
Basic attack	Make a basic attack
Bull rush	Push a target 1 square and shift into the vacated space
Charge	Move and then make a melee basic attack or a bull rush
Coup de grace	Make a critical hit against a helpless enemy
Equip or stow a shield	Use a shield or put it away
Grab	Grab an enemy
Ready an action	Ready an action to perform when a specified trigger occurs
Second wind	Spend a healing surge and gain a bonus to defenses (once per encounter)
Total defense	Gain a +2 bonus to all your defenses until the start of your next turn

MOVE ACTIONS

Action	Description
Crawl	While prone, move up to half your speed
Escape	Escape a grab and shift
Run	Move up to your speed + 2; grant combat advantage until next turn
Stand up	Stand up from prone
Shift	Move 1 square without provoking opportunity attacks
Squeeze	Reduce your space by 1, move up to half your speed, and grant combat advantage
Walk	Move up to your speed

MINOR ACTIONS

Action	Description
Draw or sheathe a weapon	You can draw or sheathe a weapon
Drink a potion	Consume a potion
Drop prone	Drop down so that you are lying on the ground
Load a crossbow	Load a crossbow so that you can fire it
Open or close a door	Open or close a door or container that isn't locked or stuck
Pick up an item	Pick up an object in your space or in an unoccupied square within reach
Retrieve or stow an Item	Retrieve or stow an item on your person

IMMEDIATE ACTION

Action	Description
Readied action	Take your readied action when its trigger occurs

OPPORTUNITY ACTION

Action	Description
Opportunity attack	Make a melee basic attack against an enemy that provokes an opportunity attack

FREE ACTIONS

Action	Description
Drop held items	Drop any items you currently hold
End a grab	Let go of an enemy
Spend an action point	Spend an action point to take an extra action (once per encounter, not in a surprise round)
Talk	Speak a few sentences

NO ACTION

Action	Description
Delay	Put off your turn until later in the initiative order

GRAB

You seize a creature bodily and keep it from moving. The creature you grab can attempt to escape on its turn (see "Escape").

GRAB: STANDARD ACTION

✦ **Target:** You can attempt to grab a creature that is smaller than you, the same size category as you, or one category larger than you. The creature must be within your melee reach (don't count extra reach from a weapon).

✦ **Strength Attack:** Make a Strength attack vs. Reflex. Do not add any weapon modifiers. You must have at least one hand free to make a grab attempt.

   Hit: The enemy is immobilized until it escapes or you end the grab. Your enemy can attempt to escape on its turn.

✦ **Sustaining a Grab:** You sustain a grab as a minor action. You can end a grab as a free action.

✦ **Effects that End a Grab:** If you are affected by a condition that prevents you from taking opportunity actions (such as dazed, stunned, surprised, or unconscious), you immediately let go of a grabbed enemy. If you move away from the creature you're grabbing, you let go and the grab ends. If a pull, a push, or a slide moves you or the creature you're grabbing out of your reach, the grab ends.

To move a grabbed target, you must succeed on a Strength attack. However, helpless allies are treated as objects; you just pick them up and move them.

MOVE A GRABBED TARGET: STANDARD ACTION

✦ **Strength Attack:** Make a Strength attack vs. Fortitude. Do not add any weapon modifiers.

   Hit: Move up to half your speed and pull the grabbed target with you.

✦ **Opportunity Attacks:** If you pull the target, you and the target do not provoke opportunity attacks from each other, and the target doesn't provoke opportunity attacks from adjacent enemies. However, if you leave a square adjacent to an enemy, that enemy can make an opportunity attack against you.

OPPORTUNITY ATTACK

Combatants constantly watch for their enemies to drop their guard. When you're adjacent to an enemy, that enemy can't move past you or use a ranged power or an area power without putting itself in danger by allowing you to take an opportunity attack against it. The most common form of opportunity action is an opportunity attack–a melee basic attack against the creature that provokes it.

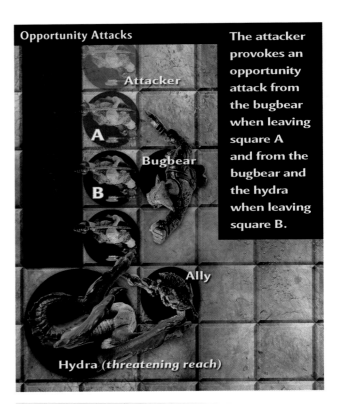

Opportunity Attacks The attacker provokes an opportunity attack from the bugbear when leaving square A and from the bugbear and the hydra when leaving square B.

Hydra *(threatening reach)*

OPPORTUNITY ATTACK: OPPORTUNITY ACTION

✦ **Melee Basic Attack:** An opportunity attack is a melee basic attack (page 287).

✦ **Moving Provokes:** If an enemy leaves a square adjacent to you, you can make an opportunity attack against that enemy. However, you can't make one if the enemy shifts or teleports or is forced to move away by a pull, a push, or a slide.

✦ **Ranged and Area Powers Provoke:** If an enemy adjacent to you uses a ranged power or an area power, you can make an opportunity attack against that enemy.

✦ **One per Combatant's Turn:** You can take only one opportunity action during another combatant's turn, but you can take any number during a round.

✦ **Able to Attack:** You can't make an opportunity attack unless you are able to make a melee basic attack and you can see your enemy.

✦ **Interrupts Target's Action:** An opportunity action takes place before the target finishes its action. After the opportunity attack, the creature resumes its action. If the target is reduced to 0 hit points or fewer by the opportunity attack, it can't finish its action because it's dead or dying.

✦ **Threatening Reach:** Some creatures have an ability called threatening reach. This lets them make opportunity attacks against nonadjacent enemies. If an enemy leaves a square that's within the creature's reach, or if an enemy anywhere within the creature's reach makes a ranged attack or an area attack, the creature can make an opportunity attack against that enemy.

READY AN ACTION

When you ready an action, you prepare to react to a creature's action or an event. Readying an action is a way of saying, "As soon as *x* happens, I'll do *y*." For instance, you could say, "As soon as the troll walks out from behind the corner, I'll use my *pinning strike* and interrupt its movement" or something like, "If the goblin attacks, I'll react with a *crushing blow*."

READY AN ACTION: STANDARD ACTION

✦ **Choose Action to Ready:** Choose the specific action you are readying (what attack you plan to use, for example) as well as your intended target. You can ready a standard action, a move action, or a minor action. Whichever action you choose, the act of readying it is a standard action.

✦ **Choose Trigger:** Choose the action that will trigger your readied action. When that action occurs, you can use your readied action. If the trigger doesn't occur or you choose to ignore it, you can't use your readied action, and you take your next turn as normal.

✦ **Immediate Reaction:** A readied action is an immediate reaction. It takes place after your enemy completes the action that triggers it.

✦ **Interrupting an Enemy:** If you want to use a readied action to attack before an enemy attacks, you should ready your action in response to the enemy's movement. That way your attack will be triggered by a portion of the enemy's move, and you will interrupt it and attack first. If you ready an action to be triggered by an enemy attack, your readied action will occur as a reaction to that attack, so you'll attack after the enemy.

  Note that an enemy might use a power that lets it move and then attack. If you readied an action to attack in response to that enemy's movement, your readied action interrupts the movement, and you can attack before the enemy does.

✦ **Reset Initiative:** After you resolve your readied action, move your place in the initiative order to directly before the creature or the event that triggered your readied action.

RUN

You can use an all-out sprint when you really need to cover ground fast. However, this is a dangerous tactic—you have to lower your guard to make your best speed, and you can't attack very well.

RUN: MOVE ACTION

✦ **Speed + 2:** Move up to your speed + 2. For example, if your speed is normally 6, you can move up to 8 squares when you run.

✦ **-5 Penalty to Attack Rolls:** You have a -5 penalty to attack rolls until the start of your next turn.

✦ **Grant Combat Advantage:** As soon as you begin running, you grant combat advantage to all enemies until the start of your next turn.

✦ **Provoke Opportunity Attacks:** If you leave a square adjacent to an enemy, that enemy can make an opportunity attack against you.

SECOND WIND

You can dig into your resolve and endurance to find an extra burst of vitality. In game terms, you spend a healing surge to regain some of your lost hit points, and you focus on defending yourself.

  Unless otherwise noted in the statistics block of a monster or a nonplayer character, this action is available only to player characters.

SECOND WIND: STANDARD ACTION

✦ **Spend a Healing Surge:** Spend a healing surge to regain hit points (see "Healing," page 293).

✦ **+2 Bonus to All Defenses:** You gain a +2 bonus to all defenses until the start of your next turn.

✦ **Once per Encounter:** You can use your second wind once per encounter and can use it again after you take a short rest or an extended rest. Some powers (either yours or another character's) allow you to spend healing surges without using your second wind.

SHIFT

Moving through a fierce battle is dangerous; you must be careful to avoid a misstep that gives your foe a chance to strike a telling blow. The way you move safely when enemies are nearby is to shift.

SHIFT: MOVE ACTION
- ✦ **Movement:** Move 1 square.
- ✦ **No Opportunity Attacks:** If you shift out of a square adjacent to an enemy, you don't provoke an opportunity attack.
- ✦ **Difficult Terrain:** Because each square of difficult terrain costs 1 extra square to enter, you can't normally shift into a square of difficult terrain, unless you're able to shift multiple squares or you're able to ignore the effects of difficult terrain.
- ✦ **Special Movement Modes:** You can't shift when using a form of movement that requires a skill check. For ex-ample, if you're climbing or swimming, you can't shift if you would need to make an Athletics check to use that kind of movement.

You might find it useful to first shift away from an adjacent enemy, then walk or run.

SQUEEZE

You can squeeze through an area that isn't as wide as the space you normally take up. Big creatures usually use this move action to fit into narrow corridors, but a Medium or a Small creature can use it to fit into a constrained space, such as a burrow.

SQUEEZE: MOVE ACTION
- ✦ **Smaller Space:** A Large, Huge, or Gargantuan creature reduces its space by 1. For example, a Large creature that squeezes has a space of 1 (1 square) instead of 2 (4 squares). A Huge creature's space changes from 3 (9 squares) to 2 (4 squares). When a Medium or smaller creature squeezes, the DM decides how narrow a space the creature can occupy. If an effect prevents a creature from leaving a square in order to squeeze, the creature cannot squeeze.
- ✦ **Half Speed:** As part of the same move action, move up to half your speed.
- ✦ **-5 Penalty to Attack Rolls:** You have a -5 penalty to attack rolls until you return to your normal space.
- ✦ **Grant Combat Advantage:** You grant combat advantage to all enemies until you return to your normal space.
- ✦ **Provoke Opportunity Attacks:** If squeezing causes any part of your space to leave a square adjacent to an enemy, that enemy can make an opportunity attack against you.

- ✦ **Ending a Squeeze:** You can end a squeeze as a free action. You return to your normal space. You have to occupy a space that includes the space you occupied when you stopped squeezing.

STAND UP

If you've been knocked prone, you need to take a move action to get back on your feet.

STAND UP: MOVE ACTION
- ✦ **Unoccupied Space:** If your space is not occupied by another creature, you stand up where you are.
- ✦ **Occupied Space:** If your space is occupied by another creature, you can shift 1 square, as part of this move action, to stand up in an adjacent unoccupied space. If your space and all adjacent squares are occupied by other creatures, you can't stand up.

TOTAL DEFENSE

Sometimes it's more important to stay alive than attack your foes, so you focus your attention on defense.

TOTAL DEFENSE: STANDARD ACTION
- ✦ **+2 Bonus to All Defenses:** You gain a +2 bonus to all defenses until the start of your next turn.

USE A POWER

The powers you know are among your most important tools in the game. Because of your at-will powers, you can potentially use a power every round.

USE A POWER: ACTION VARIES
- ✦ **Action:** Most powers require a standard action, but some require a move action, a minor action, a free action, or no action.

WALK

Walking is safe only when there are no enemies nearby. It's dangerous to walk through the middle of a pitched battle, since any enemy can take an opportunity attack as you pass by. The way you move safely when enemies are nearby is to shift instead of walk.

WALK: MOVE ACTION
- ✦ **Movement:** Move a number of squares up to your speed.
- ✦ **Provoke Opportunity Attacks:** If you leave a square adjacent to an enemy, that enemy can make an opportunity attack against you.

HEALING

Over the course of a battle, you take damage from attacks. **Hit points (hp)** measure your ability to stand up to punishment, turn deadly strikes into glancing blows, and stay on your feet throughout a battle. Hit points represent more than physical endurance. They represent your character's skill, luck, and resolve—all the factors that combine to help you stay alive in a combat situation.

When you create your character, you determine your **maximum hit points**. From this number, you derive your **bloodied** and **healing surge** values.

When you take damage, subtract that number from your current hit points. As long as your current hit point total is higher than 0, you can keep on fighting. When your current total drops to 0 or lower, however, you are dying.

Powers, abilities, and actions that restore hit points are known as **healing**. You might regain hit points through rest, heroic resolve, or magic. When you heal, add the number to your current hit points. You can heal up to your maximum hit point total, but you can't exceed it.

HIT POINTS

Damage reduces your hit points.

+ **Maximum Hit Points:** Your class, level, and Constitution score determine your maximum hit points. Your current hit points can't exceed this number.
+ **Bloodied Value:** You are bloodied when your current hit points drop to your bloodied value or lower. Your bloodied value is one-half your maximum hit points (rounded down). Certain powers and effects work only against a bloodied enemy or work better.
+ **Dying:** When your current hit points drop to 0 or lower, you fall unconscious and are dying.

HEALING SURGES

Most healing requires you to spend a healing surge. When you spend a healing surge, you restore lost hit points to your current hit point total. Once per encounter, you can use your second wind (page 291) to spend a healing surge and heal yourself. After a short rest, you can spend as many healing surges as you like outside combat. You can spend a limited number of healing surges per day. When you take an extended rest (page 263), your number of healing surges is replenished.

Some powers (either your own or those of another character) allow you to heal as if you had spent a healing surge. When you receive such healing, you don't actually spend a healing surge.

+ **Number of Healing Surges:** Your class and Constitution modifier determine how many healing surges you can use in a day.
+ **Healing Surge Value**: When you spend a healing surge, you regain one-quarter of your maximum hit points (rounded down). This number is called your healing surge value. You use it often, so note it on your character sheet.
+ **Monsters and NPCs:** As a general rule, monsters and nonplayer characters have a number of healing surges based on their tier: one healing surge at the heroic tier (1st–10th levels), two healing surges at the paragon tier (11th–20th levels), and three healing surges at the epic tier (21st–30th levels).

HEALING IN COMBAT

Even in a heated battle, you can heal. You can heal yourself by using your second wind (see page 291), an ally can use the Heal skill (see page 185) on you, and an ally can use a healing power on you.

When a power heals you, you don't have to take an action to spend a healing surge. Even if you're unconscious, the power uses your healing surge and restores hit points. And some healing powers restore hit points without requiring you to spend a healing surge.

REGENERATION

Regeneration is a special form of healing that restores a fixed number of hit points every round. Regeneration doesn't rely on healing surges.

REGENERATION

+ **Heal Each Turn:** If you have regeneration and at least 1 hit point, you regain a specified number of hit points at the start of your turn. If your current hit point total is 0 or lower, you do not regain hit points through regeneration.
+ **Limited by Maximum Hit Points:** Like most forms of healing, regeneration can't cause your current hit points to exceed your maximum hit points.
+ **Not Cumulative:** If you gain regeneration from more than one source, only the largest amount of regeneration applies.

TEMPORARY HIT POINTS

A variety of sources can grant you temporary hit points—small reservoirs of stamina that insulate you from losing actual hit points.

TEMPORARY HIT POINTS

+ **Not Real Hit Points:** Temporary hit points aren't real hit points. They're a layer of insulation that attacks have to get through before they start doing damage to you. Don't add temporary hit points to your current hit points (if your current hit points are 0, you still have 0 when you receive temporary hit points). Keep track of them as a separate pool of hit points.

✦ **Don't Count toward Maximum:** Temporary hit points don't count when you compare your current hit points to your maximum hit points, when you determine whether you're bloodied, or for other effects that depend on your current hit points.

✦ **Lose Temporary Hit Points First:** When you take damage, subtract it from your temporary hit points. If you take more damage than your temporary hit points, extra damage reduces your current hit points.

✦ **Don't Add Together:** If you get temporary hit points from different sources, use the higher value as your temporary hit point total instead of adding the values together.

✦ **Last until You Rest:** Your temporary hit points last until they're reduced to 0 by damage or until you take a rest.

DAMAGE AND HEALING IN ACTION

The 12th-level fighter Rieta is locked in combat with an otyugh, keeping it busy while her allies focus on the otyugh's mind flayer master. Rieta has 96 maximum hit points, which means she is bloodied when her current hit points drop to 48 or lower. She has ten healing surges, which restore 24 hit points apiece.

At the start of the fight, Rieta fell 20 feet into the otyugh's pit and took 16 damage. That brought her current hit point total to 80. Seeing her in danger, her warlord friend uses *bastion of defense* to grant her 8 temporary hit points. Her current hit points are still 80, but she uses the 8 temporary hit points to soak up damage before she starts subtracting hit points again.

The otyugh slams her with a tentacle, dealing 12 damage. Now she has no temporary hit points and 76 current hit points. On her turn, she strikes back.

Then the otyugh scores a critical hit, dealing 14 damage. She now has 62 hit points. On her turn, as insurance she uses *boundless endurance*, which grants her regeneration 4 when she's bloodied. The power is a minor action, so it doesn't interfere with her attack.

Then the otyugh scores another critical hit, dealing 14 damage. She's down to 48 hit points and is bloodied.

At the start of her next turn, she regains 4 hit points from the regeneration, bringing her to 52 hit points. As a standard action, she uses her second wind, which restores 24 hit points, bringing her to 76 hit points. Because using her second wind cost a healing surge, she has nine left for the day. She's not bloodied anymore, and she's ready to keep fighting.

DEATH AND DYING

In the unending exploration of the unknown and the fight against monsters, death looms as a constant danger.

DEATH AND DYING

✦ **Dying:** When your hit points drop to 0 or fewer, you fall unconscious and are dying. Any additional damage you take continues to reduce your current hit point total until your character dies.

✦ **Death Saving Throw:** When you are dying, you need to make a saving throw at the end of your turn each round. The result of your saving throw determines how close you are to death.

   Lower than 10: You slip one step closer to death. If you get this result three times before you take a rest, you die.

   10–19: No change.

   20 or higher: Spend a healing surge. When you do so, you are considered to have 0 hit points, and then your healing surge restores hit points as normal. You are no longer dying, and you are conscious but still prone. If you roll 20 or higher but have no healing surges left expressed as a negative number, your condition doesn't change.

✦ **Death:** When you take damage that reduces your current hit points to your bloodied value expressed as a negative number, your character dies.

Example: Anvil, a dwarf fighter, has a maximum hit point total of 53. He's bloodied at 26 hit points, dying at 0 hit points, and dead at -26 hit points. In a fight with an umber hulk, Anvil is reduced to 18 hit points. The monster later hits him for 33 points of damage. This reduces Anvil's current hit points to -15. He's now unconscious, dying, and only 11 points of damage away from death.

SKILLS IN COMBAT

In the heat of combat, remember to use all the tools at your disposal, including your skills. For example, you can use Athletics to jump over a chasm or leap across difficult terrain. Use skills such as Arcana and Nature to learn about your enemies' weaknesses. Clever use of Stealth can give you combat advantage. And plenty of threats that aren't monsters will give you opportunities to use Perception, Thievery, Endurance, and Acrobatics in the midst of combat. Watch for these opportunities, and be creative! Chapter 5 tells you more about how to use your skills.

Monsters and characters controlled by the Dungeon Master usually die when they reach 0 hit points, unless you choose to knock them out (see "Knocking Creatures Unconscious"). You generally don't need to stalk around the battlefield after a fight, making sure all your foes are dead.

Death is not necessarily the end in the DUNGEONS & DRAGONS game! Some powers and the Raise Dead ritual (page 311) can return a dead character to life.

Most monsters don't attack combatants who are dying; they focus on any characters still on their feet and posing a threat. But some particularly wicked monsters might attack a dying character on purpose (even using a coup de grace), and monsters make no effort to avoid including a dying character in an area attack or a close attack aimed at other characters who are still fighting.

KNOCKING CREATURES UNCONSCIOUS

When you reduce a creature to 0 hit points or fewer, you can choose to knock it unconscious rather than kill it. Until it regains hit points, the creature is unconscious but not dying. Any healing makes the creature conscious.

If the creature doesn't receive any healing, it is restored to 1 hit point and becomes conscious after a short rest.

HEALING THE DYING

When you are dying, any healing restores you to at least 1 hit point. If someone has stabilized you using the Heal skill but you receive no healing, you regain hit points after an extended rest.

HEALING A DYING CHARACTER

✦ **Regain Hit Points:** When you are dying and receive healing, you go to 0 hit points and then regain hit points from the healing effect. If the healing effect requires you to spend a healing surge but you have none left, you are restored to 1 hit point.

✦ **Become Conscious:** As soon as you have a current hit point total that's higher than 0, you become conscious and are no longer dying. (You are still prone until you take an action to stand up.)

Example: Anvil is at -15 hit points. His companion Terov, a cleric, uses *healing word* to help him. This assistance immediately raises Anvil's current hit points to 0 and allows him to spend a healing surge boosted by Terov's extra healing from *healing word* and the Healer's Lore class feature. The healing surge (13 hit points) plus Terov's boost (6 hit points) restores Anvil to consciousness and increases his current hit point total to 19.

9

CHAPTER 10

RITUALS

RITUALS ARE complex ceremonies that create magic effects. You don't memorize or prepare a ritual; a ritual is so long and complex that no one could ever commit the whole thing to memory. To perform a ritual, you need to read from a book or a scroll containing it.

A ritual book contains one or more rituals that you can use as often and as many times as you like, as long as you can spare the time and the components to perform the ritual.

A ritual scroll contains a single ritual, and you can perform the ritual from that scroll only once. After that, the magic contained in the scroll is expended, and the scroll turns to dust. Anyone can use a ritual scroll to perform the ritual it contains, as long as the appropriate components are expended.

This chapter explains the following:

- **Acquiring and Mastering a Ritual:** All about ritual books and scrolls, how you acquire them, and how you master a ritual.

- **Performing a Ritual:** How to perform a ritual, whether from a ritual book or scroll.

- **How to Read a Ritual:** The specifics on how to understand a ritual's description and effects.

- **Ritual Descriptions:** Descriptions of a wide variety of rituals, from binding rituals to warding rituals.

DAN SCOTT

Before you can perform a ritual, you need to acquire a ritual book that contains it and master the ritual, or you need to acquire a ritual scroll.

ACQUIRING A RITUAL BOOK

You can buy ritual books or find them as treasure. You can also make a copy of an existing ritual book, and some classes give you free access to a number of rituals. Wizards hold both their spells and their rituals in their spellbooks.

Buying a Ritual Book: You can buy a ritual book for 50 gp. A ritual book is 128 pages long. Each ritual takes up a number of pages equal to its level. The description of each ritual gives its market price, which is the gold piece cost for a book containing that ritual or the cost to add the new ritual to your existing ritual book or spellbook (if there's enough room in it).

Finding a Ritual Book: When you explore a ruined library, delve into a lost temple, or do away with a villainous wizard, you might discover tomes on arcane philosophy that contain rituals. Such ritual books are part of the treasure you acquire while adventuring.

Creating a Ritual Book: You can create a new ritual book by copying an existing one. You can't make a ritual book for a ritual that's higher level than you are, and you can't make a book by copying a ritual scroll, because the scroll doesn't contain the entire ritual.

When you create a ritual book or copy a ritual into an existing book, you don't just write a series of words on each page; you bind some of the ritual's magic into the book. Therefore, you need a book of the highest quality, exotic inks, and expensive components, with a total cost equal to the ritual's market price. You don't save any gold by creating a ritual book instead of buying it.

In addition to requiring gold, creating a ritual book or copying a ritual into an existing book takes time: 8 hours for a heroic tier ritual (1st–10th level), 16 hours for a paragon tier ritual (11th–20th level), and 24 hours for an epic tier ritual (21st–30th level).

If you copy a ritual that you haven't already mastered, the time you spend copying it enables you to master the ritual.

MASTERING A RITUAL

Owning a ritual book isn't enough to let you perform the ritual or rituals in it. You must first master a ritual by studying it for 8 uninterrupted hours. (If you gained a ritual by creating its book yourself or by obtaining it as a class feature, you have already mastered it.)

You must meet two requirements to master a ritual. You must have the Ritual Caster feat (clerics and wizards get this feat at 1st level), and your level must equal or exceed the ritual's level. If you meet those requirements and spend 8 hours studying a ritual, you can add it to your list of mastered rituals. As long as you have the ritual's book handy, you can perform a mastered ritual whenever you want.

There's no limit to the number of rituals you can master.

ACQUIRING A RITUAL SCROLL

A ritual scroll is a single page of parchment, vellum, or paper.

Buying a Ritual Scroll: Like a ritual book, a ritual scroll can be purchased for the given market price.

Finding a Ritual Scroll: Ritual scrolls can also be found as treasure.

Creating a Ritual Scroll: You can create a ritual scroll by transcribing a ritual you have mastered. Creating a ritual scroll takes twice the amount of time as creating a ritual book but costs the same price.

Limitation: Even though a ritual scroll lets you perform a ritual, you can neither master a ritual from a scroll nor copy a scroll into a ritual book. A scroll is a condensed version of a ritual, partially cast and primed so that it only takes up a single page.

PERFORMING A RITUAL

To perform a ritual that you have mastered, you spend a certain amount of time (specified in the ritual description) performing various actions appropriate to the ritual. The actions might include reading long passages out of the ritual book, scribing complex diagrams on the ground, burning special incense or sprinkling mystic reagents at appropriate times, or performing a long set of meticulous gestures. The specific activities required aren't described in most ritual descriptions; they're left to your imagination.

A ritual requires certain esoteric components, which you purchase before you perform the ritual and which are expended when the ritual is complete. Each ritual specifies the cost of the components you need.

If a ritual requires a skill check, the check usually determines the ritual's effectiveness. Even if the check result is low, a ritual usually succeeds, but if the result is high, you can usually achieve better effects.

ASSISTING IN A RITUAL

Unless a ritual specifies otherwise, up to four of your allies can help you perform a ritual. Everyone assisting you must be within 5 squares of you, and each assistant must actively participate in the ritual for the entire time required to complete it. Your assistants need neither the Ritual Caster feat nor knowledge of the specific ritual.

Your allies can assist you in two ways. First, if the ritual requires spending healing surges or some other resource, willing allies can contribute those resources. (Certain rituals might allow unwilling participants to pay those costs as well, but such rituals involve sacrifices to malevolent gods or demon lords and are not found in the ritual books of most player characters.)

Second, your allies can assist with the skill check you make to complete a ritual, using the normal rules for cooperating on another character's skill check (page 179).

INTERRUPTING A RITUAL

At any time before a ritual is completed, you can stop it and suffer no ill effect. You don't expend any components or pay any costs until a ritual is completed. You can't resume a ritual that was interrupted, however, so you do lose the time you spent on an interrupted ritual.

USING A RITUAL SCROLL

A ritual scroll holds one use of a particular ritual. You can perform a scroll's ritual even if you don't have the Ritual Caster feat, regardless of the level of the ritual. You still have to expend the components and supply any focus required by the ritual, and you can enlist your allies' assistance. Once you have finished performing the ritual on a scroll, the scroll turns to dust. If the ritual is interrupted, the scroll remains intact.

Time: Casting a ritual from a scroll takes half the time indicated in a ritual's description, since the creation of the scroll has primed the magic.

SELLING RITUAL BOOKS OR SCROLLS

You can sell ritual books or ritual scrolls for half the market price of the rituals they contain, assuming that the DM agrees that demand for a particular ritual exists. Although you can try to sell copies of a ritual you know, doing so offers no financial gain, and there is limited demand for ritual books or scrolls. You pay the full cost to create a scroll and can typically sell it for only half value. In addition, the number of people in the world who can afford to perform an expensive ritual and who can succeed on the necessary skill checks is small, and many of the NPCs who are skilled enough and wealthy enough to be potential customers already have collections of ritual books available to them.

HOW TO READ A RITUAL

Rituals are described in a consistent format, the elements of which are outlined below.

NAME AND FLAVOR TEXT

Beneath a ritual's name is a short passage of flavor text that tells what a ritual accomplishes, sometimes expressing that information in terms of what the ritual looks like or sounds like as it's being performed.

LEVEL

Each ritual has a level. You have to be that level or higher to perform the ritual from a book or to copy it.

CATEGORY

A ritual is classified in one or more categories, which describe the ritual's general nature and function. Each of the nine ritual categories is associated with one or more skills (given in parentheses in the following list).

Binding (Arcana or Religion): These rituals seek to lure, ensnare, control, or protect you from other beings, sometimes from other planes.

Creation (Arcana or Religion): These rituals are used to craft magic items and other special objects.

Deception (Arcana): Deception rituals cloak reality behind various facades.

Divination (Arcana, Nature, or Religion): These rituals provide advice, information, or guidance.

Exploration (Arcana, Nature, or Religion): A catch-all category, exploration rituals include a variety of effects useful in everyday adventuring.

Restoration (Heal): These rituals remove ill effects from the living or bring back the dead.

Scrying (Arcana): Scrying rituals let the caster spy on locations, objects, or creatures.

Travel (Arcana): Travel rituals transport characters from one place, or plane, to another.

Warding (Arcana): These rituals provide various forms of protection.

TIME

Performing a ritual takes the specified amount of time. Using a scroll cuts that time in half.

DURATION

This entry shows how long a ritual's effects last after the completion of the ritual. The effects of a ritual usually last longer than those of a power.

COMPONENT COST

This is the value of the components that must be expended to perform a ritual. A ritual's key skill determines the kind of components required.

- **Alchemical Reagents (Arcana):** Typically these are small vials full of powdered metals, rare earths, acids, salts, or extracts from creatures such as dragons or basilisks.
- **Mystic Salves (Heal):** Restoration rituals use mystic salves, dabbed or painted on the creatures to be healed. These salves come in small jars and include blessed oils and unguents made from rare spices.
- **Rare Herbs (Nature):** Rare herbs are usually collected and preserved during certain times of year, such as when the moon is full.
- **Sanctified Incense (Religion):** Sanctified incense is prepared during certain religious rites and is burned as a powder or a stick.
- **Residuum (Any):** The concentrated magical substance that results from performing the Disenchant Magic Item ritual, *residuum* can be used as a component for any ritual. You can't usually buy it on the open market; you acquire it by draining it out of magic items.

You can use the components associated with a key skill for any ritual that uses that skill. For example, if you stock up on alchemical reagents, you can use them when you perform any Arcana-based ritual. Ritual components are not interchangeable; you can't use alchemical reagents to perform a ritual requiring sanctified incense, for example. But you can use *residuum* for any ritual.

You can buy ritual components at some shops, your allies can provide them (sharing the cost of a ritual with you), or you might find them as treasure. However you acquire components, record their value on your character sheet. When you perform a ritual, mark off the ritual's cost from the appropriate components.

Some rituals' descriptions note other costs, including healing surges or a focus item (such as a mirror or a crystal ball for a scrying ritual). A focus item is not expended when you perform a ritual.

MARKET PRICE

This entry is the cost to purchase a ritual book containing the ritual or to copy a ritual into an existing ritual book. A scroll containing a ritual costs the same amount.

KEY SKILL

A ritual's key skill determines the type of components required to perform the ritual, and if a ritual requires a skill check, the key skill is used for the check. If this entry ends with "(no check)," then the ritual does not require a skill check.

If a ritual has more than one key skill, you choose which skill to use. Your choice determines both the components you use and the skill you use for any checks required by the ritual.

Unless a ritual's description says otherwise, you make your skill check when you finish performing a ritual. You can't take 10 on one of these skill checks.

EFFECTS

The text that follows the foregoing information describes what happens when you finish performing a ritual.

RITUAL DESCRIPTIONS

The ritual descriptions use the words "character" and "creature" interchangeably.

ANIMAL MESSENGER

You whisper to the animal before you, and it bounds off in the direction you point to carry your message.

Level: 1
Category: Exploration
Time: 10 minutes
Duration: Special
Component Cost: 10 gp
Market Price: 50 gp
Key Skill: Nature

You target a nonhostile Tiny animal, such as a sparrow, a raven, a fox, or a carp. The animal must remain within 5 squares of you for the time necessary to perform the ritual. Once the ritual is complete, you whisper a message of up to 25 words to the animal and name a recipient and a location. The animal bounds off toward the location, in search of the recipient. The animal avoids danger along its path. Upon finding the recipient, the animal approaches until it is adjacent to the recipient, and then your whisper issues from the animal's mouth, conveying the message. When the animal delivers its message or the ritual's duration ends, your influence ends and the animal reverts to its natural behavior.

Your Nature check determines how long the animal is affected by the ritual.

Nature Check Result	Duration
19 or lower	6 hours
20–29	12 hours
30–39	18 hours
40 or higher	24 hours

ARCANE LOCK

You bind a door so that intruders can't easily pass. The door is limned with amber light, which fades to a soft glow, marking it as impassible to anyone other than you and your allies.

Level: 4
Category: Warding
Time: 10 minutes
Duration: Permanent

Component Cost: 25 gp
Market Price: 150 gp
Key Skill: Arcana

You lock a door, a window, a gate, a portcullis, or some other means of ingress. You can open the door normally, but those who don't have your permission to use it find it locked.

Your Arcana check, with a +5 bonus, sets the DC for Thievery checks or Strength checks made to open the door.

When you perform the ritual, you can allow for certain other creatures or types of creatures to pass through the door normally, ignoring the ward's effect. You can choose any or all (or none) of the following options:

Password: You can set a verbal password. If uttered within 5 squares of the portal, the speaker can ignore the ward for the next minute.

Individuals: You can designate up to ten other specific individuals who can ignore the ward at all times.

Descriptions: You can describe one or more categories of creatures who can ignore the ward at all times, using specific, observable characteristics such as species, type, size, or equipment carried or worn.

The Arcane Lock remains until you dismiss it, the door is destroyed, or until the ward is defeated, such as by the Knock ritual or a successful Strength or Thievery check. Wherever you are, you instantly know if your Arcane Lock is defeated by one of these methods.

BREW POTION

Liquids brew and bubble, coalescing the raw substance of magic into a form you can drink.

Level: 5
Category: Creation
Time: 1 hour
Duration: Permanent until consumed

Component Cost: Special
Market Price: 75 gp
Key Skill: Arcana or Religion (no check)

You create a potion or an elixir (see page 255) of your level or lower. The ritual's component cost is equal to the price of the potion or the elixir you create.

RITUALS BY LEVEL

Lvl	Ritual	Key Skill
1	Animal Messenger	Nature
1	Comprehend Language	Arcana
1	Gentle Repose	Heal
1	Magic Mouth	Arcana
1	Make Whole	Arcana
1	Secret Page	Arcana
1	Silence	Arcana
1	Tenser's Floating Disk	Arcana
2	Endure Elements	Arcana or Nature
2	Eye of Alarm	Arcana
2	Water Walk	Nature
3	Detect Secret Doors	Arcana
4	Arcane Lock	Arcana
4	Enchant Magic Item	Arcana
4	Hand of Fate	Religion
4	Knock	Arcana
4	Travelers' Feast	Nature
5	Brew Potion	Arcana or Religion
5	Hallucinatory Item	Arcana
5	Magic Circle	Arcana
6	Commune with Nature	Nature
6	Cure Disease	Heal
6	Discern Lies	Religion
6	Disenchant Magic Item	Arcana
6	Leomund's Secret Chest	Arcana
6	Phantom Steed	Arcana
6	Sending	Arcana
6	Speak with Dead	Religion
8	Linked Portal	Arcana
8	Raise Dead	Heal
8	Remove Affliction	Heal
8	Water Breathing	Arcana or Nature
8	Wizard's Sight	Arcana
10	Consult Mystic Sages	Religion
10	Detect Object	Arcana
12	Drawmij's Instant Summons	Arcana
12	Hallucinatory Creature	Arcana
12	Passwall	Arcana
12	Shadow Walk	Arcana
14	Eye of Warning	Arcana
14	View Location	Arcana
16	Consult Oracle	Religion
18	Planar Portal	Arcana
18	View Object	Arcana
20	Forbiddance	Arcana
22	Loremaster's Bargain	Religion
24	Observe Creature	Arcana
26	Voice of Fate	Religion
28	True Portal	Arcana

Commune with Nature

By communing with the spirits of the land, you know exactly where to find food, shelter, or a clue to the location of the thing you seek.

Level: 6
Category: Divination
Time: 30 minutes
Duration: 10 minutes
Component Cost: 140 gp
Market Price: 360 gp
Key Skill: Nature

By communing with primal spirits of nature, you can learn a number of facts about your immediate environs (within 1 mile of you).

You can ask a number of questions, based on the result of your Nature check, about the terrain features, plants, minerals, bodies of water, creatures, and other aspects of your surroundings.

Nature Check Result	Number of Questions
9 or lower	One
10-19	Two
20-29	Three
30-39	Four
40 or higher	Five

The primal spirits you communicate with are honest but sometimes can be elusive. Most questions are answered with a yes or a no. Rarely do the spirits elaborate further, and when they do, their response is cryptic.

Comprehend Language

As you finish the ritual, the guttural language of the creatures before you clarifies into something you understand.

Level: 1
Category: Exploration
Time: 10 minutes
Duration: 24 hours
Component Cost: 10 gp
Market Price: 50 gp
Key Skill: Arcana

When beginning the ritual, choose a language you have heard or a piece of writing you have seen within the past 24 hours.

Using this ritual on a language you have heard allows you to understand it when spoken for the next 24 hours and, if your Arcana check result is 35 or higher, to speak the language fluently for the duration.

Using this ritual on a language you have seen as a piece of writing allows you to read the language for the next 24 hours and, if your Arcana check result is 35 or higher, to write the language in its native script or in any other script you know for the duration.

Using this ritual on a language you have both heard and seen as a piece of writing within the past 24 hours allows you to understand it in both forms for the next 24 hours, and an Arcana check result of 35 or higher allows you to speak and write the language.

Consult Mystic Sages

You enter a trance in which you commune with the spirits of long-dead sages and otherworldly loremasters, seeking answers to your esoteric questions.

Level: 10
Category: Divination
Time: 30 minutes
Duration: 10 minutes
Component Cost: 400 gp
Market Price: 1,000 gp
Key Skill: Religion

You ask a single question of mysterious, extraplanar presences about matters beyond your ken. Make a Religion check with a +10 bonus instead of an Arcana or a History check to uncover a clue, remember a bit of lore, or otherwise gain information about the world around you.

The ritual grants you a single piece of information. That information can take the form of a word, a name, a phrase, or even a brief story, depending on what exactly you're looking for. You can learn the name of the usurper who ended the Katerran Dynasty a thousand years ago, the burial rites of the Crimson Wolf clan, or the weaknesses of the shadow assassins who have been dogging your steps.

The ritual can't uncover information beyond the ken of the most learned sages. It's of no use if you're trying to find the magic word that unlocks the vampire's crypt, because only the vampire knows the word. Nor can the ritual tell you definitively where great stores of treasure are, but the mystic sages could tell you where a specific empress kept her treasury in ancient times or whether the treasure was looted when her empire fell.

Consult Oracle

A ghostly, shrouded figure with glowing eyes appears before you, offering brief, cryptic answers to your questions.

Level: 16
Category: Divination
Time: 1 hour
Duration: 10 minutes
Component Cost: 3,600 gp
Market Price: 9,000 gp
Key Skill: Religion

You coax forth an oracular spirit from the space between the planes. Oracles have no tangible presence and no agendas; they exist only to observe events. This makes them unparalleled sources of information because they have the potential to have seen and heard everything, even information otherwise known to only one creature.

Make a Religion check to determine how many questions you can ask an oracle before it vanishes.

Religion Check Result	Number of Questions
9 or lower	One
10-19	Two
20-29	Three
30-39	Four
40 or higher	Five

Each question is answered immediately, so you know the answer to one question before asking the next. You must phrase your question so that the oracle can answer it with a single word or a brief phrase. For the oracle to know the answer to a question, the answer must be known to at least one creature, even if that creature is no longer alive. The oracle has no foreknowledge and only a limited ability to judge what it sees. The oracle can tell you the order in which to activate the glyphs in front of the Gate of the Black Drake, but it can't answer the question "Will we do well if we venture through the gate?"

Ten minutes after you finish performing the ritual, the oracle leaves, even if you have unasked questions remaining.

CURE DISEASE

Even the most horrid affliction disappears in response to your healing touch.

Level: 6
Category: Restoration
Time: 10 minutes
Duration: Instantaneous

Component Cost: 150 gp
Market Price: 360 gp
Key Skill: Heal

The Cure Disease ritual wipes away a single disease afflicting the subject, whether the disease is active or still incubating. The subject is completely cured and loses any negative side effects and symptoms of the disease.

This ritual is physically taxing to the recipient; if used on an injured character, it can even kill him or her. Upon completing this ritual, make a Heal check, using the level of the disease as a penalty to this check. The result indicates the amount of damage the character takes. Assuming the character survives, this damage can be healed normally.

Heal Check Result	Effect on Target
0 or lower	Death
1–9	Damage equal to the target's maximum hit points
10–19	Damage equal to one-half of the target's maximum hit points
20–29	Damage equal to one-quarter of the target's maximum hit points
30 or higher	No damage

If you know that your subject is suffering from multiple diseases, you must choose which one this ritual will cure. Otherwise, the ritual affects whichever single disease you knew about. You learn the disease level when you begin the ritual, and at that point you can choose not to continue, without expending any components.

DETECT OBJECT

Lifting your finger, you point confidently at a blank stone wall. Twenty feet past it, you can sense the prince's stolen scepter.

Level: 10
Category: Exploration
Time: 10 minutes
Duration: 5 minutes

Component Cost: 400 gp
Market Price: 1,000 gp
Key Skill: Arcana

Name an object. For the duration of the ritual's effect, you can detect the direction and distance to the nearest example of that object, as long as one is within the range defined by your Arcana check result. When attempting to locate a specific object, apply the modifiers below.

Specific Object Is . . .	Modifier
Very familiar to you	0
Seen once by you	–5
Described to you	–10

Arcana Check Result	Range
9 or lower	5 squares
10–19	10 squares
20–29	30 squares
30–39	60 squares
40 or higher	100 squares

DETECT SECRET DOORS

With a smile and a wink, you show Soveliss the outline of the trapdoor he missed.

Level: 3
Category: Exploration
Time: 10 minutes
Duration: Instantaneous

Component Cost: 25 gp
Market Price: 125 gp
Key Skill: Arcana

Make an Arcana check. Use the result as a bonus to a Perception check you immediately make to find any secret or hidden doors in your line of sight. If anyone aided you while performing this ritual, they can't help you make the resulting Perception check.

DISCERN LIES

His lies quiver through the ether like water thrown on a hot griddle. The suspect doesn't even know he's giving off this signal, but to you it's clear as day.

Level: 6
Category: Divination
Time: 10 minutes
Duration: 5 minutes

Component Cost: 140 gp
Market Price: 360 gp
Key Skill: Religion

Make a Religion check. Use the result as a bonus to your Insight checks to discern any untruths spoken in your presence during the duration. If anyone aided you while performing this ritual, they can't help you make the resulting Insight checks.

DISENCHANT MAGIC ITEM

The item ignites in a brief flash of brilliant light, then crumbles to golden dust in your hands.

Level: 6
Category: Creation
Time: 1 hour
Duration: Instantaneous
Component Cost: 25 gp
Market Price: 360 gp
Key Skill: Arcana (no check)

When you finish performing this ritual, you touch a magic item and destroy it, turning it into a quantity of *residuum* valued at one-fifth of the item's price. The item must be your level or lower and must be something that can be created using the Enchant Magic Item ritual.

DRAWMIJ'S INSTANT SUMMONS

You snap your fingers, and a sword appears in your hand. The dragon's nostrils flare in irritation as it realizes you're now armed with a vorpal blade.

Level: 12
Category: Travel
Time: 1 hour
Duration: Until discharged
Component Cost: 500 gp
Market Price: 2,600 gp
Key Skill: Arcana (no check)

Use this ritual to attune one weapon, implement, or shield to yourself. At any time in the future, you can summon that object to your hands as a minor action, at which time the ritual is discharged. Through this ritual, you can have only one weapon, implement, or shield attuned to you at a time.

ENCHANT MAGIC ITEM

Magic drawn from the warp and weft of the universe infuses the item you hold in your hands.

Level: 4
Category: Creation
Time: 1 hour
Duration: Permanent
Component Cost: Special
Market Price: 175 gp
Key Skill: Arcana (no check)

You touch a normal item and turn it into a magic item of your level or lower. The ritual's component cost is equal to the price of the magic item you create.

You can also use this ritual to resize magic armor (for example, shrink a fire giant's magic armor to fit a halfling). There is no component cost for this use.

ENDURE ELEMENTS

Neither the biting cold nor the searing heat troubles you anymore. You travel in arctic or desert wastes as comfortably as in temperate climes.

Level: 2
Category: Exploration
Time: 10 minutes
Duration: 24 hours
Component Cost: 20 gp
Market Price: 100 gp
Key Skill: Arcana or Nature (no check)

The Endure Elements ritual lets you designate up to five ritual participants, including yourself, who ignore penalties associated with extremes of nonmagical weather.

An affected creature suffers no ill effects from ambient temperatures between -50 and 140 degrees Fahrenheit, and the creature's equipment is likewise protected from the ravages of these temperatures and of precipitation.

EYE OF ALARM

You conjure forth a phantasmal sentry—a slender pillar 6 feet tall, topped with a floating, unblinking eye. The eye watches over your camp as you sleep and cries out an alert if danger approaches.

Level: 2
Category: Warding
Time: 30 minutes
Duration: 24 hours (special)
Component Cost: 25 gp
Market Price: 100 gp
Key Skill: Arcana

This ritual creates watchful eyes that you place in any square within 10 squares of where you perform the ritual. Each eye is located in a particular square; it is intangible and can't be interacted with physically. The eyes are nearly invisible and have a Stealth check result of 20 + your level to avoid detection.

Your Arcana check determines how many eyes you can place and what type of vision or sensory ability they possess.

Arcana Check Result	Eyes Created	Vision or Ability
19 or lower	One	Normal
20-39	Three	Darkvision
40 or higher	Five	Darkvision and tremorsense 12 squares

The eyes do not hear, but they see well. Each uses your Perception modifier, with a +5 bonus.

If an eye sees an intruder, it emits a loud warning sound defined by you during the ritual. This sound could be anything from a stentorian "Enemies approach!" to an owl's screech to a fanfare of trumpets. The Perception DC to hear the eye's sound is 0 (modified by distance as normal).

The eyes never consider you an intruder. In addition, you can designate any number of other ritual participants as nonintruders. When you perform the ritual, you can also designate one or more categories of creatures that the eyes will ignore. You can define these categories by obvious physical characteristics (such as height, weight, or body shape), creature type (such as humanoid), creature race (such as hill giant), or obvious equipment (such as a creature carrying a shield with a flame emblazoned upon it).

The ritual's effects last for 24 hours or until you move more than 20 squares from all the eyes.

Optional Focus: You can extend the duration of this ritual indefinitely by using a focus of a small, jeweled eye made of silver and ruby, worth 100 gp. The ritual's effects last as long as the focus remains within 20 squares of any of the eyes. You can hide or protect the ritual's focus in any way you like, as long as it remains within 20 squares of the eyes.

EYE OF WARNING

You conjure forth a phantasmal sentry—a slender pillar 6 feet tall, topped with a floating, unblinking eye. The eye protects you from your enemies' efforts to scry on you, watches over your camp, and cries out an alert if danger approaches.

Level: 14	**Component Cost:** 800 gp
Category: Warding	**Market Price:** 4,200 gp
Time: 30 minutes	**Key Skill:** Arcana
Duration: 24 hours (special)	

This ritual works the same as Eye of Alarm.

In addition, an eye of warning automatically detects any scrying sensor that appears or moves within 10 squares of it, treating the sensor as an intruder. Furthermore, the eye destroys the sensor immediately after warning you unless the creator of the scrying sensor succeeds on an Arcana check (DC 20 + your level). Wherever you are, you instantly know if the eye encounters a sensor. Each round the sensor remains within 10 squares of an eye, the eye attempts to destroy it again.

Optional Focus: As with the Eye of Alarm ritual, you can extend the duration of this ritual indefinitely by keeping a focus in the vicinity. This ritual focus is a small, jeweled eye made of gold and ruby, worth 1,600 gp.

FORBIDDANCE

A powerful invisible ward protects you from your enemies' efforts to magically spy on you and from enemies who try to teleport into your presence.

Level: 20	**Component Cost:** 5,000 gp, plus 5 healing surges
Category: Warding	
Time: 30 minutes	**Market Price:** 25,000 gp
Duration: 24 hours (special)	**Key Skill:** Arcana

No scrying sensor can enter the area of Forbiddance and no creature can teleport into it, unless the sensor or the creature is higher level than the ritual caster who performed the ritual.

Your Arcana check determines the size of the warded area, which is a burst (see "Areas of Effect," page 272).

Arcana Check Result	Warded Area
9 or lower	Burst 1
10–19	Burst 3
20–29	Burst 5
30–39	Burst 8
40 or higher	Burst 12

The warding effect lasts for 24 hours, but the ritual caster (not any assistants) can extend this duration by expending a healing surge every 24 hours to sustain it. The caster does not need to be in the same area or even on the same plane to sustain the effect. If the ritual's effect is sustained without interruption for a year and a day, the effect becomes permanent.

GENTLE REPOSE

Your practiced hands perform the ritual fast enough to preserve the body for a later casting of Raise Dead.

Level: 1	**Component Cost:** 10 gp
Category: Restoration	**Market Price:** 50 gp
Time: 1 hour	**Key Skill:** Heal (no check)
Duration: Special	

This ritual is performed on an adjacent corpse. It quintuples the time the corpse can lie dead and still be affected by Raise Dead or a similar ritual. Gentle Repose also protects the corpse from being raised as an undead creature for 150 days.

HALLUCINATORY CREATURE

A few words of description, some arcane gestures, and a fearsome image appears before you.

Level: 12	**Component Cost:** 500 gp
Type: Deception	**Market Price:** 2,600 gp
Time: 10 minutes	**Key Skill:** Arcana
Duration: 24 hours	

You create the illusion of a single creature, of any size from Small to Large. It looks and smells like the creature in question. If the creature can speak or emit sounds, the illusion can do so as well, but on a limited basis (subject to the DM's judgment)—it's not possible, for instance, for the illusion to engage in an extended conversation.

You can give the illusion simple instructions, such as having it wander a set area, appear to chew on local plants, and the like. Your Arcana check determines the number of actions you can instruct the illusion to take.

Arcana Check Result	Actions
19 or lower	1 minor, 1 move
20–29	1 minor, 1 move, 1 standard
30–39	2 minor, 2 move, 1 standard
40 or higher	2 minor, 2 move, 2 standard

The illusion can perform these actions in a specific sequence, such as moving, taking a standard action, and then moving again, either in an endless loop or starting in response to a specific trigger, such as a door opening.

You can also match each action to a specific trigger. An illusion might move when a creature moves next to it or cower and scream when it is attacked.

Creatures that view or interact with the illusion are entitled to Insight checks to detect the fact that it is false. This check's DC equals your Arcana check result. A creature is allowed a check the first time it sees the illusion and each time it interacts with it. A creature that touches an illusion automatically determines that the image is a fake.

The illusion cannot travel more than 20 squares from the spot where it first appeared.

HALLUCINATORY ITEM

At your command, a phantasm of the item you've pictured in your mind shimmers into being before you. It wavers once, twice, and then seems to take on solid form.

Level: 5
Type: Deception
Time: 10 minutes
Duration: 24 hours

Component Cost: 25 gp
Market Price: 250 gp
Key Skill: Arcana

You create the illusion of a single inanimate object that appears, to all intents and purposes, to be real. You can use this ritual to create an illusory wall, door, weapon, or other object.

Your Arcana check result determines the illusion's maximum size.

Arcana Check Result	Maximum Size
19 or lower	Small
20-29	Medium
30-39	Large
40 or higher	Huge

Once you create the illusion, you cannot move it, and it can't include moving parts.

Creatures that view or interact with the illusion are entitled to Insight checks to detect the fact that it is false. This check's DC equals your Arcana check result. A creature is allowed a check the first time it sees the illusion and each time it interacts with it. A creature that touches an illusion automatically determines that the image is a fake.

HAND OF FATE

A ghostly apparition appears to give you basic guidance about a course of action.

Level: 4
Category: Divination
Time: 10 minutes
Duration: 10 minutes

Component Cost: 70 gp
Market Price: 175 gp
Key Skill: Religion (no check)

When you perform the ritual, ask up to three questions about possible courses of action. A translucent blue hand appears and indicates with a gesture what the most rewarding course of action is.

If you describe courses of action that refer to directions or specific objects, then the hand points toward the choice that bears the greatest reward. If you ask the hand, "Should we head down the stairs or through the doors?" then the hand responds by pointing either to the stairs or the doors. If you ask the hand, "Which of these three levers should we pull first?" then the hand responds by pointing to a lever.

If you describe only a single course of action, the ritual assumes that inaction is your other option. The hand either beckons you (to indicate that you should proceed) or gestures for you to halt. For example, the question "Should we explore the ruins of Solitronia?" results in the hand either beckoning you or gesturing for you to halt.

The hand can't assess events in the far future; its judgment extends only to likely events in the next hour. If the hand can't indicate a preference, the ritual has no effect and expends no components.

There are two drawbacks to using the ritual to aid your decisions. First, fate values rewards over risk, and this ritual provides guidance accordingly. It points you toward a high risk, high reward option before pointing you toward a low risk, low reward alternative. For example, if one tunnel leads to a dragon and great wealth and the other tunnel leads back to town, then the hand points toward the dragon. However, a high risk, low reward alternative is considered less rewarding than a low risk, low reward option.

Second, the hand can choose only the most rewarding course of action relative to the alternatives provided. That doesn't mean that the indicated choice is necessarily a good idea, only that it's a better idea than the other options you've indicated. In the example above, if all three levers activate traps, then the hand points toward the lever that triggers a trap less lethal than the others.

KNOCK

A blue, glowing key appears in front of the door and disappears into it. The door glows amber for a moment and then unlocks.

Level: 4   **Component Cost:** 35 gp,
Category: Exploration   plus 1 healing surge
Time: 10 minutes   **Market Price:** 175 gp
Duration: Instantaneous   **Key Skill:** Arcana

The Knock ritual allows you to open a single locked door, chest, gate, or other object. It even works against portals sealed with the Arcane Lock ritual or doors secured with bolts or bars that are on the far side, out of reach. You must defeat all the closures on a locked object to unlock it. You make one Arcana check per lock, bar, Arcane Lock, or similar closure. The object you unlock does not open automatically; you still must open it yourself after the ritual unlocks it.

Make an Arcana check with a +5 bonus in place of a Thievery check to open each lock or closure. (See the Thievery skill description, page 189, for example DCs.) To undo bolts or bars you normally couldn't reach, you must succeed on a DC 20 Arcana check.

If you use this ritual successfully against a portal protected by Arcane Lock, you destroy the Arcane Lock and its effects end.

LEOMUND'S SECRET CHEST

An ornate iron-and-silver chest fades into view in front of you.

Level: 6   **Component Cost:** 140 gp,
Category: Exploration   plus a focus worth 200 gp
Time: 10 minutes   **Market Price:** 360 gp
Duration: Until dismissed   **Key Skill:** Arcana (no check)

As part of mastering this ritual, you must create or commission a chest that bears arcane designs, and an object with personal meaning for you must be built into the chest's frame. After the chest is ready, you can store it anywhere you like. Performing this ritual then summons the chest from wherever you left it to wherever you are, along with all its contents. You can remove or add objects to the chest (subject to its natural size limitations) when it is present. Any time after summoning it, you can dismiss it back to its previous location.

Explorers use this ritual to ensure they have enough supplies or to cart treasure away from a dungeon more easily. If the chest is ever lost or destroyed, you must create a new one before you can perform this ritual again.

Focus: A chest worth at least 200 gp.

LINKED PORTAL

You create a glowing circle of sigils on the ground nearby, and you can see a hazy vision of a far-off city. You and your friends step into the circle, and you're instantly whisked away to that place.

Level: 8   **Component Cost:** 135 gp
Category: Travel   (see text)
Time: 10 minutes   **Market Price:** 680 gp
Duration: Special   **Key Skill:** Arcana

You create a shortcut across the fabric of the world, linking your location with a permanent teleportation circle somewhere else on the same plane. With a step, you can move from one circle to the other. As part of performing the ritual, you must sketch out a 10-foot-diameter circle in various rare chalks and inks. This temporary teleportation circle must exactly match the permanent teleportation circle at your destination. It disappears at the end of the portal's duration.

At the completion of this ritual, make an Arcana check. The result determines the duration that the portal remains open.

Arcana Check Result	Portal Duration
19 or lower	1 round
20-39	3 rounds
40 or higher	5 rounds

You can use a permanent teleportation circle as the origin point of this ritual, making minor temporary modifications as part of the ritual. Doing this reduces the cost to 50 gp of reagents and grants you a +5 bonus to your Arcana check.

While the portal is open, any creature that enters the circle at the origin point instantly appears at the other location, along with anything the creature holds or carries. The creature can even finish the rest of its move. Any number of creatures of any size can use an open portal; the only limitation is the number that can reach the circle before it ends.

Anyone standing in the vicinity of either end of the portal can see a haze-infused vision of the teleportation circle at the other end of the connection, as well as the environment 60 feet beyond it. Effectively, everything at the destination within this area of visibility has concealment, and the area beyond is completely fogged out (Naturally, portals that last longer give you a better opportunity to study the place you're going to before you step into the circle.). Environmental effects at one end of the connection don't affect the other end.

Most major temples, important wizards' guilds, and large cities have permanent teleportation circles, each of which has a unique set of magic sigils etched or inlaid into the ground. The exact sequence of sigils matters, because you've got to match it if you want to open a portal leading there. The sigils aren't any more complex than

remembering a string of letters and numbers. You can use Linked Portal to any permanent teleportation circle whose sequence of sigils you know. When you learn this ritual, your DM will tell you at least two such sequences. In your travels and research, you'll undoubtedly learn more.

This ritual can take you anywhere in the world, but it can't take you to other planes. Sufficiently powerful warding magic, such as the Forbiddance ritual, can block a teleportation ritual. If the location is warded in such a manner, you learn that as soon as you begin the ritual, so you can interrupt the ritual and not expend any components.

LOREMASTER'S BARGAIN

Through a significant offering, you are granted a brief magical audience with a powerful entity who possesses the information you seek.

Level: 22
Category: Divination
Time: 8 hours
Duration: Special

Component Cost: 13,000 gp
Market Price: 65,000 gp
Key Skill: Religion

Through painstaking research and preparation, you prepare a valuable offering for a powerful extraplanar entity such as an angel, a demigod, a demon, or a devil. Your offering earns you an audience with the being, which appears as a ghostly image that cannot be attacked or physically interacted with. You must succeed on a skill challenge to obtain the information you desire from that entity. You gain a +1 bonus to skill checks made in the skill challenge for every 10 points of your Religion check result (+1 for a result of 10, +2 for a result of 20, +3 for a result of 30, and so on). This challenge might be against Bluff, Diplomacy, or Intimidate, depending on the creature.

Unlike rituals that provide cryptic answers (Consult Oracle) or have limited scope (Consult Mystic Sages), the Loremaster's Bargain ritual provides contact to a creature that might be genuinely informative and helpful, provided you convince it to help. The entity begins in a neutral state—intrigued by the offering and willing to hear you out. But the entity has agendas of its own, and its nature might color the information and advice it provides.

When you complete the ritual, you can designate up to eight other ritual participants who can also speak with the entity and contribute to the skill challenge. Each one gains the same bonus to skill checks that you do.

MAGIC CIRCLE

The circle of symbols scratched into the ground glows and sparks briefly as the demon tests the boundary. "This will not save you for long!" it hisses.

Level: 5   **Component Cost:** 100 gp
Category: Binding   **Market Price:** 250 gp
Time: 1 hour   **Key Skill:** Arcana
Duration: Until broken

You inscribe a circle on the ground, a circle emblazoned with arcane symbols of protection. If drawn correctly, these symbols make it difficult for creatures of a particular origin to enter or pass. When performing the ritual, you choose aberrant, elemental, fey, immortal, natural, shadow, or all. The last option applies a –5 penalty to your check. The circle requires 1 minute to inscribe per square inside the circle (and it must be a circle).

An affected creature whose level is lower than your Arcana check result minus 10 cannot pass through the circle, affect creatures through the circle's boundary, or affect the boundary in any way. Other creatures of an affected origin take force damage equal to your Arcana check result when passing through the boundary, but doing so breaks the circle. Unaffected creatures can take a standard action to obscure the inscription and break the circle.

MAGIC MOUTH

The stone wall grinds as it reshapes into the semblance of dry, cracked lips framing teeth like canting tombstones. "Beware!" it says.

Level: 1   **Component Cost:** 10 gp
Category: Exploration   **Market Price:** 50 gp
Time: 10 minutes   **Key Skill:** Arcana (no check)
Duration: Until discharged

You bind a message into a surface you touch. When conditions you set are met, the surface manifests a mouth and conveys your message, discharging the ritual. The mouth appears to be made out of the same material as the surface, but you otherwise decide the mouth's appearance.

MAKE WHOLE

As you finish the ritual, the oaken door stands whole and unblemished as if Orten the Rager hadn't just burst through it with murder in his eyes. It's the least you can do after using the inn to ambush the infamous barbarian.

Level: 1   **Component Cost:** Special
Category: Exploration   **Market Price:** 50 gp
Time: 10 minutes   **Key Skill:** Arcana (no check)
Duration: Permanent

A single object that can fit in a 10-foot cube is completely repaired. The component cost is 20 percent of the item's cost. In cases where you attempt to repair an item not on any price list, the DM determines the cost.

OBSERVE CREATURE

You spy on a creature—whether friend, rival, or enemy—through the power of your scrying magic.

Level: 24   **Component Cost:**
Category: Scrying   21,000 gp, plus a focus
Time: 1 hour   worth 10,000 gp
Duration: Special   **Market Price:** 105,000 gp
    Key Skill: Arcana

When you perform this ritual, choose a specific creature. You create a magical sensor adjacent to that creature, and you can see and hear as if you were standing in the square where your sensor is located. You need not personally know or have ever seen the subject. However, when performing the ritual you must describe your intended subject with sufficient clarity that the ritual unambiguously knows which creature you're talking about. This ritual can show you a creature anywhere in the world, but it can't show you a creature on another plane.

ANNE STOKES

The magic of the ritual interprets your statement of intended subject in the most straightforward way possible. If your description is insufficient to determine a specific creature, the ritual fails and no components are expended. If your statement describes a subject other than the one you intended, the ritual still functions and the components are expended.

You have no inherent way to discern where the sensor is in relation to you, but careful observation might give you some clues. The sensor moves with the subject for the duration of the effect.

Your Arcana check determines how long the sensor lasts.

Arcana Check Result	Duration
19 or lower	1 round
20-24	2 rounds
25-29	3 rounds
30-39	4 rounds
40 or higher	5 rounds

You can hear through the sensor as well as see, and you have darkvision through it. Use the Perception skill to determine whether you hear quiet sounds or notice unobtrusive things while observing an area through the sensor.

Observe Creature creates a scrying sensor—a shimmer in the air—that watchful creatures might notice. Creatures must succeed on a Perception check with a DC equal to 10 + your level to notice the sensor. If the target of this ritual notices your scrying sensor, the target can use a standard action to focus its will in an attempt to destroy the sensor. Make an opposed Wisdom check; if the target's result is higher than yours, the sensor is destroyed and you spend one healing surge but regain no hit points (or take damage equal to your healing surge value if you don't have any healing surges left). The subject can repeat this effort until the sensor is destroyed or the duration ends.

Sufficiently powerful warding magic, such as the Forbiddance ritual, can block Observe Creature. If the subject's location is warded in such a manner, you learn that as soon as you begin the ritual, so you can interrupt the ritual and not expend any components.

Focus: A mirror or a crystal ball worth at least 10,000 gp. The focus conveys what you see and hear.

PASSWALL

A gap opens in the impenetrable Caldanis Fortress Wall, peeling the solid stone into a passageway as if it were a pair of tent flaps. "Come," says your guide, "we have only a short time before they notice this trick . . . or it closes on us."

Level: 12   **Component Cost:** 1,000 gp
Category: Exploration   **Market Price:** 2,600 gp
Time: 10 minutes   **Key Skill:** Arcana
Duration: 1 minute

You create a passage through any solid material. You choose the orientation of the passage relative to the surface you touch. The passage is 1 square wide and tall. The passage can be a number of squares deep equal to your Arcana check result divided by 5. This ritual does not conceal the passage from anyone or bar anyone from entering. A creature inside the passage when it closes takes 5d10 damage and is ejected to the nearest end of the passage. This ritual does not affect the structural integrity of a cavern or a wall; the passage is a twist in space, not an actual shifting of material.

PHANTOM STEED

You conjure black, ghostly horses. They sniff the air and stamp impatiently as if ready to ride like the wind. Their hooves, manes, and tails trail off into mist.

Level: 6   **Component Cost:** 70 gp
Category: Exploration   **Market Price:** 360 gp
Time: 10 minutes   **Key Skill:** Arcana
Duration: 12 hours

This ritual conjures forth up to eight horselike creatures. Each one is Large and can be ridden by you or any other character you designate during the ritual.

Your Arcana check determines the speed of the steeds you conjure and whether they have any special movement capabilities. The steeds have the special movement capabilities associated with your check result and all lower results.

Arcana Check Result	Speed	Special Movement
19 or lower	10	None
20-29	12	Ignore difficult terrain
30-39	15	Move on water as if it were solid ground
40 or higher	20	Fly (up to 10 squares above ground)

The steeds cannot attack or affect other creatures in any way other than to serve as mounts. Each steed's defense scores are equal to its rider's (or yours, if the steed has no rider). A phantom steed is immune to any effect other than damage.

A steed created by this ritual lasts for 12 hours or until it takes any damage. When the ritual ends, or when a steed is destroyed, the steed fades into nothingness and its rider lands on his or her feet in the steed's space. If a steed is flying when it disappears, the rider descends safely to the ground, landing at the start of his or her next turn.

Planar Portal

You inscribe a circle of runes on the ground. The earth shakes as the portal blazes with magical energy. A hazy image of a distant world appears within the circle's bounds.

Level: 18   **Component Cost:** 5,000 gp
Category: Travel   **Market Price:** 17,000 gp
Time: 10 minutes   **Key Skill:** Arcana
Duration: Special

This ritual works the same as Linked Portal, except that you can use it to travel to other planes. As with Linked Portal, your planar destination must have a permanent teleportation circle whose sigil sequence you have memorized.

Your Arcana check determines how long the portal remains open.

Arcana Check Result	Portal Duration
19 or lower	1 round
20–39	3 rounds
40 or higher	5 rounds

When you first learn this ritual, you learn the sigil sequences of two common planar locations, as determined by the DM.

Raise Dead

You bend over the body of your slain comrade, applying sacramental unguents. Finally his eyes flutter open as he is restored to life.

Level: 8   **Component Cost:** 500 gp
Category: Restoration   **Market Price:** 680 gp
Time: 8 hours   **Key Skill:** Heal (no check)
Duration: Instantaneous

To perform the Raise Dead ritual, you must have a part of the corpse of a creature that died no more than 30 days ago. You apply mystic salves, then pray to the gods to restore the dead creature's life. The subject returns to life as if he or she had taken an extended rest. The subject is freed of any temporary conditions suffered at death, but permanent conditions remain.

The subject returns with a death penalty: –1 to all attack rolls, skill checks, saving throws, and ability checks. This death penalty fades after the subject reaches three milestones.

You can't restore life to a creature that has been petrified or to a creature that died of old age.

The subject's soul must be free and willing to return to life. Some magical effects trap the soul and thus prevent Raise Dead from working, and the gods can intervene to prevent a soul from journeying back to the realm of the living. In all cases, death is less inclined to return paragon and epic heroes; the component cost is 5,000 gp for paragon tier characters and 50,000 gp for epic tier characters.

Remove Affliction

You undo a curse, enchantment, or madness that afflicts your subject.

Level: 8   **Component Cost:** 250 gp
Category: Restoration   **Market Price:** 680 gp
Time: 1 hour   **Key Skill:** Heal
Duration: Instantaneous

Remove Affliction wipes away a single enduring effect afflicting the subject. The ritual can remove curses, effects such as charm or domination, and fear, confusion, insanity, polymorph, and petrification effects. All effects of the curse or other effect end.

This ritual is physically taxing to the recipient; if used on an injured character, it can even kill him or her. Upon completing this ritual, make a Heal check, using the level of the effect you are trying to remove (or the level of the creature that caused the effect) as a penalty to this check. The result indicates the amount of damage the character takes. Assuming the character survives, this damage can be healed normally.

Heal Check Result	Effect on Target
0 or lower	Death
1–9	Damage equal to the target's maximum hit points
10–19	Damage equal to one-half of the target's maximum hit points
20–29	Damage equal to one-quarter of the target's maximum hit points
30 or higher	No damage

You can use this ritual on an unwilling subject (usually, a former ally who is under some enemy's influence), but you will have to restrain someone unwilling to undergo the ritual. If you know that your subject is suffering from multiple enduring effects, you must choose which one this ritual will remove. Otherwise, it affects whichever one affliction you knew about. You learn the affliction level when you begin the ritual, and you can choose not to continue, without expending any components (for example, if you determine the affliction is too powerful for you to remove).

Secret Page

You laugh through your broken teeth. The duke's impersonator might have found your journal, but he'll never see what you wrote there.

Level: 1   **Component Cost:** 10 gp
Category: Warding   **Market Price:** 50 gp
Time: 10 minutes   **Key Skill:** Arcana
Duration: Permanent

You ward writings so others cannot read them. Use of this ritual protects one page (maximum 250 words). You make the page appear not to exist, causing anyone other than you to ignore it; the page's presence is blocked from a reader's mind. You can choose instead to obscure the page with false writings, which you produce before performing the ritual. Other readers see the false text rather than the real text.

When you perform the ritual, make an Arcana check, with a +5 bonus. The result is the DC for a Perception check to notice the concealed writing (readers use passive Perception unless they are specifically looking for concealed text).

SENDING

You can see him in your mind's eye, clear as the first time you met him. Your magic lets him know that you're safe, despite encountering the followers of Thoon, and he reassures you that the red dragon caused him no harm.

Level: 6
Category: Exploration
Time: 10 minutes
Duration: Instantaneous
Component Cost: 50 gp
Market Price: 360 gp
Key Skill: Arcana

You convey a mental message of up to 25 words to a person you know. If the target is within range, he or she receives the message mentally and can respond likewise. The ritual's maximum range is determined by your Arcana check result.

Arcana Check Result	Maximum Range
9 or lower	10 miles
10–19	100 miles
20–29	500 miles
30–39	1,000 miles
40 or higher	Anywhere on the same plane

SHADOW WALK

The viscount's army is a half-day's march ahead and will beat you to Fernwich. Or would. Shadows stretch until they drape over everything as you step sideways and let the shadows lengthen your stride.

Level: 12
Category: Exploration
Time: 1 hour
Duration: 8 hours
Component Cost: 500 gp
Market Price: 2,600 gp
Key Skill: Arcana (no check)

You and your allies walk through shadows stretching out of the Shadowfell, taking advantage of the strange disparities between distance in your realm and that one to travel quickly. Multiply your overland travel speed by 5 for the duration. This ritual functions only in the natural world.

SILENCE

Straining both your patience and your keen ears, you hear nothing in the duke's private chamber. That's why you're so surprised to see the duke when you boldly enter.

Level: 1
Category: Warding
Time: 10 minutes
Duration: 24 hours
Component Cost: 30 gp
Market Price: 75 gp
Key Skill: Arcana (no check)

You ward a single room (or a burst 4 area), against eavesdropping. Creatures attempting to listen to something in the warded area from outside the area take a –10 penalty to their Perception checks.

SPEAK WITH DEAD

At your prompt, the corpse reveals its secrets to you.

Level: 6
Category: Exploration
Time: 10 minutes
Duration: 10 minutes
Component Cost: 140 gp
Market Price: 360 gp
Key Skill: Religion

You ask the corpse of an intelligent creature questions and receive answers. The corpse knows what the creature knew in life, what has occurred near the corpse, and no more; the spirit has (usually) moved on to another plane and is not present in the body.

Your Religion check result determines the number of questions you can ask.

Religion Check Result	Number of Questions
9 or lower	Zero
10–19	One
20–29	Two
30 or higher	Three

At the DM's option, questioning the departed spirit might require a skill challenge using Diplomacy.

TENSER'S FLOATING DISK

"Oh, this? It follows me everywhere, like a porter that never needs to rest."

Level: 1
Category: Exploration
Time: 10 minutes
Duration: 24 hours
Component Cost: 10 gp
Market Price: 50 gp
Key Skill: Arcana

Arcana Check Result	Maximum Load
9 or lower	250 pounds
10–24	500 pounds
25–39	1,000 pounds
40 or higher	2,000 pounds

You create a slightly concave, circular plane of force that floats a foot off the ground and can carry what you lay

upon it. The disk is 3 feet in diameter and 1 inch deep at its center. It remains stationary unless you move more than 5 squares away from it, in which case it moves with your base speed once per round until it is within 5 squares of you. You can command the disk to move up to your speed as a move action. If you are more than 5 squares from the disk for 2 consecutive rounds, the disk disappears, dropping whatever it was carrying.

Your Arcana check result determines the maximum load the disk can carry.

TRAVELERS' FEAST

Food for your entire group materializes out of the air, enough to sustain you through a long day's march.

Level: 4   **Component Cost:** 35 gp
Category: Exploration   **Market Price:** 175 gp
Time: 1 hour   **Key Skill:** Nature (no check)
Duration: 24 hours

You create food and water, enough to feed five Medium or Small creatures or two Large creatures for 24 hours. You designate the type of eaters when performing the ritual, and the ritual creates appropriate food (trail rations for people, grain for horses, and so on).

Any food or water created but uneaten disappears at the end of the duration.

TRUE PORTAL

You create a circle of glowing sigils and state your desired destination–any place you name. The circle fills with a hazy vision of the place. When you step inside the circle, you are instantly transported to your destination, no matter how far away it is.

Level: 28   **Component Cost:**
Category: Travel   50,000 gp (see text)
Time: 10 minutes   **Market Price:** 425,000 gp
Duration: Special   **Key Skill:** Arcana

This ritual works the same as Linked Portal (page 307), except as noted here.

You are not limited to teleporting to places you've seen or that have permanent teleportation circles. However, when performing the ritual, you must describe your intended destination clearly. "Lord Ambrose's audience chamber" is sufficient, as is "the nearest temple of Pelor." Your description must use only place names and other static references; you can't say "wherever Princess Katria is" or "the nearest pile of gold." The magic of the ritual interprets your intended destination in the most straightforward way possible. If your description is insufficient to determine a specific destination, the ritual fails, but no components are expended. If your description causes the portal to lead somewhere you did not intend–for example, if the nearest temple of Pelor is not in the city you'd hoped it would be–the ritual still functions, and the ritual's components are expended.

If the destination is blocked by a warding ritual, such as Forbiddance, the ritual opens the destination portal at a point along the ward's boundary. You can see through the portal before you enter, and you don't have to step through if you don't want to.

You can use a teleportation circle as the origin point of this ritual, making minor temporary modifications as part of the ritual. Using a teleportation circle reduces the ritual's component cost to 1,000 gp and grants a +5 bonus to your Arcana check.

VIEW LOCATION

The secrets of the world are yours to plumb, for your magically enhanced eyes can see into the king's chambers, the wizard's library, or the dragon's cave.

Level: 14   **Component Cost:** 1,600 gp,
Category: Scrying   plus a focus worth 1,000 gp
Time: 1 hour   **Market Price:** 4,200 gp
Duration: Special   **Key Skill:** Arcana

RAVEN MIMURA

When you perform this ritual, choose a location you have previously visited. The location must be fixed in place (for example, you can't use this to scry into the cabin of an oceangoing vessel), and it must still be at the same place (and in more or less the same shape) as when you visited. Redecorating a room won't fool View Location scrying, but destroying a tower and rebuilding it with a different layout would cause the ritual to fail (until you visit the new location). You know if the ritual has failed before you expend any components. This ritual can show you a location anywhere in the world, but it can't show you a location on another plane.

This ritual creates a scrying sensor—a shimmer in the air—that watchful creatures might notice. Creatures must succeed on a Perception check with a DC equal to 10 + your level to notice the sensor. They can't disrupt or interact with the sensor in any way.

You can hear through the sensor as well as see, and you have darkvision through it. Use the Perception skill to determine whether you hear quiet sounds or notice unobtrusive things while observing an area through the sensor.

Your Arcana check determines how long the sensor lasts.

Arcana Check Result	Duration
19 or lower	1 round
20-24	2 rounds
25-29	3 rounds
30-39	4 rounds
40 or higher	5 rounds

Sufficiently powerful warding magic, such as the Forbiddance ritual, can block View Location. If the location is warded in such a manner, you learn that as soon as you begin the ritual, so you can interrupt the ritual and not expend any components.

Focus: A mirror or a crystal ball worth at least 1,000 gp. The focus conveys what you see and hear.

VIEW OBJECT

Whether it's a magic sword, a map of the catacombs, or the jeweled cup that used to be on your mantelpiece, you can observe the location where a specific item is.

Level: 18
Category: Scrying
Time: 1 hour
Duration: Special

Component Cost: 7,000 gp, plus a focus worth 5,000 gp
Market Price: 17,000 gp
Key Skill: Arcana

When you perform this ritual, choose a specific object of up to Large size. You need not have held or viewed the object. However, when performing the ritual you must describe the object with sufficient clarity that the ritual unambiguously knows which object you're talking about. "Duke Karlerren's ancestral broadsword" is sufficient, as is "the nearest gold coin," but "the most powerful magic item nearby" is not. This ritual can show you an object

anywhere in the world, but it can't show you an object on another plane.

The magic of the ritual interprets your statement of intended object in the most straightforward way possible. If your description is insufficient to determine a specific object, the ritual fails, and no components are expended. If your statement describes an object other than the one you intended—for example, if the nearest gold coin is in your pocket, rather than in the hidden treasure vault you're looking for—the ritual still functions, and the components are expended.

You have no inherent way to discern where the object is in relation to you, but careful observation can give you some clues. If you see the duke's sword hanging on a stone wall, for example, you don't necessarily know whether that wall is across town or across the world.

This ritual creates a scrying sensor—a shimmer in the air—adjacent to the viewed object that watchful creatures might notice. Creatures must succeed on a Perception check with a DC equal to 10 + your level to notice the sensor. They can't disrupt or interact with the sensor in any way.

You can hear through the sensor as well as see, and you have darkvision through it. Use the Perception skill to determine whether you hear quiet sounds or notice unobtrusive things while observing an area through the sensor.

Your Arcana check determines how long the sensor lasts. The sensor moves with the object for this duration.

Arcana Check Result	Duration
19 or lower	1 round
20-24	2 rounds
25-29	3 rounds
30-39	4 rounds
40 or higher	5 rounds

Sufficiently powerful warding magic, such as the Forbiddance ritual, can block View Object. If the object's location is warded in such a manner, you learn that as soon as you begin the ritual, so you can interrupt the ritual and not expend any components.

Focus: A mirror or a crystal ball worth at least 1,000 gp. The focus conveys what you see and hear.

VOICE OF FATE

A booming voice heard only by the ritual participants provides guidance for your future actions.

Level: 26
Category: Divination
Time: 1 hour
Duration: Instantaneous

Component Cost: 45,000 gp, plus 5 healing surges
Market Price: 225,000 gp
Key Skill: Religion

You consult an entity of fate—perhaps a servant of Avandra, Ioun, Pelor, or the Raven Queen—for a glimpse into what the future holds. You ask questions, and a rumbling voice replies.

Your Religion check determines the number of questions you can ask.

Religion Check Result	Number of Questions
24 or lower	Three
25-29	Four
30-34	Five
35-39	Six
40 or higher	Seven

Your questions must relate to a specific goal, event, or activity that has yet to occur. Since what is yet to occur is not known by any mortal being, the answers need not be known by any creature, alive or dead. This ritual can answer only questions related to events occurring within the next 7 days. After that, the skein of possibilities is too indistinct to gain useful information.

The guidance from the entity of fate is accurate, but great heroes are capable of thwarting fate, at least for a time. If the ritual reveals that a course of action is "certain doom," you should realize that nothing is truly certain until it happens. In addition, the entity of fate assumes that you will act on its guidance completely and immediately. If you don't act on the information, or if you change the conditions in existence when you performed the ritual, then the guidance might no longer be useful.

WATER BREATHING

The cool water fills your lungs, yet you find yourself able to breathe and speak as well as you can on land.

Level: 8
Category: Exploration
Time: 10 minutes
Duration: Special
Component Cost: 135 gp
Market Price: 680 gp
Key Skill: Arcana or Nature

When you perform this ritual, you can designate up to eight participants (including yourself if you wish) who breathe water as easily as they breathe air. Furthermore, they can speak normally underwater.

Water Breathing doesn't change your ability to breathe air. It doesn't confer a greater swim speed or the ability to fight underwater unhindered. It does protect any gear you and the participants carry, such as books and scrolls, from water damage.

Your check result determines the duration of the effect.

Arcana Check Result	Duration
14 or lower	1 hour
15-19	2 hours
20-24	4 hours
25-29	8 hours
30 or higher	24 hours

WATER WALK

You walk on the water as if it were dry land.

Level: 2
Category: Exploration
Time: 10 minutes
Duration: 1 hour
Component Cost: 20 gp
Market Price: 100 gp
Key Skill: Nature (no check)

You or an ally can move on water as if it were solid ground. Rapids or choppy seas are considered difficult terrain. The target of this ritual can end its benefits as a free action. The target can immerse itself in water or swim underwater if desired without needing to end the ritual.

WIZARD'S SIGHT

You extend your senses beyond the door, looking and listening inside as if you were there.

Level: 8
Category: Scrying
Time: 10 minutes
Duration: Special
Component Cost: 270 gp, plus a focus worth 200 gp
Market Price: 680 gp
Key Skill: Arcana

When you perform a Wizard's Sight ritual, choose a square within 20 squares of you, even a square that you can't see or don't have line of effect to. You create a magical sensor in that square. You can see and hear as if you were standing there, and you have darkvision through the sensor. Use the Perception skill to determine whether you hear quiet sounds or notice unobtrusive things while observing an area through the sensor.

Your Arcana check determines how long the sensor lasts.

Arcana Check Result	Duration
19 or lower	1 round
20-24	2 rounds
25-29	3 rounds
30-39	4 rounds
40 or higher	5 rounds

The ritual creates a scrying sensor—a shimmer in the air—that watchful creatures might notice. Creatures must succeed on a Perception check with a DC equal to 10 + your level to notice the sensor. They can't disrupt or interact with the sensor in any way.

Sufficiently powerful warding magic, such as the Forbiddance ritual, can block Wizard's Sight. If the location is warded in such a manner, you learn that as soon as you begin the ritual, so you can interrupt the ritual and not expend any components.

Focus: A mirror or a crystal ball worth at least 200 gp. The focus conveys what you see and hear.

PLAYTESTER CREDITS

Aaron Moronez, Aaron Schrader, Aaron Slotness, Adam Colby, Adam Sweitzer, Adam Wojtowecz, Adrienne Mays, Alan Best, Albert Ward III, Alexander Kevin, Alexander Kiedrowicz, Algon Buechler, Allen Drees Jr., Amber Taylor, Andrew Bourne, Andrew D'Agostino, Andrew Finch, Andrew Garbade, Andrew Gately, Andrew Grimberg, Andrew Harasty, Andrew Miles, Andrew Moore, Andrew Watring, Andy Collins, Andy Lewis, Andy Reichert, Andy Scholman, Ann Troll, Arjen Laan, Arthur Doler, Barbara Cowman, Bard Lower, Bart Carroll, Bart Miller, Benjamin Harris, Benjamin Roberts, Benjamin Zimmermann, Benton Little, Bernardo Stokes, Bernd Mueller, Bill "Quill" McQuillan, Bill Benham, Bill Slavicsek, Bob Deas, Bob Rarik, Bobby Pearsall, Brad McWilliams, Brad Shugg, Brad Street, Brad Titus, Brandon Bozzi, Brandon Gehrke, BreeAnn Vosberg, Brenda Allen, Brent Michalski, Brett Stolle, Brian Benoit, Brian Booker, Brian Cortijo, Brian Farmer II, Brian Gilkison, Brian Gray, Brian Hon, Brian Jenison, Brian Mackey, Brian Martin, Brian Schoner, Bricio Rodriguez, Bruce Cordell, Bruce Jacobs, Bruce Story, Bryan Flores, Bryan Leclair, Bryant Kingry, Cal Moore, Cameron Curtis, Cameron Logan, Candy Tran, Cara Franks, Carter Wyatt, Cary Bishop, Cary Suter, Casey Hoch, Cassie Crawford, Cedric Atizado, Chad Swenson, Charles Allen, Charles Arnett, Charles Hickey, Charles Lang, Charles Speece, Charles Wartsbaugh, Chef Jannuzzi, Chet Silvers, Chisa Puckett, Chris Ballowe, Chris Corbett, Chris Gardiner, Chris Hernandez, Chris Kiritz, Chris Salter, Chris Sims, Chris Tulach, Chris Vinje, Chris Wakelin, Chris Westemeier, Chris Wilkes, Chris Youngs, Christen Sowards, Christian Alipounarian, Christian Busch, Christian Chaney, Christopher Dolunt, Christopher Groves, Christopher Hoffman, Christopher Humphries, Christopher Lindsay, Christopher Pasold, Christopher Perkins, Christopher Sparke, Christopher Ward, Christopher Wright, Chuck Arnett, Cody Judkins-Murphey, Colin Moulder-McComb, Colleen Simpson, Colton Hoerner, Conall O'Brien, Cormac Russel, Corwin Avy, Cory Brosnan, Cory Hughes, Courtney Stevenson, Craig Campbell, Craig Wright, Creighton Broadhurst, Crystal Babcock, Curt Gould, Curt Johann Steckhan, Curtis Rueden, Dagob ten Wolde, Damon Bishop, Daneen McDermott, Daniel Canper, Daniel Checchi, Daniel Sanford, Darin Briskman, Darrel Dunning, Darrell Impey, Darren Martin, Dave Russell, David Blackwell, David Christ, David Ferrell, David Guerrieri, David Kerscher, David LaMacchia, David Liliefeldt, David Napack, David Nikdol, David Noonan, David Pogue, David Smith, David Williams, David Yale, Dennis Worrell, Derek Fails, Derek Neff, Derek Schubert, Devin Low, Didier Monin, Dimas Jimenez, Dominic Hamer, Don Early, Don Frazier, Donovan Hicks, Doug Gewin, Doug La Vigne, Doug Wheeler, Ed Podsiad, Ed Stark, Edward Grant, Edward Morrow, Edward Neighbour, Elizabeth Decker, Elizabeth Merwin, Elliot Parkhurst, Eric Boughton, Eric Brittain, Eric Burk, Eric Cline, Eric Haddock, Eric Heath, Eric Kjellman, Eric Menge, Eric Moore, Erich Borchardt, Erin M. Evans, Ernest Britton III, Evan Louscher, Eve Forward, Eytan Bernstein, Farrell Hopkins, Francesco Mangiarauna, Francisco Gray, Fred Sarkis, Freek Giele, Galen Ciscell, Garin Dadson, Garth Hale-Hodgson, Gary Adkison, Gary Affeldt, Gary Simon Jr., George Smith, George Stafford, Gibbons Franks, Gordon Holcomb, Graeme Davis, Greg Bartholomew, Greg Bilsland, Greg Collins, Greg Marks, Gregg Peevers, Gregory Brooks, Gregory Marques, Gregory Martel, Gwendolyn

Kestrel, Hannu Haavisto, Hans Zimmermann, Heidi Pritchett, Henry Link II, Henry Woolsey, Hollis Lau, Ian Hardin, Ian McHugh, Ian Newborn, Ian Richards, Ian Simpson, Jacob Bonnett, James Agg, James Boyle II, James Crook, James Dempsey, James Duncan, James Durchenwald, James Hamblin, James Johnson, James Ryan, James Wyatt, Jared Farnsley, Jason Andersen, Jason Babcock, Jason Bickal, Jason Crognale, Jason Davis, Jason Farmer, Jason Feldhake, Jason Greene, Jason Hall, Jason Hrabi, Jason Lakoduk, Jason Myatt, Jason Ross, Jason Starin, Jason Stypinski, Jason Swanson, Jay Button, Jay Sheridan, Jean-Philipe Chapleau, Jeff Clare, Jeff Grubb, Jeff Quick, Jefferson Hyde, Jefferson L. Dunlap, Jeffery Dobberpuhl, Jeffery Terrill, Jeffrey Kreutz, Jeffry Clarke, Jen Alex, Jen Page, Jennifer Clarke-Wilkes, Jennifer Impey, Jennifer Overton, Jennifer Tatroe, Jeremy Crawford, Jeremy Green, Jeremy Kim, Jeremy Patrick, Jeremy Puckett, Jeremy Vosberg, Jeremy Williams, Jermone Farnsley, Jerry Aunspaw, Jesse Decker, Jesse Kindwall, Jesse Stratton, Jessica Blair, Jessica Iglehart, Jim Butzberger, Jim Hutcheson, Jim Turkowski, Jimmy Ainsworth, Joanna Chaney, Joanne Pender, Joby Walker, Jodi Murschel, Joe Cari, Joe Jannuzzi, Joe Swarner, Joe Terrenzio, Joel Kurlan, Joerg John, John Bonneau, John du Bois, John Foye Jr., John Grant, John Hanna, John Heaton, John Jones, John Kozar, John LeDonne, John Pascoe, John Rogers, John Ruff, John Wilkins, John Zamarra, Jon Cimuchowski, Jon Dobbie, Jon Machnicz, Jon Naughton, Jon Sedich, Jon Stevens, Jon Thompson, Jon Wear, Jonathan Culler, Jonathan Fish, Jonathan Pumphrey, Jonathan Tweet, Joonas Sahramaa, Jordan Deal, Jose Mercado, Joseph Bright, Joseph Guerrera, Joseph Jolly, Joseph LaMothe, Joseph Schulte, Joseph Strait, Josh Farnsley, Josh Roberts, Joshua Sipos, Jukka Sarkijarvi, Julia Martin, Julie Woolsey, Justin McGuire, Justin Muir, Katherine Fairbanks, Katherine Schubert, Keely Dolan, Keith Baker, Keith McAleer, Keith Symcox, Keith Tatroe, Keith Watson, Kelly Hoesing, Kelly Olmstead, Kelly Raynor, Kelsey Rueden, Kelsi Rarik, Ken Sams, Kenneth Goad, Kenneth Marshall, Kenneth McRowe, Kerrie Peacock, Kevin Barnsley, Kevin Downey, Kevin Lawson, Kevin Myers, Kevin Schmitt, Kevin Tatroe, Kevin Tiskja, Kierin Chase, Kimberly Anglace, Kipp Lightburn, Kolja Liquette, Konrad Brandemuhl, Lawrence Haskell, Lee Burton, Lee Thomas, Leonard Logan, Leslie Erwin, Lewis McLouth, Linae Foster, Lindsay Mohandeson, Lisa Gordon, Liz Schuh, Logan Bonner, Luc MacArthur, Lucas Wilson, Ludovic Tirtiaux, Lynn Register, Malima Wolf, Marc Russell, Mark Holdforth, Mark Jessup, Mark Jindra, Mark Knobbe, Mark Porter, Mark Somers, Mark Wheelhouse, Mark Whittaker, Marko Westerlund, Marsha Hillman, Martin Durham, Mary Toms, Mat Smith, Mathew Voster, Mathiew Booth, Matt Eddleman, Matt Howland, Matt Tabak, Matt Tyler, Matt Walters, Matthew Fuchs, Matthew Hoyt, Matthew Lund, Matthew McKitrick, Matthew Meyer, Matthew Morrissette, Matthew Sanders, Matthew Seidl, Matthew Sernett, Matthew Swetnam, Matthew Varrette, Matthew Vignan, Maureen Honore, Melanie Neumuller, Michael Adair, Michael Born, Michael Broby, Michael Brock, Michael Deal, Michael Donais, Michael Dunlap, Michael Ericson, Michael Eshleman, Michael Feuell, Michael Gersztenkorn, Michael Johnson, Michael Lang, Michael Maenza, Michael Mockus, Michael Nichols, Michael Peacock, Michael Ruble, Michael Shea, Michael Simon, Michael Tedin, Michael Turian, Michael Wells, Michael Wood, Michele Carter, Michelle Brunes, Michelle LaBolle,

Mike Barnes, Mike Fehlauer, Mike Hawkins, Mike Lescault, Mike Mearls, Mike Mohandeson, Mikko Laine, Milton Eng, Mons Johnson, Morgan Shepherd, Morschel Marcel, Murry McEntire, Nate Heiss, Nathan Barse, Nathan Hancock, Nathanael Christen, Neil Harkins, Neil Lance, Neil Topel, Neil Wright, Nicholas D'Agostino, Nicholas Impey, Nicholas Tulach, Nick Pierce, Nickey Barnard, Nigel Evans, Nina Moelker, Orren Grushkin, Osian ap Glyn, Osmond Chen, Patricia Baratta, Patrick Ellis, Paul Bazakas, Paul Casagrande, Paul Clinkingbeard, Paul Embry, Paul Hughes, Paul James, Paul Kulbitski, Paul McAinsh, Paul McCombs, Paul Sottosanti, Pete Sims, Peter Diggins, Peter Lee, Peter Schaefer, Philip Benson, Phillip Bonder, Pierre van Rooden, Pieter Sleijpen, Rachel Jones, Randall Davis, Ray Wells, Rebecca Voster, Reid Schmadeka, Renout van Rijn, Rhonda Wiese, Rich Redman, Richard Baker, Richard Brown, Richard Garfield, Richard Grogan, Richard Hudson, Richard Marflak, Richard Mickwee II, Richard Robinson, Richard Tefertiller Jr., Rick Brill, Rick Erwin, Rick Osborne, Ricky Mink, Rob Dalton, Rob Dunbar, Rob Heinsoo, Rob Lightner, Rob Watkins, Robert Altomare, Robert Bonnett, Robert Gill, Robert Gutschera, Robert Keene Jr., Robert Little, Robert Mahoney, Robert Moulton, Robert Wiese, Robert Wills, Robin MacPherson, Robin Mitra, Rodney Thompson, Roger Roberts, Roger Smith, Roland Volz, Rolando Gomez, Ron Foster, Ron Franke, Ron Janik, Ron Purvis, Ronald Frye, Ross Rushing II, Russell Olmstead, Russell Taylor, Russell Warshay, Ryan Brown, Ryan Cline, Ryan Richardson, Ryan Whelan, Rydia Vielehr, Sam E. Simpson Jr., Sampo Haarlaa, Samuel Santos, Samuel Weiss, Sara Girard, Sarah Clare, Sarah Tilson, Sarin Tatroe, Sawyer Bernath, Scott Benfield, Scott Decoursey, Scott Rosenkranz, Scott Rouse, Scott Smith, Sean Banks, Sean Croyle, Sean Dawson, Sean Hillman, Sean Lambert, Sean Molley, Shawn Blakeney, Shawn Merwin, Shawn Morris, Shawn Robbins, Shayne Schelinder, Shelly Mazzanoble, Sid Moulton, Silas Cline, Solomon Douek, Spring Koch, Stacy Longstreet, Stan!, Stanley Heston Jr., Stephen Baker, Stephen Black, Stephen Buckler, Stephen D'Agostino, Stephen Hagan, Stephen Mumford, Stephen Radney-MacFarland, Stephen Schubert, Steve Bogart, Steve Burnage, Steve Chamberlin, Steve Hipplehauser, Steve Kramer, Steve Re, Steve Warner, Steve Winter, Steve Wolbrecht, Steven Conforti, Steven Cook, Steven Montano, Stevie Hipplehauser, Sue Powell, Susan Morris, Susan Threadgill, Tamela Bangs, Teeun Medas, Teos Abadia, Terence Thambipillai, Thomas Cadwell, Thomas Christy, Thomas John, Thomas Neville, Tim Bruhn, Tim Harr, Tim Hill, Tim Sech, Timothy Houle, Timothy Stack II, Timothy Wolcott, Toby Latin-Stoermer, Todd Ammerman, Todd Iglehart, Tom Kee, Tom LaBolle, Tom Mullenger, Toni Brill, Toni Stauffer, Torry Steed, Traci Farnsley, Travis Petkovits, Travis Woodall, Trevor Doll, Trevor Kidd, Trevor Taylor, Tyson Moyer, Vernon Vincent, Vincent Price, Walter Johnson, Ward van Oosterom, Wayne Sheppard, Will Dover, William Burger Jr., William Keltner, William McConahy III, William Morrow, William Sarazin, Witney Williams, Yannik Braal, Yoerik de Voogd, Yvan Boily, Zephreum Humphreys, and all the people who attended D&D Experience 2008.

Special Thanks to Chris Tulach

INDEX

DUNGEONS & DRAGONS

CHARACTER SHEET

Player Name _____

Character Name _____

Level	Class	Paragon Path	Epic Destiny	Total XP

Race	Size	Age	Gender	Height	Weight	Alignment	Deity	Adventuring Company or Other Affiliations

INITIATIVE

SCORE		DEX	1/2 LEVEL		MISC
	Initiative				

CONDITIONAL MODIFIERS

ABILITY SCORES

SCORE	ABILITY	ABIL MOD	MOD + 1/2 LVL
	STR Strength		
	CON Constitution		
	DEX Dexterity		
	INT Intelligence		
	WIS Wisdom		
	CHA Charisma		

HIT POINTS

MAX HP

	BLOODIED	HEALING SURGES	
		SURGE VALUE	SURGES/DAY
	1/2 HP	1/4 HP	

CURRENT HIT POINTS   CURRENT SURGE USES

SECOND WIND 1/ENCOUNTER   USED ☐

TEMPORARY HIT POINTS

DEATH SAVING THROW FAILURES ☐☐☐

SAVING THROW MODS

RESISTANCES

CURRENT CONDITIONS AND EFFECTS

SKILLS

BONUS	SKILL NAME		ABIL MOD + 1/2 LVL	TRND (+5)	ARMOR PENALTY	MISC
	Acrobatics	DEX				
	Arcana	INT			n/a	
	Athletics	STR				
	Bluff	CHA			n/a	
	Diplomacy	CHA			n/a	
	Dungeoneering	WIS			n/a	
	Endurance	CON				
	Heal	WIS			n/a	
	History	INT			n/a	
	Insight	WIS			n/a	
	Intimidate	CHA			n/a	
	Nature	WIS			n/a	
	Perception	WIS			n/a	
	Religion	INT			n/a	
	Stealth	DEX				
	Streetwise	CHA			n/a	
	Thievery	DEX				

DEFENSES

SCORE	DEFENSE	10 + 1/2 LVL	ARMOR / ABIL	CLASS	FEAT	ENH	MISC	MISC
	AC							

CONDITIONAL BONUSES

SCORE	DEFENSE	10 + 1/2 LVL	ABIL	CLASS	FEAT	ENH	MISC	MISC
	FORT							

CONDITIONAL BONUSES

DEFENSE	10 + 1/2 LVL	ABIL	CLASS	FEAT	ENH	MISC	MISC
REF							

CONDITIONAL BONUSES

DEFENSE	10 + 1/2 LVL	ABIL	CLASS	FEAT	ENH	MISC	MISC
WILL							

CONDITIONAL BONUSES

ACTION POINTS

	Action Points	MILESTONES	ACTION POINTS
		0	1
		1	2
		2	3

ADDITIONAL EFFECTS FOR SPENDING ACTION POINTS

RACE FEATURES

ABILITY SCORE MODS

_____
_____
_____
_____
_____
_____
_____

CLASS / PATH / DESTINY FEATURES

_____
_____
_____
_____
_____
_____
_____
_____
_____
_____
_____
_____

LANGUAGES KNOWN

_____
_____
_____

MOVEMENT

SCORE		BASE	ARMOR	ITEM	MISC
	Speed (Squares)				

SPECIAL MOVEMENT

SENSES

SCORE	PASSIVE SENSE	BASE	SKILL BONUS
	Passive Insight	10 +	
	Passive Perception	10 +	

SPECIAL SENSES

ATTACK WORKSPACE

ABILITY:

ATT BONUS	1/2 LVL	ABIL	CLASS	PROF	FEAT	ENH	MISC
+							

ABILITY:

ATT BONUS	1/2 LVL	ABIL	CLASS	PROF	FEAT	ENH	MISC
+							

DAMAGE WORKSPACE

ABILITY:

DAMAGE	ABIL	FEAT	ENH	MISC	MISC

ABILITY:

DAMAGE	ABIL	FEAT	ENH	MISC	MISC

BASIC ATTACKS

ATTACK		DEFENSE	WEAPON OR POWER	DAMAGE
	vs			
	vs			
	vs			
	vs			

FEATS

_____
_____
_____
_____
_____
_____
_____
_____
_____
_____
_____
_____
_____
_____
_____

POWER INDEX

List your powers below.
Check the box when the power is used.
Clear the box when the power renews.

AT-WILL POWERS

ENCOUNTER POWERS

☐
☐
☐
☐
☐
☐

DAILY POWERS

☐
☐
☐
☐
☐
☐

UTILITY POWERS

☐
☐
☐
☐
☐
☐
☐
☐
☐

MAGIC ITEM INDEX

List your powers below.
Check the box when the power is used.
Clear the box when the power renews.

MAGIC ITEMS

WEAPON	☐
WEAPON	☐
WEAPON	☐
WEAPON	☐
ARMOR	☐
ARMS	☐
FEET	☐
HANDS	☐
HEAD	☐
NECK	☐
RING	☐
RING	☐
WAIST	☐
	☐
	☐
	☐
	☐
	☐
	☐
	☐
	☐
	☐
	☐

Daily Item Powers Per Day

Heroic (1-10) ☐	Milestone ☐/☐/☐/☐
Paragon (11-20) ☐☐	Milestone ☐/☐/☐/☐
Epic (21-30) ☐☐☐	Milestone ☐/☐/☐/☐

OTHER EQUIPMENT

RITUALS

COINS AND OTHER WEALTH

PERSONALITY TRAITS

MANNERISMS AND APPEARANCE

CHARACTER BACKGROUND

COMPANIONS AND ALLIES

NAME   NOTES
NAME   NOTES
NAME   NOTES
NAME   NOTES
NAME   NOTES
NAME   NOTES
NAME   NOTES
NAME   NOTES

SESSION AND CAMPAIGN NOTES

Make Your Party Even Better with the Help of Another PC